GOLF COURSES OF IRELAND

TWELFTH EDITION

Golf – Our Priceless Heritage

Can anything beat the anticipation of a good game, whilst standing on the 1st tee. Whatever your handicap the feeling of tingling anticipation is universal.

After a few holes the course may start to take its toll and you will certainly know it's winning if you can hear the ice clink in a glass by the 15th.

But regardless of the quality of your game, the quality of Ireland's courses will leave you with an invigorating satisfaction that only Nature and a good greenkeeper can provide.

In the following pages is the priceless heritage of golf in Ireland - over 360 courses that offer every golfing test imaginable. The difficulty will be deciding which to play.

BILL CAMPBELL
PUBLISHER

We have it all!

E *The* MBASSY
ROOMS

**RESTAURANT · NIGHTCLUB · LOUNGE
CONFERENCE ROOM · SNOOKER**

Located in the City Centre.
Strandhill, Rosses Point, Enniscrone
and Bundoran Golf Course nearby.

———◆———

**John F Kennedy Parade, Sligo.
Tel: (071) 61250/60650/44232
Fax: (071) 60649**

VISITORS WELCOME

E *The* MBASSY
RESTAURANT

THE
BELFRY

Lunches:
12.30pm - 2.45pm
A La Carte
Dinner Menu:
6.00pm - 10.00pm

Thurs, Fri, Sat & Sun
All Modern Lighting/
sound etc. Top DJ's
incorporating
a stylish & elegant
'Mezzanine Level'

Thomas Street
Lunch Menu
Bar Bite Menu until 9pm
'THE IMPERIAL'
Whiskey & Cigar Lounge
Snooker Rooms

HOW TO USE THIS BOOK

Ireland is divided into four ancient Provinces and these are applied in the administration of golf by the Golfing Union of Ireland. Golf Days has adopted the same geographical division. The courses in this book are grouped in Provinces, sub-divided into Counties and then listed alphabetically. The Province appears on the top left hand corner and the County name at the top right of each page.

OURSE INFORMATION

information has been provided by club and readers are advised to k details in advance as the lishers cannot guarantee to racy. Most clubs will be only too to answer queries and telephone bers for all the courses listed have included for this purpose. lephone call can save a wasted ney.

e are different area dialing codes n calling from the Republic of nd to Northern Ireland and vice . From N.Ireland dial 00 353 and the code omitting the first zero. n the Republic of Ireland replace the hern Ireland 028 code with 048.

CURRENCY

ll green Fees for Northern Ireland Counties: Down, Armagh, Antrim, ondonderry, Fermanagh and Tyrone) re in £ Sterling. Those for the Republic f Ireland are in € Euro. The currencies exchange rate between € Sterling and € Euro will fluctuate, although as a general rule € 1 is worth approximately £0.62 Sterling.

SCORE CARD

Some course cards are marked in metres, some in yards and some have both. Whatever method of distance that is currently used by each course, the same has been adopted in Golf Days to maintain the same standard of measurement. Some course lengths differ in text from course cards depending on whether Championship or Medal lengths are on the score card.

COURSE MAP

These are for general information and to provide a layout of the course. They are not intended for interpretation for scoring or competition purposes.

Published by

udor Journals Ltd
97 Botanic Avenue,
fast BT7 1JN, N. Ireland.
Tel: (028) 9032 0088.
Fax: (028) 9032 3163.
also: 74 Amiens Street Dublin1.
(01) 855 4384 Fax: (01) 855 6689
mail: info@tudorjournals.com
Web: www.tudorjournals.com
Code from Republic of Ire –
replace (028) with (048)

Original Editorial
Committee 1990
Leinster:
Kenneth W. Haughton
Ulster:
Brendan Edwards.
Munster:
J. Percy Shannon.
Connacht:
Michael P. O'Donoghue.

Provincial Introductions
Jack Magowan

Publishing Manager
Paula McVeigh

Publishing Assistants
Kelly Kirkpatrick
Adele McSherry

Production Manager
Charlene Lemon

Design & Production
Annette Mc Goldrick
Stephen Michael
Beatrix Schmalbrock

Sales Manager
Sinead Faulkner

Administration
Sheelagh Campbell

Publisher
Bill Campbell

Printed by
W & G Baird Ltd.

All contents of this publication are copyright and may not be reproduced in any form whatsoever or stored in any retrieval system without the prior written permission of the publishers.

Copyright Tudor Journals Ltd.
April 2002. ISBN 0-907520-45-6

QUICK REFERENCE GUIDE

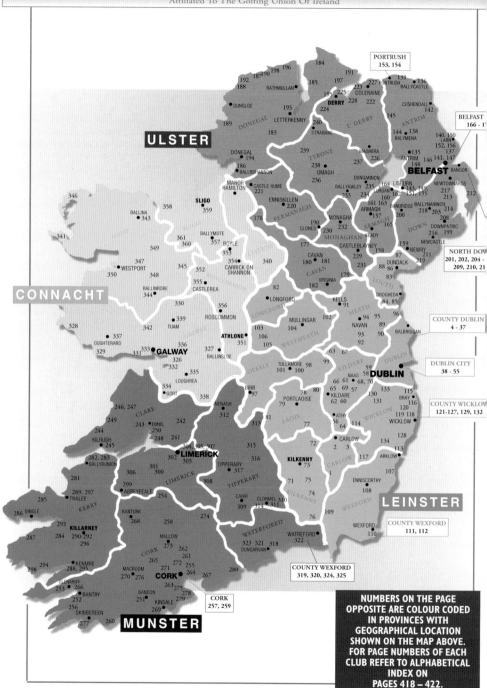

GOLF CLUBS IN IRELAND
Affiliated To The Golfing Union Of Ireland

PORTRUSH
153, 154

BELFAST
166 - 1

ULSTER

NORTH DOV
201, 202, 204 -
209, 210, 21

COUNTY DUBLIN
4 - 37

CONNACHT

DUBLIN CITY
38 - 55

COUNTY WICKLOW
121-127, 129, 132

LEINSTER

COUNTY WEXFORD
111, 112

COUNTY WEXFORD
319, 320, 324, 325

CORK
257, 259

MUNSTER

**NUMBERS ON THE PAGE
OPPOSITE ARE COLOUR CODED
IN PROVINCES WITH
GEOGRAPHICAL LOCATION
SHOWN ON THE MAP ABOVE.
FOR PAGE NUMBERS OF EACH
CLUB REFER TO ALPHABETICAL
INDEX ON
PAGES 418 – 422.**

LEINSTER

CARLOW
1 Borris
2 Carlow
3 Mount Wolseley
DUBLIN
4 Balbriggan
5 Balcarrick
6 Beaverstown
7 Beechpark
8 Blanchardstown
9 Christy O'Connor
10 City West
11 Corballis
12 Corrstown
13 Donabate
14 Dublin City
15 Dublin Mountain
16 Dun Loaghaire
17 Elmgreen
18 Forrest Little
19 Hermitage
20 Hollystown
21 Hollywood Lakes
22 Island
23 Killiney
24 Kilternan
25 Lucan
26 Malahide
27 Newlands
28 Open Golf Centre
29 Portmarnock
30 Portmarnock Links
31 Rush
32 Skerries
33 Slade Valley
34 Stepaside
35 Swords
36 Turvey
37 Westmanstown
DUBLIN CITY
38 Carrickmines
39 Castle
40 Clontarf
41 Deer Park
42 Edmonstown
43 Elm Park
44 Foxrock
45 Grange
46 Hazel Grove
47 Howth
48 Luttrellstown
49 Milltown
50 Rathfarnham
51 Royal Dublin
52 St Annes
53 St Margarets
54 Stackstown
55 Sutton
KILDARE
56 Athy
57 Bodenstown
58 Castlewarden
59 Celbridge
60 Cill Dara
61 Craddockstown
62 The Curragh
63 Highfield
64 Kilkea Castle
65 Killeen
66 The "K" Club
67 Knockanally
68 Naas
69 Newbridge
70 Woodlands
KILKENNY
71 Callan
72 Castlecomer
73 Kilkenny
74 Mountain View

75 Mount Juliet
76 Waterford
LAOIS
77 Abbeyleix
78 Heath
79 Mountrath
80 Portarlington
81 Rathdowney
LONGFORD
82 Longford
LOUTH
83 Ardee
84 Co Louth
85 Dundalk
86 Greenore
87 Killin
88 Seapoint
MEATH
89 Ashbourne
90 Black Bush
91 Headfort
92 Kilcock
93 Laytown & Bettystown
94 Navan
95 Royal Tara
96 Trim
OFFALY
97 Birr
98 Castle Barna
99 Edenderry
100 Esker Hills
101 Tullamore
WESTMEATH
102 Delvin Castle
103 Glasson
104 Moate
105 Mullingar
106 Mount Temple
WEXFORD
107 Courtown
108 Enniscorthy
109 New Ross
110 Rosslare
111 St. Helen's Bay
112 Wexford
WICKLOW
113 Arklow
114 Ballinglass
115 Blainroe
116 Bray
117 Charlestown
118 Coollattin
119 Delgany
120 Djouce Mountain
121 Druid's Glen
122 European Club
123 Glenmalure
124 Glen of the Downs
125 Greystones
126 Old Conna
127 Powerscourt
128 Rallsallagh
129 Roundwood
130 Tulfarris
131 Vartry Lake
132 Wicklow
133 Woodbrook
134 Woodenbridge

ULSTER

ANTRIM
135 Allen Park
136 Ballycastle
137 Ballyclare
138 Ballymena
139 Bushfoot
140 Cairndhu
141 Carrickfergus
142 Cushendall
143 Down Royal

144 Galgorm Castle
145 Gracehill
146 Greenacres
147 Greenisland
148 Hilton
149 Lambeg
150 Larne
151 Lisburn
152 Massereene
153 Royal Portrush
154 Royal Portrush Valley
155 Temple
156 Whitehead
ARMAGH
157 Co Armagh
158 Ashfield
159 Cloverhill
160 Edenmore
161 Loughall
162 Lurgan
163 Portadown
164 Silverwood
165 Tandragee
BELFAST CITY
166 Balmoral
167 Belvoir
168 Cliftonville
169 Dunmurry
170 Fort William
171 Knock
172 Mount Ober
173 Malone
174 Ormeau
175 Rockmount
176 Shandon
CAVAN
177 Belturbet
178 Blacklion
179 Carba Castle
180 Co Cavan
181 Slieve Russell
182 Virginia
DONEGAL
183 Ballybofey & Stranorlar
184 Ballyliffen
185 Buncrana
186 Bundoran
187 Cloughaneely
188 Cruit Island
189 Donegal
190 Dunfanaghy
191 Greencastle
192 Gweedore
193 Letterkenny
194 Narin & Portnoo
195 North West
196 Portsalon
197 Redcastle
198 Rosapenna
DOWN
199 Ardglass
200 Banbridge
201 Bangor
202 Blackwood
203 Bright Castle
204 Carnalea
205 Clandeboye
206 Clandeboye
207 Donaghadee
208 Downpatrick
209 Helens Bay
210 Holywood
211 Kilkeel
212 Kirkistown
213 Mahee Island
214 Ringdufferin
215 Royal Belfast
216 Royal Co Down
217 Scrabo
218 Spa
219 Warrenpoint

FERMANAGH
220 Castlehume
221 Enniskillen
LONDONDERRY
222 Brown Trout
223 Castlerock
224 City of Derry
225 Foyle
226 Moyola
227 Portstewart
228 Roe Park
MONAGHAN
229 Castleblayney
230 Clones
231 Nuremore
232 Rossmore
TYRONE
233 Aughnacloy
234 Benburb
235 Dungannon
236 Fintona
237 Killymoon
238 Newtown Stewart
239 Omagh
240 Strabane

MUNSTER

CLARE
241 Dromoland Castle
242 East Clare
243 Ennis
244 Kilkee
245 Kilrush
246 Lahinch Old Course
247 Lahinch
248 Shannon
249 Spanish Point
250 Woodstock
CORK
251 Bandon
252 Bantry
253 Berehaven
254 Charleville
255 Cobh
256 Coosheen
257 Cork
258 Doneraile
259 Douglas
260 Dunmore
261 East Cork
262 Fermoy
263 Fernhill
264 Fota Island
265 Frankfield
266 Glengarriff
267 Harbour Point
268 Kanturk
269 Kinsale
270 Lee Valley
271 Macroom
272 Mahon
273 Mallow
274 Mitchelstown
275 Monkstown
276 Muskerry
277 Old Head
278 Raffeen Creek
279 Skibbereen
280 Youghal
KERRY
281 Ardfert
282 Ballybunion
283 Ballybunion Cashen
284 Beaufort
285 Castlegregory
286 Ceann Sibéal
287 Dooks
288 Kenmare
289 Kerries
290 Killarney Killen

291 Killarney O'Mahoneys
292 Killarney Lackbane
293 Killorglin
294 Parknasilla
295 Ring of Kerry
296 Ross
297 Tralee
298 Waterville
LIMERICK
299 Abbeyfeale
300 Adare
301 Adare Manor
302 Castleroy
303 Killeline
304 Limerick
305 Limerick County
306 Newcastle West
307 Rathbane
TIPPERARY
308 Ballykisteen
309 Cahir Park
310 Carrick-on-Suir
311 Clonmel
312 Nenagh
313 Roscrea
314 Slievenamon
315 Templemore
316 Thurles
317 County Tipperary
WATERFORD
318 Dungarven
319 Dunmore East
320 Faithlegg
321 Gold Coast
322 Lismore
323 Tramore
324 Waterford Castle
325 West Waterford

CONNACHT

GALWAY
326 Athenry
327 Ballinasloe
328 Connemara
329 Connemara Isles
330 Dunmore
331 Galway
332 Galway Bay
333 Glenlo Abbey
334 Gort
335 Loughrea
336 Mount Bellew
337 Oughterard
338 Portumna
339 Tuam
LETRIM
340 Ballinamore
MAYO
341 Achill
342 Ashford Castle
343 Ballina
344 Ballinrobe
345 Ballyhaunis
346 Belmullet
347 Castlebar
348 Claremorris
349 Swinford
350 Westport
ROSCOMMON
351 Athlone
352 Ballaghadereen
353 Boyle
354 Carrick-on-Shannon
355 Castlerea
356 Roscommon
SLIGO
357 Ballymote
358 Co Sligo
359 Enniscrone
360 Strandhill
361 Tubbercubby

CARR GOLF
CORPORATE TRAVEL

Tee off in style

*C*arr Golf & Corporate Travel is an Irish based destination management company which is ideally positioned for the international travel company, corporate or individual group to organise and implement tailor made itineraries in Ireland.

A trip to Ireland, whether for a world class golf experience, a meeting or an incentive, Carr Golf & Corporate Travel is the solution to your requirements.

The Carr family has been welcoming golfers for over four decades and our personal involvement is essential to capture the essence of Ireland and Irish golf.

We have formed an alliance with the countries top golf courses and resorts, with whom we work to ensure that all our clients needs are being met.

We locate the right venue(s) for particular trips and all our itineraries are tailor made, according to the needs of the customer ours or yours.

MOUNT JULIET

DROMOLAND CASTLE

Accommodation, transport, tee times, sightseeing, spousal itineraries, corporate event tournament management, coupled with premier resorts and courses makes us the first and only choice for your travel plans.

For further information, reservations and enquiries please contact:

Marty Carr, Managing Director, Carr Golf & Corporate Travel, PO Box 6385, Dublin 15, Ireland.
Phone: (3531) 822 6662. **Fax:** (3531) 822 6668. **Internet Address:** www.carrgolf.com
E-mail Address: info@carrgolf.com

Introducing the new on-line booking system for golfers from Dublin & Surrounding Areas

www.golfdublin.com

Featuring 5 of Dublin's finest Pay & Play courses, with a superb mixture of links and parkland venues.

On Line Courses Include:

➤ **Elmgreen Golf Centre,** Castleknock, Dublin 15
Email: elmgreen@golfdublin.com *Phone:* (01) 820 0797
➤ **Corballis Golf Links,** Donabate, Co. Dublin
Email: corballis@golfdublin.com *Phone:* (01) 843 6583
➤ **Grange Castle Golf Course,** Clondalkin, Dublin 22
Email: grangecastle@golfdublin.com *Phone:* (01) 464 1043
➤ **Stepaside Golf Course,** Stepaside, Co. Dublin
Email: stepaside@golfdublin.com *Phone:* (01) 295 2859

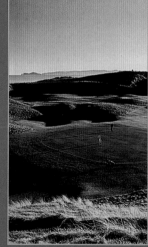

'Sunset at Corballis Golf Links'

Euro Golf Services Ltd.
Ireland's Leading Golf Course Management & Consultancy Company
Phone: (01) 822 6662 **Fax:** (01) 822 6668

Two of Ireland's great courses – Ballybunion (above) and Royal County Down.

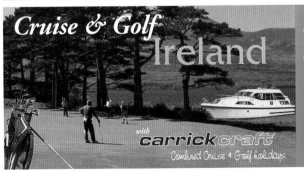

Cruise & Golf
Ireland

with
carrickcraft
Combined Cruise & Golf holidays.

This is the ideal golfers holiday that combines cruising the loveliest and most unspoilt waterways in Europe with playing at any of a host of exhilarating club courses where the golf is quite wonderful.
Please phone for a brochure.

Tel: 028 3834 4993
www.cruise-ireland.com
Carrick Craft, Kinnego Marina,
Oxford Island, Lurgan BT66 6NJ N. Ireland
Fax: 028 3834 4995

Rathsallagh GOLF CLUB

Dunlavin, Co. Wicklow
Tel: (045) 403316 Fax: (045) 403295
Email: info@rathsallagh.com Web: www.rathsallagh.com

"Rathsallagh is built on one of the finest pieces of land I have ever seen and there are some truly beautiful holes."

Peter Thomson
Five Times British Open Champion

Green Fees: Monday – Thursday € 55
Friday, Saturday & Sunday € 70

Classic Sports Travel

Packages to all major sporting events

Golf Packages both home and away
Formula One Grand Prix,
Horse Racing, Rugby Tours

Offical Agent for I.R.F.U. - Ulster

Premier League Football

Official Agent For
Manchester United

1st Floor Howard House
1 Brunswick Street
Belfast BT2 7GE
Tel: 028 9023 7222
Fax: 028 9023 8444

TIPPERARY CRYSTAL
Visitor Centre
Carrick on-Suir

TIPPERARY CRYSTAL
IRELAND'S PREMIER CRYSTAL

LOCATED ON THE N24 WATERFORD - DUBLIN ROAD,

Carrick On-Suir County Tipperary
Tel: 051 641188 Fax: 051 641190
E-Mail: sales@tipperarycrystal.com
Web: www.tipperarycrystal.com

The nine hole course at Ashford Castle on the shores of Lough Corrib and beside the village of Cong.

Visitor information at your fingertips

www.visitor**days**.com

NEXT TIME GET ALL THE INFORMATION
BEFORE YOU LEAVE HOME

GolfIreland.com

Tel: 00353 1 294 8731
Fax: 00353 1 294 3308
Email: tours@golfireland.com

The Island of Ireland offers the golfing visitor a wonderful selection of links golf courses and hotels in superb scenic and cultural environments.

We specialise in putting together the holiday combinations that best suit your particular golfing and accommodation preferences.

Member of the Ireland Golf Tour Operators Association

THE QUALITY HOTEL & SUITES
NAAS ROAD, CO. DUBLIN

• **8 miles from Dublin City Centre and 20 minutes from Dublin Airport**, the Quality Hotel & Suites offers luxury one and two bedroom suites as well as spacious bedrooms.
• **Many of our rooms are overlooking the magnificent Citywest Golf Course.**
• **Group Golf packages available.**
• **Facilities include Restaurant and Private Parking.**

FOR FURTHER DETAILS:
Tel: +353 1 458 7000 • Fax: +353 1 458 7019
Email: info@qualitycitywest.com · www.premgroup.com

Waveline Cruisers
The different way to explore the Shannon

Quigley's Marina, Killinure Point, Glasson,
Athlone, Co. Westmeath
Tel: 0902-85711 Fax: 0902-85716
e-mail: waveline@iol.ie Homepage: http://www.waveline.ie

Farm & Fun Wheels.
All Terrain Vehicle Specialists
Sales - Service - Spares

The Yamaha Golf Car delivers a level of performance, reliability and luxury no other car can match. Coiled springs and shock absorbers, an independent front suspension and our patented UltraPath rear suspension combine for a smooth, comfortable ride. And thanks to a custom made steering system, drivers have more control on hilly and uneven terrains. The car's body withstands the wear and tear of a busy golf course. Dents pop put with ease. Our exclusive energy absorbing front and rear bumpers resist repeated impacts of up to 8 km/h. Vinyl covered side sills made of heavy gage metal guard against damage. And a two part polyurethane paint protects the finish against the sun's harsh UV rays.

35 Aghnadarragh Road, Glenavy
Crumlin, Co. Antrim BT29 4QQ
Tel: (028) 9442 2231 Fax: (028) 9442 2537

Self Catering Galway

Self catering Galway offers 4 star seclusion at the Galway Bay Golf and Country club. Golfing Villa's perched on the shores of Galway Bay, 18 hole PGA Christy O'Connor Jnr. designed course adjacent to Galway Bay Hotel. Dining at AA Rosette award winning restaurant. Didean Bar. Forest walks and Galway just 10 minutes distant.

info@selfcateringgalway.com
www.selfcateringgalway.com

Reservations:
091 502 799

LEINSTER

BY JACK MAGOWAN

Jack Smith was his name, and nobody ever heard of him again. Clearly, the shock of leading a championship field by eight strokes must have been too much for this nervous young Londoner. While George Duncan, his boss at Wentworth, signed for a gale-lashed final-round 74 at Portmarnock, Smith needed seventeen shots more for a butter-fingered score of 91, and fretted all the way home.

This was 1927, the year of the first-ever Irish Open over a course made famous some years before by a couple of high-fliers who glided, in a Vickers-Vimy on to Portmarnock Strand, both fuel tanks empty, after taking off from

POWERSCOURT
GOLF CLUB
& GOLF APARTMENTS

Studio apartment accommodation is available on the Estate. They have been imaginatively converted from outbuildings adjacent to Powerscourt House and can be rented by the night or for longer periods at reduced rates.

Each apartment is beautifully finished in keeping with the character of the building and has fully equipped kitchen, a twin bedded room and ensuite bathroom.

Enjoy the tranquillity and privacy of staying in this 1,000 acre estate within strolling distance of the Golf Course and Clubhouse where restaurant and bar facilities are located.

POWERSCOURT ESTATE
ENNISKERRY CO WICKLOW
TEL: (01) 204 6033 FAX: (01) 276 1303
e-mail: golfclub@powerscourt.ie
http://www.powerscourt.ie/golfclub

TURVEY
GOLF & COUNTRY
CLUB PLC

Turvey Golf & Country Club,
Turvey Avenue, Donabate,
Co. Dublin
~ Tel: (01) 8435169
Fax: (01) 8435179 ~

Turvey Golf & Country Club, designed by Paddy McGuirk has been created in approximately 144 acres of beautiful North County Dublin countryside of undulating terrain with strong belts of mature trees. Turvey is located 8 minutes north of Dublin airport and 5 minutes from Swords. The 18 hole course provides a magnificent test for golfers of every standard. Situated on the grounds a magnificent clubhouse which will be completed August 1999.

Newfoundland the day before.

Overnight, the flagship of Leinster golf had an exciting new identity. Maggie Leonard's cow was no more, but the quickest way to get to this great links was across the estuary from Baldoyle in a row boat or horse and trap, depending on the tide. In those days, no stranger ever left Portmarnock. He may have arrived as a stranger, but by closing time he was a friend. They would ring a ship's bell to signal the departure of the last boat back to the mainland, then came the motor-car and Duncan and Mitchell and Easterbrook and Bobby Locke, all championship winners over what was then the longest and toughest links course in Europe.

The face of Portmarnock hasn't changed a great deal. Without wind, it may be like Samson shorn of his hair, yet how often do we ever get this Dublin Bay pearl bereft of wind? Even when Sandy Lyle beat a 30 year-old record with a staggering 64 on day one of the 1989 Irish Open, the burly Scot was in a cashmere sweater and cords. In Duncan's day, they usually wore oil-paper under plus -fours as protection against rain or cold.

Locke always waxed eloquent about Portmamock, and not without reason. Wasn't it there at the age of 21, and in his first season as a professional, that 'Old Muffin Face' won the Irish championship. Two years later (1940) he was flying bombing missions against Rommel in North Africa and didn't touch a golf club again until the War ended. Half-a-century later, the tournament revived by Carrolls Tobacco, and rescued by Murphy's Stout, royally hosts nearly all the game's top players before some of the biggest galleries in Europe.

A jewel in the Leinster crown is the famous Portmarnock course.

The Irish love to watch golf as well as play it, and nobody was surprised when Portmarnock had to put up 'house full' notices at the first Walker Cup match ever staged here. That was in 1991 and part of the Golfing Union's centenary celebrations, and you can be certain this glamour fixture will be back in the Emerald Isle before long. If not at Portmarnock, then almost certainly Royal County Down. Out of nearly 20 Irish courses ranked among *Golf World's* choice of the top 100 in Britain, seven still wear the Leinster label.

Arnold Palmer's baby at Naas, the fashionable K-Club, has made a quantum leap up the rankings ladder and to nobody's surprise.

This is nothing short of a superb course, tailored to a tee and possibly boasting more five-star holes than any other parkland course in the country. As club pro Ernie Jones said recently, bor-rowing a phrase from the most celebrated Jones-boy of all.

"There's not a hole here that can't be birdied if you just think. And there's not a hole that can't be double-bogied if you stop thinking!"

What a boost for Michael Smurfit, and Irish golf, it will be when the Ryder Cup comes to the K-Club in 2006! County Louth, Royal Dublin, The Island, Rosslare — all welcoming hosts and courses that have few equals in a links context. The same can be said for Pat Ruddy's wonderful new creation at Brittas Bay, the European Club. This course was only played for the first time in the summer of '94 and, like Portmarnock Links of Langer fame, is maturing fast. Already, were talking about this roller coaster gem in the same breath as Baltray, Portstewart, Ballyliffin, Sligo and others of merit.

Water, in my view, adds greatly to the

Ballsbridge, Dublin 4
Ph: 00 353 1 2838155 Fax: 00 353 1 2837877
Email: aberdeen@iol.ie   www.halpinsprivatehotels.com

Aberdeen Lodge ★★★★   Merrion Hall ★★★★

Luxury Edwardian properties in the exclusive Ballsbridge area of Dublin city. Elegant, spacious rooms and suites overlooking gardens and cricket grounds, fine food and modern comforts. Each with grand drawing rooms, Library, air-conditoned suites, Jacuzzis, four-poster beds. Private car park. Within minutes of Stephens Green, beside DART, Landsdowne Road & RDS Convention centre.

Glasson Golf Hotel & Country Club

1 1/2 hrs from Dublin / Galway / Shannon. 3hrs from Belfast.

"The Holes range from good to great and the setting is a every turn little short of enthralling."

!!HOTEL NOW OPEN!!
29 bedrooms with Magnificent Views over Lough Ree and the Golf Course.

CALL US FOR INFORMATION ON SPRING/SUMMER SPECIALS - 'PLAY & STAY'

Call: +353 (0) 902 85120
Email: info@glassongolf.ie   www.glassongolf.ie
Glasson, Athlone, Co. Westmeath.

Corrstown Golf Club

Killsallaghan, Co. Dublin, Ireland
Tel: 01 8640533 Fax: 01 8640537
info@corrstowngolfclub.com
www.corrstowngolfclub.com

Situated in North County Dublin, Corrstown Golf Club is ideally located 10 minutes north of Dublin Airport and only 30 minutes from Dublin city centre.

The Club has full bar and Restaurant facilities and our

trained staff are on hand to cater for all your needs.

Green Fee rates are available on request. Discounts given for groups and societies.

Office hours 8am - 8pm seven days a week.

SEAMUS GREEN
Resident Professional
ELM PARK GOLF CLUB.

Large selection of Golf Equipment always in stock.

Elm Park Golf Club, Nutley House, Nutley Lane, Donnybrook, Dublin 4. Telephone: 003531 – 2692650

charm and magnetism of a golf course, and there's an abundance of it at St. Margaret's, near Dublin Airport. The eighth there is one of the most genuine par-5's in the business, an exhilaratingly difficult long hole that top-girl Laura Davies clearly treated with respectful caution, even in the '95 championship she won there by a runaway 16 strokes. Laura was in orbit that week, surrendering only one shot to par in 72 holes for a World record tally of 25 – under (267) that has only once been bettered in a major ladies' tournament worldwide.

St. Margaret's is the brainchild of Ruddy and the late Tom Caddock, whose eye for what's best in golfing architecture has also put a hideaway hamlet in County Wicklow called Newtownmountkennedy firmly on the map.

Who said Valderrama was the toughest course in Europe?.

It's a pussy-cat (almost) compared to Druid's Glen, where the key is not to play all four short holes in par, but without getting that Titleist wet!

The 17th to an island green is a spectacle hole, a carbon copy of No.17 on Florida's famous Tournament Players' course, only longer.

Druid's Glen is not for everybody, not at an entrance fee of £25,000 + plus, or annual sub. of £1,500, but for sheer drama and challenge, it's something special, an examination in golf for sure.

"Our brief was to build the best inland course in the country," says Ruddy. "Clearly, there can't be many better than this."

Golf's magnetism is like the common cold – everybody gets it, but nobody can explain why. There are many permutations for a rewarding, if not inexpensive, tour of Ireland's South-East region, but

Elm Park Golf Club in Dublin – popular city parkland course with many mature trees adding to the test of golf.

Tree lined fairways at Powerscourt Golf Club in Dublin

Outstanding views from Howth Golf Course.

for one lovely lady from Baltinglass it would begin with a round at the European Club and end at Rathsallagh. Sandwiched between the two would be a visit to Woodenbridge (Arklow), Rosslare, St. Helens Bay, Faithlegg, Mount Juliet and Carlow.

Eight different courses in ten days? Sheer exhaustion, but it would be a never-to-be-forgotten experience!

To mark the Millennium, sixty top people in the game, from architects to administrators, players to writers, were invited to vote in ranking order their "100 Greatest Courses of the 20th Century".

Over 450 courses in all were nominated for selection, the majority of them known to, or played by, most of the panel.

Naturally, there was a strong preference for links golf, which is where Ireland took centre stage with no fewer than five courses in the top 25. And the choice for the No.1 spot?

You've guessed it --- Cypress Point in California, arguably the most exclusive club in the world and the pick of nearly 50 American courses on the list.

Muirfield, in Scotland, is at No.2, just ahead of Pebble Beach. Then comes Royal Co. Down at No.4 and in front of Augusta National, Royal Birkdale and formidable old Pine valley.

Not surprisingly, Ballybunion Old gets a high up rating at No.9, and Royal Portrush too, at No.13.

It speaks volumes for Irish golf that 11 courses in all are in the 100 greatest. Here they are:

At No.4 Royal Co. Down; No.9 Ballybunion Old; No.13 Royal Portrush; No.22 Portmarnock; No.24 The European Club; No.54 Waterville; No.63 Druids Glen; No.68 Lahinch; No.74 Co Louth; No.90 Co Sligo and No.92 Ballyliffin (Glashedy).

COME PLAY ONE OF
WICKLOW'S FINEST COURSES

GLEN DOWNS

Coolnaskeagh, Delgany, Co. Wicklow.
Tel: (01) 2876240 / Fax: (01) 2870063

Truly Magnificent Panoramic Views of the Wicklow Mountains & the Irish Sea.

The entire course has been built to U.S.G.A. specifications. Golfers of all standards will find the course a challenge with its natural slopes and valleys combined with it's undulating greens and some 90 bunkers.

Summer Green Fees:
Mon - Fri €65.00
Early Bird €50.00
Sat & Sun €80.00

Winter Green Fees:
Mon - Fri €50.00
Early Bird €40.00
Sat & Sun €65.00

* 18 Hole Championship Parkland Course
* Located only 35 mins from Dublin
* New 15.000 sq. ft. Pavilion complete with Bar, Restaurant, Golf Shop & Locker Rooms
* Golf clubs, buggies, caddy cars for hire
* Short game practice area

Group & Society Enquiries Welcome

Conference Leisure & Golf Resort
DUBLIN

Be it business or pleasure...Citywest Hotel has something for you

This elegant 4 star de-luxe hotel offers the ideal venue for your Corporate Event, Golf Classic/Outing or Leisure Break.

400 De-Luxe Guestrooms & Suites • 5* Health & Leisure Club with 20m Swimming Pool • Spa Areas & Beauty Salons • Two on site 18 Hole Golf Courses • Golf Academy • Extensive Conference Facilities • Elegant Terrace Restaurant & Grill Room • Lively Bars.

For further details contact:
Tel: 01 4010500 - Fax: 01 4588756
E-mail: info@citywesthotel.com • www.citywesthotel.com

Crosbie Cedars HOTEL

A Warm Welcome Awaits

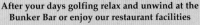

Golf Galore
- Stay & Play rates
- Special rates for hotel guests
- Associated with Rosslare Golf Club
- 5 Golf Courses within 35 mins drive.

After your days golfing relax and unwind at the Bunker Bar or enjoy our restaurant facilities

ROSSLARE, Co. WEXFORD
Tel: 053-32124 Fax: 053-32243
www.crosbiecedarshotel.com info@crosbiecedarshotel.com

KILLERIG
GOLF CLUB
CARLOW

- **Located just outside Carlow Town**
- **One hour from Dublin**
- **Par 72 Championship Course**
- **USGA Specification**
- **€32 Midweek**
- **€42 Weekends**

Tel: +353 (0) 503 63000
Fax: +353 (0) 503 63005
E-mail: contact@killerig-golf.ie
Website: www.killerig-golf.ie

Fingal, a golfer's paradise which boasts some of the country's finest courses, is located only minutes from the heart of Dublin City and is home of Dublin International Airport.

Arguably the golfing capital of Europe, Fingal offers the golfer a multitude of outstanding parkland and links courses. The picturesque open countryside and magnificent coastline of Fingal are ideal environments against which are fashioned twenty eight superb golf courses. Both experienced and novice golfers will find a course to suit their ability, taste and pocket.

Fingal Tourism
Mainscourt,
Main Street, Swords,
Fingal, Co Dublin.

For further information on courses or to receive a free Golfer's Guide to Fingal contact:

Tel +353 1 8400077
info@fingaltourism.ie
www.fingal-dublin.com

Golfing breaks at the AA/RAC ★★★★
Glenview Hotel
Only 30 mins from Dublin City Centre.

Enjoy one of the following mentioned golf courses during your stay:

Druid's Glen, Powerscourt, Glen O'The Downs, Charlesland, The European Club, Blainroe, Woodbrook, Woodenbridge and many more.

On request our hotel coach can drop you to the club of your choice. After a leisurely game, retreat to our Leisure Centre for a long swim followed by a jacuzzi and sauna.

Round off your day with a delicious dinner and superb wine in our famous Woodlands restaurant or Conservatory Bistro.

Special golf group rates available on enquiry

Glenview Hotel, Glen O'the Downs, Delgany, Co Wicklow
Tel: + 3531 287 3399 Fax: + 3531 287 7511
Email: glenview@iol.ie   Website: www.glenviewhotel.ie

County Louth links is one of the top rated courses in Ireland.

The popular Grange Golf Club in the sylvan setting of south Dublin.

THE
REGENCY HOTEL
GROUP

The Regency Hotel Group offers five hotels with strategic locations, including Dublin city centre, the environs of Dublin Airport and the South Dublin coastal resort of Bray, Co. Wicklow.

Whether on corporate business or leisure pursuits, the Regency Hotel Group has something for everyone. You are assured of a warm welcome in a relaxed and friendly atmosphere.

	2 B&B, 1 Dinner	3 nights midweek
The North Star Hotel	from Euro109	from Euro149
The Regency Hotel	from Euro109	from Euro149
The Royal Hotel	from Euro109	from Euro149
The Esplanade Hotel	from Euro109	from Euro149
The Parliament Hotel	from Euro149	from Euro179

"If you're thinking of staying in Europe's most exciting city, why not stay with us"

www.regencyhotels.com

The North Star Hotel
★★★ tel: (01) 836 3136

The Regency Airport Hotel
★★★ tel: (01) 837 3544

The Royal Hotel & Leisure Cent
★★★ tel: (01) 286 2935

The Esplanade Hotel
★★★ tel: (01) 286 2056

The Parliament Hotel
★★★ tel: (01) 670 8777

BORRIS

**Borris Golf Club, Deerpark,
Borris,
Co. Carlow.
Tel: (0503) 73143/73201.
Fax: (0503) 73750.**

Location: Outskirts of the town on the road to New Ross.
Secretary: Nollaig Lucas.

Picturesque nine hole course, sited in wooded land with an attractive backdrop of hills and mountains.

COURSE INFORMATION

**Par 70; SSS 69; Length 5,680 metres.
Visitors:** Welcome Mon – Fri.
Opening Hours: 9.00am – dark.
Avoid: Thursday afternoons, Saturdays and Sundays.
Ladies: Welcome.
Green Fees: €20, €13 with member.

Juveniles: Welcome. Caddy service available by prior arrangements.
Clubhouse Hours: 9.00am – 11.00pm.
Clubhouse Dress: Smart/casual.
Clubhouse Facilities: Bar food.

NO.	METRES	PAR	S.I.	NO.	METRES	PAR	S.I.
1	333	4	10	10	316	4	7
2	362	4	5	11	340	4	9
3	280	4	16	12	289	4	15
4	117	3	18	13	151	3	14
5	453	5	12	14	338	4	6
6	333	4	8	15	380	4	4
7	152	3	13	16	135	3	17
8	387	4	3	17	418	4	1
9	418	4	2	18	478	5	11
OUT	2,835	35		IN	2,845	35	
				TOTAL	5,572	70	
STANDARD SCRATCH				69			

BORRIS
CLUBHOUSE

Copyright Tudor Journals Ltd.

NO.	MEDAL YARDS	GEN. YARDS	PAR	S.I.	NO.	MEDAL YARDS	GEN. YARDS	PAR	S.I.
1	401	393	4	4	10	279	276	4	11
2	292	269	4	14	11	393	376	4	3
3	131	122	3	17	12	344	335	4	7
4	354	342	4	9	13	152	147	3	16
5	503	460	5	15	14	416	411	4	5
6	165	162	3	12	15	354	340	4	10
7	398	389	4	1	16	401	377	4	2
8	397	390	4	6	17	139	132	3	18
9	373	334	4	8	18	482	467	5	13
OUT	3,014	2,861	35		IN	2,960	2,861	35	
TOTAL						5,974	5,722	70	
STANDARD SCRATCH						70	70		

Deerpark, Dublin Road, Co. Carlow.
Tel: (0503) 31695 Fax: (0503) 40065.
E-mail: carlowgolfclub@tinet.ie
Website: www.carlowgolfclub.com
LOCATION: Two miles north of Carlow Town on main Dublin Road (N9).
GENERAL MANAGER: Donard Mac Sweeney
PROFESSIONAL: Andrew Gilbert. Tel: (0503) 41745.
Considered one of the best inland courses with fair but tight fairways and good greens. Its fine springy turf earns the reputation of "inland links". The course has extensive mature woods and many scenic views.

COURSE INFORMATION

Par 70; SSS 71; Length 5,974 metres.
Visitors: Welcome.
Opening Hours: Sunrise – Sunset.
Avoid: Tuesday, Saturday and Sunday.
Ladies: Welcome.
Green Fees: Mon –Fri €44, Groups (20+) €41. Weekends €57, Groups (20+) €52.
Juveniles: Restricted. Lessons available by prior arrangements. Caddy service available by prior arrangement. Handicap certificate required.
Clubhouse Hours: 9.30am – 11.30pm. Full Clubhouse Facilities.
Clubhouse Dress: Casual.
Clubhouse Facilities: Breakfast (summer), lunches, evening meals, snacks all day. Menu available on request.
Open Competitions:
Open Week: 31st May-8th June; Midland Scratch Cup: 20th & 21st April.

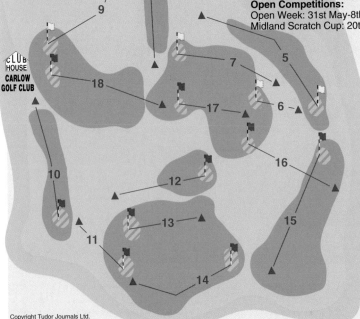

CLUB HOUSE
CARLOW GOLF CLUB

Copyright Tudor Journals Ltd.

Mount Wolseley Golf & Country Club,
Tullow, Co. Carlow.
Tel: (0503) 51674.
Fax: (0503) 52123.

LOCATION: Adjacent to Tullow town on the Ardattin Road.
SECRETARY / MANAGER: Kathy Walsh.
Tel: (0503) 51674.
CAPTAIN: Ger Curtis.

A testing 18 hole course with plenty of water hazards and bunkers. Incorporated is a good practice area consisting of finished fairways and greens situated right beside the Clubhouse.

COURSE INFORMATION

Par 72; SSS 74; Length 7,106 yards.
Avoid: Every day before 10.30am (members only).
Green Fees: €45 Mon – Thu. €65 Fri, Sat & Sun.
Clubhouse Facilities: Catering facilities available: Bar food from 10.30am, full bar menu from 12.30pm.

Restaurant a la carte from 6.30pm – 9.00pm. Carvery: 12.00am – 10pm (summer only). Breakfast for groups.
Open Competitions: Mixed open 14th June, Ladies open 26th June.

NO.	CHAMP METRES	MEDAL METRES	PAR	S.I.	NO.	CHAMP METRES	MEDAL METRES	PAR	S.I.
1	411	383	4	9	10	592	571	5	6
2	447	417	4	5	11	207	191	3	10
3	447	435	4	1	12	519	504	5	18
4	273	267	4	15	13	427	409	4	14
5	499	483	5	7	14	339	319	4	12
6	210	187	3	13	15	466	438	4	2
7	542	521	5	11	16	226	204	3	16
8	440	418	4	3	17	457	397	4	4
9	191	177	3	17	18	413	394	4	8
OUT	3,460	3,288	36		IN	3646	3,427	36	
					TOTAL	7,106	6,715	72	
					STANDARD SCRATCH	74	73		

Bunker & tree positions indicated.

MOUNT WOLSELEY CLUBHOUSE

Copyright Tudor Journals Ltd.

**Blackhall, Balbriggan,
Co. Dublin.
Tel: (01) 8412229/8412173.**

LOCATION: One mile south of
Balbriggan on Dublin /
Belfast road.
SECRETARY / MANAGER:
Michael O'Halloran.

Expanded to eighteen holes in 1985
and has been developed using an
additional 32 acres that the club
purchased which allowed for a new
clubhouse to be built in 1991 adding

to the club's many attractive features.
The new layout has made the course
more of a formidable challenge.

COURSE INFORMATION

**Par 71; SSS 71; Length
5,922 metres.
Visitors:** Welcome Monday,
Wednesday, Thursday and
Friday.
Opening Hours:
8.00am – sunset.
Avoid: Weekends and
Tuesday (Ladies day).

Juveniles: Open Week,
August.
Green Fees:€32 Mon – Fri.
€21 early bird green fee
weekdays (except Tuesdays)
before 10.00am.
Clubhouse Hours:
8.00am – 11.00pm.
Clubhouse Dress: Casual.
Clubhouse Facilities:
Snacks and meals available
from noon.
Open Competitions: Open
Week June.

NO.	METRES	PAR	S.I.	NO.	METRES	PAR	S.I.
1	365	4	6	10	417	5	15
2	504	5	16	11	184	3	7
3	357	4	4	12	368	4	3
4	321	4	18	13	308	4	13
5	384	4	2	14	358	4	5
6	180	3	10	15	392	4	1
7	339	4	14	16	130	3	11
8	171	3	12	17	323	4	9
9	360	4	8	18	461	5	17
OUT	2,981	35		IN	2,941	36	
				TOTAL	5,922	71	
STANDARD SCRATCH		71					

**BALBRIGGAN
CLUBHOUSE**

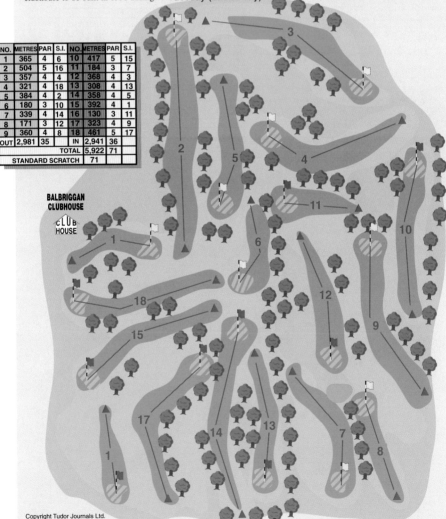

Copyright Tudor Journals Ltd.

**Balcarrick Golf Club,
Corballis, Donabate,
Co. Dublin.
Tel: (01) 8436957**

SECRETARY: Peter Quinn.
Tel: (01) 843 6957 / 843 6228.
COURSE DESIGNER: Barry Langan.

A relatively new club, founded in 1992. In 1995 it was converted to a fine 18 hole course featuring deceptive holes and water hazards creating quite a challenge. In 1997 a clubhouse was built situated on course.

COURSE INFORMATION

Par 73; SSS 72; Length 5,940 metres.
Visitors: Welcome.
Opening Hours:
Sunrise – sunset.
Ladies: Welcome.
Green Fees: Weekdays €32; weekends €40.
Juveniles: Must be accompanied by an adult.
Clubhouse Hours:
12am –11pm summer time.

Clubhouse Dress: Neat & Tidy. No denims or trainers on course or in clubhouse.
Clubhouse Facilities:
Full catering facilities. Fully licenced.
Open Competitions:
Every Thursday and Bank Holidays, Summertime
Open Week 21st - 28th July.

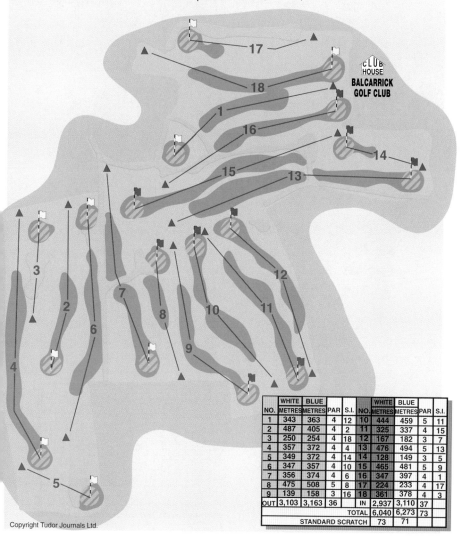

NO.	WHITE METRES	BLUE METRES	PAR	S.I.	NO.	WHITE METRES	BLUE METRES	PAR	S.I.
1	343	363	4	12	10	444	459	5	11
2	487	405	4	2	11	325	337	4	15
3	250	254	4	18	12	167	182	3	7
4	357	372	4	4	13	476	494	5	13
5	349	372	4	14	14	128	149	3	5
6	347	357	4	10	15	465	481	5	9
7	356	374	4	6	16	347	397	4	1
8	475	508	5	8	17	224	233	4	17
9	139	158	3	16	18	361	378	4	3
OUT	3,103	3,163	36		IN	2,937	3,110	37	
					TOTAL	6,040	6,273	73	
					STANDARD SCRATCH	73	71		

Copyright Tudor Journals Ltd.

**Beaverstown, Donabate,
Co. Dublin.
Tel: (01) 8436439.
Fax: (01) 8435059.**

LOCATION: 6 miles north of
Dublin Airport.
ARCHITECT: Eddie Hackett.
MANAGER: Declan Monaghan
PROFESSIONAL: Anthony Schweppe
Tel: (01) 8434655.

Beaverstown is sited in an attractive
orchard setting. The main feature of
the course is its proximity to deep
water which is a hazard on as many as
ten of the eighteen holes.

COURSE INFORMATION

**Par 71; SSS 70; Length
5,874 metres.
Visitors:** Welcome.
Opening Hours:
8.00am – sunset.
Avoid: Wed, Sat and Sun.
Ladies: Welcome.

Juveniles: Must be
accompanied by an adult.
Green Fees: €50 Mon – Fri;
€65 Sat / Sun.
Clubhouse Hours: 8.00am
to closing time.
Clubhouse Dress: Neat
dress essential, no denim.
Clubhouse Facilities: Bar
and restaurant from
10.30am.
Open Competitions: As per
list published by G.U.I.
Open Weekend: April and
September.
Open Week: May.

NO.	MEDAL METRES	GEN. METRES	PAR	S.I.	NO.	MEDAL METRES	GEN. METRES	PAR	S.I.
1	295	295	4	15	10	328	274	4	16
2	294	283	4	9	11	165	157	3	8
3	161	150	3	13	12	303	294	4	14
4	320	306	4	7	13	308	297	4	12
5	418	408	4	1	14	469	462	5	4
6	375	369	4	3	15	445	439	5	10
7	125	114	3	17	16	385	333	4	2
8	368	313	4	5	17	157	122	3	18
9	452	443	5	11	18	469	461	5	6
OUT	2,808	2,681	35		IN	3,029	2,839	37	
					TOTAL	5,837	5,520	71	
					STANDARD SCRATCH	70	70		

Copyright Tudor Journals Ltd.

BEECH PARK

Johnstown, Rathcoole, Co. Dublin.
Tel: (01) 4580100/4580522.

LOCATION: 2 miles from Rathcoole village on Kilteel Road.
GENERAL MANAGER: Paul Muldowney.
ARCHITECT: Eddie Hackett.

The course is in a setting of natural beauty with mature beech trees in abundance. Holes 9, 10, 11, 12 & 13 have a combination of mature trees and water providing difficulty, particularly in the drives.

COURSE INFORMATION

Par 72; SSS 70; Length 6,268 yds; 5,730 metres.
Visitors: Welcome Mon, Thurs & Fri.
Opening Hours: 8.00am – Sunset.
Avoid: Tues, Wed, and weekends.
Ladies Day: Tuesday.
Juveniles: Must be accompanied by an adult.
Green Fees: €38

Juveniles €8.
Clubhouse Hours: 9.00am – midnight.
Clubhouse Dress: Collar and tie after 8.00pm. No jeans or sneakers.
Clubhouse Facilities: 11.30am – 10.30pm.
Open Competitions: Open Week 8th – 16th June.

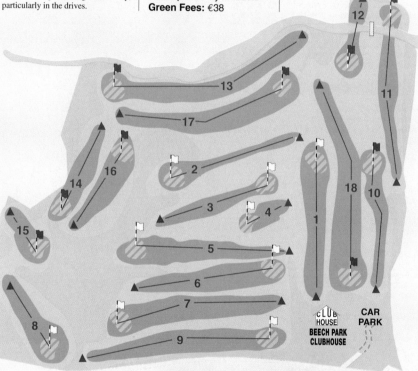

NO.	MEDAL METRES	GEN. METRES	PAR	S.I.	NO.	MEDAL METRES	GEN. METRES	PAR	S.I.
1	315	306	4	15	10	331	319	4	4
2	353	342	4	3	11	281	269	4	12
3	349	337	4	9	12	171	153	3	8
4	120	110	3	17	13	471	459	5	6
5	351	321	4	1	14	293	282	4	10
6	360	329	4	5	15	130	118	3	18
7	500	457	5	7	16	346	333	4	14
8	150	137	3	13	17	450	438	5	16
9	476	435	5	11	18	371	359	4	2
OUT	3,035	2,774	36		IN	2,844	2,729	36	
					TOTAL	5,730	5,503	72	
					STANDARD SCRATCH	70	69		

Copyright Tudor Journals Ltd.

**Blanchardstown Golf Centre,
Tyrrelstown House,
Mulhuddart, Co. Dublin.
Tel: (01) 821 3206.
www.blanchardstowngolf.com**

LOCATION: 2 miles
Blanchardstown town centre, off
N3 near Mulhuddart Cemetary.
SECRETARY: Noelle McClenahan
PROFESSIONAL: Kevin Garvey.
ARCHITECT: Johnny Young.

North Leinsters longest par 3 (which
has not been parred). Set in mature
parkland around a beautiful all timber
public golf practice range, which is
floodlit with white lighting. Includes
excellent practice bunkers. We
specialise in group lessons for adult &
juniors (during school holidays) and
corporate groups which include clinic
and round of golf.

COURSE INFORMATION

**Par 54; SSS 56; Length
2,769 yards; 2,531 metres.
Visitors:** Public pay & play all
welcome.
Opening Hours:
9am – 10pm Mon – Fri. All year.
9am – 8pm. Sat & Sun
Summertime. 9am – 6pm. Sat
& Sun Wintertime.
Avoid: No restrictions.
Green Fees: Mon – Fri €10;
Sat & Sun €12.50, Bank
Holidays €15.
Juveniles: Accompanied.
Clubhouse Hours:
Up to 10pm midweek; 8pm
weekends and 6pm
weekends in Wintertime.
Clubhouse Dress:
Casual smart
Clubhouse Facilities:
Coffee Shop,
sandwich bar.
No alcohol.

NO.	METRES	YARDS	S.I.	NO.	METRES	YARDS	S.I.
1	114	127	7	10	132	147	1
2	92	102	17	11	116	129	1
3	126	140	11	12	129	143	5
4	104	115	5	13	152	169	1
5	95	105	15	14	134	149	1
6	180	200	1	15	135	150	5
7	98	109	9	16	131	145	1
8	95	106	13	17	153	170	7
9	153	170	3	18	113	126	9
OUT						TOTAL	2,502

Bunker and tree positions indicated.

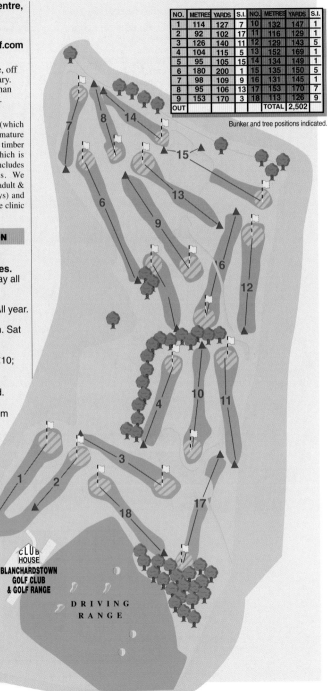

CLUB HOUSE
BLANCHARDSTOWN
GOLF CLUB
& GOLF RANGE

DRIVING
RANGE

Copyright Tudor Journals Ltd.

Silloge Park Golf Course, Ballymun Road, Swords, Co. Dublin.
Tel: (01) 8620 464/8620 440
Email:christyo@indigo.ie
www.christyo'connor.com

LOCATION: Co. Dublin
SECRETARY: Denis Darcy
PROFESSIONAL: Peter O'Connor
& Christopher O'Connor

NO.	METRES	PAR	S.I.	NO.	METRES	PAR	S.I.
1	381	4	4	10	392	4	2
2	162	3	10	11	360	4	8
3	424	5	7	12	508	5	3
4	347	4	12	13	156	3	13
5	505	5	5	14	317	4	14
6	296	4	16	15	351	4	11
7	124	3	15	16	374	4	9
8	411	4	1	17	307	4	18
9	120	3	17	18	370	4	6
OUT	2,770	35		IN	3,135	36	
				TOTAL	5,924	70	
				STANDARD SCRATCH	69		

18 hole parkland. Inland tree-lined course. SS of 69 makes this a long demanding course. Mostly flat over undulating hills. The feature hole is the 8th, 411 metres Par 4, index 1 over a small river and uphill dog-leg left. This course is very mature with tall tree features on numerous holes on the golf course.

COURSE INFORMATION

Par 71; SSS 70; Length 5,924 metres.
Ladies Day: Monday.
Green Fees: €13.97 weekdays, €15.24 weekends.
Juveniles: Welcome.
Clubhouse Dress: Casual
Clubhouse Facilities: Changing rooms, showers, soup/sandwiches etc, caddy cars available.

Tree positions indicated.
Copyright Tudor Journals Ltd.

Citywest Hotel Conference, Leisure & Golf Resort, Saggart, Co. Dublin.
Tel: (01) 401 0500.
Fax: (01) 458 0945.

LOCATION: On N7, off M50, 20 mins from Dublin Airport & Dublin City.
GOLF DIRECTOR: Barry Phelan.

ARCHITECT: Christy O'Connor Jnr. International championship golf course recognised as being one of the most outstanding. Sergio Garcia and Jose Maria Olazabal, who visited Citywest, were lavish in their praise and admiration of the Club and the excellent standard of the practice facilities.

COURSE INFORMATION
Par 70; Length 6,691 yards.

Visitors: Always welcome.
Opening Hours: 7am – Sunset.
Green Fees: (18 hole) €38 Mon – Thurs; Fri – Sun & Bank Holidays €45. (9 Hole) €20 Mon – Thurs; Fri – Sun & Bank Holidays €25. (36 hole) €57 Mon – Thurs; Fri – Sun & Bank Holidays €76.
Juveniles: Welcome – €20. Golf clubs, trolleys, buggies, locker and caddies available. Professional tuition and golf schools available by appointment.
Clubhouse Dress: Casual/Neat.
Facilities: Restaurant, bar food, grill room, carvery. Conference facilities up to 6,500, banqueting 2000. Deluxe guestrooms, Health & Leisure Club with 20m pool. Golf Academy.

NO.	CHAMP YARDS	MEDAL YARDS	PAR	S.I.	NO.	CHAMP YARDS	MEDAL YARDS	PAR	S.I.
1	386	366	4	9	10	200	181	3	10
2	197	171	3	13	11	369	349	4	12
3	541	516	5	7	12	400	385	4	4
4	220	211	3	11	13	555	539	5	8
5	398	374	4	15	14	178	156	3	18
6	454	423	4	1	15	536	496	5	14
7	380	367	4	17	16	397	381	4	6
8	457	432	4	3	17	158	139	3	16
9	430	414	4	5	18	435	414	4	2
OUT	3,463	3,274	35		IN	3,228	3,040	35	
					TOTAL	6,691	6,314	70	

TO DUBLIN

16
12
17
13
15
18
11
14
10
DRIVING RANGE
CLUB HOUSE
CITYWEST CLUBHOUSE
1
2
8
9
6
5
7
3
4
TO NAAS

Bunker and tree positions indicated.
Copyright Tudor Journals Ltd.

Citywest Hotel Conference, Leisure & Golf Resort, Saggart, Co. Dublin.
Tel: (01) 401 0500.
Fax: (01) 458 0945.

LOCATION: On N7, off M50, 20 mins from Dublin Airport & Dublin City.
GOLF DIRECTOR: Barry Phelan.
ARCHITECT: Christy O'Connor Jnr.

Designed by Christy O' Connor Jnr. and based on the popular US concept this new 'Executive' course is already rated as one of the finest courses around. With a unique par 65 design, incorpotating magnificient greens and some fantastically laid out holes, this 'Executive' course has quickly gained admiration from the serious golf enthusiast.

COURSE INFORMATION

Par 65; Length 5,154 yards.
Visitors: Always welcome.
Opening Hours: 7am – Sunset.
Green Fees: Mon –Thurs €38 resident €32 Fri – Sun €45 resident €38. Spring Weekend Specal 4 ball; €120
Juveniles: Welcome – €20.
Golf clubs, trolleys, buggies,

locker and caddies available. Professional tuition and golf schools available by appointment.
Clubhouse Dress: Casual/Neat.
Facilities: Restaurant, bar food, grill room, carvery. Conference facilities up to 6,500, banqueting 2000. Deluxe guestrooms, Health & Leisure Club with 20m pool. Golf Academy.

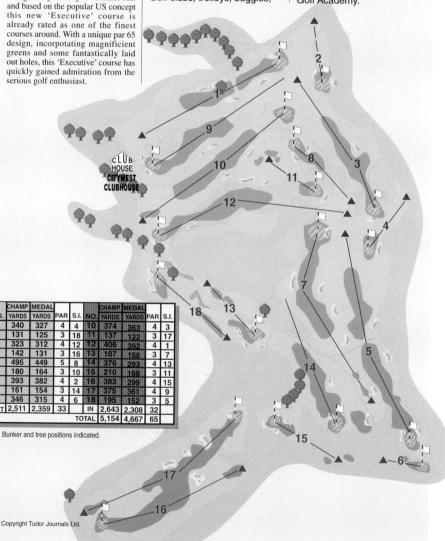

NO.	CHAMP YARDS	MEDAL YARDS	PAR	S.I.	NO.	CHAMP YARDS	MEDAL YARDS	PAR	S.I.
1	340	327	4	4	10	374	363	4	3
2	131	125	3	18	11	137	122	3	17
3	323	312	4	12	12	406	392	4	1
4	142	131	3	16	13	187	158	3	7
5	495	449	5	8	14	376	293	4	13
6	180	164	3	10	15	210	168	3	11
7	393	382	4	2	16	383	299	4	15
8	161	154	3	14	17	375	361	4	9
9	346	315	4	6	18	195	152	3	5
OUT	2,511	2,359	33		IN	2,643	2,308	32	
					TOTAL	5,154	4,667	65	

Bunker and tree positions indicated.

Copyright Tudor Journals Ltd.

CORBALLIS

NO.	YARDS	PAR	S.I.	NO.	YARDS	PAR	S.I.
1	155	3	12	10	132	3	15
2	251	4	18	11	374	4	9
3	465	4	2	12	405	4	3
4	155	3	16	13	264	4	17
5	389	4	4	14	191	3	11
6	183	3	6	15	196	3	5
7	188	3	8	16	392	4	1
8	264	4	14	17	140	3	13
9	494	5	10	18	333	4	7
OUT	2,544	33		IN	2,427	32	
				TOTAL	4,971	65	
				STANDARD SCRATCH	64		

Corballis Public Golf Course, Donabate, Co. Dublin. Tel: (01) 8436583.

LOCATION: North County Dublin on the coast.
MANAGER: P. J. Boylan.
Tel: (01) 8436583/8436781.
ARCHITECT: Dublin County Council.

A links course situated adjacent to Corballis Beach, Donabate. Aquired and redeveloped by Dublin County Council in 1973. A very popular and challenging Par 65 course which attracts large numbers of golfers particularly during the winter months.

COURSE INFORMATION

Par 65; SSS 64; Length 4,971 yards.
Visitors: Welcome.
Opening Hours: Weekends 7.00am; Weekdays 8.00am.
Ladies: Welcome.
Green Fees: €9 Mon – Fri; €14 Sat/Sun; Juveniles, Senior Citizens and unemployed €9 (Mon–Fri before 2.30pm).
Juveniles: Welcome.
Clubhouse Hours: Open normal hours.
Clubhouse Dress: Casual/neat.

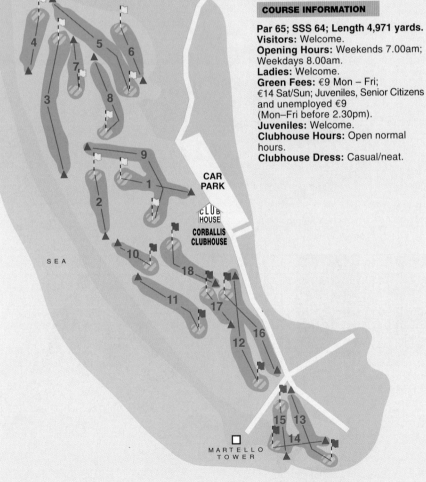

Copyright Tudor Journals Ltd.

**Corrstown Golf Club,
Kilsallaghan, Co Dublin.
Tel: (01) 8640533.**

LOCATION: North West Dublin
Airport - 6 minutes.
SECRETARY: Jason Kelly. (Admin)
Tel: (01) 864 0533.
Fax: (01) 864 0537.
PROFESSIONAL: Pat Gittens.
ARCHITECT: Eddie Connaughton
B. Sc. – Designer Agronomist.
Course: Grass Technology
International.

27 holes – 9 hole course (Orchard
Course) 18 hole course (River Course).
Both parkland courses. 18 hole course

contains a river with island green and
water features throughout the course.

COURSE INFORMATION

**Par 72; SSS 71; Length;
6,298 metres (River Course);
5,584
metres (Orchard Course).
Visitors:** Welcome weekdays
before 3pm (ring for booking).
Opening Hours: 7.00am.
Avoid: Wednesdays.
Green Fees: 18 Hole Course
Midweek €35, Weekend €45
Members & Guests: Midweek
€15, Weekend €20. Society €26
(midweek only)

9 Hole Course Midweek €18,
Weekends €23. Members &
Guests: Midweek €8, Weekends
€10. Society Midweek €15,
Weekend €18
Juveniles: Usually accompanied
with an adult.
Clubhouse Hours:
11.30am – 11.30pm; pub hours in
summer.
Clubhouse Dress: Informal.
Clubhouse Facilities: Full
catering and bar facilities.
Open Competitions:
Interm. Scratch Cup 25th May.
Junior Scratch Cup: 29th June.
Seniors Open - 4th July.

NO.	GENTS Metres	PAR	S.I.	NO.	LADIES Metres	PAR	S.I.
1	298	4	16	1	278	4	16
2	356	4	2	2	326	4	2
3	125	3	18	3	105	3	18
4	323	4	12	4	300	4	12
5	387	4	4	5	365	5	4
6	140	3	8	6	130	3	8
7	448	5	10	7	400	5	10
8	332	4	14	8	310	4	14
9	383	4	6	9	318	4	6
OUT	2,792	35		IN	2,532	36	
				TOTAL	5,324	72	
				STANDARD SCRATCH	71		

ORCHARD COURSE

PRACTICE AREA

CORRSTOWN HOUSE

CLUB HOUSE CORRSTOWN CLUBHOUSE

NO.	MEDAL METRES	GEN. METRES	PAR	S.I.	NO.	MEDAL METRES	GEN. METRES	PAR	S.I.
1	144	138	3	10	10	319	314	4	15
2	518	504	5	2	11	538	526	5	5
3	372	361	4	12	12	476	463	5	17
4	507	497	5	6	13	415	387	4	1
5	454	446	5	16	14	178	169	3	13
6	153	144	3	18	15	410	384	4	7
7	395	388	4	4	16	421	395	4	9
8	292	286	4	14	17	174	163	3	11
9	150	141	3	8	18	382	371	4	3
OUT	2,985	2,905	36		IN	3,313	3,172	36	
					TOTAL	6,298	6,077	72	
					STANDARD SCRATCH	72	71		

RIVER COURSE

Bunker and tree positions indicated.
Copyright Tudor Journals Ltd.

DONABATE

Balcarrick, Donabate, Co. Dublin.
Tel: (01) 8436346

LOCATION: 12 miles north of Dublin city.
SECRETARY / MANAGER: Brian Judd.
Tel: (01) 8436346.
PROFESSIONAL: Hugh Jackson.
Tel: (01) 8436346.

Flat parkland with tree lined fairways -all 27 greens now reconstructed to USPGA spec.

COURSE INFORMATION

Par 72; SSS 73; Length 6,534 yards. (red/yellow)
Visitors: Mon, Tues ;a/noon, Thurs-Sun;a/noon,
Opening Hours: 7.30am – sunset.
Avoid: Wednesday, and Bank Holidays.
Ladies: Welcome.
Green Fees: €40 daily (€13 with member); €45 Sat/Sun. €35 9-40 people, €30 40·

Juveniles: Welcome if accompanied by an adult. Club Hire and Caddy carts available by prior arrangements.
Clubhouse Hours: 8.00am – 11.30pm.
Clubhouse Dress: Casual / neat (no jeans or trainers).
Clubhouse Facilities: Snacks available at all times; a la carte from 5pm, bar also.
Open Competitions: Scratch Cups - June 3; Cotter Cup - July 6: Open Week - August 4-11.

NO.	MEDAL METRE	GEN. METRES	PAR	S.I.	NO.	MEDAL METRE	GEN. METRE	PAR	S.I.	NO.	MEDAL METRE	GEN. METRE	PAR	S.I.
1	162	147	3	7	1	365	338	4	8	1	375	366	4	2
2	444	435	5	11	2	178	167	3	14	2	450	430	5	18
3	375	356	4	3	3	316	309	4	16	3	154	130	3	12
4	137	128	3	15	4	377	352	4	4	4	385	360	4	4
5	310	395	4	11	5	321	309	4	12	5	360	340	4	8
6	356	342	4	1	6	347	335	4	6	6	375	366	4	10
7	272	251	4	17	7	258	248	4	18	7	191	176	3	6
8	167	155	3	13	8	467	458	5	10	8	315	296	4	14
9	449	435	5	9	9	408	380	4	2	9	452	438	5	16
OUT	2,903	2,778	36		OUT	3,037	2,896	36		TOTAL	3,057	2,092	36	

CLUB HOUSE
DONABATE CLUBHOUSE

Copyright Tudor Journals Ltd.

Ballinascorney, Dublin 24,
Tel: (01) 4516430/4512028.
Fax: (01) 459 8445.
Email: info@dublincitygolf.com
www.dublincitygolf.com

LOCATION: Approx. ten miles south west of Dublin. 10mins from M50 motorway.
MANAGER: Frank Bagnill.
Tel: (01) 4516430.

Dublin Cty Golf Club is set in the beautiful valley of Glen Na Smil (The valley of the thrush) overlooking the lakes and the river Dodder. The Course was Originally Designed by the late Eddie Hackett, with redesign work by Frank Clarke. The course would be described as parkland and the layout has been dictated by the terrain. The designers have taken full dvantage of the varied terrain and produced a great variety of golf holes with very few parallel holes. Players never get bored with a new challange around every corner.

COURSE INFORMATION

Par 71; SSS 67; Length 5,464 metres.
Visitors: Welcome 7 days a week (phone in advance) societies welcome.
Opening Hours: Sunrise – sunset.
Ladies: Welcome Tuesdays.
Green Fees: €25 (weekdays) €35 (weekends).
Juveniles: Welcome.
Clubhouse Hours: 8.00am – 11.00pm.
Clubhouse Dress: Smart / casual (no denim).
Clubhouse Facilities: Snacks and full catering available. Trolly buggy & club hire available.

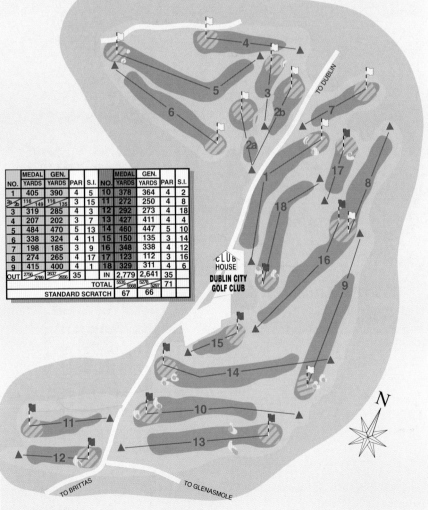

NO.	MEDAL YARDS	GEN. YARDS	PAR	S.I.	NO.	MEDAL YARDS	GEN. YARDS	PAR	S.I.
1	405	390	4	5	10	378	364	4	2
2a 2b	116 149	116 135	3	15	11	272	250	4	8
3	319	285	4	3	12	292	273	4	18
4	207	202	3	7	13	427	411	4	4
5	484	470	5	13	14	460	447	5	10
6	338	324	4	11	15	150	135	3	14
7	198	185	3	9	16	348	338	4	12
8	274	265	4	17	17	123	112	3	16
9	415	400	4	1	18	329	311	4	6
OUT	2756 2789	2637 2656	35		IN	2,779	2,641	35	
					TOTAL	5535 5568	5278 5297	71	
			STANDARD SCRATCH			67	66		

CLUB HOUSE
DUBLIN CITY GOLF CLUB

TO DUBLIN

N

TO BRITTAS   TO GLENASMOLE

Copyright Tudor Journals Ltd.

**Gortlum, Brittas,
Co. Dublin
Tel: (01) 458 2622.
Fax: (01) 458 2048.**

LOCATION: Just outside the village of Brittas, on the Main N81.10 mins from Tallaght, South Dublin.
CAPTAIN: Tony Sunderland.
LADY CAPTAIN: Margaret Macardle.
HON. SECRETARY: Pat O' Rourke
SECRETARY MANAGER: Fiona Carolan

COURSE INFORMATION

**Par 71; SSS 69; Length 5,635 yards.
Opening Hours:** Dawn – Dusk
Avoid: Saturday & Sunday mornings.
Green Fees: Weekdays €14; weekends €18.
Facilities: Caddy Hire,

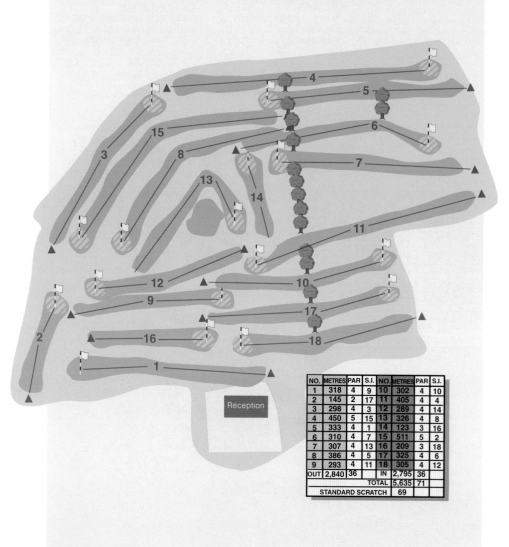

NO.	METRES	PAR	S.I.	NO.	METRES	PAR	S.I.
1	318	4	9	10	302	4	10
2	145	2	17	11	405	4	4
3	298	4	3	12	289	4	14
4	450	5	15	13	326	4	8
5	333	4	1	14	123	3	16
6	310	4	7	15	511	5	2
7	307	4	13	16	209	3	18
8	386	4	5	17	325	4	6
9	293	4	11	18	305	4	12
OUT	2,840	36		IN	2,795	36	
				TOTAL	5,635	71	
				STANDARD SCRATCH		69	

Copyright Tudor Journals Ltd.

Bunker & tree positions indicated.

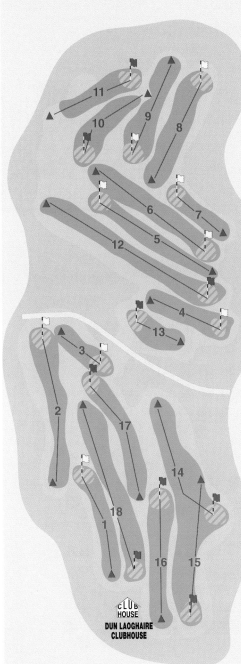

**Dun Laoghaire Golf Club,
Eglinton Park, Tivoli Road,
Dun Laoghaire.
Tel: (01) 2803916.
Fax: (01) 2804868.**

LOCATION: 7 miles South of Dublin.
GENERAL MANAGER: Dennis Peacock.
Tel: (01) 2803916.
PROFESSIONAL: Vincent Covey.
Tel: (01) 2801694.

A relatively short course in the quiet suburbs
of Dun Laoghaire, but with some interesting
holes requiring accurate club selection.

COURSE INFORMATION

**Par 69; SSS 68; Length
5,313 metres.
Visitors:** Welcome Monday,
Tuesdays & Friday.
Opening Hours: 8.00am – sunset.
Green Fees: €50 each round.
Juveniles: Welcome.
Lessons available by prior
arrangements. Club Hire available.
Clubhouse Hours: 10.00am –
11.00pm.
Clubhouse Dress: Casual. Jacket
and tie after 8.00pm.
Clubhouse Facilities: 10.00am –
10.00pm/ Snack service April – Oct/
6.00pm – 10.00pm Restaurant April
– Oct/ 10.00am – 6.00pm Snack
service Nov – March.

NO.	MEDAL METRES	GEN. METRES	PAR	S.I.	NO.	MEDAL METRES	GEN. METRES	PAR	S.I.
1	304	291	4	11	10	183	174	3	12
2	332	323	4	5	11	241	233	4	16
3	148	139	3	9	12	440	430	5	18
4	173	164	3	7	13	149	137	3	14
5	392	376	4	1	14	368	359	4	2
6	284	275	4	15	15	331	323	4	8
7	114	107	3	17	16	337	329	4	6
8	367	360	4	3	17	328	318	4	4
9	343	336	4	13	18	479	471	5	10
OUT	2,457	2,371	33		IN	2,856	2,774	36	
					TOTAL	5,313	5,145	69	
					STANDARD SCRATCH	72	71		

**CLUB HOUSE
DUN LAOGHAIRE
CLUBHOUSE**

Copyright Tudor Journals Ltd.

Castleknock,
Dublin 15.
Tel: (01) 8200 797.
Fax: (01) 822 6668

LOCATION: Situated just off the
Navan Road, a minutes drive
from Castleknock roundabout.
SECRETARY: Gerry Carr.
PROFESSIONAL: Paul
McGahan/Arnold O'Connor/
Joe Murray/Carl Kelly.

Located 15 minutes from Dublin City.
This is a very pleasant parkland
course. The 17th hole Par 3 is an

exceptional hole played against the
backdrop of the Wicklow Mountains.

COURSE INFORMATION

**Par 71; SSS 68; Length
5,796 Yards.**
Visitors: Welcome anytime.
Telephone for booking.
Opening Hours:
Dawn 'till Dusk.
Ladies: Welcome Anytime.
Green Fees: €18 Weekdays.
€25 Weekends.
Juveniles: Welcome anytime.

Clubhouse Facilities:
Changing Rooms / Showers.
Coffee Shop, restaurant.
Open Competitions: Varied
contact club.

NO.	YARDS	PAR	S.I.	NO.	YARDS	PAR	S.I.
1	269	4	9	10	300	4	10
2	476	5	13	11	121	3	18
3	118	3	17	12	350	4	12
4	383	4	11	13	401	4	2
5	478	5	5	14	332	4	14
6	308	4	7	15	337	4	8
7	397	4	1	16	509	5	6
8	153	3	15	17	177	3	16
9	289	4	3	18	398	4	4
OUT	2,871	36		IN	2,925	35	
				TOTAL	5,796	71	
				STANDARD SCRATCH		68	

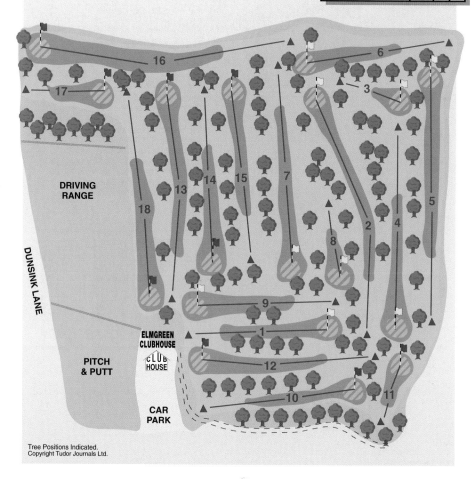

Tree Positions Indicated.
Copyright Tudor Journals Ltd.

Cloghran.
Co. Dublin.
Tel: (01) 8401183 / 8401763.

NO.	MEDAL METRES	GEN. METRES	PAR	S.I.	NO.	MEDAL METRES	GEN. METRES	PAR	S.I.
1	291	278	4	7	10	349	334	4	12
2	377	353	4	5	11	160	143	3	8
3	354	342	4	11	12	324	309	4	4
4	413	374	4	1	13	351	335	4	16
5	171	156	3	9	14	183	170	3	10
6	460	446	5	15	15	450	432	5	18
7	149	126	3	17	16	346	332	4	6
8	400	386	4	3	17	320	304	4	14
9	349	338	4	13	18	418	402	4	2
OUT	2,964	2,799	35		IN	2,901	2,761	35	
					TOTAL	5,865	5,560	70	
STANDARD SCRATCH						70	69		

LOCATION: Beside Dublin Airport.
SECRETARY / MANAGER: Tony Greany.
Tel: 8401763.
PROFESSIONAL: Tony Judd.
Tel: 407670.

One of the pre-qualifying courses for the Irish Open. A parkland course sited close to Dublin Airport.

COURSE INFORMATION

Par 70; SSS 70; Length 5,865 metres.
Visitors: Welcome Mon – Fri. Societies Mon – Thur.
Opening Hours: 8.00am – sunset.
Green Fees: €40 daily.
Avoid: Wed & Fri afternoons. Telephone appointment required.
Ladies & Juveniles: Welcome. Handicap Certificate required. Lessons, Club Hire and caddy cars available. Ladies day Tuesday. Juveniles must be off the course by 3pm.
Clubhouse Hours: 8.00am – midnight.
Clubhouse Dress: Casual (no jeans).
Clubhouse Facilities: Tues & Wed evenings & weekends, full catering and bar.

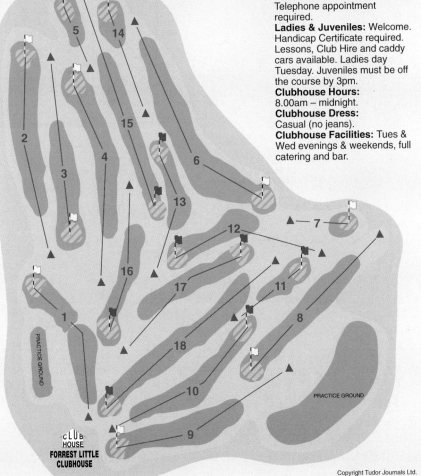

FORREST LITTLE CLUBHOUSE

PRACTICE GROUND

PRACTICE GROUND

Copyright Tudor Journals Ltd.

**Ballydowd, Lucan,
Co. Dublin.
Tel: (01) 6268491.**

LOCATION: 8 miles from Dublin
city, on the N4.
GENERAL MANAGER: Patrick
Maguire. Tel: (01) 6268491.
PROFESSIONAL: Simon Byrne.
Tel: (01) 6268072.

This course has a fairly flat front nine
and an undulating back nine. The 10th
hole is the most scenic, followed by

an extremely difficult par 5, bordered
on right by the River Liffey and on the
left by woodland. USGA spec greens.

COURSE INFORMATION

**Par 71; SSS 71; Length
6,032 metres.
Visitors:** Welcome Monday
– Friday mornings (except
Tuesday).
Opening Hours: 8.00am –
Sunset.
Avoid: Weekends.

Ladies Day: Tuesday.
Juveniles: Must be
accompanied by an adult, tel.
appointment required. Caddy
service available; club hire and
lessons available by prior
arrangement.
Green Fees: €70 Mon – Fri.
Clubhouse Hours: 9.00am –
midnight.
Clubhouse Dress: Casual. No
jeans or shorts. Tie after 8pm.
Clubhouse Facilities: Snacks
from 10am; full restaurant from
12.30pm – 9.30pm everyday.

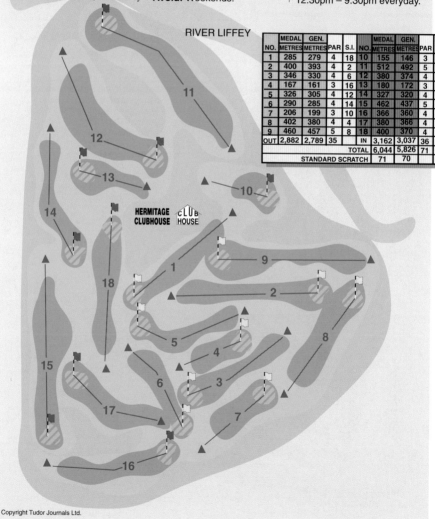

RIVER LIFFEY

NO.	MEDAL METRES	GEN. METRES	PAR	S.I.	NO.	MEDAL METRES	GEN. METRES	PAR	S.I.
1	285	279	4	18	10	155	146	3	15
2	400	393	4	2	11	512	492	5	9
3	346	330	4	6	12	380	374	4	1
4	167	161	3	16	13	180	172	3	13
5	326	305	4	12	14	327	320	4	7
6	290	285	4	14	15	462	437	5	17
7	206	199	3	10	16	366	360	4	3
8	402	380	4	4	17	380	366	4	11
9	460	457	5	8	18	400	370	4	5
OUT	2,882	2,789	35		IN	3,162	3,037	36	
					TOTAL	6,044	5,826	71	
					STANDARD SCRATCH	71	70		

HERMITAGE CLUBHOUSE   CLUB HOUSE

Copyright Tudor Journals Ltd.

**Hollystown Golf Club,
Hollystown, Holywood
Rath, Dublin 15.
Tel: (01) 8207444
Fax: (01) 8207447**

LOCATION: 10km from Dublin
City.
MANAGER: Oliver Barry.
PROFESSIONAL: Brian Boshell.
ARCHITECT: Eddie Hackett.

Set in Dublin countryside, Hollystown
was designed by one of Ireland's most
celebrated golf architects, Eddie
Hackett, and was opened in 1992.

Recognition for the Golf Course came
in 1997 when hosting the Golfing
Union of Ireland, Leinster Youths
Golf Championship. An additional
nine holes was opened in August 1999
complementing the existing eighteen
holes. "The 4th on the red course at
234 yards is one of the best Par 3 in
any part of the country" said Christy
O'Connor Snr who also singled out
the 1st on the blue course. The
facilities include a fine new pavilion
and is 20 minutes from Dublin's city
centre.

COURSE INFORMATION

Visitors: Welcome.
Opening Hours: Daylight
Hours.
Ladies: Welcome.
Green Fees: €25 weekdays,
€35 weekends.
Juveniles: Welcome.
Clubhouse Hours: Daylight
Hours.
Clubhouse Dress: Casual.
Clubhouse Facilities: Full
facilities including bar and
catering.

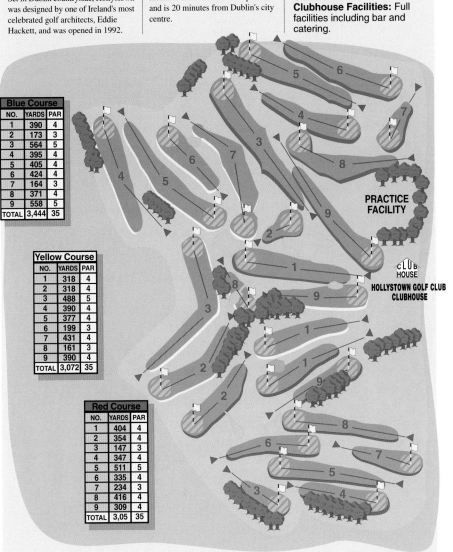

Blue Course

NO.	YARDS	PAR
1	390	4
2	173	3
3	564	5
4	395	4
5	405	4
6	424	4
7	164	3
8	371	4
9	558	5
TOTAL	3,444	35

Yellow Course

NO.	YARDS	PAR
1	318	4
2	318	4
3	488	5
4	390	4
5	377	4
6	199	3
7	431	4
8	161	3
9	390	4
TOTAL	3,072	35

Red Course

NO.	YARDS	PAR
1	404	4
2	354	4
3	147	3
4	347	4
5	511	5
6	335	4
7	234	3
8	416	4
9	309	4
TOTAL	3,05	35

PRACTICE
FACILITY

CLUB
HOUSE
HOLLYSTOWN GOLF CLUB
CLUBHOUSE

Hollywood Lakes Golf Club, Ballyboughal, Co.Dublin. Tel: (01) 8433407, (01) 8433002.

LOCATION: 12 miles north of Dublin Airport.
SECRETARY: A.C. Brogan
Tel: (01) 8433407.
ARCHITECT: M. Flanagan

Parkland course featuring many lakes, large greens and the longest par 5 in Ireland at 581 metres. A long course demanding accuracy from the tee.

COURSE INFORMATION

Par 72; SSS 72; Length 6,870 yards.
Visitors: Welcome.
Opening Hours: Dawn – dusk.
Avoid: Weekends before 1.00pm / Wed after 4.00pm.
Ladies: Welcome.
Green Fees: Weekdays €30 and weekends €35.
Juveniles: Welcome.
Clubhouse Hours: 10.30am– 11.30pm.

Clubhouse Dress: Casual – no denim.
Clubhouse Facilities: Bar / Lounge / Restaurant.
Open Competitions: Senior Open: 28th May, 30th July and 24th September. Open Mens' Weekend: 8th & 9th June.

NO.	CHAMP YARDS	MEDAL YARDS	PAR	S.I.	NO.	CHAMP YARDS	MEDAL YARDS	PAR	S.I.
1	321	299	4	8	10	365	345	4	3
2	379	373	4	4	11	166	158	3	11
3	358	330	4	12	12	337	323	4	17
4	129	120	3	14	13	366	360	4	9
5	449	431	5	18	14	581	534	5	7
6	166	156	3	10	15	481	465	5	15
7	373	364	4	2	16	389	381	4	5
8	350	318	4	6	17	185	164	3	13
9	438	429	5	16	18	413	359	4	1
OUT	2,963	2,820	36	36	IN	3,283	3,089	36	
					TOTAL	6,246	5,909	72	
					STANDARD SCRATCH		72		

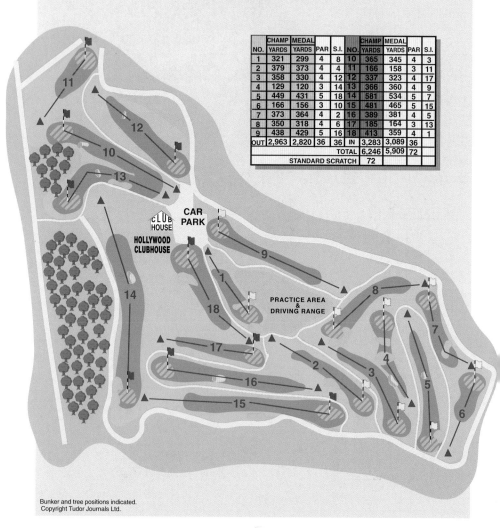

Bunker and tree positions indicated.
Copyright Tudor Journals Ltd.

Island Golf Club, Corballis, Donabate, Co. Dublin
Tel: (01) 8436462.
Fax: (01) 8436860.
Email: islandgc@iol.ie
www.theislandgolfclub.com

LOCATION: Corballis.
ARCHITECT: 1990 Redesign, F. Hawtree & E. Hackett.

Enveloped on three sides by the sea, this is a naturally true links course. The 1st, 3rd and 7th are probably the best holes on the outward nine but the most spectacular are to be found on the inward half. The 12th needs an excellent drive while the 13th is a superb par 3 of 190 metres, requiring a long iron or wood shot to reach a naturally well protected green. The 425 metre par 4 18th offers an excellent challenge with imposing sandhills on both sides.

COURSE INFORMATION

Par 71; SSS 72; Length 6,053 metres.
Visitors: Welcome Mon, Tues & Fridays, Wed & Thurs pm.
Opening Hours: 7.30am – sunset.

Ladies: Welcome Thurs (pm).
Green Fees: €100 Mon - Fri
Juveniles: Welcome.
Clubhouse Hours: 7.00am – 12.00 midnight (summer); 8am – close (winter).
Clubhouse Dress: Casual. No denims or training shoes.
Clubhouse Facilities: 10.30am – 6pm winter. 8.00am - 11.30pm summer.
Competitions: Irish Close Championship in 1998. Irish PGA 1999.

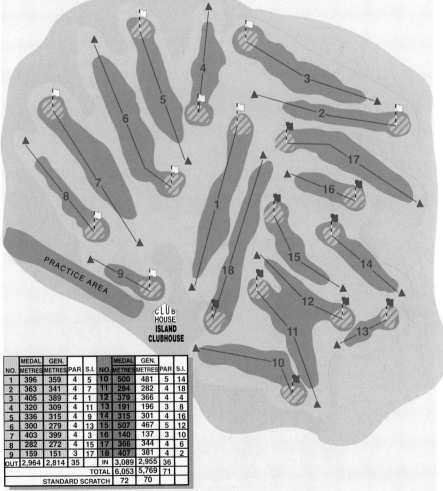

NO.	MEDAL METRES	GEN. METRES	PAR	S.I.	NO.	MEDAL METRES	GEN. METRES	PAR	S.I.
1	396	359	4	5	10	500	481	5	14
2	363	341	4	7	11	284	282	4	18
3	405	389	4	1	12	379	366	4	4
4	320	309	4	11	13	191	196	3	8
5	336	315	4	9	14	315	301	4	16
6	300	279	4	13	15	507	467	5	12
7	403	399	4	3	16	140	137	3	10
8	282	272	4	15	17	366	344	4	6
9	159	151	3	17	18	407	381	4	2
OUT	2,964	2,814	35		IN	3,089	2,955	36	
					TOTAL	6,053	5,769	71	
		STANDARD SCRATCH	72			70			

Copyright Tudor Journals Ltd.

**Killiney Golf Club,
Balinclea Road,
Killiney,
Co. Dublin.
Tel: (01) 2851027/2852823.
Fax: (01) 2856294.**

LOCATION: Killiney.
PROFESSIONAL: Paddy O'Boyle.
Tel: (01) 2856294.
SECRETARY: Michael Walsh.

This parkland course is on the southern side of Killiney Hill, the most scenic area of Co. Dublin. The local terrain while hilly is not too difficult.

COURSE INFORMATION

**Par 70; SSS 70; Length 5,723 metres.
Visitors:** Welcome Monday and Tuesday morning; Wednesday, Friday and Sunday afternoons subject to availability.
Opening Hours: 8.30am – sunset.
Avoid: Thursdays, Saturdays, Sunday mornings and Tuesday pm.
Green Fees: €40 (€20 with member).

Juveniles: Welcome. Must be accompanied by an adult. Lessons available by prior arrangements; Club Hire available.
Clubhouse Hours: 8.30am – Dark.
Clubhouse Dress: Casual / Neat (no jeans, T-shirts or trainers).
Clubhouse Facilities: Bar snacks 10am – 11pm everyday.

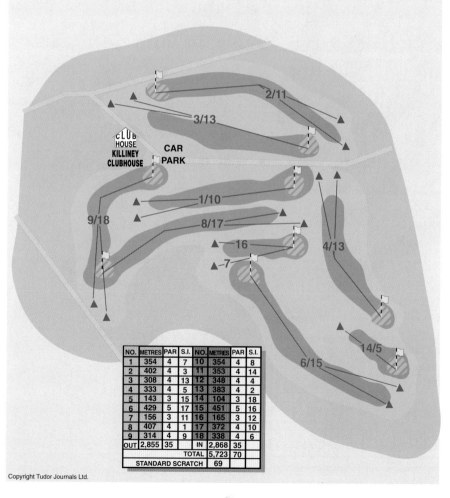

NO.	METRES	PAR	S.I.	NO.	METRES	PAR	S.I.
1	354	4	7	10	354	4	8
2	402	4	3	11	353	4	14
3	308	4	13	12	348	4	4
4	333	4	5	13	383	4	2
5	143	3	15	14	104	3	18
6	429	5	17	15	451	5	16
7	156	3	11	16	165	3	12
8	407	4	1	17	372	4	10
9	314	4	9	18	338	4	6
OUT	2,855	35		IN	2,868	35	
				TOTAL	5,723	70	
				STANDARD SCRATCH		69	

Copyright Tudor Journals Ltd.

Kilternan Golf & Country Club, Kilternan, Co. Dublin.
Tel: (01) 2955559
Fax: (01) 2955670.

LOCATION: Kilternan, Co. Dublin.
SECRETARY: Mr Jimmy Kinsella.
PRO-SHOP: Tel: (01) 2952986.

A challenging course with spectacular views over Dublin Bay, "Offers every golf shot in the book."

COURSE INFORMATION

Par 68; SSS 66; Length 5,223 yards.
Visitors: Welcome by booking outside competition hours.
Opening Hours: Operates on time sheet only.
Ladies: Welcome.
Green Fees: Mon – Fri €25; Sat / Sun €32.
Juveniles: Welcome. Buggy Hire available by prior arrangements.

Clubhouse Hours: Monday – Sunday 10.00am – 11.00pm. Full clubhouse facilities.
Clubhouse Dress: Smart / casual, no jeans or training shoes.
Clubhouse Facilities: Food available everyday – 10am to 9.30pm.

Hotel closed for retrofit.

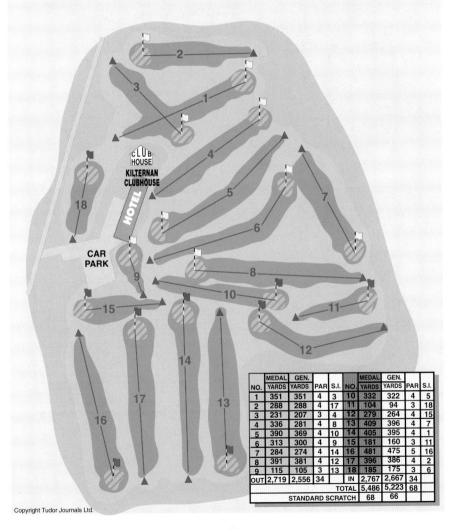

NO.	MEDAL YARDS	GEN. YARDS	PAR	S.I.	NO.	MEDAL YARDS	GEN. YARDS	PAR	S.I.
1	351	351	4	3	10	332	322	4	5
2	288	288	4	17	11	104	94	3	18
3	231	207	3	4	12	279	264	4	15
4	336	281	4	8	13	409	396	4	7
5	390	369	4	10	14	405	395	4	1
6	313	300	4	9	15	181	160	3	11
7	284	274	4	14	16	481	475	5	16
8	391	381	4	12	17	396	386	4	2
9	115	105	3	13	18	185	175	3	6
OUT	2,719	2,556	34		IN	2,767	2,667	34	
					TOTAL	5,486	5,223	68	
					STANDARD SCRATCH		68	66	

Copyright Tudor Journals Ltd.

Lucan, Co. Dublin.
Tel: (01) 6280246.

LOCATION: 10 miles from Dublin City
on Cellbridge Road.
SECRETARY/MANAGER: Tom O'Donnell.
Tel: (01) 6282106.
CADDYMASTERS: Martin Furey &
Christy Dobbs. Tel: (01) 6280246.

Lucan Golf Course has an undulating first
nine. The first and seventh providing a good
test. The back nine which was added in 1988
is fairly flat and has a fine finishing 18th hole
of 530 metres.

COURSE INFORMATION

**Par 71; SSS 71; Length
5,888 metres.**
Visitors: Monday, Tuesday, Fridays,
Wednesdays to 1.00pm.
Opening Hours: Sunrise – sunset.
Avoid: Weekends.
Green Fees: €40.
Juveniles: Must be accompanied by
a member. Telephone appointment
required; Club Hire available; Caddy
service available by prior
arrangements.
Clubhouse Hours: 9.00am – 12.00
midnight. Full clubhouse facilities.
Clubhouse Dress: No denims on
Course. Neat dress in clubhouse.
Clubhouse Facilities: Full bar &
restaurant facilities. Bar food available.

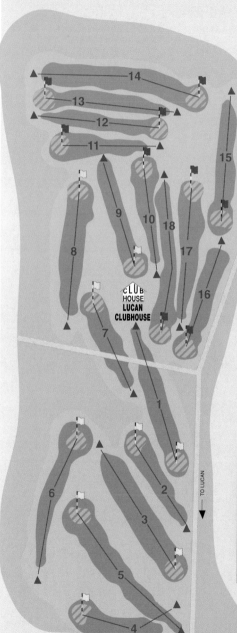

NO.	MEDAL METRES	GEN. METRES	PAR	S.I.	NO.	MEDAL METRES	GEN. METRES	PAR	S.I.
1	364	369	4	6	10	358	371	4	3
2	304	332	4	8	11	156	169	3	7
3	411	416	4	4	12	279	292	4	15
4	143	107	3	12	13	317	330	4	11
5	431	435	5	16	14	402	415	4	1
6	268	279	4	18	15	321	334	4	13
7	124	138	3	10	16	172	185	3	9
8	346	366	4	2	17	426	439	5	17
9	310	344	4	14	18	518	531	5	5
OUT	2,701	2,786	35		IN	2,949	3,066	36	
					TOTAL	5,650	5,852	71	
					STANDARD SCRATCH	71	70		

Copyright Tudor Journals Ltd.

MALAHIDE

L E I N S T E R

DUBLIN

Beechwood, The Grange, Malahide, Co. Dublin.
Tel: (01) 8461611
/8461270/8461642.
Fax: (01) 8461270.

Location: Malahide.
Secretary / Manager: Mr John McCormack.
Professional: John Murray.
Tel: 01 8460002.
Architect: E. Hackett.

A championship standard course, which opened to 27 holes in 1990. This parkland course has water as a feature of a number of the holes.

COURSE INFORMATION

Par 71; SSS 72; Length 6,066 metres
Visitors: Welcome.
Opening Hours: Sunrise – sunset.
Ladies: Welcome. Telephone appointment required.
Green Fees: €50 Mon – Fri; Weekends & Holidays €85

Clubhouse Hours: 9.00am – 12.30am.
Clubhouse Facilities: Full catering and bar facilities.
Clubhouse Dress: Dining room, Lounge and bar – casual but neat.
Open Competitions: August Bank Holiday week.

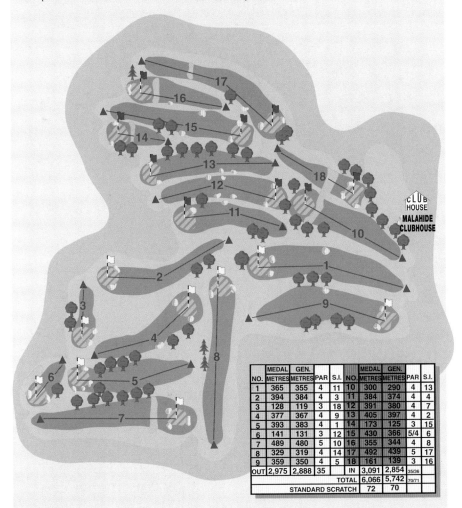

NO.	MEDAL METRES	GEN. METRES	PAR	S.I.	NO.	MEDAL METRES	GEN. METRES	PAR	S.I.
1	365	355	4	11	10	300	290	4	13
2	394	384	4	3	11	384	374	4	4
3	128	119	3	18	12	391	380	4	7
4	377	367	4	9	13	405	397	4	2
5	393	383	4	1	14	173	125	3	15
6	141	131	3	12	15	430	366	5/4	6
7	489	480	5	10	16	355	344	4	8
8	329	319	4	14	17	492	439	5	17
9	359	350	4	5	18	161	139	3	16
OUT	2,975	2,888	35		IN	3,091	2,854	35/36	
					TOTAL	6,066	5,742	70/71	
					STANDARD SCRATCH	72	70		

Copyright Tudor Journals Ltd.

Bunker and tree positions indicated.

**Clondalkin,
Dublin, 22.
Tel: (01) 4592903/4593157.
Fax: (01) 4593498.**

LOCATION: Dublin.
SECRETARY / MANAGER:
A.T. O'Neill.
Tel: 4593157/4593498.
ARCHITECT: James Braid.
PROFESSIONAL: Karl O'Donnell.

Attractive, mature parkland course. The careful placing of trees, bunkers and other hazards soon dispels any feeling of complacency, even with the most accomplished of players.

COURSE INFORMATION

Par 71; SSS 70; Length 5,714 metres.
Visitors: Welcome Monday, Wednesday (am), Thursday, Friday.
Opening Hours: 9.00am – Sunset.
Avoid: Tuesday, Saturday, Sunday.
Ladies Day: Tuesdays.
Juveniles: Must be accompanied by an adult after 6pm. Lessons and club hire available; telephone appointment required.

Green Fees: €55
Mon – Fri (€25 with member).
Societies €50.
Clubhouse Hours:
7.30am – 12.30pm.
Full clubhouse facilities.
Clubhouse Dress: Casual.
Jacket and tie in Dining Room after 8pm.
Clubhouse Facilities:
Full catering and bar;
Summer 10.00am – 9.30pm;
Winter 10.00am – 6.00pm.
Open Competitions:
Husband and wife mixed foursomes – June.

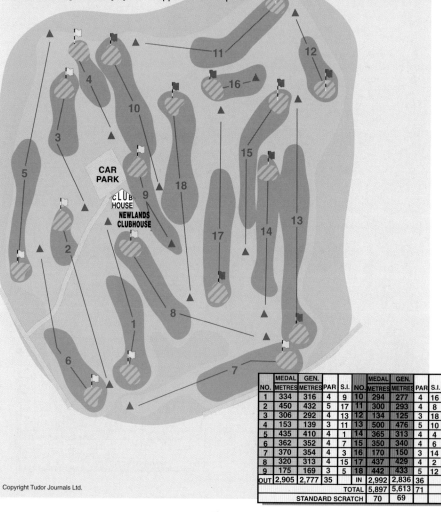

NO.	MEDAL METRES	GEN. METRES	PAR	S.I.	NO.	MEDAL METRES	GEN. METRES	PAR	S.I.
1	334	316	4	9	10	294	277	4	16
2	450	432	5	17	11	300	293	4	8
3	306	292	4	13	12	134	125	3	18
4	153	139	3	11	13	500	476	5	10
5	435	410	4	1	14	365	313	4	4
6	362	352	4	7	15	350	340	4	6
7	370	354	4	3	16	170	150	3	14
8	320	313	4	15	17	437	429	4	2
9	175	169	3	5	18	442	433	5	12
OUT	2,905	2,777	35		IN	2,992	2,836	36	
					TOTAL	5,897	5,613	71	
					STANDARD SCRATCH	70	69		

Copyright Tudor Journals Ltd.

**Newtown House,
St. Margaret's, Co. Dublin.
Tel: (01) 8640324.**

LOCATION: Between Derry Rd,
N2 and the St. Margaret's Rd,
by Dublin Airport.
SECRETARY: Karen Yates
PROFESSIONAL: Mr R. Yates.
Tel: (01) 8640324.
ARCHITECT: Martin Hawtree.

Parkland course with large well guarded greens. Driving range and large tuition staff – excellent pro shop. Full range of hire equipment and full tee time reservation system.

COURSE INFORMATION

Par 71; SSS 69; Length 6,532 yards.
Visitors: Welcome at any time. Bookings may be made 48hrs in advance by telephone.

Ladies: Welcome at any time.
Juveniles: Welcome (limited times) £5 Midweek.
Green Fees: €16 midweek €24 weekends & Bank Holidays (18 holes) Club hire available.
Clubhouse Dress: Casual.
Facilities: Golf shop and coffee shop. Driving range.

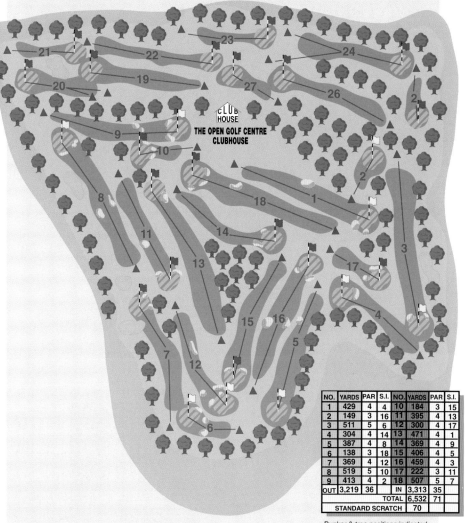

NO.	YARDS	PAR	S.I.	NO.	YARDS	PAR	S.I.
1	429	4	4	10	184	3	15
2	149	3	16	11	395	4	13
3	511	5	6	12	300	4	17
4	304	4	14	13	471	4	1
5	387	4	8	14	369	4	9
6	138	3	18	15	406	4	5
7	369	4	12	16	459	4	3
8	519	5	10	17	222	3	11
9	413	4	2	18	507	5	7
OUT	3,219	36		IN	3,313	35	
				TOTAL	6,532	71	
STANDARD SCRATCH				70			

Bunker & tree positions indicated.

Copyright Tudor Journals Ltd.

Portmarnock, Co. Dublin.
Tel: (01) 8462968 Fax: 8462601.
Email:
secretary@portmanockgolfclub.ie
www.portmarnockgolfclub.ie

LOCATION: North east of Dublin city.
SECETARY/MANAGER: John Quigley.
Tel: (01) 8462968.
ARCHITECT: W. C. Pickeman.

One of the premium links courses in the country. Venue for the Irish Open Championship and given world championship ranking by many critics. The sandy soil of the Portmarnock peninsula makes it ideal for golf. Now has 27 holes with room for more. Its potential as a golf links was realised in 1894. Within two years of the opening of the 18 hole course, Portmarnock hosted its first tournament, the Irish Open Amateur Championship and has hosted the prestigious Irish Open Championship many times since then and was also host for the Walker Cup. New computerised irrigation system.

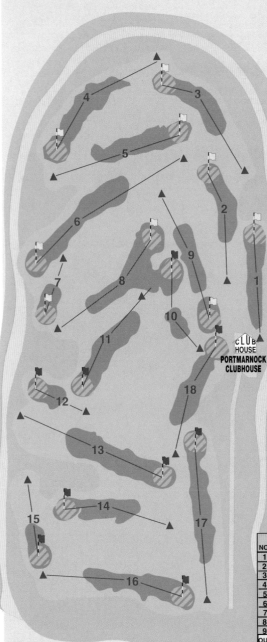

COURSE INFORMATION

Par 72; SSS 74; Length 7,321 yards.
Visitors: Welcome.
Opening Hours: 8am – sunset. Lessons available on weekdays by prior arrangements. Caddy service available by prior arrangement. Handicap Certificate required. Prior arrangement preferred.
Green Fees:
Mon – Fri €130 (not Wednesday); Sat, Sun & Bank Holidays €160.
Clubhouse Hours:
8.00am – close.
Clubhouse Dress:
Jacket and tie for dining room and members bar. Casual attire for Harry Bradshaw Room.
Clubhouse Facilities: Changing rooms and showers.

NO.	MEDAL METRES	GEN METRES	PAR	S.I.	NO.	MEDAL METRES	GEN METRES	PAR	S.I.
1	304	320	4	14	10	467	484	5	15
2	305	329	4	10	11	406	419	4	1
3	172	178	3	12	12	316	329	4	5
4	512	527	5	6	13	135	137	3	17
5	409	431	4	2	14	312	317	4	13
6	462	486	5	18	15	352	364	4	7
7	405	412	4	4	16	354	371	4	11
8	323	342	4	8	17	171	185	3	9
9	139	156	3	16	18	365	408	4	3
OUT	3,031	3,181	36		IN	2,878	3,014	35	
					TOTAL	7,321	6,175	72	
					STANDARD SCRATCH	74	73		

Copyright Tudor Journals Ltd.

NO.	CHAMP METRES	MEDAL METRES	PAR	S.I.	NO.	CHAMP METRES	MEDAL METRES	PAR	S.I.
1	354	320	4	14	10	484	467	5	15
2	360	350	4	10	11	419	406	4	1
3	178	172	3	12	12	329	316	4	5
4	527	512	5	6	13	137	135	3	17
5	431	409	4	2	14	317	312	4	13
6	486	462	5	18	15	364	352	4	7
7	412	405	4	4	16	371	354	4	11
8	342	323	4	8	17	185	171	3	9
9	156	139	3	16	18	408	365	4	3
OUT	3,246	3,092	36		IN	3,014	2,878	35	
					TOTAL	6,260	5,970	71	
					STANDARD SCRATCH		73	72	

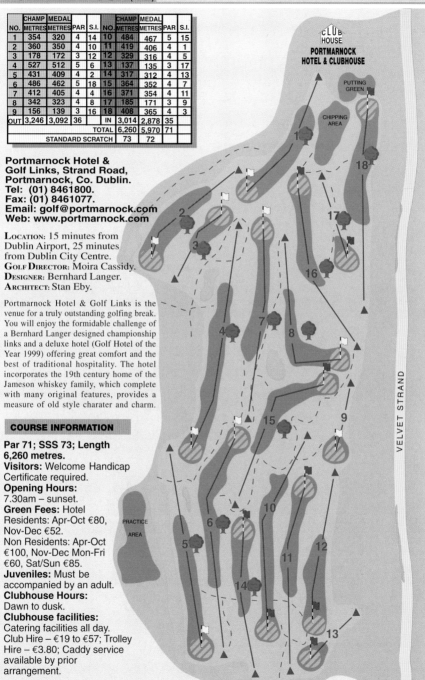

CLUB HOUSE

PORTMARNOCK HOTEL & CLUBHOUSE

PUTTING GREEN

CHIPPING AREA

VELVET STRAND

PRACTICE AREA

Portmarnock Hotel & Golf Links, Strand Road, Portmarnock, Co. Dublin.
Tel: (01) 8461800.
Fax: (01) 8461077.
Email: golf@portmarnock.com
Web: www.portmarnock.com

LOCATION: 15 minutes from Dublin Airport, 25 minutes from Dublin City Centre.
GOLF DIRECTOR: Moira Cassidy.
DESIGNER: Bernhard Langer.
ARCHITECT: Stan Eby.

Portmarnock Hotel & Golf Links is the venue for a truly outstanding golfing break. You will enjoy the formidable challenge of a Bernhard Langer designed championship links and a deluxe hotel (Golf Hotel of the Year 1999) offering great comfort and the best of traditional hospitality. The hotel incorporates the 19th century home of the Jameson whiskey family, which complete with many original features, provides a measure of old style charater and charm.

COURSE INFORMATION

Par 71; SSS 73; Length 6,260 metres.
Visitors: Welcome Handicap Certificate required.
Opening Hours: 7.30am – sunset.
Green Fees: Hotel Residents: Apr-Oct €80, Nov-Dec €52. Non Residents: Apr-Oct €100, Nov-Dec Mon-Fri €60, Sat/Sun €85.
Juveniles: Must be accompanied by an adult.
Clubhouse Hours: Dawn to dusk.
Clubhouse facilities: Catering facilities all day. Club Hire – €19 to €57; Trolley Hire – €3.80; Caddy service available by prior arrangement.

Copyright Tudor Journals Ltd.

Rush, Dublin.
Tel: (01) 8437548.
Fax: (01) 8438177.

LOCATION: Seaside.
SECRETARY: Paul Connolly
Tel: (01) 8438177.

Links course which is playable all year round. Good greens protected by pot bunkers, with undulating fairways. Alternate tees except on two par 3's.

COURSE INFORMATION

Par 70; SSS 69; Length 5,598 metres.
Visitors: Welcome Monday, Tuesday, Friday.
Opening Hours: 8.00am – sunset.
Avoid: Wednesday, Thursday, weekends.
Ladies: Welcome.

Green Fees: €29 (€15 with member).
Clubhouse Hours: 11.00am – 11.00pm.
Clubhouse Dress: Casual. No jeans or shorts allowed.
Clubhouse Facilities: Available on request.
Open Competitions: Seniors only on fourth Friday in May each year.

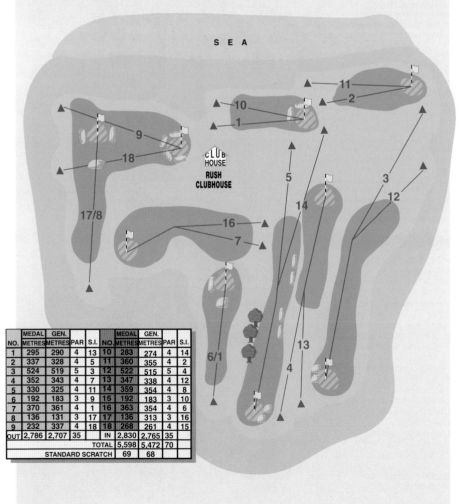

NO.	MEDAL METRES	GEN. METRES	PAR	S.I.	NO.	MEDAL METRES	GEN. METRES	PAR	S.I.
1	295	290	4	13	10	283	274	4	14
2	337	328	4	5	11	360	355	4	2
3	524	519	5	3	12	522	515	5	4
4	352	343	4	7	13	347	338	4	12
5	330	325	4	11	14	359	354	4	8
6	192	183	3	9	15	192	183	3	10
7	370	361	4	1	16	363	354	4	6
8	136	131	3	17	17	136	313	3	16
9	232	337	4	18	18	268	261	4	15
OUT	2,786	2,707	35		IN	2,830	2,765	35	
					TOTAL	5,598	5,472	70	
	STANDARD SCRATCH					69	68		

Copyright Tudor Journals Ltd.

NO.	MEDAL METRES	GEN. METRES	PAR	S.I.	NO.	MEDAL METRES	GEN. METRES	PAR	S.I.
1	370	369	4	3	10	354	346	4	6
2	154	147	3	15	11	267	256	4	18
3	393	386	4	1	12	131	122	3	16
4	419	410	5	17	13	366	357	4	4
5	393	383	4	5	14	449	438	5	14
6	470	465	5	7	15	144	133	3	12
7	144	135	3	13	16	372	362	4	8
8	479	470	5	9	17	485	481	5	10
9	320	311	4	11	18	371	362	4	2
OUT	3,142	3,076	37		IN	2,939	2,857	36	
					TOTAL	6,081	5,933	73	
	STANDARD SCRATCH					72	71		

**Hacketstown, Skerries,
Co. Dublin.
Tel: (01) 8491567/8491204.
Fax: (01) 8491591.**

LOCATION: 20 miles north of Dublin.
MANAGER: Aiden Burns.
Tel: (01) 8491567.
PROFESSIONAL: Jimmy Kinsella.
Tel: (01) 8490925.

**SKERRIES
CLUBHOUSE**

A rolling parkland course with splendid views
of the coastline. Many of the holes demand
accuracy from the tee to the green. The 12th
(par 3) and 18th (par 4) are particularly
attractive holes. The newer 4th (par 5), 6th
(par 5) and 7th (par 3) have enhanced the
course as a good test of golf.

COURSE INFORMATION

**Par 73; SSS 72; Length
6,097 metres.
Visitors:** Welcome Mon – Fri.
Avoid: Wednesday afternoons,
weekends after competition times,
Tuesday after 4.30pm. Members hour
1pm – 2pm (Mon, Thurs, Fri).
Opening Hours:
Sunrise – sunset.
Ladies Day: Tuesday.
Green Fees: €40 weekdays
and €45 weekends.
Juveniles: Must be accompanied
by an adult.
Clubhouse Hours:
9.00am – 11.30pm.
Clubhouse Dress: Casual.
Clubhouse Facilities: Snacks
lunches, dinner available daily.
Open Competitions:
Junior Scratch Cup – May;
Intermediate Scratch Cup – June;
Open Week – July.

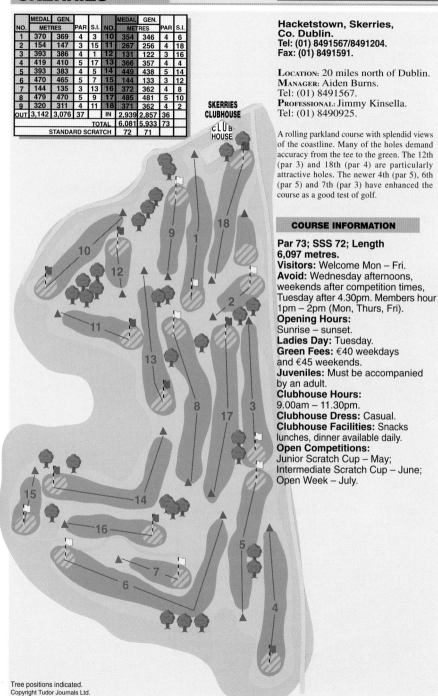

Tree positions indicated.
Copyright Tudor Journals Ltd.

NO.	MEDAL METRES	GEN. METRES	PAR	S.I.	NO.	MEDAL METRES	GEN. METRES	PAR	S.I.
1	400	369	4	4	10	395	383	4	3
2	168	162	3	12	11	373	371	4	1
3	330	324	4	10	12	330	115	4	15
4	251	243	4	16	13	125	115	3	17
5	119	100	3	14	14	285	279	4	13
6	276	251	4	5	15	335	325	4	9
7	440	423	5	18	16	356	344	4	7
8	280	275	4	8	17	170	164	3	11
9	395	383	4	2	18	384	375	4	5
OUT	2,659	2,530	35		IN	2,716	2,676	34	
				TOTAL	5,412	5,206	69	
				STANDARD SCRATCH	68	67		

Lynch Park, Brittas,
Co. Dublin.
Tel: (01) 4582207 /4582183.

SECRETARY: Micheal Downes.
Tel: 01 4582183.
ARCHITECT: W. Sullivan &
D. O'Brien.
PROFESSIONAL: John Dignam.

Not a particularly demanding course, but the scenic views make for a very pleasant and relaxing game with some interesting holes. A "take it easy" course.

COURSE INFORMATION

Par 69; SSS 68; Length 5,412 Metres.
Visitors: Welcome Monday to Friday.
Opening Hours: Sunrise – Sunset.
Avoid: Weekends.
Ladies Day: Tuesday.
Green Fees: Weekdays – €25 (€12.50 with a member).
Juveniles: Welcome.
Clubhouse Hours: 8.30am – 12.00 midnight; Full clubhouse facilities.
Clubhouse Dress: Neat dress.
Clubhouse Facilities: All day.

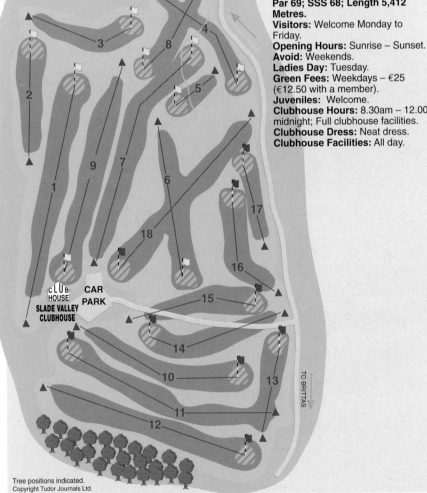

Tree positions indicated.
Copyright Tudor Journals Ltd.

Kilternan, Co. Dublin.
Tel: (01) 2952859.
E-mail:
stepaside@golfdublin.com
www.golfdublin.com

Location: Eight miles south
of Dublin City.
Secretary: Mark Keogh.
Tel: (01) 2952859.
Architect: E. Hackett.

This course was constructed in

1981 by the joint efforts of the Dublin
County Council and G.U.I. who
contributed to the construction costs
of the course. It is popular both from
the availability and the standard of
the course.

COURSE INFORMATION

**Par 74; SSS 70; Length
5,848 metres.**
Visitors: Welcome.

Opening Hours:
8.00am – sunset.
Green Fees: €13.50 Mon –
Fri; €20 Sat/Sun. Senior
Citizens, Students and
unemployed €9.
Juveniles: Welcome.
Clubhouse Hours:
8.00am – sunset.
Clubhouse Dress: Casual.
Clubhouse Facilities: Snacks
available.

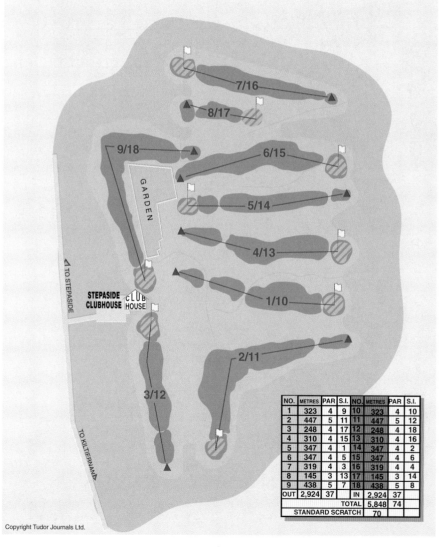

NO.	METRES	PAR	S.I.	NO.	METRES	PAR	S.I.
1	323	4	9	10	323	4	10
2	447	5	11	11	447	5	12
3	248	4	17	12	248	4	18
4	310	4	15	13	310	4	16
5	347	4	1	14	347	4	2
6	347	4	5	15	347	4	6
7	319	4	3	16	319	4	4
8	145	3	13	17	145	3	14
9	438	5	7	18	438	5	8
OUT	2,924	37		IN	2,924	37	
				TOTAL	5,848	74	
				STANDARD SCRATCH	70		

Copyright Tudor Journals Ltd.

Swords Open Golf Course, Balheary Avenue, Swords, Co. Dublin.
Tel: (01) 840 9819
Email: swordsgc@indigo.ie

SECRETARY: Orla McGuinness.
ARCHITECT: Tommy Halpin.

Set along the banks of the Broad Meadow River, Swords Open Golf

Course offers a unique golfing experience to all golfers.

COURSE INFORMATION

Par 71; SSS 70; Length 5612 metres.
Green Fees: €13 Midweek, €20 Weekend.

Clubhouse Hours: Dawn to Dusk.
Clubhouse Dress: Neat.
Clubhouse Facilities: Coffee Shop, Clubhire, Changing Rooms, Showers, Putting Green.

NO.	METRES	PAR	NO.	METRES	PAR
1	135	3	10	360	4
2	487	5	11	320	4
3	120	3	12	440	5
4	460	5	13	180	3
5	345	4	14	350	4
6	360	4	15	145	3
7	470	5	16	315	4
8	255	4	17	170	3
9	400	4	18	300	4
OUT	3,032	37	IN	2,580	34
			TOTAL	5,677	71
			STANDARD SCRATCH	70	

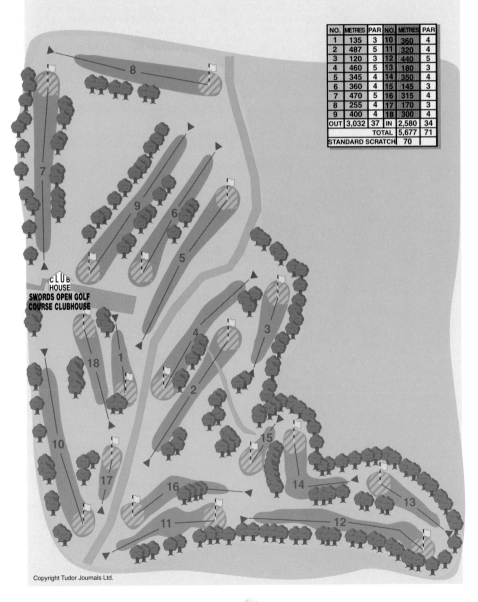

CLUB HOUSE
SWORDS OPEN GOLF COURSE CLUBHOUSE

Copyright Tudor Journals Ltd.

TURVEY

Turvey Golf & Country Club Plc. Turvey Avenue, Donabate, Co. Dublin. Tel: (01) 8435169/179.

LOCATION: 700 yards from Dublin/Belfast Road on A126 Portrane to Donabate Road. MANAGER: Maura Hegarty.

Opened in 1993, this 18 hole golf course is set in 144 acres of beautiful north County Dublin countryside. The tree lined course provides a good challenge for golfers of all standards to test their skills and improve their game. Clubhouse opened in August 1999 provides many welcome features.

COURSE INFORMATION

Par 71; SSS 72; Length 6658 metres. Visitors: Welcome. **Opening Hours:** 8.00am to sunset. **Green Fees:** Mon – Fri €25 Sat/Sun & Bank Holidays €31.

€15 when playing with a member. **Clubhouse Hours:** 8.00am – 10.00pm. **Clubhouse Dress:** Casual. **Clubhouse Facilities:** Snacks and meals available.

NO.	MEDAL METRES	GEN.	PAR	S.I.	NO.	MEDAL METRES	GEN.	PAR	S.I.
1	350	348	4	3	10	311	296	4	9
2	485	480	5	7	11	366	359	4	12
3	315	301	4	13	12	376	365	4	6
4	384	362	4	10	13	172	166	3	11
5	354	344	4	5	14	400	381	4	1
6	289	281	4	16	15	173	159	3	17
7	165	146	3	18	16	503	486	5	14
8	383	368	4	2	17	482	469	5	8
9	175	147	3	15	18	385	366	4	4
OUT	2,900	2,777	35		IN	3,168	3,047	36	
					TOTAL	6,068	5,824	71	
					STANDARD SCRATCH	71	72		

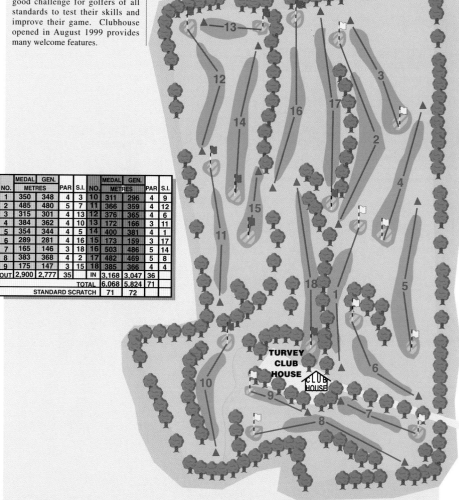

Bunker & tree positions indicated.
Copyright Tudor Journals Ltd.

Westmanstown, Clonsilla, Dublin 15.
Tel: (01) 8205817.
Fax: (01) 8205858.

LOCATION: Two miles from Lucan Village.
HON: SECRETARY: Michael O'Shea.
Tel: (01) 8205817.
ARCHITECT: Mr Eddie Hackett.

Short flat parkland course which has recently undergone additional development.

COURSE INFORMATION

Par 71; SSS 70; Length 5,848 metres.
Visitors: Welcome Sat and Sun - phone for appointment.
Opening Hours:
8am – Sunset.
Ladies: Welcome Tuesdays.
Green Fees: Weekdays €35; Sat, Sun & Bank Hols €40, €15 with member.
Clubhouse Hours:
7.30am – 12.30pm.

Clubhouse Dress: Neat dress essential on course.
Clubhouse Facilities: Full bar and catering facilities all year round.
Open Competitiions: Invitation Four Ball every Wednesday.
Open week: 29th July – 4th August.

NO.	BLUE METRES	WHITE METRES	PAR	S.I.	NO.	BLUE METRES	WHITE METRES	PAR	S.I.
1	394	279	4	16	10	476	466	5	11
2	335	327	4	8	11	268	258	4	17
3	152	143	3	12	12	136	125	3	13
4	397	377	4	6	13	492	483	5	3
5	367	360	4	4	14	364	356	4	7
6	140	118	3	10	15	422	394	4	1
7	491	483	5	14	16	180	161	3	5
8	387	379	4	2	17	435	430	5	15
9	150	142	3	18	18	340	332	4	9
OUT	2,713	2,608	34		IN	2,713	3,005	37	
					TOTAL	5,826	5,613	71	
		STANDARD SCRATCH	71			71			

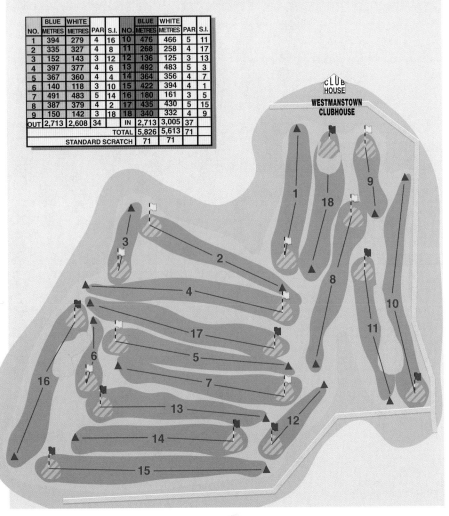

CLUB HOUSE
WESTMANSTOWN CLUBHOUSE

CARRICKMINES   L E I N S T E R   DUBLIN CITY

**Carrickmines,
Dublin 18.
Tel: (01)
2955972/2955941.**

LOCATION: Carrickmines.
SECRETARY: T.J.B. Webb.
Tel: (01) 2882930.

Nine hole inland course situated on hilly country approximately six miles from Dublin. Alternate tees are used.

COURSE INFORMATION

Par 71; SSS 69; Length 6,063 yards.
Visitors: Welcome.
Opening Hours: 8.30am – Sunset.
Avoid: Saturday and Wednesday, & Bank Holidays.
Ladies: Welcome.
Green Fees: 18 hole course €33 week days; €38 Sundays.

9 hole course: €19 weekdays, €22 Sundays.
Juveniles: Must be accompanied by a responsible adult.
Clubhouse Hours: 8.30am – 11.30pm.
Clubhouse Dress: Smart casual.
Clubhouse Facilities: Limited.

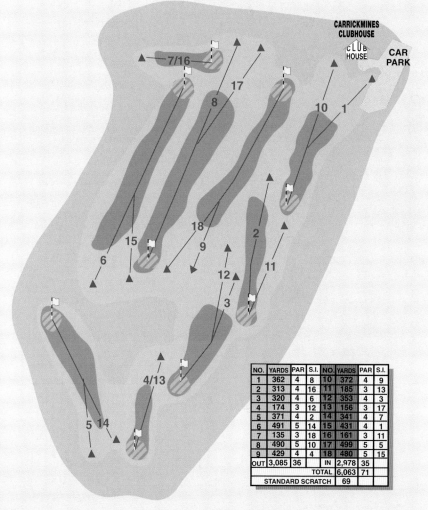

NO.	YARDS	PAR	S.I.	NO.	YARDS	PAR	S.I.
1	362	4	8	10	372	4	9
2	313	4	16	11	185	3	13
3	320	4	6	12	353	4	3
4	174	3	12	13	156	3	17
5	371	4	2	14	341	4	7
6	491	5	14	15	431	4	1
7	135	3	18	16	161	3	11
8	490	5	10	17	499	5	5
9	429	4	4	18	480	5	15
OUT	3,085	36		IN	2,978	35	
				TOTAL	6,063	71	
				STANDARD SCRATCH		69	

Copyright Tudor Journals Ltd.

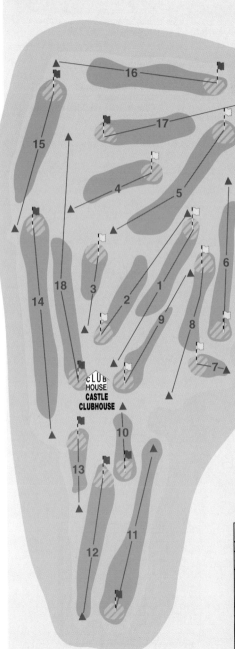

Castle Golf Club, Woodside Drive, Rathfarnham, Dublin 14. Tel: (01) 4904207.

LOCATION: Between Rathfarnham & Churchtown.
SECRETARY: L. Blackburne.
Tel: 4905835.
PROFESSIONAL: D. Kinsella.
Tel: 4920272.
ARCHITECT: Barcroft Pickman & Hood.

Very tight fairways – the Par 4 6th hole regarded as one of the most difficult and yet attractive golf holes. Spectacular views from the Clubhouse.

COURSE INFORMATION

Par 70; SSS 70; Length 5,653 metres.
Visitors: Welcome Monday, Thursday, Friday.
Opening Hours: Sunrise – Sunset.
Avoid: Tuesday, Wednesday afternoons and weekends.
Ladies: Tuesdays. Lessons available by prior arrangements; Caddy trolleys available; telephone appointment required 01 492 2000.
Green Fees: €56.
Juveniles: As Visitors. Lessons available by prior arrangements; Caddy trolleys available; telephone appointment required 01 492 2000.
Clubhouse Hours: 8.30am – 11.30pm; Full clubhouse facilities.
Clubhouse Dress: Casual dress in clubhouse.
Clubhouse Facilities: 10.00am – 10.30pm, lunch, dinner, snacks & bar everyday.
Open Competitions: Ladies Opens; April, July & Aug; Father & Son – July.

NO.	MEDAL YARDS	GEN. YARDS	PAR	S.I.	NO.	MEDAL YARDS	GEN. YARDS	PAR	S.I.
1	492	482	5	9	10	234	216	3	6
2	433	420	4	5	11	401	391	4	2
3	149	130	3	17	12	348	333	4	14
4	317	307	4	13	13	132	122	3	18
5	372	362	4	7	14	371	358	4	8
6	418	401	4	1	15	187	180	3	10
7	177	157	3	15	16	529	509	5	12
8	347	326	4	11	17	500	487	5	16
9	452	440	4	3	18	411	403	4	4
OUT	3,157	3,025	35		IN	3,113	2,999	35	
					TOTAL	6,270	6,024	70	
					STANDARD SCRATCH	68	67		

Copyright Tudor Journals Ltd.

**Clontarf Golf Club,
Donnycarney House,
Malahide Road, Dublin 3.
Tel: (01) 8331892.**

LOCATION: Two miles from city
Centre.
PROFESSIONAL: Mark Callan.
Tel: (01) 331877.
HON. SECRETARY: Brian Curran.
ARCHITECT: Harry Colt.

A pleasant parkland course with a
quarry hole as a special feature.
Convenient city course with good
access.

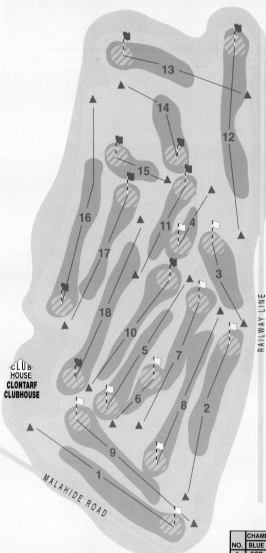

COURSE INFORMATION

**Par 69; SSS 68; Length
5,317 metres.**
Visitors: Welcome Mon – Fri
(telephone first).
Avoid: Monday.
Ladies: Welcome.
Ladies Day: Monday.
Green Fees: €25 Winter, €50
Weekends. €38 Summer, €50
Weekends.
Juveniles: Must be
accompanied by an adult
member if not before 10.00am.
Clubhouse Hours:
9.00am – 12.00pm; full
clubhouse facilities.
Clubhouse Dress:
Casual (no jeans / sneakers).
Collar and tie for dining room
after 8pm preferred.
Clubhouse Facilities: Catering
facilities: meals and snacks
every day.
Open Competitions:
AIB Lord Mayors Cup (Junior
Matchplay) August; Open
Week – June;
Seniors May/Aug

NO.	CHAMP BLUE	SOCIETY GREEN	PAR	S.I.	NO.	CHAMP BLUE	SOCIETY GREEN	PAR	S.I.
1	302	296	4	10	10	361	355	4	7
2	407	399	4	2	11	182	175	3	11
3	284	278	4	14	12	334	328	4	1
4	138	124	3	12	13	248	246	4	13
5	342	335	4	6	14	317	310	4	3
6	130	119	3	18	15	142	134	3	17
7	332	322	4	8	16	353	344	4	5
8	352	347	4	4	17	351	344	4	9
9	289	281	4	16	18	453	447	5	15
OUT	2,576	2,501	34		IN	2,741	2,683	35	
					TOTAL	5,317	5,184	69	
					STANDARD SCRATCH	68	67		

Copyright Tudor Journals Ltd.

**Deer Park Hotel,
Howth, Co. Dublin.
Tel: (01) 8322624/8320273.
Fax: (01) 8392405**
LOCATION: Howth Head.
SECRETARY: David Tighe.

A busy course with both visitors and holiday makers, especially during August, well served by the adjacent Deer Park Hotel – another 18 hole and a 9 hole course are also included as part of the Hotel facilities.

COURSE INFORMATION

**Par 72; SSS 73; Length 6,174 Metres.
Visitors:** Welcome.
Opening Hours: 7.30am – Sunset (weekdays) & 6.30 – Sunset (weekends).
Ladies: Welcome.
Green Fees: €15.50 Mon – Fri; €21.50 Sat / Sun (18 holes).

Juveniles: Welcome. Club Hire and caddy trolleys available.
Clubhouse Hours: Sunrise – Sunset.
Clubhouse facilities: Full catering and bar facilities available at Hotel – other leisure facilities also.

DEER PARK COURSE
18 HOLES

NO.	METRES	PAR	NO.	METRES	PAR
1	382	4	10	399	4
2	203	3	11	178	3
3	322	4	12	360	4
4	335	4	13	292	4
5	372	4	14	510	5
6	190	3	15	153	3
7	467	5	16	312	4
8	395	4	17	393	4
9	477	5	18	503	5
			TOTAL	6,830	72
			SSS	73	

GRARCE O'MALLEY 9
18 HOLES

NO.	METRES	PAR	NO.	METRES	PAR
1	308	4	10	562	5
2	355	4	11	425	4
3	180	3	12	375	4
4	370	4	13	374	4
5	174	3	14	376	4
6	371	4	15	400	4
7	435	4	16	154	3
8	560	5	17	355	4
9	350	4	18	442	5
TOTAL	3,130	35	TOTAL	3,373	37
			SSS	73	

SHORT COURSE
12 HOLES

NO.	METRES	PAR	NO.	METRES	PAR
1	154	3	7	116	3
2	151	3	8	224	3
3	140	3	9	150	3
4	205	3	10	95	3
5	99	3	11	137	3
6	206	3	12	133	3
			TOTAL	1,810	36
			SSS	73	

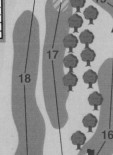

Bunker & tree positions indicated.

Copyright Tudor Journals Ltd.

**Edmondstown Golf Club, Edmondstown, Dublin 16.
Tel: (01) 4931082.**

MANAGER: Selwyn S. Davies.
HON. SECRETARY:
Peter Galbraith.
Tel: (01) 4931082.
PROFESSIONAL: A. Crofton.
Tel: (01) 4941049.

An elevated parkland course with a fair but testing reputation, situated in the Dublin suburbs. Now of Championship standard.

COURSE INFORMATION

Par 71; SSS 71; Length 6,130 metres; 5,892 metres.
Visitors: Welcome to play Monday – Friday.
Opening Hours:
8.00am – 11.30pm.

Ladies: Welcome
Green Fees: Mon – Fri €55; Sat / Sun €65 (by appointment). Lessons and electric caddy service available by prior arrangement. 8th – 13th in July is Invitation Week.
Juveniles: Welcome. Must be accompanied by an adult.
Clubhouse Hours:
8.00am – 11.30pm.
Clubhouse Dress: Collar and tie in restaurant. Neat casual dress on course.
No denims.
Clubhouse Facilities:
Coffee and snacks available 9.00am onwards.
Lunch: 12.30pm – 2.00pm.
Dinner: 6.30pm –11.00pm, to order if later.

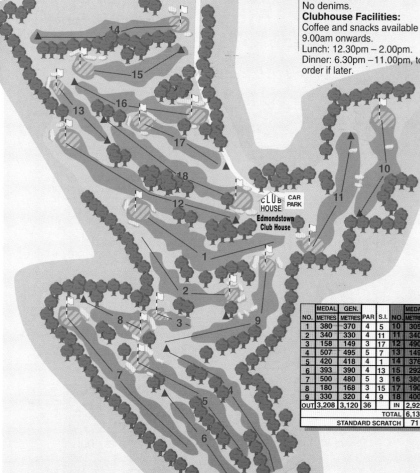

NO.	MEDAL METRES	GEN. METRES	PAR	S.I.	NO.	MEDAL METRES	GEN. METRES	PAR	S.I.
1	380	370	4	5	10	305	298	4	12
2	340	330	4	11	11	340	333	4	4
3	158	149	3	17	12	490	475	5	8
4	507	495	5	7	13	149	140	3	18
5	420	418	4	1	14	376	368	4	2
6	393	390	4	13	15	292	285	4	16
7	500	480	5	3	16	380	330	4	10
8	180	168	3	15	17	190	155	3	14
9	330	320	4	9	18	400	388	4	6
OUT	3,208	3,120	36		IN	2,922	2,772	35	
					TOTAL	6,130	5,892	71	
					STANDARD SCRATCH	71	70		

Bunker & tree positions indicated.
Copyright Tudor Journals Ltd.

ELM PARK

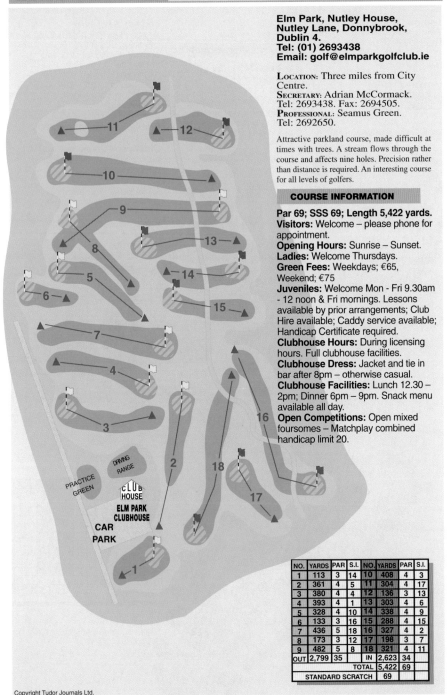

**Elm Park, Nutley House,
Nutley Lane, Donnybrook,
Dublin 4.
Tel: (01) 2693438
Email: golf@elmparkgolfclub.ie**

LOCATION: Three miles from City
Centre.
SECRETARY: Adrian McCormack.
Tel: 2693438. Fax: 2694505.
PROFESSIONAL: Seamus Green.
Tel: 2692650.

Attractive parkland course, made difficult at
times with trees. A stream flows through the
course and affects nine holes. Precision rather
than distance is required. An interesting course
for all levels of golfers.

COURSE INFORMATION

Par 69; SSS 69; Length 5,422 yards.
Visitors: Welcome – please phone for
appointment.
Opening Hours: Sunrise – Sunset.
Ladies: Welcome Thursdays.
Green Fees: Weekdays; €65,
Weekend; €75
Juveniles: Welcome Mon - Fri 9.30am
- 12 noon & Fri mornings. Lessons
available by prior arrangements; Club
Hire available; Caddy service available;
Handicap Certificate required.
Clubhouse Hours: During licensing
hours. Full clubhouse facilities.
Clubhouse Dress: Jacket and tie in
bar after 8pm – otherwise casual.
Clubhouse Facilities: Lunch 12.30 –
2pm; Dinner 6pm – 9pm. Snack menu
available all day.
Open Competitions: Open mixed
foursomes – Matchplay combined
handicap limit 20.

NO.	YARDS	PAR	S.I.	NO.	YARDS	PAR	S.I.
1	113	3	14	10	408	4	3
2	361	4	5	11	304	4	17
3	380	4	4	12	136	3	13
4	393	4	1	13	303	4	6
5	328	4	10	14	338	4	9
6	133	3	16	15	288	4	15
7	436	5	18	16	327	4	2
8	173	3	12	17	198	3	7
9	482	5	8	18	321	4	11
OUT	2,799	35		IN	2,623	34	
				TOTAL	5,422	69	
				STANDARD SCRATCH		69	

Copyright Tudor Journals Ltd.

Torquay Road, Foxrock, Dublin 18.
Tel: (01) 2893992 /2895668.

LOCATION: South Dublin.
SEC/MANAGER: William Daly.
Tel: 2893992. Fax: 2894943.
PROFESSIONAL: David Walker.
Tel: 2893414.
CAPTAIN: J. K. Woods.

Foxrock is a very flat course but it nonetheless provides a reasonable test of golf ability.

COURSE INFORMATION

Par 70; SSS 69; Length 5,667 metres.
Visitors: Welcome Monday, Thursday and Friday mornings.
Opening Hours: 8.00am – Sunset.
Avoid: Tues, Wed, weekends.
Ladies: Welcome.
Lessons and Caddy service available by prior arrangement; Club Hire available.
Juveniles: Welcome. Must be accompanied by an adult

after 5.00pm.
Green Fees: €40, €15 with member.
Clubhouse Hours: 8.30am – 11.30pm.
Clubhouse Dress: Smart/Casual. Jacket and tie after 7pm in the Dining Room.
Clubhouse Facilities: Snacks in the bar; meals on Wednesdays and Saturdays.

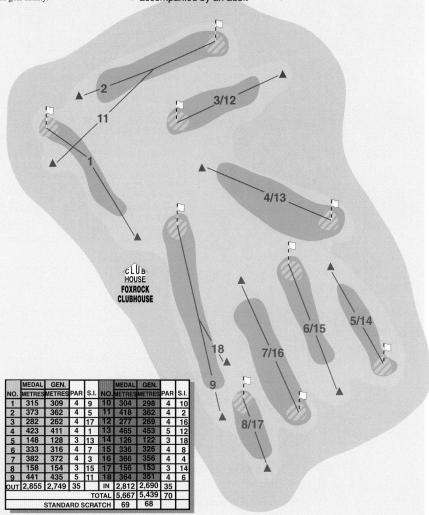

FOXROCK CLUBHOUSE

	MEDAL	GEN.				MEDAL	GEN.		
NO.	METRES	METRES	PAR	S.I.	NO.	METRES	METRES	PAR	S.I.
1	315	309	4	9	10	304	298	4	10
2	373	362	4	5	11	418	362	4	2
3	282	262	4	17	12	277	269	4	16
4	423	411	4	1	13	465	453	5	12
5	148	128	3	13	14	126	122	3	18
6	333	316	4	7	15	336	326	4	8
7	382	372	4	3	16	366	356	4	4
8	158	154	3	15	17	156	153	3	14
9	441	435	5	11	18	364	351	4	6
OUT	2,855	2,749	35		IN	2,812	2,690	35	
					TOTAL	5,667	5,439	70	
			STANDARD SCRATCH			69	68		

Copyright Tudor Journals Ltd.

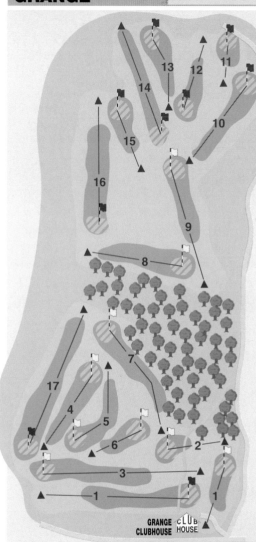

Whitechurch Road, Rathfarnham, Dublin 16.
Tel: (01) 4932889.

LOCATION: South West of Dublin City, four miles from City Centre.
SECRETARY: J. A. O'Donaghue.
Tel: (01) 4932889.
PROFESSIONAL: Dedon Leigh.
Tel: (01) 4932299.

Interesting and popular parkland course, with tree-lined fairways being a major feature, which is both attractive yet challenging.

COURSE INFORMATION

Par 69; SSS 70; Length 5,686 metres.
Visitors: Welcome to play during the week.
Opening Hours: Sunrise – sunset.
Avoid: Weekends (Members Only).
Ladies: Welcome Tuesdays.
Green Fees: €57 Mon – Fri. €45 Weekends.
Juveniles: Welcome. Must be accompanied by an adult after 12.00 noon. Lessons available by prior arrangement; Caddy service available by prior arrangement; telephone appointment advisable.
Clubhouse Hours: 8.00am – 12.30 noon.
Clubhouse Facilities: Full bar and catering facilities.
Clubhouse Dress: Casual / neat (summer). Collar and tie (winter).

NO.	MEDAL METRES	GEN. METRES	PAR	S.I.	NO.	MEDAL METRES	GEN. METRES	PAR	S.I.
1	203	195	3	7	1	390	385	4	2
2	122	111	3	1	1	182	177	3	8
3	389	384	4	7	1	292	287	4	1
4	383	378	4	1	1	329	324	4	6
5	306	301	4	5	1	487	483	5	1
6	170	165	3	1	1	150	145	3	0
7	388	383	4	3	1	385	380	4	1
8	193	188	3	1	1	467	462	5	4
9	319	315	4	5	1	362	357	4	1
OUT	2,47	2,24	3		IN	3,04	3,00	3	
					TOTAL	4	0	6	
					STANDARD SCRATCH	5,51	5,42		

Copyright Tudor Journals Ltd.

Mount Seskin Road, Jobstown, Tallaght, Dublin 24.
Tel: 4520911/4512010.

LOCATION: Tallaght, Blessington Road.
SECRETARY / MANAGER: Mr. Foley. Tel: 4520911.
ARCHITECT: Watty Sullivan & Eddie Hackett.

One of the few courses in Dublin which will give you a full panoramic view of the city. This is a course that appears easy on first sight but can be unexpectedly difficult.

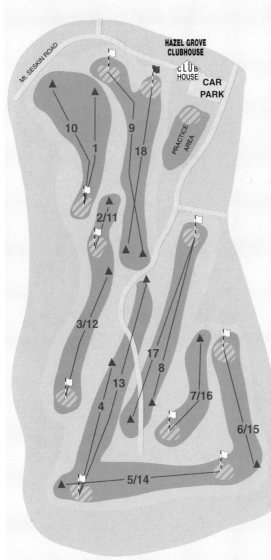

COURSE INFORMATION

Par 69; SSS 67; Length 5,077 metres.
Visitors: Welcome Mon – Fri.
Opening Hours: 8.30am – Sunset.
Green Fees: Mon – Fri €13 (9 holes) €18 (18 holes). Weekends €15 (9 holes) €20 (18 holes).
Avoid: Sat, Sun, Tues afternoon and Thurs mornings.
Juveniles: Welcome. Lessons available by prior arrangement; telephone appointment required.
Clubhouse Hours: 8.30am – 11.30pm.
Clubhouse Dress: Neat / Casual.
Clubhouse Facilities: Full clubhouse facilities. Catering facilities by prior arrangement – Bar snacks throughout the day.
Open Competitions: Tuesday, Fourballs from April – Sept; Open Week June.

NO.	METRES	PAR	S.I.	NO.	METRES	PAR	S.I.
1	306	4	10	10	292	4	11
2	81	3	18	11	110	3	17
3	300	4	7	12	300	4	8
4	352	4	2	13	390	4	1
5	144	3	9	14	322	4	4
6	200	3	12	15	206	3	13
7	242	4	15	16	242	4	16
8	371	4	5	17	431	4	3
9	507	5	14	18	429	4	6
OUT	2,503	34		IN	2,722	34	
				TOTAL	5,225	69	
				STANDARD SCRATCH	67		

Copyright Tudor Journals Ltd.

HOWTH

LEINSTER   **DUBLIN CITY**

St. Fintan's, Carrickbrack Road, Sutton, Dublin 13. Tel: (01) 832 3055.

LOCATION: Nine miles north east of city centre, two miles from Sutton Cross on Sutton side of hill of Howth.
SECRETARY: Ann MacNeice. Tel: 8323055.
PROFESSIONAL: John McGuirk. Tel: 8393895.
ARCHITECT: James Braid.

Moorland course with scenic views of Dublin Bay. Very hilly – a challenge for the athletic golfer.

COURSE INFORMATION

Par 71; SSS 69; Length 5,672 metres.
Visitors: Welcome weekdays except Wednesday.
Opening Hours: 8.30am – 4.00pm.
Avoid: 1.00pm – 2.00pm; All day Wednesday, Thursday afternoons. Lessons available by prior arrangements; Caddy service available by prior arrangements.
Green Fees: €50 daily.

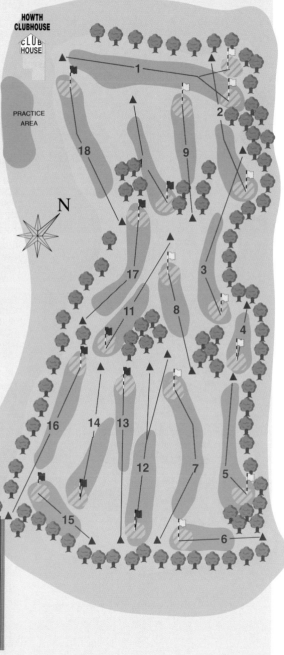

NO.	MEDAL METRES	GEN. METRES	PAR	S.I.	NO.	MEDAL METRES	GEN. METRES	PAR	S.I.
1	313	304	4	10	10	455	446	5	15
2	313	306	4	4	11	395	384	4	1
3	413	407	5	14	12	326	318	4	11
4	150	143	3	8	13	137	133	3	17
5	410/352	345	4	2	14	299	291	4	9
6	281	266	4	12	15	360	345	4	5
7	482	477	5	6	9	253	245	4	18
8	143	131	3	16	17	308	304	4	7
11	314	310	4	3	18	320	311	4	13
OUT	2,819	2,689	36		IN	2,853	2,777	36	
					TOTAL	5,672	5,466	72	
					STANDARD SCRATCH	69	69		

Copyright Tudor Journals Ltd.

Tree positions indicated.

Luttrellstown Castle Golf & Country Club, Castleknock, Dublin 15.
Tel: (01) 808 9988
Email: golf@luttrellstown.ie
www.luttrellstown.ie

LOCATION: West of Dublin City.
SECRETARY: Marty Crawford.
PROFESSIONAL: Edward Doyle.
ARCHITECT: Eddie Conaughton and Nick Bielenberg.

Located just 20 minutes from Dublin city centre. This course is well manicured and regarded as having one of the best putting surfaces. "A Must" for the discerning golfer".

COURSE INFORMATION

Par 72; SSS 73; Length 7,021 Yards.
Ladies Day: Tuesday.

Visitors: Welcome every day.
Green Fees: Mon - Fri. €80, Sat/ Sun. €85.
Juveniles: €30
Clubhouse Hours:
8am-12am in Summer, Winter times vary.
Clubhouse Dress:
Neat dress - no denims.
Clubhouse facilities:
Spike bar, restaurant, pro shop, meeting facilities, function room.

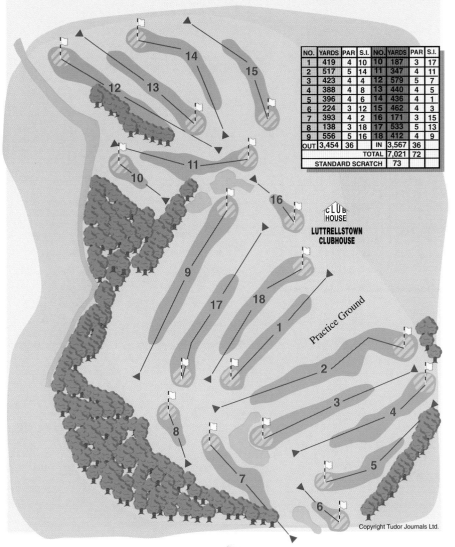

NO.	YARDS	PAR	S.I.	NO.	YARDS	PAR	S.I.
1	419	4	10	10	187	3	17
2	517	5	14	11	347	4	11
3	423	4	4	12	579	5	7
4	388	4	8	13	440	4	5
5	396	4	6	14	436	4	1
6	224	3	12	15	462	4	3
7	393	4	2	16	171	3	15
8	138	3	18	17	533	5	13
9	556	5	16	18	412	4	9
OUT	3,454	36		IN	3,567	36	
				TOTAL	7,021	72	
				STANDARD SCRATCH	73		

CLUB HOUSE
LUTTRELLSTOWN CLUBHOUSE

Practice Ground

Copyright Tudor Journals Ltd.

Lower Churchtown Road, Dublin 14.
Tel: (01) 4976090.
Fax: (01) 4976008.

LOCATION: South Dublin three miles from the city centre.
GENERAL MANAGER: Eamonn Lawless.
PROFESSIONAL: John Harnett.
Tel: (01) 4977072.
ARCHITECT: Freddie Davis.

Well established parkland course on the suburbs of Dublin. One of the many Dublin clubs that provide convenient locations.

COURSE INFORMATION

Par 71; SSS 69; Length 5,638 metres.
Visitors: Welcome.
Opening Hours: Sunrise – Sunset.
Avoid: Weekends.
Ladies: Welcome.
Green Fees: €80 Mon – Fri.
Juveniles: Welcome.
Lessons available by prior arrangement; club hire available; caddy service

available by prior arrangement. Telephone appointment advisable.
Handicap Certificate required.
Clubhouse Hours: 9.00am – 11.30pm.
Clubhouse Dress: Neat/casual.
Clubhouse Facilities: Full clubhouse and catering facilities.

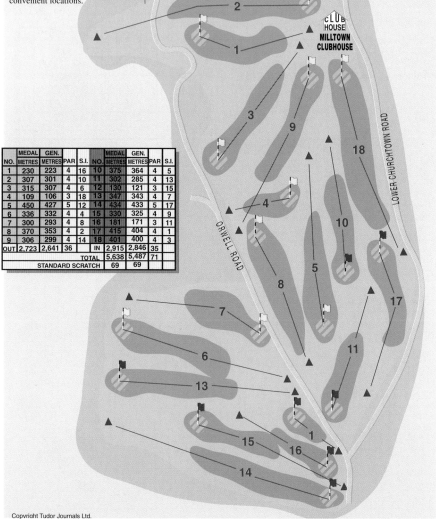

	MEDAL	GEN.				MEDAL	GEN.		
NO.	METRES	METRES	PAR	S.I.	NO.	METRES	METRES	PAR	S.I.
1	230	223	4	16	10	375	364	4	5
2	307	301	4	10	11	302	285	4	13
3	315	307	4	6	12	130	121	3	15
4	109	106	3	18	13	347	343	4	7
5	450	427	5	12	14	434	433	5	17
6	336	332	4	4	15	330	325	4	9
7	300	293	4	8	16	181	171	3	11
8	370	353	4	2	17	415	404	4	1
9	306	299	4	14	18	401	400	4	3
OUT	2,723	2,641	36		IN	2,915	2,846	35	
					TOTAL	5,638	5,487	71	
					STANDARD SCRATCH	69	69		

Copyright Tudor Journals Ltd.

**Newtown, Rathfarnham,
Dublin 16
Tel: (01) 4931201.**

LOCATION: Two miles from Rathfarnham
Village.
SECRETARY/MANAGER: C Mc Inerny.
PROFESSIONAL: Brian O'Hara.
Tel: (01) 4931201.
ARCHITECT: John Jacob.

Parkland course, with attractive
scenery, mature trees and spinneys.
Greens are built on the natural lie of
the ground.

COURSE INFORMATION

**Par 71; SSS 70; Length
5,815 metres.
Visitors:** Welcome Monday,
Wednesday & Friday.
Opening Hours: 8.30am –
Sunset.
Avoid: Tues, Sat, Sun & Bank
Holidays.
Ladies: Welcome (Handicap
Certificate required).
Green Fees: €15 Mon – Fri
(€30 without member); €38
Sun (with a member).
Juveniles: Welcome with
member only. Lessons
available by prior
arrangements.
Clubhouse Hours: 10.30am –
11.00pm.
Clubhouse Dress: Jacket and
tie after 7.30pm.
Clubhouse Facilities: Light
snacks daily; meals by prior
arrangements.

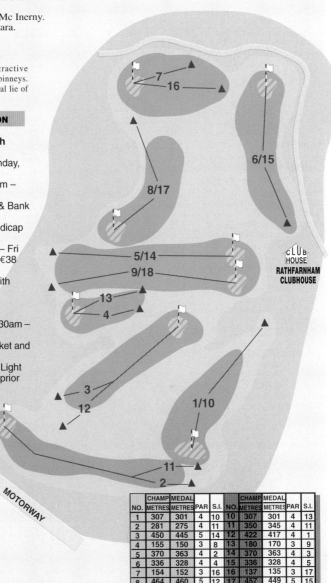

NO.	CHAMP METRES	MEDAL METRES	PAR	S.I.	NO.	CHAMP METRES	MEDAL METRES	PAR	S.I.
1	307	301	4	10	10	307	301	4	13
2	281	275	4	11	11	350	345	4	11
3	450	445	5	14	12	422	417	4	1
4	155	150	3	8	13	180	170	3	9
5	370	363	4	2	14	370	363	4	3
6	336	328	4	15	15	336	328	4	5
7	154	152	3	16	16	137	135	3	17
8	464	460	5	12	17	457	449	5	15
9	375	371	4	6	18	343	340	4	7
OUT	2,892	2,845	36		IN	2,902	2,848	35	
					TOTAL	5,794	5,693	71	
					STANDARD SCRATCH	70	70		

Copyright Tudor Journals Ltd.

Dollymount, Dublin 3.
Tel: (01) 833 6346/833 1262.
Fax: (01) 833 6504

Location: Three miles north east from the city centre along the coast road.
Secretary: John A. Lambe.
Tel: (01) 833 6346.
Professional: Leonard Owens.
Tel: (01) 833 6477.
Architect: H. S. Colt.

The links is 6,922 yards (6,330 metres) in length and is laid out in the old traditional links style resembling St Andrews. Fine fescue grasses provide an ideal basis for greens and fairways and a wandering wind adds that extra hazard. Fine bunkers, close lies and subtle trapping are all features of Royal Dublin.

COURSE INFORMATION

Par 72; SSS 73; Length 6,330 Metres.
Visitors: Please telephone for availability.
Opening Hours: 8am – Sunset.
Avoid: Wed. and Saturday.
Ladies: Welcome. Lessons available by prior arrangements; Club Hire available; Caddy service available by prior arrangements. Telephone appointment required.
Green Fees: €100 Mon – Thur; €115 Fri/Sat/Sun.
Clubhouse Hours: 8am – midnight.
Clubhouse Dress: Jacket and tie in Clubhouse; Casual in Grill Room and Christy O'Connor Room.
Clubhouse Facilities: Full facilities available.

ROYAL DUBLIN CLUB
CLUBHOUSE HOUSE

NO.	METRES	PAR	S.I.	NO.	METRES	PAR	S.I.
1	361	4	7	10	427	4	3
2	445	5	17	11	493	5	13
3	363	4	4	12	188	3	10
4	163	3	12	13	425	4	1
5	423	4	2	14	455	5	15
6	180	3	16	15	397	4	6
7	338	4	9	16	245	4	18
8	465	5	11	17	345	4	8
9	164	3	14	18	453	4	5
OUT	2,902	35		IN	3,428	37	
				TOTAL	6,330	72	
				STANDARD SCRATCH		73	

Copyright Tudor Journals Ltd.

Bunker positions indicated.

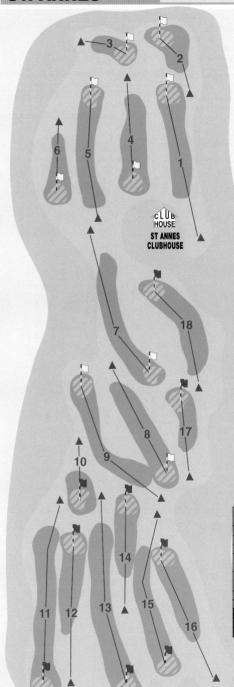

North Bull Island Nature Reserve, North Bull Island, Dublin, 5.
Tel: 8336471 Fax: 8334618

LOCATION: Five miles north east of Dublin.
MANAGER/SECRETARY: Shirley Sleator.
ARCHITECT: E. Hackett and Committee.

This links course is located in the heart of one of the finest bird sanctuaries in Ireland. The rich wildlife adds an additional dimension to the enjoyment of golf.

COURSE INFORMATION

Par 70; SSS 70; Length 5,669 metres.
Visitors: Welcome any time except during Gents or Ladies Competitions.
Opening Hours: 8.30am – 7.00pm.
Avoid: Days of Competitions.
Ladies: Welcome.
Green Fees: Weekdays – €45, weekends and Bank Holidays – €60.
Clubhouse Hours: 8.30am – 11.00pm.
Clubhouse Dress: Casual/Neat.
Clubhouse Facilities: Full bar and catering. Catering Tel: 8332797. Bar Tel: 8331797.
Open Competitions: Open weeks – July & December.

NO.	CHAMP METRES	MEDAL METRES	PAR	S.I.	NO.	CHAMP METRES	MEDAL METRES	PAR	S.I.
1	446	437	5	15	10	139	134	3	16
2	334	329	4	11	11	477	472	5	10
3	139	134	3	17	12	359	354	4	6
4	353	348	4	7	13	419	414	5	8
5	349	344	4	5	14	196	191	3	12
6	153	148	3	13	15	363	358	4	2
7	432	427	4	1	16	285	280	4	18
8	342	337	4	3	17	172	167	3	14
9	348	343	4	9	18	363	358	4	4
OUT	2,896	2,847	35		IN	2,773	2,728	35	
					TOTAL	5,669	5,575	70	
					STANDARD SCRATCH		70	69	

Copyright Tudor Journals Ltd.

ST. MARGARET'S

**St Margarets Golf &
Country Club, St.
Margarets, Co. Dublin.
Tel: (01) 864 0400.
Fax: (01) 864 0289.
Email:
sales@stmargarets.net
www.st-margarets.net**

LOCATION: Eight miles north of
city centre.
CHEIF EXECUTIVE:**Brian Begley**
RESERVATIONS MANAGER:
Gillian Harris.
ARCHITECT: Tom Craddock &
Pat Ruddy

Home to the Women's Irish Open and
the PGA Irish Seniors Open, St
Margaret's measures just under 7,000
yards off the back tees and the modern
design approach makes use of water
hazards and sculptured mounding on a
level new to Irish golf. Every effort has
been made to make the course a
challenge full of variety and drama but
very playable by all standards of
player. 15 mins from city centre.

COURSE INFORMATION

**Par 73; SSS 73; Length
6,917 yards.**

Visitors: Welcome everyday.
Opening Hours: Sunrise –
Sunset.
Ladies: Welcome.
Green Fees:
Mon – Wed €45(L) £60(H),
Thurs & Sun €55(L) £70(H),
Fri & Sat €65(L) £75(H),
Juveniles: Welcome.
Clubhouse Hours: 8.00am –
11.00pm.
Clubhouse Dress: Neat.
Clubhouse Facilities: Full
catering facilities available.
Cobra Golf Academy.

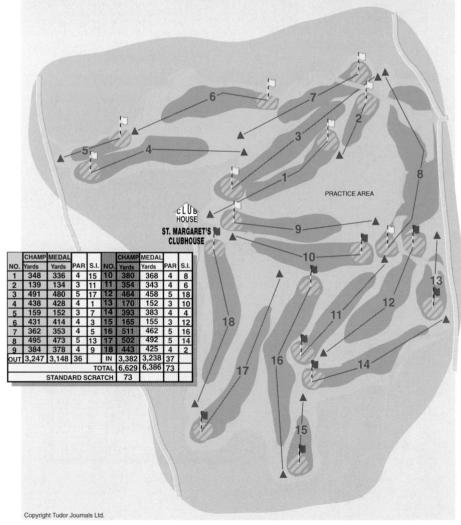

NO.	CHAMP Yards	MEDAL Yards	PAR	S.I.	NO.	CHAMP Yards	MEDAL Yards	PAR	S.I.
1	348	336	4	15	10	380	368	4	8
2	139	134	3	11	11	354	343	4	6
3	491	480	5	17	12	464	458	5	18
4	438	428	4	1	13	170	152	3	10
5	159	152	3	7	14	393	383	4	4
6	431	414	4	3	15	165	155	3	12
7	362	353	4	5	16	511	462	5	16
8	495	473	5	13	17	502	492	5	14
9	384	378	4	9	18	443	425	4	2
OUT	3,247	3,148	36		IN	3,382	3,238	37	
					TOTAL	6,629	6,386	73	
	STANDARD SCRATCH						73		

Copyright Tudor Journals Ltd.

STACKSTOWN

**Kellystown Road,
Rathfarnham, Dublin 16.
Tel: (01) 494 2338.**
Email: stackstowngc@eircom.net
www.stackstowngolfclub.com

LOCATION: South West Dublin,
2kms after exit 13, M50.
SECRETARY: Paul Kennedy.
Tel: (01) 494 1993.
ARCHITECT: Shaffreys.

A parkland course in the foothills of
the Dublin mountains, affording
breathtaking views of the city & bay.

COURSE INFORMATION

**Par 72; SSS 68; Length
5,952 metres.**
Visitors: Welcome Monday,
Thursday, Friday & Saturday.
Opening Hours: Sunrise –
Sunset.
Avoid: Sundays(pm) and Bank
holidays.
Green Fees: €30 Mon – Fri;
Sun; €38.
Clubhouse Hours: 8.30am –
11.30pm.
Clubhouse Dress:
Neat dress essential.
Clubhouse Facilities: Full bar,
catering & function facilities
available. Societies/ groups at
reduced fees.
Open Competitions:
Open Week – Last week in May

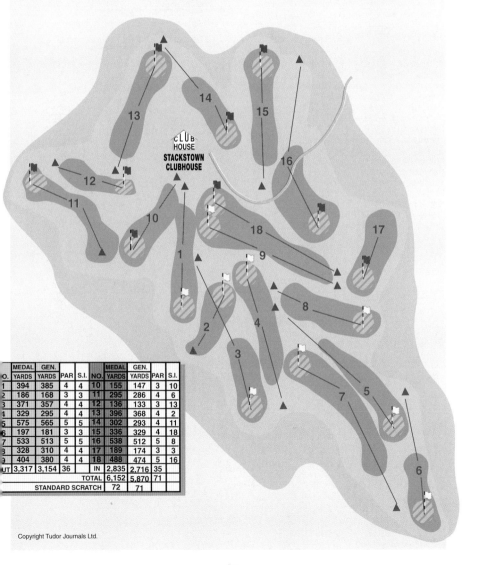

NO.	MEDAL YARDS	GEN. YARDS	PAR	S.I.	NO.	MEDAL YARDS	GEN. YARDS	PAR	S.I.
1	394	385	4	4	10	155	147	3	10
2	186	168	3	3	11	295	286	4	6
3	371	357	4	4	12	136	133	3	13
4	329	295	4	4	13	396	368	4	2
5	575	565	5	5	14	302	293	4	11
6	197	181	3	3	15	336	329	4	18
7	533	513	5	5	16	538	512	5	8
8	328	310	4	4	17	189	174	3	3
9	404	380	4	4	18	488	474	5	16
OUT	3,317	3,154	36		IN	2,835	2,716	35	
					TOTAL	6,152	5,870	71	
					STANDARD SCRATCH		72	71	

Copyright Tudor Journals Ltd.

SUTTON

L E I N S T E R **DUBLIN CITY**

**Cush Point, Sutton,
Dublin 13.
Tel: (01) 8323013.**

LOCATION: Ten minutes from City centre.
HONORARY SECRETARY: Seamus Carroll.
Tel: (01) 8322965.
PROFESSIONAL: N. Lynch.
Tel: (01) 8321703.
MANAGER: Micheal Healy.

Links course with very narrow fairways and one of the main features is that the course is surrounded by water.

NO.	YARDS	PAR	S.I.	NO.	YARDS	PAR	S.I.
1	310	4	13	10	310	4	14
2	346	4	15	11	346	4	16
3	514	5	11	12	514	5	12
4	320	4	5	13	320	4	2
5	171	3	7	14	171	3	8
6	107	3	17	15	107	3	18
7	351	4	9	16	351	4	10
8	387	4	3	17	387	4	4
9	383	4	1	18	383	4	6
OUT	2,889	35		IN	2,889	35	
				TOTAL	5,778	70	
STANDARD SCRATCH							

COURSE INFORMATION

Par 70; SSS 67; Length 5,718 yards.
Visitors: Welcome.
Opening Hours: 9.00am – sunset.
Avoid: Tuesday and Saturday.
Green Fees: €35 Mon – Fri (€20 with member); €45 Sat, Sun & Bank Holidays.
Juveniles: Welcome no weekend play. Lessons by prior arrangments. Caddy cars available.
Clubhouse Hours: 9.00am onwards.
Clubhouse Dress: Casual, no denims or trainers.
Clubhouse Facilities: Full clubhouse facilities, by arrangement.

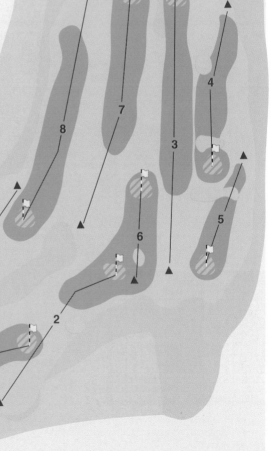

N

cLUb
HOUSE
**SUTTON
CLUBHOUSE**

Copyright Tudor Journals Ltd.

76

**Geraldine, Athy,
Co. Kildare.
Tel: (0507) 31729.
Fax: (0507) 34710.
www.athygolfclub.com.**

LOCATION: Off the Kildare Road.
SECRETARY: Pat Fleming.
Tel: (0507) 31729.
PUBLIC RELATIONS OFFICE:
Ger Ennis. Tel: (087) 2481471.

The club was founded in 1906 as a 9 hole course and extended to 18 holes in 1993 among the features of this parkland course is a river which comes into play in four holes. All the new greens are totally sand based. Two of the par three's are over 200 yards long.The 16th hole has a deep "valley of sin" to the right and is 420 yards long. Heading for home the 17th is a unique dog-leg to the right down a hill to a two-tier elevated green.

COURSE INFORMATION

**Par 71; SSS 69;
Length 6,340 yards.
Visitors:** Welcome Mon – Fri.
Avoid: Weekends and Bank holidays.
Ladies: Thursday.

Green Fees: 20 Mon – Fri; 30 Sat & Sun, Bank Holidays.
Juveniles: Wed & Fri mornings during holiday periods.
Clubhouse Hours: Mon–Sun 10am–11pm.
Clubhouse Dress: Casual.
Clubhouse Facilities: By arrangement.
Open Competitions: Open Week – mid June; Husband and Wife – August.

NO.	CHAMP YARDS	MEDAL YARDS	PAR	S.I.	NO.	CHAMP YARDS	MEDAL YARDS	PAR	S.I.
1	354	349	4	6	10	402	384	4	3
2	176	162	3	14	11	336	329	4	15
3	301	291	4	18	1	203	188	3	9
4	369	356	4	8	13	487	478	5	13
5	154	147	3	10	14	217	203	3	7
6	421	411	4	2	15	365	356	4	11
7	373	364	4	4	16	423	413	4	1
8	503	499	5	16	17	387	374	4	5
9	362	354	4	12	18	507	501	5	17
OUT	3,013	2,933	35		IN	3,327	3,226	36	
					TOTAL	6,340	6,159	71	
					STANDARD SCRATCH	70	69		

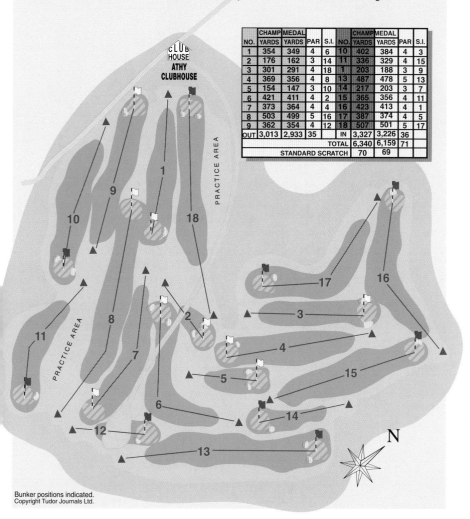

Bunker positions indicated.
Copyright Tudor Journals Ltd.

BODENSTOWN

Sallins, Co. Kildare.
Tel: (045) 897096.
Fax: (045) 898126.

LOCATION: Four miles outside
Naas near Bodenstown
graveyard.
SECRETARY: Bernadette Mather.
Tel: (045) 897096.

The Old Course in Bodenstown, with
its ample fairways and large greens,
some of which are raised, provides
more than a fair test of golf. The

Ladyhill Course, also at Bodenstown,
is a little shorter but still affords a fair
challenge.

COURSE INFORMATION

Par 72; SSS 70; Length
6,132 yards (Old Course).
Visitors: Welcome.
Opening Hours:
Sunrise – sunset.
Avoid: Main course at
weekends. Ladyhill course
available.

Ladies: Welcome Mondays.
Green Fees: €17 Main
Course; €14 Ladyhill Course.
Juveniles: Welcome.
Clubhouse Hours: 9am –
11pm. Full clubhouse facilities.
Clubhouse Dress: Informal.
Clubhouse Facilities: Full
catering available.
Open Competitions: Open
Week – June.

NO.	CHAMP METRES	MEDAL METRES	PAR	S.I.	NO.	CHAMP METRES	MEDAL METRES	PAR	S.I.
1	317	277	4	13	10	338	322	4	10
2	363	354	4	3	11	161	133	3	12
3	484	459	5	15	12	366	348	4	2
4	382	359	4	5	13	336	320	4	16
5	384	363	4	1	14	145	137	3	8
6	153	137	3	7	15	476	446	5	18
7	336	308	4	17	16	359	316	4	6
8	186	172	3	11	17	370	347	4	4
9	468	440	5	14	18	508	488	5	9
OUT	3,073	2,869	36		IN	3,059	2,857	36	
					TOTAL	6,132	5,726	72	
		STANDARD SCRATCH	71	70					

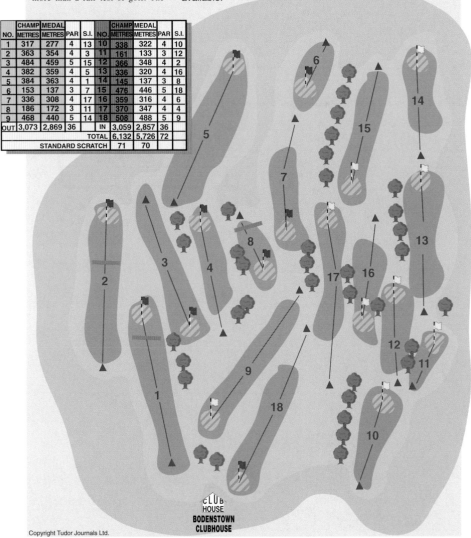

CLUB
HOUSE
BODENSTOWN
CLUBHOUSE

Copyright Tudor Journals Ltd.

Castlewarden, Straffan, Co. Kildare.
Tel: Dublin (01) 4588218 (clubhouse).
Email: castlewarden@clubi.ie
www.castlewardengolfclub.com
LOCATION: Between Naas and Newlands Cross.
SECRETARY:Fiona Kane.
Tel: (01) 4589254 (office).
PROFESSIONAL: Gerry Egan.
Tel: (01) 4588219.

Throughout this relatively new course there are several scenic views of both the Dublin and Wicklow mountains.

The course features gently-contoured greens, with elevated tees and water hazards.

COURSE INFORMATION

Par 72; SSS 70; Length 6,624 yards.
Visitors: Welcome to play.
Opening Hours: Daylight to dusk.
Avoid: Saturdays and Sundays.
Ladies: Welcome.
Green Fees: Weekdays – €25 (€16 with a member –

max. of 3 guests); weekend – €33.50 (€22 with a member). Lessons available by prior arrangement. Club Hire available also.
Clubhouse Hours:
1.00pm – 11.30pm (weekdays) & 11.00am – 11.30pm (weekends).
Clubhouse Dress: Neat.
Clubhouse Facilities: Available on request.

NO.	CHAMP YARDS	MEDAL YARDS	PAR	S.I.	NO.	CHAMP YARDS	MEDAL YARDS	PAR	S.I.
1	506	488	5	7	10	262	255	4	18
2	185	180	3	15	11	378	366	4	12
3	445	439	4	1	12	400	394	4	8
4	333	320	4	11	13	153	148	3	14
5	399	391	4	9	14	392	387	4	6
6	408	403	4	3	15	398	384	4	10
7	374	365	4	5	16	420	410	4	2
8	530	480	5	17	17	172	166	3	16
9	379	372	4	13	18	553	548	5	4
OUT	3,562	3,438	37		IN	3,128	3,058	35	
					TOTAL	6,690	6,496	72	
					STANDARD SCRATCH	71	70		

CLUB HOUSE
CASTLEWARDEN CLUBHOUSE
PUTTING GREEN
PRACTICE AREA

Bunker & Tree positions indicated.
Copyright Tudor Journals Ltd.

Celbridge Elm Hall Golf Club, Celbridge, Co. Kildare. Tel: (01)6288208.

LOCATION: 1km of the Lucan/Celbridge Road. GENERAL MANAGER: Seamus Lawless. Tel: (01) 628 8208.

Beautiful parkland course with mature trees and outstanding fairways. The excellent quality of the greens at Celbridge Elm Hall are already legendary amongst the golfing fraternity of County Kildare and the surrounding counties.

Three lakes are a major feature and make the course an interesting and challenging one to play.

COURSE INFORMATION

Par 70; SSS 70; Length 5,922 yards.
Visitors: Welcome.
Opening Hours: Sunrise/sunset.
Avoid: Early Sat/Sun.
Green Fees: Weekdays €14 (9 holes) & €21 (18 holes).

Weekends/Bank Holidays €16 (9 holes) & €25 (18 holes). Guests, Seniors and Juniors discounted.
Ladies: No restrictions.
Juveniles: Restricted.
Clubhouse Hours: Weekdays 9am – sunset & Weekends 7.30am – sunset.
Clubhouse Facilities: Bar, catering & showers etc.
Also available: 18 hole par 3 and 18 hole pitch & put.

NO.	YARDS	PAR	S.I.	NO.	YARDS	PAR	S.I.
1	161	3	13	10	161	3	16
2	475	5	12	11	424	4	2
3	285	4	4	12	385	4	18
4	337	4	11	13	337	4	12
5	419	4	1	14	462	5	4
6	380	4	6	15	360	4	8
7	384	4	8	16	361	4	10
8	132	3	17	17	132	3	14
9	315	4	16	18	315	4	6
OUT	2,695	35		IN	2,957	35	
				TOTAL	5,922	70	
	STANDARD SCRATCH				70		

CAR PARK

PITCH & PUTT

CELBRIDGE CLUB HOUSE

CLUB HOUSE

Bunker & tree positions indicated.
Copyright Tudor Journals Ltd.

**Little Curragh, Kildare,
Co. Kildare.
Tel: (045)**

LOCATION: One mile west of Kildare town.
Hon. SECRETARY: Frank Curran.
PROFESSIONAL: Mark O'Boyle.
Tel: (045) 521295.

A course which is typical to many in the area with all the colour of the gorse and heather. Flat and relatively straight forward to play. A good choice for the middle and high handicappers.

COURSE INFORMATION

**Par 71; SSS 70; Length
5,738 metres.
Visitors:** Welcome.
Opening Hours: Sunrise – sunset.
Avoid: Wednesday, Sundays (Club Competitions).
Ladies Day: Wednesday.

Green Fees: €20 Weekday €10 with member; €25 Weekend €15 with member.
Juveniles: Welcome.
Club Hire available; telephone appointment required.
Clubhouse Hours: 11.00am – 11.30pm.
Clubhouse Dress: Casual.
Clubhouse Facilities: 9.00am – 10.30pm daily (full facilities).

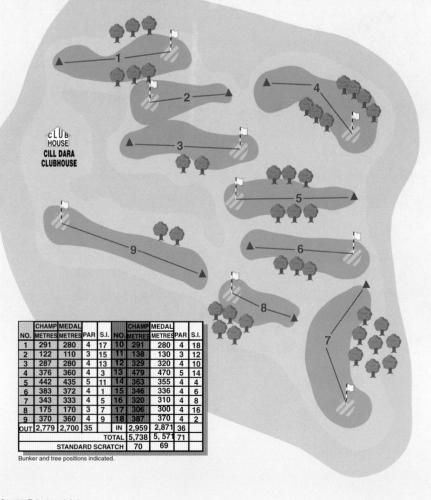

CILL DARA
CLUBHOUSE

NO.	CHAMP METRES	MEDAL METRES	PAR	S.I.	NO.	CHAMP METRES	MEDAL METRES	PAR	S.I.
1	291	280	4	17	10	291	280	4	18
2	122	110	3	15	11	138	130	3	12
3	287	280	4	13	12	329	320	4	10
4	376	360	4	3	13	479	470	5	14
5	442	435	5	11	14	363	355	4	4
6	383	372	4	1	15	346	336	4	6
7	343	333	4	5	16	320	310	4	8
8	175	170	3	7	17	306	300	4	16
9	370	360	4	9	18	387	370	4	2
OUT	2,779	2,700	35		IN	2,959	2,871	36	
					TOTAL	5,738	5,571	71	
	STANDARD SCRATCH					70	69		

Bunker and tree positions indicated.

Copyright Tudor Journals Ltd.

**Craddockstown Golf Club,
Blessington Road,
Naas, Co. Kildare.
Tel: (045) 897610.**

Location: 11/2 miles from Naas town.
Manager: Gay Nolan.
Tel: (045) 897610.
Architect: A. Spring.

Testing, spacious course with young parkland trees, which when mature will increase accuracy needed. Greens well protected and some fairways include tricky water hazards.

COURSE INFORMATION

**Par 71; SSS 70; Length
6,134 metres.
Visitors:** Welcome any day.
Opening Hours:
Sunrise to Sunset.
Avoid: Saturdays and Sundays until 3.00pm.
Ladies: Tuesdays, Saturdays* & Sundays* (*limited tee times).
Green Fees: Mon-Thurs:€28
Fri/Sat/Sun : €35
Juveniles: €7
Clubhouse Hours:
9.30am – 11.30pm.

Clubhouse Dress:
Smart and neat, casual.
Clubhouse Facilities:
Changing rooms, showers, bar and catering by arrangement.
Open Competitions:
Semi-Opens Wednesdays; Open Week July.

NO.	METRES	PAR	S.I.	NO.	METRES	PAR	S.I.
1	358	4	4	10	327	4	15
2	191	3	13	11	180	4	7
3	444	5	10	12	319	3	17
4	382	4	5	13	416	4	1
5	367	4	6	14	297	4	11
6	180	3	18	15	208	5	5
7	388	4	2	16	328	4	9
8	460	5	14	17	361	3	3
9	400	4	8	18	519	5	13
OUT	3,170	36		IN	2,955	35	
				TOTAL	6,125	71	
				STANDARD SCRATCH		70	

CLUB
HOUSE
**CRADDOCKSTOWN
GOLF CLUB**

Bunker & tree positions indicated.
Copyright Tudor Journals Ltd.

Curragh, Co. Kildare.
Tel: (045) 441714/441238.

LOCATION: Thirty two miles
south east of Dublin.
SECRETARY: Ann Culleton.
Tel: (045) 441714.
PROFESSIONAL: G.Burke.
Tel: (045) 441896.

A long testing course of over 6,000
meters. Hazards include tree lined
fairways, furze bushes and grazing
sheep. Every hole presents a separate
and distinctive challenge. A scenic
course with panoramic views of
Kildare and the Wicklow Mountains.

COURSE INFORMATION

**Par 72; SSS 71; Length
6,001 metres.**
Visitors: Welcome, advance
enquires are essential.
Opening Hours: Sunrise –
Sunset.
Avoid: Tuesdays, Sat & Sun.
Ladies: Tuesday.

Green Fees: €30 Mon – Fri;
€35 Sat & Sun.
Juveniles: Welcome but must
be accompanied by an adult.
Lessons & club hire available by
prior arrangement with the Club
Professional; telephone for
appointment.
Clubhouse Hours: 10am –
10pm (all year).
Clubhouse Dress: Neat.
Club Competitions: June &
July.

NO.	CHAMP METRES	MEDAL METRES	PAR	S.I.	NO.	CHAMP METRES	MEDAL METRES	PAR	S.I.
1	477	473	5	11	10	170	160	3	10
2	335	325	4	3	11	400	392	4	4
3	272	267	4	17	12	391	361	4	6
4	187	179	3	5	13	285	275	4	18
5	322	313	4	15	14	460	449	5	16
6	341	334	4	7	15	459	451	5	14
7	483	473	5	13	16	124	105	3	18
8	166	156	3	9	17	412	407	4	2
9	407	404	4	1	18	344	343	4	6
OUT	2,290	2,924	36		IN	3,045	2,943	36	
					TOTAL	6,035	5,867	72	
	STANDARD SCRATCH		71	70					

Tree positions indicated.

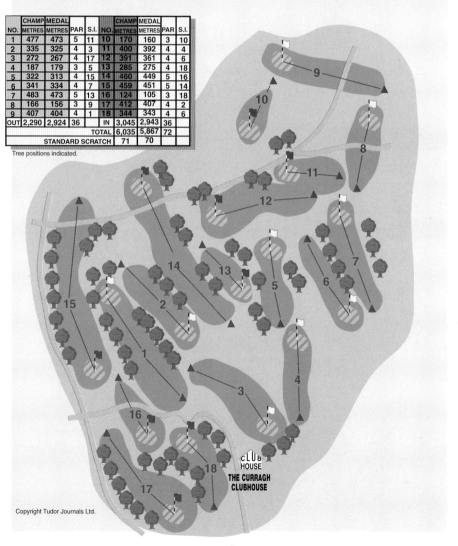

Copyright Tudor Journals Ltd.

Highfield Golf Club, Carbury, Co. Kildare.
Tel: (0405) 31021.

LOCATION: North Kildare. Within one hour of Dublin, via M4 motorway.
SECRETARY: Margaret Duggan.
Tel: (0405) 31021.
ARCHITECT: Alan Duggan.

Attractive 18 hole parkland course, set in a quiet country area, featuring leisurely fairways and mature sycamore, beech & chestnut trees.

COURSE INFORMATION

Par 72; SSS 69; Length 6,277 yards.
Visitors: Welcome.
Opening Hours: Sunrise – sunset.
Avoid: Early Saturday & Sunday.
Ladies: Welcome.
Green Fees: Mon – Fri €20 (€16 with member); Sat / Sun / Bank Holidays €30 (€16 with member).
Juveniles: Must be accompanied by an adult.

Clubhouse Hours: 8.30am – sunset.
Clubhouse Dress: Smart / casual.
Clubhouse Facilities: Available everyday – reception; Restaurant.
Open Competitions: Contact club for details.

	CHAMP METRES	MEDAL METRES	PAR	S.I.	NO.	CHAMP METRES	MEDAL METRES	PAR	S.I.
1	300	270	4	6	10	454	404	5	10
2	472	422	5	2	11	323	283	4	8
3	135	105	3	14	12	323	273	4	13
4	517	467	5	3	13	262	247	4	16
5	321	281	4	9	14	205	165	3	5
6	120	95	3	18	15	312	262	4	11
7	460	420	5	4	16	302	282	4	12
8	275	237	4	15	17	295	275	4	17
9	400	325	4	1	18	189	157	3	7
OUT	3,000	2,622	37		IN	2,665	2,348	35	
					TOTAL	5,665	4,970	72	
		STANDARD SCRATCH				69	67		

Bunker and tree positions indicated.

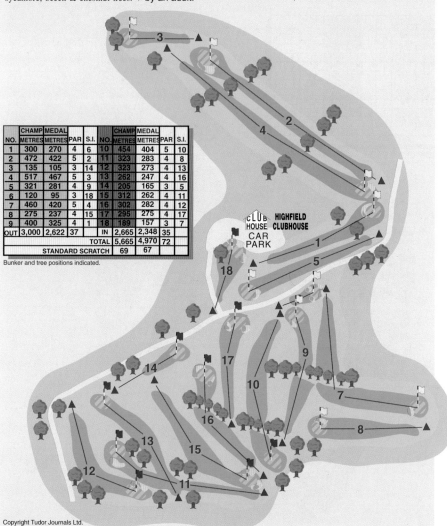

Copyright Tudor Journals Ltd.

**Kilkea Castle, Castledermot,
Co. Kildare.
Tel: (0503) 45555.
Fax: (0503) 45505.
Email: kilkeagolfclub@eircom.net
www.kilkeacastlehotelgolf.com**

LOCATION: 40 miles from Dublin.
GOLF MANAGER : Adeline Molloy.
Tel: (0503) 45555.

A parkland course which surrounds the oldest inhabited castle in Ireland. The River Griese comes into play on ten of the holes.

COURSE INFORMATION

**Par 70; SSS 71; Length
6,128 Metres.**
Visitors: Welcome to play every day. Reserve tea time.
Opening Hours: Sunrise – Sunset.
Ladies: Welcome.
Green Fees: €38 Mon-Fri, €45 Fri-Sun.
Hotel Residents: €32.

Juveniles: Welcome only when accompanied by adults.
Clubhouse Hours: 10.00am - 11.30pm.
Clubhouse Dress: Neat.
Clubhouse Facilities: Bar, restaurant, pro-shop, putting green and pitching green. Conference facilities.

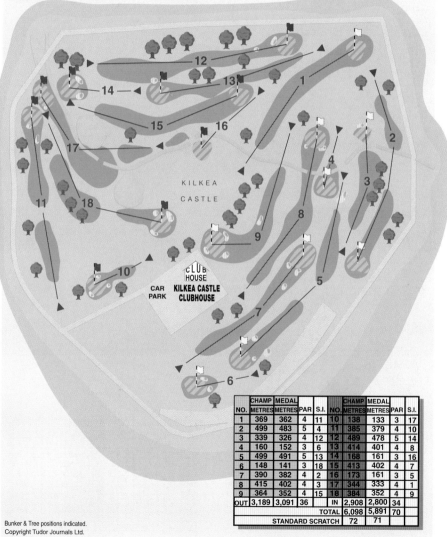

NO.	CHAMP METRES	MEDAL METRES	PAR	S.I.	NO.	CHAMP METRES	MEDAL METRES	PAR	S.I.
1	369	362	4	11	10	138	133	3	17
2	499	483	5	4	11	385	379	4	10
3	339	326	4	12	12	489	478	5	14
4	160	152	3	6	13	414	401	4	8
5	499	491	5	13	14	168	161	3	16
6	148	141	3	18	15	413	402	4	7
7	390	382	4	2	16	173	161	3	5
8	415	402	4	3	17	344	333	4	1
9	364	352	4	15	18	384	352	4	9
OUT	3,189	3,091	36		IN	2,908	2,800	34	
					TOTAL	6,098	5,891	70	
					STANDARD SCRATCH	72	71		

Bunker & Tree positions indicated.
Copyright Tudor Journals Ltd.

Killeen Golf Club,
Kill, County Kildare,
Tel: (045) 866003.
Fax: (045) 875881.
Email: admin@kilkeengc.ie

LOCATION: Two miles west of Kill village, off N7 Dublin – Cork Road.
SECRETARY / MANAGER: Maurice Kelly. Tel: (045) 866003.
ARCHITECT: Tom Craddock & 1995 saw the introduction of six magnificent holes that feature all the elements associated with Craddock and Ruddy designs in recent years ... broad sweeping fairways, boldly shaped and placed fairways, water hazards that are very much in play and also perfectly conditioned greens

COURSE INFORMATION

Par 71; SSS 71; Length 5,526 yards.
Visitors: Welcome weekdays and at weekends.
Opening Hours: Summer 7.00am – 12.00pm; winter 8.00am – 6.00pm.
Avoid: Sat / Sun up to 4.00pm. At weekends telephone, appointments essential.
Ladies: Welcome Tuesday and Thursday.
Green Fees: €26 Mon – Thu; €28 Fri; €32 Sat & Sun. €13 with member. Caddy car hire available.
Clubhouse Hours: Summer 9.00am – 12 midnight; winter 9.00am – 6.00pm.
Clubhouse Dress: Neat.
Clubhouse Facilities: Golf shop open everyday. Licensed restaurant and bar.

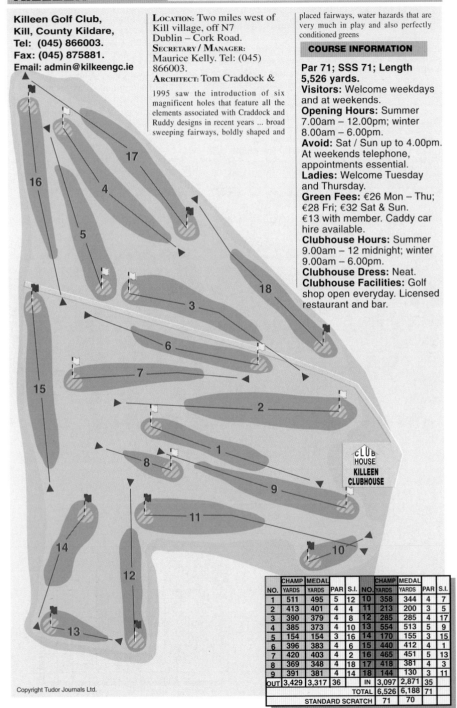

KILLEEN CLUBHOUSE

	CHAMP	MEDAL				CHAMP	MEDAL		
NO.	YARDS	YARDS	PAR	S.I.	NO.	YARDS	YARDS	PAR	S.I.
1	511	495	5	12	10	358	344	4	7
2	413	401	4	4	11	213	200	3	5
3	390	379	4	8	12	285	285	4	17
4	385	373	4	10	13	554	513	5	9
5	154	154	3	16	14	170	155	3	15
6	396	383	4	6	15	440	412	4	1
7	420	403	4	2	16	465	451	5	13
8	369	348	4	18	17	418	381	4	3
9	391	381	4	14	18	144	130	3	11
OUT	3,429	3,317	36		IN	3,097	2,871	35	
					TOTAL	6,526	6,188	71	
					STANDARD SCRATCH		71	70	

Copyright Tudor Journals Ltd.

THE 'K' CLUB

**Kildare Hotel & Country Club
Straffan, Co. Kildare.
Tel: (01) 6017300. Fax (01) 6017299
Email: resortsales@kclub.ie
Web: www.kclub.ie**

LOCATION: Co. Kildare.
GOLF DIRECTOR / MANAGER: Paul Crowe.
PROFESSIONAL: Ernie Jones.
ARCHITECT: Arnold Palmer.

A world class major championship designed golf course by Arnold Palmer. Eleven man made lakes, large sand bunkers, large mounds both sides of fairways. The River Liffey runs alongside four holes with the 16th green on the far side of the river. Large quantity of 300 year old trees.

COURSE INFORMATION

Par 72; SSS 74; Length 6,368 metres.
Visitors: Welcome.
Opening Hours: 8.00am (summer), 8.30am (winter).
Avoid: Contact (01) 6017300 for details.
Ladies: Welcome.
Green Fees: €245 (summer), €110 (winter). Lessons available by prior arrangement. Club Hire and Caddy service available. No Open Competitions.
Juveniles: Must be accompanied by an adult.
Clubhouse Dress: Jacket and tie after 7.00pm – otherwise casual but strictly no jeans.
Clubhouse Hours: 8.30am – 10pm (summer), 9pm (winter).
Clubhouse Facilities: Bar, snack bar, restaurant. Snack bar 9am–9pm. Bar & Restaurant 11am–9pm everyday.

NO.	MEDAL YARDS	GEN YARDS	PAR	S.I.	NO.	MEDAL YARDS	GEN YARDS	PAR	S.I.
1	418	401	4	5	10	584	561	5	6
2	413	399	4	9	11	408	382	4	12
3	170	157	3	17	12	173	164	3	18
4	568	545	5	7	13	402	386	4	10
5	416	402	4	15	14	213	197	3	2
6	447	412	4	11	15	446	407	4	4
7	395	371	4	3	16	606	581	5	8
8	173	155	3	13	17	375	364	4	16
9	434	427	4	1	18	537	518	5	14
OUT	3,434	3,269	35		IN	3,744	3,560	37	
						TOTAL	7,178	6,829	72
						STANDARD SCRATCH	74		

PRACTICE AREA

Bunker & Tree positions indicated.
Copyright Tudor Journals Ltd.

KNOCKANALLY

Donadea, North Kildare.
Tel: (045) 869322.

LOCATION: North Kildare.
SECRETARY: Noel Lyons.
Tel: (045) 869322.
Fax: (045) 869322.
ARCHITECT: Noel Lyons.

A popular parkland course which is basically flat, and has several water hazards. Christy O'Connor Senior once described the first hole as "the most difficult opening hole in golf".

Home of the Irish International Professional Matchplay Championship. Palladian old world clubhouse is also an interesting feature.

COURSE INFORMATION

Par 72; SSS 72; Length 6,424 yards.
Visitors: Welcome. Telephone in advance.
Opening Hours: Sunrise – sunset.
Avoid: Saturday mornings.
Ladies: Welcome Tuesday and Thursday mornings.

Green Fees: Mon – Fri €28 (with member €15); Sat, Sun & Bank Hols €40 (with member €15).
Juveniles: Welcome. Lessons available by prior arrangement.
Clubhouse Hours: 8.30am – 12.00 midnight.
Clubhouse Dress: Smart / casual (no jeans).
Clubhouse Facilities: Available everyday. Members bar, restaurant, professional shop, offices, games rooms.

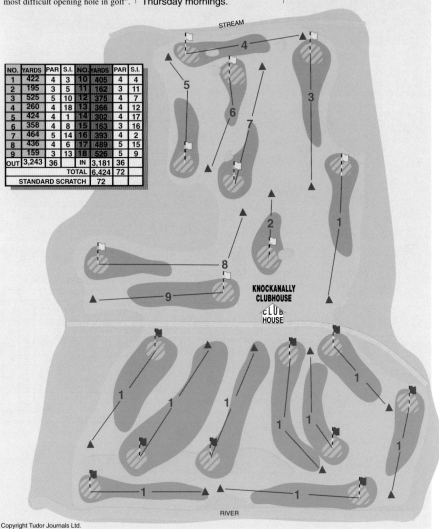

NO.	YARDS	PAR	S.I.	NO.	YARDS	PAR	S.I.
1	422	4	3	10	405	4	4
2	195	3	5	11	162	3	11
3	525	5	10	12	375	4	7
4	260	4	18	13	366	4	12
5	424	4	1	14	302	4	17
6	358	4	8	15	163	3	16
7	464	5	14	16	393	4	2
8	436	4	6	17	489	5	15
9	159	3	13	18	526	5	9
OUT	3,243	36		IN	3,181	36	
				TOTAL	6,424	72	
				STANDARD SCRATCH		72	

Copyright Tudor Journals Ltd.

Kerdiffstown, Naas, Co. Kildare.
Tel: (045) 897509.

LOCATION: Beside Naas/Dublin dual carriageway on Johnstown /Sallins road.
SECRETARY: Denis A. Mullins.
Tel: (045) 897509.

A pleasant parkland course where each hole has its features providing a keen golfing challenge.

COURSE INFORMATION

Par 71; SSS 69; Length 6,232 yards.
Visitors: Welcome Mon, Wed, Fri and Sat.
Opening Hours: Sunrise – Sunset.
Ladies: Welcome.
Green Fees: €27 Mon – Fri; €35 Sat.
Juveniles: Welcome
Clubhouse Hours: 8.00am – 11.30pm.
Clubhouse Dress: Neat.
Clubhouse Facilities: Catering.
Open Competitions: April, June & August.

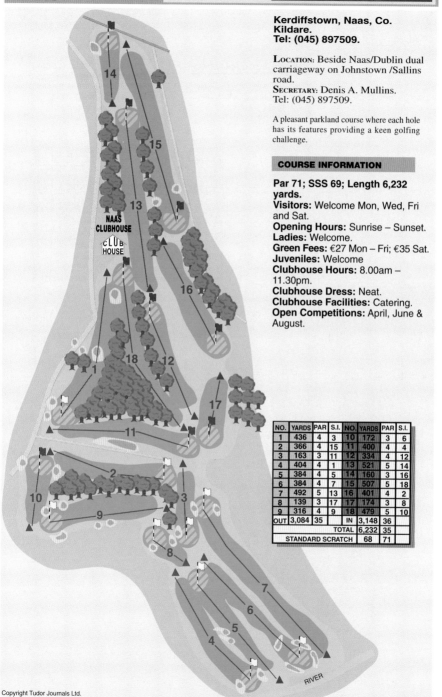

NO.	YARDS	PAR	S.I.	NO.	YARDS	PAR	S.I.
1	436	4	3	10	172	3	6
2	366	4	15	11	400	4	4
3	163	3	11	12	334	4	12
4	404	4	1	13	521	5	14
5	384	4	5	14	160	3	16
6	384	4	7	15	507	5	18
7	492	5	13	16	401	4	2
8	139	3	17	17	174	3	8
9	316	4	9	18	479	5	10
OUT	3,084	35		IN	3,148	36	
				TOTAL	6,232	35	
				STANDARD SCRATCH	68	71	

Copyright Tudor Journals Ltd.

Barretstown, Newbridge.
Co. Kildare.
Tel: (045) 486110.
Tel/Fax: (045) 431289.

LOCATION: Down M7 from Dublin
OWNER: Eddie Stafford.
MANAGER: Jamie Safford.
PROFESSIONAL: Available

18 hole Parklands course with many water features. Green Fees and Societies welcome.

COURSE INFORMATION

Par 72; SSS 72; Length 5,835 metres.
Visitors: Welcome.
Opening Hours:
8am – Sunset.

Green Fees: €19 weekend;
€16 weekdays;
Clubhouse Hours: 8am – 8pm.
Clubhouse Dress: Casual.
Clubhouse Facilities:
Snack all the time / no bar.
Open Competitiions:
Various throughout year.

NO.	BLUE METRES	WHITE METRES	PAR	S.I.	NO.	BLUE METRES	WHITE METRES	PAR	S.I.
1	435	421	5	15	10	420	415	4	12
2	312	276	4	16	11	172	165	3	18
3	208	199	3	4	12	295	290	4	6
4	506	500	5	11	13	356	359	4	8
5	323	322	4	7	14	185	174	3	16
6	140	120	3	18	15	286	293	4	2
7	352	368	4	9	16	384	374	4	14
8	344	360	4	2	17	322	297	4	4
9	45	448	5	6	18	463	454	5	10
OUT	3,077	3,014	37		IN	2,883	2,821	35	
					TOTAL	5,960	5,835	72	
					STANDARD SCRATCH	72	72		

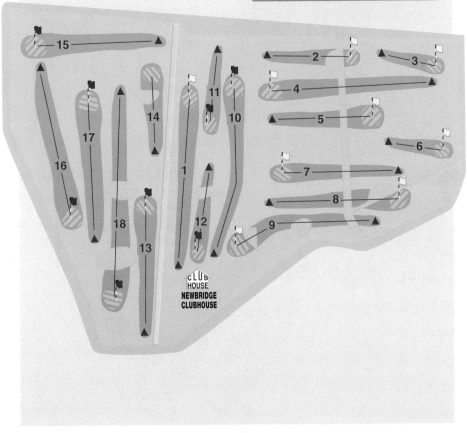

CLUB HOUSE
NEWBRIDGE CLUBHOUSE

WOODLANDS

**Woodlands Golf Club,
Coill Duth, Naas,
Co. Kildare
Tel: (045) 860777.**

SECRETARY: John Noone
FACILITIES MANAGER:
George Connolly
ARCHITECT: Tommy Halpin.
Woodlands Golf Course offers an
attractive setting with a reasonable
golf challenge.

COURSE INFORMATION

**Par 72; SSS 71; Length
6,020 metres.
Avoid:** Saturday/ Sunday -
available for green fees from
2.30pm.
Ladies Day: Wednesday.
Green Fees: Midweek €16,
Weekend €20.
Clubhouse Dress: Neat.

Clubhouse Facilities:
Dressing/ Locker Rooms,
Shower facilities.
Clubhouse Hours:
11am to closing.
Open Competitions:
Open week 27th July
- 4th August

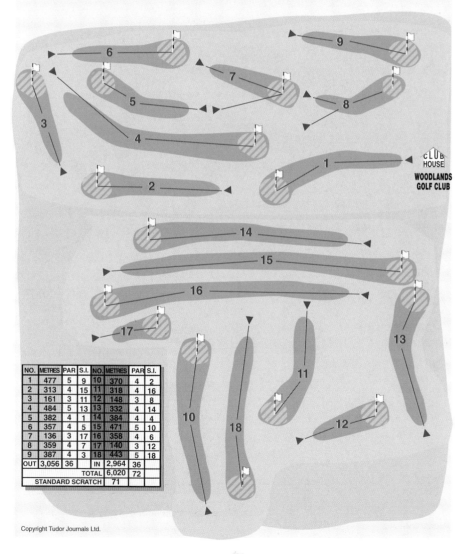

WOODLANDS
GOLF CLUB

NO.	METRES	PAR	S.I.	NO.	METRES	PAR	S.I.
1	477	5	9	10	370	4	2
2	313	4	15	11	318	4	16
3	161	3	11	12	148	3	8
4	484	5	13	13	332	4	14
5	382	4	1	14	384	4	4
6	357	4	5	15	471	5	10
7	136	3	17	16	358	4	6
8	359	4	7	17	140	3	12
9	387	4	3	18	443	5	18
OUT	3,056	36		IN	2,964	36	
				TOTAL	6,020	72	
				STANDARD SCRATCH	71		

Copyright Tudor Journals Ltd.

CALLAN

**Geraldine, Callan,
Co. Kilkenny.
Tel: (056)
25136/25949.**

LOCATION: One mile from town of Callan on Knocktopher road.
HONORARY SECRETARY:
Murt Duggan.

Stream comes into play on six holes with the par 3 10th requiring 155 yard carry over water to the green. In addition there are well placed spinneys to catch wayward drives. There is also a pond left of line of drive on the 6th. All greens are bunkered and well protected.

COURSE INFORMATION

Par 72; SSS 70; Length 6,422 yards.
Visitors: Welcome to play.
Opening Hours: Daylight hours.
Avoid: Sundays a.m, Saturdays p.m. Prior arrangement preferred.
Green Fees: €25 all week. Caddy service and Club Hire available.

Juveniles: Welcome if accompanied by an adult. Must be off the course by 6.00pm. Allocated days for juveniles, phone clubhouse for details.
Clubhouse Hours: 9am-11pm.
Clubhouse Dress: Neat/Casual.
Clubhouse Facilities: Bar open 9.00am – 11.00pm. Full catering facilities. Golf Shop open everyday.
Open Week: 8th - 16th June

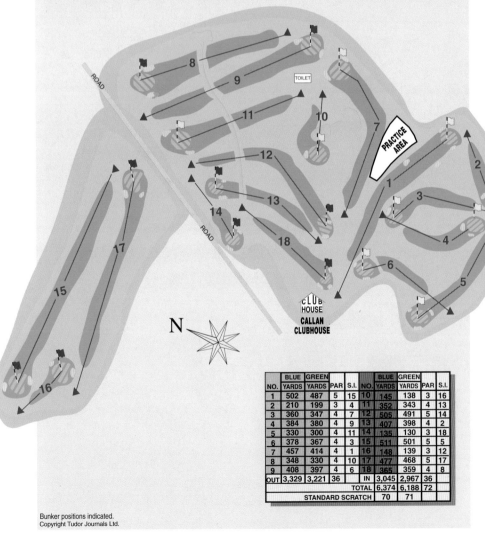

NO.	BLUE YARDS	GREEN YARDS	PAR	S.I.	NO.	BLUE YARDS	GREEN YARDS	PAR	S.I.
1	502	487	5	15	10	145	138	3	16
2	210	199	3	4	11	352	343	4	13
3	360	347	4	7	12	505	491	5	14
4	384	380	4	9	13	407	398	4	2
5	330	300	4	11	14	135	130	3	18
6	378	367	4	3	15	511	501	5	5
7	457	414	4	1	16	148	139	3	12
8	348	330	4	10	17	477	468	5	17
9	408	397	4	6	18	365	359	4	8
OUT	3,329	3,221	36		IN	3,045	2,967	36	
					TOTAL	6,374	6,188	72	
					STANDARD SCRATCH	70	71		

Bunker positions indicated.
Copyright Tudor Journals Ltd.

**Drumgoole, Castlecomer,
Co. Kilkenny.
Tel: (056) 41139.**

LOCATION: Edge of town on
Kilkenny road.
HON. SECRETARY: Matt Dooley.
Tel: (056) 41139.
ARCHITECT: Pat Ruddy.

This course is in a sylvan setting
bounded on one side by the River Deen.
A long course considered a good test of
golf, it is the third longest nine hole
course in Ireland.

COURSE INFORMATION

**Par 71; SSS 71; Length 5,547
metres.
Visitors:** Welcome.
Opening Hours: Sunrise – Sunset.
Avoid: All Sundays.
Ladies: Welcome.
Green Fees: €20 per day.
Juveniles: Welcome.
Clubhouse Hours: Sunrise –
Sunset.
Clubhouse Dress: Casual.
Clubhouse Facilities: Full
clubhouse facilities (by request for
groups).
Open Competitions:
Open Week July / Aug.

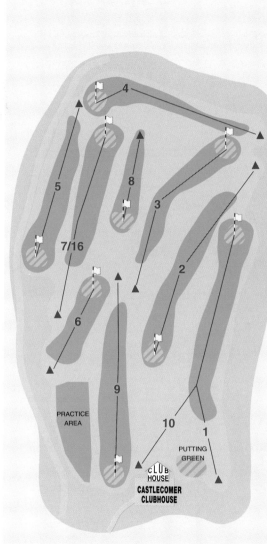

NO.	METRES	PAR	S.I.	NO.	METRES	PAR	S.I.
1	464	5	11	10	375	5	12
2	365	4	7	11	344	4	8
3	363	4	5	12	363	4	6
4	253	4	13	13	253	4	14
5	353	4	3	14	353	4	4
6	132	3	17	15	132	3	18
7	347	4	9	16	368	4	2
8	123	3	15	17	123	3	16
9	396	4	1	18	440	5	10
OUT	2,796	35		IN	2,751	36	
				TOTAL	5,547	71	
				STANDARD SCRATCH		71	

Copyright Tudor Journals Ltd.

Glendine, Kilkenny.
Tel: (056) 65400.
Members: (056) 22125.

LOCATION: One mile outside the city – off Castlecomer road.
SECRETARY: Ms. Anne O'Neill.
PROFESSIONAL: Jimmy Bolger.
Tel: (056) 61730.

Parkland course with plenty of trees throughout the fairways which provide a good test of golf. GUI Irish finals are held here from time to time.

COURSE INFORMATION

Par 71; SSS 70; Length 5,925 metres.
Visitors: Welcome to play Mon – Fri, weekends by prior arrangement.
Opening Hours: Daylight hours.
Avoid: Saturday and Sunday – prior arrangement preferred.
Ladies: Welcome.

Green Fees: €35 weekdays and €40 weekends. Club hire and Lessons available. Caddy service available by prior arrangement.
Clubhouse Hours: As per licensing law.
Clubhouse Dress: Neat.
Clubhouse Facilities: Bar, food, snooker and pool.

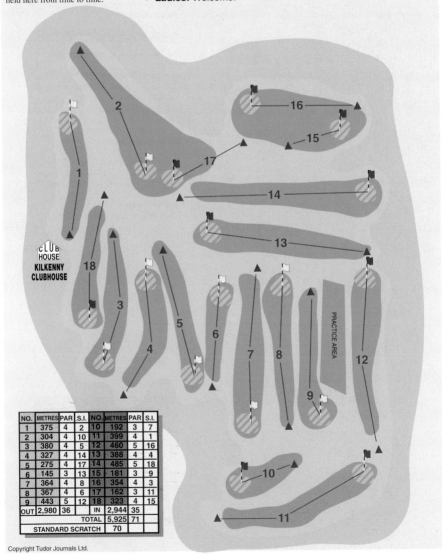

NO.	METRES	PAR	S.I.	NO.	METRES	PAR	S.I.
1	375	4	2	10	192	3	7
2	304	4	10	11	399	4	1
3	380	4	5	12	460	5	16
4	327	4	14	13	388	4	4
5	275	4	17	14	485	5	18
6	145	3	13	15	181	3	9
7	364	4	8	16	354	4	3
8	367	4	6	17	162	3	11
9	443	5	12	18	323	4	15
OUT	2,980	36		IN	2,944	35	
				TOTAL	5,925	71	
				STANDARD SCRATCH	70		

Copyright Tudor Journals Ltd.

**Kiltorcan, Ballyhale,
Co. Kilkenny
Tel: (056) 68122.**

LOCATION: South Kilkenny
SECRETARY: Pat 'O Hanlon.
ARCHITECT: John O'Sullivan.

A picturesque 18 hole course situated in south Kilkenny offering (as its name suggests) a wide panoramic view of the surrounding areas.

COURSE INFORMATION

Par 70; SSS 67; Length 5,496 yards.
Visitors: Welcome, pre-booking of time appreciated.
Opening Hours: Daily from 8.00am.
Green Fees: Weekdays; €15 (€13 with a member).
Weekends; €20 (€15 with a member).
Juveniles: €10.
Clubhouse Hours:
8am - 11.30pm.
Clubhouse Dress:
Neat dress required.
Open Competitions:
Open Week - 25th Aug to 3rd September.

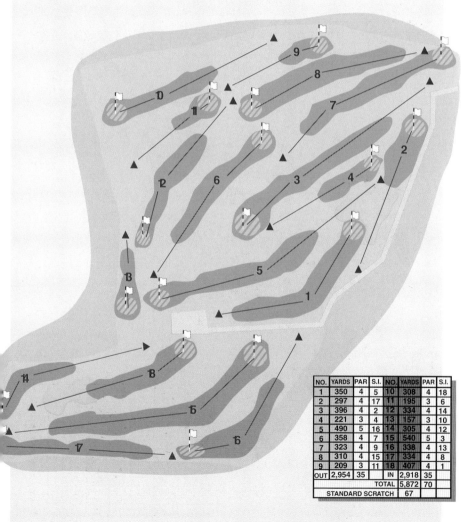

NO.	YARDS	PAR	S.I.	NO.	YARDS	PAR	S.I.
1	350	4	5	10	308	4	18
2	297	4	17	11	195	3	6
3	396	4	2	12	334	4	14
4	221	3	4	13	157	3	10
5	490	5	16	14	305	4	12
6	358	4	7	15	540	5	3
7	323	4	9	16	338	4	13
8	310	4	15	17	334	4	8
9	209	3	11	18	407	4	1
OUT	2,954	35		IN	2,918	35	
				TOTAL	5,872	70	
	STANDARD SCRATCH				67		

Copyright Tudor Journals Ltd.

Thomastown, Co. Kilkenny.
Tel: (056) 24725
Fax: (056) 24828.
Email: info@mountjuliet.ie
www.mountjuliet.com

LOCATION: Main Dublin – Waterford road, ten miles from Kilkenny.
SECRETARY: Myra Phelan.
GOLF MANAGER: Frances Reynolds.
ARCHITECT: Jack Nicklaus.

The only Jack Nicklaus designed course in Ireland, it features old specimen trees, water hazards and bunkers. It is set in a beautiful old 1500 acre estate and appeals to all levels and standards of golfers. Accommodation is available in both Mount Juliet House and the clubhouse. New 18 hole putting course featuring par 2, 3 and 4, also with water features and bunkers.

COURSE INFORMATION

Par 72; SSS 72; Length 7112 yards.
Visitors: Welcome. Prior arrangement required. Handicap certificate required.
Opening Hours: Daily from 7.30am – 8.00pm.
Ladies: Welcome.
Green Fees: Summer – midweek €135 & Fri-Sun €150. Apr/Oct – midweek €110 & Fri-Sun €120. Nov-Mar – midweek €75 & Fri-Sun €85. Lessons available by prior arrangement. Club hire and caddy service available.

Juveniles: Welcome (no reduction in green fees).
Clubhouse Hours: 8.00am – 11.30pm.
Clubhouse Facilities: Changing rooms, Bar, Restaurant. 8.00am – 9.00pm (Must be booked in advance).

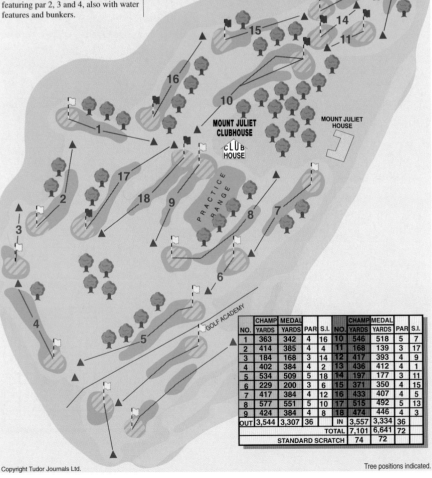

NO.	CHAMP YARDS	MEDAL YARDS	PAR	S.I.	NO.	CHAMP YARDS	MEDAL YARDS	PAR	S.I.
1	363	342	4	16	10	546	518	5	7
2	414	385	4	4	11	168	139	3	17
3	184	168	3	14	12	417	393	4	9
4	402	384	4	2	13	436	412	4	1
5	534	509	5	18	14	197	177	3	11
6	229	200	3	6	15	371	350	4	15
7	417	384	4	12	16	433	407	4	5
8	577	551	5	10	17	515	492	5	13
9	424	384	4	8	18	474	446	4	3
OUT	3,544	3,307	36		IN	3,557	3,334	36	
					TOTAL	7,101	6,641	72	
					STANDARD SCRATCH	74	72		

Tree positions indicated.

Copyright Tudor Journals Ltd.

**Newrath,
Waterford.
Tel: (051) 876748.**

LOCATION: Newrath.
SECRETARY: Joseph Condon.
Tel: (051) 876748.
ARCHITECT: James Braid.

A parkland course with good views of the countryside. The course character is as the undulating countryside around Newrath and will appeal to low and middle handicappers.

COURSE INFORMATION

Par 71; SSS 70; Length 5,722 metres.
Visitors: Welcome by prior arrangement.
Opening Hours: 8.00am – Sunset.
Avoid: Tue/Wed afternoons; all day Sunday.
Ladies: Welcome.
Ladies Day: Tuesday.
Green Fees: €35 Mon – Fri; €45 Sat/Sun/Bank Holidays.

Club Hire available; Caddy service also available during the summer months; Handicap certificate required for open competitions.
Clubhouse Hours: 8.00am – 12.00 midnight.
Clubhouse Dress: Casual.
Clubhouse Facilities: Bar and snacks; full catering from 12 noon during the summer.
Open Competitions:
Waterford Crystal Open Fortnight – July / Aug.

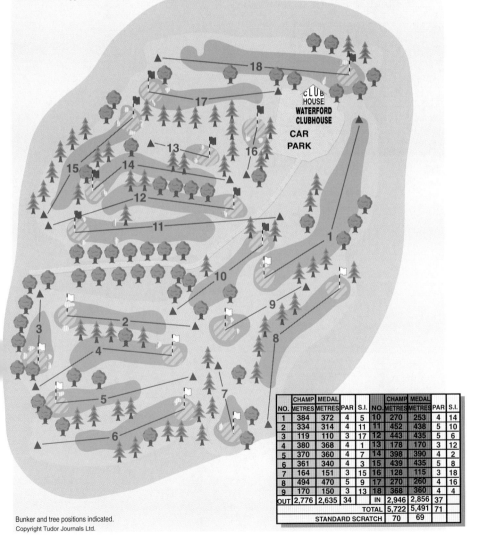

NO.	CHAMP METRES	MEDAL METRES	PAR	S.I.	NO.	CHAMP METRES	MEDAL METRES	PAR	S.I.
1	384	372	4	5	10	270	253	4	14
2	334	314	4	11	11	452	438	5	10
3	119	110	3	17	12	443	435	5	6
4	380	368	4	1	13	178	170	3	12
5	370	360	4	7	14	398	390	4	2
6	361	340	4	3	15	439	435	5	8
7	164	151	3	15	16	128	115	3	18
8	494	470	5	9	17	270	260	4	16
9	170	150	3	13	18	368	360	4	4
OUT	2,776	2,635	34		IN	2,946	2,856	37	
					TOTAL	5,722	5,491	71	
					STANDARD SCRATCH	70	69		

Bunker and tree positions indicated.
Copyright Tudor Journals Ltd.

Rathmoyle, Abbeyleix, Portlaoise, Co Laois
Tel: (0502) 31450
Fax: (0502) 31608

LOCATION: Less than one mile north of the town on Stradbally road.
SECRETARY: Micheal Martin. Tel: (0502) 31546.

Abbeyleix has just constructed a new 9 hole extension which opened on 1st April 2001. The new course features some great water hazards and natural contours which make it challenging to any golfer. Visitors are most welcome to play this new amenity and will surely come away enriched by the experience.

COURSE INFORMATION

Par 72; SSS 70; Length 5,557 metres.
Visitors: Welcome to play on weekdays.
Opening Hours: Sunrise – Sunset.
Ladies: Welcome.
Green Fees: €17 Weekdays, €22 Weekends.

Juveniles: Only when accompanied by adults.
Clubhouse Hours: Open 7 days a week.
Clubhouse Dress: Informal but respectable.
Clubhouse Facilities: General. Catering facilities and times; by prior arrangement.
Open Competitions: Open Week 2nd weekend & 3rd week of July; Open Hampers October and November.

NO.	CHAMP YARDS	MEDAL YARDS	PAR	S.I.	NO.	CHAMP YARDS	MEDAL YARDS	PAR	S.I.
1	570	517	5	11	10	406	348	4	6
2	515	477	5	7	11	412	382	4	8
3	121	121	3	15	12	267	212	4	18
4	307	307	4	9	13	376	376	4	4
5	379	379	4	3	14	136	136	3	16
6	145	145	3	17	15	499	468	5	14
7	262	262	4	5	16	495	495	5	12
8	467	412	4	1	17	235	210	3	10
9	347	347	4	13	18	426	426	4	2
OUT	3,113	2,967	36		IN	3,252	3,053	36	
					TOTAL	6,365	6,020	72	
					STANDARD SCRATCH	74	72		

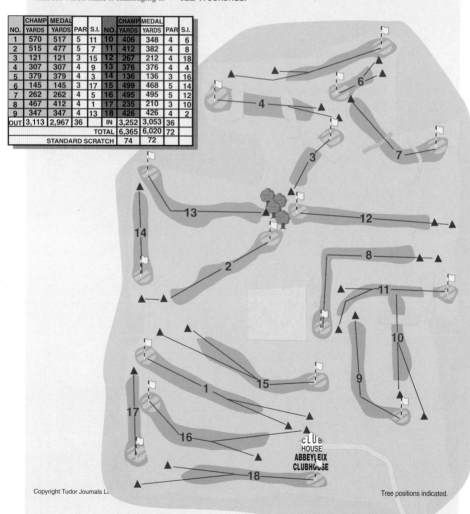

Tree positions indicated.

Copyright Tudor Journals L

The Heath, Portlaoise, Co. Laois.
Tel: (0502) 46533.
Fax: (0502) 46866

LOCATION: Three miles north east Portlaoise town.
ADMINISTRATOR: Elaine Crofton.
Tel: (0502) 46533.
PROFESSIONAL: Eddie Doyle.
Tel: (0502) 46622.

This Par 71 course is playable all year round and is exceptionally dry in wintertime. Set in picturesque surroundings with views of the rolling hills of Laois, the course incorporates three natural lakes. Noted for its rough of heather and gorse furze it is a challenge for any golfer. The Heath Golf Club is the seventh oldest Golf Club in Ireland, founded in November 1889.

COURSE INFORMATION

Par 71; SSS 70; Length 5,854 metres.
Visitors: Welcome, please book.
Opening Hours: Sunrise – sunset.
Avoid: Weekends unless with advance booking.
Ladies: Welcome.
Green Fees: €13 Mon – Fri; €26 Sat / Sun / Bank Hols. Societies welcome. Special offer weekdays: golf and steak dinner €25.40.
Juveniles: Welcome. Lessons available by prior arrangement; Club Hire available; Caddy service available by prior arrangement; telephone appointment required.
Clubhouse Hours: 10.30am – 11.30pm Mon – Sat; 10.30am – 11.00pm Sundays.
Clubhouse Dress: Casual (Neat).
Clubhouse Facilities:
Full catering facilities.
Floodlit 10 bay driving range.
Open Competitions: Open Week August. Other various days. Contact Administrator for details.

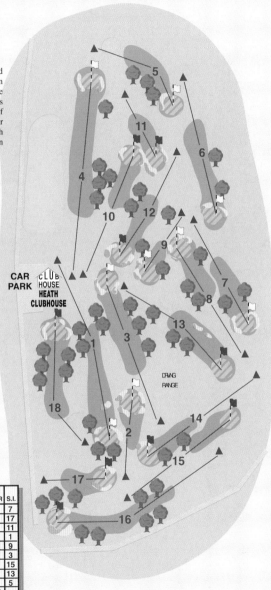

NO.	MEDAL METRES	GREEN METRES	PAR	S.I.	NO.	MEDAL METRES	GREEN METRES	PAR	S.I.
1	450	442	5	16	1	341	330	4	7
2	160	150	3	12	11	139	132	3	17
3	350	339	4	4	12	341	332	4	11
4	458	452	5	10	13	388	381	4	1
5	286	286	4	14	14	352	346	4	9
6	359	341	4	6	15	367	344	4	3
7	347	330	4	8	16	482	473	5	15
8	351	334	4	2	17	171	162	3	13
9	167	148	3	18	18	345	335	4	5
OUT	2,928	2,820	36		IN	2,926	2,835	35	
					TOTAL	5,854	5,655	71	
	STANDARD SCRATCH		70				69		

Copyright Tudor Journals Ltd.

Tree positions indicated.

Knockinina, Mountrath, Co. Laois.
Tel: (0502) 32558.

Location: Two miles Limerick side of Mountrath – just off the main Dublin/Limerick road.
Secretary: Tom O' Grady.

This is a pleasant 18 hole course set on gently rolling land with the river Nore and an old Mill stream flowing through and coming into play on a number of holes. Lush fairways and good greens which are well bunkered make it an excellent test of golf.

COURSE INFORMATION

Par 71; SSS 69; Length 5,493 metres.
Visitors: Welcome.
Ladies: Welcome Tuesdays.
Opening Hours: Sunrise – sunset.
Avoid: Saturday or Sunday mornings (check in clubhouse).
Green Fees: €20 per round Monday – Friday; Sat/Sun €20.
Clubhouse Hours: Evening service available full time.
Clubhouse Dress: Casual.
Clubhouse Facilities: Catering facilities by prior arrangment.

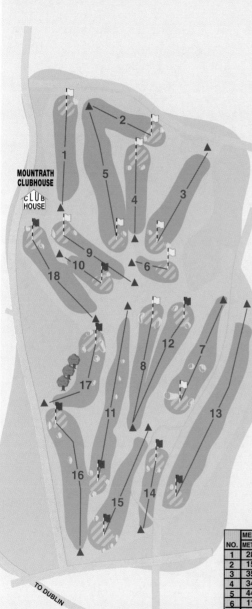

NO.	MEDAL METRES	GEN. METRES	PAR	S.I.	NO.	MEDAL METRES	GEN. METRES	PAR	S.I.
1	288	374	4	3	10	127	117	3	17
2	154	142	3	12	11	445	430	5	11
3	352	298	4	1	12	373	350	4	2
4	347	329	4	6	13	463	440	5	8
5	440	418	5	13	14	177	140	3	5
6	111	105	3	16	15	290	268	4	9
7	270	250	4	18	16	378	360	4	4
8	337	320	4	7	17	269	248	4	15
9	287	283	4	10	18	285	265	4	14
OUT	2,686	2,519	35		IN	2,807	2,618	36	
					TOTAL	5,493	5,137	71	
					STANDARD SCRATCH	69	68		

Copyright Tudor Journals Ltd.

Garryhinch, Portarlington, Co. Laois.
Tel: (0502) 23115.
Fax: (0502) 23044
Email: portarlingtongc@eircom.net
www.portarlingtongc.com
LOCATION: Three miles from Portarlington.
HON. SECRETARY: Tom Kennedy
Tel: (0502) 23351.

The course has recently undergone extensive development from a nine hole course to an eighteen hole course. The new course was completed in November 1992 and provides a fresh test of skill and ability.

COURSE INFORMATION

Par 71; SSS 71; Length 5,872 metres.
Visitors: Welcome as members of societies and as individuals.
Opening Hours: 8.00am – sunset.
Avoid: Weekends.
Ladies: Tuesday.
Green Fees: Mon – Fri, €20 Saturday / Sunday / holidays €25. 50% with member

Juveniles: Welcome. Handicap Certificate required for Open Competitions.
Clubhouse Hours: 8.00am – 11.00pm.
Clubhouse Dress: Casual.
Clubhouse Facilities: By prior arrangement.

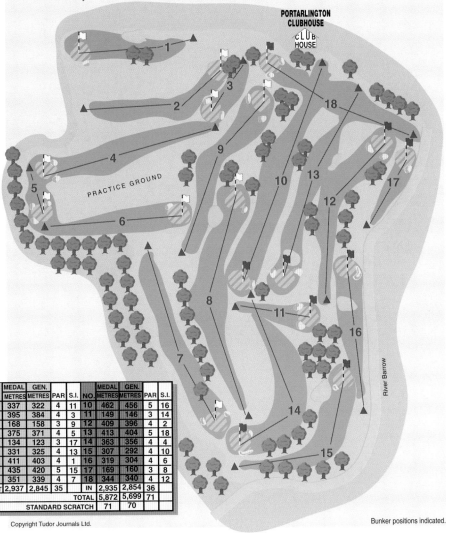

PORTARLINGTON CLUBHOUSE

MEDAL METRES	GEN. METRES	PAR	S.I.	NO.	MEDAL METRES	GEN. METRES	PAR	S.I.
337	322	4	11	10	462	456	5	16
395	384	4	3	11	149	146	3	14
168	158	3	9	12	409	396	4	2
375	371	4	5	13	413	404	5	18
134	123	3	17	14	363	356	4	4
331	325	4	13	15	307	292	4	10
411	403	4	1	16	319	304	4	6
435	420	5	15	17	169	160	3	8
351	339	4	7	18	344	340	4	12
2,937	2,845	35		IN	2,935	2,854	36	
				TOTAL	5,872	5,699	71	
			STANDARD SCRATCH		71	70		

Copyright Tudor Journals Ltd.

Bunker positions indicated.

**Coulnaboul West,
Rathdowney,
Co. Laois.
Tel: (0505) 46170.
Tel/Fax: (0505) 46065.**

LOCATION: Less than one mile
east of Rathdowney.
SECRETARY: Sean Bolger.

This inland course was redeveloped to
eighteen holes in 1997 and provides
the golfer with a varied game, testing
flexibility.

COURSE INFORMATION

**Par 71; SSS 70; Length
5,864 metres.**
Visitors: Welcome all times.
Opening Hours:
Sunrise – sunset.
Avoid: Bank Holidays,
Sundays, 1st week in July.
Ladies Day: Wednesday.
Green Fees: €20 Weekdays
€25 Sat & Sun.
Juveniles: Welcome

before 6.00pm.
Clubhouse Hours:
11.00am – 11.30pm.
Clubhouse Dress: Casual.
Clubhouse Facilities: Bar
open weekends and most
week nights; meals by prior
arrangement.
Open Competitions: Ard
Junior Intermediate Scratch
Cup May. Open Week in July;
Open Hampers in October.

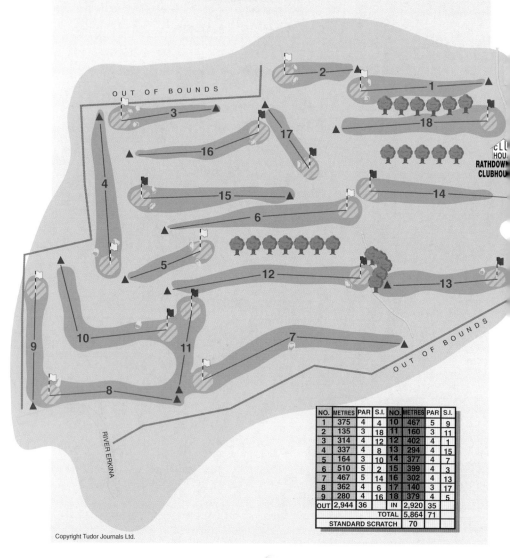

NO.	METRES	PAR	S.I.	NO.	METRES	PAR	S.I.
1	375	4	4	10	467	5	9
2	135	3	18	11	160	3	11
3	314	4	12	12	402	4	1
4	337	4	8	13	294	4	15
5	164	3	10	14	377	4	7
6	510	5	2	15	399	4	3
7	467	5	14	16	302	4	13
8	362	4	6	17	140	3	17
9	280	4	16	18	379	4	5
OUT	2,944	36		IN	2,920	35	
				TOTAL	5,864	71	
				STANDARD SCRATCH		70	

Copyright Tudor Journals Ltd.

Glack, Dublin Road, Longford, Co. Longford
Tel: (043) 46310.
Fax: (043) 47082
Email:colonggolf@eircom.net

LOCATION: Dublin Road, Longford.
SECRETARY: Dan Rooney.
ARCHITECT: E. Hackett

An elevated parkland course, overlooking Longford Town and surrounding countryside.

COURSE INFORMATION

Par 70; SSS 69; Length 6,044 yards.
Visitors: Welcome.
Opening Hours: Sunrise – Sunset (closed mon. in winter)
Avoid: Weekends and Tuesdays.
Ladies Day: Tuesday.
Green Fees: €16 Mon – Fri (€13 with member); €20 Sat/Sun (€17 with member on a one to one basis).

Juveniles: Welcome. Lessons available; Club Hire and caddy cars also available.
Clubhouse Hours: 12noon – 11pm.
Clubhouse Dress: Neat / Casual.
Clubhouse Facilities: Meals snacks and bar.
Open Competitions: Open week July / August.

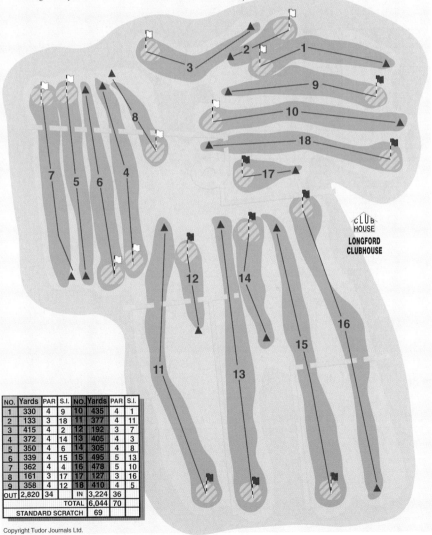

NO.	Yards	PAR	S.I.	NO.	Yards	PAR	S.I.
1	330	4	9	10	435	4	1
2	133	3	18	11	377	4	11
3	415	4	2	12	192	3	7
4	372	4	14	13	405	4	3
5	350	4	6	14	305	4	8
6	339	4	15	15	495	5	13
7	362	4	4	16	478	5	10
8	161	3	17	17	127	3	16
9	358	4	12	18	410	4	5
OUT	2,820	34		IN	3,224	36	
				TOTAL	6,044	70	
				STANDARD SCRATCH	69		

Copyright Tudor Journals Ltd.

Townparks, Ardee, Co. Louth.
Tel: (041) 6853227.

Location: Just north of Ardee town.
Secretary Manager: M.P. Conoulty.
Tel: (041) 6853227.
Architect: Mr Eddie Hackett.

A very fair test of golf and also a very pleasant walk with some beautiful old trees on this parkland course.

COURSE INFORMATION

Par 70; SSS 69/71; Length 6,438 yards.
Visitors: Welcome.
Avoid: Sat & Sun mornings, Societies only.
Ladies: Welcome.
Green Fees: €35 Mon – Fri. Sat €50. No Green Fees Sun.
Juveniles: Welcome Mondays. Any other time adult company. Caddy Service

by prior arrangements.
Clubhouse Hours: 10.00am – 11.30pm.
Clubhouse Dress: Casual.
Clubhouse Facilities: Catering facilities available at all times.
Open Competitions: Several dates throughout year. Open Week – June.

NO.	CHAMP YARDS	MEDAL YARDS	PAR	S.I.	NO.	CHAMP YARDS	MEDAL YARDS	PAR	S.I.
1	354	331	4	6	10	313	301	4	15
2	180	154	3	14	11	337	337	4	17
3	364	364	4	12	12	372	343	4	9
4	317	305	4	18	13	200	191	3	5
5	191	175	3	16	14	545	518	5	1
6	386	378	4	10	15	408	378	4	11
7	407	393	4	4	16	365	335	4	13
8	437	417	4	2	17	409	376	4	3
9	387	359	4	8	18	376	366	4	7
OUT	3,023	2,876	34		IN	3,325	3,145	36	
					TOTAL	6,438	6,021	70	
		STANDARD SCRATCH	71			69			

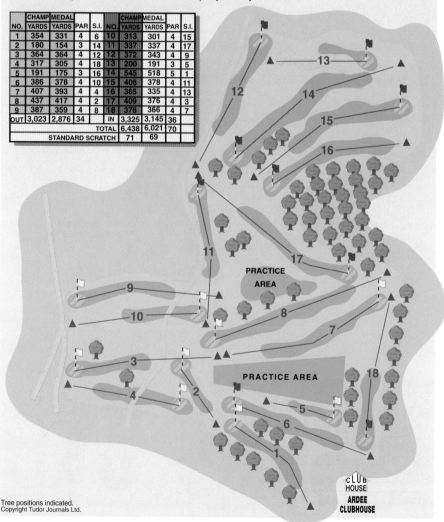

PRACTICE AREA

PRACTICE AREA

CLUB HOUSE
ARDEE CLUBHOUSE

Tree positions indicated.
Copyright Tudor Journals Ltd.

COUNTY LOUTH

Balltray, Co. Louth.
Tel: (041) 9881530.

LOCATION: Five miles north east Drogheda.
SECRETARY: Michael Delany.
Professional: Paddy McGuirk.
Tel: (041) 9881536.
ARCHITECT: Tom Simpson.

A championship links which can be enjoyed by every category of golfer which is not as well known as some of the other links courses. Baltray's demands are stern but its rewards are many, not least in the fun and enjoyment it evokes and the sense of freshness that prevails.

COURSE INFORMATION

Par 73; SSS 72; Length 6,783 metres.
Visitors: Welcome by prior arrangement.
Opening Hours: Winter 8.30am – Sunset; Summer 7.30am – Sunset.
Avoid: Weekends and Tuesdays.
Ladies: By prior arrangement.
Green Fees: €80 Mon – Fri; €100 Sat & Sun.

Juveniles: Restricted. Lessons available by prior arrangement; Club Hire available; Caddy service available by prior arrangement; telephone appointment required.
Clubhouse Hours: 10.30am – 12.00 midnight.
Clubhouse Dress: Casual.
Clubhouse Facilities: 9.00am – 8.00pm (winter); 9.00am – 10.00pm (summer).

NO.	CHAMP METRES	MEDAL METRES	PAR	S.I.	NO.	CHAMP METRES	MEDAL METRES	PAR	S.I.
1	433	423	4	3	10	398	388	4	4
2	462	476	5	17	11	481	476	5	16
3	544	534	5	9	12	410	410	4	2
4	344	334	4	15	13	421	408	4	6
5	158	148	3	13	14	332	322	4	12
6	531	521	5	7	15	152	142	3	18
7	163	453	3	5	16	388	375	4	8
8	407	397	4	11	17	179	169	3	10
9	419	409	4	1	18	541	527	5	14
OUT	3,481	3,395	37		IN	3,302	3,302	36	
					TOTAL	6,783	6,783	73	
					STANDARD SCRATCH	72	72		

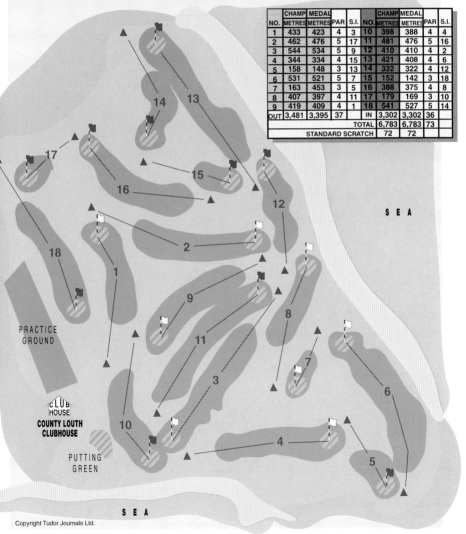

SEA

PRACTICE GROUND

CLUB HOUSE
COUNTY LOUTH CLUBHOUSE

PUTTING GREEN

SEA

Copyright Tudor Journals Ltd.

DUNDALK

Blackrock, Dundalk, Co. Louth.
Tel: (042) 9321731
Fax: (042) 9322022.
Email: dkgc@iol.ie
www.eiresoft.com/dundalkgc/
LOCATION: Three miles south of Dundalk at Blackrock Village.
SECRETARY: Terry Sloane.
PROFESSIONAL: Leslie Walker.
Tel: (042) 9322102.
ARCHITECTS: Dave Thomas

Top ranking course with excellent facilities and catering. Hosted all Ireland finals in 1997 and 2000. Attracts country's top players to senior Scratch Cup. Hosts major PGA pro-Am.

COURSE INFORMATION

Par 72; SSS 72; Length 6,160 metres.
Visitors: Welcome.
Opening Hours: Sunrise – Sunset.
Avoid: Tuesdays and Sundays. Prior appointment preferable but not essential.
Ladies: Welcome except Tuesdays and Sundays.

Green Fees: €45 Mon – Fri (€13 with member)
Juveniles: Before 6.00pm, not Tuesdays or weekends. Lessons available by prior arrangement; Club hire and Caddy service available by prior arrangement.
Clubhouse Hours: Sunrise to midnight.
Clubhouse Dress: Informal.
Clubhouse Facilities: Snacks & full meals any time.
Open Competitions: May 19th-26th, July 14th-21st

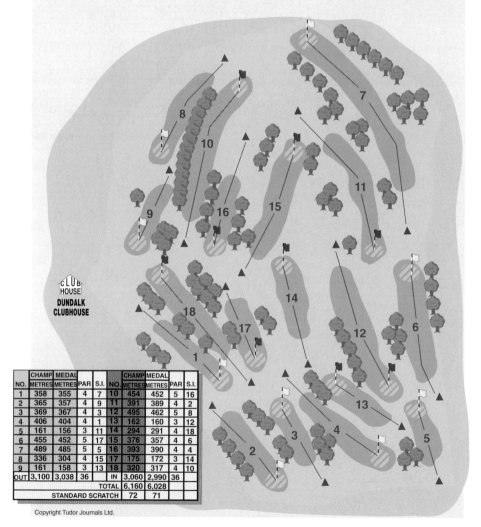

DUNDALK CLUBHOUSE

NO.	CHAMP METRES	MEDAL METRES	PAR	S.I.	NO.	CHAMP METRES	MEDAL METRES	PAR	S.I.
1	358	355	4	7	10	454	452	5	16
2	365	357	4	9	11	391	389	4	2
3	369	367	4	3	12	495	462	5	8
4	406	404	4	1	13	162	160	3	12
5	161	156	3	11	14	294	291	4	18
6	455	452	5	17	15	376	357	4	6
7	489	485	5	5	16	393	390	4	4
8	336	304	4	15	17	175	172	3	14
9	161	158	3	13	18	320	317	4	10
OUT	3,100	3,038	36		IN	3,060	2,990	36	
					TOTAL	6,160	6,028		
					STANDARD SCRATCH	72	71		

Copyright Tudor Journals Ltd.

Greenore, Co. Louth.
Tel: (042) 9373212/
9373678.
Fax: (042) 9383898.

LOCATION: Travelling form Dublin
– proceed through Drogheda and
Dundalk and take the first turn
right on the Newry road out of
Dundalk and proceed to Greenore
– fifteen minutes.
SECRETARY: Connie O'Connor.
ARCHITECT: Eddie Hackett.

An inland course with a links nature
on the shores of Carlingford Lough.
The course enjoys scenic views of
both the Lough and the Mountains of
Mourne. An unusual feature are the

tall pine trees, a rare sight on a semi-
links course, which come into play on
seven holes. The 14th or "pigs back"
is the most famous hole in Greenore, a
par 3 to an elevated green.

COURSE INFORMATION

Par 71; SSS 73; Length
6,647 yards.
Visitors: Welcome to play
weekdays and weekends, but
appointment is recommended for
weekends.
Opening Hours: 8.00am (or
earlier by appointment) – Sunset.
Green Fees: €32 Mon – Fri

(€13 with a member); €45 Sat
& Sun & Bank Holidays (€20
with a member).
Students half price.
Clubhouse Hours:
9am – 6pm (winter);
8am – 11.30pm (summer).
Clubhouse Dress: Informal.
Clubhouse Facilities: All days.
Open Competitions:
Open Week –
5th/14th July 2002.

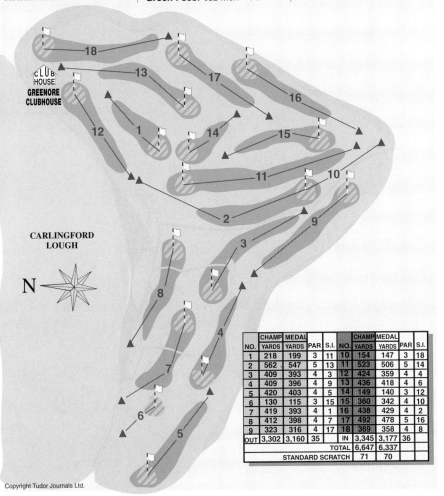

NO.	CHAMP YARDS	MEDAL YARDS	PAR	S.I.	NO.	CHAMP YARDS	MEDAL YARDS	PAR	S.I.
1	218	199	3	11	10	154	147	3	18
2	562	547	5	13	11	523	506	5	14
3	409	393	4	3	12	424	359	4	4
4	409	396	4	9	13	436	418	4	6
5	420	403	4	5	14	149	140	3	12
6	130	115	3	15	15	360	342	4	10
7	419	393	4	1	16	438	429	4	2
8	412	398	4	7	17	492	478	5	16
9	323	316	4	17	18	369	358	4	8
OUT	3,302	3,160	35		IN	3,345	3,177	36	
					TOTAL	6,647	6,337		
					STANDARD SCRATCH	71	70		

CARLINGFORD
LOUGH

N

Copyright Tudor Journals Ltd.

**Killin Park Golf &
Country Club, Killin,
Dundalk, Co. Louth.
Tel: (042) 9339303.**

LOCATION: Three miles from
Dundalk town centre, off the
Castleblayney road.
MANAGER: Pat Reynolds.
ARCHITECT: Eddie Hacket.

Killin Park is a privately owned
course situated in rolling parkland
with mature trees and scenic views
of the Mourne Mountains. Bordered
by Killin Wood and the Castletown
River, this exceptionally free
draining course has American style

greens. Noted for its 6th hole which
resmbles the 10th at the Belfry, this
course offers a challenge even to the
most experienced golfer.

COURSE INFORMATION

**Par 69; SSS 65;
Length 5,388 yards.
Visitors:** Welcome all times.
Ladies: Welcome.
Green Fees: €18 Mon – Fri; €23
weekends & public holidays.
Juveniles: Welcome any time
Mon - Fri, after 2pm Sat, Sun &
Bank Holidays.

Clubhouse Hours:
Sunrise – sunset.
Clubhouse Dress: Neat dress.
Clubhouse Facilities: Bar
snacks available everyday
from 8.30am. Full catering
facilities by prior arrangement.
Club hire available.
Open Competitions: Various
Open Days throughout the
year, telephone Club for
details.

NO.	CHAMP YARDS	MEDAL YARDS	PAR	S.I.	NO.	CHAMP YARDS	MEDAL YARDS	PAR	S.I.
1	114	109	3	16	10	280	277	4	17
2	360	351	4	3	11	161	161	3	4
3	196	177	3	5	12	177	160	3	6
4	358	354	4	1	13	476	473	5	8
5	310	305	4	14	14	396	382	4	2
6	312	307	4	9	15	310	310	4	11
7	492	487	5	10	16	291	291	4	7
8	280	268	4	18	17	160	160	3	15
9	261	244	4	13	18	359	342	4	12
OUT	2,683	2,602	35		IN	2,610	2,556	34	
					TOTAL	5,293	5,158	69	
					STANDARD SCRATCH	65	64		

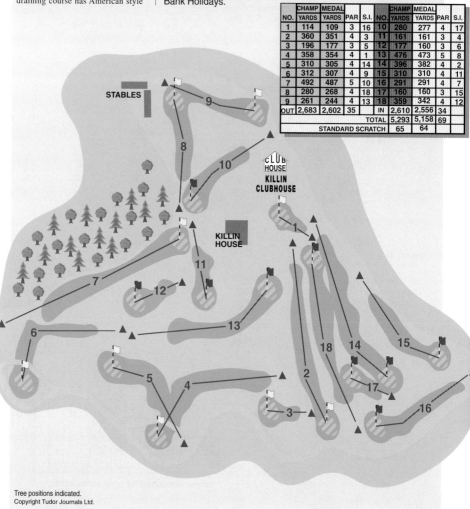

STABLES

CLUB HOUSE

KILLIN
CLUBHOUSE

KILLIN
HOUSE

Tree positions indicated.
Copyright Tudor Journals Ltd.

**Termonfeckin,
Co. Louth.
Tel: (041) 982 2333.
Fax: (041) 982 2331.
Email:
golflinks@seapoint.ie
www.seapointgolfclub.com**

LOCATION: The golf club at
Seapoint lies by the mouth of
the Boyne, near to the historic
town of Drogheda which is just
under one hour from Dublin.
SECRETARY: Kevin Carrie.
PROFESSIONAL: David Carroll
Tel: (041) 9881066

Inland, the Boyne Valley hosts
numerous historic treasures, from the
beautiful medieval abbeys at
Mellifontfamed battlefield of 1690 to
the and Monasterboice.

COURSE INFORMATION

**Par 36; SSS 74; Length
7,100 Yards.
Opening Hours:**
Daily at 9.00am.
Ladies: Welcome Anytime.

Green Fees: €40 Mon – Thu;
€50 Fri; €60 Weekends.
Clubhouse Facilities: Full
bar and restaurant facilities.
Pro shop, club hire, caddy
car & bugie hire.
Open Competitions: Open
week last week in July.
Contact Kevin Carrie
Tel: (041) 9822333.

NO.	BLUE METRES	WHITE METRES	PAR	S.I.	NO.	BLUE METRES	WHITE METRES	PAR	S.I.
1	354	329	4	7	10	480	441	5	18
2	141	134	3	11	11	368	344	4	10
3	347	340	4	15	12	419	392	4	8
4	402	388	4	3	13	412	370	4	4
5	385	353	4	1	14	401	384	4	2
6	484	469	5	17	15	154	138	3	12
7	404	384	4	5	16	342	338	4	16
8	505	494	5	13	17	171	156	3	14
9	186	168	3	9	18	465	453	5	6
OUT	3,208	3,059	36		IN	3,212	3,016	36	
					TOTAL	6,420	6,075		
				STANDARD SCRATCH		74	72		

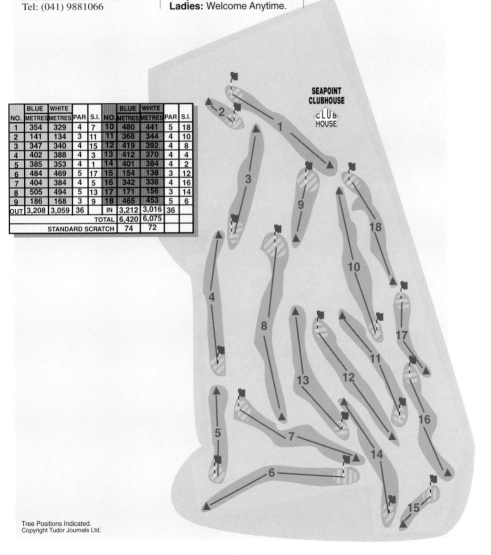

SEAPOINT
CLUBHOUSE

Tree Positions Indicated.
Copyright Tudor Journals Ltd.

**Ashbourne Golf Club,
Ashbourne, Co Meath.
Tel: (01) 835 2005.
Fax: (01) 835 2561**

LOCATION: One mile from
Ashbourne, 12 miles (20 mins
drive) from Dublin.
SECRETARY: Aidan Punch.
Tel: (01) 835 2005.
ARCHITECT: Des Smyth.

Undulating parkland course with
great variety incorporated in design.
Water comes into play at eight holes
in the form of the Broadmeadow
River and a number of lakes on the

course. A fine blend of established and
younger trees contributes to the players
overall enjoyment of this peaceful
countryside course.

COURSE INFORMATION

**Par 71; SSS 70; Length
6,420 yards.**
Visitors: Welcome Mon – Fri and
Sat/Sun afternoons.
Opening Hours: 9.00am – dusk.
Ladies: No restrictions.
Green Fees: Mon-Fri €35
Sat./Sun/Bank Holidays €45.

Juveniles: Must be
accompanied by an adult.
Clubhouse Hours:
Normal licensing hours.
Clubhouse Dress:
Neat casual dress required.
Clubhouse Facilities:
Lounge bar, bar food and full
restaurant.
Open Competitions:
Regularly during summer
months – Open Week mid
June.

NO.	MEDAL METRES	GEN. METRES	PAR	S.I.	NO.	MEDAL METRES	GEN. METRES	PAR	S.I.
1	274	270	4	10	10	170	149	3	9
2	155	147	3	16	11	362	347	4	3
3	330	322	4	2	12	358	350	4	1
4	450	440	5	6	13	140	133	3	15
5	144	136	3	18	14	471	454	5	5
6	487	477	5	12	15	322	314	4	11
7	356	346	4	8	16	138	131	3	17
8	405	396	4	4	17	489	481	5	7
9	346	334	4	14	18	320	314	4	13
OUT	2,947	2,868	36		IN	2,770	2,673	35	
					TOTAL	5,717	5,541	71	
					STANDARD SCRATCH	70	69		

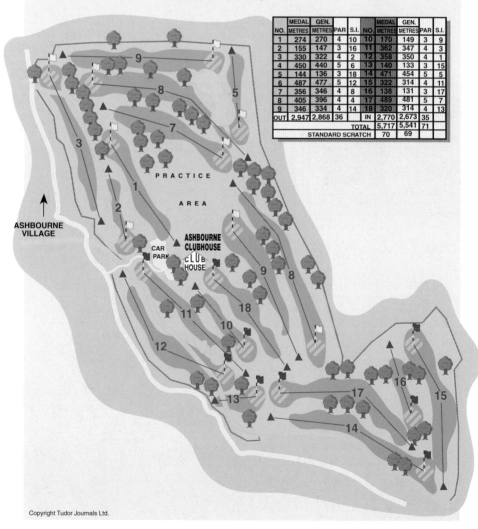

Copyright Tudor Journals Ltd.

**Thomastown,
Dunshaughlin, Co. Meath.
Tel: (01) 8250021.
Fax (01) 8250400.**

LOCATION: 1 mile from Dunshaughlin – off Ratoath road.
HON. SECRETARY: Micheal Fogarty.
Tel: (01) 8250021.
ARCHITECT: R. J. Browne.
CLUB ADMINISTRATOR: Kate O' Rourke.

A new 27 hole course which opened in June 1990. It is situated in a beautiful parkland setting, with a memorable 1st hole playing over the lake. There is also a driving range available and a new nine hole course was opened in August 1992.

COURSE INFORMATION

**27 Hole: Par 73; SSS 72;
Length 6,849 yards.**

Visitors: Welcome any day.
Opening Hours: Sunrise – Sunset.
Avoid: Saturday and Sunday mornings (18 hole course only).
Ladies: Welcome.
Green Fees: €26 Mon – Thurs; €32 Fri – Sun.
Juveniles: Must be accompanied by an adult. Telephone appointment required for weekend play.
Clubhouse Hours: 8.00am – midnight.
Clubhouse Dress: Casual.

Clubhouse Facilities: Dining room, snack bar and a la carte available all day. Pro Shop, Services professional, SOG practice balls, driving range & lessons Tel: 8250793
Open Competitions: Various open days in May, June and July; Open week – August.

COURSE A & B

CHAMP YARDS	MEDAL YARDS	PAR	S.I.	NO.	CHAMP YARDS	MEDAL YARDS	PAR	S.I.
548	539	5	9	10	490	481	5	16
162	156	3	15	11	378	370	4	8
577	536	5	3	12	386	386	4	4
200	192	3	11	13	153	153	3	18
443	379	4	1	14	421	410	4	2
380	367	4	7	15	395	385	4	6
427	419	4	5	16	177	167	3	16
338	322	4	13	17	380	370	4	12
462	462	5	17	18	562	559	5	10
3,507	3,372	37		IN	3,342	3,281	36	
				TOTAL	6,849	6,653	73	
				STANDARD SCRATCH	71	71		

COURSE B & C

CHAMP YARDS	MEDAL YARDS	PAR	S.I.	NO.	CHAMP YARDS	MEDAL YARDS	PAR	S.I.
490	481	5	12	10	344	322	4	11
378	370	4	14	11	182	175	3	7
386	366	4	4	12	514	507	5	13
153	153	3	18	13	368	361	4	5
421	410	4	2	14	432	425	4	1
395	385	4	8	15	339	339	4	15
177	157	3	6	16	138	138	3	17
380	370	4	16	17	393	385	4	3
562	559	5	10	18	382	376	4	9
3,342	3,281	36		IN	3,092	3,028	35	
				TOTAL	6,434	6,309	71	
				STANDARD SCRATCH	70	69		

COURSE A & C

CHAMP YARDS	MEDAL YARDS	PAR	S.I.	NO.	CHAMP YARDS	MEDAL YARDS	PAR	S.I.
344	322	4	12	10	548	539	5	11
182	175	3	6	11	162	156	8	15
514	507	5	14	12	577	536	5	5
368	361	4	6	13	200	192	3	9
432	425	4	2	14	413	379	4	1
339	339	4	16	15	380	367	4	7
138	138	3	16	16	427	419	4	3
393	385	4	4	17	338	322	4	18
382	376	4	10	18	462	462	5	17
3,092	3,028	35		IN	3,507	3,372	37	
				TOTAL	6,599	6,400	72	
				STANDARD SCRATCH	71	70		

COURSE A

BLACK BUSH CLUBHOUSE

CLUB HOUSE

COURSE C

COURSE B

BLACK BUSH CLUBHOUSE   CLUB HOUSE

Copyright Tudor Journals Ltd.

Kells, Co. Meath.
Tel: (046) 40146.
Fax: (046) 49282.
LOCATION: Kells/Navan road – within one mile of town.
HON. SECRETARY: Micheal O' Grady. Tel: (046) 40146.
PROFESSIONAL: Brendan McGovern. Tel: (046) 40639.

Generally accepted as a first class parkland course, the Headfort Club is set in the rolling countryside of Kells. Two 18-hole Courses. New course designed by Christy O' Connor Jnr. Expect a stroke saver shortly for the new course.

COURSE INFORMATION

Par 72; SSS 71; Length 6,007 metres.
Visitors: Welcome.
Opening Hours: Sunrise – Sunset.
Ladies: Welcome. Ladies day; Tuesday (mostly old course)
Green Fees: Old Course €35 Midweek; £40 Weekends New Course €50
Juveniles: Must be accompanied by an adult (adults with juveniles must give way). Lessons available by prior arrangement; Club hire available; Caddy service available by prior arrangments; Telephone appointment required.
Clubhouse Hours: 9.00am – 11.30pm.
Clubhouse Dress: Casual.
Clubhouse Facilities: Full facilities in new clubhouse.

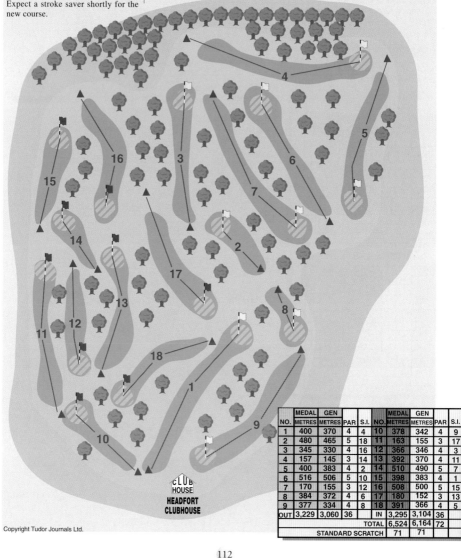

HEADFORT
CLUBHOUSE

NO.	MEDAL METRES	GEN METRES	PAR	S.I.	NO.	MEDAL METRES	GEN METRES	PAR	S.I.
1	400	370	4	4	10	378	342	4	9
2	480	465	5	18	11	163	155	3	17
3	345	330	4	16	12	366	346	4	3
4	157	145	3	14	13	392	370	4	11
5	400	383	4	2	14	510	490	5	7
6	516	506	5	10	15	398	383	4	1
7	170	155	3	12	16	508	500	5	15
8	384	372	4	6	17	180	152	3	13
9	377	334	4	8	18	391	366	4	5
OUT	3,229	3,060	36		IN	3,295	3,104	36	
					TOTAL	6,524	6,164	72	
					STANDARD SCRATCH	71	71		

Copyright Tudor Journals Ltd.

**Gallow, Kilcock,
Co. Meath.
Tel: (01) 6287592.
Fax: (01) 6287283.**

LOCATION: South Meath.
SECRETARY: Brendon Tyrrell.
MANAGER: Seamus Kelly.
ARCHITECT: Eddie Hackett.

A relatively easy course for experienced players. Large greens and tees. Generally flat but slopes into a centre stream that features in the course. The club has 400 members and all visitors are welcome. An extra nine holes, recently constructed to the west of the 6th green, create more of a challenge now. What is shown as the 7th, 8th, and 9th, are now the 16th, 17th, and 18th. The new nine holes (not shown in the diagram below) are similar to the original nine holes and include two par 5's.

COURSE INFORMATION

**Par 71; SSS 70; Length 5,801 metres.
Visitors:** Welcome except Sunday morning. Saturday by prior arrangement.
Opening Hours: Sunrise – sunset.

Ladies: Welcome.
Green Fees: €20 Mon – Fri; €25 Sat / Sun,€13 with member; €8 Juveniles.
Juveniles: Welcome (must be accompanied by an adult).
Clubhouse Dress: Neat.
Clubhouse Facilities: Bar open everyday. Catering by prior arrangement.
Open Competitions: Open Weekends – July. Various other Open Days throughout the summer.

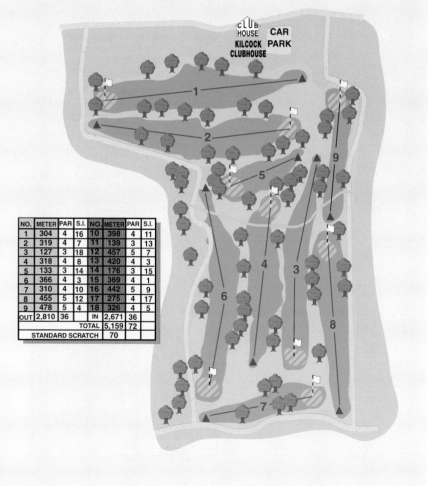

NO.	METER	PAR	S.I.	NO.	METER	PAR	S.I.
1	304	4	16	10	398	4	11
2	319	4	7	11	139	3	13
3	127	3	18	12	457	5	7
4	318	4	8	13	420	4	3
5	133	3	14	14	176	3	15
6	366	4	3	15	369	4	1
7	310	4	10	16	442	5	9
8	455	5	12	17	275	4	17
9	478	5	4	18	326	4	5
OUT	2,810	36		IN	2,671	36	
				TOTAL	5,159	72	
	STANDARD SCRATCH				70		

Copyright Tudor Journals Ltd.

Bettystown, Co. Meath.
Tel: (041) 9827170
/ 9827534 / 9827563.

Location: Thirty miles north of
Dublin.
Secretary: Helen Finnegan.
Tel: (041) 9827170.
Professional: Robert J Browne.
Tel: (041) 9828793.

This is a traditional links course with the
reputation of a tough par of 70. It has
produced many fine players, the best known
of whom is Des Smyth.

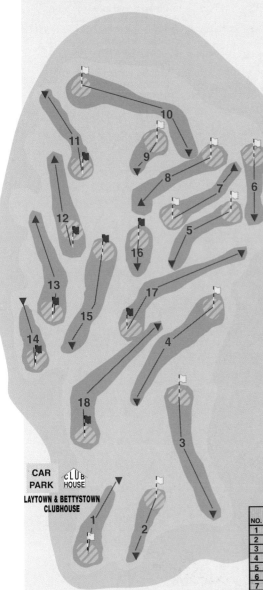

COURSE INFORMATION

Par 71; SSS 72; Length 5,852
metres.
Visitors: Welcome Mon – Fri.
Opening Hours: 8.30am – Sunset.
Avoid: Weekends am.
Ladies: Welcome.
Ladies Days: Mon. and Thurs.
Green Fees: €45 Mon – Fri;
€55 Weekend. Ring for societiy rates
Juveniles: Welcome – must be
accompanied by an adult before
6pm. Lessons available by prior
arrangement; Club Hire available.
Clubhouse Hours: 10.30am –
licencing hours.
Clubhouse Dress: Neat Dress.
Clubhouse Facilities: Full bar and
catering facilities available everyday.
Open Competitions:
Open weeks June, July & August.
Booking through office only –
Tel: (041) 9827170.

NO.	WHITE METRES	GREEN METRES	PAR	S.I.	NO.	WHITE METRES	GREEN METRES	PAR	S.I.
1	294	288	4	12	10	382	375	4	3
2	309	296	4	10	11	347	337	4	7
3	372	362	4	4	12	421	410	4	1
4	443	434	5	17	13	354	345	4	6
5	333	325	4	9	14	312	307	3	16
6	153	142	3	13	15	361	352	4	8
7	361	350	4	2	16	176	172	3	11
8	361	353	3	5	17	278	271	4	18
9	163	153	4	14	18	432	423	5	15
OUT	2,789	2,703	35		IN	3,063	2,994	35	
					TOTAL	5,852	5,697	71	
	STANDARD SCRATCH					72			

Copyright Tudor Journals Ltd.

**Navan Golf Club,
Proudstown, Navan,
Co. Meath. Tel: (046) 72888.**

SECRETARY: Francis Duffy.
ARCHITECT: Bobby Browne.
SUPERINDENT: Donal Curtis.
PROFFESSIONAL: Emmanuel Riblet.

Parkland course featuring 9 holes within racetrack and 9 outer holes. Excellent sand based greens with a number of water features. 15 bay

driving range open 8am – 9.30pm.

COURSE INFORMATION

Par 72; SSS 72; Length 6,728 yards.
Visitors: Welcome.
Opening Hours:
Dawn to Dusk.
Green Fees: €22 mid-week & €27 weekends & Bank Holidays.
Juveniles: €11 mid-week &

€15 weekends & Bank Holidays.
Clubhouse Hours:
10.00am – 11.30pm.
Clubhouse Dress:
As per course.
Clubhouse Facilities: Public bar and restaurant.
Golf lessons by appointment.
Open Competitions:
Phone club for details.

MEDAL METRES	GEN METRES	PAR	S.I.	NO.	MEDAL METRES	GEN METRES	PAR	S.I.
85	396	4	7	10	406	463	5	6
24	164	3	15	11	318	375	4	16
38	381	4	3	12	124	148	3	12
63	440	5	5	13	300	359	4	18
79	333	4	1	14	122	158	3	14
14	403	4	13	15	276	358	4	4
57	336	4	17	16	310	376	4	8
06	152	3	9	17	310	363	4	10
00	474	5	11	18	359	435	5	2
27	3,146	36		IN	2,482	2,968	36	
				TOTAL	5,109	6,114	72	
STANDARD SCRATCH		72	72					

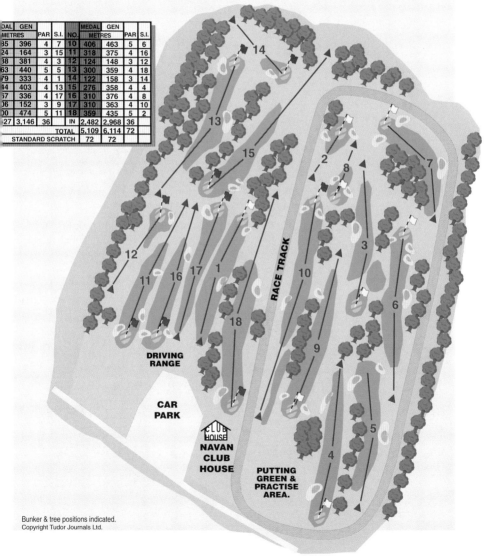

DRIVING RANGE

CAR PARK

CLUB HOUSE
NAVAN CLUB HOUSE

RACE TRACK

PUTTING GREEN & PRACTISE AREA.

Bunker & tree positions indicated.
Copyright Tudor Journals Ltd.

Bellinter, Navan, Co. Meath.
Tel: (046) 25244/25508.
LOCATION: Twenty miles north of Dublin
off National Primary Route N 3.
HON. SECRETARY: Mr Paddy O'Brien.
Tel: (046) 25508.
PROFESSIONAL: Mr Adam Whiston.
Tel: (046) 26009.
ARCHITECT: Des Smyth Golf Design Ltd.

Parkland course situated in the heart of Co.
Meath adjacent to the Hill of Tara, ancient
home of the high kings of Ireland. A pleasant
tree-lined course of average length with various
degrees of difficulty. New clubhouse planned
for 2000.

COURSE INFORMATION

**Par 72; SSS 71; Length 5,904
metres.**
Visitors: Welcome.
Opening Hours: 8.00am – 4.00pm.
Avoid: Ladies Day (Tuesday).
Ladies: Welcome.
Green Fees: €35 Mon – Fri;
€40 Sat / Sun.
Juveniles: Welcome. Lessons
available by prior arrangement; Club
Hire available; Caddy service
available by prior arrangements;
Telephone appointment required.
Clubhouse Hours: 10.30am –11.00pm.
Clubhouse Dress: Neat / smart.
Clubhouse Facilities: 10.00am –
10.30pm (summer); 12.00 noon –
6.00pm (winter). Full catering

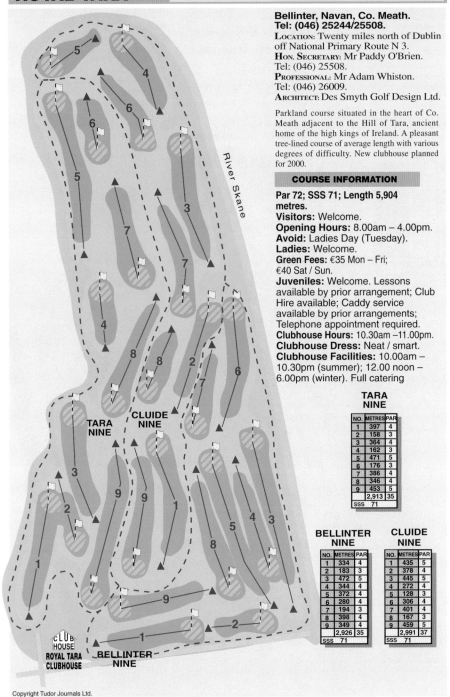

TARA NINE

NO.	METRES	PAR
1	397	4
2	158	3
3	364	4
4	162	3
5	471	5
6	176	3
7	386	4
8	346	4
9	453	5
	2,913	35
SSS	71	

BELLINTER NINE

NO.	METRES	PAR
1	334	4
2	183	3
3	472	5
4	344	4
5	372	4
6	280	4
7	194	3
8	398	4
9	349	4
	2,926	35
SSS	71	

CLUIDE NINE

NO.	METRES	PAR
1	435	5
2	378	4
3	445	5
4	272	4
5	128	3
6	306	4
7	401	4
8	167	3
9	459	5
	2,991	37
SSS	71	

River Skane

TARA NINE

CLUIDE NINE

ROYAL TARA CLUBHOUSE

CLUB HOUSE

BELLINTER NINE

Copyright Tudor Journals Ltd.

Newtownmoynagh, Trim, Co. Meath.
Tel: (046) 31463.

LOCATION: Three miles from Trim on Longwood road
SECRETARY: Jerry Kearney. Tel: (046) 31463/(086) 2749859.
ARCHITECT: E. Hackett and Tom Craddock.
PROFESSIONAL: Robin Machin

Originally a pleasing nine hole course which has been recently developed into eighteen holes. Work was completed on the course in 1990.

COURSE INFORMATION

Par 73; SSS 72; Length 6,720 yards.
Visitors: Welcome.
Opening Hours: 8.00am – Sunset.
Avoid: Thursday.
Ladies: Welcome.
Ladies Day: Thursday.

Green Fees: €30 Mon – Thurs; €35 Fri/Sat/Sun
Juveniles: Welcome.
Clubhouse Hours: 10.30am – 11.30pm.
Clubhouse Dress: Casual.
Clubhouse Facilities: Full catering facilities.

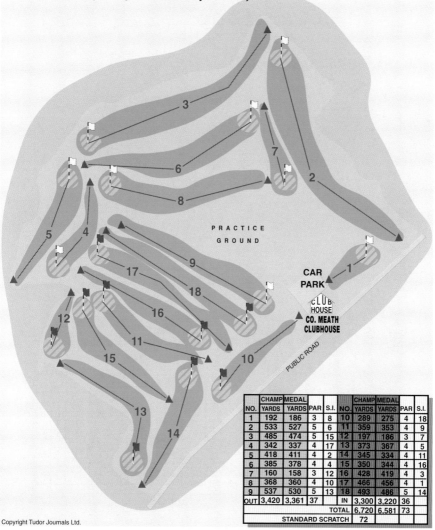

NO.	CHAMP YARDS	MEDAL YARDS	PAR	S.I.	NO.	CHAMP YARDS	MEDAL YARDS	PAR	S.I.
1	192	186	3	8	10	289	275	4	18
2	533	527	5	6	11	359	353	4	9
3	485	474	5	15	12	197	186	3	7
4	342	337	4	17	13	373	367	4	5
5	418	411	4	2	14	345	334	4	11
6	385	378	4	4	15	350	344	4	16
7	160	158	3	12	16	428	419	4	3
8	368	360	4	10	17	466	456	4	1
9	537	530	5	13	18	493	486	5	14
OUT	3,420	3,361	37		IN	3,300	3,220	36	
					TOTAL	6,720	6,581	73	
					STANDARD SCRATCH	72			

Copyright Tudor Journals Ltd.

The Glenns, Birr, Co. Offaly.
Tel: (0509) 20082.

LOCATION: Two miles west of Birr.

Hon. SECRETARY: Mary O'Gorman.

OFFICE SECRETARY: Joan Grimes

Undulating parkland course with sandy sub-soil, the greatest difficulties being "blind" shots and the strategic placing of pines.

COURSE INFORMATION

Par 70; SSS 70; Length 5,727 metres.
Visitors: Welcome, limited to 11.00am – 12.00 noon on Sundays.
Opening Hours: Sunrise – sunset.
Avoid: Weekends if possible.

Green Fees: Mon – Fri €23, Sat / Sun / Bank Hols €32.
Juveniles: Welcome.
Clubhouse Hours: 10.00am – 12.00 midnight.
Clubhouse Dress: Neat/Casual.
Clubhouse Facilities: Food available every day.

NO.	CHAMP METRES	MEDAL METRES	PAR	S.I.	NO.	CHAMP METRES	MEDAL METRES	PAR	S.I.
1	311	300	4	13	10	325	313	4	7
2	324	319	4	15	11	390	363	4	2
3	130	126	3	17	12	356	340	4	10
4	325	319	4	8	13	364	349	4	5
5	461	453	5	18	14	174	160	3	14
6	438	432	5	9	15	226	217	3	6
7	369	359	4	3	16	302	285	4	16
8	169	163	3	12	17	350	306	4	11
9	413	407	4	1	18	397	380	4	4
OUT	2,940	2,878			IN	2,884	2,713		
					TOTAL	5,824	5,535		
					STANDARD SCRATCH				

Copyright Tudor Journals Ltd.

**Castle Barna Golf Club,
Daingean, Co. Offaly.
Tel: (0506) 53384.**

LOCATION: 8 miles south of main Dublin to Galway road (N6). One hour from Dublin.
SECRETARY: Evelyn Mangan.
Tel: (0506) 53384.
ARCHITECT: Alan Duggan.

18 hole parkland course, with rolling parkland and natural water hazards making it an interesting course to play. The 9th hole (par 3) set alongside the Grand Canal is a real challenge.

COURSE INFORMATION

Par 72; SSS 69; Length 6,200 yards.
Visitors: Welcome.
Opening Hours: Sunrise – sunset.
Ladies: Welcome every day.
Green Fees: Weekdays €15; weekends €20.
Juveniles: Weekdays €5; Weekends €5.
Clubhouse Hours: 8.00am – sunset.

Clubhouse Dress: Neat.
Clubhouse Facilities: Coffee shop, golf clubs for hire, golf shop, bar.
Open Competitions: June, July and August.

NO.	MEDAL METRES	FWARD METRES	PAR	S.I.	NO.	MEDAL METRES	FWARD METRES	PAR	S.I.
1	326	310	4	6	10	425	405	5	15
2	277	275	4	14	11	170	146	3	13
3	163	153	3	8	12	296	290	4	9
4	268	255	4	12	13	270	245	4	17
5	158	155	3	4	14	325	305	4	7
6	478	458	5	10	15	365	345	4	1
7	402	390	5	16	16	456	435	5	11
8	375	365	4	2	17	384	374	4	3
9	119	114	3	18	18	393	373	4	5
OUT	2,566	2,475	35		IN	3,084	2,918	37	
					TOTAL	5,650	5,393	72	
					STANDARD SCRATCH	69	68		

CASTLE BARNA CLUBHOUSE

GRAND CANAL

Bunker and tree positions indicated.
Copyright Tudor Journals Ltd.

**Kishawanny, Edenderry,
Co. Offaly.
Tel: (0405) 31072.
Fax: (0405) 33911.
www.edenderrygolfclub.com**

LOCATION: Just under a mile from the town centre.
HON. SECRETARY: Pat O'Conell.
ARCHITECT: Havers (original nine hole). E. Hackett (new nine holes).

Unique in so much that it is built almost entirely on fen peat. An attractive 18 hole course,the par 3's in particular being challenging. Trees and traps are ideally located.

COURSE INFORMATION

**Par 72; SSS 72; Length 6,029 metres.
Visitors:** Welcome (Weekends Limited).
Opening Hours: 8.30am – Sunset.
Avoid: Thursdays (Ladies Comp. Day).

Green Fees: Weekend €35, Weekday €30. Reductions for groups and societies.
Juveniles: Must be accompanied by an adult.
Clubhouse Hours: 11.00am – 11.00pm March – October.
Clubhouse Dress: Casual.
Clubhouse Facilities: Full bar & catering facilities.
Open Competitions: First week in August & most Bank Holidays.

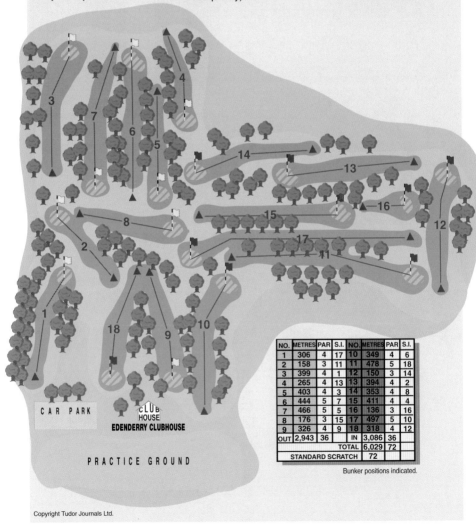

EDENDERRY CLUBHOUSE

CAR PARK

PRACTICE GROUND

NO.	METRES	PAR	S.I.	NO.	METRES	PAR	S.I.
1	306	4	17	10	349	4	6
2	158	3	11	11	478	5	18
3	399	4	1	12	150	3	14
4	265	4	13	13	394	4	2
5	403	4	3	14	353	4	8
6	444	5	7	15	411	4	4
7	466	5	5	16	136	3	16
8	176	3	15	17	497	5	10
9	326	4	9	18	318	4	12
OUT	2,943	36		IN	3,086	36	
				TOTAL	6,029	72	
STANDARD SCRATCH					72		

Bunker positions indicated.

Copyright Tudor Journals Ltd.

Esker Hills Golf Club,
Ballykilmurray,
Tullamore,Co. Offaly.
Tel: (0506) 55999.
Fax: (0506) 55021.
Email: info@eskerhillsgolf.com
www.eskerhillsgolf.com
LOCATION: Three miles from Tullamore town, off the main Tullamore – Clara road.
DIRECTOR: Donal Molloy.
Tel: (0506) 55999
Tel: (087) 2677567.
ARCHITECT: C. O'Connor Jnr.

The course has a series of valleys and plateaux, part of the Esker Riada which together with the natural lakes and woodlands makes for an amazing variety of challenging golf holes. "A great test of golf to all who care to challenge it."

"Esker Hills is one of Ireland's finest Golf Courses. If you are a golfer, never ever pass this place"
    -*David Walshe, The Sunday Times.*

COURSE INFORMATION

Par 71; SSS 71; Length 6,669 yards.

Visitors: Welcome every day. Booking required.
Opening Hours:
Summer: 8am – sunset.
Winter: 9am – 5pm.
Green Fees: €27 weekdays; €37 weekends/Bank Holidays.
Clubhouse Dress:
Smart / Casual.
Additional Facilities:
Esker Hills is situated in the heart of Ireland where a golfing paradise awaits you!

NO.	MEDAL METRES	GEN. METRES	PAR	S.I.	NO.	MEDAL METRES	GEN. METRES	PAR	S.I.
1	493	475	5	17	10	307	299	4	18
2	355	337	4	11	11	390	371	4	4
3	490	459	4	1	12	396	349	4	6
4	393	358	4	5	13	201	166	3	16
5	171	161	3	15	14	360	344	4	10
6	535	511	5	9	15	191	176	3	8
7	428	395	4	3	16	580	540	5	14
8	355	333	4	13	17	450	427	4	2
9	181	163	3	7	18	393	376	4	12
OUT	3,401	3,192	36		IN	3,268	3,048	35	
					TOTAL	6,669	6,240	71	
					STANDARD SCRATCH	71	71		

Bunker and tree positions indicated.

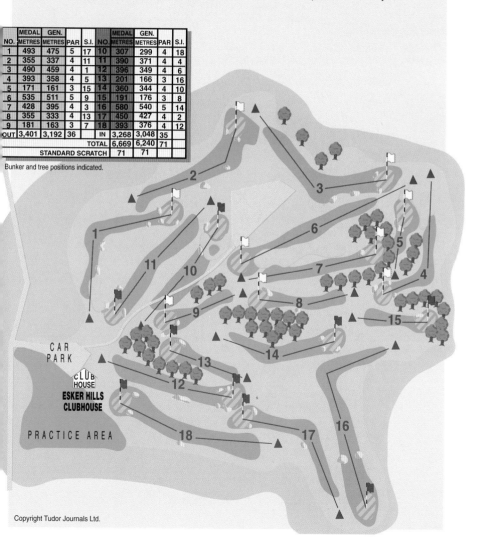

CAR PARK

CLUB HOUSE
ESKER HILLS CLUBHOUSE

PRACTICE AREA

Copyright Tudor Journals Ltd.

**Brookfield, Tullamore,
Co. Offaly.
Tel: (0506) 21439.**
Tullamoregolfclub@eircom.net
www.tullamoregolfclub.ie

LOCATION: Three miles south of
Tullamore town.
HON SECRETARY: Jo Barber-
Loughnane.
Tel: (0506) 29959.
PROFESSIONAL: Donagh MacArdle.
Tel: (0506) 51757.
ARCHITECT: James Braid, Paddy
Merrigan.

Parkland course situated in a very
attractive tree lined setting on the
outskirts of Tullamore.

COURSE INFORMATION

**Par 70; SSS 71; Length
6,457 yards.**

Visitors: Welcome. Tel
Professional for tee-times.
Societies contact Hon.
Secretary well in advance.
Opening Hours: Sunrise –
sunset.
Avoid: Tuesday.
Ladies: Tuesday. Lessons
available, Club hire & Caddy
service available, telephone
appointment required for
groups only. (Advised for other
days).
Green Fees: Mon - Fri €32;
weekends €40.

Clubhouse Hours: 8.30am –
11.30pm.
Clubhouse Dress: Neat /
casual.
Clubhouse Facilities: Full
bar and catering facilities.
Open Competitions: Open
Charity Fourball -
March/August; Open Week -
June; Mixed - July;
Intermediate Scratch Cup –
September; Mixed Hamper –
October; Men's Foursomes
Hamper – November.

NO.	YARDS	PAR	S.I.	NO.	YARDS	PAR	S.I.
1	359	4	8	10	382	4	9
2	177	3	14	11	325	4	17
3	429	4	4	12	197	3	11
4	492	5	6	13	387	4	13
5	439	4	2	14	474	4	1
6	189	3	10	15	548	5	7
7	489	5	12	16	419	4	3
8	338	4	16	17	184	3	15
9	148	3	18	18	452	4	5
OUT	3,060	35		IN	3,368	35	
				TOTAL	6,428	70	
				STANDARD SCRATCH		70	

OUT OF BOUNDS

CLUB
HOUSE
TULLAMORE
CLUBHOUSE

Copyright Tudor Journals Ltd.

Delvin, Co Westmeath
Tel: (044) 64315.

LOCATION: In the village of Delvin on the N52 road from the North Dundalk to the West.
MANAGER: Fiona Dillon.
PROFESSIONAL: David Keenaghan.
ARCHITECT: John Day.

Set in the Parkland of Clonyn Castle, this course provides a challenging test of Golf amid an unique historic setting. A Ruined castle provides the focus of the back nine. The course opened in 1992 and has an active club membership. There are full bar and restaurant facilities.

COURSE INFORMATION

Par 70; SSS 68; Length 0,000 metres.
Visitors: Welcome, prior reservation at weekends necessary
Opening Hours: Daylight hours.
Ladies: Welcome
Green Fees: €24 (weekdays) €26 (weekends).
Juveniles: Welcome.
Clubhouse Hours: Daylight hours.
Clubhouse Dress: casual
Clubhouse Facilities: Full bar and restaurant facilities.

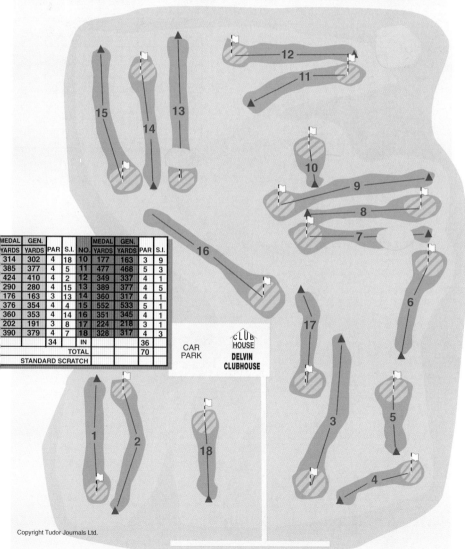

	MEDAL YARDS	GEN. YARDS	PAR	S.I.	NO.	MEDAL YARDS	GEN. YARDS	PAR	S.I.
	314	302	4	18	10	177	163	3	9
	385	377	4	5	11	477	468	5	3
	424	410	4	2	12	349	337	4	1
	290	280	4	15	13	389	377	4	5
	176	163	3	13	14	360	317	4	1
	376	354	4	4	15	552	533	5	1
	360	353	4	14	16	351	345	4	1
	202	191	3	8	17	224	218	3	1
	390	379	4	7	18	328	317	4	3
			34		IN			36	
					TOTAL			70	
					STANDARD SCRATCH				

CAR PARK

CLUB HOUSE
DELVIN CLUBHOUSE

Copyright Tudor Journals Ltd.

Glasson Golf Hotel and Country Club, Glasson, Athlone, Co. Westmeath.
Tel: (0902) 85120. (Office)
(Clubhouse)
Fax: (0902) 85444.
Email: info@glassongolf.ie
Web: www.glassongolf.ie
LOCATION: 6 miles north of Athlone Town on the N55.
SECRETARY: Fidelma Reid.
Tel: (0902) 85120.
ARCHITECT: Christy O'Connor Jnr.

A Christy O'Connor Jnr. design that has golfers talking. Every hole is fascinating and measuring over 7000 yds from the championship tees it is a true test for all golfing standards. Magnificent new on site hotel now open -treat yourself 'play and stay'.

COURSE INFORMATION

Par 72; SSS 74; Length 7,120 Yards.
Visitors: Welcome anyday.

Opening Hours: Sunrise – Sunset.
Green Fees: €45 Mon – Thur, €50 Fri & Sun, €60 Sat. Caddies available on request.
Clubhouse Facilities: Catering facilities available at all times.
Open Competitions: Easter weekend.
Hotel: 29 Bedrooms beautiful views, call for details.

NO.	CHAMP YARDS	MEDAL YARDS	PAR	S.I.	NO.	CHAMP YARDS	MEDAL YARDS	PAR	S.I.
1	396	373	4	15	10	513	476	5	18
2	552	536	5	7	11	183	165	3	14
3	219	190	3	5	12	406	380	4	16
4	406	384	4	9	13	397	369	4	6
5	199	177	3	17	14	566	521	5	12
6	559	535	5	13	15	185	170	3	8
7	410	386	4	1	16	452	417	4	4
8	432	404	4	11	17	450	432	4	2
9	412	377	4	3	18	383	361	4	10
OUT	3,585	3,362	36		IN	3,535	3,291	36	
					TOTAL	7,120	6,653	72	
					STANDARD SCRATCH	74	72		

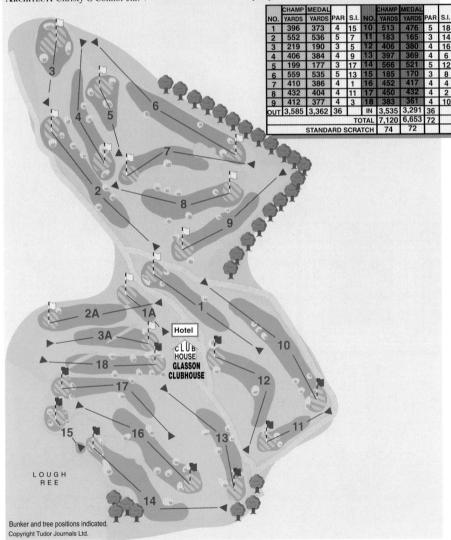

Bunker and tree positions indicated.
Copyright Tudor Journals Ltd.

**Aghanargit, Moate,
Co. Westmeath.
Tel: (0902) 81271.
Email:
moategolfclub@eircom.net**

LOCATION: Access via town centre.
HON SECRETARY: P.J. Higgins.
Tel: (0902) 36198.
PRESIDENT: Anita Mc Loughlin.
CAPTAIN: Louis Cunningham

A narrow course which adds to the degree of difficulty. An 18 hole parkland course. It enjoys good drainage which means it is not affected by heavy rainfall and is playable throughout the winter.

COURSE INFORMATION

**Par 72; SSS 70; Length 6,287 yards.
Visitors:** Welcome.
Opening Hours: Sunrise – sunset.
Avoid: Sunday.
Ladies: Welcome. Letter of introduction / handicap certificate for Open Competitions.
Green Fees: Mon – Fri €20; €25 Saturday, Sunday & Bank Holiday Weekends; €12 with Member anytime.

Juveniles: Welcome. Caddy service available by prior arrangement; handicap certificate required for open competitions; telephone appointment required.
Clubhouse Hours: 8.30am – 11.00 pm.
Clubhouse Dress: Casual.
Clubhouse Facilities: New clubhouse with full catering and bar facilities at all times.
Open Competitions: Contact (0902) 81271 for details.

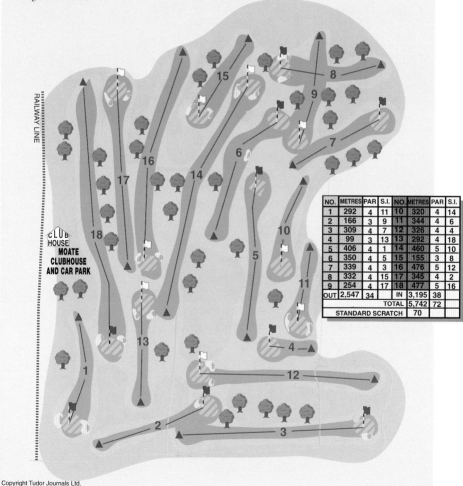

NO.	METRES	PAR	S.I.	NO.	METRES	PAR	S.I.
1	292	4	11	10	320	4	14
2	166	3	9	11	344	4	6
3	309	4	7	12	326	4	4
4	99	3	13	13	292	4	18
5	406	4	1	14	460	5	10
6	350	4	5	15	155	3	8
7	339	4	3	16	476	5	12
8	332	4	15	17	345	4	2
9	254	4	17	18	477	5	16
OUT	2,547	34		IN	3,195	38	
				TOTAL	5,742	72	
			STANDARD SCRATCH	70			

Copyright Tudor Journals Ltd.

**Belvedere, Mullingar,
Co. Westmeath.
Tel: (044) 40085.**

LOCATION: Three miles south
of Mullingar.
HON. SECRETARY: John Wims.
Tel: (044) 42753 (H).
SECRETARY / MANAGER:
Anne Scully. Tel: (044) 48366.
Fax: (044) 41499.
PROFESSIONAL: John Burns.
Tel: (044) 40085.

This parkland golf at its most
sublime. Generous, rolling fairways
wind their paths through mature

timbers. It hosts an important amateur
events in Britain and Ireland annually
in the shape of the Mullingar Scratch
Cup.

COURSE INFORMATION

**Par 72; SSS 71; Length
6,198 metres.**
Visitors: Welcome. Prior
arrangement required for
weekends.
Opening Hours:
8.00am – sunset.
Avoid: Wednesday and
weekends.

Green Fees: €32 Mon –
Fri; €38 weekends. Sun-
members only.
Ladies: Welcome.
Juveniles: Welcome.
Clubhouse Hours:
10.00am – 11.30pm.
Clubhouse Dress:
Casual, no shorts.
Clubhouse Facilities:
Bar food.

NO.	METRES	PAR	S.I.	NO.	METRES	PAR	S.I.
1	332	4	1	1	421	4	2
2	182	3	0	1	360	4	9
3	379	4	7	1	139	3	1
4	480	5	4	1	360	4	6
5	173	3	1	1	470	5	5
6	313	4	4	1	154	3	1
7	444	4	1	1	485	5	7
8	329	4	2	1	371	4	1
9	330	4	1	1	476	5	3
OUT	2,96	3		IN	3,23	3	
				TOTAL		6	7
				STANDARD SCRATCH		6,19	

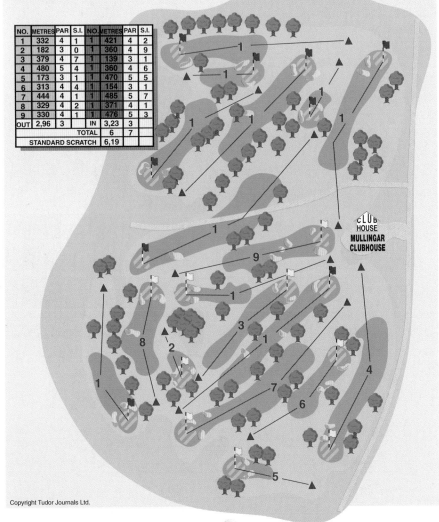

CLUB
HOUSE
MULLINGAR
CLUBHOUSE

Copyright Tudor Journals Ltd.

**Mount Temple Golf Club,
Mount Temple Village,
Moate, Co. Westmeath.
Tel: (0902) 81841/81545.
Fax: (0902) 81957.
Web: www.emerald-golf.com**

LOCATION: 4 1/2 miles east of Athlone, 4 1/2 miles west of Moate, just over 1 hour from Dublin and the K-Club and 5 miles east of Glasson.
SECRETARY: Michelle Allen.
Tel: (0902) 81841 clubhouse, (0902) 81545 office,
Internet: Mttemple@iol.ie
PROFESSIONAL: David Kinahan.
ARCHITECT: Michael Dolan.

Traditional built 18 hole championship course with links and parkland features incorporating calibre and character. Natural water hazards come into play on five holes. Panoramic views of the Midlands and playable all year.

COURSE INFORMATION

Par 72; SSS 72; Length 5,872 metres.
Visitors: Welcome.
Opening Hours: Sunrise – sunset.
Avoid: Playable all week, but check weekends.
Ladies: Welcome.

Green Fees: €25 weekdays; €32 weekends and public holidays.
Juveniles: Welcome.
Lessons and caddy service available by prior arrangement.
Clubhouse Hours: 8.30am – 11.30pm.
Clubhouse Dress: Neat and casual.
Clubhouse Facilities: Farmhouse cuisine in oldtime clubhouse atmosphere.

NO.	MEDAL METRES	METRES	PAR	S.I.	NO.	MEDAL METRES	METRES	PAR	S.I.
1	125	161	3	17	10	260	397	4	1
2	300	326	4	12	11	458	458	5	15
3	320	348	4	4	12	310	372	4	5
4	415	435	5	14	13	320	398	4	2
5	320	364	4	6	14	300	363	4	7
6	320	320	4	13	15	118	118	3	18
7	300	350	4	3	16	435	453	5	9
8	183	183	3	8	17	120	143	3	11
9	230	288	4	16	18	395	450	5	10
OUT	2,513	2,775	35		IN	2,716	3,152	37	
					TOTAL	5,229	5,927	72	
					STANDARD SCRATCH		72		

EGAN'S BAR

MOATE ►

CAR PARK

CLUB HOUSE

MOUNT TEMPLE CLUBHOUSE

◄ GLASSON

Copyright Tudor Journals Ltd.
Bunker and tree positions indicated.

Courtown Golf Club
Kiltennel, Gorey,
Co. Wexford
Tel: (055) 25166.
Fax: (055) 25553.

LOCATION: 3 miles from Gorey.
SECRETARY / MANAGER: David Cleere.
Tel: (055) 25166.
PROFESSIONAL: John Coone.
Tel: (055) 25860 / 25166.

This is a heavily wooded parkland course. Features are the 4 par 3's, particularly the nerve wracking 18th. Top class bar and catering facilities complement this excellent course.

The newly refurbished clubhouse has panoramic views across the course and the Irish Sea.

COURSE INFORMATION

**Par 71; SSS 71; Length
5,898 metres.**
Visitors: Welcome except on major competition days and Tuesdays.
Opening Hours: Sunrise – sunset.
Ladies: Welcome. Lessons available; Club Hire available; Caddy cars available.

Green Fees:

	Weekdays	weekends /Bank hols
Oct-Mar	€30	€36
Apr-Sept	€36	€42

Clubhouse Hours:
10.30am – 11.30pm.
Clubhouse Dress:
Casual/Neat.
Clubhouse Facilities:
April – October full catering available.
Open Competitions: Open Week June.

NO.	MEDAL METRES	GEN. METRES	PAR	S.I.	NO.	MEDAL METRES	GEN. METRES	PAR	S.I.
1	288	278	4	18	10	439	436	5	17
2	393	340	4	4	11	389	379	4	1
3	155	145	3	14	12	512	485	5	11
4	302	292	4	16	13	347	337	4	9
5	311	301	4	10	14	183	173	3	7
6	294	284	4	12	15	352	342	4	5
7	389	369	4	2	16	294	284	4	11
8	166	156	3	8	17	370	360	4	3
9	516	516	5	6	18	152	142	3	13
OUT	2,814	2,681	35		IN	3,038	2,938	36	
					TOTAL	5,898	5,619	71	
					STANDARD SCRATCH	70	69		

Copyright Tudor Journals Ltd.

Knockmarshall, Enniscorthy, Co. Wexford.
Tel: (054) 33191.
Fax: (054) 37637.

LOCATION: 2 miles from Enniscorthy post office off main New Ross Road.
SECRETARY: John Maguire.
Tel: (054) 33191. Fax: (054) 37637.
PROFESSIONAL: Martin Sludds.
ARCHITECT: E. Hackett.

A course of the highest quality. Excellent Greens. Enjoyable for all handicap players.

COURSE INFORMATION

Par 72; SSS 72; Length 6,115 metres.
Visitors: Welcome.
Opening Hours: Sunrise – Sunset.
Avoid: Sundays (telephone first).
Ladies: Welcome.
Juveniles: Welcome. Telephone appointment required for open competitions.
Green Fees: €25 weekdays, €34 weekends
Clubhouse Hours: 11.00am – 11.00pm; Full clubhouse facilities; Catering facilities up to 9pm daily.
Clubhouse Dress: Neat/casual.

NO.	CHAMP METRES	MEDAL METRES	PAR	S.I.	NO.	CHAMP METRES	MEDAL METRES	PAR	S.I.
1	166	156	3	14	10	484	447	5	9
2	352	327	4	6	11	506	490	5	17
3	131	121	3	18	12	165	155	3	15
4	488	448	5	12	13	343	330	4	7
5	468	448	5	8	14	350	336	4	5
6	178	154	3	10	15	402	390	4	1
7	387	375	4	4	16	314	304	4	13
8	363	348	4	2	17	367	357	4	3
9	333	314	4	16	18	318	308	4	11
OUT	2,866	2,691	35		IN	3,249	3,117	37	
					TOTAL	6,115	5,808	72	
					STANDARD SCRATCH	72	70		

Copyright Tudor Journals Ltd.

Tinneranny, New Ross, Co. Wexford.

LOCATION: Tinneranny.
HONORARY SECRETARY: Bill Hurley.
SECRETARY / MANAGER: Kathleen Daly.
Tel: (051) 421433.

Pleasant, well kept 18 hole golf course. Straight hitting and careful placing of shots is very important as the fairways are tight and allow little room for errors.

COURSE INFORMATION

Par 71; SSS 70; Length 5,751 metres.
Visitors: Welcome weekdays and Saturdays.
Avoid: Sundays.
Ladies Day: Wednesday.
Juveniles: Welcome – mornings.

Green Fees: €20 Mon – Fri; €30 Sat / Sun.
Clubhouse Hours:
8am – 11.30pm (summer);
9am – 10.30pm (winter).
Clubhouse Dress:
Neat / Casual.
Clubhouse Facilities:
Full catering by arrangement and bar every day.
Open competitions:
Open Week 8th-18th June,
Open Team Event 5th-6th Aug.

NO.	MEDAL METRES	GEN. METRES	PAR	S.I.	NO.	MEDAL METRES	GEN. METRES	PAR	S.I.
1	334	329	4	6	10	475	465	5	5
2	171	158	3	10	11	169	169	3	9
3	290	272	4	18	12	301	293	4	17
4	420	408	5	14	13	470	434	5	15
5	332	309	4	12	14	163	152	3	11
6	323	309	4	2	15	363	343	4	1
7	335	321	4	8	16	329	309	4	13
8	366	350	4	4	17	357	347	4	7
9	148	139	3	16	18	405	388	4	3
OUT	2,719	2,595	35		IN	3,032	2,900	36	
					TOTAL	5,751	5,495	71	
					STANDARD SCRATCH	70	69		

CLUB HOUSE

NEW ROSS CLUBHOUSE
CAR PARK

Bunker & Hedge positions indicated.
Copyright Tudor Journals Ltd.

Rosslare, Co. Wexford.
Tel: (053) 32203.

LOCATION: In the village of Rosslare.
SECRETARY: Emily Ward
MANAGER: James F. Hall.
PROFESSIONAL: Johnny Young.
Tel: (053) 32032.

Pleasant links which provides a good test of golf. An enjoyable course for both the good and not so good golfer.

COURSE INFORMATION

Par 72; SSS 72;
Length 6,608 yards.
Visitors: Welcome.
Opening Hours:
Sunrise – Sunset.
Avoid: No particular day.
Telephone first to avoid disappointment.
Ladies: Welcome.
Ladies Day Tuesday.
Juveniles: Welcome, must be accompanied by an adult.
Lessons available by prior arrangement; Club Hire available; Caddy service available by prior arrangment;

Green Fees: €35 Mon – Fri;
€50 Sat / Sun.
Clubhouse Hours: 9.00am – 11.30pm. Full clubhouse facilities; Full catering facilities.
Clubhouse Dress: Casual / neat.
Open Competitions: Most Sundays. In high season open to visitor paying green fees.

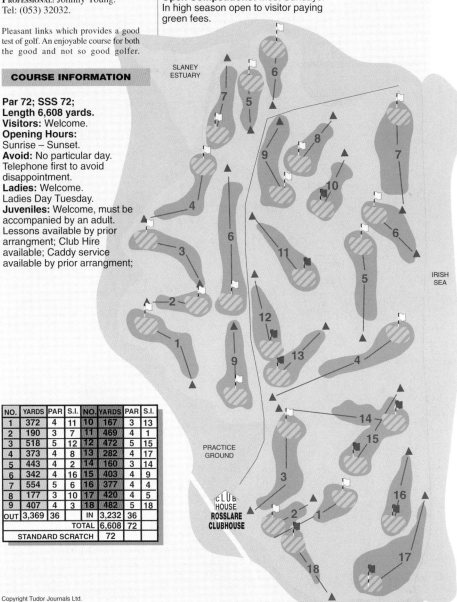

NO.	YARDS	PAR	S.I.	NO.	YARDS	PAR	S.I.
1	372	4	11	10	167	3	13
2	190	3	7	11	469	4	1
3	518	5	12	12	472	5	15
4	373	4	8	13	282	4	17
5	443	4	2	14	160	3	14
6	342	4	16	15	403	4	9
7	554	5	6	16	377	4	4
8	177	3	10	17	420	4	5
9	407	4	3	18	482	5	18
OUT	3,369	36		IN	3,232	36	
				TOTAL	6,608	72	
STANDARD SCRATCH					72		

Copyright Tudor Journals Ltd.

NO.	CHAMP METRES	MEDAL METRES	PAR	S.I.	NO.	CHAMP METRES	MEDAL METRES	PAR	S.I.
1	410	399	5	17	10	488	463	5	4
2	379	367	4	6	11	175	164	3	12
3	192	183	3	10	12	406	386	4	1
4	288	280	4	18	13	419	405	4	5
5	305	298	4	8	14	299	290	4	14
6	308	296	4	16	15	567	482	5	9
7	165	159	3	13	16	368	360	4	11
8	412	400	4	2	17	192	186	3	3
9	478	461	5	7	18	240	234	4	15
OUT	2,937	2,843	36		IN	3,154	2,970	36	
					TOTAL	6,091	5,813	72	
		STANDARD SCRATCH	72	71					

St. Helen's, Kilrane,
Rosslare Harbour,
Co. Wexford.
Tel: (053) 33234/33669.
Fax: (053) 33803.
Email:sthelens@iol.ie

LOCATION: 2 miles from Rosslare Port; 10 miles from Wexford; 90 miles from Dublin.
SECRETARY: Larry Byrne.
Public Tel: (053) 33806.
COURSE DESIGN / ARCHITECT: Philip Walton.

Set in the beautiful location beside St. Helen's Bay, 14 holes of the course overlook the coast and Tuskar Lighthouse. It is a design, by Philip Walton, which takes full advantage of the onshore winds and gently sloping rural land, totally at one with nature. There are nine water features and 5,000 trees, as well as strategically lined bunkers.

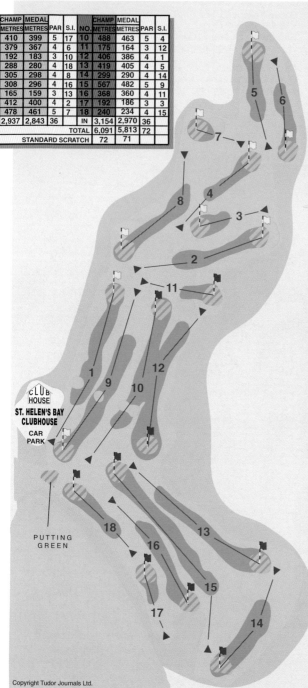

COURSE INFORMATION

Par 72; SSS 72; Length 6,091 Metres.
Type: Parkland / Links course.
Opening Hours: Daylight Hours
Avoid: None.
Green Fees: Low Season – €25 Mon-Fri, €32 weekends; Mid Season – €32 Mon-Fri, €38 weekends; High Season – €35 Mon-Fri, €40 weekends. Club hire and Caddie Service available.
Clubhouse Hours: Licencing Hours.
Clubhouse Dress: Neat, casual dress.
Clubhouse Facilities: Full catering and clubhouse facilities available. Tel Caterer: Ext. 21. Accommodation available on site.
Open Competitions: Various Open Days throughout the year

ST. HELEN'S BAY CLUBHOUSE
CAR PARK
PUTTING GREEN

Copyright Tudor Journals Ltd.

Mulgannon, Co. Wexford.
Tel: (053) 42238.
Fax: (053) 42243
Web: www.wexfordgolfclub.ie
Email: info@wexfordgolfclub.ie
LOCATION: Wexford Town.
HON. SECRETARY: Pat Daly.
ARCHITECT: H. Stutt & Co.
          D. Branigan
PROFESSIONAL: Damien McGraine.
Tel: (053) 46300

Parkland course with many mature trees. The location has beautiful views of County Wexford, including the Saltee Islands, Bletchin Mountains and Wexford Harbour.

COURSE INFORMATION

Par 72; SSS 70;
Length 6,306 yards, 5,734 metres.
Visitors: Welcome (except on Sundays). Should book in advance.
Opening Hours: Sunrise – sunset.
Avoid: Sunday.
Ladies Day: Thursday.
Juveniles: Lessons available by prior arrangments; Club Hire available; Caddy service available by prior arrangments; Telephone appointment required.
Green Fees: Weekdays €28 (summer) €23 (winter); Sat, Sun & Bank Hols €32 (all year round).
Clubhouse Hours: 8am – 11.30pm (summer).
Clubhouse Dress: Casual.
Clubhouse Facilities: Bar snacks available all day every day. Full catering available by arrangement.

NO.	YARDS	PAR	S.I.	NO.	YARDS	PAR	S.I.
1	190	3	6	10	340	4	9
2	317	4	14	11	505	5	11
3	395	4	7	12	166	3	12
4	348	4	13	13	491	5	16
5	386	4	4	14	451	4	3
6	151	3	8	15	134	3	17
7	263	4	18	16	399	4	1
8	540	5	10	17	462	5	15
9	433	4	2	18	335	4	5
OUT	3,023	35		IN	3,283	37	
				TOTAL	6,306	72	
	STANDARD SCRATCH					70	

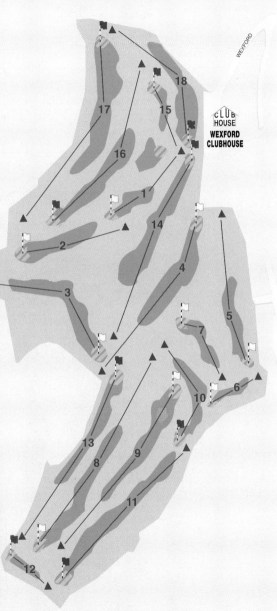

Copyright Tudor Journals Ltd.

Abbeylands, Arklow, Co Wicklow.
Tel: (0402) 32492.
Fax: (0402) 91604
Email:
arklowgolflinks@eircom.net
LOCATION: Just south of the town centre.
SECRETARY: Mr Brendan Timmons.(0402)32971after 5pm
ADMINISTRATOR: Mrs. Linda Timmons.(0402)32492between 9/1pm
A typical links course with majestic scenery and the opportunity to play throughout the year. Sited just outside the townland of Arklow.

COURSE INFORMATION

Par 69; SSS 69; Length 5,665 metres.
Visitors: Welcome.
Opening Hours:
9am – 6pm in Winter,
8am – Sunset in Summer.
Avoid: Weekends.
Ladies: Welcome Mondays.
Juveniles: Must by accompanied by an adult.
Handicap Certificate required for Open Competitions.
Green Fees:
Individual - €40, Husband and Wife - €65 (Mon - Fri only)

Student - €20 (must present student card, Mon - Fri) Juvenile €13 (In company of an adult Mon - Fri) With Member €20 (Mon - Fri)
Clubhouse Hours:
Winter: 9am – 6pm.
Summer: 8am – Sunset.
Clubhouse Dress: No denims, shorts etc allowed on course or in clubhouse.
Clubhouse Facilities: Full bar and restaurant open all year round.
Open Competitions: Open Week July / August.

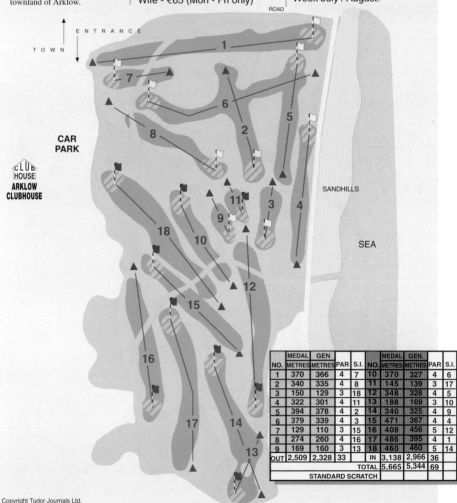

NO.	MEDAL METRES	GEN METRES	PAR	S.I.	NO.	MEDAL METRES	GEN. METRES	PAR	S.I.
1	370	366	4	7	10	370	327	4	6
2	340	335	4	8	11	145	139	3	17
3	150	129	3	18	12	348	328	4	5
4	322	301	4	11	13	188	169	3	10
5	394	378	4	2	14	340	325	4	9
6	379	339	4	3	15	471	367	4	4
7	129	110	3	15	16	408	456	5	12
8	274	260	4	16	17	486	395	4	1
9	169	160	3	13	18	460	460	5	14
OUT	2,509	2,328	33		IN	3,138	2,966	36	
					TOTAL	5,665	5,344	69	
					STANDARD SCRATCH				

Copyright Tudor Journals Ltd.

Stratford Lodge,
Baltinglass
Co. Wicklow.
Tel: (0508) 81031
Fax: (0508 82842

LOCATION: Baltinglass.
SECRETARY: Owen Codney.
Tel: (0508) 81609.
ARCHITECT: Lionel Hewtson.
CAPTAIN: Fintan J. Doyle

Nine hole course at present - new 9-hole development now completed and due to open in Summer/Autumn 2002. Societies welcome.

NO.	MEDAL METRES	MEDAL METRES	PAR	S.I.	NO.	MEDAL METRES	MEDAL METRES	PAR	S.I.
1	367	362	4	3	10	356	352	4	4
2	325	321	4	11	11	314	310	4	12
3	137	133	3	17	12	133	128	3	18
4	395	390	4	5	13	391	387	4	6
5	366	359	4	7	14	366	359	4	8
6	418	411	4	1	15	409	404	4	2
7	148	142	3	15	16	143	136	3	16
8	339	333	4	9	17	332	323	4	10
9	314	309	4	8	18	301	297	4	14
OUT	2,809	2,760	34		IN	2,745	2,696	34	
					TOTAL	5,554	5,456	68	
					STANDARD SCRATCH	72			

Bunker and tree positions indicated.

COURSE INFORMATION

Par 68; SSS 69; Length 6,072 yards, 5,549 metres.
Visitors: Welcome.
Opening Hours: 9.00am – Sunset.
Avoid: Competition dates, weekends and Thursdays.
Ladies: Welcome. Ladies Day Thursday.
Green Fees: Mon – Fri €16 (€10 with a member); Sat/Sun/Bank Holidays €20 (€16 with a member).
Juveniles: Welcome. Caddy service available by prior arrangement, telephone appointment required.
Clubhouse Dress: Neat/Casual.
Clubhouse Facilities: Catering by previous arrangements except at weekends.
Clubhouse Facilities: 9.00am – 6.00pm (winter) 9.00am – 11.00pm (summer).
Open Competiions: Open Week June/July.

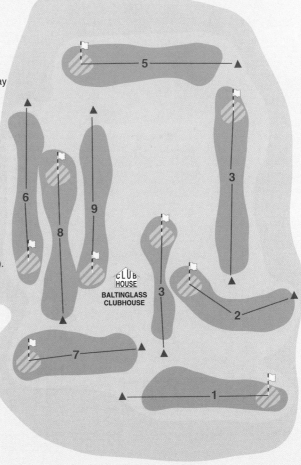

Copyright Tudor Journals Ltd.

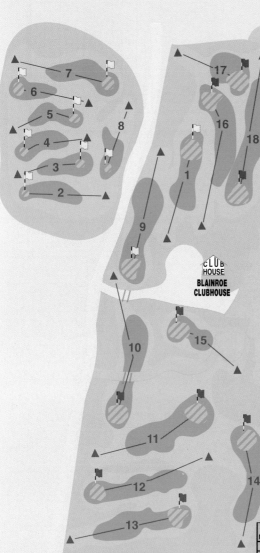

Blainroe, Co Wicklow.
Tel: (0404) 68168.
Fax: (0404) 69369.

LOCATION: 4 miles south of Wicklow Town; 35 miles south of Dublin.
SECRETARY / MANAGER: W. O'Sullivan.
Tel: (0404) 68168.
PROFESSIONAL: J. McDonald.
Tel: (0404) 68168.
ARCHITECT: Fred Hawtree.

This is a parkland course overlooking the sea. Two holes worth noting are the 14th, which is played from the cliff peninsula, and the par 3 15th hole over the lake. There is a total of 58 sand bunkers which makes it a very challenging test to all golfers.

COURSE INFORMATION

Par 72; SSS 72;
Length 6,171 metres.
Visitors: Welcome.
Opening Hours: Sunrise – Sunset.
Avoid: Weekends.
Ladies: Welcome.
Juveniles: Welcome. Lessons available by prior arrangements; Club Hire available; Caddy cars available by prior arrangements.
Green Fees: €41 Mon – Fri; €53 Sat/Sun/Bank Holidays.
Clubhouse Hours: 11.00am – 11.00pm. Full Clubhouse facilities.
Clubhouse Dress: Neat dress essential.
Clubhouse Facilities: Available in season and weekends.

NO.	MEDAL METRES	GEN METRES	PAR	S.I.	NO.	MEDAL METRES	GEN METRES	PAR	S.I.
1	331	326	4	7	10	347	339	4	6
2	392	387	4	1	11	351	346	4	12
3	384	378	4	5	12	392	388	4	2
4	481	475	5	11	13	362	351	4	10
5	444	440	5	15	14	303	296	4	17
6	339	335	4	13	15	209	199	3	8
7	337	332	4	9	16	418	408	4	1
8	192	188	3	13	17	111	108	3	18
9	335	329	4	17	18	447	445	5	16
OUT	3,235	3,190	37		IN	2,940	2,880	35	
					TOTAL	6,175	6,070	72	
					STANDARD SCRATCH	72	71		

Copyright Tudor Journals Ltd.

Ravenswell Road, Bray, Co Wicklow.

LOCATION: Bray Town.
SECRETARY / MANAGER:
G. Montgomery.
Tel: (01) 2862484.
PROFESSIONAL: Michael Walby.
Tel: (01) 2760057.

Relatively short nine holes with separate tees for 1st and 2nd nine. A mostly flat inland course, but still a reasonable test of golf.

COURSE INFORMATION

Par 70; SSS 70; Length 5,784 metres.
Visitors: Welcome.
Opening Hours: 8.am – Sunset.
Avoid: Weekends and Mondays.
Ladies Day: Monday.
Lessons available by prior arrangment.
Green Fees: €30.

Clubhouse Hours: 8.30am – Sunset.
Bar open 11.00am.
Clubhouse Dress: No Jeans or trainers on course or in clubhouse; proper golf attire on course.
Clubhouse Facilities: Bar & bar snacks.

NO.	MEDAL METRES	GEN. METRES	PAR	S.I.	NO.	MEDAL METRES	GEN. METRES	PAR	S.I.
1	335	327	4	5	10	357	344	4	3
2	477	453	5	13	11	424	378	4	1
3	339	326	4	6	12	334	311	4	9
4	148	138	3	14	13	138	132	3	17
5	374	351	4	4	14	354	327	4	7
6	155	142	3	11	15	172	162	3	10
7	334	321	4	15	16	312	300	4	16
8	420	392	4	2	17	445	397	5/4	18
9	324	311	4	12	18	340	317	4	8
OUT	2,908	2,761	35		IN	2,876	2,668	35	
					TOTAL	5,784	5,429	70/69	
					STANDARD SCRATCH	70	68		

CLUB HOUSE
BRAY CLUBHOUSE

Tree positions indicated.
Copyright Tudor Journals Ltd.

Greystones, Co Wicklow.
Tel: (01) 2874350.
Fax: (01) 2874360.
Email:
teetimes@charlesland.com
www.charlesland.com

LOCATION: 18 Miles south of Dublin.
GOLF ADMINISTRATION: Rosaleen Casey.
Tel: (01) 2878200.
GENERAL MANAGER: Mr. Patrick
Bradshaw
PROFESSIONAL: Peter Duignan
ARCHITECT: Eddie Hackett.

Parkland course in a superb setting on a delightfully rolling terrain, sweeping towards the Irish Sea. Well bunkered, with water hazards on seven of the holes. An all weather course playable twelve months of the year.

COURSE INFORMATION

Par 72; SSS 72; Length 6,169 metres.
Visitors: Welcome.
Opening Hours: Sunrise – Sunset.
Juveniles: Welcome with adult or handicap certificate. Lessons available by prior arrangement.
Green Fees: 1 Apr - 31 Oct Mon - Thurs €45; Fri - Sun €57.
Clubhouse Dress: Neat dress essential.
Clubhouse Facilities: Full facilities available. Bar food menu and Dining room available every day. Also 12 en-suite bedrooms.
Competitions:
Open Week – August.

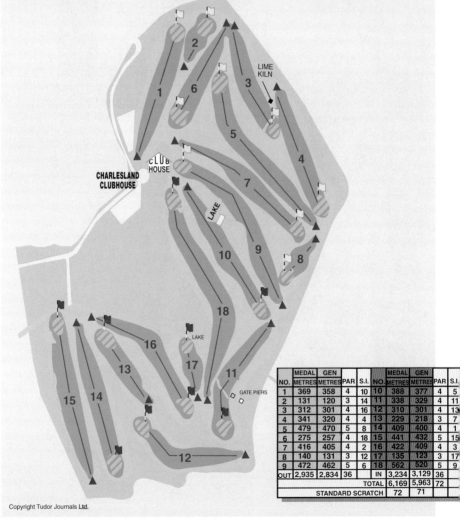

NO.	MEDAL METRES	GEN METRES	PAR	S.I.	NO.	MEDAL METRES	GEN METRES	PAR	S.I.
1	369	358	4	10	10	388	377	4	5
2	131	120	3	14	11	338	329	4	11
3	312	301	4	16	12	310	301	4	13
4	341	320	4	4	13	229	218	3	7
5	479	470	5	8	14	409	400	4	1
6	275	257	4	18	15	441	432	5	15
7	416	405	4	2	16	422	409	4	3
8	140	131	3	12	17	135	123	3	17
9	472	462	5	6	18	562	520	5	9
OUT	2,935	2,834	36		IN	3,234	3,129	36	
					TOTAL	6,169	5,963	72	
					STANDARD SCRATCH	72	71		

Copyright Tudor Journals Ltd.

138

Shillelagh, Co. Wicklow.
Tel: (055) 29125.

LOCATION: South Wicklow.
HON. SECRETARY: Dennis Byrne.
Tel: (054) 77314.
ARCHITECT: Peter McAvoy.

A picturesque parkland course with
excellent fairways and greens. The
large number of trees of different
varieties add greatly to the character
of the course. Part of the Old
Fitzwilliam Solate, set in lovely
countryside. New 18 hole course
opened in March 1998, built to
U.S.G.A. standards.

COURSE INFORMATION

Par 70; SSS 69; Length
6,148 yards.
Visitors: Welcome.
Opening Hours: Sunrise –
Sunset.
Avoid: Weekends.
Green Fees: €30 Mon – Fri;
€40 weekends. 10% discount
for groups of 20+.
Clubhouse Hours:
12pm – close. All day
Saturday / Sunday.
Clubhouse Dress:
Casual.
Clubhouse Facilities:
Full clubhouse facilities.
Open Competitions:
Open Week July.

Copyright Tudor Journals Ltd.

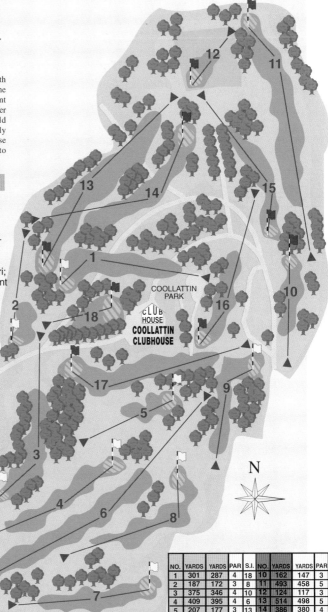

NO.	YARDS	YARDS	PAR	S.I.	NO.	YARDS	YARDS	PAR	S.I.
1	301	287	4	18	10	162	147	3	7
2	187	172	3	8	11	493	458	5	12
3	375	346	4	10	12	124	117	3	14
4	409	395	4	6	13	514	498	5	9
5	207	177	3	13	14	386	380	4	3
6	583	561	5	11	15	390	376	4	5
7	398	390	4	2	16	267	246	4	17
8	344	314	4	15	17	469	459	4	1
9	372	358	4	4	18	167	150	3	16
OUT	3,176	3,000	35		IN	2,972	2,831	35	
					TOTAL	6,148	5,831	70	
					STANDARD SCRATCH	69	68		

DELGANY

Delgany, Co Wicklow.
Tel: (01) 2874536.
Fax: (01) 287 3977.
Email: delganygolf@eircom.net

LOCATION: Delgany Village.
SECRETARY / MANAGER:
R.J. Kelly.
Tel: (01) 2874536.
PROFESSIONAL: Gavin
Kavanagh.
Tel: (01) 2874697.

Slightly hilly parkland course with beautiful scenery and views, situated in the attractive village of Delgany.

COURSE INFORMATION

Par 69; SSS 68; Length 5,474 metres.
Visitors: Welcome Monday, Thursday and Friday. Weekends by arrangment only.
Opening Hours: 8.00am – Sunset.
Avoid: Tuesday and Wednesday.
Ladies: Welcome.
Juveniles: Welcome.
Lessons available by prior

arrangements; Club hire available; Caddy service available prior arrangements; Telephone appointment required.
Green Fees: €38 Mon – Fri; €44 Sat/Sun.
Clubhouse Hours: 8.30am – close.
Clubhouse Dress: Neat/casual.
Clubhouse Facilities: Snacks & bar food from 11am. Dining room from 1pm.

NO.	Metres	PAR	S.I.	NO.	Metres	PAR	S.I.
1	367	4	4	10	437	5/4	9
2	276	4	12	11	159	3	7
3	344	4	2	12	395	4	1
4	352	4	16	13	294	4	15
5	178	3	6	14	163	3	11
6	359	4	8	15	346	4	13
7	302	4	10	16	153	3	17
8	126	3	18	17	367	4	3
9	368	4	14	18	488	5	5
OUT	2,672	34		IN	2,802	35	
				TOTAL	5,474	69	
				STANDARD SCRATCH		69	

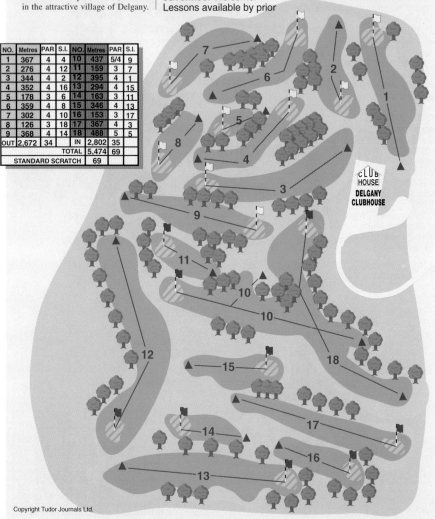

Copyright Tudor Journals Ltd.

**Djouce Golf Club,
Roundwood, Co. Wicklow.
Tel: (01) 2818585.**

LOCATION: 50 mins from Dublin city.
Turn right at Kilmacanogue on N11.
SECRETARY: Anne Farrelig.
Tel: (01) 2818585.
MANAGER/PROPRIETOR:
Donal McGullycuddy.
ARCHITECT: Eddie Hackett.

Very level with testing tight fairways.
Panoramic views with the course
surrounded by the Dublin and Wicklow
Mountains.

COURSE INFORMATION

**Par 71; SSS 70; Length 6,296
yards.**
Visitors: Welcome. Except
Tuesday and Sunday mornings.
Opening Hours:
8.00am onwards.
Visitors: Welcome.
Green Fees: Weekdays €12
(9 holes) / €15 (18 holes);
weekends & Bank Holidays
€15 (9 holes) / €20(18 holes).
Juveniles: Welcome.
Clubhouse Hours:
9.00am – closing.
Clubhouse Dress:
Smart / casual.
Clubhouse Facilities:
Snack bar, teas/coffees.
Open Competitons:
Please check details with club.

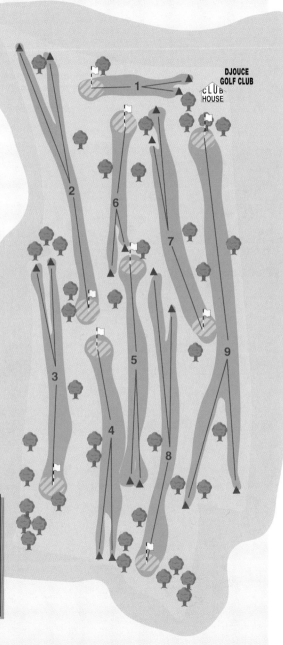

NO.	YARDS	METRES	PAR	S.I.	NO.	YARDS	METRES	PAR	S.I.
1	194	177	3	9	1	179	164	3	11
2	401	367	4	2	1	420	384	4	11
3	376	344	4	12	1	365	334	4	15
4	307	280	4	16	1	262	240	4	18
5	343	314	4	10	1	342	313	4	8
6	165	151	3	14	1	204	188	3	13
7	419	483	4	7	1	383	350	4	6
8	454	415	5	17	1	390	356	4	5
9	552	504	5	3	1	540	494	5	4
OUT	3,211	2,937	36		IN	3,085	2,823	35	
					TOTAL	6,296	5,760	71	
STANDARD SCRATCH			69						

Copyright Tudor Journals Ltd.

Newtownmountkennedy, Co. Wicklow.
Tel: (01) 2873600.
Fax: (01) 2873699.

LOCATION: Twenty-three miles south of Dublin City. Two miles east of Newtownmountkennedy off the N11.
Tel: (01) 2873600
PROFESSIONAL: Eamonn Darcy.
COURSE DESIGNERS: Pat Ruddy & Tom Craddock.

Druids Glen situated on the ancestral estate of Sir Thomas Wentworth is already an acknowledged masterpiece and had the honour of hosting the Murphy's Irish Open Championship in 1996, 1997, 1998 and 1999.

COURSE INFORMATION

Par 71; Length 7,026 yards.
Visitors: Welcome – tee times by arrangement.
Opening Hours: 8.00am – Sunset.

Green Fees: Mid October – mid April €82.53 includes breakfast, €107.93 with dinner. Early Bird mid April – mid October €125.
Clubhouse Hours: 8.00am – onwards.
Clubhouse Dress: Neat Casual.
Clubhouse Facilities: Snacks, Lunch, Dinner and conference facilities available. Caddies available by prior arrangement. Hotel on site.

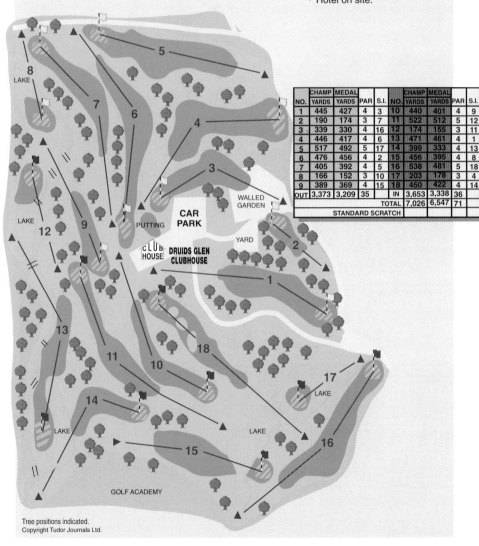

NO.	CHAMP YARDS	MEDAL YARDS	PAR	S.I.	NO.	CHAMP YARDS	MEDAL YARDS	PAR	S.I.
1	445	427	4	3	10	440	401	4	9
2	190	174	3	7	11	522	512	5	12
3	339	330	4	16	12	174	155	3	11
4	446	417	4	6	13	471	461	4	1
5	517	492	5	17	14	399	333	4	13
6	476	456	4	2	15	456	395	4	8
7	405	392	4	5	16	538	481	5	18
8	166	152	3	10	17	203	178	3	4
9	389	369	4	15	18	450	422	4	14
OUT	3,373	3,209	35		IN	3,653	3,338	36	
					TOTAL	7,026	6,547	71	
					STANDARD SCRATCH				

DRUIDS GLEN CLUBHOUSE

Tree positions indicated.
Copyright Tudor Journals Ltd.

Brittas Bay, Wicklow.
Tel: (0404) 47415.
Fax: (0404) 47449.

LOCATION: 45 minutes from city centre via the Bray – Shankill Bypass.

SECRETARY / MANAGER: Pat & Sidon Ruddy.

ARCHITECT: Mr. Pat Ruddy.

The links offers a rare variety of golf challenges and awesome scenery as the holes plunge into deep valleys in the sand dunes, run on a sand spit through age old marshlands and along and up into the rugged cliffs of Mizen Head. The Irish sea can be seen from every hole on the links and the Wickow Hills complete the scenic cocktail inland.

COURSE INFORMATION

Par 71; SSS 72; Length 7,089 yards.
Visitors: Welcome.
Opening Hours: Summer: 8am – 5pm; Winter: 8.30am – 12.30pm (tee times).

Ladies: Welcome.
Juveniles: Must be accompanied by an adult and have playing skills.
Green Fees: €100 Apr1- Oct31 €75 Nov1- Mar31
Clubhouse Hours: Open 8.00am until dusk.
Clubhouse Dress: Smart / casual.
Clubhouse Facilities: Full clubhouse and catering facilities. Caddy car hire available.

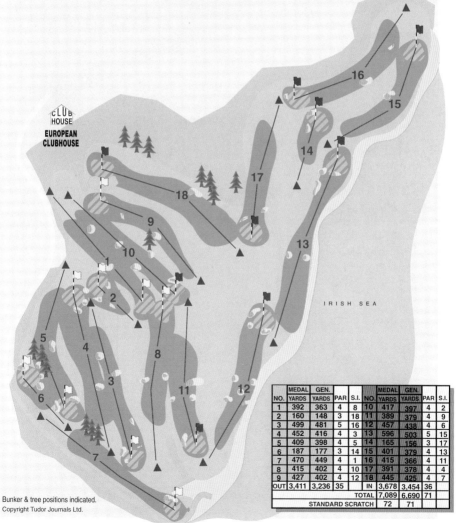

NO.	MEDAL YARDS	GEN. YARDS	PAR	S.I.	NO.	MEDAL YARDS	GEN. YARDS	PAR	S.I.
1	392	363	4	8	10	417	397	4	2
2	160	148	3	18	11	389	379	4	9
3	499	481	5	16	12	457	438	4	6
4	452	416	4	3	13	596	503	5	15
5	409	398	4	5	14	165	156	3	17
6	187	177	3	14	15	401	379	4	13
7	470	449	4	1	16	415	366	4	11
8	415	402	4	10	17	391	378	4	4
9	427	402	4	12	18	445	425	4	7
OUT	3,411	3,236	35		IN	3,678	3,454	36	
					TOTAL	7,089	6,690	71	
					STANDARD SCRATCH		72	71	

Bunker & tree positions indicated.
Copyright Tudor Journals Ltd.

**Glenmalure Golf Club,
Greenane, Rathdrum,
Co. Wicklow.
Tel: (0404) 46679.**

LOCATION: Greenane, Glenmalure, 2½ miles west of Rathdrum (35 miles south of Dublin via N11).
SECRETARY: Brian Lahane.
ARCHITECT: P.Suttle & Sporting Concepts Ltd.

Set in a beautiful location overlooking the Glenmalure & Vale of Avoca in the Wicklow Hills. Delightful course with inclines, a plateau and downhill. Accommodation available in lodges on site.

COURSE INFORMATION

**Par 71; SSS 66; Length 5,384 yards.
Visitors:** Welcome.
Opening Hours:
8.00am – dusk.
Ladies: ILGU affiliated.
Green Fees: €25 weekdays; €35 weekends.

Juveniles: €10.
Clubhouse Hours: Normal licencing hours.
Clubhouse Dress: No special requirements.
Clubhouse Facilities: Full bar and catering available.
Buggy hire available.
Open Competitions:
March 29th - 31st. May 4th - 8th Mixed. Aug 3rd - 4th. Sep 7 - 8th Team.

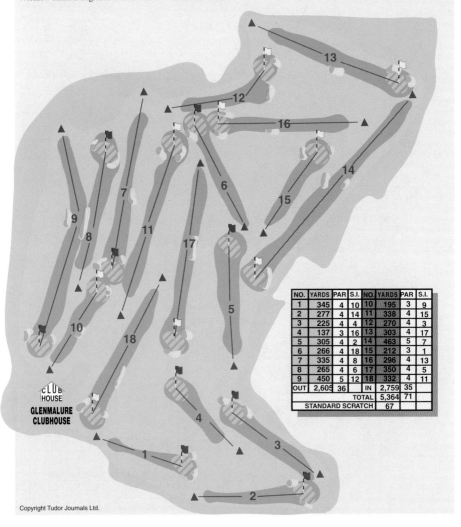

NO.	YARDS	PAR	S.I.	NO.	YARDS	PAR	S.I.
1	345	4	10	10	195	3	9
2	277	4	14	11	338	4	15
3	225	4	4	12	270	4	3
4	137	3	16	13	303	4	17
5	305	4	2	14	463	5	7
6	266	4	18	15	212	3	1
7	335	4	8	16	296	4	13
8	265	4	6	17	350	4	5
9	450	5	12	18	332	4	11
OUT	2,605	36		IN	2,759	35	
				TOTAL	5,364	71	
				STANDARD SCRATCH	67		

CLUB HOUSE
GLENMALURE CLUBHOUSE

Copyright Tudor Journals Ltd.

Glen of the Downs Golf Club, Coolnaskeagh, Delgany, Co. Wicklow.
Tel: (01) 2876240
Fax: (01) 2870063
Email: info@glenofthedowns.com
www.glenofthedowns.com

LOCATION: Off the N11 Main Dublin, Wexford Road.(approx. 30 mins from Dublin Centre)
GOLF DIRECTOR: Derek Murphy.
ARCHITECT: Peter McEvoy/ Paddy Governey.

Located in the 'Garden of Ireland' at the foot of the Sugarloaf Mountain. It boasts spectacular views of the Wicklow Mountains and the Irish Sea. The course has been designed and built to USGA standard with sand based greens and tees. Golfers will find Glen of the Downs a challenge with its natural slopes and valleys combined with its fairway bunkering and lakes.

COURSE INFORMATION

Par 71; SSS 70; Length 5,980 yards.
Green Fees: €65 Midweek, €80 Weekend. €50 before 10am midweek.
Restrictions: Soft spikes only.
Clubhouse Hours: 8 am - Sunset.
Clubhouse Dress: Neat dress essential/ no denim.
Clubhouse Facilities: New Clubhouse (15,000 sq ft) opened May 2001, with extensive facilities.

NO.	YARDS	PAR	S.I.	NO.	YARDS	PAR	S.I.
1	360	3	14	10	361	4	5
2	385	4	4	11	366	4	9
3	373	4	8	12	305	4	15
4	166	3	10	13	528	5	1
5	427	4	2	14	167	3	11
6	471	5	12	15	489	5	7
7	438	3	16	16	159	3	13
8	367	4	6	17	385	4	3
9	466	3	18	18	267	4	17
OUT	2,953	35		IN	3,027	36	
				TOTAL	5,980	71	
			STANDARD SCRATCH	70			

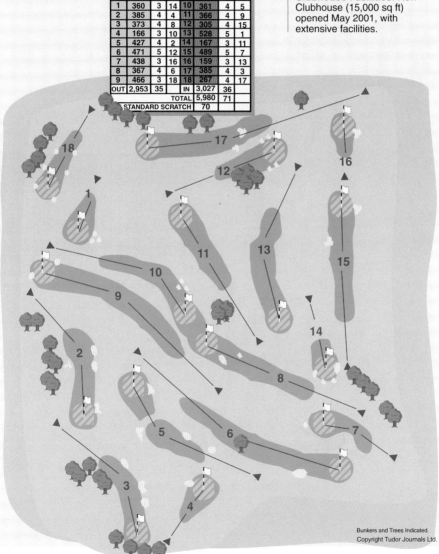

Bunkers and Trees Indicated.
Copyright Tudor Journals Ltd.

Greystones, Co Wicklow.
Tel: (01) 2876624.
LOCATION: 20 miles south of Dublin.
GENERAL MANAGER: Jim Melody.
OFFICE Tel: (01) 2874136.
GOLF SHOP: Tel (01) 2875308.

A parkland course with considerable contrasts. The first nine holes are hilly with some spectacular views, which is in stark contrast to the more level second nine holes. A new Cluhouse, incorporating an old Georgian Manor House, opened in 1991, completes this very attractive package.

COURSE INFORMATION

Par 69; SSS 69; Length 5,322 metres.
Visitors: Welcome Mon, Tues and Friday mornings.
Opening Hours: 9.00am – Sunset.
Avoid: Wed, Thurs and Weekends.
Ladies: Welcome.
Green Fees: €40 weekdays (n/a weekends).
Clubhouse Hours: 9.00am – 12.00 midnight.
Clubhouse Dress: Casual. No jeans or sneakers.
Clubhouse Facilities: By prior arrangment.
Open Competitions: Open Week July; Intermediate Scratch Cup July. Junior Scratch Cup; July.

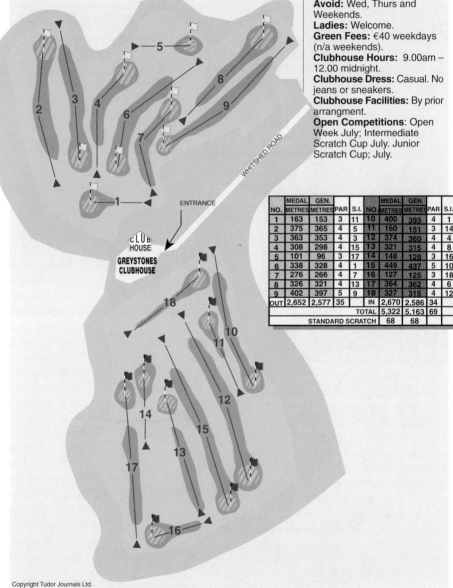

NO.	MEDAL METRES	GEN. METRES	PAR	S.I.	NO.	MEDAL METRES	GEN. METRES	PAR	S.I.
1	163	153	3	11	10	400	393	4	1
2	375	365	4	5	11	160	151	3	14
3	363	353	4	3	12	374	360	4	4
4	308	298	4	15	13	321	315	4	8
5	101	96	3	17	14	148	128	3	16
6	338	328	4	1	15	449	437	5	10
7	276	266	4	7	16	127	125	3	18
8	326	321	4	13	17	364	362	4	6
9	402	397	5	9	18	327	315	4	12
OUT	2,652	2,577	35		IN	2,670	2,586	34	
					TOTAL	5,322	5,163	69	
					STANDARD SCRATCH	68	68		

ENTRANCE

CLUB HOUSE

GREYSTONES CLUBHOUSE

WHITSHED ROAD

Copyright Tudor Journals Ltd.

**Old Conna Golf Club,
Ferndale Road, Bray,
Co Wicklow.
Tel: (01) 2826055/2826766.
Fax: (01) 2825611.**

LOCATION: Two miles north of
Bray.
SECRETARY: Dave Diviney.
Tel: (01) 2826055/2826766.
ARCHITECT: E. Hackett

Situated twelve miles south of Dublin
in the Bray area, Old Conna is a testing
18 hole parkland course with
panoramic views of the Irish Sea and
Wicklow mountains. Set in wooded
terrain, otralegically placed hazards
and mature trees ensure a challenging

round for even the most accomplished
golfer.
This attractive layout should become
one of the regions premier inland
courses in the not too distant future.

COURSE INFORMATION

**Par 72; SSS 71; Length
6,551 yards.
Visitors:** Welcome Mon – Fri
9.00am – 4.00pm (closed
12.30pm – 1.30pm).
Opening Hours:
Sunrise – sunset.
Avoid: Tuesday, Wednesday,
Saturday & Sunday.
Green Fees: €45 weekdays.

Juveniles: Must be over 12 yrs
old. Lessons available by prior
arrangement; Caddy Service /
Cars and Club Hire available
by prior arrangement.
Clubhouse Hours: 10.30am –
11.30pm; Full clubhouse
facilities.
Clubhouse Dress: Neat attire
essential (no jeans / T-shirts).
Clubhouse Facilities: Bar
snacks and full catering
everyday. Menu available
12.00 noon – 9.30pm. Phone:
(01) 2820038.

NO.	MEDAL YARDS	GEN YARDS	PAR	S.I.	NO.	MEDAL YARDS	GEN YARDS	PAR	S.I.
1	376	362	4	10	10	354	334	4	15
2	236	221	3	4	11	351	339	4	5
3	320	305	4	12	12	163	149	3	11
4	546	532	5	14	13	565	551	5	7
5	582	568	5	2	14	292	278	4	13
6	373	354	4	8	15	470	461	4	1
7	382	358	4	6	16	434	424	4	3
8	112	98	3	18	17	160	146	3	9
9	346	332	4	16	18	500	476	5	17
OUT	3,264	3,130	36		IN	3,289	3,158	36	
					TOTAL	6,553	6,288	72	
			STANDARD SCRATCH	71					

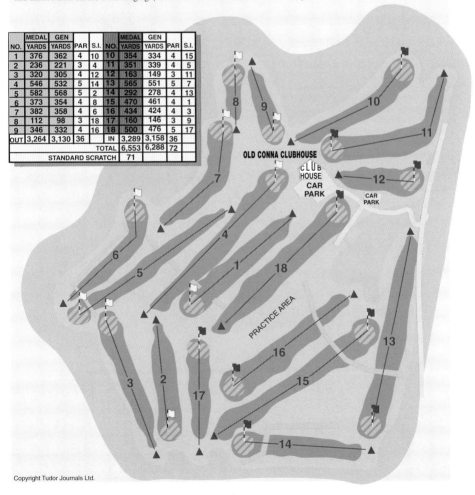

OLD CONNA CLUBHOUSE

Copyright Tudor Journals Ltd.

**Powerscourt Golf Club PLC,
Powerscourt Estate, Enniskerry,
Co. Wicklow.
Tel: (01) 2046033. Fax: (01) 2761303.**

LOCATION: Set in Powerscourt Estate with its world famous Gardens, 4 miles west of Bray. Powerscourt is 25 minutes from Dublin City Centre adjacent to Enniskerry village.
MANAGER: Bernard Gibbons.
Tel: (01) 2046033.
PROFESSIONAL: Paul Thompson.

Powerscourt is a free draining course with links characteristics. Built to championship standard, with top quality tees and exceptional tiered greens, it is set in some of Ireland's most beautiful parkland. The course has an abundance of mature trees and natural features, with stunning views to the sea and Sugar Loaf Mountain.

COURSE INFORMATION

Par 72; SSS 74; Length 6,421 metres.
Visitors: Welcome.
Opening Hours: 8.00am – sunset.
Ladies: Welcome.
Juveniles: With handicap welcome,
Caddies, club and trolley hire available,
practice range and short game practice
area also available.
Green Fees: €100 all week;
Group rates on request
Clubhouse Hours: 8.00am – 12.00pm.
Clubhouse Dress: Casual. No jeans.
Clubhouse Facilities: Golf shop,
restaurant and full bar facilities.

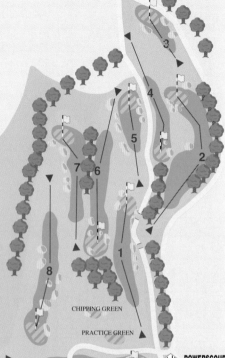

CHIPPING GREEN

PRACTICE GREEN

CLUB POWERSCOURT
HOUSE CLUBHOUSE

PRACTICE GROUND

Bunkers and trees positions indicated.
Copyright Tudor Journals Ltd.

NO.	CHAMP METRES	MEDAL METRES	PAR	S.I.	NO.	CHAMP METRES	MEDAL METRES	PAR	S.I.
1	401	384	4	12	10	387	351	4	3
2	461	444	5	8	11	382	354	4	11
3	154	131	3	14	12	498	485	5	15
4	332	295	4	6	13	156	156	3	9
5	216	191	3	10	14	350	309	4	17
6	484	461	5	16	15	357	333	4	7
7	383	336	4	4	16	145	134	3	5
8	422	401	4	2	17	544	488	5	1
9	348	306	4	18	18	390	371	4	13
OUT	3,201	2,949	36		IN	3,209	2,981	36	
					TOTAL	6,421	5,930	72	
					STANDARD SCRATCH	74	72		

NO.	MEDAL YARDS	GEN YARDS	PAR	S.I.	NO.	MEDAL YARDS	GEN YARDS	PAR	S.I.
1	571	506	5	10	10	465	438	4	1
2	454	436	4	2	11	519	510	5	11
3	400	367	4	18	12	390	355	4	7
4	173	158	3	12	13	153	134	3	15
5	396	373	4	16	14	351	332	4	17
6	502	490	5	8	15	382	374	4	9
7	176	177	3	14	16	536	516	5	5
8	382	351	4	6	17	169	170	3	13
9	447	386	4	4	18	450	426	4	3
OUT	3,501	3,244	36		IN	3,415	3,255	36	
					TOTAL	6,916	6,499	72	
	STANDARD SCRATCH		74			72			

**Rathsallagh Golf Club,
Dunlavin, Co. Wicklow.
Tel: 045 403316.
Fax: 045 403295.
Email: info@rathsallagh.com
Web: www.rathsallagh.com**

LOCATION: 15 miles south-east of Naas.
DIRECTOR OF GOLF: Joe O'Flynn.
PROFESSIONAL: Brendan McDaid.
ARCHITECT: Peter McEvoy/
Christy O'Connor Jnr.

Rathsallagh is a Championship Parkland
Course set on 252 acres with thousands of
mature trees with breathtaking views across
the Wicklow mountains. Arguably the best
greens in Ireland! Accommodation is
available on site at the award winning 4
star Rathsallagh Country House.

COURSE INFORMATION

Par 72; Length 6,920 yards.
Visitors: Welcome.
Opening Hours: 7.30am – Sunset.
Ladies: No restrictions.
Green Fees: April to October €55
Mon – Thur; €70 Fri to Sun & Bank
Hols. Nov to March €45 Mon-Thur;
€55 Fri/Sun & Bank Hols.
Juveniles: With handicaps.
Clubhouse Dress: Smart/Casual.
Facilities: Full restaurant and bar.
Golf shop, Caddies, Golf Buggies,
Trolley hire. Flood lit driving range
with heated covered bays, two
pitching greens, putting green and
three practice bunkers.

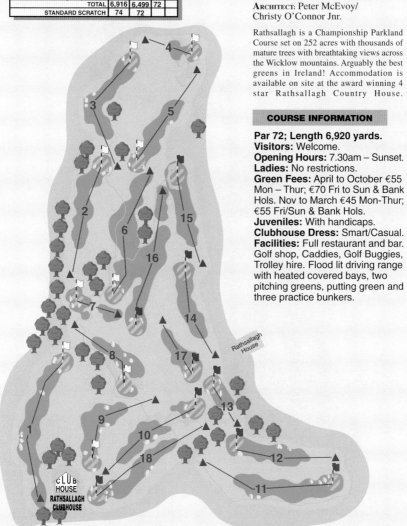

Copyright Tudor Journals Ltd.

Bunker and tree positions indicated.

**Roundwood Golf Club,
Newtownmountkennedy, Co.
Wicklow.
Tel: (01) 281 8488.
Fax: (01) 284 3642.
Email: rwood@indigo.ie
www.roundwoodgolf.com**

LOCATION: 2.5 miles from
Newtownmountkennedy on
Glendalough/Roundwood Road (N765).
SECRETARY: Mr Michael McGuirk
and Angela Brady.
ARCHITECT: Consortium.

All sand greens built to U.S.P.G.A. standards.
Water hazards and forestry. Heathland plays
like links. Magnificent views of coast,
mountains and Roundwood lakes.

COURSE INFORMATION

Par 72; Length 6,685 yards.
Visitors: Welcome.
Opening Hours: 8am – sunset.
Juveniles: Restricted.
Green Fees: €33 weekdays;
€45 weekends & holidays.
Society Rates available.
Clubhouse Dress:
Smart / Casual.
Clubhouse Facilities:
Restaurant food available
Tel: (01) 2818500.
Motorised Buggy,
Hand Cart,
Trolley & Clubs
available for hire.

NO.	MEDAL YARDS	GEN. YARDS	PAR	S.I.	NO.	MEDAL YARDS	GEN. YARDS	PAR	S.I.
1	413	379	4	12	10	182	172	3	7
2	176	166	3	10	11	397	382	4	9
3	480	470	5	16	12	435	420	4	3
4	427	383	4	2	13	184	146	3	13
5	556	541	5	8	14	320	300	4	17
6	347	337	4	6	15	501	481	5	5
7	125	119	3	18	16	446	360	4	1
8	381	371	4	4	17	211	183	3	15
9	515	505	5	14	18	589	579	5	11
OUT	3,420	3,271	37		IN	3,265	3,023	35	
					TOTAL	6,685	6,294	72	
					STANDARD SCRATCH				

Copyright Tudor Journals Ltd.

Bunker and tree positions indicated.

TULFARRIS

L E I N S T E R   **WICKLOW**

**Blessington Lakes,
Co Wicklow.
Tel: (045) 864574.**

LOCATION: 5 miles from
Blessington.
GOLF MANAGER: Adrian
Williams. Tel: (045) 867644.
ARCHITECT: Patrick F. Merrigan

Designed by Patrick F. Merrigan (Old
Head of Kinsale, Slieve Russell,
Woodenbridge) situated on a 200 acre
site overlooking Poulaphuca and
Blessington Lakes at the foothills of the

Wicklow mountains. The course
which measures over 7100 yards from
the back tees has been designed to be
challenging and enjoyable for golfers
of all levels. The tees, fairways, and
sand based greens have been
manicured to a high standard.

COURSE INFORMATION

**Par 72; SSS 74; Length
7,116 yards.
Visitors:** Welcome.
Opening Hours: Sunrise to
sunset.
Ladies: Welcome.

Juveniles: Under 12's not
allowed on the course.
Green Fees: €65 weekdays.
€80 weekends.
Clubhouse Hours:
6am - 10pm.
Clubhouse Dress:
Neat dress essential.
Clubhouse Facilities:
Bar Snacks 10am - 10pm.
Courtyard Restaurant
7pm – 10pm.

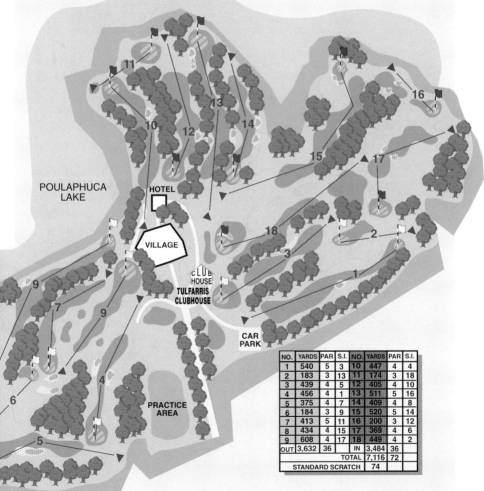

NO.	YARDS	PAR	S.I.	NO.	YARDS	PAR	S.I.
1	540	5	3	10	447	4	4
2	183	3	13	11	174	3	18
3	439	4	5	12	405	4	10
4	456	4	1	13	511	5	16
5	375	4	7	14	409	4	8
6	184	3	9	15	520	5	14
7	413	5	11	16	200	3	12
8	434	4	15	17	369	4	6
9	608	4	17	18	449	4	2
OUT	3,632	36		IN	3,484	36	
				TOTAL	7,116	72	
				STANDARD SCRATCH	74		

Copyright Tudor Journals Ltd.

Vartry Lakes Golf Course, Roundwood, Co. Wicklow.
Tel: (01) 2817006

LOCATION: 24 miles south of Dublin.
SECRETARY: Anne McDonald.
Tel: (01) 2817006.

This course is in the Wicklow Mountains and situated alongside the beautiful Vartry Lakes with spectacular scenic views off every hole. A well designed course, it has proved a tough test for all golfers.

COURSE INFORMATION

Par 70; SSS 70; Length 5,250 metres.
Visitors: Welcome.
Opening Hours:
7am – sunset.
Avoid: Sunday mornings.
Juveniles: Welcome with an adult.

Green Fees: €15; 9-holes €19; 18-holes.
Clubhouse Hours:
7.00am – sunset.
Clubhouse Dress:
Neat dress.
Clubhouse Facilities:
All day.

NO.	METRES	PAR	S.I.	NO.	METRES	PAR	S.I.
1	144	3	11	10	144	3	12
2	369	4	3	11	369	4	4
3	377	4	1	12	377	4	2
4	146	3	15	13	146	3	16
5	448	5	7	14	448	5	8
6	282	4	5	15	282	4	6
7	294	4	9	16	294	4	10
8	282	4	17	17	282	4	18
9	283	4	13	18	283	4	14
OUT	2,625	35		IN	2,625	35	
				TOTAL	5,250	70	
	STANDARD SCRATCH					70	

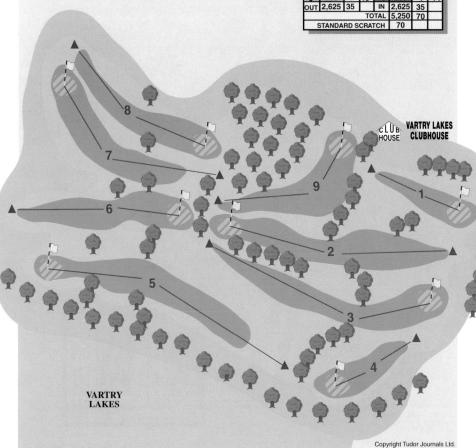

VARTRY LAKES CLUBHOUSE

VARTRY LAKES

Copyright Tudor Journals Ltd.

Dunbur Road, Wicklow.
Tel: (0404) 67379

LOCATION: Wicklow town; 30 miles south of Dublin city.
HONORARY SECRETARY: J Kelly. Tel: (0404) 69386.
PROFESSIONAL: Darren Mc Loughlin.
Tel/Fax: (0404) 66122.

The course makes full use of the natural contours and features of the terrain, creating a challenging and spectacular test of golf.

COURSE INFORMATION

Par 71; SSS 70; Length 5,695 metres.
Visitors: Welcome.
Opening Hours: Sunrise – Sunset.
Avoid: Wednesday and Sunday.
Ladies: Ladies Day Wednesday.
Juveniles: Must be accompanied by an adult.

Green Fees: €35 daily.
Clubhouse Hours: 9.00am Normal Licensing hours.
Clubhouse Dress: Neat, no jeans after 7pm.
Clubhouse Facilities: New clubhouse opening end of June.
Open Competitions: Regularly throughout the season. Visitors welcome with prior arrangement.

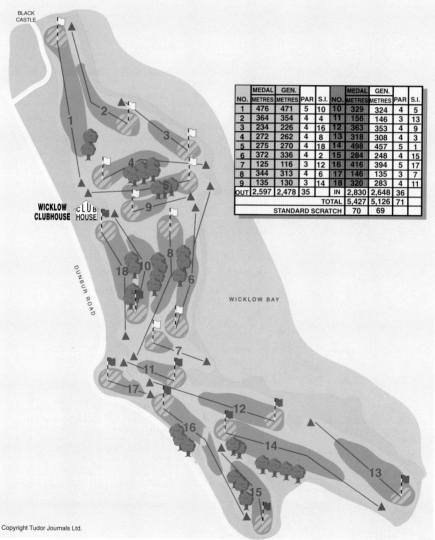

NO.	MEDAL METRES	GEN. METRES	PAR	S.I.	NO.	MEDAL METRES	GEN. METRES	PAR	S.I.
1	476	471	5	10	10	329	324	4	5
2	364	354	4	4	11	156	146	3	13
3	234	226	4	16	12	363	353	4	9
4	272	262	4	8	13	318	308	4	3
5	275	270	4	18	14	498	457	5	1
6	372	336	4	2	15	284	248	4	15
7	125	116	3	12	16	416	394	5	17
8	344	313	4	6	17	146	135	3	7
9	135	130	3	14	18	320	283	4	11
OUT	2,597	2,478	35		IN	2,830	2,648	36	
					TOTAL	5,427	5,126	71	
					STANDARD SCRATCH	70	69		

BLACK CASTLE

WICKLOW CLUBHOUSE

CLUB HOUSE

DUNBUR ROAD

WICKLOW BAY

Copyright Tudor Journals Ltd.

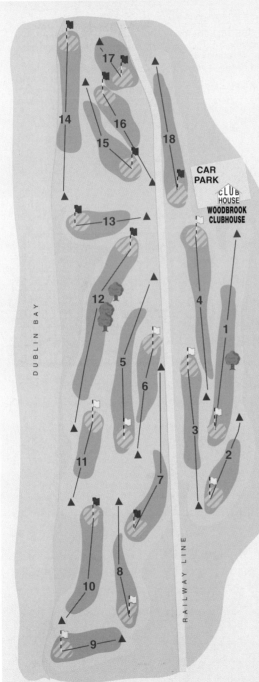

Woodbrook Golf Club, Dublin Road, Bray, Co. Wicklow Tel: (01) 2824799.

LOCATION: Eleven Miles south of Dublin City on N11.
GENERAL MANAGER: Patrick F. Byrne Tel: 2824799 Fax: 2821950.
PROFESSIONAL: Billy Kinsella.

Newly constructed layout with 18 new sand based greens and whilst beside the sea it is not a links course. The return of the course to Championship status will offer an excellent test of golf for all handicaps and with its traditional heritage, atmosphere and ambience, it is the perfect location for golf and hospitality.

COURSE INFORMATION

Par 72; SSS 72; Length 6,863 yards.
Visitors: Welcome weekdays and occasional weekends.
Opening Hours: Sunrise – Sunset.
Avoid: Tuesdays and Bank Holidays.
Ladies: Welcome.
Green Fees: €75 Mon - Fri or €60 before 10am; €85 Sat/Sun & Public Holidays.
Juveniles: Welcome. Lessons available; Club hire; Caddy service available by prior arrangement; Letter of introduction required (if possible); Handicap certificate required; Telephone appointment required.
Clubhouse Hours: 8am-12 midnight.
Clubhouse Dress: Jacket and tie in restaurant after 7pm.
Clubhouse Facilities: 10am - 9pm (with some exceptions in winter); Full restaurant facilities.

NO.	YARDS	PAR	S.I.	NO.	YARDS	PAR	S.I.
1	506	5	17	10	443	4	4
2	194	3	9	11	175	3	10
3	383	4	11	12	542	5	14
4	392	4	3	13	230	3	6
5	576	5	7	14	551	5	12
6	401	4	13	15	447	4	2
7	467	4	1	16	507	5	16
8	385	4	5	17	136	3	18
9	157	3	15	18	371	4	8
OUT	3,461	36		IN	3,402	36	
				TOTAL	6,863	72	
				STANDARD SCRATCH		72	

Copyright Tudor Journals Ltd.

154

**Woodenbridge, Arklow,
Co Wicklow.
Tel: (0402) 35202.
Fax: (0402) 35754
Email: wgc@eircom.net**
LOCATION: 4 miles west of
Arklow town.
SECRETARY / MANAGER:
Henry Crummy.
HON. SECRETARY:
Brian Hurley.
Tel: (0402) 39855 (o)
(0402) 32973 (h)

An 18 hole level parkland course,
renowned for the quality of its greens.
Carefully appointed trees and bunkers
demand accurate shots.

Sitting scenically in the beautiful Vale
of Avoca, crouched under hills of
magnificent forests and encircled by
the meandering Rivers Avoca &
Aughrim, it possesses a charm and
character very special to
Woodenbridge.

COURSE INFORMATION

**Par 71; SSS 70; Length
6,400 yards.
Visitors:** Welcome all week
except Thursday and
Saturday.
Opening Hours:
Sunrise – sunset.
Avoid: Thursdays and
Saturdays.

Ladies Day: Thursdays.
Juveniles: Welcome.
Green Fees: €51 weekdays,
€63 Sundays/ Bank Holidays.
Clubhouse Hours:
8.00am – 11.00pm.
Clubhouse Dress:
Informal – neat and tidy.
Clubhouse Facilities:
Full clubhouse facilities.
Mid-day – 9.00pm. Dinner
menu and a la carte. Prior
telephone call for special
service.

NO.	YARDS	PAR	S.I.	NO.	YARDS	PAR	S.I.
1	362	4	9	10	455	4	2
2	419	4	3	11	194	3	4
3	377	4	13	12	353	4	16
4	186	3	11	13	386	4	10
5	410	4	5	14	295	4	18
6	437	4	1	15	500	5	12
7	324	4	15	16	357	4	14
8	123	3	17	17	167	3	6
9	502	5	7	18	553	5	8
OUT	3,140	35		IN	3,260	36	
				TOTAL	6,400	71	
STANDARD SCRATCH					70		

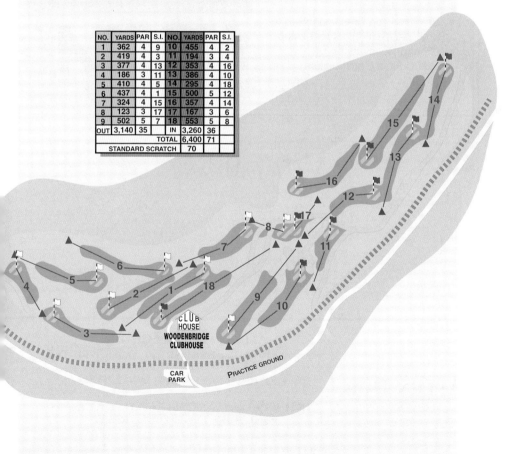

Copyright Tudor Journals Ltd.

The choice of the professionals

- 2.0m & 1.6m Verti Drains
- Multi - Core
- Core Harvestor
- Hydroject
- Drill and Fill Aerator
- Shattermaster
- Proseed
- Top Dresser
- Rotorake (Scarifier)
- Slitter
- Ground-Breaker
- Sand Spreading
- Direct Seeding
- Sterilised Top Dressing mixed to any specification, as requested.
- Ground Renovations
- Golf Course Construction

HORTA SOILS LTD. 4 Carn Court Road, Portadown, Co. Armagh, BT63 5YX. Tel: (028) 3833 7160. Fax: (028) 3833 7161

Website: www.hortasoils.co.uk
Email: Hortasoilslimited@btinternet.com

NUREMORE
H O T E L

18 Hole Championship Course
Resident PGA Professional
Classic Bedrooms ❖ *Exquisite Restaurant*
Extensive Leisure Facilities
Society Day Outings
Weekend & Midweek Golf Breaks
Carrickmacross, Co Monaghan.
Telephone: (042) 9661438. Fax: (042) 9661853.

ALLEN PARK GOLF CENTRE,
45 Castle Road (Randalstown Road), Antrim, BT41 4NA.

—— **TELEPHONE: (028) 9442 9001.** ——

18 Hole Parkland Golf Course (with U.S.G.A Greens)
and 20-Bay Floodlit Driving Range.
Open for visitors and special rates available for Societies.
• **Open Daily (dawn to dusk)** • **Clubs and Trolleys Available For Hire.**

BY JACK MAGOWAN

Peter Dobereiner never tried to keep it a secret. His love affair with Irish golf, and the Royal Co. Down links in particular, never waned one iota in all of his years as Europe's most erudite and best read writer on the game.

It was this wartime fighter pilot turned law student, then golf scribe, who first announced that Royal Co. Down was the best course in the world outside America, and nobody in the Press tent had more front door keys to more top clubs in the Emerald Isle.

For me, Dobereiner's death left a void that may never be filled. Ireland was where there were six days in the week, plus one for Guinness and golf. "It's informal and welcoming", he would say. "And the welcome is genuine because clubs there actually like visitors".

Peter must have told the story a thousand times, yet I, for one, never tired of hearing it.... of how the former U.S. Ryder Cup ace, Mike Souchak, lost all awareness of time and place on a visit to Killarney some years ago.

For business reasons, Souchak had to be back in New York as quickly as possible after filming ended in one of Shell's 'Wonderful World' matches.

Mike was still in spiked shoes as he set off by taxi for a speedy ride to Shannon Airport. Aer Lingus was alerted and the ground-staff briefed to expect a last-minute VIP. In fact, they even agreed to hold the flight for Mike.

Alas, it was three days later when the burly American checked in. If Dobers says he was singing a song about Rafferty's pig as he boarded the aircraft, you had better believe it.

Nobody ever got to hear exactly what happened to Souchak, but you can be sure that the taxi driver had a hand in it somehow. He could have had a cousin who lived close to Shannon and made only the best poteen in his own private still. Would Mike like to sample a quick toot? "Sure now, we've plenty of time to spare, and this is a grand car, to be sure."

Life had nothing richer to offer, so Souchak unwittingly said 'yes', a decision he never regretted.

They say the gifts of the Irish have enriched other nations more than their own, but in golf it's different. Here the game so many of us get a kick out of playing badly has everything going for it, a wide and exciting choice of courses, close to 30 on Dublin's doorstep alone; weather

Malone Golf Course in County Down – one the most attractive and popular of the inland courses.

One of the top courses in the world – Royal County Down set at the foot of the Mourne Mountains.

A wide range of accommodation.
Expert advice on where to go and stay.
An instant live booking service.

00800 668 668 66 (IRL., UK & Europe)
011 800 668 668 66 (USA & Canada)
+353 66 9792084 (all other countries)

www.discovernorthernireland.com

Gulliver Ireland
The Swift Way to Get Away

Northern Ireland
Tourist Board
www.discovernorthernireland.com

Bord Fáilte
Irish Tourist Board
www.ireland.travel.ie

North Coast Hotels Ltd

Bayview Hotel ★★★

2 Bayhead Road, Portballintrae, Bushmills, Co. Antrim, BT57 8RZ
Tel: 028 2073 4100 Fax: 028 2073 4330
Email: info@bayviewhotelni.com   www.bayviewhotelni.com

Opened the 4th December 2001 the 3 star Bay View Hotel is situated in the heart of the picturesque harbour village of Portballintrae, one mile from Bushmills. Overlooking the Atlantic Ocean and close to the Giants Causeway and Old Bushmills Distillery. 25 luxurious bedrooms with spacious Standard. Superior and Premier Rooms available, lift and private car park. The Porthole Restaurant and Bar with its open fire is the perfect meeting place. This small luxury hotel is the ideal destination for golfing at Royal Portrush, Portstewart, Castlerock, Ballycastle and Galgom Castle golf courses.

Comfort Hotel Portrush ★★★

73 Main Street, Portrush, Co. Antrim, BT56 8BN
Tel: 028 7082 6100 Fax: 028 7082 6160
Email: info@comforthotelportrush.com
www.comforthotelportrush.com

The 3 star Comfort Hotel Portrush opened 31st January 2001 situated overlooking the Atlantic Ocean in the centre of Portrush. 50 ensuite rooms; lift and private car park. The Counties Cafe Bar and Restaurant with its lively atmosphere is a popular meeting place. Ideal base for golfing at Royal Portrush, Portstewart, Castlerock, Ballycastle and Galgom Castle golf courses.

Dufferin
COACHING INN

The Inn has been operating since 1803 and is located in the midst of County Down golf country, surrounded by no less than 23 golf courses, topped by the Royal County Down championship course, all within 30 mins drive. Special rates for golf societies and groups. All golf can be reserved in advance. Transport can be arranged on request.

For further information & bookings please contact:
31 High Street, Killyleagh, Co. Down, BT30 9QF.
Tel: (028) 4482 8229. Fax: (028) 4482 8755.

Website: www.dufferincoachinginn.co.uk
Email: dufferin@dial.pipex.com

INISHOWEN GATEWAY H O T E L

This contemporary style 63 room Hotel is located on the shores of the Lough Swilly in the bustling seaside town of Buncrana. Ideally placed for golfers, overlooking both the North West Links and the ancient Buncrana Golf Course, the Inishowen Gateway Hotel is just a short drive from the two Championship Links courses at Ballyliffin. The Hotel offers excellent Leisure facilities and Golf Breaks are available all year round.

Railway Road,
Buncrana,
Inishowen,
Co. Donegal
Tel: 077 61144
Fax: 077 62278

info@inishowengateway.com
www.inishowengateway.com

conditions that can be uncharitable but never hazardous, and the kind of friendship and hospitality Souchak and a multitude of others have found so hard to resist.

It was in August 1981 that Royal Belfast celebrated its centenary as Ireland's oldest club. Rasputin was a thorn in the flesh of the Czar and a gallon of whisky cost 24 shillings (£1.20) when the game perfected by Scots was played for the first time over a course at Carnalea.

No competition could begin until the 11 o'clock train arrived from Belfast. The ladies of the club had their own wooden clubhouse built and furnished for less than £100, but without the modern-day luxury of a warm shower. There were rocks nearby, so quite few of the pretty young set would go bathing to cool off after their round. Subject to one condition, that is.

"Would ladies kindly refrain from passing the main clubhouse window in swim attire while the men are at lunch", said a notice bolted to the wooden fence.

It was in the mid-20's that Royal Belfast moved to Craigavad, £6,000 – that's how much they paid for the handsome Victorian manor and 140-acre estate which is now home to one of the most celebrated clubs in the game.

First Royal Belfast, then Royal Dublin, Royal Curragh, Mullingar, Royal Portrush, Aughnacloy and Royal County Down. By the time the Golfing

The wooded fairways of Royal Belfast to the east of the city, on the shores of Belfast Lough.

Hilton Templepatrick,
Castle Upton Estate,
Templepatrick,
Co. Antrim. BT39 0DD
Tel: (028) 9443 5500
Fax: (028) 9443 5511

www.hilton.com

Belfast has a great range of golf courses including the Hilton Templepatrick, a four star hotel and golf course set in 220 acres of the historic Castle Upton Estate, just 5 minutes from Belfast International Airport

18 Hole Championship golf course designed by David Jones and David Feherty

Putting Green • Practice range • PGA tuition

Ideal for Golf weekends. Societies and groups welcome.

Livingwell Health Club with gym, pool, steam and sauna.

For an information pack on Belfast contact:
The Belfast Welcome Centre,
Tel: (028) 9024 6609 or www.gotobelfast.com

THE BALMORAL
H·O·T·E·L

• 44 En suite Bedrooms
• Food served all day
• Conference & Banqueting suites
• Convenient to Belfast's finest golf courses, Malone, Dunmurry, Balmoral

Blacks Road, Dunmurry, BT10 0NF
Tel: (028) 9030 1234 Fax: (028) 9060 1455
E-mail: info@balmoralhotelbelfast.co.uk

LA MON
HOTEL & COUNTRY CLUB

Set in the heart of County Down

Family-run hotel with excellent cuisine and service

70 contemporary en-suite bedrooms

Superb health & leisure facilities with 15 metre pool, sauna, jacuzzi, steam-room, gymnasium

Choice of twelve 18 hole golf courses in local area (5 links)

All golfing arrangements can be made in advance by the hotel

41 Gransha Road, Comber, County Down.
Tel: 028 90448631
Website: www.lamon.co.uk   email: golf@lamon.co.uk

ACKNOWLEDGMENTS

GOLF DAYS WOULD LIKE TO RECORD ITS THANKS AND APPRECIATION TO THE MANY GOLF CLUBS AND STAFF WHO GREATLY ASSISTED THE PUBLISHERS IN COMPILING THIS BOOK. THE PUBLISHER'S ALSO ACKNOWLEDGE THE SUPPORT OF THE MANY ADVERTISERS THROUGHOUT THE JOURNAL AND WOULD RECOMMEND THEIR SERVICES TO READERS.

The lush greenery of the Lisburn course, in the Lagan Valley.

Union was born in 1891, there were twenty-one golf clubs in Ireland, half of them Ulster clubs. In fact, the GUI is the grandfather of all national golf Unions, older than the United States Golf Association by three years and the Welsh Union by four.

Remarkably, the Scottish Union wasn't formed until 1920, probably because of the Royal and Ancient Club's influence there and it was four years after that again before England had a ruling body.

What a virtuoso role Royal Portrush has played in the game. Hosts to more major championships and tournaments than they can count, the club's roll-call is dotted with players of distinction, names like Fred Daly, Joe Carr, Catherine Lacoste, Max Faulkner and Garth McGimpsey, not forgetting such legends of the past as Hughie McNeill, Anthony Babington, Rhona Adair, Zara Bolton and the Hezlet sisters.

Like Sir Anthony, P. G. Stevenson was a pillar of the great club for over half a century. And a fine teacher, clubmaker and storyteller, too. Nobody could remember Faulkner's historic 'Open' victory better than Stevie, or when Sunday golf there was outlawed as a sin, and the par for Dunluce was 81, repeat 81!. A milestone, surely, in the chequered history of Ulster golf.

A recent poll of Ireland's top 30 courses listed six in the North with probably only two notable omissions, Clandeboye and Belvoir Park. Portstewart and Malone were there (naturally!), and Slieve Russell, and Donegal as well.

Malone came in for a shower of kudos from Gary Player even before his victory in the Irish Seniors' championship of '93, and like good wine, he seems to improve with age.

Nobody attracted a bigger gallery in

Foyle is a parkland course which takes full advantage of its natural setting.

the British Seniors' Open at Dunluce than South Africa's knight in black, winner in 1997.

After the K-Club, Mount Juliet and Druid's Glen, Malone could be the pick of Ireland's best inland courses, and some of them are very good indeed.

It was an American writer of hard-boiled detective stories who compared golf in Ireland to playing poker with nothing wild. "It's the real thing," declared Larry Ferguson after a month-long safari here. "Irish golf is not for players who like to be petted and protected. It's for pulling on a sweater, feeling the spray in your face, then boring long irons under winds that may keep the Coast Guard in port!"

Is it possible that globe-trotter Ferguson may have played Portrush or Newcastle on a bad day in March? It's not that Irish weather can't be trusted.

There's just so much of it, that's all!

There are some places you have to come back to in order to discover them for the first time, wrote Tom Callahan, in *Golf Digest* after a visit to Ulster, and we know he'll be back to the course he rates the best in Ireland.

"Tom Watson cleaves to Ballybunion," says Callahan. "He agrees the front nine at Newcastle is close to perfection, but suggests that the closing couple of holes are not up to the rest of the course's extreme standard." A view shared by most critics, perhaps, before they did such a good job of re-modelling the long 18th.

To the west in Donegal, superb scenery goes in harmony with some great golf, especially on the Inishowen as well as Fanad Peninsulas. And what they say of the natives there is true. They are the salt of the earth!

Allen Park Golf Centre, 45 Castle Road (Randalstown Rd), Antrim, BT41 4NA. Tel: (028) 9442 9001.

LOCATION: 2₁/₂ miles from Antrim town centre on the road from Antrim to Randalstown.
MANAGER: Marie Agnew.
ARCHITECT: Mr T. McAuley.

The course opened in Spring 1996. This gently undulating parkland course will test the skill and ability of even the more experienced golfer. The shortest hole is 196 yards with the longest being 559 yards. 3 lakes provide interesting features in the front nine holes.

COURSE INFORMATION

Par 72; SSS 72;
Length 6,683 yards.

Visitors: Welcome.
Opening Hours: Dawn–Dusk
Green Fees: Mon/Fri – £15: Adults, £9: Senior Citizen (Over 60), £6:Junior (Under 18). Weekends & Holidays – £17: Adults, £11: Senior Citizen (Over 60), £7: Junior (under 18).
Juveniles: Welcome.
Clubhouse Dress: Casual.
Clubhouse Facilities: Locker rooms, Snooker table and catering facilities.

MEDAL YARDS	GEN. YARDS	PAR	S.I.	NO	MEDAL YARDS	GEN. YARDS	PAR	S.I.
419	347	4	5	10	427	360	4	3
197	175	3	7	11	290	252	4	16
396	322	4	9	12	319	277	4	13
477	407	5	18	13	306	259	4	15
559	479	5	14	14	503	452	5	17
196	175	3	6	15	555	463	5	12
364	320	4	11	16	203	181	3	8
201	179	3	4	17	445	365	4	1
388	332	4	10	18	438	373	4	2
3,197	2,736	35		IN	3,486	2,982	37	
				TOTAL	6,683	5,718	72	
STANDARD SCRATCH					72			

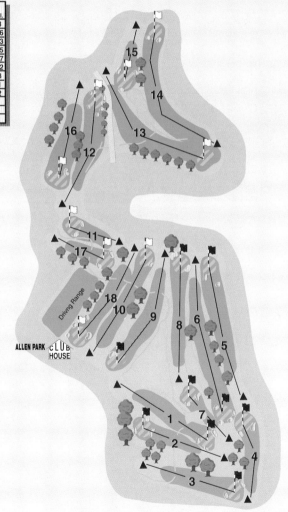

Bunker and tree positions indicated.
Copyright Tudor Journals Ltd.

**Cushendall Road,
Ballycastle, Co. Antrim
BT54 6QP.
Tel: (028) 2076 2536.**

LOCATION: On the north coast of Antrim at the eastern end of the Causeway Coast — adjacent to the Glens of Antrim.
SECRETARY: Brian Dillon.
PROFESSIONAL: Ian McLaughlin.
Tel: (028) 2076 2506.

The opening five holes are parkland bordered by the Margy and Carey Rivers and played around the ruins of a 13th Century Friary. The Warren area of four holes is true links and the final nine are played in an adjacent upland, giving panoramic views including Mull of Kintyre, Rathlin Island and Ballycastle Bay. Accurate iron play is essential for good scoring.

COURSE INFORMATION

Par 71; SSS 70; Length 5,927 yards.
Visitors: Welcome.
Opening Hours:
Summer 9.00am – 9.00pm;
Winter 9.00am – 3.00pm.
Avoid: Sat and Sun morning.
Ladies Day: Friday.
Green Fees: £20 (£10 with member) Mon – Fri; £30 (£15 with member) Sat / Sun and public holidays. Juveniles under 18 years – 1/2 rates.

Juveniles: Welcome before 6.00pm in July and August. Lessons by prior arrangement; Club hire and Caddy service available by prior arrangement.
Clubhouse Hours:
11.30am – 11pm (July & August); Restricted in winter.
Clubhouse Dress: Casual.
Clubhouse Facilities: Bar snacks and meals throughout the day. Evening meals by prior arrangement.
Open Competitions: Open Week – July; other competitions throughout the season.

NO.	YARDS	METRES	PAR	S.I.	NO.	YARDS	METRES	PAR	S.I.
1	456	415	5	9	10	115	105	3	12
2	358	326	4	3	11	346	315	4	4
3	168	153	3	13	12	495	450	5	14
4	410	373	4	1	13	138	126	3	16
5	264	240	4	17	14	363	330	4	2
6	310	282	4	15	15	409	372	4	8
7	416	379	4	7	16	298	271	4	18
8	331	301	4	11	17	180	164	3	6
9	359	327	4	5	18	511	465	5	10
OUT	3,072	2,796	36		IN	2,855	2,598	35	
					TOTAL	5,927	5,391	71	
					STANDARD SCRATCH		70		

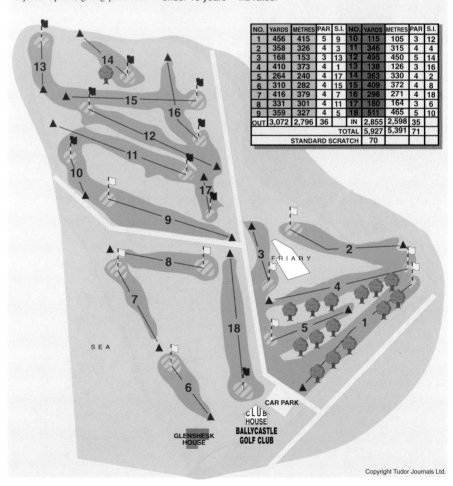

SEA

FRIARY

CAR PARK

CLUB HOUSE
GLENSHESK HOUSE
BALLYCASTLE GOLF CLUB

Copyright Tudor Journals Ltd.

**25 Springvale Road,
Ballyclare, Co. Antrim.
Tel: (028) 9332 2696.**

LOCATION: Two miles north of
Ballyclare.
SECRETARY: H. McConnell.
Tel: (028) 9332 2696.
ARCHITECT: T. McCauley.

Parkland course which makes good use of
the local river and streams. The fairways
are tree-lined and as expected, accurate
driving is required for a good score.

COURSE INFORMATION

**Par 71; SSS 71; Length
5,745 metres.**
Visitors: Welcome Mon, Tues,
Wed, Fri, & Sun.
Opening Hours: Dawn–Dusk.
Avoid: Sunday mornings,
Thursdays from 1.30pm and
Saturdays.
Ladies: Welcome.
Green Fees: £18 Mon – Fri;
£24 Sunday/Bank Holidays.

Juveniles: Mon – Fri before
4.30pm; Sat/Sun after
4.30pm.
Clubhouse Hours: 12.30 –
11.30pm.
Clubhouse Dress: Jacket
and tie after 7.00pm.
Clubhouse Facilities: Meals
from 12.30pm unless by prior
arrangement.

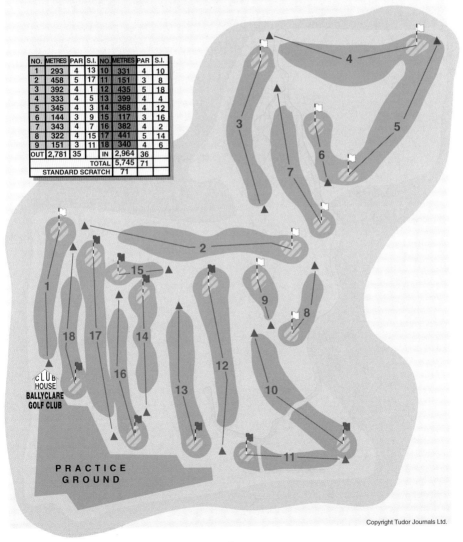

NO.	METRES	PAR	S.I.	NO.	METRES	PAR	S.I.
1	293	4	13	10	331	4	10
2	458	5	17	11	151	3	8
3	392	4	1	12	435	5	18
4	333	4	5	13	399	4	4
5	345	4	3	14	368	4	12
6	144	3	9	15	117	3	16
7	343	4	7	16	382	4	2
8	322	4	15	17	441	5	14
9	151	3	11	18	340	4	6
OUT	2,781	35		IN	2,964	36	
				TOTAL	5,745	71	
	STANDARD SCRATCH				71		

CLUB
HOUSE
**BALLYCLARE
GOLF CLUB**

**P R A C T I C E
G R O U N D**

Copyright Tudor Journals Ltd.

NO.	MEDAL METRES	GEN. METRES	PAR	S.I.	NO.	MEDAL METRES	GEN. METRES	PAR	S.I.
1	323	315	4	10	10	187	177	3	9
2	163	154	3	8	11	406	395	4	1
3	448	440	5	14	12	381	354	4	5
4	138	126	3	16	13	271	261	4	17
5	350	338	4	6	14	200	191	3	13
6	354	323	4	2	15	360	321	4	3
7	103	92	3	18	16	188	180	3	7
8	345	337	4	4	17	333	323	4	11
9	449	437	5	12	18	300	290	4	15
OUT	2,673	2,562	35		IN	2,626	2,492	33	
					TOTAL	5,299	5,054	68	
			STANDARD SCRATCH			68	68		

**128 Raceview Road, Ballymena.
Tel: (028) 2586 1487.**

LOCATION: Three miles east of
Ballymena.
SECRETARY:Seamus Crummey.
Tel: (028) 2586 1487.
PROFESSIONAL: Ken Revie.

A flat course comprised mainly of heathland
with numerous bunkers. The Glens of Antrim
lie to the northeast and Slemish Mountain is
clearly visible to the east.

COURSE INFORMATION

**Par 68; SSS 68; Length 5,299
Metres.
Visitors:** Welcome.
Men's Competitions – Saturdays.
Ladies: Tuesdays.
Green Fees: Adults: £17 Mon – Fri;
£22 Sat /Sun. Societies 10% discount
for parties of 20 or more.
Juveniles: Weekdays before 6.00pm;
Sat after 6.00pm; Sunday all day.
Lessons by prior arrangement.
Club Hire and Caddy Cars available.
Clubhouse Dress: Casual except
function nights.
Clubhouse Facilities: Catering facilities:
bar snacks; restaurant 11.30am –
9.00pm everyday except Mon in winter.
Open competions:
Open Week; 21st-27th July. Open
Stableford; 6th & 17th Mar, 7th & 24th
April, 9th June (ladies & gents), 17th,
20th July & 25th Aug. Open Stroke; 23rd
Mar, 10th Apr, 4th May, 30th June, 14th
& 18th Aug, 1st Sept. Mixed foursomes;
4th Aug.

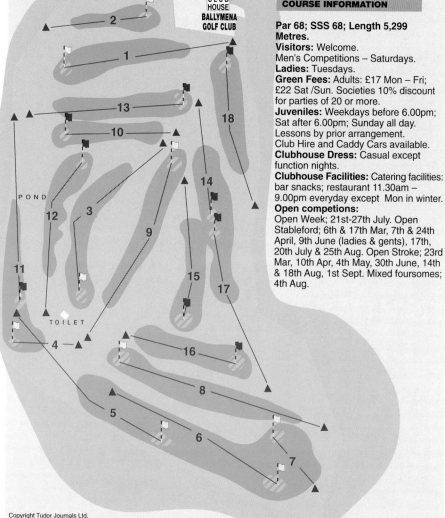

Copyright Tudor Journals Ltd.

NO.	MEDAL YARDS	GEN. YARDS	PAR	S.I.	NO.	MEDAL YARDS	GEN. YARDS	PAR	S.I.
1	408	419	4	4	10	445	458	4	1
2	157	169	3	7	11	128	135	4	7
3	299	306	4	15	12	347	354	3	1
4	339	347	4	6	13	354	362	4	7
5	377	386	4	2	14	377	386	3	3
6	483	490	5	10	15	493	499	4	1
7	156	160	3	12	16	182	190	4	3
8	323	328	4	17	17	323	338	5	5
9	327	337	4	13	18	327	337	4	1
OUT	2,869	2,942	35		IN	2,869	3,059	35	5
					TOTAL	5,845	6,001	70	
					STANDARD SCRATCH		68		

50 Bushfoot Road, Portballintrae, Bushmills, Co Antrim BT57 8RA.
Tel: (028) 2073 1317.

LOCATION: Two miles from Bushmills beside Portballintrae village.
SECRETARY/MANAGER: J. Knox Thompson.
Tel: (028) 2073 1317.
Fax:(028) 2073 1852.

Links course laid around the estuary of the River Bush. Quite a short course with the river playing a prominent part of the challenge. The clubhouse offers good views of the Causeway Coast and on a clear day Scotland is visible.

COURSE INFORMATION

Par 70; SSS 68; Length 6,001 Yards.
Visitors: Welcome Mon – Fri.
Avoid: Saturday or Sunday unless guest of a member.
Ladies: Welcome any time.
Green Fees: £14 Mon – Fri; £18 Bank & Public Holidays; Sat/Sun £12 with a member only.
Juveniles: Under 10 with an adult. July & August must be off the course by 6.00pm. Handicap Certificate required. Prior arrangement preferable.
Clubhouse Dress: Acceptable Casual.
Clubhouse Facilities: Full meals, snacks Tue – Sat 12.00 noon – 3.00pm and 5.00pm – 9.00pm.

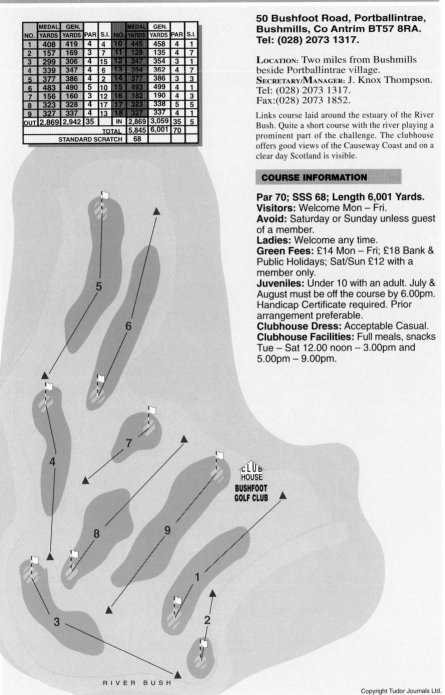

CLUB HOUSE
BUSHFOOT GOLF CLUB

RIVER BUSH

Copyright Tudor Journals Ltd.

**192 Coast Road,
Ballygally, Larne.
Tel: (028) 2858 3324.**

LOCATION: Four miles north of Larne.
SECRETARY/MANAGER: Nat Moore
Tel: (028) 2858 3324.
PROFESSIONAL: Mr R. Walker.
Tel: (028) 2858 3417.

Parkland course built on the face of a hill known as Ballygally Head. One of the more scenic courses in Ireland, views to Scotland, down the coast to Carnlough and Antrim Hills. From the third tee which is 200ft above sea level beware of the hazardous valley on the right hand side and the rocks in

front. Your drive has to carry 175 yards to the fairway — apart from the level of difficulty this is one of the most scenic holes.

COURSE INFORMATION

Par 70; SSS 69; Length 5,611 metres.
Visitors: Welcome any day except Saturday.
Opening Hours: From 9.00am.
Green Fees: £20 Mon – Fri;
£25 Sun. Ladies £15 (Sun £20)
Ladies: Mon – Fri £10.
Sun £15.
Juveniles: 9.00am – 6.00pm
Monday – Friday; Saturday after

7.00pm; Sunday after 6.00pm.
Club Hire available.
Clubhouse Hours: 8.00am –
11.00pm.
Clubhouse Dress: No Denims or tracksuits. Collar and tie.
Clubhouse Facilities: Catering facilities: bar and restaurant 5.00pm – 11.00pm. Outside these hours, by prior arrangement.
Open Competitions:
Open Week – July.

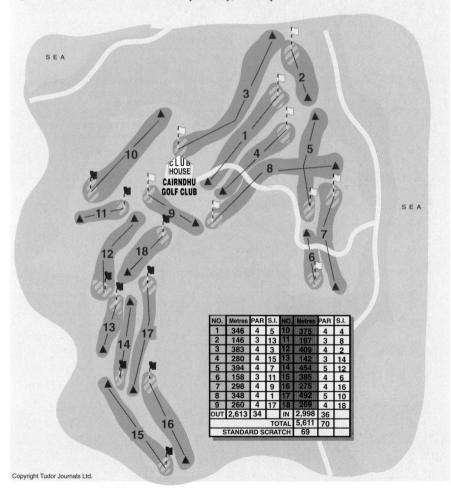

NO.	Metres	PAR	S.I.	NO.	Metres	PAR	S.I.
1	346	4	5	10	375	4	4
2	146	3	13	11	197	3	8
3	383	4	3	12	409	4	2
4	280	4	15	13	142	3	14
5	394	4	7	14	454	5	12
6	158	3	11	15	385	4	6
7	298	4	9	16	275	4	16
8	348	4	1	17	492	5	10
9	260	4	17	18	269	4	18
OUT	2,613	34		IN	2,998	36	
				TOTAL	5,611	70	
				STANDARD SCRATCH	69		

Copyright Tudor Journals Ltd.

35 North Road, Carrickfergus, BT38 8LP.
Tel: (028) 9336 3713.
Email: carrickfergusgc@talk21.com

LOCATION: On outskirts of town.
SECRETARY / MANAGER: John Thomson.
PROFESSIONAL: Colin P. Farr.

A parkland course with a spectacular first hole. The first drive, from an elevated tee is over the infamous dam which is full of water and quite intimidating! Although a reasonably flat course there are several demanding holes to be tackled. The Par 4, 6th hole is a dog-leg left playing to a hidden green beside the dam. The course is well maintained throughout the year and there are some very pleasant views across the Belfast Lough to Co. Down.

NO.	MEDAL YARDS	GEN. YARDS	PAR	S.I.	NO.	MEDAL YARDS	GEN. YARDS	PAR	S.I.
1	418	416	4	8	10	444	439	4	1
2	107	104	3	16	11	409	405	4	7
3	384	376	4	4	12	167	154	3	17
4	122	118	3	18	13	436	426	4	3
5	322	312	4	10	14	197	186	3	13
6	426	421	4	2	15	355	353	4	5
7	139	124	3	14	16	301	300	4	15
8	283	273	4	12	17	490	488	5	9
9	440	400	4	6	18	328	320	4	11
OUT	2,641	2,544	33		IN	3,127	3,071	35	
					TOTAL	5,768	5,615	68	
					STANDARD SCRATCH			68	

COURSE INFORMATION

Par 68; SSS 68; Length 5,752 Yards.
Visitors: Welcome any day during the week. Sunday after 12 noon.
Avoid: Tuesday, Saturday and Sunday.
Ladies: Tuesdays.
Green Fees: £19.50 Mon – Fri (£11 with member); £26.50 Sat / Sun/Bank Holidays (£16.50 with a member).
Juveniles: Up to 4pm – restricted times at weekends.
Clubhouse Dress: Jacket and tie in Dinning Room after 7pm – otherwise neat / casual.
Clubhouse Facilities: Catering facilities: bar snacks, meals 12 noon – 9pm everyday except Mondays.
Open Competitons:
Open Week – July / Aug.

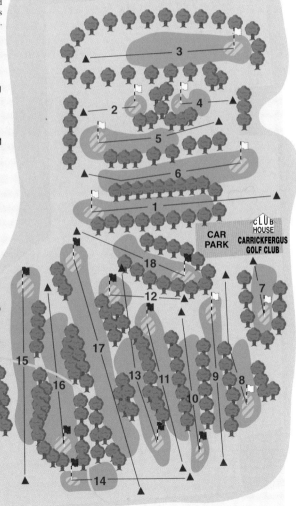

Copyright Tudor Journals Ltd.

21 Shore Road, Cushendall, Co. Antrim.
Tel: (028) 2177 1318.

LOCATION: In Cushendall village on road to beach.
SECRETARY: Shaun McLaughlin.
Tel: (028) 2175 8366.
ARCHITECT: Dan Delargy.

Beautifully situated course where the River Dall winds through the fairways in seven of the nine holes. Cushendall is quite a short course, it has three par 3's and no par 5's, but it requires great accuracy as it is possible to go out of bounds at every hole.

COURSE INFORMATION

Par 66; SSS 63; Length 4,386 metres.
Visitors: Check with club in advance.
Avoid: Sundays anytime (time sheet).
Ladies: Any time but not Sunday before 1.00pm. Priority on Thursdays.
Green Fees: £13 Mon – Fri; £18 Sat / Sun / Bank Holidays.
Juveniles: Weekdays up to 5.00pm. Must be off course

by 1.00pm Sat and no play on Sun. Lessons can be arranged.
Clubhouse Dress: Casual.
Clubhouse Facilities: Full bar and Catering available at all times during summer.
Open Competitions: Glens of Antrim mixed foursomes – May / June. Most weekends. Handicap Certificate required for Open Competitions.

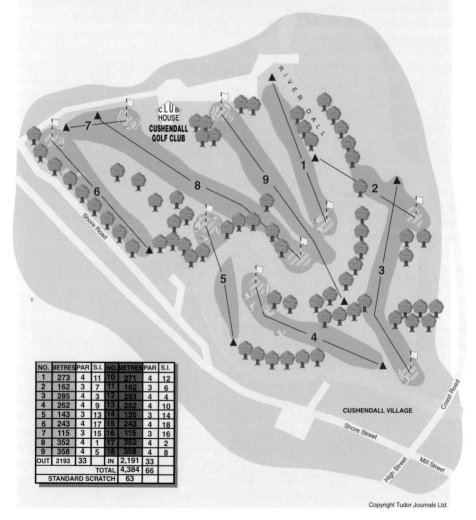

NO.	METRES	PAR	S.I.	NO.	METRES	PAR	S.I.
1	273	4	11	10	271	4	12
2	162	3	7	11	162	3	6
3	285	4	3	12	293	4	4
4	262	4	9	13	262	4	10
5	143	3	13	14	135	3	14
6	243	4	17	15	243	4	18
7	115	3	15	16	115	3	16
8	352	4	1	17	352	4	2
9	358	4	5	18	358	4	8
OUT	2193	33		IN	2,191	33	
				TOTAL	4,384	66	
				STANDARD SCRATCH	63		

CUSHENDALL VILLAGE

Copyright Tudor Journals Ltd.

Dunygarton Road, Maze, Lisburn, BT27 5RT.
Tel: (028) 9262 1339.

LOCATION: Within the Maze racecourse.
SECRETARY / MANAGER: Mr. J. Tinnion.
Tel: (028) 9262 1339.
ARCHITECT: Golf Design Associates.

Situated in the Lagan Valley amid pleasant rural surroundings the course is conveniently situated to many of the major provincial towns. Set in 150 acres of rolling heathland with gorse lined fairways within the Down Royal (Maze) Racecourse. The nature of the soil being sandy loam ensures the course is playable all year round. The course is in two loops of nine and a classical Par 72, with four Par 5's, four Par 3's and ten Par 4's.

COURSE INFORMATION

Par 72; SSS 72; Length 6,824 Yards.

Visitors: Welcome.
Ladies: Welcome.
Green Fees: £15 Mon – Fri; £17 Sat; £20 Sun / Bank Holidays. £12 off-peak.
Juveniles: Must be accompanied by an adult.
Clubhouse Dress: Smart – collar and tie after 7.00pm.
Clubhouse Facilities: Licensed restaurant nearby – open everyday.

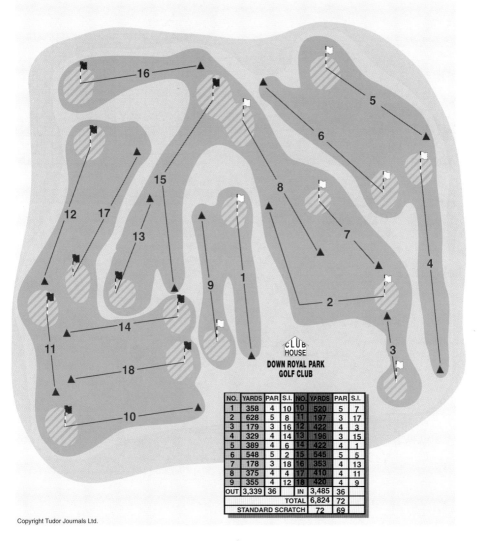

DOWN ROYAL PARK
GOLF CLUB

NO.	YARDS	PAR	S.I.	NO.	YARDS	PAR	S.I.
1	358	4	10	10	520	5	7
2	628	5	8	11	197	3	17
3	179	3	16	12	422	4	3
4	329	4	14	13	196	3	15
5	389	4	6	14	422	4	1
6	548	5	2	15	545	5	5
7	178	3	18	16	353	4	13
8	375	4	4	17	410	4	11
9	355	4	12	18	420	4	9
OUT	3,339	36		IN	3,485	36	
				TOTAL	6,824	72	
				STANDARD SCRATCH		72	69

Copyright Tudor Journals Ltd.

**Galgorm Castle,
Galgorm Road,
Ballymena, BT42 1HL.
Tel: (028) 2564 6161.**

LOCATION: Galgorm, Ballymena.
SECRETARY: Barbara McGeown.
ARCHITECT: Simon Gidman.

18 hole championship course set in 220 acres of mature parkland in the grounds of Galgorm Castle. The course is bordered by the rivers Main and Braid which come into play and include a magnificent oxbow feature and five landscape lakes. A stimulating challenge and memorable round for both novice and low handicap golfers.

COURSE INFORMATION

Par 72; SSS 72; Length 6,736 yards.
Visitors: Welcome.
Opening Hours: 8am – 10pm. Saturday, ring to book.
Green Fees: Weekdays £23; weekends £28. No metal spikes.

Ladies: Welcome.
Juveniles: Welcome, ring in advance.
Clubhouse Hours:
8.00am – 10.00pm.
Clubhouse Dress: Casual.
Facilities: Pavilion licenced bar and restaurant with wonderful views of the course. P.G.A. staffed Academy. Floodlit covered driving range. Golf School. Golf shop.

NO.	CHAMP YARDS	MEDAL YARDS	PAR	S.I.	NO.	CHAMP YARDS	MEDAL YARDS	PAR	S.I.
1	464	423	4	6	10	510	483	5	9
2	302	302	4	16	11	475	443	4	1
3	475	475	5	14	12	169	150	3	17
4	323	301	4	10	13	376	350	4	3
5	206	176	3	8	14	177	147	3	13
6	415	371	4	4	15	382	342	4	11
7	141	141	3	18	16	409	362	4	7
8	409	352	4	2	17	446	404	4	5
9	507	484	5	12	18	550	524	5	15
OUT	3,242	3,025	36		IN	3,494	3,205	36	
					TOTAL	6,736	6,230	72	
					STANDARD SCRATCH	72	72		

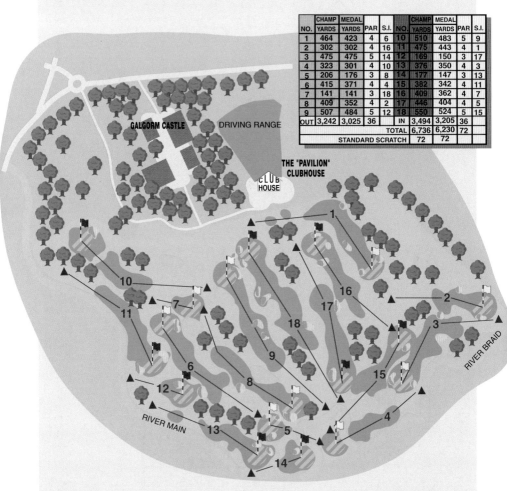

GALGORM CASTLE   DRIVING RANGE

THE "PAVILION"
CLUBHOUSE
CLUB HOUSE

RIVER BRAID

RIVER MAIN

Copyright Tudor Journals Ltd.   Bunker & tree positions indicated.

**141 Ballinlea Road,
Stranocum, Ballymoney,
Co. Antrim, BT53 8PX.
Tel: (028) 7075 1209.**

LOCATION: Seven miles north of Ballymoney, forty five minutes from Belfast International Airport and ten minutes from the Causeway Coast.
PROPRIETORS: J&M Gillan.
ARCHITECT: Frank Ainsworth.

Gracehill opened in July 1995 and is a very challenging parkland course which will provide a stern test for even the best golfers. Some of the holes are played over water and many mature trees also come into play. Considered to be one of the best 18 hole golf courses in all of Ulster, if not all of Ireland.

COURSE INFORMATION

Par 72; SSS 73; Length 6,600 yards.
Opening Hours: 8am–Sunset.
Green Fees: £16 Mon – Fri; £22 Sat/Sun.

Juveniles: Must be accompanied by an adult.
Clubhouse Hours: 8am – Sunset.
Clubhouse Dress: Smart / Casual.
Clubhouse Facilities: Catering available from 12 noon - 5.30pm or later for party bookings.

NO.	YARDS	PAR	S.I.	NO.	YARDS	PAR	S.I.
1	336	4	8	10	455	4	2
2	356	4	15	11	161	3	13
3	378	4	14	12	482	5	10
4	492	5	11	13	425	4	1
5	442	4	4	14	235	3	6
6	375	4	9	15	500	5	3
7	188	3	12	16	145	3	18
8	386	4	7	17	359	4	17
9	486	5	16	18	405	4	5
OUT	3,439	37		IN	3,167	35	
				TOTAL	6,606	72	
	STANDARD SCRATCH	71					

Copyright Tudor Journals Ltd.

Bunker and tree positions indicated.

**Greenacres Golf Centre,
153 Ballyrobert Road,
Ballyclare, Co. Antrim.
Tel: (028) 9335 4111.
Fax: (028) 9335 4166.**

LOCATION: 8 miles from Belfast
city centre.
SECRETARY: Peter Watson.
Tel: (028) 9335 4111.
PROFESSIONAL: Ray Skillon.

A challenging parkland course
designed to fit in with the natural
rolling countryside of Co.Antrim.

COURSE INFORMATION

**Par 70; SSS 69; Length
5,839 yards.
Visitors:** Welcome.
Opening Hours:
8.00am – 9.00pm.
Avoid: Saturday mornings.
Green Fees: £12 Mon - Fri,
£18 Sat/Sun/Bank & Public hols.
Ladies: Welcome.
Juveniles: Welcome if
accompanied by an adult.
Clubhouse Dress:
Smart / Casual.

Clubhouse Facilities:
Full restaurant facilities and bar.
Weekend booking advisable. Tel.
Barnaby's (028) 9335 4151.
20 bay full flood-lit driving range.
Open Competitions: June.

NO.	YARDS	PAR	S.I.	NO.	YARDS	PAR	S.I.
1	279	4	16	10	372	4	5
2	354	4	4	11	135	3	15
3	171	3	14	12	396	4	1
4	330	4	18	13	182	3	13
5	380	4	6	14	340	4	7
6	158	3	8	15	290	4	17
7	457	4	2	16	185	3	11
8	494	5	10	17	351	4	3
9	486	5	12	18	479	5	9
OUT	3,109	36		IN	2,730	34	
				TOTAL	5,839	70	
			STANDARD SCRATCH		69		

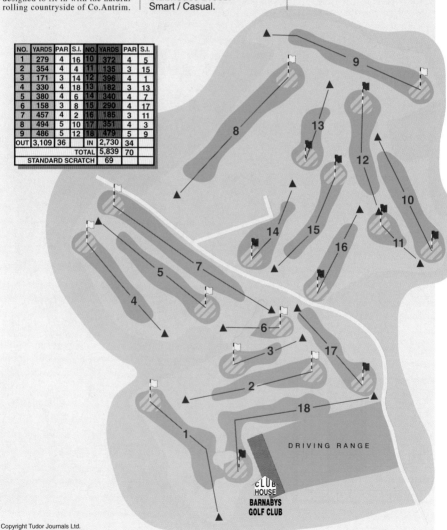

DRIVING RANGE

cLUB
HOUSE
BARNABYS
GOLF CLUB

Copyright Tudor Journals Ltd.

GREENISLAND   U L S T E R   **ANTRIM**

**156 Upper Road,
Greenisland, Carrickfergus,
BT38 8RW.
Tel: (028) 9086 2236.**

Location: Eight miles north of Belfast, and two miles from Carrickfergus.
Hon. Secretary: J Mc Laughlin.
Tel: (028) 9086 2236.

The course is nestled at the foot of the Knockagh Hill and situated on the edge of Carrickfergus town. One of its features is the scenic views over Belfast Lough.

COURSE INFORMATION

Par 71; SSS 68; Length 5,536 Metres.
Visitors: Welcome.
Opening Hours: Sunrise – Sunset.
Avoid: Saturdays until 5.00pm and Thursdays.
Ladies Day: Thursday.
Green Fees: £12 Mon – Fri (£6 with a member); £18 Sat/Sun/All Public Holidays (£9 with a member).
Juveniles: Saturdays after

5.30pm. Must be accompanied by an adult. Prior arrangement is required for societies.
Clubhouse Hours: 12.00pm – 11.00pm (summer). Full clubhouse facilities.
Clubhouse Dress: Bar area — casual; Dinning room — jacket, collar and tie.
Clubhouse Facilities: Lunch and evening meals, bar snacks.
Open Competitions:
Men's Open – June.
Mixed foursomes – May.

MEDAL METRES	GEN. METRES	PAR	S.I.	NO.	MEDAL METRES	GEN. METRES	PAR	S.I.
312	308	4	3	10	323	308	4	2
348	337	4	7	11	360	337	4	6
449	443	5	11	12	437	443	5	12
304	283	4	13	13	296	283	4	14
389	374	4	1	14	484	374	5	8
191	170	3	9	15	173	170	3	10
326	332	4	5	16	336	332	4	4
92	97	3	17	17	87	97	3	18
306	286	4	15	18	310	286	4	16
2,717	2,630	35		IN	2,806	2,630	35	
				TOTAL	5,523	5,260	71	
				STANDARD SCRATCH		69	68	

Bunker and tree positions indicated.

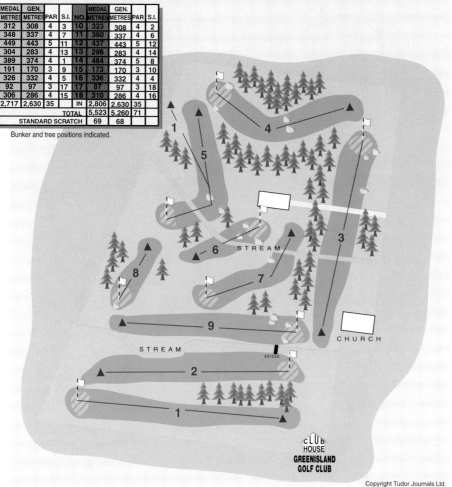

STREAM

STREAM   BRIDGE

CHURCH

CLUB HOUSE
GREENISLAND GOLF CLUB

Copyright Tudor Journals Ltd.

Hilton Templepatrick Golf Club, Castle Upton Estate, Templepatrick, BT39 ODD
Tel: (028) 9443 5510
Email:
golf.manager@park.stakis.co.uk

LOCATION: 3 miles from Int. Airport and 10 miles from Belfast.
MANAGER: Bill Donald
PROFESSIONAL: Eamonn Logue & Lynn McCool
ARCHITECT: David Jones & David Feherty

220 acres of parkland provide the setting for an exciting new course in County Antrim. The mature woodlands of the Castle Upton Estate come in to play, and also act as a backdrop to the championship standard golf course. Water punctuates the course with a number of lakes and rivers making shot and club selection the key to the course. The 18th hole with the Hilton Hotel as a backdrop allows the golfer to play safe or take on the challenge of the lake in front of the green.

COURSE INFORMATION
Par 71; SSS 72; Length 7,012 yards.
Avoid: Sat & Sun am.
Green Fees: £40 Midweek; £45 Weekend; £20. Residents £25
Juveniles: £12.
Clubhouse Dress: No restriction.
Additional Facilities:
130 Bedroom Hotel - Treffners Restaurant & Kinahans Brasserie - Livingwell Health Club
Open Competitions:
Easter, 12th July week, Halloween, Christmas.

HOTEL

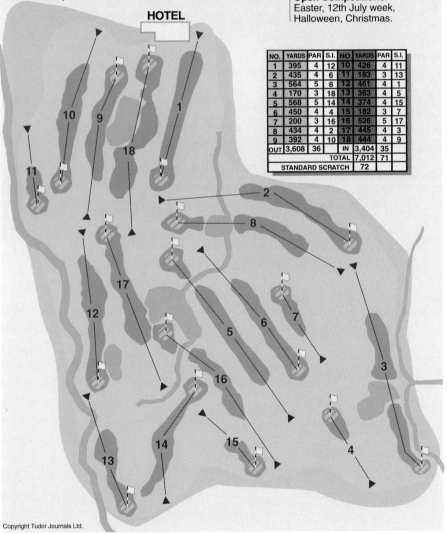

NO.	YARDS	PAR	S.I.	NO.	YARDS	PAR	S.I.
1	395	4	12	10	426	4	11
2	435	4	6	11	183	3	13
3	564	5	8	12	461	4	1
4	170	3	18	13	363	4	5
5	568	5	14	14	374	4	15
6	450	4	4	15	182	3	7
7	200	3	16	16	526	5	17
8	434	4	2	17	445	4	3
9	392	4	10	18	444	4	9
OUT	3,608	36		IN	3,404	35	
				TOTAL	7,012	71	
STANDARD SCRATCH			72				

Copyright Tudor Journals Ltd.

Aberdelghy, Bells Lane, Lambeg, Lisburn.
Tel: (028) 9266 2738.

LOCATION: Two miles from Lisburn town centre, off the main Lisburn / Belfast Road.
HON. SECRETARY: Brian Jackson.
PROFESSIONAL: Ian Murdock.
Tel: (028) 9266 2738.

This parkland course is ideal for medium and high handicap golfers. An interesting feature is the par three 5th which straddles a reservoir. The course was recently upgraded to 18 holes.

COURSE INFORMATION

Par 66; SSS 62; Length 4,139 metres.
Visitors: Welcome. Municiple course for public use.

Opening Hours: 8am – dusk.
Avoid: Saturday Morning.
Ladies: Welcome.
Green Fees: Mon – Fri £10.50; Sat / Sun / Public Holidays £12.50.
Clubhouse Facilities: Limited – no bar. Lessons available by prior arrangement. Club Hire available. Well stocked golf shop.

NO.	METRES	PAR	S.I.	NO.	METRES	PAR	S.I.
1	283	4	15	10	339	4	4
2	180	3	5	11	324	4	10
3	340	4	1	12	99	3	16
4	208	4	11	13	260	4	6
5	118	3	13	14	119	3	14
6	257	4	7	15	339	4	2
7	218	4	3	16	103	3	18
8	93	3	17	17	282	4	12
9	322	4	9	18	255	4	8
OUT	2,019	33		IN	2,120	33	
				TOTAL	4,139	66	
				STANDARD SCRATCH	62		

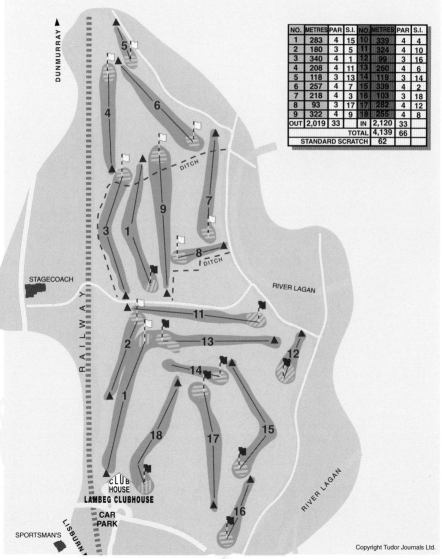

STAGECOACH

RIVER LAGAN

CLUB HOUSE
LAMBEG CLUBHOUSE

CAR PARK

SPORTSMAN'S

RIVER LAGAN

Copyright Tudor Journals Ltd.

**54 Ferris Bay Road, Islandmagee, Larne, Co. Antrim BT40 3RT.
Tel: (028) 9338 2228.**

LOCATION: Six miles north of Whitehead.
HON. SECRETARY: Mr Ian Johnston.
Tel: (028) 9338 2228.
ARCHITECT: G. L. Bailie.

This course is part links, meadowland with good views of Larne Lough to the Maidens. The first five holes are fairly 'open', and from the 6th the course becomes tighter with the 7th, 8th and 9th being 'sterner' tests along the shore. Greens are varied. The 8th is the most difficult, spoiling many good cards.

COURSE INFORMATION

Par 70; SSS 70; Length 6,288 yards.
Visitors: Welcome.
Opening Hours: Sunrise – sunset.
Avoid: Friday & Saturday.
Ladies: Welcome Fridays.
Green Fees: £10 Mon – Fri (with member £5); £18 Sat / Sun / Bank Hols (w/m £10). Saturdays – members only.
Juveniles: Mon – Fri before 5.00pm. Not at weekends.
Clubhouse Hours: Mon – Fri 1pm – 11.00pm; Sat 12 noon – 11pm, Sun 12.30pm – 2.30pm and 5.00pm – 8.00pm. Full clubhouse facilities.
Clubhouse Dress: Casual, (no denims). Jacket and tie for evening.
Clubhouse Facilities: Mon – Fri meals after 5.00pm by arrangement. Sunday – as bar hours.

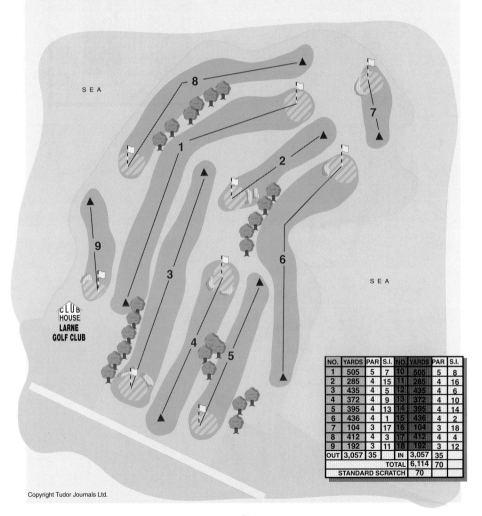

NO.	YARDS	PAR	S.I.	NO.	YARDS	PAR	S.I.
1	505	5	7	10	505	5	8
2	285	4	15	11	285	4	16
3	435	4	5	12	435	4	6
4	372	4	9	13	372	4	10
5	395	4	13	14	395	4	14
6	436	4	1	15	436	4	2
7	104	3	17	16	104	3	18
8	412	4	3	17	412	4	4
9	192	3	11	18	192	3	12
OUT	3,057	35		IN	3,057	35	
				TOTAL	6,114	70	
				STANDARD SCRATCH		70	

Copyright Tudor Journals Ltd.

**68 Eglantine Road,
Lisburn, Co. Antrim.
Tel: (028) 9267 7216.**

LOCATION: Two miles south of Lisburn off A1 to Hillsborough.
SECRETARY / MANAGER: George McVeigh.
Tel: (028) 9267 7216.
PROFESSIONAL: S. Hamill.
Tel: (028) 9267 7217.
ARCHITECT: F. Hawtree.

Mixture of parkland and meadowland with reasonably flat terrain which has an abundance of trees, some of which have not yet reached maturity. Landscaped in recent years, many shrubs are beginning to feature and enhance the course. Again, this is a course of championship standard with a very difficult finish at 16, 17 and 18, with the last hole being a spectacular downhill Par 3 of 195 metres.

COURSE INFORMATION

Par 72; SSS 72; Length 6,647 yards.
Visitors: Welcome. Mon, Wed, Thurs, Fri. Must commence before 3.00pm. Members only Tue & Sat.
Green Fees: £30 Mon – Fri (with member £10); £35 Sat / Sun / Bank Holidays (with member £12).
Juveniles: Mon – Fri £12.50 (with member £5), Sat / Sun / Bank Holidays £15 (with member £6). Lessons by prior arrangements. Club Hire available. Caddy trolleys available prior arrangement required. Telephone club for details on restricted hours of play.
Clubhouse Dress: Jacket and tie after 7.30pm.
Clubhouse Facilities: Snacks and meals all day.

NO.	MEDAL YARDS	GEN. YARDS	PAR	S.I.	NO.	MEDAL YARDS	GEN. YARDS	PAR	S.I.
1	479	465	5	6	10	461	448	4	3
2	360	344	4	16	11	401	385	4	5
3	375	330	4	10	12	493	484	5	11
4	157	140	3	18	13	160	152	3	17
5	349	344	4	4	14	505	488	5	13
6	164	150	3	12	15	367	358	4	15
7	465	449	4	1	16	375	355	4	7
8	500	488	5	8	17	449	379	4	2
9	370	335	4	14	18	217	200	3	9
OUT	3,219	3,045	36		IN	3,428	3,249	36	
					TOTAL	6,647	6,294	72	
					STANDARD SCRATCH	72	70		

ENTRANCE

PRACTICE GROUND

CLUB HOUSE
LISBURN GOLF CLUB

Copyright Tudor Journals Ltd.

51 Lough Road, Antrim BT41 4DQ.
Tel: (028) 9442 8096.

LOCATION: Two miles from Antrim town centre.
SECRETARY/MANAGER: S. Greene.
Tel: (028) 9442 8096
PROFESSIONAL: Jim Smyth.
Tel: (028) 9446 4074.
ARCHITECT: Mr F. Hawtree.

The first nine holes could be described as parkland in character with trees and indigenous scrub. The second nine holes are adjacent to the shore of Lough Neagh and are sandy in nature resembling a links course. The most difficult holes on the course are the long Par 4's at the 6th and 17th. A true golf shot from the tee is

essential at the Par 3, 11th which is well bunkered. The view from the course takes in Lough Neagh and Shanes Castle.

COURSE INFORMATION

Par 72; SSS 71; Length 6,614 Yards.
Visitors: Welcome.
Opening Hours: 7.30am – 8.00pm (summer); 8.00am – 4.00pm (winter).
Avoid: Sat & Fri mornings.
Ladies: Fridays.
Green Fees: £25 Mon – Fri; £30 Sat/Sun; Ladies £17 Mon – Fri; £20 Sat/Sun; Juveniles £5 Mon – Fri; £8 Sat/Sun.

No teeing off after 4.45pm unless with an adult. Lessons available by prior arrangement. Club hire available. Societies only need prior arrangement.
Clubhouse Hours: 11.30am – 11.00pm. Full clubhouse facilities.
Clubhouse Dress: Casual – no denims.
Clubhouse Facilities: Catering facilities: snack meals and dining room meals 10.30am – 9.30pm (summer); 11.30am – 5.00pm (winter).
Open Competitions: Open Week: first week in June. Other Opens throughout the year.

NO.	MEDAL YARDS	GEN YARDS	PAR	S.I.	NO.	MEDAL YARDS	GEN YARDS	PAR	S.I.
1	374	350	4	5	10	510	480	5	14
2	400	384	4	3	11	205	189	3	10
3	130	118	3	17	12	341	329	4	8
4	363	346	4	7	13	415	425	4	2
5	376	360	4	9	14	135	126	3	18
6	460	436	4	1	15	392	377	4	6
7	554	538	5	11	16	496	480	5	16
8	196	187	3	15	17	436	420	4	4
9	329	313	4	13	18	502	487	5	12
OUT	3,182	3,032	35		IN	3,432	3,313	37	
					TOTAL	6,614	6,345	72	
					STANDARD SCRATCH	72	71		

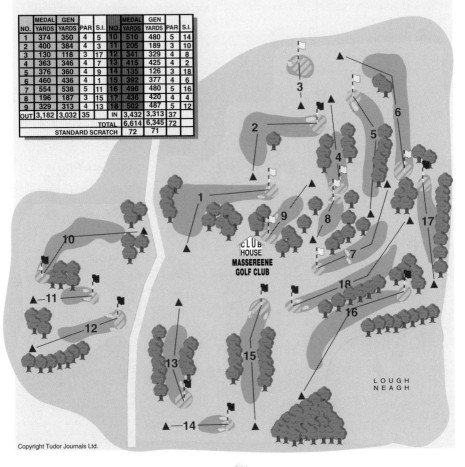

MASSEREENE GOLF CLUB

LOUGH NEAGH

Copyright Tudor Journals Ltd.

ROYAL PORTRUSH

Bushmills Road, Portrush, Co. Antrim BT56 8JQ. Tel: (028) 7082 2311.

LOCATION: One mile from Portrush town towards Bushmills.
SECRETARY: Wilma Erskine.
Tel: (028) 7082 2311.
Fax: (028) 7082 3139.
PROFESSIONAL: Gary McNeill.
Tel: (028) 7082 3335.
ARCHITECT: Harry Colt.

One of Ireland's most famous links courses. The course is laid out in a marvellous stretch of natural golfing country. Through a tangle of sandhills the course threads its way, with the sweeping contours of dunes lending infinite variety of the game. Situated east of Portrush occupying a triangle of giant sandhills, from the highest point of which is an amazing varied prospect. The hills of Donegal in the west, the Isle of Islay and southern Hebrides in the north with the Giants Causeway and the Skerries to the east.

COURSE INFORMATION

Par 73; SSS 73; Length 6,641 yards.
Visitors: Welcome on any week day.
Opening Hours: Sunrise – sunset.
Avoid: Wed, Fri pm, Saturday.
Ladies: Welcome.
Green Fees: Mon – Fri £85 (£40 additional round); Sat / Sun / Bank Hols £95.
Juveniles: Play with a member.
Lessons by prior arrangements.

Club Hire available; Caddy service available by prior arrangement. A letter of introduction is required and Handicap Certificate required.
Clubhouse Hours: 9am – 11pm. Full clubhouse facilities.
Clubhouse Dress: Casual acceptable; jacket & tie for functions.
Clubhouse Facilities: Limited snacks.
Open Competitions: Antrim Cup: May (Mixed foursomes); Lifeboat Trophy: June; Irish Cup: August (Mixed foursomes); Scott Cup: Sept (Mixed foursomes).

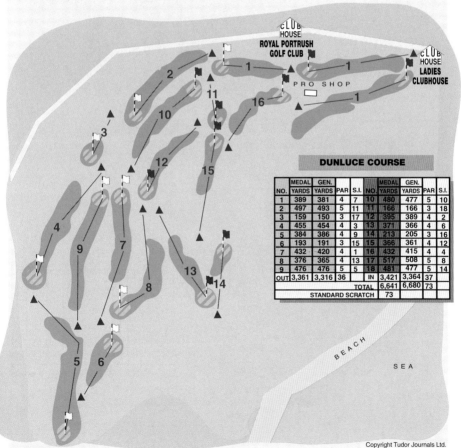

DUNLUCE COURSE

NO.	MEDAL YARDS	GEN. YARDS	PAR	S.I.	NO.	MEDAL YARDS	GEN. YARDS	PAR	S.I.
1	389	381	4	7	10	480	477	5	10
2	497	493	5	11	11	166	166	3	18
3	159	150	3	17	12	395	389	4	2
4	455	454	4	3	13	371	366	4	6
5	384	386	4	9	14	213	205	3	16
6	193	191	3	15	15	366	361	4	12
7	432	420	4	1	16	432	415	4	4
8	376	365	4	13	17	517	508	5	8
9	476	476	5	5	18	481	477	5	14
OUT	3,361	3,316	36		IN	3,421	3,364	37	
						TOTAL	6,641	6,680	73
						STANDARD SCRATCH	73		

Copyright Tudor Journals Ltd.

Bushmills Road, Portrush, Co. Antrim. BT56 8JQ. Tel: (028) 7082 2311.

LOCATION: One mile from Portrush town towards Bushmills.
SECRETARY: Wilma Erskine.
Tel: (028) 7082 2311.
Fax: (028) 7082 3139.
PROFESSIONAL: Gary McNeill.
Tel: (028) 7082 3335.
ARCHITECT: Harry Colt.

The Valley lies between the East Strand and the Dunluce course. It is the home of Royal Portrush Ladies Club and the affiliated Rathmore Club. Its characteristics are very much that of a links, undulating sandhills, remarkably dry and in some places below sea level.

COURSE INFORMATION

Par 70; SSS 71: Length 6,273 Yards.
Visitors: Welcome every day except mornings and weekends.
Opening Hours: Dawn – Dusk.
Avoid: Wed (pm); Sat (am) & Sun (before 10.00am).

Ladies: Saturday mornings.
Green Fees: £30 Mon – Fri (additional round £15); £37.50 Sat/Sun/Bank Hols.
Juveniles: Play with a member.
Clubhouse Hours: 9am – 11pm.
Clubhouse Dress: Smart casual at all times. Jacket and tie required for functions.
Clubhouse Facilities: Full clubhouse facilities. Catering facilities: snacks. R.P.G.C.

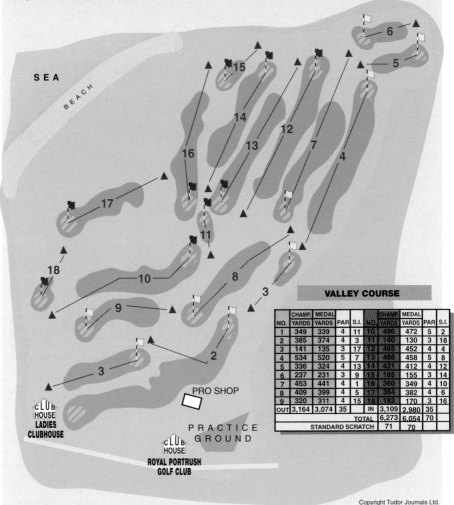

	CHAMP. YARDS	MEDAL YARDS	PAR	S.I.		CHAMP. YARDS	MEDAL YARDS	PAR	S.I.
1	349	339	4	11	10	496	472	5	2
2	385	374	4	3	11	140	130	3	18
3	141	135	3	17	12	465	452	4	4
4	534	520	5	7	13	486	458	5	8
5	336	324	4	13	14	421	412	4	12
6	237	231	3	9	15	165	155	3	14
7	453	441	4	1	16	360	349	4	10
8	409	399	4	5	17	384	382	4	6
9	320	311	4	15	18	192	170	3	16
OUT	3,164	3,074	35		IN	3,109	2,980	35	
					TOTAL	6,273	6,054	70	
	STANDARD SCRATCH					71	70		

VALLEY COURSE

PRO SHOP

CLUB HOUSE
LADIES CLUBHOUSE

PRACTICE GROUND
CLUB HOUSE
ROYAL PORTRUSH GOLF CLUB

SEA
BEACH

Copyright Tudor Journals Ltd.

Temple Golf & Country Club, 60 Church Road, Boardmills, Lisburn, Co Antrim, BT27 6UP.
Tel: (028) 9263 9213.
Fax: (028) 9263 8637.
Email: david@templegolf.com

LOCATION: Situated within easy access to Belfast / Lisburn.
SECRETARY: David Kinnear.
Tel: (028) 9263 9213.
ARCHITECT: Paddy Johnson.

A 9 hole challenging golf course with a new innovation of 18 tees, designed to incorporate the panormic views of the Mourne Mountains and the Dromara Hills. Good natural drainage will ensure all year round golf.

COURSE INFORMATION

Par 68; SSS 68; Length 2,552 yards.
Visitors: Welcome every day except Saturday mornings.
Opening Hours: Mon – Fri 9am – 8pm; Sat & Sun 8am – 8pm.
Avoid: Saturday mornings.
Ladies: Welcome.
Green Fees: Weekdays £6 (9 holes), £10 (18 holes); weekends/ Bank Holidays £8 (9 holes), £14 (18 holes).
Juveniles: Permitted to play until 5.30pm Mon – Fri.

Clubhouse Hours: Daily 9am – 9pm; Saturday night licenced bar hours.
Clubhouse Dress: Smart / casual.
Clubhouse Facilities: Fitness suite, tennis courts, licenced bar & restaurant with conference & function facilities.
Open Competitions: Varies year to year. Contact Club for details.

NO.	YARDS	PAR	S.I.	NO.	YARDS	PAR	S.I.
1	164	3	15	10	126	3	16
2	361	4	13	11	346	4	14
3	199	3	8	12	199	3	7
4	374	4	4	13	381	4	3
5	321	4	10	14	345	4	9
6	325	4	12	15	325	4	11
7	395	4	2	16	401	4	1
8	281	4	18	17	293	4	17
9	303	4	6	18	312	4	5
OUT	2,723	34		IN	2,728	34	
				TOTAL	5,451	68	
				STANDARD SCRATCH		69	

Bunker & tree positions indicated.

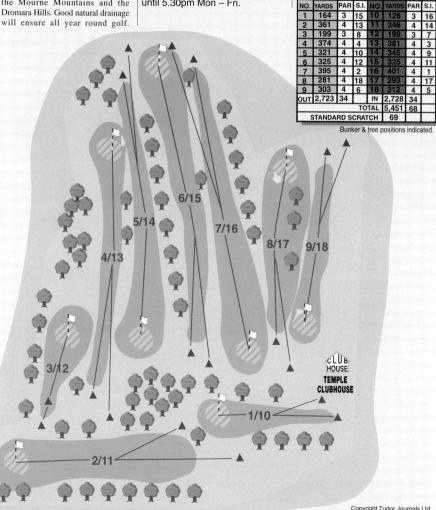

6/15
5/14
7/16
4/13
8/17
9/18
3/12
CLUB HOUSE
TEMPLE CLUBHOUSE
1/10
2/11

Copyright Tudor Journals Ltd.

**McCrae's Brae,
Whitehead, Carrickfergus,
Co. Antrim BT38 9NZ.
Tel: (028) 9337 0826.
Fax: (028) 9337 2825.**

LOCATION: Co.Antrim coast. 18
miles north of Belfast, between
Carrickfergus and Larne.
PRO SHOP: C. Farr.
Tel: (028) 9337 0821.

Parkland course overlooking
Blackhead and the Irish Sea. The
views from the 4th tee are superb and
include Fairhead in the north, the
Mourne Mountains to the south and
Ailsa Craig to the east.

COURSE INFORMATION

**Par 70; SSS 68; Length
6,050 Yards.**
Visitors: Welcome Mon – Fri,
Sunday with a member only.
Opening Hours:
9am – 6pm (April & Sept);
9am - 5pm (Winter).
Avoid: Saturdays.
Ladies: Welcome.
Competition Day – Thursday.
Green Fees: £15 Mon – Fri
(£9 with a member) £20 Sun,
& Public Holidays (£11 with
member).

Juveniles: Mon – Fri before
4.15pm. Must be off by
6pm. Sunday after 2.30pm.
(under 18) £8 Mon – Fri (£6
with a member); £11
Sat/Sun/All Public Holidays
(with a member only). Parties
20 plus: £13 Mon – Fri; £20
Sat/Sun/All Public Holidays.
Clubhouse Hours: 12am –
11.30pm.
Clubhouse Dress: Casual,
Open Competitions:
August – McKenna Scratch &
Open mixed foursomes.
Open week June/July .

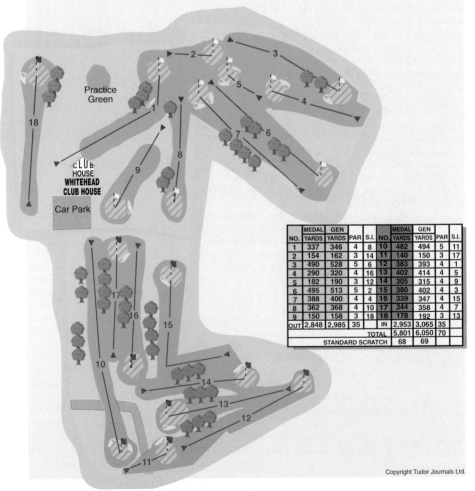

NO.	MEDAL YARDS	GEN YARDS	PAR	S.I.	NO.	MEDAL YARDS	GEN YARDS	PAR	S.I.
1	337	346	4	8	10	482	494	5	11
2	154	162	3	14	11	140	150	3	17
3	490	528	5	6	12	383	393	4	1
4	290	320	4	16	13	402	414	4	5
5	182	190	3	12	14	305	315	4	9
6	495	513	5	2	15	380	402	4	3
7	388	400	4	4	16	339	347	4	15
8	362	368	4	10	17	344	358	4	7
9	150	158	3	18	18	178	192	3	13
OUT	2,848	2,985	35		IN	2,953	3,065	35	
					TOTAL	5,801	6,050	70	
					STANDARD SCRATCH	68	69		

Copyright Tudor Journals Ltd.

The Demense, Newry Road, Armagh.
Tel: (028) 3752 2501.

SECRETARY: June McParland.
Tel: (028) 3752 5861.
PROFESSIONAL: Alan Rankin.
Tel: (028) 3752 5864.

This wooded parkland course, established in 1893, has nice views from the Obelisk built by Primate Robinson in 1700's. While the 16th might be considered the most difficult, the fifth requires an accurate drive and then an even more accurate second shot down an alley of mature trees, which should be the most rewarding hole to play well.

COURSE INFORMATION

Par 70; SSS 69; Length 6,212 Yards.
Visitors: Welcome Mon – Fri (contact Secretary's office for weekends).
Opening Hours: Sunrise – Sunset.
Avoid: Tues evenings and Thurs (Ladies Day).
Green Fees: £15 weekdays, (£10 with member) £20 weekends (£16 with member). Prior arrangement required if possible. Lessons available by prior arrangement. Caddy cars available.
Ladies Day: Thursday.
Juveniles: Monday – Friday with adult evenings and weekends.
Clubhouse Hours: 9.30am – 11.30pm.
Clubhouse Dress: Smart and neat (no denims or football garments).
Clubhouse Facilities: Full catering and bar facilities except Monday, bar snacks and a la carte available until 9.00pm.
Open Competitions: Numerous through the year, contact club for details.

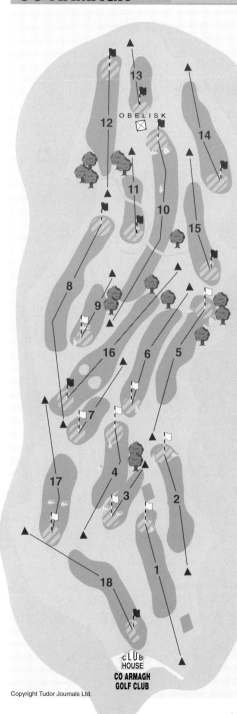

NO.	METRES	PAR	S.I.	NO.	METRES	PAR	S.I.
1	366	4	3	10	473	5	4
2	330	4	10	11	160	3	12
3	131	3	13	12	436	5	18
4	354	4	5	13	164	3	15
5	368	4	2	14	335	4	9
6	305	4	17	15	307	4	14
7	136	3	16	16	408	4	1
8	486	5	8	17	358	4	7
9	172	3	11	18	370	4	6
OUT	2,649	34		IN	3,009	36	
				TOTAL	5,658	70	
				STANDARD SCRATCH	69		

Bunker and tree positions indicated.

CLUB HOUSE
CO ARMAGH
GOLF CLUB

Copyright Tudor Journals Ltd.

**Freeduff, Cullyhanna,
Co. Armagh.
Tel: (028) 3086 8180.
Fax:(028) 3086 8611.**

LOCATION: Two miles from
Crossmaglen.
SECRETARY: James and
Elizabeth Quinn.
PROFESSIONAL: Erill Maney.
ARCHITECT: Frank Ainsworth.

An interesting eighteen hole course
situated in attractive rural
surroundings. Advance notice is
recommended before turning up at
weekends. There are over one
hundred new trees of mature variety
and a man-made lake, and bunkers on
the 17th, 4th, 1st 3rd and 8th.

COURSE INFORMATION

**Par 69; SSS 70; Length
5,616 yards.
Visitors:** Welcome.
Telephone appointment
preferred.
Opening Hours:
Summer 8am – 10pm.

Green Fees: £10 Mon – Fri;
£12 Sat / Sun. Special
reductions for juveniles,
students, senior citizens,
handicapped persons and
unemployed persons.Special
rates for societies.
Juveniles: Welcome. Lessons
by prior arrangment. Club Hire
available.
Clubhouse Hours:
8am – 10pm.
Clubhouse Dress: Informal.
Clubhouse Facilities: Meals
and snacks available.

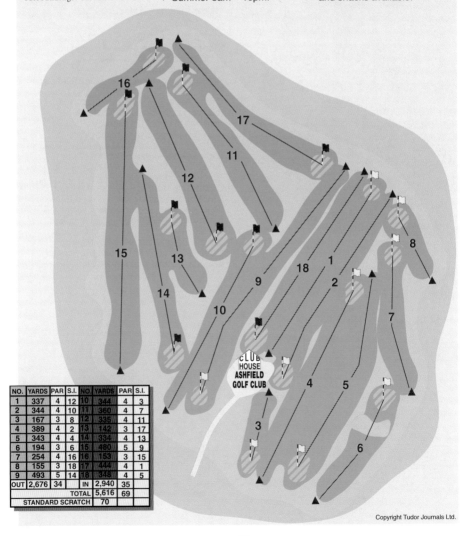

NO.	YARDS	PAR	S.I.	NO.	YARDS	PAR	S.I.
1	337	4	12	10	344	4	3
2	344	4	10	11	360	4	7
3	167	3	8	12	335	4	11
4	389	4	2	13	142	3	17
5	343	4	4	14	384	4	13
6	194	3	6	15	480	5	9
7	254	4	16	16	153	3	15
8	155	3	18	17	444	4	1
9	493	5	14	18	348	4	5
OUT	2,676	34		IN	2,940	35	
				TOTAL	5,616	69	
				STANDARD SCRATCH	70		

Copyright Tudor Journals Ltd.

**Mullaghbawn, Newry,
Co. Armagh.
Tel: (028) 3088 8380/
(028) 3088 9374
Email: info@cloverhillgc.com
www.cloverhillgc.com**

LOCATION: In scenic area of the
Ring of Gullion in south
Armagh.
SECRETARY: Joe Pilkington
PROFESSIONAL: Joe Frawley
CONTACTS: Pat or Margaret Smyth
Tel: (028) 3088 8380/ 3088 9374
Fax: (028) 3088 9199

9 hole golf course (18 hole from 1st
July 2002) situated in the scenic area
of the Ring of Gullion. 10 miles south

of Newry, 8 miles from Dundalk. The
course has very good greens and
maintained to a high standard.

COURSE INFORMATION

**Par 70; SSS 69; Length
6,090 yards.
Green Fees:** £10 every day
Juveniles: £4
Clubhouse Hours: From
8:00am. Full club facilities.
Additional Dress:
Smart/ Casual
Clubhouse Facilities:
Licensed club house with full
changing facilities. Snacks
available. Open 7 days. Golf
clubs and trolleys for hire.

NO.	YARDS	PAR	NO.	YARDS	PAR
1	390	4	10	323	4
2	277	4	11	392	4
3	558	5	12	183	3
4	143	3	13	465	4
5	335	4	14	122	3
6	347	4	15	588	5
7	513	5	16	260	3
8	229	4	17	437	4
9	152	4	18	376	4
OUT	2,944	36	IN	3,246	34
			TOTAL	6,090	70
		STANDARD SCRATCH		69	

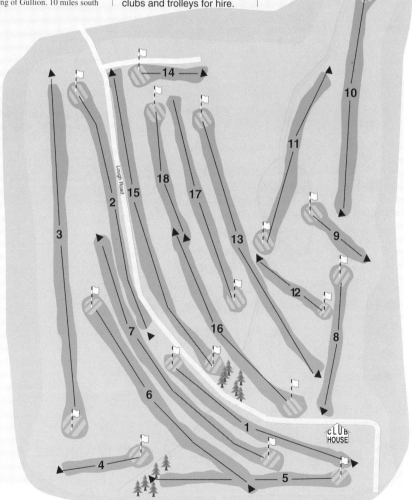

NO.	MEDAL YARDS	GEN YARDS	PAR	S.I.	NO.	MEDAL YARDS	GEN YARDS	PAR	S.I.
1	550	531	5	5	10	530	502	5	4
2	426	368	4	1	11	186	160	3	10
3	358	330	4	17	12	284	270	4	18
4	168	148	3	13	13	481	470	5	12
5	403	373	4	3	14	401	380	4	2
6	382	372	4	9	15	424	380	4	6
7	195	170	3	11	16	289	269	4	16
8	311	285	4	15	17	184	174	3	8
9	342	322	4	7	18	330	320	4	14
OUT	3,135	2,899	35		IN	3,109	2,925	36	
					TOTAL	6,244	5,824	71	
	STANDARD SCRATCH					70	68		

Drumnabreeze Road, Magheralin, Craigavon, Co. Armagh.
Tel: (028) 9261 9241.
Fax: (028) 9261 3310.

LOCATION: Twenty miles from Belfast, five minutes from Moira roundabout. Signposted from Magheralin on main Moira - Lurgan Road.
SECRETARY: Robert McDowell.

COURSE INFORMATION

Par 71; SSS 70; Length 6,244 yds.
Visitors: Very welcome.
Opening Hours: 8am – Sunset.
Avoid: Saturdays before 2pm.
Ladies: Welcome.
Green Fees: Mon-Fri £14; Saturdays/ Bank Holidays £18.
Juveniles: Welcome.
Lessons can be arranged, telephone for details.
Clubhouse Dress: Smart.
Clubhouse Facilities:
Old Yard Restaurant (closed Sun), Showers available.

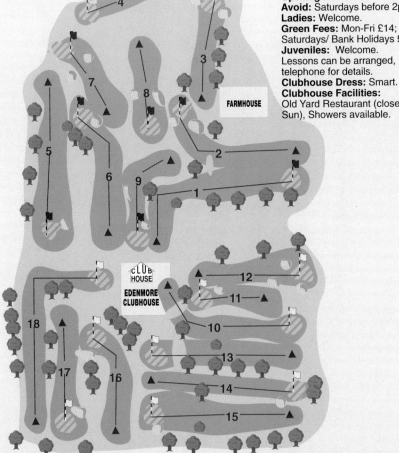

Copyright Tudor Journals Ltd. Bunker positions indicated.

11 - 14 Main Street,
Loughall, BT61 8HZ
Tel: (028) 38892900.
Fax: (028) 38392902.
Email: info@armagh.gov.uk
www.armagh.gov.uk

Location: Situated within Country
Park in the centre of Loughall

village approximately 6 miles
from Armagh and 8 miles from
Portadown.
Manager: Greg Ferson

COURSE INFORMATION

Par 72; SSS 70; Length
6,229 metres.
Visitors: Welcome to play;
muncipal course for public use.

Opening Hours: Mon - Fri 9am
- Dusk. Sat/Sun 7.30am -
Dusk.
Green Fees: £14 weekdays;
£16 Sat/Sun & Bank Holidays.
Juveniles: £5 Mon - Fri, £9
Sat/Sun & Bank Holidays.
Concession rates available
Mon- Fri.
Clubhouse Facilities:
Tea/Coffee and refreshments
in on site shop.

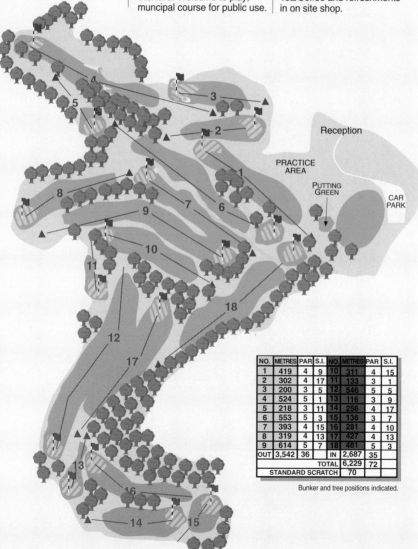

NO.	METRES	PAR	S.I.	NO.	METRES	PAR	S.I.
1	419	4	9	10	311	4	15
2	302	4	17	11	133	3	1
3	200	3	5	12	546	5	5
4	524	5	1	13	116	3	9
5	218	3	11	14	256	4	17
6	553	5	3	15	136	3	7
7	393	4	15	16	281	4	10
8	319	4	13	17	427	4	13
9	614	5	7	18	481	5	3
OUT	3,542	36		IN	2,687	35	
				TOTAL	6,229	72	
				STANDARD SCRATCH		70	

Bunker and tree positions indicated.

Copyright Tudor Journals Ltd.

NO.	MEDAL METRES	GEN. METRES	PAR	S.I.	NO.	MEDAL METRES	GEN. METRES	PAR	S.I.
1	258	233	4	13	10	298	272	4	14
2	214	194	3	5	11	158	143	3	15
3	113	107	3	18	12	355	345	4	2
4	371	354	4	3	13	448	430	5/4	12
5	387	374	4	9	14	376	365	4	8
6	504	490	5	7	15	394	374	4	4
7	390	368	4	1	16	410	395	4	6
8	152	150	3	16	17	125	114	3	17
9	528	513	5	11	18	355	340	4	10
OUT	2,917	2,783	35		IN	2,919	2,778	35/34	
					TOTAL	5,836	5,561	70/69	
					STANDARD SCRATCH	70	69		

The Demense, Lurgan BT67 9BN.
Tel: (028) 3832 2087.

LOCATION: One to two miles from the town centre.
HONORARY SECRETARY: Mr S. McClean.
SECRETARY/MANAGER: Mrs G. Turkington.
Tel: (028) 3832 2087.
PROFESSIONAL: Des Paul.

Parkland course bordering on Lurgan Lake. Well wooded and greens well trapped. Pond on 7th and 17th fairways, internal out-of-bounds (on some holes), quite a few dog-legs, long straight driving essential. Considered quite a difficult course and well suited for low and middle handicappers.

COURSE INFORMATION

Par 70; SSS 70; Length 6,257 yards.
Visitors: Welcome Mon – Fri.
Opening Hours: 9.00am – 6.00pm.
Avoid: Wednesday (playing by arrangement) and Saturday.
Ladies: £12 (£6 with member).
Green Fees: £15 Mon – Fri (£7.50 with member); £20 Sat / Sun / Bank Holidays (£10 with member).
Juveniles: £5 Must give way to adult members and visitors.
Student: £10 (£5 with member).
Clubhouse Hours: 8.00am – 11.30pm. Professional shop open 9.00am – 6.00pm.
Clubhouse Dress: Smart / casual.
Clubhouse Facilities: Catering facilities: Bar snacks and full menu. Mon: closed; Tues & Thurs 12.00 – 9.00pm; Wed, Fri, Sat and Sun 12.00 – 9.00pm.
Open Competitions: Open week normally May. Handicap certificate required for Open Competition only.

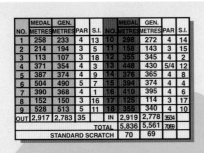

16
15
14
13
4
6
5
7
17
12
8
11
18
3
2
10
9
1

PARK LAKE

CLUB HOUSE
LURGAN GOLF CLUB

Copyright Tudor Journals Ltd.

192 Gilford Road, Portadown.
Tel: (028) 3835 5356.
Fax: (028) 3839 1394

LOCATION: On Gilford Road out of Portadown, approx. 34 miles from Belfast.
SECRETARY: Mrs. Holloway.
Tel: (028) 3835 5356.
PROFESSIONAL: Mr. Paul Stevenson.
Tel: (028) 3833 4655.

Situated on the edge of Portadown this parkland course has one of the holes actually played over the River Bann (9th). Trees come into play on many of the holes, and the course is generally flat.

COURSE INFORMATION

Par 70; SSS 70; Length 5,621 Metres.
Visitors: Welcome.
Opening Hours: 9.00am – 9.30pm.
Ladies: Tuesday (No green fees on Tuesdays).
Green Fees: Mon – Fri £18 Male, £16 Female (£12 with member); Sat / Sun, Bank Holidays; Male £23 Female £21(£13 with member); Juveniles: 50% off listed price.
Juveniles: Mon, Wed, Fri until 4pm; Thur after 12.00 noon Sat before 5pm; resricted on Sun. Club Hire available.
Clubhouse Hours:
Office: 9am – 5pm. Bar: 12 noon – 11pm. Full Clubhouse facilities.
Clubhouse Dress: Neat dress essential. No jeans, shorts or sleeveless shirts both on the course or clubhouse.
Clubhouse Facilities: Full catering, á la carte, snacks and functions 12 – 9pm. Closed Mondays.
Open Competitions: Opens run throughout the season.

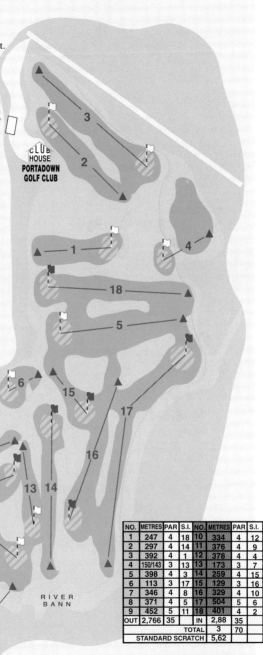

NO.	METRES	PAR	S.I.	NO.	METRES	PAR	S.I.
1	247	4	18	10	334	4	12
2	297	4	14	11	376	4	9
3	392	4	1	12	378	4	4
4	150/143	3	13	13	173	3	7
5	398	4	3	14	259	4	15
6	113	3	17	15	129	3	16
7	346	4	8	16	329	4	10
8	371	4	5	17	504	5	6
9	452	5	11	18	401	4	2
OUT	2,766	35		IN	2,88	35	
					TOTAL	3	70
				STANDARD SCRATCH		5,62	

Copyright Tudor Journals Ltd.

**Tormoyra Lane, Silverwood,
Lurgan, BT66 6NG.
Tel: (028) 3832 6606.**

LOCATION: The Golf/Ski Centre is
located at Silverwood, just off the
M1 Lurgan roundabout.
MANAGER: Geoff Coupland.
PROFESSIONAL: Part-time, Mr D. Paul.
Tel: (028) 3832 6606.

The course has sand-based, well irrigated
greens making ideal winter putting conditions
and is ideally suited for the middle and high
handicap golfers. One of it's main features are
the lakes which are incorporated into the third
and tenth holes. The course has already proved
extremely popular with golfing societies for
tournaments.

COURSE INFORMATION

**Par 72; SSS 72; Length 6,496
yards.
Visitors:** Welcome to play: municipal
course for public use.
Opening Hours: Daylight hours.
Green Fees: £13.50 Monday – Friday;
£17 Saturday, Sunday & Bank Hols.
Club Hire available.
Clubhouse Hours: Mon – Fri 9.00am –
9.30pm. Sat/Sun 9am – 7pm.
Clubhouse Facilities: Full restaurant
available. Driving range Par 3 Course and
Pitch and Putt. Ski centre on site.
Open Competitions: June / July.

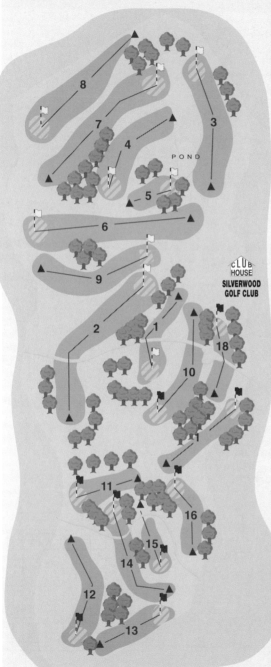

NO.	YARDS	PAR	S.I.	NO.	YARDS	PAR	S.I.
1	401	4	5	10	484	5	11
2	529	5	9	11	188	3	10
3	390	4	8	12	369	4	6
4	320	4	16	13	284	4	17
5	161	3	18	14	464	4	1
6	433	4	4	15	212	3	3
7	444	4	2	16	321	4	13
8	387	4	7	17	326	4	15
9	477	5	12	18	306	4	14
OUT	3,542	37		IN	2,954	35	
				TOTAL	6,496	72	
				STANDARD SCRATCH		72	

Copyright Tudor Journals Ltd.

TANDRAGEE

Markethill Rd, Tandragee.
Tel: (028) 3884 0727.

LOCATION: Six miles from
Portadown, 15 miles from
Newry.
SECRETARY/MANAGER: David
Clayton. Tel: (028) 3884 1272.
PROFESSIONAL: Paul Stevenson.
Tel: (028) 3884 1761.

Parkland course — complete with
beautiful old trees and pleasant
views of the Mourne Mountains and
South Armagh hills.

COURSE INFORMATION

Par 71; SSS 70; Length
5,589 metres.
Visitors: Welcome.
Opening Hours: Dawn – dusk.
Avoid: Thursdays and
Saturdays.
Green Fees: £15 weekdays;
£20 Sat / Sun / Public Holidays.
Ladies: £11 weekdays; £18
weekends.
Juveniles: £5 daily.

Clubhouse Hours:
9.00am – 11.00pm. Full
clubhouse facilities.
Clubhouse Dress: Casual;
jacket & tie on function nights.
Clubhouse Facilities: Full
catering from 12.30pm. Last
orders 9pm. No catering on
Monday.
Open Competitions: Contact
professional for details.

NO.	METRES	PAR	S.I.	NO.	METRES	PAR	S.I.
1	346	4	4	10	305	4	15
2	273	4	14	11	380	4	1
3	490	5	6	12	350	4	5
4	307	4	18	13	363	4	9
5	168	3	11	14	140	3	17
6	322	4	16	15	304	4	7
7	388	4	2	16	157	3	10
8	456	5	12	17	474	5	13
9	182	3	8	18	342	4	3
OUT	2,932	36		IN	2,815	35	
				TOTAL	5,747	71	
				STANDARD SCRATCH	70		

Bunker and tree positions indicated.

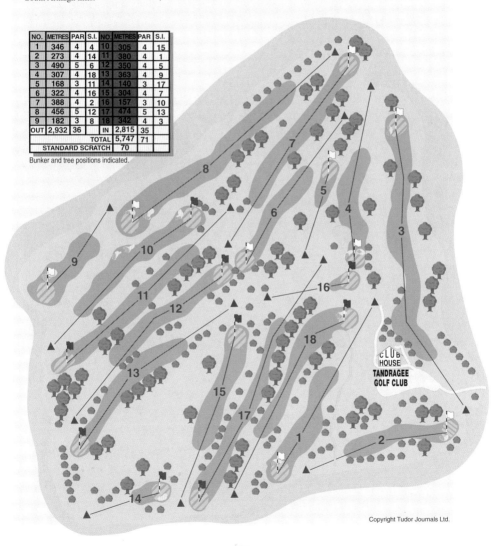

TANDRAGEE
GOLF CLUB

Copyright Tudor Journals Ltd.

518 Lisburn Road, Belfast BT9 6GX.
Tel: (028) 9038 1514.

LOCATION: Two to three miles south of Belfast City Centre on main Lisburn Road, next to King's Hall.
MANAGER: R. McConkey.
PROFESSIONAL: G. Bleakley.
Tel: (028) 9066 7747.

A flat undulating course with thirty plus bunkers, and a stream to contend with when playing. The greens are generally excellent and approached by tree-lined fairways.

Situated beside the Royal Ulster Agricultural Society, the course is particularly convenient to Belfast city centre.

COURSE INFORMATION

Par 69; SSS 70;
Length 5,702 Metres.
Visitors: Welcome.
Green Fees: £20 Mon – Fri (£24 Wed.) £10 with member. £30 weekends & public holidays (£10 with a member).
Ladies: £16 Mon - Fri; £20 weekends; £9 with a member / Public holidays.

Juveniles: £7 and restricted on weekends. Lessons by prior arrangement.
Clubhouse Hours: 9.00am - 11.00pm
Clubhouse Dress: Smart casual (no jeans) up to 8.00pm. After 7.30pm jacket and tie for gentlemen.
Catering Facilities: Lunch 12.30pm - 2.30pm; Evening meal 6.30pm-10pm. Full á la carte menu. (Last orders 9.30pm).
Open Competitions: Several throughout the golfing season.

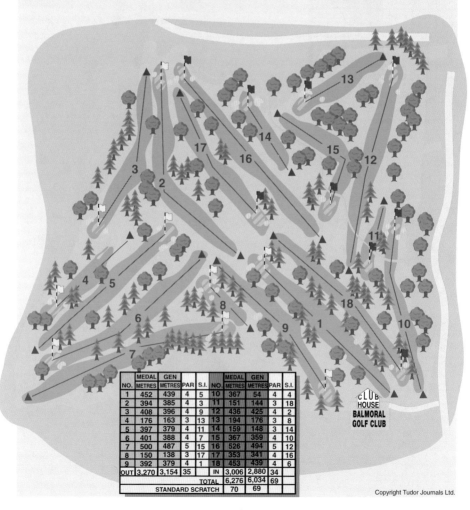

NO.	MEDAL METRES	GEN METRES	PAR	S.I.	NO.	MEDAL METRES	GEN METRES	PAR	S.I.
1	452	439	4	5	10	367	54	4	4
2	394	385	4	3	11	151	144	3	18
3	408	396	4	9	12	436	425	4	2
4	176	163	3	13	13	194	176	3	8
5	397	379	4	11	14	159	148	3	14
6	401	388	4	7	15	367	359	4	10
7	500	487	5	15	16	526	494	5	12
8	150	138	3	17	17	353	341	4	16
9	392	379	4	1	18	453	439	4	6
OUT	3,270	3,154	35		IN	3,006	2,880	34	
					TOTAL	6,276	6,034	69	
					STANDARD SCRATCH		70	69	

CLUB HOUSE
BALMORAL GOLF CLUB

Copyright Tudor Journals Ltd.

BELVOIR

**Newtownbreda, Belfast
BT8 7AN.
Tel: (028) 9049 1693.
Fax: (028) 9064 6113.**

LOCATION: Four miles south of city centre.
SECRETARY: Ann Vaughan.
PROFESSIONAL: Maurice Kelly.
Tel: (028) 9064 6714.

Considered one of the best inland courses with fair but tight fairways and good greens. Rarely closed due to water logging. The course has extensive mature woods and many scenic views.

COURSE INFORMATION

Par 71; SSS 71; Length 6,476 Yards.
Visitors: Welcome Mon, Tues, Thur and Sun.
Opening Hours: 8am – dusk.
Avoid: Wednesday & Saturday (competiton days). Friday is Ladies Day, prior arrangement is preferred.
Ladies Day: Friday.
Green Fees: Weekdays excluding Wed – £35.
Weekends and Bank Hols – £40.

Clubhouse Dress: Jacket, collar and tie after 7.30pm.
Clubhouse Facilities: Catering facilities 10.30am – 9.30pm.
Open Competitions: Mixed foursomes in June; Open week – July.
Clubhouse Hours: 10am – 11pm.

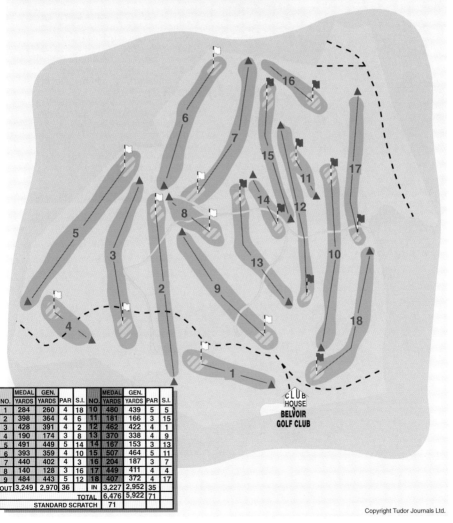

BELVOIR
GOLF CLUB

NO.	MEDAL YARDS	GEN. YARDS	PAR	S.I.	NO.	MEDAL YARDS	GEN. YARDS	PAR	S.I.
1	284	260	4	18	10	480	439	5	5
2	398	364	4	6	11	181	166	3	15
3	428	391	4	2	12	462	422	4	1
4	190	174	3	8	13	370	338	4	9
5	491	449	5	14	14	167	153	3	13
6	393	359	4	10	15	507	464	5	11
7	440	402	4	3	16	204	187	3	7
8	140	128	3	16	17	449	411	4	4
9	484	443	5	12	18	407	372	4	17
OUT	3,249	2,970	36		IN	3,227	2,952	35	
					TOTAL	6,476	5,922	71	
					STANDARD SCRATCH	71			

Copyright Tudor Journals Ltd.

CLIFTONVILLE ULSTER BELFAST

NO.	YARDS	PAR	S.I.	NO.	YARDS	PAR	S.I.
1	181	3	7	10	181	3	8
2	406	4	1	11	406	4	2
3	327	4	13	12	327	4	14
4	137	3	15	13	137	3	16
5	341	4	3	14	341	4	4
6	350	4	9	15	350	4	10
7	331	4	5	16	331	4	6
8	439	5	17	17	439	5	18
9	324	4	11	18	324	4	12
OUT	2,836	35		IN	2,836	35	
				TOTAL	5,672	70	
				STANDARD SCRATCH		70	

Bunker and tree positions indicated.

**44 Westland Road, Belfast
BT14 6NH.
Tel: (028) 9074 4158.**

LOCATION: Situated between Cavehill
Road and Cliftonville Circus.
Hon Treasurer: Ronnie Greg.
SECRETARY: J. M. Henderson.
Tel: (028) 9074 6595.
PROFESSIONAL: Ricky Duckett.
PRO-SHOP: Tel: (028) 9022 8585.

Parkland course on rising ground with
exstensive views of Belfast Lough. Course is
played around the waterworks complex.

COURSE INFORMATION

**Par 70; SSS 70; Length 5,672 Yards.
Visitors:** Welcome to play up to 5pm.
Opening Hours: 8.30am – sunset.
Avoid: Tuesday afternoons and
Sunday mornings. Members only —
Saturday, (visitors can only be
accompanied by a member after 6pm.
Ladies Day: Tuesday.
Green Fees: £14 weekdays (with
member £10); £20 Sat, Sun / Bank
Holidays (with member £12).
Juveniles: £7 weekdays only, until 6pm.
Clubhouse Hours: 8.30am – 11pm.
Clubhouse Dress: No denims.
Jacket and tie in lounge after 9pm.
Clubhouse Facilities: Snacks,
meals 12 - 3pm and á la carte 5pm -
9pm. No catering on Monday except
by arrangement.

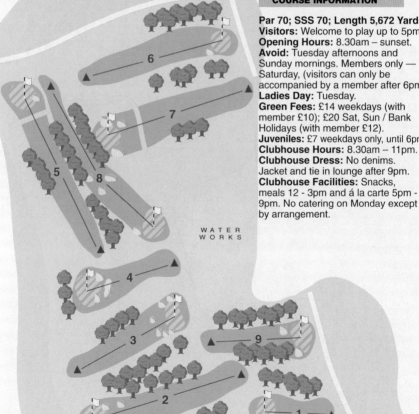

WATER
WORKS

CLUB
HOUSE
CLIFTONVILLE
GOLF CLUB

Copyright Tudor Journals Ltd.

91 Dunmurry Lane, Dunmurry, Belfast.
Tel: (028) 9061 0834.

LOCATION: Between Upper Malone Road and Lisburn Rd.
GOLF MANAGER: Tony Cassidy.
Tel: (028) 9061 0834.
PROFESSIONAL: J. Dolan.
ASSISTANT: N.Dunlop.
Tel: (028) 9062 1314.

The course lies astride Dunmurry Lane and consists of rolling parkland in all directions. Since its opening in 1983 it has matured well and is a popular venue for many golfers. The lake at the tenth makes it a very interesting hole.

COURSE INFORMATION

Par 69; SSS 68; Length 5,832 Yards.
Visitors: Welcome Mon – Thur by arrangement.
Opening Hours: Dawn to dusk.
Ladies: Welcome Friday.
Green Fees: £25 weekdays; £35 weekends.
Juveniles: Must be accompanied by an adult. Lessons, Club Hire and Caddy trolleys (limited) available.

Clubhouse Dress: Jacket and tie all day Sunday in restaurant, otherwise smart / casual.
Clubhouse Facilities: Full clubhouse facilities all week during summer months. Snacks and meals: at certain times during the winter. No catering on Mon during the winter.
Open Competitions: Open Week: First week in Aug. Various other semi opens during the summer.

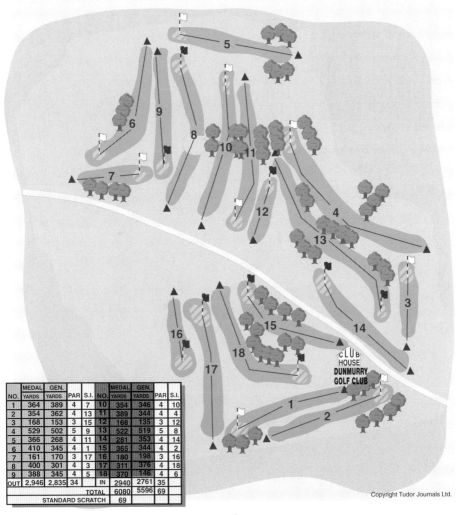

NO.	MEDAL YARDS	GEN. YARDS	PAR	S.I.	NO.	MEDAL YARDS	GEN. YARDS	PAR	S.I.
1	364	389	4	7	10	354	346	4	10
2	354	362	4	13	11	389	344	4	4
3	168	153	3	15	12	168	135	3	12
4	529	502	5	9	13	522	519	5	8
5	366	268	4	11	14	281	353	4	14
6	410	345	4	1	15	365	344	4	2
7	161	170	3	17	16	180	198	3	16
8	400	301	4	3	17	311	376	4	18
9	388	345	4	5	18	370	146	4	6
OUT	2,946	2,835	34		IN	2940	2761	35	
					TOTAL	6080	5596	69	
					STANDARD SCRATCH		69		

Copyright Tudor Journals Ltd.

**Downview Avenue,
Belfast BT15 4EZ.
Tel: (028) 9037 0770.
www.fortwilliam.co.uk**

LOCATION: Off Antrim Road, Belfast.
HONORARY SECRETARY: Michael Purdy.
Tel: (028) 9037 0770.
PROFESSIONAL: Peter Hanna.
Tel: (028) 9077 0980.
ARCHITECT: H. Colt.

The course is dominated by the picturesque and heavily wooded 'Cavehill' which rises to over 1,000 feet above sea level, making an attractive background to many shots throughout the round. There is quite a height difference between the top and bottom of the course, which in itself is divided into two parts by Grays Lane.

COURSE INFORMATION

Par 70; SSS 69; Length 5,993 Yards.
Visitors: Mon–Fri, Sunday.
Opening Hours: 8.30 – Dusk.
Ladies: £20 Mon – Fri (£12 with a member) £24 Sat / Sun / Bank holidays (£14 with a member).
Ladies Day: Monday & Friday.
Green Fees: £22 Mon – Fri (£13 with a member) £29 Sat / Sun / Bank holidays (£14 with a member).
Juveniles: Can play all day Mon, Tues, Thur, Fri & Sun. Restricted hours Wed & Sat – telephone club for details.
Clubhouse Hours: 9.00am – 11.30pm everyday.
Clubhouse Dress: October – March jacket and tie after9.00pm. April - September casual smart dress (no denims).
Open Competitions: Open Week – August; plus various other open competitions.

NO.	MEDAL YARDS	GEN YARDS	PAR	S.I.	NO.	MEDAL YARDS	GEN YARDS	PAR	S.I.
1	421	412	4	7	10	195	188	3	10
2	329	298	4	9	11	381	362	4	8
3	437	418	4	1	12	131	129	3	18
4	314	291	4	4	13	377	358	4	2
5	474	442	4	17	14	502	491	5	12
6	186	153	5	5	15	315	312	4	14
7	311	292	3	15	16	345	331	4	4
8	421	402	4	11	17	150	140	3	16
9	272	260	4	13	18	432	404	4	6
OUT	3,165	2,968	36		IN	2,828	2,715	34	
					TOTAL	5,993	5,688	70	
					STANDARD SCRATCH	69	68		

CLUB HOUSE
FORTWILLIAM GOLF CLUB

Copyright Tudor Journals Ltd.

NO.	MEDAL YARDS	GEN YARDS	PAR	S.I.	NO.	MEDAL YARDS	GEN YARDS	PAR	S.I.
1	328	319	4	11	10	493	483	5	12
2	379	370	4	16	11	417	413	4	5
3	457	452	4	2	12	147	130	3	15
4	136	122	3	17	13	377	367	4	10
5	374	364	4	9	14	447	440	4	1
6	453	447	4	3	15	403	393	4	4
7	368	358	4	7	16	185	178	3	14
8	409	400	4	6	17	270	260	4	18
9	363	353	4	13	18	396	389	4	8
OUT	3,267	3,185	35		IN	3,135	3,053	35	
					TOTAL	6,402	6,238	70	
					STANDARD SCRATCH	71	70		

**Summerfield, Dundonald, Belfast. BT16 2QX.
Tel: (028) 9048 2249.**

LOCATION: Five miles east of Belfast onthe Upper Newtownards Road.
SECRETARY/MANAGER: Mrs Anne Armsrong. Tel: (028) 9048 3251.
PROFESSIONAL: Gordon Fairweather. Tel: (028) 9048 3825.

Parkland course with numerous large and small trees with the additional hazard of several deep bunkers. The 8th is an interesting hole with a river immediately fronting the green. The course is situated on the eastern suburbs of the city adjacent to Dundonald village.

COURSE INFORMATION

Par 70; SSS 71; Length 6,435 Yards.
Visitors: Welcome Mon – Fri & Sun.
Avoid: Tuesday & Saturday.
Ladies: After 4pm Sat, before 2pm Wed.
Ladies Day: Tuesday.
Green Fees: £20 Mon – Fri;
£25 Sun & Public Holidays.
Juveniles: Anytime except after 4pm Wed & before 4pm Sat. unless handicap is less than 12. Lessons by prior arrangement. Club hire available.
Clubhouse Dress: Smart casual dress throughout the clubhouse, except after 7.00pm on Saturdays when jacket and tie are required in main lounge.
Clubhouse Facilities: Full catering facilities. Snacks and meals available.
Open Competitions: Open week June.

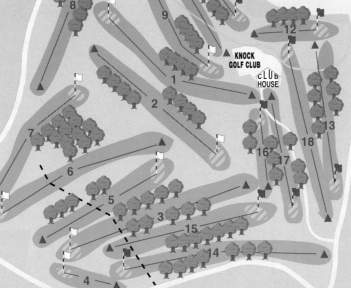

KNOCK GOLF CLUB

CLUB HOUSE

Copyright Tudor Journals Ltd.

Mount Ober Golf and Country Club,
24 Ballymaconaghy Road, Knockbracken, Belfast.
Tel: (028) 9079 2108.
Fax: (028) 9070 5862.
Location: 15 minutes from the city centre, off the Saintfield Road.
Secretary/Manager: E.Williams.
Professional: Geoff Loughrey.

Undulating parkland course with narrow, but open fairways. It has

several other sporting facilities on location. There is a large Golf Driving Range at the complex, which is ideal for practice and a Golf Academy with shop and teaching professionals.

COURSE INFORMATION

Par 67; SSS 66; Length 5,448 Yards.
Visitors: Welcome anytime.
Avoid: Saturday all day and Sunday 8am – 10.30am.
Ladies: Welcome anytime.

Green Fees: £14 Mon - Fri; £16 Sun.
Juveniles: Weekdays and after 3pm Sat & Sun. Lessons by prior arrangements. Club Hire available. Caddy cars are also available.
Clubhouse Dress: Smart casual wear.
Clubhouse Facilities: Full clubhouse facilities.Snacks and meals all day for up to 100 people. All weather barbecue available also.

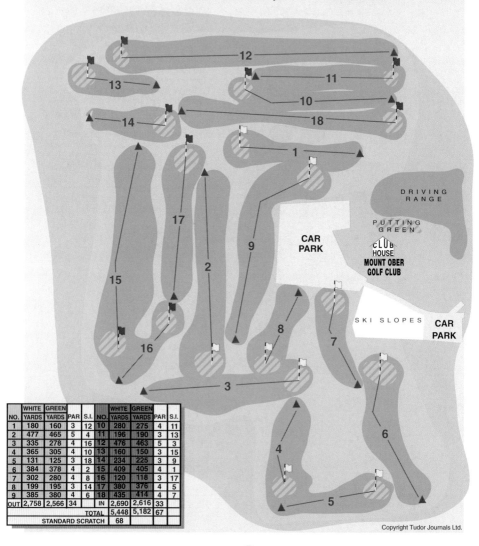

NO.	WHITE YARDS	GREEN YARDS	PAR	S.I.	NO.	WHITE YARDS	GREEN YARDS	PAR	S.I.
1	180	160	3	12	10	280	275	4	11
2	477	465	5	4	11	196	190	3	13
3	335	278	4	16	12	476	463	5	3
4	365	305	4	10	13	160	150	3	15
5	131	125	3	18	14	234	225	3	9
6	384	378	4	2	15	409	405	4	1
7	302	280	4	8	16	120	118	3	17
8	199	195	3	14	17	380	376	4	5
9	385	380	4	6	18	435	414	4	7
OUT	2,758	2,566	34		IN	2,690	2,616	33	
					TOTAL	5,448	5,182	67	
					STANDARD SCRATCH	68			

Copyright Tudor Journals Ltd.

240 Upper Malone Road, Dunmurry, Belfast BT17 9LB.
Tel: (028) 9061 2758.

LOCATION: Five miles from centre of Belfast.
HON. SECRETARY: M H Turnbull.
Tel: (028) 9061 2758.
MANAGER: Nick Agate.
PROFESSIONAL: Michael McGee.
Tel: (028) 9061 4917.
CATERER: (028) 9061 4916.

One of the most picturesque inland golf courses in the Province with many mature trees and flowering shrubs. This course is of championship standard and has a very high standard of course maintenance. The greens on the course are large with many undulations and an exceptionally good putting surface. The course is quite long and demanding and is classed as one of the best inland courses in Ireland. A real pleasure to play. Malone is now a 27 hole golf club.

COURSE INFORMATION

Par 71; SSS 71; Length 6,599 Yards.
Visitors: Welcome, although letter of introduction or handicap preferred.
Opening Hours: 8am – Dusk.
Avoid: Wednesday pm – members only. No visitors before 3pm Sat.
Ladies Day: Tuesday.
Green Fees: £40 Mon – Fri (£15 with member); £45 Sat / Sun & Bank Holidays (£17 with member). Lessons by prior arrangements. Caddy trolleys available. Society & Company book through office Mon & Thurs only.
Juveniles: Restricted on main course.
Clubhouse Hours: From 8.00am. Full club facilities when with a member.
Clubhouse Dress: Jacket and tie in upstairs lounge, otherwise smart / casual. No denim, tee shirts or training shoes on main course.
Clubhouse Facilities: Full catering by arrangement with caterer. Lunch and bar snacks.
Open Competitions: Open Week: July. Open Scratch Foursomes in June.

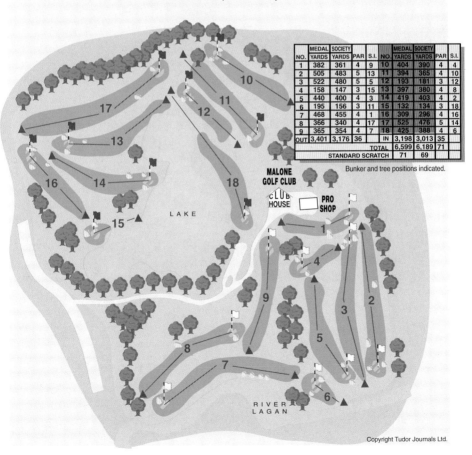

NO.	MEDAL YARDS	SOCIETY YARDS	PAR	S.I.	NO.	MEDAL YARDS	SOCIETY YARDS	PAR	S.I.
1	382	361	4	9	10	404	390	4	4
2	505	483	5	13	11	394	365	4	10
3	522	480	5	5	12	193	181	3	12
4	158	147	3	15	13	397	380	4	8
5	440	400	4	3	14	419	403	4	2
6	195	156	3	11	15	132	134	3	18
7	468	455	4	1	16	309	296	4	16
8	366	340	4	17	17	525	476	5	14
9	365	354	4	7	18	425	388	4	6
OUT	3,401	3,176	36		IN	3,198	3,013	35	
					TOTAL	6,599	6,189	71	
					STANDARD SCRATCH	71	69		

MALONE GOLF CLUB

CLUB HOUSE   PRO SHOP

Bunker and tree positions indicated.

LAKE

RIVER LAGAN

Copyright Tudor Journals Ltd.

**50 Park Road,
Belfast
BT7 2FX.
Tel: (028) 9064 0700.
Fax: (028) 9064 6250.**

LOCATION: Alongside Ravenhill
Road and Park Road, adjacent
to Ormeau Road.
SECRETARY / MANAGER:
William Lynn.
SHOP MANAGER: Bertie Wilson.
Tel: (028) 9064 0999.

A parkland setting on the edge of
Ormeau Park, this course is tree-lined
on all holes, with a realistic out of
bounds on eight of the nine holes.

Nearest golf course to Belfast city
centre, although situated in a quiet
residential area. New clubhouse
recently constructed.

COURSE INFORMATION

**Par 68; SSS 66; Length
5,308 Yards, 4,850 Metres.
Visitors:** Welcome every day
except Tuesdays after 4pm and
Saturdays between 8am - 6pm
Opening Hours: 8.00am –
11.00pm seven days per week.
Ladies Day: Tuesday (pm).
Gents day: Saturday

Green Fees: £14 Weekdays;
£16.50 Weekends. Tel for
special offers – golfers free fry
etc.
Juveniles: Welcome, but
restrictions apply.
Clubhouse Hours:
Mon – Sat 11.30am – 11pm.
Sun 12.30pm – 10pm.
Clubhouse Dress: Smart /
casual. Jacket, collar and tie
after 7pm on Sat.
Clubhouse Facilities:
Restaurant, lounge bar &
snooker.

NO.	METRES	PAR	S.I.	NO.	METRES	PAR	S.I.
1	261	4	15	10	261	4	16
2	265	4	13	11	265	4	14
3	465	5	3	12	465	5	4
4	92	3	17	13	92	3	18
5	414	4	1	14	414	4	2
6	173	3	7	15	173	3	8
7	274	4	9	16	274	4	10
8	202	3	5	17	202	3	6
9	279	4	11	18	279	4	12
OUT	2,425	34		IN	2,425	34	
				TOTAL	4,850	68	
STANDARD SCRATCH		66					

Bunkers and tree positions indicated.

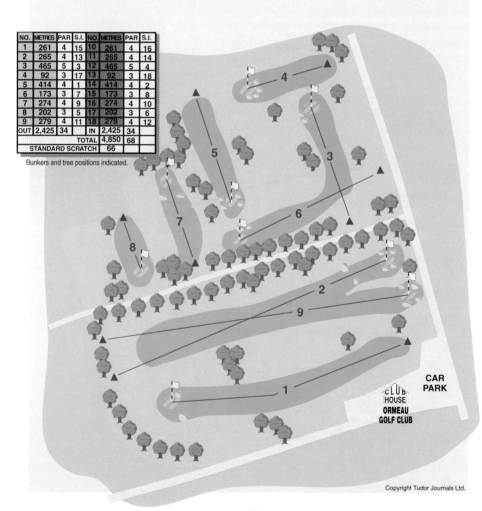

CAR
PARK

CLUB
HOUSE
ORMEAU
GOLF CLUB

Copyright Tudor Journals Ltd.

**28 Drumalig Road,
Carryduff, Belfast.
Tel: (028) 9081 2279.
Fax: (028) 9081 5851.**
Email: rockmountgc@btconnect.com
www.rockmountgolfclub.co.uk

LOCATION: Seven miles south of Belfast.
SECRETARY: R & D. Patterson.
Tel: (028) 9081 2279.

18 hole Drumlin Course set in the beauty and quiet of the countryside with scenic views of the Mourne Mountains. The course has been designed to ensure that the land's natural features are incorporated throughout the 18 holes.

COURSE INFORMATION

Par 72; SSS 71; Length 6,410 yards.
Opening Hours: 8am – Dusk.
Avoid: Saturday – (as it is members only).
Ladies: Welcome.
Green Fees: Mon – Fri £20 and Sunday £24.
Visitors: Welcome any day (except Saturday).

Juveniles: Must be accompanied by an adult.
Clubhouse Facilities: Restaurant open to the public. Function room for hire. Shop.
Clubhouse Dress: Smart casual, No Denims, no tracksuits.

NO.	CHAMP YARDS	MEDAL YARDS	PAR	S.I.	NO.	CHAMP YARDS	MEDAL YARDS	PAR	S.I.
1	301	289	4	12	10	358	345	4	5
2	496	485	5	4	11	397	381	4	2
3	213	199	3	6	12	157	147	3	15
4	324	305	4	16	13	353	340	4	9
5	541	513	5	8	14	361	343	4	11
6	489	473	5	18	15	554	511	5	7
7	410	384	4	1	16	193	157	3	17
8	349	338	4	10	17	360	336	4	13
9	129	121	3	14	18	425	412	4	3
OUT	3,215	3,082	37		IN	3,158	2,972	35	
					TOTAL	6,410	6,079	72	
					STANDARD SCRATCH	71	72		

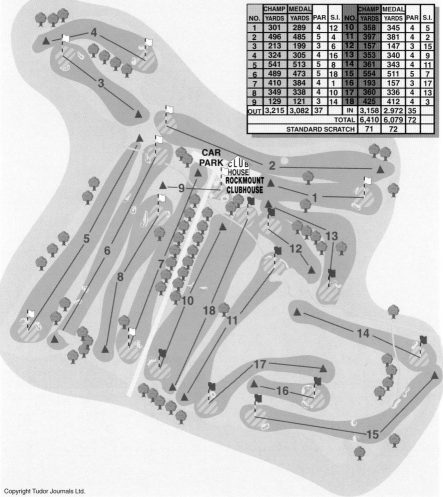

Copyright Tudor Journals Ltd.

**73 Shandon Park,
Belfast, BT5 6NY.
Tel: (028) 90805030.
Fax: (028) 90805999.**

LOCATION: Three miles from city centre.
GENERAL MANAGER: David Jenkins.
Tel: (028) 90805030.
PROFESSIONAL: B. Wilson.
Tel: (028) 90805031.

Situated in eastern suburbs of Belfast this is a well known lush parkland course with true greens. Irrespective of handicap, golfers will find that it offers an enjoyable challenge to their golfing prowness. The course is generally flat and trees come into play on some of the holes.

COURSE INFORMATION

Par 70; SSS 70; Length 6,282 yards.
Visitors: Welcome.
Opening Hours: 8.30am – sunset.

Avoid: Saturdays and Wednesdays.**Ladies:** Welcome Tuesdays.
Green Fees: £28 Mon – Fri; £36 Sat / Sun / all Public Holidays.
Juveniles: Accompanied by a member. Lessons by prior arrangement.
Clubhouse Dress: Casual Jacket and tie in Restaurant.
Clubhouse Facilities: 12.00 – 11.00pm.
Open Competitions: Open Week; 20th – 27th July.

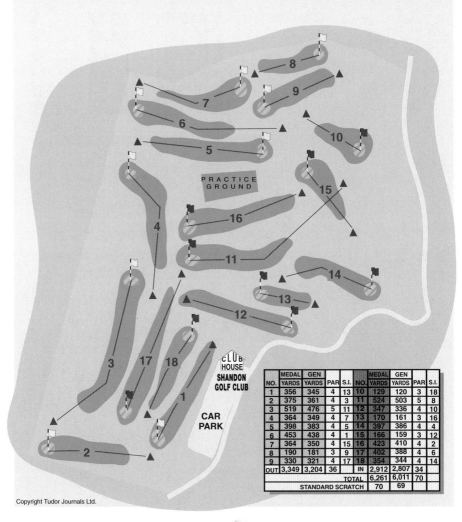

NO.	MEDAL YARDS	GEN YARDS	PAR	S.I.	NO.	MEDAL YARDS	GEN YARDS	PAR	S.I.
1	356	345	4	13	10	129	120	3	18
2	375	361	4	3	11	524	503	5	8
3	519	476	5	11	12	347	336	4	10
4	364	349	4	7	13	170	161	3	16
5	398	383	4	5	14	397	386	4	4
6	453	438	4	1	15	166	159	3	12
7	364	350	4	15	16	423	410	4	2
8	190	181	3	9	17	402	388	4	6
9	330	321	4	17	18	354	344	4	14
OUT	3,349	3,204	36		IN	2,912	2,807	34	
					TOTAL	6,261	6,011	70	
					STANDARD SCRATCH	70	69		

SHANDON GOLF CLUB

CLUB HOUSE

CAR PARK

Copyright Tudor Journals Ltd.

**Erne Hill, Belturbet,
Co. Cavan.
Tel: (049) 9522287.
or (049) 9524044.**

LOCATION: Just outside town on main Cavan Road.
SECRETARY: Peter Coffey.
Tel: (049) 9522498.

Most of the holes at Belturbet are played to elevated greens. Out of the eighteen holes the 5th, 7th and 9th holes are considered to be the toughest on the whole course.

COURSE INFORMATION

Par 72; SSS 65; Length 5,180 yards.
Visitors: Welcome any day, including weekends.
Opening Hours: 9.00am – dusk each day.
Avoid: Major club competitions and selected Open Competitions.
Green Fees: €15 Mon – Sun. Letter of introduction required, or Handicap Certificate required

if wishing to compete in Open Competitions.
Clubhouse Hours: Normal bar hours except mornings.
Clubhouse Dress: Informal.
Clubhouse Facilities: Snooker, darts. Catering facilities by arrangement.
Open Competitions: Contact club for details.

NO.	YARDS	PAR	S.I.	NO.	YARDS	PAR	S.I.
1	277	4	15	10	277	4	16
2	378	4	3	11	378	4	4
3	477	5	11	12	477	5	12
4	175	3	7	13	175	3	8
5	340	4	5	14	340	4	6
6	115	3	17	15	115	3	18
7	415	4	1	16	415	4	2
8	272	4	13	17	272	4	14
9	141	3	9	18	141	3	10
OUT	2,590	34		IN	2,590	34	
				TOTAL	5,180	72	
	STANDARD SCRATCH					65	

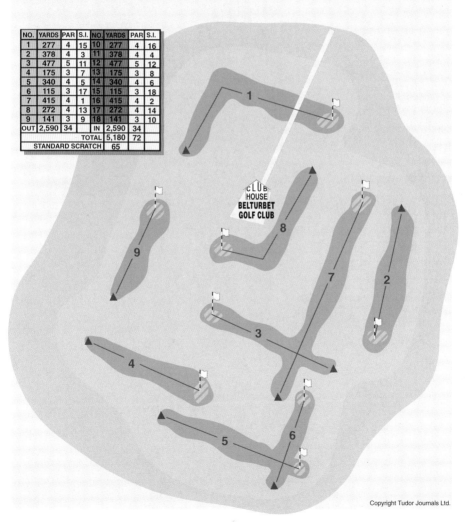

CLUB HOUSE
BELTURBET GOLF CLUB

Copyright Tudor Journals Ltd.

BLACKLION

CAVAN

Toam, Blacklion,
Co. Cavan.
Tel: (072) 53024.
Fax/Tel: (072) 53481.

LOCATION: At Blacklion
Village on the main
Enniskillen – Sligo Road
(A4 / N15).
HON. SECRETARY:
Pat Gallery.
ARCHITECT: E. Hackett.

The course is bordered on two sides
by Lough McNean which can come
into play on three holes. Typical inland
course, which is playable all year. Out
of bounds on two holes, some thick
shrubbery comes into play on two
holes. Reasonably easy for the straight
hitter!

COURSE INFORMATION

Par 72; SSS 69; Length
6,170 yards, 5,642
metres.
Visitors: Welcome any day,
but prior arrangement is
preferred. Limited at
weekend.

Opening Hours:
Sunrise – sunset.
Avoid: Sunday morning and
early afternoon. Certain club
competitions, which are
posted in clubhouse.
Ladies: Welcome Thursdays.
Green Fees: €15 weekdays
€20 Sat / Sun and all public
holidays.
Juveniles: Welcome when
accompanied by an adult.
Lessons available by prior
arrangement.
Clubhouse Hours:
Summer 10am - Close.

Winter 1pm - Close
Clubhouse Dress: Informal.
Clubhouse Facilities:
Snacks and meals available
throughout the day.
Open Competitions: Bush
Cup Ladies May 2nd. Bush
Cup Men May 5th. Blacklion
Golf Classic May 13th-19th.
Open Week June 8th - 16th.
Open Weekend Singles Aug
4th & 5th. Seniors Open Aug
14th. Open 4 Ball 21st-23rd,
25th-28th Aug. Ladies Open
Day Aug 24th.

NO.	METRES	PAR	S.I.	NO.	METRES	PAR	S.I.
1	320	4	11	10	320	4	12
2	337	4	3	11	337	4	4
3	108	3	18	12	136	3	13
4	306	4	9	13	306	4	10
5	445	5	7	14	445	5	8
6	138	3	15	15	138	3	14
7	457	5	16	16	457	5	17
8	346	4	1	17	346	4	2
9	350	4	5	18	350	4	6
OUT	2,807	36		IN	2,835	36	
				TOTAL	5,642	72	
	STANDARD SCRATCH	69					

Bunker and tree positions indicated.

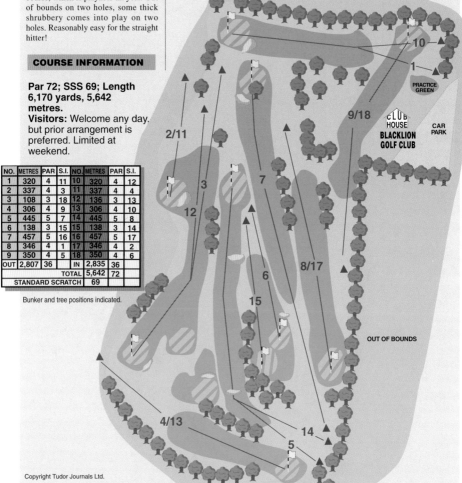

Copyright Tudor Journals Ltd.

Kingscourt, Co. Cavan.
Tel: (042) 67030.

LOCATION: Kingscourt,
Co Cavan.
SECRETARY / MANAGER: Howard
Corscadden.
Tel: (042) 67030.
Fax: (042) 67039.

Cabra Castle Golf Club may not be the hardest golf course that you will play, but it can be surprisingly difficult and will provide a reasonable test of golf.

COURSE INFORMATION

Par 70; SSS 68; Length 5,308 Metres.
Visitors: Welcome to play at all times.
Opening Hours: Daylight.
Avoid: Sunday morning and Tuesday.
Ladies Day: Tuesday.

Green Fees: €11.50 Mon – Fri; €11.50 Sat / Sun.Green Fees: £11.50 Mon – Fri; €11.50 Sat / Sun.
Juveniles: Must be accompanied by an adult.
Clubhouse Hours: Cabra Castle Hotel 7am – 12 midnight.
Clubhouse Dress: Casual.
Clubhouse Facilities: Full catering and bar facilities.
Open Competitions: Open Week – June 10th – 16th.

NO.	METRES	PAR	S.I.	NO.	METRES	PAR	S.I.
1	315	4	7	10	315	4	8
2	186	3	11	11	186	3	12
3	346	4	5	12	346	4	6
4	114	3	15	13	114	3	16
5	347	4	1	14	347	4	2
6	275	4	17	15	275	4	18
7	452	5	9	16	452	5	10
8	275	4	13	17	275	4	14
9	344	4	3	18	344	4	4
OUT	2,654	35		IN	2,654	35	
				TOTAL	5,308	70	
	STANDARD SCRATCH				68		

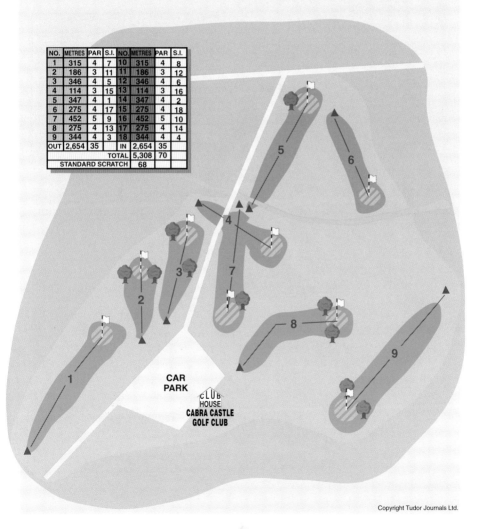

CAR PARK

CLUB HOUSE
CABRA CASTLE GOLF CLUB

Copyright Tudor Journals Ltd.

Arnmore House, Drumelis, Cavan, Co. Cavan.
Tel: (049) 31283.

LOCATION: One mile from Cavan town, on the Killeshandra Road.
SECRETARY: Brian Fitzsimons.
Tel: (049) 4331541.

A Parkland course in the suburbs of Cavan town that offers a good test of golf, with several interesting holes a feature of the course. Three of the holes (12th, 13th and 14th) have recently been modified.

COURSE INFORMATION

Par 70; SSS 69; Length 5,634 metres.
Visitors: Welcome to play at any time.
Opening Hours: Daylight hours.
Avoid: Sundays and Wednesdays.
Ladies: Welcome Wednesdays.
Green Fees: €20 Mon – Fri; €25 Sat / Sun & Public Holidays.
Juveniles: Must be accompanied by an adult. Club Hire and Caddy cars

available by prior arrangement.
Clubhouse Hours: Normal licensing hours.
Clubhouse Dress: Casual.
Clubhouse Facilities: Bar, meals. Catering facilities available any day May – Sep. (prior arrangements may be made with resident steward or caterer).
Open Competitions: Open Week – July; Open Junior Scratch Cup – Sep; Open Intermediate Scratch Cup – Sep.

NO.	CHAMP YARDS	MEDAL YARDS	PAR	S.I.	NO.	CHAMP YARDS	MEDAL YARDS	PAR	S.I.
1	288	283	4	6	10	189	179	3	11
2	291	291	4	16	11	303	298	4	13
3	371	371	4	2	12	341	341	4	9
4	161	154	3	18	13	133	133	3	17
5	350	340	4	4	14	381	376	4	5
6	312	312	4	14	15	377	367	4	1
7	488	476	5	12	16	358	353	4	3
8	326	321	4	10	17	447	437	5	15
9	171	150	3	8	18	347	341	4	7
OUT	2,758	2,698	35		IN	2,758	2,698	36	
					TOTAL	5,634	5,525	72	
				STANDARD SCRATCH		74	72		

CLUB HOUSE
COUNTY CAVAN GOLF CLUB

14 15 16 17 18 10 9 11 13 12 1 2 7 8 6 5 4 3

Copyright Tudor Journals Ltd.

**The Slieve Russell,
Golf and Country Club,
Ballyconnell, Co. Cavan.
Tel: (049) 9526444.
Fax: (049) 9526640**

LOCATION: Two hours from both
Dublin and Belfast.
GOLF DIRECTOR:
Ivan Hewson.
ARCHITECT: Paddy Merrigan.
PROFESSIONAL: Liam McCool.
HON. SECRETARY:
Cathal Brady.

An 18 hole championship course is set in
300 acres of parkland including 50 acres of
lake. The unique style of the Slieve Russell
fits and complements the Cavan Drumlin
landscape multiple tee positions facilitate all
categories of golfer.

COURSE INFORMATION

**Par 72; SSS 72; Length
7,053 yards.
Visitors:** Welcome.
Opening Hours: 8am –11pm
(seasonal opening times).
Avoid: Saturday.
Ladies: Welcome.
Juveniles: Over 12yrs full green
fees payable.
Green Fees: Non-resident rates
–€50 (Sun – Fri) & €65 (Sat).
Clubhouse Hours:
10am –11pm.
Clubhouse Dress: Dress code
in operation.
Clubhouse Facilities:
Restaurant and bar also
available.
Additional Facilities:
9 hole Par 3 course; Flood lit
driving range; Golf Tuition
available. Adjacent to Slieve
Russell Hotel.

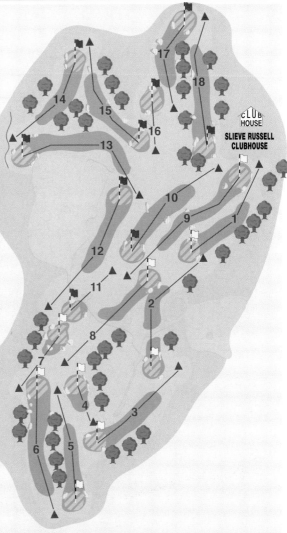

SLIEVE RUSSELL
CLUBHOUSE

NO.	CHAMP YARDS	MEDAL YARDS	PAR	S.I.	NO.	CHAMP YARDS	MEDAL YARDS	PAR	S.I.
1	428	399	4	10	10	411	393	4	2
2	434	407	4	1	11	193	168	3	1
3	398	371	4	6	12	442	434	4	3
4	167	159	3	16	13	529	502	5	4
5	436	412	4	3	14	374	356	4	1
6	512	491	5	18	15	453	326	4	2
7	220	196	3	8	16	176	165	3	1
8	389	338	4	14	17	399	369	4	6
9	552	509	5	12	18	540	519	5	5
OUT	3,536	3,282	36		IN	3,517	3,333	3	
					TOTAL	7,053	6,615	6	
		STANDARD SCRATCH				74	72		

Copyright Tudor Journals Ltd.

Bunker & tree positions indicated.

Virginia, Co Cavan.
Tel: (049) 8548066.

LOCATION: Fifty miles N.W. of Dublin on Virginia – Ballyjamesduff Road on the grounds of the Park Hotel. SECRETARY: Seamus Kearney.

A compact nine hole course situated adjacent to the picturesque Lough Ramor. Fairways are narrow and divided by trees. Involves accuracy and a delicate touch around the greens. The course is located in the grounds of the Park Hotel.

COURSE INFORMATION

Par 64; SSS 62; Length 4,139 Metres.
Visitors: Welcome to play on any day except Ladies Day on Thurs.
Opening Hours: Daylight hours.
Avoid: Sunday mornings – Men's competitions.

Ladies: Welcome Thursdays (except on Competition Days).
Green Fees: €15, €8 with a member.
Ladies day: Thursday.
Juveniles: Not allowed after 5.00pm or on Sun. or Thur. Club Hire and Caddy service available by prior arrangement.
Clubhouse Facilities: Available in the Park Hotel.
Open Competitions: Open Week: last week in June.

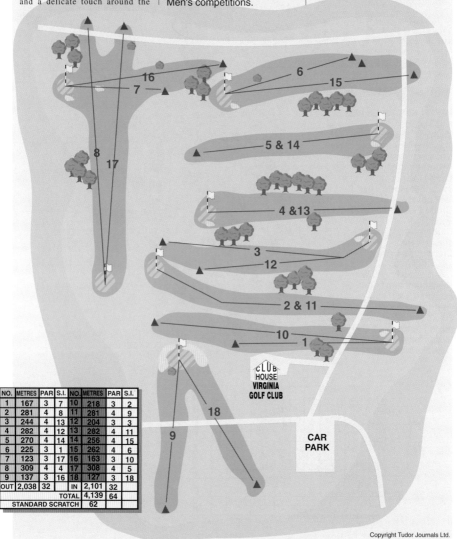

NO.	METRES	PAR	S.I.	NO.	METRES	PAR	S.I.
1	167	3	7	10	218	3	2
2	281	4	8	11	281	4	9
3	244	4	13	12	204	3	3
4	282	4	12	13	282	4	11
5	270	4	14	14	256	4	15
6	225	3	1	15	262	4	6
7	123	3	17	16	163	3	10
8	309	4	4	17	308	4	5
9	137	3	16	18	127	3	18
OUT	2,038	32		IN	2,101	32	
				TOTAL	4,139	64	
			STANDARD SCRATCH		62		

CLUB
HOUSE
VIRGINIA
GOLF CLUB

CAR
PARK

Copyright Tudor Journals Ltd.

Ballybofey, Co. Donegal.
Tel: (074) 31093.
Fax: (074) 30158.

LOCATION: Lough Alan, Stranorlar, off Strabane/Stranorlar main road.
HON SECRETARY: John Mc Caughan. Tel: (074) 31228.
PRESIDENT: Drew Brogan.
ARCHITECT: P.C. Carr.
CAPTAIN: John Reid.
LADY CAPTAIN: Ann Mc Granaghan.

Undulating parkland course with picturesque views of the Donegal Hills and Valley of River Finn. The course, is located on the shores of Lough Alan yet follows the rolling contours of the surrounding countryside. A satisfying course and one that is popular with societies.

COURSE INFORMATION

Par 68; SSS 69; Length 5,399 metres.
Visitors: Welcome. Booking essential for weekends. Please telephone (074) 31093.
Opening Hours: 9.00am – sunset. New shop.

Avoid: Mon & Tue evenings from 4.30pm.
Green Fees: €25 Weekends €20 Mon – Fri; €22 Societies.
Clubhouse Hours: 12 noon – 11pm.
Clubhouse Dress: Informal.
Clubhouse Facilities: A new clubhouse with full facilities.
Open Competitions: Annual Open Week 26th May – 5th June.

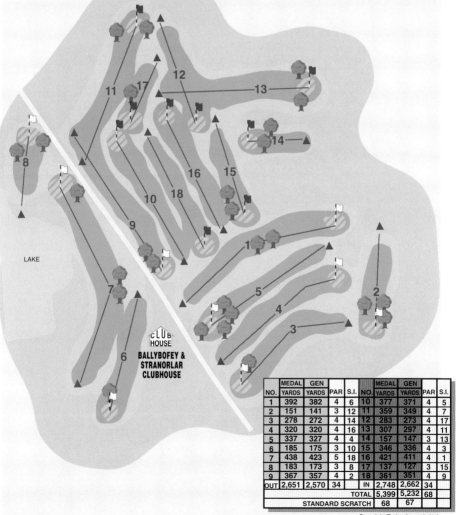

LAKE

CLUB HOUSE
BALLYBOFEY & STRANORLAR CLUBHOUSE

NO.	MEDAL YARDS	GEN YARDS	PAR	S.I.	NO.	MEDAL YARDS	GEN YARDS	PAR	S.I.
1	392	382	4	6	10	377	371	4	5
2	151	141	3	12	11	359	349	4	7
3	278	272	4	14	12	283	273	4	17
4	320	320	4	16	13	307	297	4	11
5	337	327	4	4	14	157	147	3	13
6	185	175	3	10	15	346	336	4	3
7	438	423	5	18	16	421	411	4	1
8	183	173	3	8	17	137	127	3	15
9	367	357	4	2	18	361	351	4	9
OUT	2,651	2,570	34		IN	2,748	2,662	34	
					TOTAL	5,399	5,232	68	
					STANDARD SCRATCH		68	67	

Copyright Tudor Journals Ltd.

**Ballyliffin Golf Club, Clonmany, Co. Donegal.
Tel: (077) 76119.
Fax: (077) 76672.**

LOCATION: 6 miles from Cardonagh.
HON. SECRETARY: Des Kemmy.
ARCHITECT: Tom Craddock & Pat Ruddy.

To play The Old Links at Ballyliffin is to experience golf on one of natures most beautiful stages. All around are dramatic hills and mountains with magnificent views of the bay, the ocean and the course. The Glashedy Links was opened in 1995, designed by Tom Craddock & Pat Ruddy is 7,000 yards of sweeping fairways, undulating Greens and cavanous Bunkers - A real professional test.

COURSE INFORMATION

**Par 72; SSS 73; Length 6,837 yards.
Visitors:** Welcome.
Opening Hours: Daylight.
Avoid: Sat & Sun afternoons.
Ladies: Welcome Tuesdays and 4.00pm – 6.00pm Sat & Sun.

Green Fees: Old Links: Mon – Fri €38. Weekend €42.
Glashedy: Mon – Fri €57. Weekend €64.
Juveniles: By arrangement. Caddy service available by prior arrangement.
Clubhouse Hours: 9.00am – 11.30pm.
Clubhouse Facilities: Bar, snacks, showers. Catering facilities by arrangement and most weekends.
Open Competitions: Contact office for details.

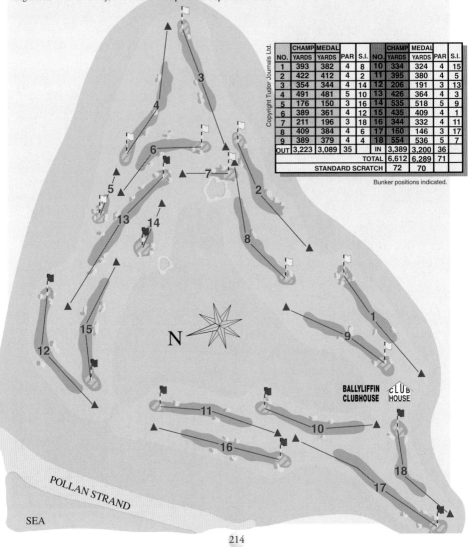

Copyright Tudor Journals Ltd.

	CHAMP	MEDAL				CHAMP	MEDAL		
NO.	YARDS	YARDS	PAR	S.I.	NO.	YARDS	YARDS	PAR	S.I.
1	393	382	4	8	10	334	324	4	15
2	422	412	4	2	11	395	380	4	5
3	354	344	4	14	12	206	191	4	13
4	491	481	5	10	13	426	364	4	3
5	176	150	3	16	14	535	518	5	9
6	389	361	4	12	15	435	409	4	1
7	211	196	3	18	16	344	332	4	11
8	409	384	4	6	17	160	146	3	17
9	389	379	4	4	18	554	536	5	7
OUT	3,223	3,089	35		IN	3,389	3,200	36	
					TOTAL	6,612	6,289	71	
					STANDARD SCRATCH	72	70		

Bunker positions indicated.

N

BALLYLIFFIN CLUBHOUSE　CLUB HOUSE

POLLAN STRAND

SEA

Railway Road, Buncrana, Co. Donegal.
Tel: (077) 62279.

LOCATION: Buncrana Town.
SECRETARY: Francis McGrory.
Tel: (028) 9338 2228.

Buncrana golf course is the oldest 9-hole course in Ireland. It offers an attractive setting beside the sea, with a reasonable golf challenge.

COURSE INFORMATION

Par 62; SSS 60; Length 4,250 yards.
Visitors: Welcome any time - phone for teetimes at weekends.
Opening Hours: Sunrise – sunset.
Ladies: Welcome anytime, Ladies day Friday.
Green Fees: €13 Gents, €8 Ladies, €5 Juveniles.

Juveniles: Must be accompanied by an adult after 6pm and at weekends.
Clubhouse Hours: 9am – closing.
Clubhouse Dress: Casual.
Clubhouse Facilities: Golf shop.
Open Competitions: All year. Handicap certificate required for competitions.

NO.	YARDS	PAR	S.I.	NO.	YARDS	PAR	S.I.
1	280	4	7	10	280	4	8
2	159	3	15	11	159	3	16
3	240	3	9	12	240	3	10
4	176	3	11	13	176	3	12
5	357	4	3	14	357	4	4
6	128	3	13	15	128	3	14
7	320	4	5	16	320	4	6
8	370	4	1	17	370	4	2
9	95	3	17	18	95	3	18
OUT	2,125	31		IN	2,125	31	
				TOTAL	4,250	62	
	STANDARD SCRATCH				60		

3/12

2/11

1/10

CLUB HOUSE
BUNCRANA GOLF CLUB

4/13

7/16

5/14

9/18

8/17

6/15

Copyright Tudor Journals Ltd.

**Bundoran, Co. Donegal.
Tel: (072) 41302.**

LOCATION: 22 miles North of Sligo on coast.
SECRETARY: John McGagh.
Tel: (072) 41302.
PROFESSIONAL: David Robinson.
Tel: (072) 41302.
ARCHITECT: Harry Vardon.

A combination of links and a treeless parkland course in undulating terrain. The greens and approaches are well protected by bunkers. A picturesque course with the middle holes playing alongside the impressive Atlantic coast and beautiful strands. The course is sited on the edge of Bundoran and literally surrounds the Great Northern Hotel.

COURSE INFORMATION

Par 70; SSS 70; Length 5,689 metres.
Visitors: Welcome to play especially on weekdays.
Opening Hours: 9.00am – 6.00pm (winter) 8.00am – 8.00pm (summer).
Green Fees: €30 Mon – Fri;

€40 at weekends. Club Hire available.
Clubhouse Hours: Bar 4.30pm – 11.30pm (winter) 12noon – 11.30pm (summer).
Clubhouse Dress: Casual.
Clubhouse Facilities: Snacks only. Open all day, snacks available. Hotel on course.
Open Competitions: All weekends from May to October. Open Week. Letter of introduction required for competitions.

NO.	BLUE METRES	YELLOW METRES	PAR	S.I.	NO.	BLUE METRES	YELLOW METRES	PAR	S.I.
1	333	324	4	8	10	367	358	4	1
2	470	442	5	16	11	382	374	4	5
3	115	105	3	18	12	316	307	4	11
4	331	291	4	6	13	214	178	3	9
5	286	279	4	10	14	373	355	4	7
6	146	141	3	2	15	390	375	4	3
7	324	279	4	12	16	142	137	3	17
8	359	328	4	4	17	458	404	5/4	15
9	363	351	4	13	18	319	310	4	14
OUT	2,727	2,540	35		IN	2,961	2,798	35/34	
					TOTAL	5,688	5,338	69/68	
					STANDARD SCRATCH	70	68		

SEA

GREAT NORTHERN HOTEL

CLUB HOUSE　BUNDORAN CLUBHOUSE

Copyright Tudor Journals Ltd.

Cloughaneely Golf Club, Ballyconnell, Falcarragh, Co. Donegal.
Tel: (074) 65416.

LOCATION: Ballyconnell, Falcarragh, Co. Donegal.
SECRETARY: Noel 'O Gallchóir.
ARCHITECT: Michael Doherty.

Opened in 1997 this is an undulating inland course set in an old estate with mature woodlands.

COURSE INFORMATION

Par 70; SSS 69; Length 6,088 yards.
Visitors: Welcome.
Opening Hours: 8.30am – 10.00pm.
Avoid: Sunday mornings.
Green Fees: Weekdays €13; weekends / Bank Holidays €15.
Juveniles: Welcome.
Clubhouse Hours: 9.00am – 11.00pm.
Clubhouse Dress: Informal.

Clubhouse Facilities:
Tea, coffee, sandwiches and snacks. Full catering by arrangement.
Nearby accommodation in Ostan Lough Altan Gortahork.
Open Competitions:
Bank Holiday weekends / Open Week July.

NO.	YARDS	PAR	S.I.	NO.	YARDS	PAR	S.I.
1	408	4	1	10	408	4	2
2	195	3	15	11	195	3	16
3	334	4	13	12	334	4	14
4	345	4	9	13	345	4	10
5	381	4	11	14	381	4	12
6	362	4	5	15	362	4	6
7	147	3	17	16	147	3	18
8	501	5	7	17	501	5	8
9	371	4	3	18	371	4	4
OUT	3,044	35		IN	3,044	35	
					TOTAL	6,088	70	
				STANDARD SCRATCH		69	

OUT OF BOUNDS

OUT OF BOUNDS

9

1

8

7

BALLYCONNELL HOUSE

CLUB HOUSE CLOUGHANEELY CLUBHOUSE

2

LODGE

3

6

4

5

LODGE

MAIN ENTRANCE

TO FALCARRAGH (1/2 MILE)

Copyright Tudor Journals Ltd.

Tree positions indicated.

Kincasslagh, Co Donegal.
Tel: (075) 43296.

LOCATION: Two miles outside village of Kincasslagh.
SECRETARY: Dermot Devenney.
Tel: (075) 48872.

A breathtaking 9 hole links course perched precariously on the edge of the Atlantic Ocean and accessible only by a bridge which joins it to the mainland and the village of Kincasslagh. The crowning glory of the course is the magnificent Par 3 6th hole where nerves of steel are required

to hit over a deep cove and land on a small green which as a sheer drop into the sea behind for anyone who over clubs it.

COURSE INFORMATION

Par 68; SSS 66; Length 5,141 metres.
Visitors: Welcome anytime. Prior arrangement required for parties in excess of 12 people.
Avoid: Club Competitions Sunday mornings; Ladies Competitions Thursday.

Green Fees: €20 weekdays; Groups over 10 €15
Juveniles: Welcome. No restrictions.
Clubhouse Hours:
June/Sept 10.00am – dusk.
Clubhouse Facilities:
Bar, locker rooms. Trolley hire. Catering facilities, meals available. Prior arrangement required for larger parties.

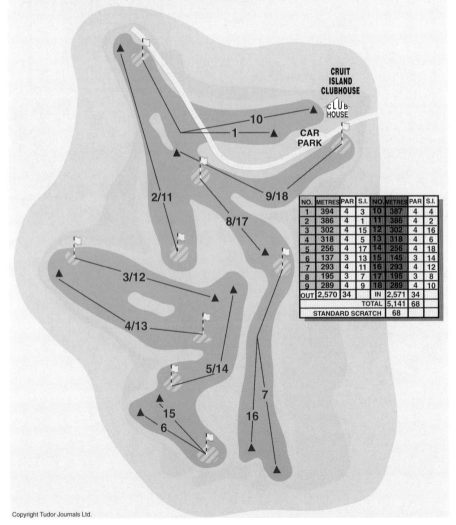

NO.	METRES	PAR	S.I.	NO.	METRES	PAR	S.I.
1	394	4	3	10	387	4	4
2	386	4	1	11	386	4	2
3	302	4	15	12	302	4	16
4	318	4	5	13	318	4	6
5	256	4	17	14	256	4	18
6	137	3	13	15	145	3	14
7	293	4	11	16	293	4	12
8	195	3	7	17	195	3	8
9	289	4	9	18	289	4	10
OUT	2,570	34		IN	2,571	34	
				TOTAL	5,141	68	
STANDARD SCRATCH		68					

Copyright Tudor Journals Ltd.

Murvagh, Laghey, Ballintra, Co Donegal
Tel: (073) 34054
Fax: (073) 34377.

LOCATION: Halfway between Rossnowlagh & Donegal Town.
ADMINISTRATOR: John McBride.
ARCHITECT: Eddie Hackett.

Challenging links course fit to test the best. Superbly scenic between sea and mountains, the holes are a mixture of testing Par 5's, tricky Par 4's and memorable Par 3's.

COURSE INFORMATION

Par 73; SSS 73; Length 6,249 metres.
Visitors: Welcome. Every day except special events as per fixture card.
Opening Hours: Dawn – dusk.
Avoid: Sunday.
Ladies: Welcome Mondays.
Green Fees: €40 Mon-Thur; €55 Fri-Sun and bank holidays.

Juveniles: Welcome 1/2 price – restrictions at weekends.
Clubhouse Hours: 9.00am – 11.00pm.
Clubhouse Dress: Informal but neat.
Clubhouse Facilities: Available to visitors, include buggy hire, caddy carts, bar, locker rooms and showers. Snacks available at all times full meals by prior arrangement with caterer.
Open Competitions: Phone for details.

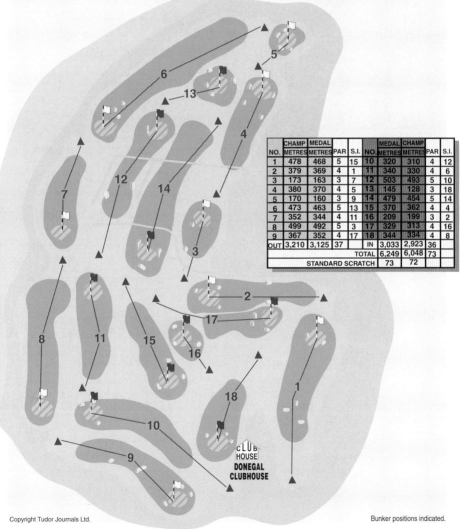

NO.	CHAMP METRES	MEDAL METRES	PAR	S.I.	NO.	MEDAL METRES	CHAMP METRES	PAR	S.I.
1	478	468	5	15	10	320	310	4	12
2	379	369	4	1	11	340	330	4	6
3	173	163	3	7	12	503	493	5	10
4	380	370	4	5	13	145	128	3	18
5	170	160	3	9	14	479	454	5	14
6	473	463	5	13	15	370	362	4	4
7	352	344	4	11	16	209	199	3	2
8	499	492	5	3	17	329	313	4	16
9	367	352	4	17	18	344	334	4	8
OUT	3,210	3,125	37		IN	3,033	2,923	36	
					TOTAL	6,249	6,048	73	
					STANDARD SCRATCH	73	72		

DONEGAL CLUBHOUSE

Copyright Tudor Journals Ltd.

Bunker positions indicated.

Kill, Dunfanaghy.
Tel/Fax: (074) 36335/36488.
Email: dunfanaghygolf@ eirom.net
Web: www.dunfanaghy.com

LOCATION: Within walking distance
of the Village of Dunfanaghy on
the main Letterkenny Road.
SECRETARY / MANAGER: Michael
McGinley

Beautiful seaside links course located on
the western shores of "Sheep Haven Bay".
The course offers an enjoyable challenge
for golfers of every ability. Memorable
holes include the 7th, 9th, 10th and a superb
finishing five holes.

DUNFANAGHY
CLUBHOUSE

COURSE INFORMATION

Par 68; SSS 66; Length
5,066 metres.
Visitors: Very welcome. Please
check time sheet for weekends.
Opening Hours: Dawn - Dusk.
Ladies: Welcome.
Green Fees: Mon – Fri €22;
€27 Sat, Sun & Bank Hols. Special
rates for societies and local hotel
residents (including most weekends).
Juveniles: Welcome.
Clubhouse Hours:
9.00am onwards.
Clubhouse Dress: Informal but neat.
Clubhouse Facilities: Bar and
snacks available all day. Clubs and
trolleys available for hire.
Open Competitions:
The club organise open competitions
throughout the year. Open week is
held over the last week in July and
first weekend in August. Please phone
for further details.

NO.	METRES	PAR	S.I.	NO.	METRES	PAR	S.I.
1	306	4	12	10	228	4	13
2	143	3	15	11	280	4	17
3	351	4	1	12	332	4	2
4	336	4	4	13	141	3	14
5	325	4	11	14	322	4	3
6	305	4	8	15	358	4	7
7	205	3	5	16	466	5	6
8	277	4	16	17	156	3	9
9	120	3	18	18	325	4	10
OUT	2,336	33		IN	2,638	35	
				TOTAL	5,066	68	
			STANDARD SCRATCH			66	

Copyright Tudor Journals Ltd.

**Greencastle Golf Club,
Greencastle, Co Donegal
Tel: (077) 81013.
Fax: (077) 81015
Email: b_mc_caul@yahoo.com
www.derry.net/greencastle**

LOCATION: 23 miles North of Derry on Moville road.
HON. SECRETARY: Billy McCaul. Tel: (028) 7126 0396.
ARCHITECT: E. Hackett.

A very picturesque course with panoramic views of Inishowen and Lough Foyle. Challenging without being truly tiring.

COURSE INFORMATION

**Par 69; SSS 69; Length 5,211 metres.
Visitors:** Welcome.
Opening Hours: 8am to dark.
Ladies Day: Thursday.
Green Fees: €20 Mon –Fri, (€15 with member); €26 Sat / Sun & Bank Hols (€22 with member).

Juveniles: Welcome.
Clubhouse Hours: 12 noon to after dark.
Clubhouse Dress: G.U.I. dress code
Clubhouse Facilities: Bar. Catering Thur, Fri, Sat, Sun or by arrangement.
Open Competitions: Open Week 8th-16th June. Open Competitions on various weekends.

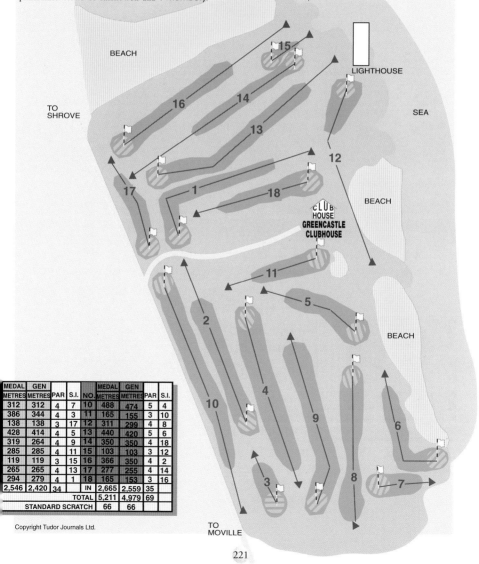

MEDAL	GEN	PAR	S.I.	NO.	MEDAL	GEN	PAR	S.I.
METRES	METRES				METRES	METRES		
312	312	4	7	10	488	474	5	4
386	344	4	3	11	165	155	3	10
138	138	3	17	12	311	299	4	8
428	414	4	5	13	440	420	5	6
319	264	4	9	14	350	350	4	18
285	285	4	11	15	103	103	3	12
119	119	3	15	16	366	350	4	2
265	265	4	13	17	277	255	4	14
294	279	4	1	18	165	153	3	16
2,546	2,420	34		IN	2,665	2,559	35	
				TOTAL	5,211	4,979	69	
				STANDARD SCRATCH	66	66		

Copyright Tudor Journals Ltd.

GWEEDORE   ULSTER   DONEGAL

**Maghergallon, Derrybeg,
Letterkenny, Co Donegal.
Tel: (075) 31140.**

LOCATION: North west of
Letterkenny.
SECRETARY / MANAGER:
Noel O'Fearraigh.

An attractive nine hole, seaside course
which is quite challenging for players
of all handicaps. The course is not
physically taxing and the setting is
attractive.

COURSE INFORMATION

**Par 71; SSS 69; Length
6,201 metres.
Visitors:** Welcome.
Opening Hours: All day.
Ladies: Welcome.
Green Fees: €12 Weekdays
Weekends & Bank Hols €15
(with member £5). Caddy
service available by prior
arrangement.

Juveniles: Sat mornings.
Clubhouse Hours: Normally
10am – 12 midnight.
Clubhouse Dress: Informal.
Clubhouse Facilities:
Showers, Cloakrooms.
Catering facilities; daily during
summer months. Weekends
for remainder of the year.

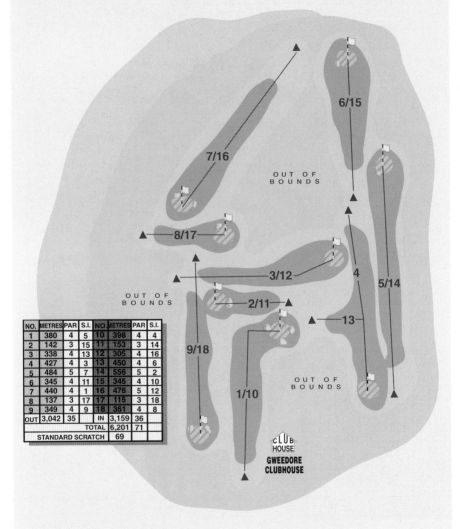

NO.	METRES	PAR	S.I.	NO.	METRES	PAR	S.I.
1	380	4	5	10	398	4	4
2	142	3	15	11	153	3	14
3	338	4	13	12	305	4	16
4	427	4	3	13	450	4	6
5	484	5	7	14	556	5	2
6	345	4	11	15	345	4	10
7	440	4	1	16	476	5	12
8	137	3	17	17	115	3	18
9	349	4	9	18	361	4	8
OUT	3,042	35		IN	3,159	36	
				TOTAL	6,201	71	
STANDARD SCRATCH		69					

GWEEDORE
CLUBHOUSE

Copyright Tudor Journals Ltd.

NO.	MEDAL METRES	GEN. METRES	PAR	S.I.	NO.	MEDAL METRES	GEN. METRES	PAR	S.I.
1	368	354	4	14	10	396	384	4	9
2	530	516	5	12	11	415	397	4	2
3	364	354	4	8	12	343	343	4	11
4	362	352	4	6	13	209	195	3	7
5	138	128	3	18	14	337	325	4	13
6	423	413	4	2	15	420	406	4	5
7	388	378	4	4	16	151	151	3	17
8	170	170	3	16	17	400	368	4	1
9	370	354	4	10	18	508	508	5	15
OUT	3,113	3,019	35		IN	3,179	3,077	35	
					TOTAL	6,292	6,096	70	
					STANDARD SCRATCH	71	70		

Barnhill, Letterkenny Co Donegal. Tel: (074) 21150.

LOCATION: One – two miles from outskirts of Letterkenny town on Ramelton Road.
SECRETARY: Barry Ramsay.
Tel: (074) 21150 (home) (074) 24491.

An attractive eighteen hole golf course in which the first eleven holes are played on relatively flat ground, the remaining seven holes are played on a plateau above the others. The course is a good challenge with a demanding finishing hole. New Clubhouse opened 1998. Hosted the 1999 Donegal Irish Ladies Open – European Ladies Tour Event.

COURSE INFORMATION

Par 70; SSS 71; Length 6,292 metres.
Visitors: Welcome.
Opening Hours:
Call in advance to check.
Avoid: Tuesdays and Wednesdays after 5pm. Timesheets in use most weekends.
Ladies: Welcome Anyday. Ladies competitions Tuesdays, Thursday and occasionally at Weekends.
Green Fees: €25 weekdays & €35 weekends.
Juveniles: Welcome. Lessons by appointment. Club Hire and trolleys available.
Clubhouse Hours: 12noon – 11.30pm.
Clubhouse Dress: Informal.
Clubhouse Facilities: New clubhouse opened 1998. Full catering and bar facilities all week during summer (only at weekends in winter).
Open Competitions: Weekends in summer. Open Week – June. Phone clubhouse for further details.

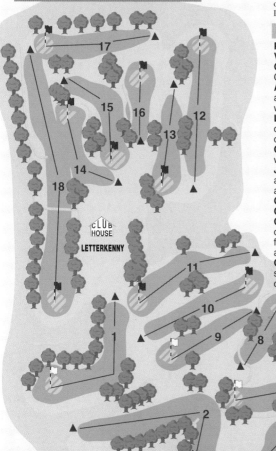

LETTERKENNY

Copyright Tudor Journals Ltd.

Narin, Portnoo, Co Donegal.
Tel: (074) 45107.
Email: Narinportnoo@eircom.net

LOCATION: Narin / Portnoo, Co
Donegal.
SECRETARY: Enda Bonner.
Tel: (074) 24668.
PROFESSIONAL: None.
ARCHITECT: P Carr, Ballybofey.

Beautiful scenery and a quiet course, although
it is particularly popular in the summer
months as it is located in a holiday area. Set
amidst beautiful scenery on the extreme west
coast of Donegal, providing well deserved
praise from both low and high handicappers.
A very popular location with the best of links
and inland characteristics.

COURSE INFORMATION

**Par 69; SSS 68; Length
5,766 yards.**
Visitors: Welcome.
Opening Hours: Daylight hours.
Avoid: Sunday (sometimes available
– ring before).
Ladies: Welcome.
Green Fees: €25 daily, €30
weekends.
Juveniles: Welcome.
Clubhouse Hours:
9.00am – 12.00pm.
Clubhouse Dress: Casual.
Clubhouse Facilities: Bar and light
refreshments.
Open Competitions: 2 mini open
weeks – July & August. Open
competitions regular during Summer.

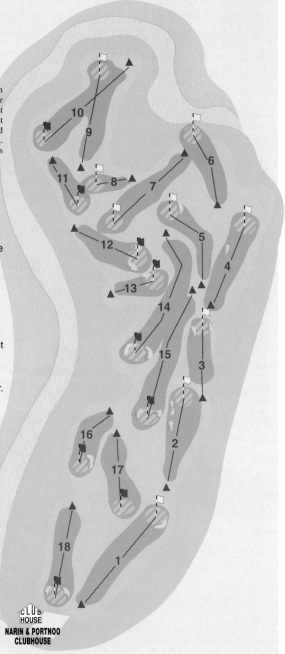

**NARIN & PORTNOO
CLUBHOUSE**

NO.	YARDS	PAR	S.I.	NO.	YARDS	PAR	S.I.
1	313	4	17	10	386	4	2
2	486	5	6	11	195	3	5
3	185	3	12	12	328	4	11
4	450	4	1	13	184	3	16
5	386	4	7	14	516	5	10
6	202	3	9	15	488	5	8
7	316	4	3	16	120	3	18
8	140	3	13	17	402	4	4
9	319	4	15	18	348	4	14
OUT	2,801	34		IN	2,965	35	
				TOTAL	5,766	69	
	STANDARD SCRATCH				68		

Copyright Tudor Journals Ltd.

Lisfannon, Fahan,
Co. Donegal.
Tel: (077)
61027/61715.

LOCATION: At Lisfannon which
is two miles from Buncrana
and eight miles from Derry.
SECRETARY: Dudley Coyle.
PROFESSIONAL: Seamus
McBriarty.

The course lies between the sea and
the picturesque Mouldy Mountain.
The holes are varied, with many
sandy knolls and pleasing
undulations, but the general tendency
is flattish. There are two loops of nine
holes, each loop terminating at the
Clubhouse.

COURSE INFORMATION

**Par 70; SSS 69; Length
6,239 yards.**
Visitors: Welcome Mon-Fri
and Weekends by
arrangement.
Opening Hours: 8.00am
till dark.
Avoid: Weekends during
October – March, 12.00 –
2.00pm Saturday and 8.30am
– 11pm Sunday's.
Ladies: Welcome.
Green Fees: €21 weekdays,
€28 weekends & Bank Hols

(£15 with member). Caddy
cars always available. Lessons
available by prior arrangement.
Juveniles: Welcome.
Clubhouse Dress: Casual.
Clubhouse Facilities: Locker
room, showers. Catering
facilities all week at 1.00pm.
Open Competitions: Whit
Open May; Open Week July.
Handicap certificate required.

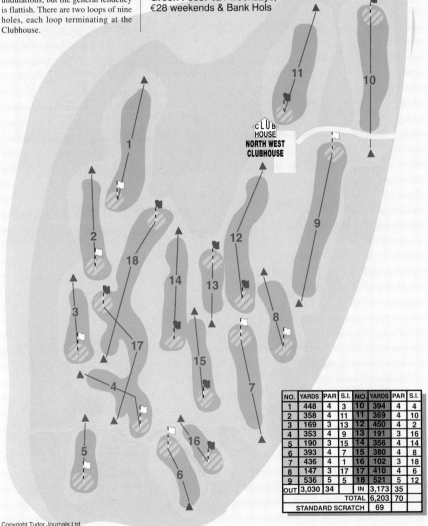

NO.	YARDS	PAR	S.I.	NO.	YARDS	PAR	S.I.
1	448	4	3	10	394	4	4
2	358	4	11	11	369	4	10
3	169	3	13	12	450	4	2
4	353	4	9	13	191	3	16
5	190	3	15	14	356	4	14
6	393	4	7	15	380	4	8
7	436	4	1	16	102	3	18
8	147	3	17	17	410	4	6
9	536	5	5	18	521	5	12
OUT	3,030	34		IN	3,173	35	
				TOTAL	6,203	70	
				STANDARD SCRATCH	69		

Copyright Tudor Journals Ltd.

**Portsalon, Letterkenny,
Co. Donegal.
Tel: (074) 59459.
Fax: (074) 59919.**

LOCATION: Twenty miles north
of Letterkenny on western
shore of Lough Swilly.
SECRETARY: Peter Doherty.
Tel: (074) 59459.

A popular seaside links with quite
narrow fairways. Greens are well
protected with bunkers, streams and
natural sand dunes all coming into
play. Course runs in clockwise
direction, so the out-of-bounds is
generally on left. The club celebrated
its Centenary in 1991 and in the same
year built a new clubhouse. The 7th,
8th and 9th holes have been modified.

COURSE INFORMATION

**Par 68; SSS 66; Length
5,208 metres.**
Visitors: Welcome (ring in
advance).
Opening Hours: Sunrise –
Sunset.
Green Fees: €30 weekdays,
€35 weekends & bank hols,
weekly tickets on request.
Ladies: Welcome.
Juveniles: Should be
accompanied by an adult.
Clubhouse Hours: 8.30 –
11.30pm.
Clubhouse Facilities: Bar
snacks and meals available
everyday (April – October).
Normal clubhouse facilities.
Open Competitions:
Open Week 28th Jun –
7th July 2002.

NO.	METRES	PAR	S.I.	NO.	METRES	PAR	S.I.
1	340	4	2	10	190	3	7
2	180	3	12	11	296	4	15
3	320	4	14	12	170	3	11
4	316	4	4	13	391	4	1
5	167	3	10	14	142	3	13
6	327	4	8	15	356	4	9
7	472	5	6	16	260	4	17
8	150	3	18	17	479	5	5
9	291	4	16	18	371	4	3
OUT	2,569	34		IN	2,639	34	
				TOTAL	5,208	68	
				STANDARD SCRATCH	66		

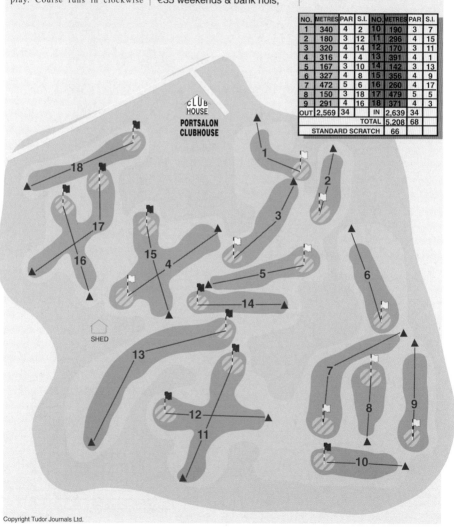

PORTSALON
CLUBHOUSE

Copyright Tudor Journals Ltd.

**Redcastle, Moville,
Co. Donegal.
Tel: (077) 82073.**

LOCATION: Beside hotel.
SECRETARY: Danny McCartney.
Tel: (048) 7135 0510.

Difficult course set in a picturesque area on the shores of Lough Foyle, with the advantage of its own hotel. The two Par 3 holes are quite difficult and should be approached with the necessary respect.

COURSE INFORMATION

Par 72; SSS 69; Length 6,142 yards.
Visitors: Welcome to play midweek.
Opening Hours: All day, all year.
Ladies: Welcome.
Green Fees: €15 Mon – Fri (€13 with member); €20 Sat / Sun & Bank Holidays (€18 with member).

Juveniles: Welcome if accompanied by an adult. Half Price.
Clubhouse Hours: 9.00am – 11.30pm.
Clubhouse Dress: Casual
Clubhouse Facilities: Bar and catering from 11.30am – 7pm.
Open Competitions: Various throughout the season. Information on request.

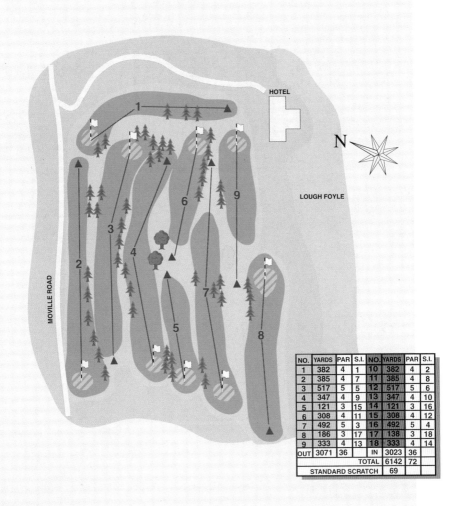

NO.	YARDS	PAR	S.I.	NO.	YARDS	PAR	S.I.
1	382	4	1	10	382	4	2
2	385	4	7	11	385	4	8
3	517	5	5	12	517	5	6
4	347	4	9	13	347	4	10
5	121	3	15	14	121	3	16
6	308	4	11	15	308	4	12
7	492	5	3	16	492	5	4
8	186	3	17	17	138	3	18
9	333	4	13	18	333	4	14
OUT	3071	36		IN	3023	36	
				TOTAL	6142	72	
STANDARD SCRATCH					69		

Copyright Tudor Journals Ltd.

ROSAPENNA

**Rosapenna Golf Club,
Downings.
Co. Donegal.
Tel: (074) 55301.
Fax: (074) 55128
Email: rosapenna@eircom.net
Web: www.rosapenna.ie**

LOCATION: Two miles north of Carrigart.
SECRETARY: Frank Casey.
ARCHITECT: Original Course (1893) – Tom Morris.

This championship length links course is set in north west Donegal at Downings. The first nine are played along a majestic stretch of beach and have many large sandhills with some bunkers. The second nine begins and ends with a second shot over the main Downings–Carrigart Road. Looping around a large bluff the second nine have inland characteristics. Very popular with visiting societies as the Rosapenna Golf Hotel is situated on the course and and offers special golf breaks. A new alternative back eight was added in 1997 that double back behind the giant dunes. The new holes are more in the links character of the first 10.

Visitors: Welcome.
Opening Hours: Dawn to Dusk. **Ladies:** Welcome.
Green Fees: €40 weekdays; €45 Saturday and Sunday/Bank Holidays.
Juveniles: Must be accompanied by an adult.
Clubhouse Facilities: Full catering facilities at Rosapenna Golf Hotel.
Open Competition: Open week 11th – 18th August.

COURSE INFORMATION

Old course distances; Par 70; SSS 71; Length 5,719 metres.

OLD COURSE CARD

NO.	YARDS	PAR	S.I.	NO.	YARDS	PAR	S.I.
1	298	4	11	10	543	5	10
2	428	4	5	11	427	4	2
3	446	4	1	12	342	4	14
4	386	4	9	13	455	4	6
5	255	4	15	14	128	3	18
6	167	3	17	15	418	4	4
7	367	4	3	16	216	3	16
8	485	5	7	17	358	4	12
9	185	3	13	18	367	4	8
OUT	3,017	35		IN	3,254	35	
				TOTAL	6,271	70	
STANDARD SCRATCH					71		

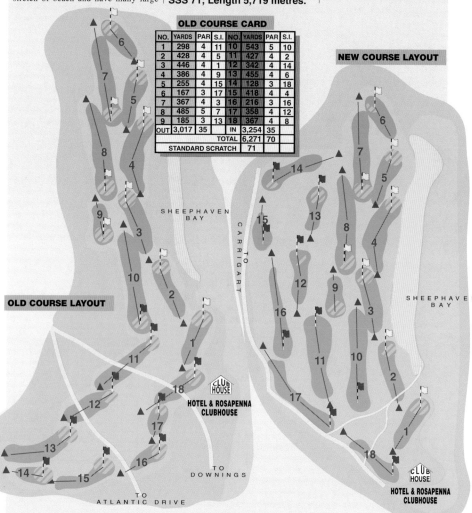

OLD COURSE LAYOUT

NEW COURSE LAYOUT

SHEEPHAVEN BAY

TO CARRIGART

SHEEPHAVEN BAY

HOTEL & ROSAPENNA CLUBHOUSE

TO DOWNINGS

TO ATLANTIC DRIVE

HOTEL & ROSAPENNA CLUBHOUSE

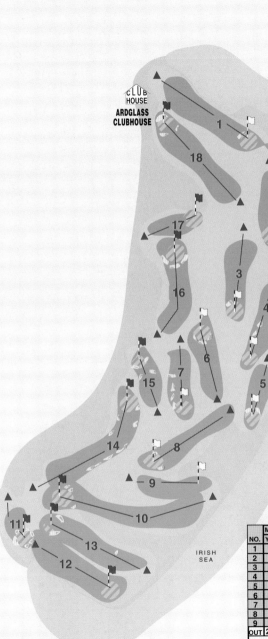

**Castle Place, Ardglass.
Co. Down.
Tel: (028) 4484 1219.
Fax: (028) 4484 1219.**

LOCATION: Approx 7 miles from Downpatrick on B1.
CLUB MANAGER: Debbie Polly.
Tel: (028) 4484 1219.
PROFESSIONAL: Philip Farrell.
Tel: (028) 4484 1022.

A seaside course with superb views over St. Johns Point, Killough Harbour and lying to the west, the Mourne Mountains. The 2nd (Howds) hole a 147 Metres, Par 3 is played over a gaping gorge to an elevated green. Another Par 3, the 11th is played from an elevated tee looking down to Coney Island. Both provide two memorable golf holes.

COURSE INFORMATION

Par 70; SSS 69; Length 5776 yards.
Visitors: Welcome Monday, Tuesday, Thursday & Friday.
Avoid: Arrangement only Wednesday, Saturday, Sunday.
Green Fees: £22 Mon – Fri; £28.50 weekends.
Ladies Day: Wednesday.
Clubhouse Dress: Smart dress.
Clubhouse Facilities: Snacks are available during the day. Evening meals by prior arrangement.

NO.	MEDAL YARDS	GEN YARDS	PAR	S.I.	NO.	MEDAL YARDS	GEN YARDS	PAR	S.I.
1	326	292	4	10	10	439	430	4	1
2	161	173	3	6	11	181	142	3	5
3	334	269	4	14	12	397	371	4	7
4	363	351	4	4	13	382	362	4	11
5	144	135	3	12	14	490	480	5	13
6	494	485	5	16	15	392	384	4	3
7	514	507	5	18	16	361	361	4	9
8	404	394	4	2	17	119	114	3	17
9	219	205	3	8	18	345	321	4	15
OUT	2,959	2,811	35		IN	3,106	2,965	35	
					TOTAL	6,065	5,776	70	
					STANDARD SCRATCH	69	68		

IRISH SEA

Bunker positions indicated.
Copyright Tudor Journals Ltd.

**Huntly Road, Banbridge.
Co. Down. BT32 3UR
Tel: (028) 4066 2211 /
4062 6189.**

LOCATION: 1 mile from town
centre on Huntly Road.
HON SEC: Tom Mulholland.
SECRETARY / MANAGER:
Mrs J. Anketell
ADMINISTRATOR:
Mrs W. Cull
Tel: (028) 4066 2211.

The course is a mature parkland
course set in the rolling drumlins of
Co. Down. Signature holes are the
6th hole with it's menacing pond and
the par 3,210 yrd. The 10th hole
where playing for a safe 4 is usually
the best option! The course provides
a challenge to all golfers whether
scratch or 24 handicaps, without
being intimidating.

COURSE INFORMATION
**Par 69; SSS 67; Length
5,590 metres.**

Visitors: Welcome to play on
most days, contact office to
make arrangements.
Green Fees: £17 Mon – Fri
(£10 with member); Weekends
£22 (£12 with member).
Ladies £14 (£10 with member)
Juveniles £6. Students £10.
Ladies Day: Tuesday.
Clubhouse Dress: Casual.
Clubhouse Facilities: Well
stocked Pro Shop, superb
luxurious clubhouse,
restaurant & conference room
Open Competitions:
Telephone Club for details.

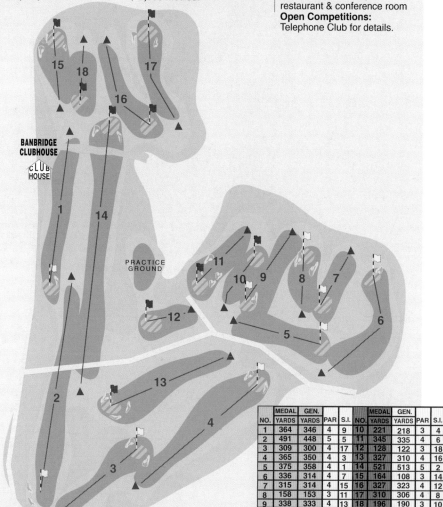

BANBRIDGE
CLUBHOUSE

PRACTICE
GROUND

NO.	MEDAL YARDS	GEN. YARDS	PAR	S.I.	NO.	MEDAL YARDS	GEN. YARDS	PAR	S.I.
1	364	346	4	9	10	221	218	3	4
2	491	448	5	5	11	345	335	4	6
3	309	300	4	17	12	128	122	3	18
4	365	350	4	3	13	327	310	4	16
5	375	358	4	1	14	521	513	5	2
6	336	314	4	7	15	164	108	3	14
7	315	314	4	15	16	327	323	4	12
8	158	153	3	11	17	310	306	4	8
9	338	333	4	13	18	196	190	3	10
OUT	3,051	2,916	36		IN	2,539	2,425	33	
					TOTAL	5,590	5,341	69	
					STANDARD SCRATCH	69	68		

Copyright Tudor Journals Ltd.

MEDAL YARDS	GEN. YARDS	PAR	S.I.	NO.	MEDAL YARDS	GEN. YARDS	PAR	S.I.
351	341	4	14	10	438	417	4	3
493	482	5	10	11	319	309	4	15
359	339	4	18	12	194	175	3	7
471	461	5	6	13	384	374	4	5
463	455	4	2	14	175	163	3	13
354	344	4	16	15	408	398	4	1
192	182	3	12	16	510	482	5	11
409	391	4	4	17	159	149	3	17
392	384	4	8	18	339	323	4	9
3,484	3,379	37		IN	2,926	2,790	34	
				TOTAL	6,410	6,169	71	
STANDARD SCRATCH					71	70		

Bunker and tree positions indicated.

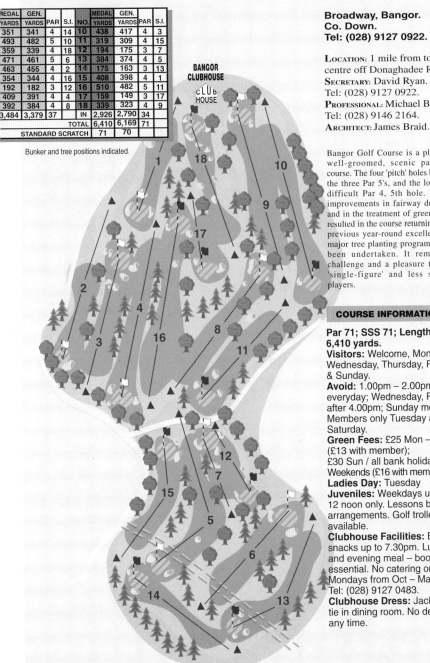

BANGOR CLUBHOUSE

Broadway, Bangor.
Co. Down.
Tel: (028) 9127 0922.

LOCATION: 1 mile from town centre off Donaghadee Road.
SECRETARY: David Ryan.
Tel: (028) 9127 0922.
PROFESSIONAL: Michael Barron.
Tel: (028) 9146 2164.
ARCHITECT: James Braid.

Bangor Golf Course is a pleasant, well-groomed, scenic parkland course. The four 'pitch' holes balance the three Par 5's, and the long and difficult Par 4, 5th hole. Recent improvements in fairway drainage and in the treatment of greens have resulted in the course returning to its previous year-round excellence. A major tree planting programme has been undertaken. It remains a challenge and a pleasure to both 'single-figure' and less serious players.

COURSE INFORMATION

Par 71; SSS 71; Length 6,410 yards.
Visitors: Welcome, Monday, Wednesday, Thursday, Friday & Sunday.
Avoid: 1.00pm – 2.00pm everyday; Wednesday, Friday after 4.00pm; Sunday morning. Members only Tuesday and Saturday.
Green Fees: £25 Mon – Fri (£13 with member); £30 Sun / all bank holidays. Weekends (£16 with member).
Ladies Day: Tuesday
Juveniles: Weekdays up to 12 noon only. Lessons by prior arrangements. Golf trolleys available.
Clubhouse Facilities: Bar snacks up to 7.30pm. Lunch and evening meal – booking is essential. No catering on Mondays from Oct – Mar. Tel: (028) 9127 0483.
Clubhouse Dress: Jacket and tie in dining room. No denim at any time.

Copyright Tudor Journals Ltd.

**Crawfordsburn Rd,
Clandeboye, Co. Down,
BT19 1GB.
Tel: (028) 9185 2706.**

LOCATION: Ten miles from Belfast –
three miles from Bangor, Co. Down.
GENERAL MANAGER: Richard Gibson.
Tel: (028) 9185 3581.
PROFESSIONAL: Debbie Hanna.
Tel: (028) 9185 2706.
ARCHITECT: Simon Gidman.

Blackwood Golf Centre is Ulster's foremost
pay and play golf facility. Opened in 1994,
the centre comprises Hamilton course – an
eighteen hole championship standard
course, Temple course – an eighteen hole,
par 3 course, plus a twenty bay covered,
floodlit driving range. The centre also
boasts Shanks Restaurant, bar & grill and a
salon privé (private function room)
sponsored by Guinness Northern Ireland.

COURSE INFORMATION

**HAMILTON COURSE SSS 70
Par 71; Length 6,304 yards.
Visitors:** Welcome.
Opening Hours: 8am – 10pm.
Green Fees: £19 midweek & £25
weekends and Bank Holidays
(booking advised).

**TEMPLE COURSE
Par 54; Length 2,492 yards.
Greens Fees:** £11 midweek & £13
weekends and Bank Holidays.
Opening hours: 8 a.m –10 p.m.
Golf Centre Hours: 10am –11pm.
Golf Centre Dress: Smart /casual.
Golf Centre Facilities: Top rated
restaurant (telephone booking for
evening service is recommended),
bar and grill (with lunch menu) and
private function room – available for
private hire.

NO.	MEDAL YARDS	GEN. YARDS	PAR	S.I.	NO.	MEDAL YARDS	GEN. YARDS	PAR	S.I.
1	354	343	4	12	10	436	421	4	3
2	540	529	5	4	11	354	341	4	15
3	212	206	3	6	12	166	152	3	9
4	306	295	4	18	13	436	415	4	1
5	419	398	4	2	14	491	475	5	11
6	332	321	4	14	15	404	385	4	7
7	165	165	3	16	16	180	164	3	5
8	325	305	4	10	17	355	340	4	13
9	480	471	5	8	18	349	331	4	17
OUT	3,133	3,033	36		IN	3,171	3,024	35	
					TOTAL	6,304	6,057	71	
		STANDARD SCRATCH							

NO.	YARDS	PAR	S.I.	NO.	YARDS	PAR	S.I.
1	75	3	16	10	185	3	4
2	182	3	6	11	101	3	13
3	108	3	14	12	176	3	3
4	83	3	18	13	129	3	15
5	116	3	8	14	154	3	7
6	116	3	12	15	125	3	11
7	147	3	4	16	163	3	9
8	177	3	2	17	129	3	17
9	132	3	10	18	174	3	5
OUT	1,136	27		IN	1,356	27	
				TOTAL	2,492	54	
STANDARD SCRATCH							

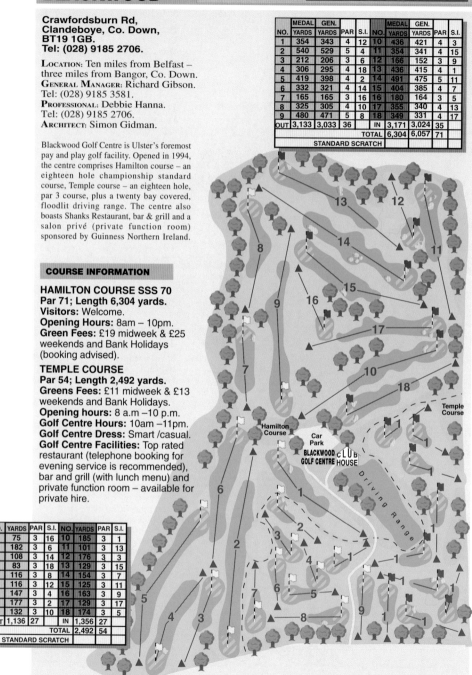

Temple Course

Hamilton Course

Car Park

BLACKWOOD GOLF CENTRE
CLUB HOUSE

Driving Range

Bunker and tree positions indicated.

Copyright Tudor Journals Ltd.

**14 Coniamstown Road, Bright, Downpatrick, Co. Down.
Tel: (028) 4484 1319.**

LOCATION: 5 miles south of Downpatrick off B1 to Ardglass, take road to Bright.
SECRETARY: John McCaul.
Tel: (028) 4484 1319.
ARCHITECT: Mr A. Ennis (Sen).

Inland course on high ground with splendid views of the Mourne Mountains from the 2nd green. A long course with four Par 5's, and an abundance of young trees which are maturing well. Stamina is important on this course.

COURSE INFORMATION

Par 73; SSS 73; Length 7,143 yards.

Visitors: Welcome anytime.
Opening Hours:
Sunrise – sunset.
Green Fees: £11 Mon – Fri; £14 Sat / Sun / Bank Holidays. Easter - Sept, Mon - Fri after 5.30pm £8.
Clubhouse Dress: Casual.
Clubhouse Facilities: New clubhouse with bar and restaurant facilities opening April 2002. Food available by prior arrangement.
Open Competitions:
Various dates throughout the year.

NO.	YARDS	PAR	S.I.	NO.	YARDS	PAR	S.I.
1	550	5	8	10	565	5	13
2	560	5	2	11	345	4	11
3	475	4	6	12	455	4	1
4	440	4	4	13	455	4	5
5	285	4	16	14	320	4	7
6	340	4	12	15	210	3	15
7	330	4	14	16	735	6	3
8	355	4	10	17	395	4	9
9	140	3	18	18	188	3	17
OUT	3,475	37		IN	3,668	37	
				TOTAL	7,143	74	
			STANDARD SCRATCH		74		

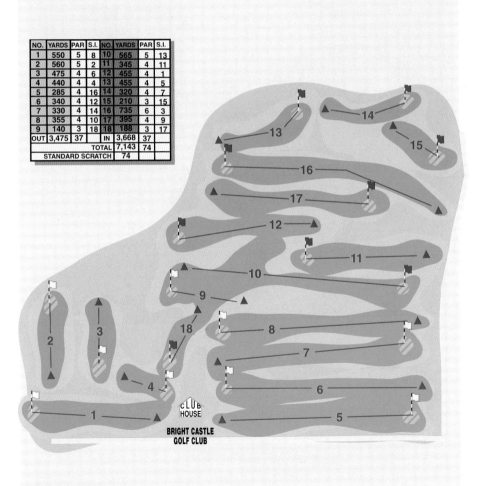

BRIGHT CASTLE
GOLF CLUB

Copyright Tudor Journals Ltd.

Station Road, Bangor, Co. Down.
Tel: (028) 9146 5004.
Fax: (028) 9127 3989

LOCATION: 2 Miles West of Bangor.
SECRETARY: Gary Steele.
Tel: (028) 9127 0368.

The course is situated on rising ground by the shores of Belfast Lough and the turf is of inland variety. The railway line runs parallel and adjacent to the 1st hole so one has to be careful not to be playing three off the tee! If your game is not working on all cylinders you can enjoy the scenery instead.

COURSE INFORMATION

Par 69; SSS 67; Length 5,647 yards.
Visitors: Welcome any day.
Avoid: Saturday.
Ladies: Welcome.

Green Fees: £16.50 Mon - Fri; £21 Sat / Sun.
Juveniles: Must be accompanied by an adult. Lessons available by prior arrangement. Club Hire and trollys available.
Clubhouse Dress: Informal except Saturday night. Jacket and tie after 8.00pm.
Clubhouse Facilities:
Full facilities. Lunches, snacks 11.30am - 2.30pm. Snacks, high tea, á la carte 5pm to 10pm.

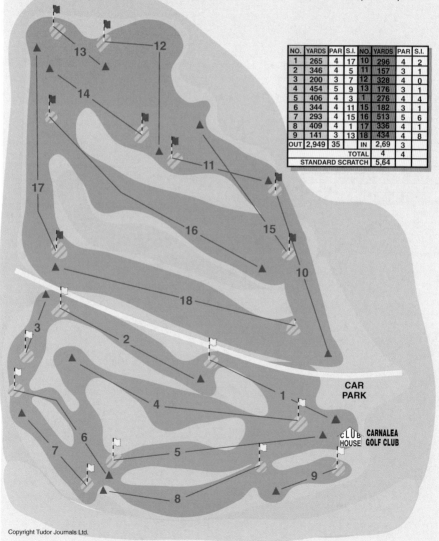

NO.	YARDS	PAR	S.I.	NO.	YARDS	PAR	S.I.
1	265	4	17	10	296	4	2
2	346	4	5	11	157	3	1
3	200	3	7	12	328	4	0
4	454	5	9	13	176	3	1
5	406	4	3	1	276	4	4
6	344	4	11	15	182	3	1
7	293	4	15	16	513	5	6
8	409	4	1	17	336	4	1
9	141	3	13	18	434	4	8
OUT	2,949	35		IN	2,69	3	
				TOTAL		4	4
				STANDARD SCRATCH		5,64	

CAR PARK

CLUB HOUSE   **CARNALEA GOLF CLUB**

Copyright Tudor Journals Ltd.

**Tower Road, Conlig,
Newtownards. BT23 3PN.
Tel: (028) 9127 1767.**

LOCATION: Above Conlig Village off
A21 between Bangor and
Newtownards.
GENERAL MANAGER: Rhonda Eddis.
PROFESSIONAL: Peter Gregory.
Tel: (028) 9127 1750.
ARCHITECT: William Rennick
Robinson, Dr Von Limburger.

The second course at Clandeboye, the Ava,
although much shorter than the 'Dufferin' is a
complete contrast and is different in its own
right. The 2nd hole is considered one of the
most attractive in Irish golf and is a true test
of any players game.

NO.	MEDAL YARDS	GEN YARDS	PAR	S.I.	NO.	MEDAL YARDS	GEN YARDS	PAR	S.I.
1	346	335	4	9	10	175	150	3	12
2	524	506	5	1	11	432	421	4	2
3	166	156	3	7	12	178	167	3	10
4	319	274	4	5	13	495	479	5	14
5	310	303	4	17	14	359	345	4	4
6	183	171	3	15	15	131	120	3	18
7	312	305	4	3	16	317	303	4	6
8	542	496	5	13	17	329	315	4	16
9	309	294	4	11	18	328	317	4	8
OUT	3,011	2,840	36		IN	2,744	2,625	34	
					TOTAL	5,755	5,465	70	
			STANDARD SCRATCH			68	67		

COURSE INFORMATION

Par 70; SSS 68; Length 5,755 yards.
Visitors: Welcome on weekdays.
Must be with member at weekends.
Green Fees: £22 Mon - Fri (with
member £13); £27.50 Sat/Sun £27.50
Or £16 with member. £40 day
ticket.Lessons available by prior
arrangment. Club Hire and Caddy
cars also available.
Clubhouse Dress: Smart / Casual.
Clubhouse Facilities: Full facilities
(except during the winter closed on
Mon). Prior arrangement required.
Snacks, meals 10.00am - 10.00pm.
Open Competitions: Numerous
throughout the year. Letter of
introduction required, if possible.

AVA COURSE

CLUB HOUSE CLANDEBOYE CLUBHOUSE

Copyright Tudor Journals Ltd.

Tower Road, Conlig, Newtownards. BT23 3PN.
Tel: (028) 9127 1767.

LOCATION: Above Conlig Village off A21 between Bangor and Newtownards.
GENERAL MANAGER: Rohnda Eddis.
PROFESSIONAL: Peter Gregory. Tel: (028) 9127 1750.
ARCHITECT: William Rennick Robinson, Dr Von Limburger.

One of North Down's most popular golf clubs, Clandeboye, has two courses – the Ava and the Dufferin. The latter being the Championship one, the short Par 4, 1st giving no indication of the stern test ahead. The course is laid out on the hills above Conlig village and has superb views over Belfast Lough and the Irish Sea. This course is now recognised as one of the great inland golfing experiences in Ireland.

COURSE INFORMATION

Par 71; SSS 71; Length 6,548 yards.
Visitors: Welcome on weekdays. Must be with member at weekends.
Green Fees: £27.50 Mon – Fri (with member £16).

£33 Sat /Sun/Bank Holidays (£21 with member) Lessons available by prior arrangement. Club Hire and Caddy cars available.
Clubhouse Facilities: Full facilities. Prior arrangement required. Snacks, meals 10.00am – 10.00pm.
Open Competitions: Numerous throughout the year contact: (028) 9127 1767. Letter of introduction required, if possible, for open competitons.

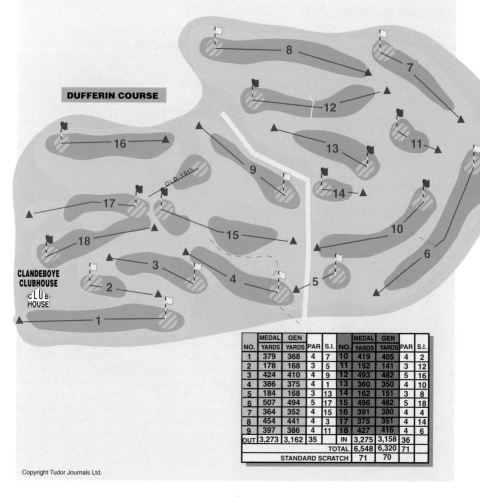

DUFFERIN COURSE

CLANDEBOYE CLUBHOUSE

NO.	MEDAL YARDS	GEN YARDS	PAR	S.I.	NO.	MEDAL YARDS	GEN YARDS	PAR	S.I.
1	379	368	4	7	10	419	405	4	2
2	178	168	3	5	11	152	141	3	12
3	424	410	4	9	12	493	482	5	16
4	386	375	4	1	13	360	350	4	10
5	184	168	3	13	14	162	151	3	8
6	507	494	5	17	15	496	482	5	18
7	364	352	4	15	16	391	380	4	4
8	454	441	4	3	17	375	351	4	14
9	397	386	4	11	18	427	416	4	6
OUT	3,273	3,162	35		IN	3,275	3,158	36	
					TOTAL	6,548	6,320	71	
					STANDARD SCRATCH	71	70		

Copyright Tudor Journals Ltd.

84 Warren Road, Donaghadee, Co. Down. BT21 0PQ
Tel: (028) 9188 3624.

LOCATION: 5 miles south of Bangor on A2 on Coast Road.
GENERAL MANAGER: Ron Thomas.
Tel: (028) 9188 3624.
PROFESSIONAL: Gordon Drew.

A part links and part inland open course with little rough but several water hazards which can catch the unthinking shot. The 18th with out-of-bounds on both left and right can be intimidating. Lovely views over the Copeland Islands to the Scottish Coast, particularly from the 16th tee. Well appointed clubhouse.

COURSE INFORMATION

Par 71; SSS 69; Length 5,570 metres.
Visitors: Welcome on any weekday and Sunday. Members only on Saturday.
Avoid: Saturdays and Bank Holidays.
Ladies: Welcome Tuesday.
Green Fees: £22 Mon – Fri; £25 Sunday. Special rates for societies. Special offers to include food/drink
Juveniles: Mon – Fri and Sun. Must be accompanied by an adult. Lessons available by prior arrangement. Club Hire available also.
Clubhouse Dress: Saturday after 8.00pm in mixed lounge and dining room – jacket and tie. Otherwise smart / casual (no denims).
Clubhouse Facilities: Full facilities; 11.00am – 9.00pm Tues – Sun during winter; 7 days a week in summer.
Open Competitions: Open week: 1st–8th June; Youth Tournament: 12th–16th Aug. Various others throughout the season; telephone club for details.

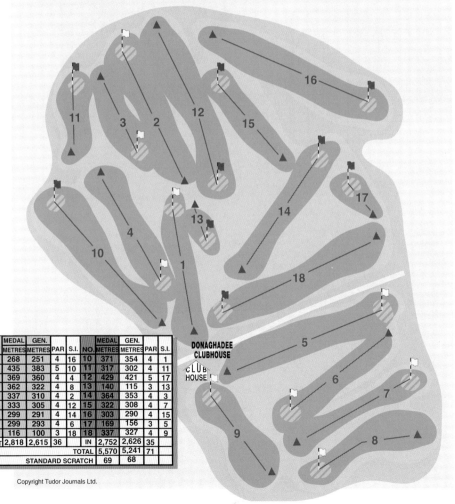

NO.	MEDAL METRES	GEN. METRES	PAR	S.I.	NO.	MEDAL METRES	GEN. METRES	PAR	S.I.
1	268	251	4	16	10	371	354	4	1
2	435	383	5	10	11	317	302	4	11
3	369	360	4	4	12	429	421	5	17
4	362	322	4	8	13	140	115	3	13
5	337	310	4	2	14	364	353	4	3
6	333	305	4	12	15	322	308	4	7
7	299	291	4	14	16	303	290	4	15
8	299	293	4	6	17	169	156	3	5
9	116	100	3	18	18	337	327	4	9
T	2,818	2,615	36		IN	2,752	2,626	35	
					TOTAL	5,570	5,241	71	
	STANDARD SCRATCH		69				68		

DONAGHADEE CLUBHOUSE

Copyright Tudor Journals Ltd.

43 Saul Road, Downpatrick,
Co. Down BT30 6PA
Tel: (028) 4461
2152/5947.

LOCATION: 25 miles south of
Belfast on (A7) and 1 1/2 miles
south east of Downpatrick
town centre.
SECRETARY: Joe McCoubrey.
Tel: (028) 4461 5947.
ARCHITECT: Martin Hawtree.

Recently upgraded, challenging
parkland course. 5th hole particularly
challenging. Excellent drainage so open
all year round.

COURSE INFORMATION

**Par 69; SSS 69; Length
6,100 yards.**
Visitors: Welcome any day
by prior arrangment.
Ladies: Any weekday.
Green Fees: £15 Mon – Fri;
£25 Sat / Sun.
Juveniles: No non - members
allowed on course. Lessons
available. Club Hire and
Caddy cars available.
Clubhouse Hours:
11.00am – 11.00pm.

Clubhouse Dress: Jacket and
tie after 7pm.
Clubhouse Facilities: Full
facilities snooker, bowls, TV
lounge. Meals available all
day; everyday (except
Monday) during season.
Winter months 12pm – 3pm.
Open Competitions:
Bank of Ireland – May;
Guinness Open – July;
Heart of Down – September.

NO.	MEDAL YARDS	GEN. YARDS	PAR	S.I.	NO.	MEDAL YARDS	GEN. YARDS	PAR	S.I.
1	374	368	4	3	10	362	326	4	10
2	298	293	4	1	11	181	170	3	12
3	506	500	5	7	12	544	538	5	4
4	176	166	3	1	13	390	379	4	6
5	457	457	4	1	14	424	390	4	2
6	330	324	4	1	15	171	168	3	16
7	437	427	4	3	16	364	338	4	14
8	135	129	3	5	17	278	270	4	18
9	337	325	4	9	18	336	330	4	8
OUT	3050	2989	35		IN	3050	2909	34	
					TOTAL	6100	5898	69	
					STANDARD SCRATCH		69		

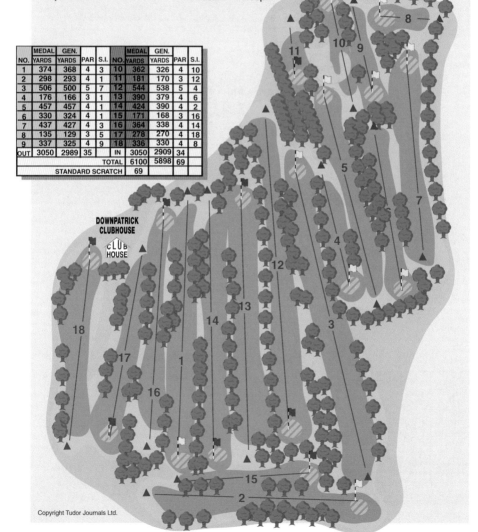

DOWNPATRICK
CLUBHOUSE

CLUB
HOUSE

Golf Road, Helens Bay, Bangor, Co Down.
Tel: (028) 9185 2601.

LOCATION: 9 miles east of Belfast on A2.
SECRETARY: Peter Clarke.
Tel: (028) 9185 2815.
Fax: (028) 9185 2815.

This popular course is compact with the layout encircling the Clubhouse. The turf is of the inland variety, greens are small making scoring more difficult than first impressions would suggest. There are extensive views of the Antrim Hills across Belfast Lough. The 4th hole, a short pitch over trees to a green protected by bunkers on three sides, is a particularly interesting one.

COURSE INFORMATION

Par 68; SSS 67; Length 5,176 metres.
Visitors: Welcome to play; Mon, Wed, Thurs up to 1.30pm. Fri and Sun. (Fri Jul/Aug after 11.30am).
Avoid: Tue, Thur (after 1.30pm) Sat before 6.00pm. Tuesday – members only.
Green Fees: £17 Mon - Thurs; £20 Fri / Public Holidays.
Juveniles: Under 18's must be accompanied by an adult and unable to play after 6.00pm Mon – Fri.

Clubhouse Hours: 9.00am – 11.30am.
Clubhouse Dress: Smart casual dress is permitted until 7.30pm. After 7.30pm gentlemen must wear a jacket, collar and tie. Tee shirts or denim jeans are not acceptable on the course or in the Clubhouse.
Clubhouse Facilities: Full facilities. Evening meals until 9.00pm.
Open Competitions: Open week; July. Numerous other competitions – telephone for details.

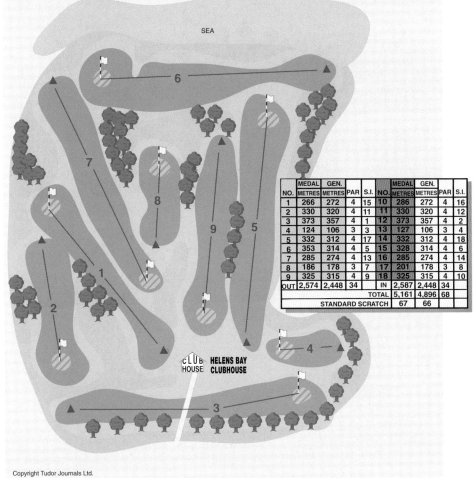

NO.	MEDAL METRES	GEN. METRES	PAR	S.I.	NO.	MEDAL METRES	GEN. METRES	PAR	S.I.
1	266	272	4	15	10	286	272	4	16
2	330	320	4	11	11	330	320	4	12
3	373	357	4	1	12	373	357	4	2
4	124	106	3	3	13	127	106	3	4
5	332	312	4	17	14	332	312	4	18
6	353	314	4	5	15	328	314	4	6
7	285	274	4	13	16	285	274	4	14
8	186	178	3	7	17	201	178	3	8
9	325	315	4	9	18	325	315	4	10
OUT	2,574	2,448	34		IN	2,587	2,448	34	
					TOTAL	5,161	4,896	68	
					STANDARD SCRATCH	67	66		

SEA

HELENS BAY CLUBHOUSE

Copyright Tudor Journals Ltd.

**Demense Road,
Holywood, Co Down.**

LOCATION: 5 miles east of Belfast on A2.
GENERAL MANAGER: Gerry Fyfe.
Tel: (028) 9042 3135.
PROFESSIONAL: Paul Gray.
Tel: (028) 9042 5503.

Hilly parkland course over-looking Holywood, and with excellent views over Belfast Lough. The first nine play on the slopes of the Holywood Hills, whilst the back nine are more varied with some interesting tee shots and some steep hills and valleys. Most of the greens run toward the sea. The back nine are a strenuous test begining with a very steep climb to the 10th green.

COURSE INFORMATION

Par 69; SSS 68; Length 5,480 metres.
Opening hours: Sunrise - Sunset.
Visitors: Welcome to play; (members only 1.30pm - 2.15pm and 5-7pm weekdays.)
Avoid: Public holidays and Thursdays.
Ladies: Welcome Thursday.
Green Fees: €26 Mon / Fri, Ladies €16 Mon / Fri, €40 Sun/Societies/Visitors
Juveniles: Lessons available by prior arrangments. Club Hire and Caddy service available.

Clubhouse Hours:
9.00am 11.30pm.
Clubhouse Dress:
Smart / casual, no denims or training shoes on course.
Clubhouse Facilities:
Full facilities. Snacks, evening meals all day everyday (except Monday).
Open Competitions:
Open Week in June. Various other open competitions throughout the summer – telephone club for details.

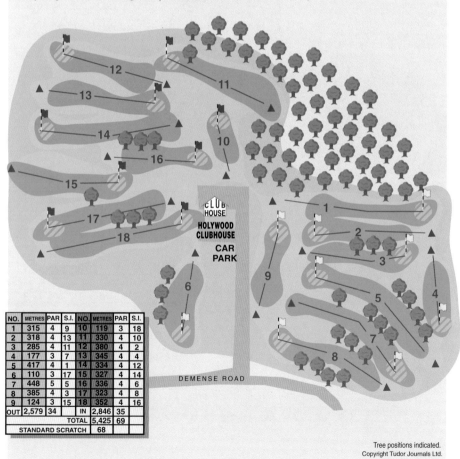

NO.	METRES	PAR	S.I.	NO.	METRES	PAR	S.I.
1	315	4	9	10	119	3	18
2	318	4	13	11	330	4	10
3	285	4	11	12	380	4	2
4	177	3	7	13	345	4	4
5	417	4	1	14	334	4	12
6	110	3	17	15	327	4	14
7	448	5	5	16	336	4	6
8	385	4	3	17	323	4	8
9	124	3	15	18	352	4	16
OUT	2,579	34		IN	2,846	35	
				TOTAL	5,425	69	
		STANDARD SCRATCH				68	

DEMENSE ROAD

Tree positions indicated.
Copyright Tudor Journals Ltd.

**Mourne Park, Kilkeel,
Co Down.
Tel: (028) 4176 5095.
Fax: (028) 4176 5579.**

Location: Three miles from Kilkeel on main Newry Road.
Secretary: S. C. McBride.
Tel: (028) 4176 5095.
Architect: Lord Justice Babington (original nine holes); Mr. E. Hackett (new development).

Situated at the foot of Knockcree Mountain, the course is ringed by woodlands and masses of rhododendron shrubs in an area that might well be described as the Garden of Mourne. The course was enlarged in 1993 from 9 holes to 18 holes.

COURSE INFORMATION

**Par 72; SSS 72; Length 6,579 yards.
Opening hours:** Sunrise – sunset.
Visitors: Welcome Mon, Wed, Thurs, Fri and Sun.
Avoid: Tues & Sat.

Ladies Day: Tuesday.
Green Fees: £18 Mon – Fri; £22 weekends.
Juveniles: up to 5.00pm. Caddy cars available by prior arrangment.
Clubhouse Dress: Jacket and tie in main lounge.
Clubhouse Facilities: Full facilities. Snacks, evening meals all day during summer or by prior arrangment.
Open Competitions: Several throughout the year.

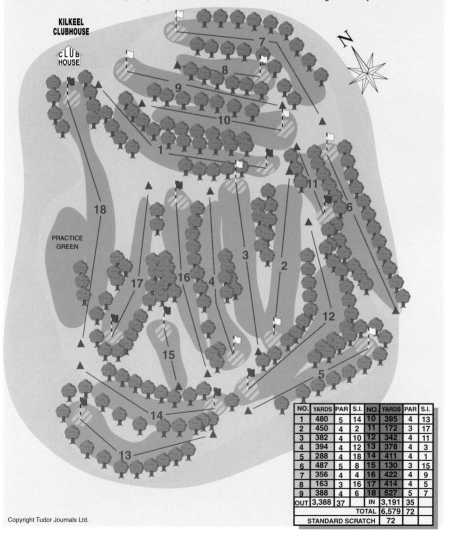

NO.	YARDS	PAR	S.I.	NO.	YARDS	PAR	S.I.
1	480	5	14	10	395	4	13
2	450	4	2	11	172	3	17
3	382	4	10	12	342	4	11
4	394	4	12	13	378	4	3
5	288	4	18	14	411	4	1
6	487	5	8	15	130	3	15
7	356	4	16	16	422	4	9
8	163	3	16	17	414	4	5
9	388	4	6	18	527	5	7
OUT	3,388	37		IN	3,191	35	
				TOTAL	6,579	72	
				STANDARD SCRATCH		72	

Copyright Tudor Journals Ltd.

**142 Main Road, Cloughey,
Co Down, BT22 1JA.
Tel: (028) 4277 1233
Fax: (028) 4277 1699
Email: kirkstown@aol.com
www.kcgc.org**

LOCATION: Approx. 45 mins. from Belfast, 16 miles from Newtownards on the A2.
CLUB ADMIN: Rosemary Coulter.
PROFESSIONAL: J. Peden.
Tel: (028) 4277 1004.
ARCHITECT: J Braid.

This fine old links course, designed by the legendary course architect Jim Braid on the coast of County Down has a tremendous variety of holes. The long 397 metre, par 4 10th plays like a par 5 when into the wind. A true and fair test of golf catering for low and high handicappers alike. You will find a warm and friendly atmosphere the clubhouse. This course dries so quickly after bad weather that it is usually open when other courses are closed.

COURSE INFORMATION

**Par 69; SSS 70; Length 5,596 metres.
Opening hours:** 8am - Dusk.
Visitors: Welcome any day except Saturday.
Avoid: Friday mornings.
Green Fees: £18.75 Mon – Fri; (£10.75 with a member); £25.75 Sat / Sun / All public holidays (£13.75 with a member).

Juveniles: £4.75 Mon – Fri; £5.75 – Sat / Sun, must be accompanied by an adult. Can play anytime.
Clubhouse Hours: 9am – 10.30pm.
Clubhouse Dress: Casual, jacket and tie after 7.30pm.
Clubhouse Facilities: Trolleys and Golf Clubs for hire. Bar & catering facilities daily. Evening meals must be ordered before commencing play.
Open Competitions: Throughout the season. Open Week June/July.

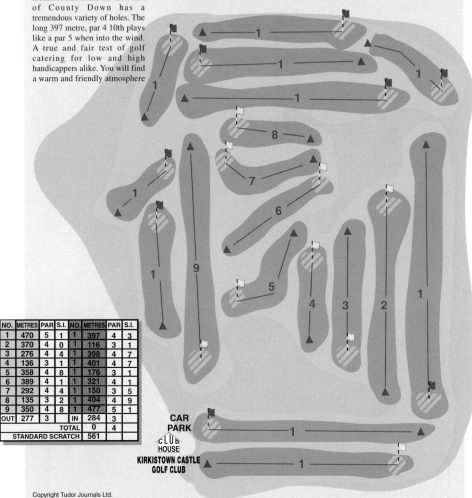

NO.	METRES	PAR	S.I.	NO.	METRES	PAR	S.I.
1	470	5	1	1	397	4	3
2	370	4	0	1	116	3	1
3	276	4	4	1	398	4	7
4	136	3	1	1	401	4	7
5	358	4	8	1	176	3	1
6	389	4	1	1	321	4	1
7	292	4	4	1	150	3	5
8	135	3	2	1	404	4	9
9	350	4	8	1	477	5	1
OUT	277	3		IN	284	3	
	TOTAL	0				4	
STANDARD SCRATCH		561					

CAR PARK

cLUB HOUSE

KIRKISTOWN CASTLE GOLF CLUB

Copyright Tudor Journals Ltd.

**Comber, Newtownards,
Co Down.
Tel: (028) 9754 1234.**

LOCATION: Take Killyleagh
Road from Comber, in less than
a mile take a road to left,
signposted Ardmillan. Bear left
for 6 miles to Mahee Island.
SECRETARY: Mr Marshall.
Tel: (028) 9754 1234.
SHOP: Mr McCracken.
Tel: (028) 9754 1234.
ARCHITECT: Mr Robinson,
Bangor.

A nine hole course sited on an island
in Strangford Lough with excellent
views for 360 degrees. The course is
parkland with luscious fairways and
well manicured greens. The
undulating fairways and tricky
approach shots make this a good test
of golf. The course record stands at
63 so it is no pushover. One to visit,
not only for the golf enthusiast, but
for the views.

COURSE INFORMATION

**Par 68; SSS 68; Length 5,588
yards 5,108 metres.
Opening hours:**
9.00am – 9.00pm.
Visitors: Welcome to play.
Avoid: Sat before 4.30pm and
Wed after 4.30pm.

Ladies: Welcome Mondays.
Green Fees: £10 Mon – Fri;
£15 Sat / Sun / Bank hols.
Juveniles: Juveniles
competition day Thursday.
Handicap Certificate required
for Open Competitions only.
Prior arrangement required.
Clubhouse Hours:
9.00am – 5.30pm.
Clubhouse Dress: Casual to
7pm. Jacket and tie at
all functions.
Clubhouse Facilities: Meals
by prior arrangement. No bar.
Open Competitions:
Open week July.

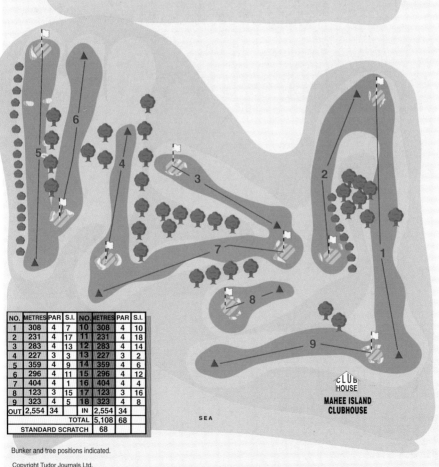

NO.	METRES	PAR	S.I.	NO.	METRES	PAR	S.I.
1	308	4	7	10	308	4	10
2	231	4	17	11	231	4	18
3	283	4	13	12	283	4	14
4	227	3	3	13	227	3	2
5	359	4	9	14	359	4	6
6	296	4	11	15	296	4	12
7	404	4	1	16	404	4	4
8	123	3	15	17	123	3	16
9	323	4	5	18	323	4	8
OUT	2,554	34		IN	2,554	34	
				TOTAL	5,108	68	
	STANDARD SCRATCH				68		

CLUB HOUSE

**MAHEE ISLAND
CLUBHOUSE**

SEA

Bunker and tree positions indicated.

Copyright Tudor Journals Ltd.

**Ringdufferin Road, Toye, Killyleagh, Co Down.
Tel: (028) 4482 8812.**

LOCATION: Three miles north of Killyleagh off Comber Road.
SECRETARY: Helen Lindsay.
Tel: (028) 4482 8812.

An 18 hole course with excellent views. The course runs over drumlins (rounded hills) with undulating fairways and tricky approach shots which make this a testing course to play on. Idyllic views over Strangford Lough from some of the elevated tees.

COURSE INFORMATION

Par 68; SSS 66; Length 4,698 metres.
Visitors: Welcome.
Opening Hours:
8.00am – 9.00pm.
Avoid: Telephone for available tee times on Saturday.
Ladies: Welcome.

Green Fees: £7 Mon – Fri (9 holes), £10 (18 holes); Sat & Sun £8 (9 holes), £12 (18 holes).
Juveniles: Permitted.
Clubhouse Hours:
8.00am – 9.00pm.
Clubhouse Dress: Casual.
Clubhouse Facilities:
Licensed restaurant.
Open week: June

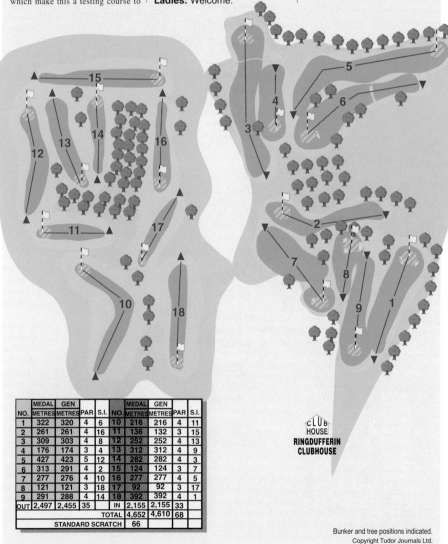

RINGDUFFERIN CLUBHOUSE

NO.	MEDAL METRES	GEN METRES	PAR	S.I.	NO.	MEDAL METRES	GEN METRES	PAR	S.I.
1	322	320	4	6	10	216	216	4	11
2	261	261	4	16	11	136	132	3	15
3	309	303	4	8	12	252	252	4	13
4	176	174	3	4	13	312	312	4	9
5	427	423	5	12	14	282	282	4	3
6	313	291	4	2	15	124	124	3	7
7	277	276	4	10	16	277	277	4	5
8	121	121	3	18	17	92	92	3	17
9	291	288	4	14	18	392	392	4	1
OUT	2,497	2,455	35		IN	2,155	2,155	33	
					TOTAL	4,652	4,610	68	
					STANDARD SCRATCH		66		

Bunker and tree positions indicated.
Copyright Tudor Journals Ltd.

Station Road, Craigavad, Holywood, Co Down.
Tel: (028) 9042 8165.

LOCATION: 7 miles east of Belfast on A2.
SECRETARY: Susanna Morrison. Tel: (028) 9042 8165.
PROFESSIONAL: Chris Spence. Tel: (028) 9042 8586.
ARCHITECT: H. C. Colt.

Eighteen hole parkland course rolls gently to the shores of Belfast Lough. The course is very picturesque with many mature trees and many carefully placed bunkers. The greens are undulating and generally run towards the sea. A very pleasant course that presents a challenge to any handicap of golfer.

COURSE INFORMATION

Par 70; SSS 71; Length 6,274 yards.
Visitors: Welcome any day except Wednesday, Saturday before 4.30pm and the 1st Mon of each month
Opening Hours: 8.30am – 7.30pm.

Avoid: Wednesday.
Ladies: Welcome Wednesday, Saturdays after 4.30pm and the 1st Mon of each month.
Green Fees: £40 Mon – Fri; £50 Saturday / Sunday / all public holidays.
Clubhouse Dress: Smart / casual.
Juveniles: Must be accompanied by an adult. Lessons available by prior arrangement.
Clubhouse Facilities: Full catering and bar.

NO.	MEDAL YARDS	GEN YARDS	PAR	S.I.	NO.	MEDAL YARDS	GEN YARDS	PAR	S.I.
1	417	414	4	7	10	303	299	4	14
2	404	400	4	3	11	165	162	3	8
3	372	359	4	13	12	433	430	4	4
4	143	140	3	15	13	360	357	4	12
5	555	550	5	9	14	187	184	3	10
6	351	348	4	11	15	410	407	4	2
7	184	164	3	17	16	485	476	5	16
8	394	392	4	5	17	193	190	3	18
9	409	406	4	1	18	509	506	5	6
OUT	3,229	3,173	35		IN	3,045	3,011	35	
					TOTAL	6,274	6,184	70	
					STANDARD SCRATCH	71	70		

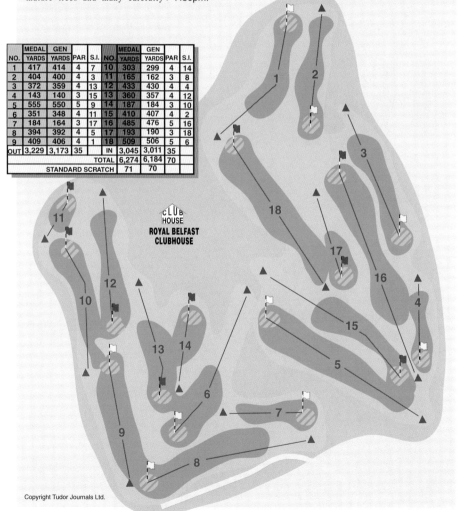

ROYAL BELFAST CLUBHOUSE

Copyright Tudor Journals Ltd.

ROYAL COUNTY DOWN   ULSTER   DOWN

NO.	C'SHIP YARDS	GEN. YARDS	PAR	S.I.	NO.	C'SHIP YARDS	GEN. YARDS	PAR	S.I.
1	506	502	5	13	10	197	189	3	14
2	421	385	4	9	11	448	425	4	8
3	474	474	4	3	12	525	479	5	10
4	212	212	3	15	13	443	421	4	2
5	438	416	4	7	14	213	203	3	12
6	396	369	4	11	15	464	450	4	4
7	145	135	3	17	16	276	265	4	18
8	429	425	4	1	17	427	400	4	16
9	486	425	4	5	18	547	547	5	6
OUT	3,507	3,343	35		IN	3,530	3,379	36	
					TOTAL	7,037	6,722	71	
					STANDARD SCRATCH	74	73		

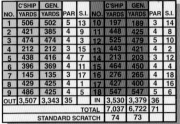

ROYAL COUNTY
DOWN
GOLF CLUB

CLUB HOUSE

PRO SHOP

Newcastle, Co. Down.
Tel: (028) 43723314.
Fax: (028) 4372 6281.
Email: golf@royalcountydown.org
www.royalcountydown.org

LOCATION: 30 miles south of Belfast, 1 mile from Newcastle.
HON / SECRETARY: Mr D. Nicholson.
SECRETARY: P. E. Rolph.
Tel: (028) 4372 3314.
PROFESSIONAL: Kevan J. Whitson.
Tel: (028) 4372 2419.
ARCHITECT: Tom Morris.

Founded in 1889, the course offers an exhilerating challenge to even the most experienced golfers. The setting of this links course is continually remarked upon for its outstanding beauty. The Mountains of Mourne in all their glory rise up from the Irish Sea. The fact that this course has five blind tee shots and several partially obscured approach shots makes it all the more formidable challenge to play. This is in addition to its well positioned bunkers. Professional golfers from all over the world rate Royal County Down as one of the best.

COURSE INFORMATION

Par 71; SSS 74; Length 7,037 yards.
Visitors: Welcome to play every weekday, except Wed; Sun, make prior arrangements.
Opening Hours: 8am – sunset.
Avoid: Saturdays & Wednesdays (members only).
Ladies: Welcome.
Green Fees: Summer; €90 Mon – Fri; €100 Weekends. Winter; €40 Mon – Fri; €45 Weekends.
Reduced green fees with a member. Club Hire available, Caddy service available by prior arrangement. No open competitions.
Juveniles: Accompanied by an adult only.
Clubhouse Hours: 8am – 9pm except at weekends when members only. (Centenary Room; 9am – 9pm).
Clubhouse Dress: Jacket and tie at all times except in the Centenary Room where casual dress is permitted.
Clubhouse Facilities: Available in the Centenary Room from 9.30am – 9pm weekdays.

Copyright Tudor Journals Ltd.

**233 Scrabo Road,
Newtownards, Co Down.
BT23 4SL.
Tel: (028) 9181 2355.
Fax: (028) 9182 2919.
Email: scrabo@compuserve.com**

LOCATION: 10 miles from Belfast off the main Belfast to Newtownards carriageway, (follow signs for scrabo country park).
SECRETARY: Christine Hamill.
Tel: (028) 9181 2355.
PROFESSIONAL: Paul McCrystal.
Tel: (028) 9181 7848.

The course winds its way around Scrabo Hill and Tower, one of the well-known Co Down landmarks. Fabulous views over Strangford Lough and MourneMountains (the 2nd hole is called Mourne View). Narrow fairways bordered by health and gorse call for accurate driving. The terrain around Scrabo Hill makes it a strenuous course for golfers.

COURSE INFORMATION

Par 71; SSS 71; Length 6,227 yards.
Visitors: Welcome.
Opening Hours: 9am – sunset.
Avoid: Saturday & Wednesday afternoons.
Ladies: Anyday except Sat.
Green Fees: £15.00 Mon – Fri; £20.00 weekend.

Juveniles: Not to play after 5.30pm. Must be accompanied by an adult member. Lessons and Caddy service available by prior arrangements. Club Hire available also by prior arrangements.
Clubhouse Hours: 8.30am – 12 midnight. Full clubhouse facilities.
Clubhouse Dress: Informal. Jacket & Tie after 7.30pm in Dining Room. No Denim.
Catering Facilities: Tues 11.30am – 2.30pm; Wed – Fri 11.30am – 2.30pm & 6pm – 9.30pm. Sat/ Sun 11.30am – 9.30pm. Excellent Cuisine.
Tel: (028) 9181 5048

	WHITE	GREEN				WHITE	GREEN		
NO.	YARDS	YARDS	PAR	S.I.	NO.	YARDS	YARDS	PAR	S.I.
1	459	404	4	1	10	322	319	4	16
2	163	127	3	9	11	474	464	5	14
3	415	409	4	3	12	443	441	4	2
4	128	122	3	17	13	204	182	3	8
5	555	501	5	7	14	364	375	4	10
6	313	305	4	15	15	378	374	4	6
7	320	320	4	11	16	345	342	4	4
8	318	315	4	13	17	145	121	3	18
9	565	561	5	5	18	296	296	4	12
OUT	3,236	3,064	36		IN	2,991	2,914	35	
					TOTAL	6,227	5,978	71	
					STANDARD SCRATCH	71	70		

Copyright Tudor Journals Ltd.

**20 Grove Road,
Ballynahinch, Co. Down.
Tel: (028) 9756 2365.**

LOCATION: 11 miles south of Belfast on the main road to Newcastle.
HON. SECRETARY: Norman Morrow. Tel: (028) 9756 2365.
SECRETARY / MANAGER: Terry Magee.

Each fairway is lined with trees, and several high points on the course give scenic views of the countryside. The 8th and 17th give panoramic views of the Mourne Mountains. This is a relatively new eighteen hole golf course which has been laid out adjacent to the Monalto Estate. Not physically demanding and many of the views on the course overlook the Mourne Mountains. Wildlife is also a great feature of the course.

COURSE INFORMATION

Par 72; SSS 72; Length 6,003 metres.
Visitors: Welcome any day except Saturdays.
Green Fees: £15.00 Mon – Fri; £20.00 Sun / Bank Holidays.
Ladies: Welcome.
Ladies: Competition – Friday.
Juveniles: Must be accompanied by an adult at weekends and off the course by 6.00pm during weekdays.
Clubhouse Hours: 8.30am – 11.30pm.
Clubhouse Facilities: Full clubhouse facilities all week. Bar snacks from 12noon – 3.00pm. Arrangements for parties.
Clubhouse Dress: Casual – no denims.
Open Competitions: Open Week; 3rd – 11th Aug. Open Stroke 6th & 20th June.

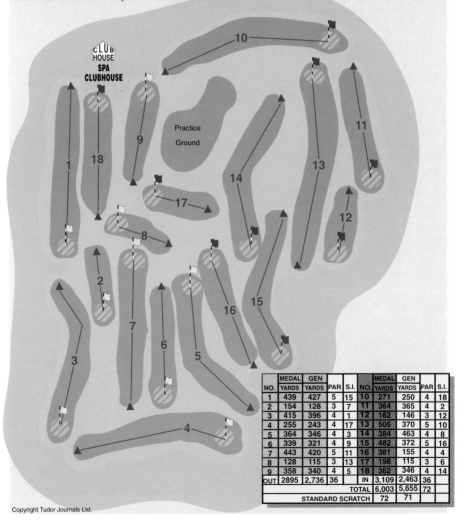

NO.	MEDAL YARDS	GEN YARDS	PAR	S.I.	NO.	MEDAL YARDS	GEN YARDS	PAR	S.I.
1	439	427	5	15	10	271	250	4	18
2	154	128	3	7	11	364	365	4	2
3	415	396	4	1	12	162	146	3	12
4	255	243	4	17	13	505	370	5	10
5	364	346	4	3	14	384	463	4	8
6	339	321	4	9	15	482	372	5	16
7	443	420	5	11	16	381	155	4	4
8	128	115	3	13	17	198	115	3	6
9	358	340	4	5	18	362	346	4	14
OUT	2895	2,736	36		IN	3,109	2,463	36	
					TOTAL	6,003	5,655	72	
					STANDARD SCRATCH	72	71		

Copyright Tudor Journals Ltd.

WARRENPOINT ULSTER DOWN

Lower Dromore Road, Warrenpoint, Co. Down.
Tel: (028) 4177 53695.

SECRETARY / MANAGER:
Marian Trainor.
Tel: (028) 4177 53695.
PROFESSIONAL: Nigel Shaw.
Tel: (028) 4177 52371.

The course is set in parkland with picturesque views of the Carlingford Mountains. Although not a long course, it demands from the golfer straight driving and skill around the greens. There are five par 3's and four par 5's so it offers plenty of variety.

COURSE INFORMATION

Par 71; SSS 70; Length 5,618 metres.
Visitors: Welcome Mon, Thurs & Fri. By arrangement Wed & Sun.
Avoid: Tues & Sat.
Green Fees: £20 Mon – Fri; £27 Sat / Sun / Bank Holidays.
Juveniles: Must be accompanied by an adult. Lessons available. Club Hire and Caddy Cars available by prior arrangement.

Clubhouse Hours: 8.30am – 12midnight.
Clubhouse Facilities: Full clubhouse facilities everyday. Catering 10.30am – 9.30pm.
Clubhouse Dress: Respectable dress essential.
Open Competitions: Open Week June. Handicap certificate is required for open competitions.

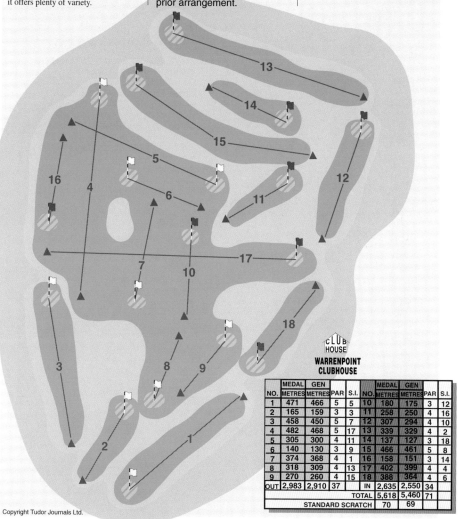

WARRENPOINT CLUBHOUSE

NO.	MEDAL METRES	GEN METRES	PAR	S.I.	NO.	MEDAL METRES	GEN METRES	PAR	S.I.
1	471	466	5	5	10	180	175	3	12
2	165	159	3	3	11	258	250	4	16
3	458	450	5	7	12	307	294	4	10
4	482	468	5	17	13	339	329	4	2
5	305	300	4	11	14	137	127	3	18
6	140	130	3	9	15	466	461	5	8
7	374	368	4	1	16	158	151	3	14
8	318	309	4	13	17	402	399	4	4
9	270	260	4	15	18	388	364	4	6
OUT	2,983	2,910	37		IN	2,635	2,550	34	
					TOTAL	5,618	5,460	71	
					STANDARD SCRATCH	70	69		

Copyright Tudor Journals Ltd.

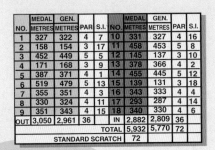

NO.	MEDAL METRES	GEN. METRES	PAR	S.I.	NO.	MEDAL METRES	GEN. METRES	PAR	S.I.
1	327	322	4	7	10	331	327	4	16
2	158	154	3	17	11	458	453	5	8
3	452	449	5	5	12	145	137	3	10
4	171	168	3	9	13	378	366	4	2
5	387	371	4	1	14	455	445	5	12
6	519	479	5	13	15	139	131	3	18
7	355	351	4	3	16	343	333	4	4
8	330	324	4	11	17	293	287	4	14
9	351	343	4	15	18	340	330	4	6
OUT	3,050	2,961	36		IN	2,882	2,809	36	
					TOTAL	5,932	5,770	72	
	STANDARD SCRATCH		72						

Castle Hume, Enniskillen, Co. Fermanagh.

LOCATION: A few minutes drive from Enniskillen on the A46 Belleek/Donegal Road.
MARKETING: Pat Duffy
OFFICE ADMINISTRATOR: Wilma Connor
Tel: (028) 6632 7077
Fax: (028) 6632 7076

Castle Hume Championship Golf Course is situated within the grounds of old Ely Estate, surrounded by Castle Hume Lake and Lower Lough Erne. It is one of the most scenic parkland areas in Fermanagh lovely Lakeland. Hospitality service for cruising golfers from local Carrick Reagh Jetty. Castle Hume Golf Course has hosted the Ulster Professional Golf Association Championship in 1996, 1997 and 1998.

COURSE INFORMATION

Par 72; SSS 71; Length 5,932 metres.
Visitors/Groups: Welcome
Opening Hours: Dawn – Dusk.
Green Fees: Mon – Fri £20 €35; Weekends/Bank Holidays £25 €40 Reduced rates for groups of 16+
Clubhouse Facilities: New 10,000 sq.ft Colonial style clubhouse opening April 2002, complete with full bar/catering facilities. Hospitality Conference room available.
Open Competitions: Open Week 27th May-2nd June. Erne Waterways 14th-16th June. PGA Ulster Lakeland Classic-21st June. Lakeland Open 27th-28th July

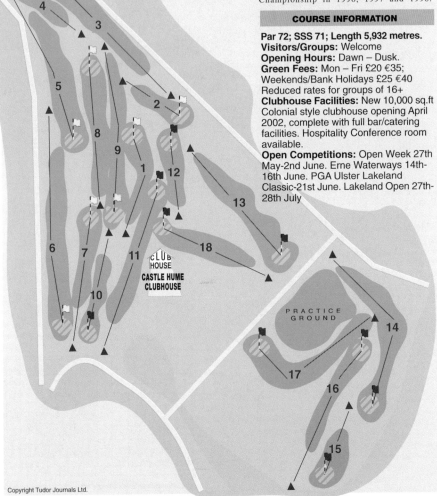

CASTLE HUME
CLUBHOUSE

PRACTICE GROUND

Copyright Tudor Journals Ltd.

Castlecoole Rd, Enniskillen, Co. Fermanagh.
Tel: (028) 6632 5250.

LOCATION: Beside Castlecoole Estate.
SECRETARY: Russel Ferguson.
Tel: (028) 6638 7794.

The first nine holes of this course are developing well with plenty of new young trees, shrubs and new drainage while the back nine offers a different challenge with a more mature landscape.

COURSE INFORMATION

Par 71; SSS 69; Length 6,189 yards (medal).
Visitors: Welcome to play.
Opening Hours: Daylight hours.
Avoid: Tuesday – all day, and Saturday afternoons.
Ladies Day: Tuesday.
Green Fees: £15 Weekdays; £18 weekends and bank hols. Half price with member, one visitor per member.

Juveniles: Not allowed on course after 5pm, unless accompanied by an adult.
Clubhouse Hours: 9.00am – 11.00pm.
Clubhouse Facilities: All refurbished. Snooker and table-tennis. Snacks and catering available everyday by prior arrangement.
Open Competitions: On a regular basis.

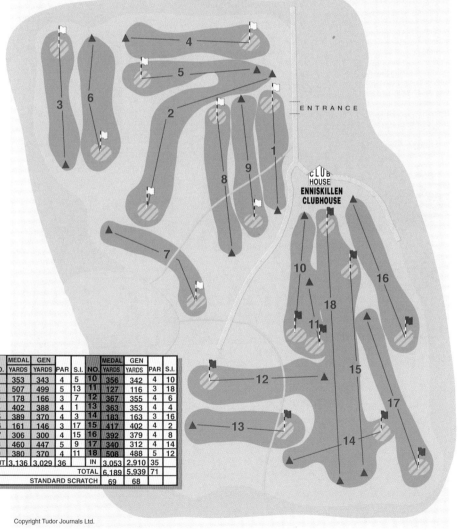

NO.	MEDAL YARDS	GEN YARDS	PAR	S.I.	NO.	MEDAL YARDS	GEN YARDS	PAR	S.I.
1	353	343	4	5	10	356	342	4	10
2	507	499	5	13	11	127	116	3	18
3	178	166	3	7	12	367	355	4	6
4	402	388	4	1	13	363	353	4	4
5	389	370	4	3	14	183	163	3	16
6	161	146	3	17	15	417	402	4	2
7	306	300	4	15	16	392	379	4	8
8	460	447	5	9	17	340	312	4	14
9	380	370	4	11	18	508	488	5	12
UT	3,136	3,029	36		IN	3,053	2,910	35	
					TOTAL	6,189	5,939	71	
	STANDARD SCRATCH					69	68		

Copyright Tudor Journals Ltd.

BROWN TROUT

ULSTER   **L/DERRY**

**Brown Trout Golf Club,
209 Agivey Road,
Aghadowey, Co. L/Derry.**
Email: bill@browntroutinn.com
www.browntroutinn.com

LOCATION: 7 miles from Coleraine
on A54/B66 intersection.
SECRETARY / MANAGER:
Bill O'Hara. Tel: (028)7086 8209
PROFESSIONAL: Ken Revie
ARCHITECT: Bill O'Hara Snr.

A nine hole parkland course which
crosses water seven times and is heavily
wooded. The feature hole is the 2nd, a
170 yard carry across the Agivey River.

COURSE INFORMATION

**Par 70; SSS 68; Length
5,510 yards.**
Visitors: Always welcome.
Opening Hours:
7.00am – sunset.
Ladies: No restrictions.
Green Fees: Mon – Fri £10;
weekends / holidays £15.
Juveniles: Must be
accompanied by an adult on
weekends / holidays /
Wednesday & Thursday
evenings.

Clubhouse Hours:
7.00am – midnight.
Clubhouse Dress: Casual.
Clubhouse Facilities:
15 bedroom hotel, gym and
full bar / restaurant.
Four 5 star cottages.
Open Competitions:
1st Friday of month May –

NO.	YARDS	PAR	S.I.	NO.	YARDS	PAR	S.I.
1	466	5	15	10	466	5	16
2	189	3	3	11	189	3	4
3	286	4	9	12	286	4	10
4	155	3	11	13	155	3	12
5	492	5	1	14	492	5	2
6	313	4	7	15	313	4	8
7	345	4	5	16	345	4	6
8	345	4	13	17	345	4	14
9	164	3	17	18	164	3	18
OUT	2,755	35		IN	2,755	35	
				TOTAL	5,510	70	
			STANDARD SCRATCH		68		

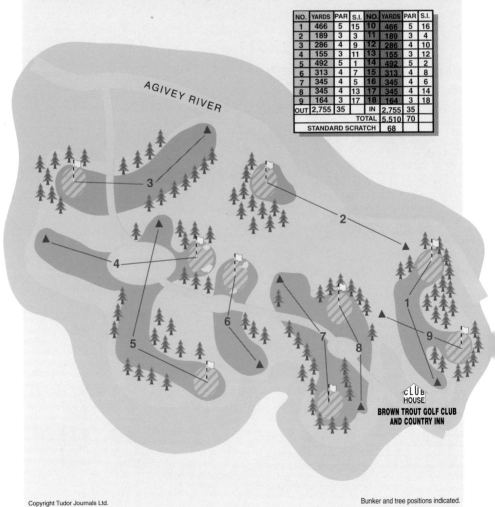

AGIVEY RIVER

CLUB
HOUSE
**BROWN TROUT GOLF CLUB
AND COUNTRY INN**

Copyright Tudor Journals Ltd.

Bunker and tree positions indicated.

**65 Circular Road, Castlerock.
Tel: (01265) 848314.**

LOCATION: Six miles north-west
of Coleraine.
SECRETARY: Mark Steen.
Tel: (028) 7084 8314.
PROFESSIONAL: Mr Bobby Kelly.
Tel: (028) 7084 8314.
ARCHITECT: Ben Sayers.

A true links course, with two courses —
eighteen holes and nine holes. Main feature is
the 4th hole with a burn on left and a railway
on the right! The club claims the best greens
in Ireland twelve months of the year.
Castlerock can sometimes be underestimated,
or not appreciated for the magnificent links
course that it is. There are also superb views
to Donegal and over to Scotland.

COURSE INFORMATION

Par 73; SSS 72; Length 6,499 Yards.
Visitors: Welcome.
Opening Hours: Sunrise – sunset.
Weekends by arrangement Sat/Sun from
3pm and Sun 9.30-10.15 am.
Ladies Day: Friday.
Green Fees: Mon – Fri £35,
Weekends £60.
Juveniles: Lessons by prior
arrangements; Club Hire available.
Caddy service available by prior
arrangements.
Clubhouse Hours: 8am – 12 midnight.
Clubhouse Facilities: Full clubhouse
facilities; Snacks; meals by arrangement.
Clubhouse Dress: Neat (no denims /
trainers) jacket & tie for functions.
Open Competitions: Open Week – July.

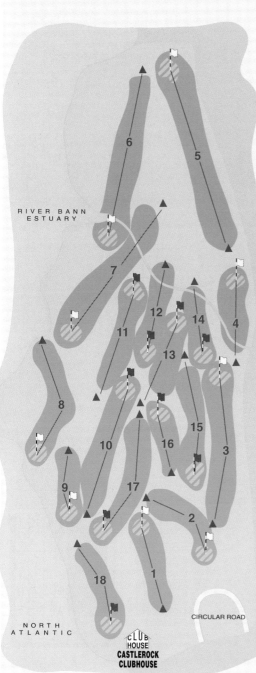

RIVER BANN ESTUARY

NORTH ATLANTIC

CIRCULAR ROAD

CLUB HOUSE
CASTLEROCK CLUBHOUSE

NO.	MEDAL YARDS	COMP YARDS	PAR	S.I.	NO.	MEDAL YARDS	COMP YARDS	PAR	S.I.
1	343	348	4	5	10	386	391	4	4
2	366	375	4	13	11	485	509	5	16
3	493	509	5	11	12	420	430	4	1
4	184	200	3	8	13	363	379	4	14
5	472	477	5	15	14	182	192	3	9
6	336	347	4	7	15	510	518	5	6
7	407	409	4	2	16	145	157	3	18
8	400	411	4	3	17	485	493	5	12
9	193	200	3	17	18	330	342	4	10
OUT	3,194	3,276	36		IN	3,305	3,411	37	
					TOTAL	6,499	6,687	73	
					STANDARD SCRATCH	72	71		

Copyright Tudor Journals Ltd.

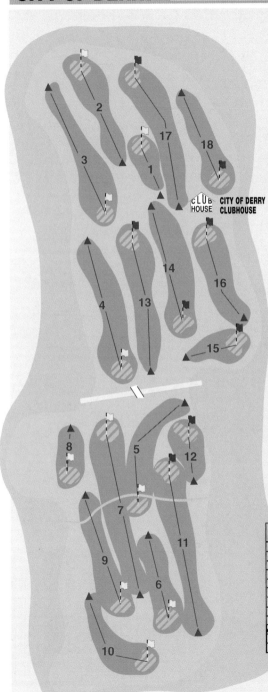

CLUB HOUSE — CITY OF DERRY CLUBHOUSE

49 Victoria Road, Londonderry, BT47 2PU.
Tel: (028) 71346369
Fax: (028) 7131 0008.
Email: cityofderry@aol.com

LOCATION: Three miles from city centre on A5 to Strabane, turn left.
HON. SECRETARY: Hugh Doherty.
PROFESSIONAL: Michael Doherty.
Tel: (028) 7131 1496.

Parkland course overlooking River Foyle with views towards Donegal. Undulating terrain well lined by plenty of trees. There is also an easy nine hole course which is very suitable for those beginning golf.

COURSE INFORMATION

Par 71; SSS 71; Length 6,429 yards.
Visitors: Welcome anytime. Weekends – please check with the club professional. Contact club for booking.
Opening Hours: Sunrise – sunset.
Avoid: Tuesday (ladies day).
Green Fees: £20 Monday – Friday; Saturday, Sunday & Bank Holidays £25. 9 hole is £6 daily. Members half price. Handicap certificate required.
Juveniles: Handicap 12 and under anytime, otherwise with adult only. 9 hole course £3. Lessons by prior arrangement. Full clubhouse facilities.
Clubhouse Hours: 8.00am – 12.00 midnight.
Clubhouse Dress: Smart / casual (no jeans).
Clubhouse Facilities: Bar snacks, full meals everyday except Monday. Handicap Certificate is required for Open competitions.

NO.	MEDAL YARDS	GEN. YARDS	PAR	S.I.	NO.	MEDAL YARDS	GEN. YARDS	PAR	S.I.
1	222	212	3	12	10	362	342	4	13
2	381	374	4	4	11	507	495	5	7
3	540	516	5	8	12	175	166	3	11
4	441	431	4	2	13	412	404	4	3
5	370	362	4	6	14	435	427	4	1
6	338	328	4	16	15	142	130	3	17
7	488	478	5	10	16	299	289	4	15
8	165	154	3	18	17	401	393	44	5
9	379	369	4	14	18	349	341	35	9
OUT	3,324	3,224	36		IN	3,082	2,987	71	
					TOTAL	6,406	6,211		
					STANDARD SCRATCH	71	70		

Copyright Tudor Journals Ltd.

Foyle International Golf Centre, 12 Alder Road, Londonderry. BT48 8DB.
Tel: (028) 7135 2222.
Fax: (028) 7135 3967.
www.foylegolfcentre.co.uk

LOCATION: One mile from Foyle Bridge heading for Moville turn left.
SECRETARY: Margaret Lapsley.
ARHITECT: Frank Ainsworth.
PROFESSIONAL: Kieran McLaughlin.

Foyle consists of an 18 hole par 72 course, nine hole par 3, 25 bay driving range and Golf Academy with indoor video teaching facilities. The parkland course is designed at championship standard with water coming into play on three of the 18 holes.

COURSE INFORMATION

Par 72; SSS 71; Length 6,678 Yards.
Visitors: Welcome at any time. Guaranteed tee times due to computerised booking system.
Opening Hours: Dawn – Dusk.
Juveniles: Handicap 12 and under anytime, otherwise with an adult.

Green Fees: £12 weekdays, £15 weekends & Bank Holidays.
Clubhouse Hours: 8.00am – late.
Clubhouse Dress: Informal.
Clubhouse Facilities: Licensed bar & restaurant with food available every day, a fully stocked golf shop, lockers and changing rooms.
Open Competitions: Regular open competitions during the Summer.
Open week- 15th - 20th July.

NO.	MEDAL YARDS	GEN YARDS	PAR	S.I.	NO.	MEDAL YARDS	GEN YARDS	PAR	S.I.
1	397	381	4	6	10	375	353	4	3
2	536	519	5	12	11	382	359	4	7
3	186	166	3	10	12	359	335	4	13
4	295	284	4	18	13	178	174	3	9
5	342	326	4	14	14	501	472	5	11
6	405	388	4	2	15	439	404	4	1
7	389	378	4	8	16	352	336	4	15
8	150	133	3	16	17	539	499	5	17
9	412	396	4	4	18	441	409	4	5
OUT	3,112	2,971	35		IN	3,566	3,341	37	
					TOTAL	6,678	6,312	72	
					STANDARD SCRATCH	72	71		

Bunker positions indicated.
Copyright Tudor Journals Ltd.

Shanemullagh, Castledawson, Co. Londonderry.
Tel: (028) 7946 8468.
Email: golf@moyola-park-n-ireland.freeserve.co.uk

LOCATION: 40 miles north of Belfast, via M2.
SECRETARY: Frank Kearney.
PROFESSIONAL: Bob Cockroft.
Tel: (028) 7946 8830.
CATERING TEL: (028) 7946 8270.
ARCHITECT: Don Patterson.

The course demands long accurate driving on most holes and the strategic use of large mature trees emphasises the need for well placed approach shots. The 8th hole is a ninety degree dog-leg which features a difficult pitch shot to the green across the Moyola River.

COURSE INFORMATION

Par 71; SSS 71; Length 6,519 yards.
Visitors: Welcome mid-week. Weekends by prior arrangement.
Opening Hours: Dawn – Dusk Monday – Sunday.
Avoid: Tuesday and Wednesday evenings in Summer; Saturday in Winter.
Ladies: Welcome.

Green Fees: £20 Mon – Fri (£12 with member); £30 Weekend.
Juveniles: Mon – Fri; after 4.30pm on Sat / Sun. Lessons by prior arrangement.
Clubhouse Hours: 12noon – 11pm. Full clubhouse facilities.
Clubhouse Facilities: 12noon – 9pm. A la carte by prior arrangement. Buggies availabel for hire.
Clubhouse Dress: Smart/casual, no denims.
Open Competitions: Open Week – July; usually monthly in summer (mixed opens).

NO.	WHITE YARDS	YELL. YARDS	PAR	S.I.	NO.	WHITE YARDS	YELL. YARDS	PAR	S.I.
1	438	406	4	7	10	348	341	4	12
2	418	409	4	5	11	377	370	4	4
3	346	303	4	13	12	200	191	3	10
4	152	140	3	15	13	494	476	5	18
5	521	515	5	17	14	417	404	4	2
6	430	423	4	3	15	320	312	4	14
7	391	387	4	11	16	177	167	3	6
8	421	410	4	1	17	128	128	3	16
9	379	363	4	9	18	562	554	5	8
OUT	3,496	3,356	36		IN	3,023	2,943	35	
TOTAL						6,519	6,299	71	
STANDARD SCRATCH						71	70		

Bunker positions indicated.

RIVER MOYOLA

MOYOLA CLUBHOUSE   CLUB HOUSE

Copyright Tudor Journals Ltd.

**117 Strand Road,
Portstewart, Co. L/Derry.
Tel: (028) 7083 2015.**

LOCATION: Four miles north west
of Coleraine on the north coast.
MANAGER: Michael Moss.
Tel: (028) 7083 2015 / 3839.
PROFESSIONAL: Alan Hunter.
Tel: (028) 7083 2601.
Fax: (028) 7083 4097.

Difficult, but open links course giving
magnificent views of Donegal Hills,
the rolling Atlantic, Strand Beach and
the River Bann, especially from the 1st,
5th and 12th tees. Greens are fast

and true. The Strand Course has
hosted many championships. An
outstanding test.

COURSE INFORMATION

**Par 72; SSS 73; Length 6,784
yards (Strand Course).
Par 64; Length 4,730 yards.
(Old Course).
Par 64; Length 5,324 yards.
(Riverside Course).
Visitors:** Booking necessary.
Avoid: Weekends and Bank Hols
Ladies: Priority on
Wednesdays..

Green Fees: Strand Course – £60
Mon–Fri; £80 Sat / Sun. Old
Course – £10 Mon–Fri; £14 Sat /
Sun. Riverside Course – £12
Mon–Fri; £17 Sat / Sun.
Juveniles: Must be accompanied
by an adult. Lessons by prior
arrangements. Club Hire &
Caddy trolleys available.
Clubhouse Hours:
All day everyday.
Clubhouse Facilities:
Bar / Bar Food.
Clubhouse Dress: Casual/Neat.
Open Competitons:
Open Week 6th – 13th July.

STRAND COURSE

NO.	YARDS	PAR	S.I.	NO.	YARDS	PAR	S.I.
1	425	4	7	10	393	4	10
2	366	4	15	11	370	4	4
3	207	3	11	12	166	3	18
4	535	5	5	13	500	5	12
5	456	4	1	14	485	5	14
6	140	3	17	15	169	3	16
7	511	5	13	16	422	4	6
8	384	4	9	17	434	4	2
9	352	4	3	18	464	4	8
OUT	3,376	36		IN	3,403	36	
				TOTAL	6,779	72	
				STANDARD SCRATCH		73	

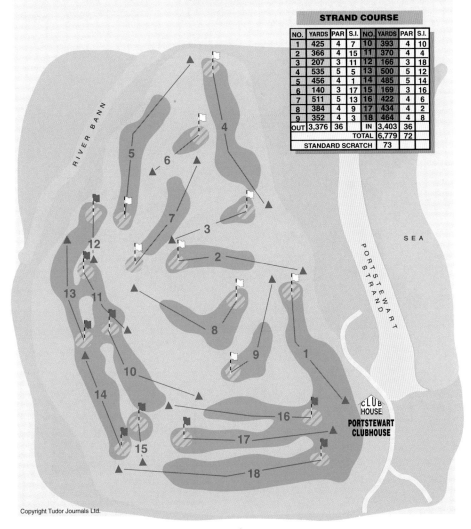

Copyright Tudor Journals Ltd.

**Radisson Roe Park Hotel
and Golf Resort,
Roe Park. Limavady,
Co. Londonderry.
BT49 9LB.
Tel: (028) 7772 2222.
Fax: (028) 7772 2313.**

LOCATION: In the picturesque
Roe Valley, one mile west of
Limavady, adjacent to Roe
Valley Country Park.
GOLF / LEISURE MANAGER: Don
Brockerton.
Tel: (015 047) 60105.
ARHITECT: Frank Ainsworth.
PROFESSIONAL: Seamus Duffy.
Tel: (015 047) 60105.

The 18 hole parkland course takes full
advantage of this beautiful riverside estate
setting, with Lough Foyle and the
Inishowen Peninsula providing a dramatic
backdrop. Water comes into play on five
holes, and with a challenging par four 18th
to finish, the golfer can enjoy the game to
the full.

COURSE INFORMATION

**Par 70; SSS 71; Length
6,318 Yards.
Visitors:** Welcome.
Opening Hours: 8am – Dusk.
Avoid: Weekends 8 – 10am
and 1 – 2pm (members only).

Ladies: Welcome.
Juveniles: Permitted.
Green Fees: £20 midweek (£15
with member), £25 Sat/Sun (£16
with member)
Coach House Hours: Open
every day from 10.00am until
late.
Coach House Dress: Smart
casual.
Coach House Facilities:
International menu available all
day in the Coach House.
Flood-lit and covered Driving
Range open to the public. Golf
Acadamy & full leisure facilities
on site. 4 Star luxury hotel on site.

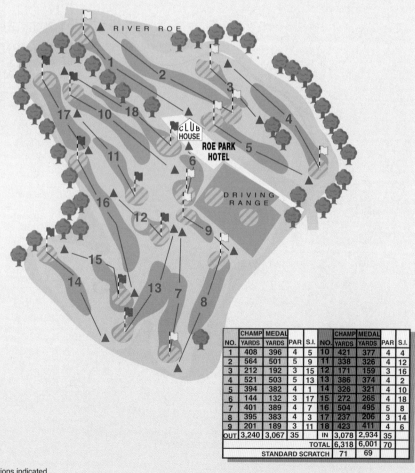

NO.	CHAMP YARDS	MEDAL YARDS	PAR	S.I.	NO.	CHAMP YARDS	MEDAL YARDS	PAR	S.I.
1	408	396	4	5	10	421	377	4	4
2	564	501	5	9	11	338	326	4	12
3	212	192	3	15	12	171	159	3	16
4	521	503	5	13	13	386	374	4	2
5	394	382	4	1	14	326	321	4	10
6	144	132	3	17	15	272	265	4	18
7	401	389	4	7	16	504	495	5	8
8	395	383	4	3	17	237	206	3	14
9	201	189	3	11	18	423	411	4	6
OUT	3,240	3,067	35		IN	3,078	2,934	35	
					TOTAL	6,318	6,001	70	
					STANDARD SCRATCH	71	69		

Tree positions indicated.
Copyright Tudor Journals Ltd.

**Onomy, Castleblayney,
Co. Monaghan.**

LOCATION: Hope Castle Estate,
Castleblayney.
SECRETARY: Raymond Kernan.
Tel: (042) 9740451.
ARCHITECT: R.J. Browne.

The course enjoys a scenic setting beside lake and forest. Hilly in character yet convenient (approx. 500 yards) to town centre the course is enjoyable for all levels of handicappers.

COURSE INFORMATION

**Par 68; SSS 66; Length
5,378 yards.**
Visitors: Welcome at all times.
Opening Hours: Sunrise –
sunset.
Ladies: Welcome Thursdays.
Green Fees: €10 Mon – Fri;
€12 Sat / Sun / all Public
Holidays.
Juveniles: Monday, Tuesday,
Thursday, Friday up to 5.00pm;
weekends after 6.00pm.
Clubhouse Hours: Daylight
hours in summer.
Clubhouse Dress: Casual
but neat.
Clubhouse Facilities:
Restaurant and bar facilities
everyday all day. Restaurant
in Hope Castle.
Open Competitions:
Open Week in June.

NO.	YARDS	PAR	S.I.	NO.	YARDS	PAR	S.I.
1	336	4	6	10	356	4	5
2	186	3	10	11	170	3	11
3	302	4	12	12	335	4	7
4	381	4	4	13	381	4	3
5	315	4	14	14	325	4	13
6	389	4	2	15	389	4	1
7	126	3	18	16	126	3	17
8	317	4	16	17	317	4	15
9	311	4	8	18	316	4	9
OUT	2,663	34		IN	2,715	34	
				TOTAL	5,378	68	
				STANDARD SCRATCH	66		

CASTLEBLAYNEY
CLUBHOUSE

CLUB
HOUSE

HOPE
CASTLE

7 & 16

10

1

2 & 11

3 & 12

WHITE
ISLAND

6

8 & 17

15

9 & 18

4 & 13

MUCKNO
LAKE

5 & 14

Copyright Tudor Journals Ltd.

NO.	METRES	PAR	S.I.	NO.	METRES	PAR	S.I.
1	161	3	13	10	426	5	14
2	414	5	17	11	370	4	18
3	159	3	9	12	204	3	10
4	321	4	3	13	366	4	4
5	370	4	1	14	382	4	2
6	383	4	15	15	129	3	16
7	344	4	11	16	347	4	12
8	324	4	5	17	336	4	6
9	179	3	7	18	334	4	8
OUT	2,655	34		IN	2,894	35	
				TOTAL	5,549	69	
	STANDARD SCRATCH				68		

Hilton Park, Clones, Co. Monaghan.
Tel: (047) 56017.

LOCATION: Scotshouse Road, Clones.
HON. SECRETARY: M. Taylor.

The course is usually playable all year round. It is parkland and set in Hilton Park estate and with its hills, forts, lakes and streams provides a very scenic backdrop for a good test of golf.

COURSE INFORMATION

Par 69; SSS 68; Length 5,549 yards.
Visitors: Welcome at all times.
Opening Hours: Sunrise – sunset.
Ladies: Welcome.
Green Fees: €20
Juveniles : Up to 5pm Weekdays
       After 6pm Weekends
Clubhouse Hours: 2pm – 11.30pm.
Clubhouse Dress: Informal.
Clubhouse Facilities: Full clubhouse facilities, evening meals, snacks, etc
Open Competitions:
Open Weekend –13th & 14th April
Open Week – 1st to 9th June
Open Weekend – 20th & 21thJuly
Open Weekend –10th & 11th August
Open Weekend – 7th & 8th September

TO CLONES

CLUB HOUSE CLONES CLUBHOUSE

DEER PARK

Copyright Tudor Journals Ltd.

Carrickmacross, Co. Monaghan.
Tel: (042) 9661438/9664016.
Fax: (042) 9661853.

LOCATION: On the Dublin road,
one mile from Carrickmacross.
PROFESSIONAL: Maurice Cassidy.

Panoramic views over counties Monaghan,
Cavan, Louth, Armagh and Meath. A new
eighteen hole championship course opened
in August 1991.

COURSE INFORMATION

Par 71; SSS 69; Length 5,870 metres.
Visitors: Welcome everyday.
Opening Hours: Daylight hours.
Avoid: Prior arrangement is preferred.
Green Fees: €30 Weekdays,
€37 weekends.
Clubhouse Dress: Casual.
Clubhouse Facilities:
Full bar and dining facilities available.
Open Competitions:
Open Week – August.

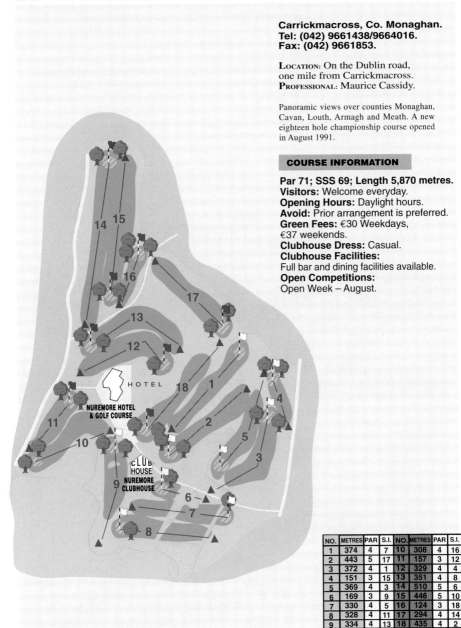

NO.	METRES	PAR	S.I.	NO.	METRES	PAR	S.I.
1	374	4	7	10	308	4	16
2	443	5	17	11	157	3	12
3	372	4	1	12	329	4	4
4	151	3	15	13	351	4	8
5	369	4	3	14	510	5	6
6	169	3	9	15	446	5	10
7	330	4	5	16	124	3	18
8	328	4	11	17	294	4	14
9	334	4	13	18	435	4	2
OUT	2,868	36		IN	2,954	36	
					TOTAL	5,900	71
				STANDARD SCRATCH		69	

Copyright Tudor Journals Ltd.

**Cootehill Road, Monaghan,
Co. Monaghan.
Tel: (047) 81316.**

LOCATION: Two miles south of
Monaghan town on the
Cootehill Road.
SECRETARY: Jimmie McKenna.
PROFESSIONAL: Gareth McShea
Tel: (047) 71222.
ARCHITECT: Des Smith Golf
Design Ltd.

The club has recently undergone an
extensive development from a shortish
nine hole course to a 6,000 yard
eighteen hole course, which is now in
operation.

COURSE INFORMATION

**Par 70; SSS 68; Length
5,605 metres.
Visitors:** Welcome – at all
times except on days of major
competitions.
Opening Hours: Sunrise –
sunset.
Ladies: Welcome – have
priority on Wednesdays.
Green Fees: €25 Mon-Fri,
€32 Sat/Sun. With member
€15 Mon-Fri, €20 Sat/Sun
Juveniles: Welcome any day
except Open Days and Major
Competition days.

Clubhouse Hours:
6 pm – 11 pm Mon;
12 noon – 12 pm Tues – Sun;
Full clubhouse facilities.
Clubhouse Dress: Casual.
Clubhouse Facilities: Full
catering available from 1.00pm
(except Mondays); large parties
by prior arrangement.
Open Competitions:
Open Week – July;
Open Weekends – April, May,
June & August.

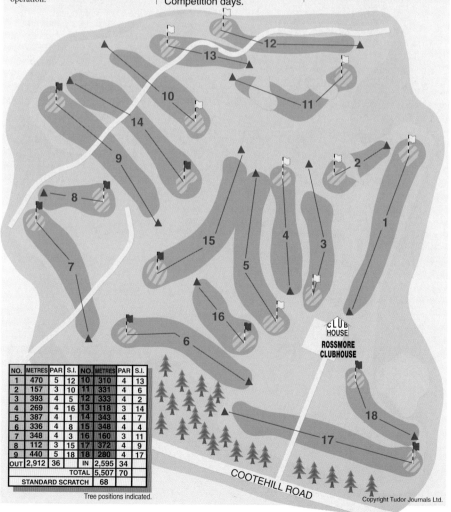

NO.	METRES	PAR	S.I.	NO.	METRES	PAR	S.I.
1	470	5	12	10	310	4	13
2	157	3	10	11	331	4	6
3	393	4	5	12	333	4	2
4	269	4	16	13	118	3	14
5	387	4	1	14	343	4	7
6	336	4	8	15	348	4	3
7	348	4	3	16	160	3	11
8	112	3	15	17	372	4	9
9	440	5	18	18	280	4	17
OUT	2,912	36		IN	2,595	34	
				TOTAL	5,507	70	
	STANDARD SCRATCH			68			

Tree positions indicated.

ROSSMORE
CLUBHOUSE

CLUB
HOUSE

COOTEHILL ROAD

Copyright Tudor Journals Ltd.

**Aughnacloy Golf Club,
99 Tullyvar Road,
Aughnacloy, Co. Tyrone.**

Location: Co. Tyrone.
Secretary: S.J. Houston
Tel: (028) 8555 7050.

9 hole inland course situated close to the Ballygawley roundabout. Includes a driving range.

COURSE INFORMATION

Par 68; SSS 67; Length 5,017 metres.
Visitors: Welcome.
Opening Hours: All day.
Ladies: Welcome.
Green Fees: Mon – Fri £12; Sat /Sun £15. Special rates for golfing societies.

Juveniles: Welcome.
Clubhouse Hours: 9.00 a.m.– late.
Clubhouse Dress: Casual.
Clubhouse Facilities: Bar, changing room, pool, meals.
Open Competitions: Several. Contact club for details.

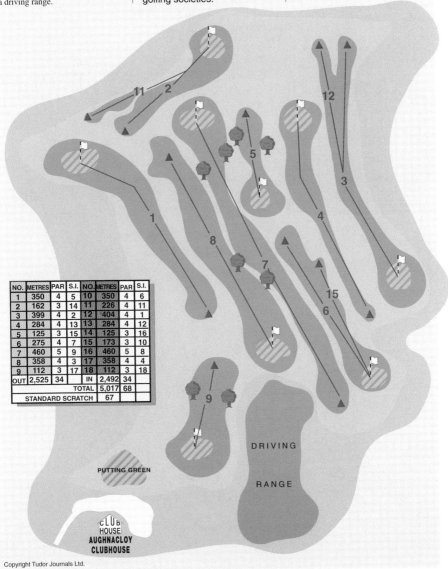

NO.	METRES	PAR	S.I.	NO.	METRES	PAR	S.I.
1	350	4	5	10	350	4	6
2	162	3	14	11	226	4	11
3	399	4	2	12	404	4	1
4	284	4	13	13	284	4	12
5	125	3	15	14	125	3	16
6	275	4	7	15	173	3	10
7	460	5	9	16	460	5	8
8	358	4	3	17	358	4	4
9	112	3	17	18	112	3	18
OUT	2,525	34		IN	2,492	34	
				TOTAL	5,017	68	
	STANDARD SCRATCH				67		

DRIVING

RANGE

PUTTING GREEN

CLUB HOUSE
**AUGHNACLOY
CLUBHOUSE**

Copyright Tudor Journals Ltd.

Benburb Valley Golf Course, Maydown Road, Benburb. BT71 7LJ
Tel: (028) 3754 9868

LOCATION: 8 miles from Armagh & Dungannon. 8 miles from M1 junction 14.
SECRETARY: Neville Pogue. Tel: (028) 3754 9868.
ARCHITECT: Robert Irwin.

Parkland course in a beautiful secluded rural setting with large undulating greens. Bounded on one side by the river Blackwater and maintained to a high standard. The club house is in a tastefully restored stone built corn mill.

COURSE INFORMATION

Par 72; SSS 70; Length 6,404 yards.
Visitors: Individuals & societies welcome 7 days a week.
Opening Hours: Dawn – Dusk.
Green Fees: £10 Mon – Fri; £13 Sat.Sun/Holidays.
Juveniles: Welcome at weekend.

Clubhouse Hours: 12 noon – 12 midnight.
Clubhouse Dress: Smart/Casual.
Clubhouse Facilities: Full pub and restaurant open to the public. Private function room with bar and food, for societies.
Open Competitions: Phone for details.

NO.	MEDAL YARDS	GEN. YARDS	PAR	S.I.	NO.	MEDAL YARDS	GEN. YARDS	PAR	S.I.
1	518	508	5	17	10	518	508	5	18
2	347	338	4	13	11	347	338	4	14
3	134	128	3	03	12	134	128	3	04
4	403	331	4	11	13	403	331	4	12
5	147	140	3	07	14	147	140	3	08
6	350	341	4	09	15	350	341	4	10
7	333	322	4	01	16	333	322	4	02
8	546	520	5	15	17	546	520	5	16
9	424	413	4	05	18	424	413	4	06
OUT	3202	3041	36		IN	3202	3041	36	
					TOTAL	6404	6082	72	
					STANDARD SCRATCH	70	70		

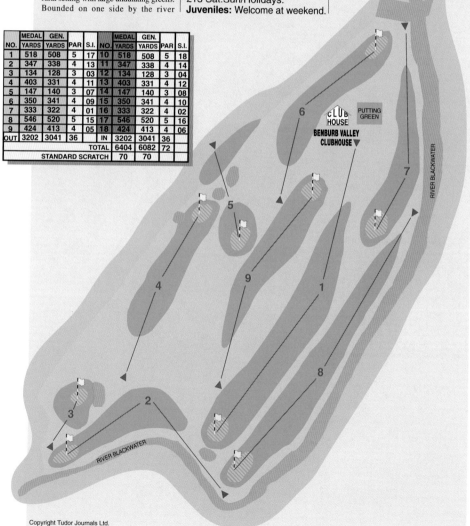

CLUB HOUSE
PUTTING GREEN
BENBURB VALLEY CLUBHOUSE
RIVER BLACKWATER

Copyright Tudor Journals Ltd.

**34 Springfield Lane,
Dungannon, Co. Tyrone
BT70 1QX.
Tel: (028) 8772 2098.**

LOCATION: 40 miles west of Belfast. 1 mile from Dungannon off B43 Donaghmore Road.
SECRETARY: Mr N. McGrath.

The Dungannon Golf Club founded in 1890 is a parkland course with tree – lined fairways. Here, golf is flourishing with a membership of about 600. A challenging and pleasant course and today the visitor could reiterate the entry in the old handbook that the greens are 'very good'.

COURSE INFORMATION

Par 72; SSS 69; Length 5,433 metres.
Visitors: Welcome any time.
Opening Hours: 9.00am – sunset.
Avoid: Saturday.
Ladies: Tuesday.
Green Fees: £18 Mon – Fri; £22 Sat / Sun / all public holidays. Ladies £16 Mon – Fri; £20 Sat / Sun / all public holidays. £4 Juveniles.
Juveniles: Mon – Fri before 5.00pm. Sat / Sun play after 4.00pm.

Clubhouse Dress: Casual.
Clubhouse Facilities:
Open every day
12.00noon – 11.00pm.
Open Competitions:
May – Aughnacloy putter.

NO.	METRES	PAR	S.I.	NO.	METRES	PAR	S.I.
1	477	5	11	10	347	4	12
2	161	3	15	11	183	3	8
3	558	5	1	12	492	5	16
4	341	4	7	13	338	4	2
5	332	4	13	14	379	4	6
6	129	3	5	15	283	4	14
7	488	5	17	16	90	3	18
8	390	4	3	17	554	5	4
9	146	3	9	18	358	4	10
OUT	3,022	36		IN	3,024	36	
				TOTAL	6,046	72	
				STANDARD SCRATCH	69		

DUNGANNON CLUBHOUSE

Copyright Tudor Journals Ltd.

**1 Kiln Street, Ecclesville
Demesne, Fintona,
Co. Tyrone.
Tel: (028) 8284 0777.
Fax: (028) 8284 1480.**

LOCATION: 8 miles from
Omagh.
HON. SECRETARY:
Vincent McCarney.

An attractive parkland course, its main
feature being a trout stream which
meanders through the course causing
many problems for badly executed
shots. Rated one of the top nine hole
courses in the province.

COURSE INFORMATION

**Par 72; SSS 70; Length
5,766 metres.**
Visitors: Welcome Mon – Fri.
Sat by arrangement.
Opening Hours: Daylight.
Ladies: Welcome Mondays.

Green Fees: £15 weekdays,
weekends, bank holidays;
£10 with member.
Juveniles: Welcome.
Saturday by prior arrangement.
Clubhouse Dress: Casual.
Clubhouse Facilities:
Full clubhouse facilities. Bar
snacks available. Meals on
request.
Open Competitions:
Telephone club for details.

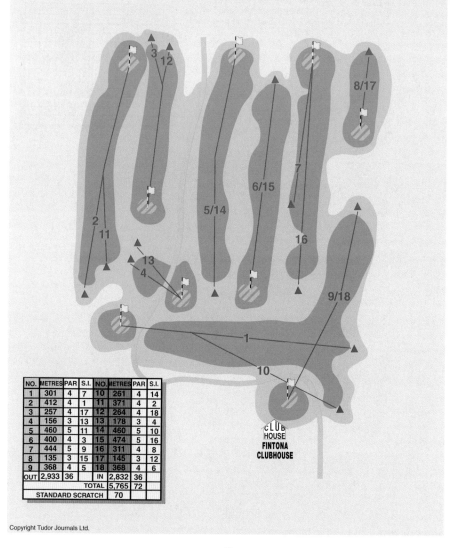

NO.	METRES	PAR	S.I.	NO.	METRES	PAR	S.I.
1	301	4	7	10	261	4	14
2	412	4	1	11	371	4	2
3	257	4	17	12	264	4	18
4	156	3	13	13	178	3	4
5	460	5	11	14	460	5	10
6	400	4	3	15	474	5	16
7	444	5	9	16	311	4	8
8	135	3	15	17	145	3	12
9	368	4	5	18	368	4	6
OUT	2,933	36		IN	2,832	36	
				TOTAL	5,765	72	
STANDARD SCRATCH		70					

CLUB
HOUSE
**FINTONA
CLUBHOUSE**

Copyright Tudor Journals Ltd.

200 Killymoon Road, Cookstown, Co. Tyrone BT80 8TW.
Tel/Fax: (028) 86763762
Email:
kgc1@btopenworld.com

LOCATION: South end of Cookstown, 1 mile from Dungannon roundabout.
HON. SECRETARY: Tom Doonan.
Tel: (028) 8676 3762 / 2976
PROFESSIONAL: Garry Chambers
GOLF SHOP: (028) 8676 3460.

A parkland course set on high ground with the soil being a sandy consistency. The 1st is the most picturesque hole, which is a dog leg skirting the woods of Killymoon Castle.

COURSE INFORMATION

Par 70; SSS 69; Length 5,488 metres.
Visitors: Welcome Tuesday to Friday all day, Saturday and Sunday. Must have current handicap. Members only Saturday before 3pm.
Ladies: Have priority on Thursdays.
Green Fees: £28 Tue – Fri all day (£20 with member); £22 Sat (after 3pm) & Sun (£14 with member). Juniors £6.

Juveniles: Monday – Friday £10 all day / 18 holes £6. Handicap Certificate required for open competitions. Society rates available.
Clubhouse Dress: Smart and casual.
Clubhouse Facilities: Full catering and bar facilities available.

NO.	WHITE METRES	YELL. METRES	PAR	S.I.	NO.	WHITE METRES	YELL. METRES	PAR	S.I.
1	472	467	5	10	10	343	317	4	11
2	143	139	3	16	11	171	158	3	7
3	458	436	5	2	12	391	382	4	3
4	331	323	4	14	13	156	143	3	17
5	301	292	4	6	14	444	435	5	15
6	281	268	4	18	15	478	470	5	1
7	181	172	3	4	16	175	163	3	13
8	153	139	3	8	17	359	345	4	5
9	332	314	4	12	18	327	300	4	9
OUT	2,652	2,550	35		IN	2,844	2,713	35	
					TOTAL	5,496	5,263	70	
					STANDARD SCRATCH	69	68		

KILLYMOON CLUBHOUSE

Copyright Tudor Journals Ltd.

**38 Golf Course Road,
Newtownstewart, Omagh,
Co. Tyrone BT78 4HU.
Tel: (028) 8166 1466.
Fax: (028) 8166 2506.**

LOCATION: 2 miles west of
Newtownstewart.
SECRETARY: Diane Cooke.
Tel: (028) 8166 1466.

Newtownstewart, although only an hour
and a half from Belfast lies in a different
world in the west of Tyrone. The course
is positioned at the confluence of the
Strule and the Glenelly rivers and at the
foot of the Sperrin Mountains.

COURSE INFORMATION

**Par 70; SSS 69; Length
5,341 metres.
Visitors:** Welcome any day
(telephone first).
Opening Hours: 8.30am – 8.30pm.
Avoid: Saturday and Sunday.
Ladies: Welcome Thursdays.
Green Fees: £12 Mon – Fri;
£17 Sat / Sun / all public holidays.
Juveniles: Welcome.
Clubhouse Dress: Casual except on
competition evenings.
Clubhouse Facilities: By prior
arrangements. Bar & Restaurant.
Open Competitions:
Open week: 20th – 28th July.
Competitions throughout the season,
ie. April–Sept.

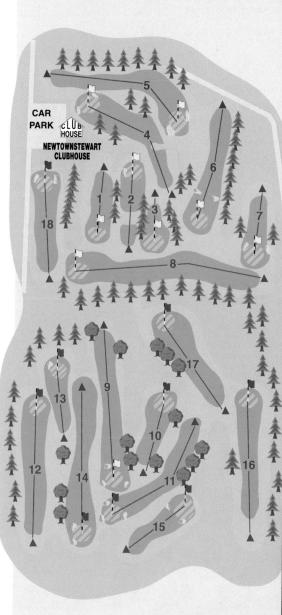

NO.	METRES	PAR	S.I.	NO.	METRES	PAR	S.I.
1	277	4	14	10	132	3	18
2	279	4	17	11	321	4	4
3	127	3	15	12	349	4	7
4	347	4	8	13	178	3	13
5	270	4	10	14	460	5	2
6	354	4	1	15	142	3	16
7	194	3	6	16	454	5	9
8	343	4	3	17	332	4	12
9	421	5	11	18	361	4	5
OUT	2,612	35		IN	2,729	35	
				TOTAL	5,341	70	
				STANDARD SCRATCH	69		

Copyright Tudor Journals Ltd.

Bunker and tree positions indicated.

NO.	MEDAL METRES	GEN. METRES	PAR	S.I.	NO.	MEDAL METRES	GEN. METRES	PAR	S.I.
1	316	324	4	7	10	139	147	3	16
2	283	281	4	17	11	250	257	4	14
3	188	198	3	13	12	280	305	4	10
4	440	467	5	11	13	115	147	3	8
5	348	377	4	3	14	385	390	4	2
6	483	506	5	5	15	471	484	5	6
7	322	335	4	9	16	298	305	4	4
8	362	380	4	1	17	155	164	3	12
9	261	310	4	15	18	268	273	4	18
OUT	3,003	3,178	37		IN	2,361	2,472	34	
					TOTAL	5,364	5,650		
					STANDARD SCRATCH	68	70		

**83a Dublin Road, Omagh,
Co. Tyrone, BT78 1HQ.
Tel: (028) 8224 3160 / 8224
1442.**

LOCATION: 1 mile from town centre
on main Omagh – Dublin Road.
HON. SECRETARY:
Joseph A. McElholm.
SECRETARY: Florence Caldwell.
ARCHITECT: Don Patterson.

Attractive course with four of the holes
bordering the River Drumragh. The
course is split on either side by the
Dublin road.

COURSE INFORMATION

**Par 71; SSS 70; Length
5,650 metres.**
Visitors: Individuals or societies
welcome.
Avoid: Tuesdays and Saturdays
Ladies: Ladies have priority on the
1st Tee all day Tuesday.
Green Fees: £12 Mon – Fri (£10 with
member) ; £18 Sat / Sun (£13 with
member). O.A.P and students £6
weekdays and £9 weekends.
Reduced rates for societies.
Clubhouse Hours: 11.30am – 1.30pm
and 4.30pm – 11.00pm.
Clubhouse Dress: Casual / neat.
Clubhouse Facilities:
Bar snacks available. Full catering by
arrangement with caterer.
Open Competitions: Open Week –
27th July – 4th Aug , plus various
other Open Days, (telephone for
details).

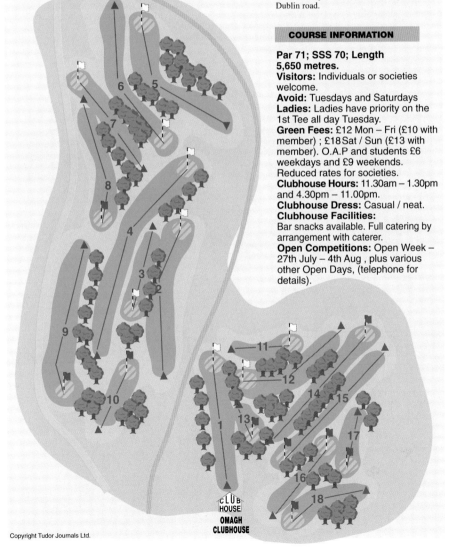

CLUB
HOUSE
**OMAGH
CLUBHOUSE**

Copyright Tudor Journals Ltd.

33 Ballycolman Road, Strabane, Co. Tyrone, BT82 9PH.
Tel: (028) 7138 2271/2007.
LOCATION: 1 mile from Strabane on the Dublin Road.
HON SECRETARY: Gerry Glover.
CLUB SECRETARY: Claire McNamee.
ARCHITECT: Desmond Hackett.

Rolling parkland intersected by the River Mourne, which runs alongside the 9th fairway, making the 9th one of the most picturesque and feared holes. The course is at the foothills of the Sperrin Mountains which provide an attractive i back-drop to the river falls. Agreed by professionals and low handicapped players as an excellent test of golf.

COURSE INFORMATION

Par 69; SSS 69; Length 5,610 metres.
Visitors: Welcome. Telephone appointment advisable.
Opening Hours: 8.00am – dusk.
Avoid: Saturday.
Ladies: Tuesday.
Green Fees: £15 Monday – Friday; (£12 with member); £17 Sat / Sun/ Public holidays (£15 with member). Societies by arrangement.

Juveniles: Welcome. Caddy service available by prior arrangement. Under 18's not allowed in clubhouse. Handicap Certificate required for competition.
Clubhouse Hours: Mon – Fri 2pm – 11pm, Saturday 11am – 11pm, Sunday 12noon – 10pm.
Clubhouse Dress: Informal but respectable.
Clubhouse Facilities: Cateing by arrangement only. Full bar.
Open Competitions: Many throughout the year, telephone for details.

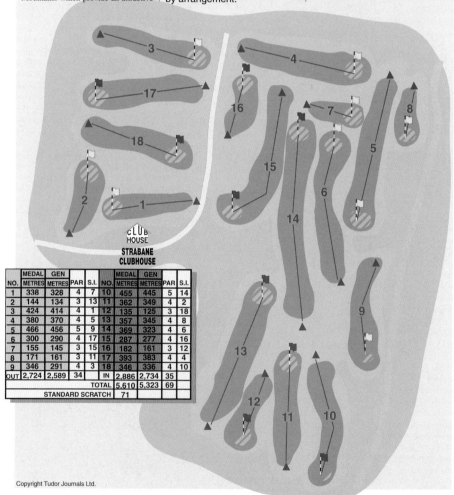

STRABANE CLUBHOUSE

NO.	MEDAL METRES	GEN METRES	PAR	S.I.	NO.	MEDAL METRES	GEN METRES	PAR	S.I.
1	338	328	4	7	10	455	445	5	14
2	144	134	3	13	11	362	349	4	2
3	424	414	4	1	12	135	125	3	18
4	380	370	4	5	13	357	345	4	8
5	466	456	5	9	14	369	323	4	6
6	300	290	4	17	15	287	277	4	16
7	155	145	3	15	16	182	161	3	12
8	171	161	3	11	17	393	383	4	4
9	346	291	4	3	18	346	336	4	10
OUT	2,724	2,589	34		IN	2,886	2,734	35	
					TOTAL	5,610	5,323	69	
	STANDARD SCRATCH					71			

Copyright Tudor Journals Ltd.

MUNSTER

BY JACK MAGOWAN

I f ever there was a name that sounded Irish, it's Ballybunion. And if ever there was a no-frills, absolutely true test of links golf, it is to be found on both Ballybunion courses lapped by the Atlantic and swept by winds off an exposed, sometimes inhospitable Shannon Estuary.

Asked to choose one course on which he would be happy to play for the rest of his life, Bob Sommers, a former editor of the U.S. *Golf Journal*, didn't hesitate.

"I'm still working on it," he declared. "But there are two in Ireland high up on my list – Ballybunion and Royal Co. Down. Both are rare jewels (and) difficult to separate. Ballybunion may be the more spectacular test, but County Down is the more relentlessly demanding. It never stops asking for first-class shot-making."

(continued on Page 275).

Great Southern Hotels

SHANNON

115 En-Suite Bedrooms with all modern
facilities for your comfort
Restaurant & Bar
Residents Car Park

Because of the Hotel's convenient location
to the passenger terminal at Shannon Airport,
this luxurious Hotel offers an ideal base for
golf enthusiasts visiting the Shannon region:

Within walking distance of Shannon Golf Club,
with Special Green Fee Rates available to Hotel guests.
Six miles from Dromoland Golf Club
Thirty miles from Lahinch Golf Club
Tel: (061) 471122 Fax: (061) 471982
E-Mail: res@shannon.gsh.ie

KILLARNEY

180 En-Suite Bedrooms with all modern facilities for
your comfort
Two Restaurants, including The new 'Peppers' á la
carte restaurant, Bar
Residents Car Park
Leisure Centre

Built in 1854 this elegant and old world Hotel
is located in the heart of Killarney town. The Hotel
is located:
Two miles from Killarney Golf Club
(Green fee concessions available Monday - Friday)
Seven miles from Beaufort Golf Club
Forty miles from Ballybunion Golf Club
Forty miles from Waterville Golf Club
Twenty eight miles from Tralee Golf Club

Tel: (064) 31262 Fax: (064) 31642
E-Mail: res@killarney.gsh.ie

Ballybunion's natural terrain makes it one of the top courses in Ireland and top ten in the world.

Mahon

Opening Hours:
Sunrise to Sunset
Green Fees:
€18.00 Monday - Friday
€19.00 Weekends/Bank Holidays
Pensioners €8.00 Monday - Friday
Juveniles: €8.00 Monday - Friday
Juniors: €8.00 Monday - Friday
Club hire available.
Clubhouse Facilities:
Bar and catering facilities available at
The Blackrock Inn.
Open throughout the year
Visitors welcome and should ring in advance
Telephone: (021) 4294280

CORK CITY COUNCIL
City Hall, Cork

The Celtic Ross Hotel,
Conference & Leisure Centre
"Simply Special"
Rosscarbery, West Cork
Overlooking Rosscarbery Bay

*67 Graciously Appointed Guest Rooms, Leisure Facilities,
Druids Restaurants, Library Bar, Old Forge Pub & Eaterie
Only 50 Minutes from Cork City on the N71.*

Quality 18 Hole Courses on our Doorstep Include:
The Newly Developed Old Head Golf Links - Par72
Skibbereen, Excellent for the High Handicapper - Par 71
Bandon, Beautiful Parkland Course - Par 70
Ideal for Midweek & Weekend Golf Breaks. Tailored packages
available. Green fees start from €25 (ex. Old Head, Kinsale).

*The Celtic Ross Hotel, Conference & Leisure Centre,
Rosscarbery, West Cork.*

*Tel: 023-48722. lo-call: 1850-272737 Fax: 023-48723.
e-mail: reservations@celticross.com www.celticrosshotel.com*

CORK & KERRY.
BEAT THE CLOCK!

WEEKEND RETURN FROM €195 CAR & FIVE ADULTS

SLEEP OVER ARRIVING AT 7am

SAVE OVER 400 MILES OF DRIVING

For ferry passage, holiday brochure and reservations, telephone

— 01792 —
456116
or contact your local travel agent

SWANSEA CORK FERRIES
MILES AHEAD OF THE THE REST

Mountain View Guesthouse & Apartments

The highest standard of accommodation by friendly and efficient staff.

- Close to town centre.
- All Guest bedrooms en-suite, satellite T.V., Tea/coffee.
- Two bedroom self contained apartments.
- On the Ring of Kerry scenic route.
- Close to Killeen, O'Mahony's Point, Lackbane, Beaufort, Ross and Dunloe golf course.

Muckross Road, Killarney, Co Kerry
Tel: 064 33293 Fax: 064 37295 OR
Tel: 051 877910 Fax: 051 844499
E-mail: tguerin@indigo.ie

AA ☆☆☆ **TRIDENT HOTEL KINSALE** **RAC** ☆☆☆

Three Star, 58 bedroom Hotel, splendidly located on the waterfront of Kinsale.

Old Head Golf Links Championship Course and Kinsale Golf Club's 18 and 9 hole courses less than 8 miles from the Trident Hotel. Fota Island, Douglas and Lee Valley Golf Clubs within easy driving distance.

All inclusive packages available with reduced Green Fees.

The Trident Hotel, World's End, Kinsale, Co. Cork.
Tel: (0035321) 4772301 Fax: (0035321) 4774173
www.tridenthotel.com • E-mail: info@tridenthotel.com

Sommers then agreed with me on one score. To play golf at Ballybunion is to slide into a blissful vacuum happy in the knowledge that if you hear the phone ring, you'll know the call will be for somebody else! Waterville, Killarney, Lahinch, Tralee, Adare, Ballybunion and now the Head of Kinsale ... they string out like green pearls on a jeweller's tray as the loveliest, most inviting part of Munster welcomes more and more golfers every season.

Today, Ireland's South-West is as closely linked to the Royal and Ancient game as The Curragh is to horses, or Blarney to the Stone. Like O'Connell Street at rush-hour, I once said of the first tee at Killarney, and nothing has changed. The Killeen and Mahony's Point courses now host 40,000 visitors a year, a record for any European club and worth a staggering £1 million-plus in green fees alone. Small wonder some less

Waterside tranquillity at Kenmare Golf Club.

𝓑𝓻𝓸𝓸𝓴 𝓛𝓸𝓭𝓰𝓮 𝓗𝓸𝓽𝓮𝓵
KILLARNEY

Where a warm and friendly welcome awaits you...

Situated in the heart of Killarney town – off High Street. Family owned and run, on over an acre of landscaped gardens with private parking on grounds.

The Counihan family offer traditional hospitality, delivered by professionals.

Unwind and enjoy an aperitif before dinner in our Residents Bar. The Brook Restaurant boasts a fine and varied menu to suit all tastes.

Lift and wheelchair facilities.

High Street, Killarney, Co. Kerry.
Tel: (064) 31800 Fax: (064) 35001
Email: brooklodgekillarney@eircom.net   www.brooklodgekillarney.com

AGHADOE HEIGHTS HOTEL
Lakes of Killarney – County Kerry

Golf Spoken Nightly

Overlooking Killarney Golf Club and within driving distance of Ballybunion, Old Head, Waterville, Tralee and Dooks, this award winning Five Star hotel offers the epitome in Luxury, Fine Dining and Personal Service. A dedicated staff are on hand to ensure every golfing need, from tee times to the 19th Hole, are anticipated.

"Enhancing a Tradition of Excellence"
RAC Blue Ribbon

Lakes of Killarney, Co. Kerry, Ireland
Tel: 064 31766. Fax: 064 31345
info@aghadoeheights.com

KILLIMER TARBERT FERRIES   Shannon Ferry Ltd.

When touring Ireland's Shannon Region remember that a 20 minute journey by ferry will take you from Tarbert in County Kerry across the Shannon estuary to Killimer in County Clare, or vice versa, saving you 137km (85 miles) from ferry terminal to terminal. The ferry leaves Killimer every hour on the hour and Tarbert every hour on the half hour. No reservations are necessary and you buy your ticket onboard.

From Killimer, County Clare		Sailing Times		From Tarbert, County Kerry		Sailing Times	
Departure on the hour		*First*	*Last*	**Departure on the half hour**		*First*	*Last*
April to September	Weekdays	07.00H	21.00H	April to September	Weekdays	07.30H	21.30H
	Sundays	09.00H	21.00H		Sundays	09.30H	21.30H
October to March	Weekdays	07.00H	19.00H	October to March	Weekdays	07.30H	19.30H
	Sundays	10.00H	19.00H		Sundays	10.30H	19.30H

Over 30 sailings a day • Sailings everyday of the year except Christmas Day •
The direct route to and from Kerry and Clare • Visitor Centre • Shop • Restaurant • Bridging the Best of Ireland's West

Telephone: 065–905 3124. Facsimile 065-905 3125. Email: enquiries@shannonferries.com Web: shannonferries.com

glamorous neighbours must be green with envy.

Irish golf has a liberating sense of space and freedom, never more so than on the first course Arnold Palmer built outside America – Tralee. It's new, it's scenic, it's tough, and the wind is as fresh as tomorrow's milk. Banna Strand, where *Ryan's Daughter* was filmed, is only a nine iron shot away from the third green, an elusive target on what is the classiest of short holes. Tralee's wind-swept dunes are impressive, yet no bigger than a mole hill compared to those at Ballybunion. Here, as *Golf World* once said, "you're driving over them, into them, up them, and on to them," which might have prompted King Christy's famous remark: "Anybody who breaks 70 on either of these courses on a windy day is playing better than he knows how!".

Full marks, then, to a couple of amateurs called Mulcare and McGimpsey. Record-holder Pat Mulcare (66) was the only man ever to better McGimpsey's gale-lashed round of 67 in the Irish Championship of 1979, the day on which Garth shot five birdies on his way to a flawless outward half of 31. Freak stuff.

Tom Watson fell in love with Ballybunion the first time he ever saw it, and so did the late, great Jimmy Bruen. A burly, overweight Bruen was only 17 and still at school when he won the 'Close' there about 12 months before playing in Britain's winning Walker Cup side of 1938. Like Mulcare he lost a grave fight against cancer and died at the age of 50.

Nobody ever swung a golf club the way Bruen did, or with such stunning effect.

Park Hotel Kenmare

KENMARE, CO. KERRY, IRELAND
TELEPHONE: 064-41200, FAX: 064-41402
E-mail: info@parkkenmare.com.   www.parkkenmare.com

18 hole Golf Course on site.
Ring of Kerry Golf and Country Club 4 miles.
Ideal base for Waterville, Old Head and Killarney.

TODDIES
RESTAURANT & SUITES

Toddies – Kinsale's best restaurant is a must before or after your visit to the old head. Also suites with harbour views for your overnight stay.

TODDIES RESTAURANT & SUITES
Eastern Road · Kinsale · Co. Cork
Telephone: 00 353 (0) 21 4777769
E-mail: toddies@eircom.net
Website: toddieskinsale.com/

Killeen House Hotel

If there were no such thing as Golf, there would be no such place as the Killeen House Hotel!

This 23-bedroom (8 of them deluxe 'Championship' rooms), 3 star Hotel specialises in Golf to such an extent that it has the only Pub in the World that accepts Golf balls as Legal Tender! The Award-winning Dining room will serve full Irish Breakfast and Dinner at any hour to suit Golfer's tee-times.

Located less than 10 minutes drive from Killarney Town centre, the Killeen House is the ideal place to base yourself when playing such magnificent Courses as Killarney, Ballybunion, Waterville, Tralee and Dooks. We would even be delighted to book all your Golf needs for you!

Go on, do the smart thing and contact us today for full details.

We look forward to extending the 'Hostility of the House' to you!

KILLEEN HOUSE HOTEL
Aghadoe, Lakes of Killarney, Co. Kerry
Tel: 353-64-31711 Fax: 353-64-31811
e-mail: charming@indigo.ie
www.killeenhousehotel.com

Castlerosse GOLF CLUB
HOTEL AND LEISURE CENTRE
Lower Lake, Killarney, Co. Kerry.
Tel: 064-31144 / 31031.
Email: castler@iol.ie.
Web: www.castlerosse-killarney.com

Set on mature parkland, the course commands majestic views of Lough Leane, Killarney's lower lake and the Magillicuddys Ireland's highest mountains

The golf shop and locker rooms are located right beside the 20 metre swimming pool and fitness centre at the Castlerosse Hotel and Mulligan's Pub, overlook the course.

Eviston House Hotel, Killarney
"The Best Value in Town"

Located in the centre of Killarney yet only minutes from championship golf the Eviston House is the ideal location for a golfing holiday.

• Special rates for golfers • Late bar & early breakfast!
• Tee times & transport arranged
• Luxuriously appointed ensuite rooms
• Enjoy traditional music in the famous Danny Mann pub

Tel: 353 64 31640
Fax: 353 64 33685
Email: evishtl@eircom.net

Best Western
A Best Western Hotel

The parkland course of Kinsale Golf Club.

"Hogan and Cotton could stir the imagination and command attention," wrote Pat Ward-Thomas in *Masters Of Golf*. "And Thomson and Snead could create an awareness of beauty ...... but the golf of none of these mortals had a greater dramatic appeal for me than that of James Bruen, citizen of Cork."

Ballesteros, Nicklaus, Woods, John Daly — Bruen would have matched them all for magnetism and power-play. Jimmy hit the ball like he had a grudge against it, and in a style that was entirely his own. The 'Bruen loop' was his copyright, club-head drawn back so much outside the line of flight that at the top of the swing it would be pointed in the direction of the tee-box. The club was then whipped inside and down into the hitting area with animal ferocity.

It's no exaggeration to say there must have been a foot or more between Bruen's arcs. Anybody who didn't know who he was would have been inclined to scoff, Ward-Thomas used to say, but not for long. The action of his hands was identical to that of cracking a whip and was the source of tremendous power.

(continued on Page 283).

Kenny

Knitwear Manufacturers

Stockists of Waterford Crystal, Galway Irish Dreselen, Belleek, Donegal, Royal Tara, Aynsley, Jewellery and Pottery. Art Gallery, Irish Furniture.

A Family Factory Outlet
Mail Order Specialists

**Kenny Woollen Mills,
Main St., Lahinch, Co. Clare.**
Tel: 065-7081400 Fax: 065-7081473
E-mail: klahinch@iol.ie

Crystal Springs

AA

❖ All rooms with private bathrooms, TV, radio, tea/coffee facilities, hairdryers, iron press, mini fridge and direct dial phones, all non smoking.
❖ Close to Killarney town centre (10 mins. walk)
❖ Local attractions are Muckross House and Gardens, Torc Waterfall, Ross Castle, Ladies View, Moll's Gap and the Gap of Dunloe near Kate Karney's Cottage, all 10-15 mins.
❖ For a close up view of Crystal Springs please see our website at:
http://homepage.eircom.net/~doors/
❖ Ample safe parking (off street), Golf Courses, Riding Stables close by, Fishing on location
❖ Traditional bars and Restaurants
❖ Trout River running behind B&B

Ballycasheen, Killarney, Co. Kerry.
Tel: 064 33272.
Email: info@crystalspringsbb.com
crystalsprings@eircom.net

Woodville Lodge

◉ Luxury Guest Accommodaion in scenic Fossa, approx. 2 miles from Killarney
◉ 5 minutes from Golf Club
◉ Beautiful views of Killarney lakes & mountains
◉ All rooms en suite with TV, Tea/Coffee making facilities
◉ Breakfast menu

Fossa, Killarney, Co. Kerry
☎ 064 36381 © 087 6179347
ⓔ woodvillelodge@eircom.net

Garnish House

A delightful Victorian style home located on Western Road, Cork City. 5 min. walk from the City Centre.

Luxury rooms (some with jacuzzi baths), all en suite with colour T.V. and tea-making facilities. Self-catering suites & studios also available Car parking provided.

Superb cuisine is always on offer with 30 different breakfast options.

Western Road, Cork City.
Opposite University College Cork.
Tel: 021-4275111 Fax: 021-4273872
E-mail: garnish@iol.ie
Web: www.garnish.ie
Reg. I.T.B. & A.A. R.A.C. 4 diamond.

Waterville, situated at the furthest extent of Kerry's peninsulas,
has possibly the best par-5 hole (11th) in Ireland.

Dromoland Golf & Country Club

Built in the late 16th century, Dromoland Castle forms a majestic backdrop to the very challenging and most enjoyable course that bears its name.

Dromoland Golf & Country Club is situted on 375 unspoilt acres of lush wooded parkland enhanced by the rushing River Rine which becomes the out of bounds for three of the course's most breathtaking holes.

An 18 hole course since 1985 with a par of 71, Dromoland Golf & Country Club has earned an enviable reputation both for the quality of golf and for the amenities at the new Club House which include a fully equipped Health & LeisureCentre and the brasserie style Fig Tree Restaurant. The golf course at Dromoland is a mere 10 minute drive from Shannon Airport.

Newmarket-on-Fergus, Co. Clare.
Tel: (061) 368 444

The Lost Ball
B E D & B R E A K F A S T

❖ Situated 2km west of Killarney Town on Ring of Kerry Road
❖ Guest Accommodation
❖ Rooms ensuite
❖ TV and Tea/Coffee
❖ Private Parking ❖ Adjacent to one of Killarney's three 18 Hole Championship Golf Courses, Riding Stables, Leisure Centre, Boating, Walking, Fishing, 5 minutes drive from Town Centre.

Gortoe, Killarney, Co. Kerry.

T: 064-37449
email:thelostball@eircom.net
website:www.thelostball.com

The John Barleycorn Hotel

A fine 18th century, residence beside Cork city yet where country charm abounds.

Riverstown, Glanmire, Cork.

Tel: (021) 482 1499 Fax: (021) 482 1221

19TH C Subtropical Gardens
❖
Extensive Collection of Exotic Plants
❖
Open: Daily 11am - 5pm from Easter until end September or by arrangement
❖
Beautiful walks for all the family
❖
Admission: Adults €4.50 OAP/Student €3.50 Children €2.50
❖
Vegtables and fruit from our organic garden
❖
Bed & Breakfast available. Houses for rent on estate - all modern facilities

For further details:
Tel: 066-76176
Fax: 066-76108
Email: info@glanleam.com

GLANLEAM HOUSE
SUBTROPICAL GARDENS
Once the seat of the Knights of Kerry

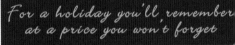

For a holiday you'll remember at a price you won't forget

With hotels from Mayo to Galway to Clare to Limerick to Kerry Lynch Hotels' Golf Inclusive breaks have never been such great value

Choose between city breaks, country retreats and coastal havens with prices from €163 per person sharing for 2 nights Bed and Breakfast, 1 Dinner and 1 Round of Golf.

Located throughout the West of Ireland, Lynch Hotels offer you a choice of superb hotels, each partnered with a choice of superior 18-hole golf courses guaranteed to challenge even the most experienced golfer!!!

Golf Inclusive Breaks

 LYNCH HOTELS
www.lynchotels.com

For further details and reservations 'phone Lynch Hotels on 065 68 2300 (open 7 days) or email us golf@lynchotels.com

WEST COUNTY HOTEL, ENNIS. CLARE INN HOTEL, DROMOLAND.
OCEAN COVE HOTEL, KILKEE BAY. SOUTH COURT HOTEL, LIMERICK.
HAYDEN'S GATEWAY HOTEL, BALLINASLOE.
GALWAY BAY GOLF & COUNTRY CLUB HOTEL, ORANMORE.
BREAFFY HOUSE HOTEL, CASTLEBAR.
ASSOCIATE HOTELS: RATHKEALE HOUSE HOTEL, RATHKEALE.
VICTORIA HOUSE HOTEL, KILLARNEY.

Henry Cotton once asked Bruen to try swinging normally, and Jimmy hit the ball as well as any scratch player would. Not with the same clubhead speed, however, the key to his great length, especially off the tee.

No rough or hazard was ever tough enough to bold Bruen, yet you could never have said he was erratic.

"There was an almost hypnotic quality about his play," wrote Ward-Thomas. "Its very strangeness was compelling; its power and unusual beauty fascinating. No course, however long or difficult, was safe from destruction when Bruen teed it up. There will never be another like him!"

It was soon after winning the Amateur Championship in 1946 at Royal Birkdale that Jimmy felt a sudden pain in his right wrist while lifting tiles in his garden at home. The explosive violence of a unique but gifted swing had taken its toll. He was never the same player again, and quit tournament golf on the day he lost to Joe Carr in the semi-finals of the Irish Amateur at Killarney. The year: 1963.

All great golf courses are remorseless in the face of sloppy play. Hit the ball badly and the likes of Ballybunion, Lahinch, Waterville or Adare will devour you. Hit it

(continued on Page 287).

Famous and challanging test of golf – Lahinch, Co. Clare.

Adare Manor

HOTEL & GOLF RESORT

Enjoy the glamourous life of Adare Manor, a RAC 5 Star hotel. Home for the past two centuries to the Earls of Dunraven, Adare Manor has been lovingly transformed into a world-class hotel with sixty-four luxury bedrooms. Located only 20 miles from Shannon Airport in Ireland's most picturesque village of Adare, the Manor offers the finest of Irish hospitality. Relax with afternoon tea in the drawing room, a candlelit dinner in the dining room, or simply enjoy fireside drinks in the library or Tack Room.

Adare Golf Club is just a nine iron from the front door of the Manor. An 18 hole course designed by Robert Trent Jones, Sr, it measures 7,138 yards from the championship tees. The golf course has three lakes, including a 14 acre lake that anchors the front nine, while the River Maigue meanders through the back nine creating a sense of beauty and challenge.

Within the 840 acre estate of Adare Manor, the indoor facilities include a heated swimming pool & fitness centre. Outdoor activities include horseriding, clay pigeon shooting & fishing. The 'Spa @ Adare Manor' is the latest addition to this 5 star Resort.

Come and experience the beauty and challenge of Adare Manor. Whether it's a fairytale holiday or long weekend, let us pamper you in old world style.

Tel: (353) 6139 6566, Fax: (353) 6139 6124
RAC & Bord Failte ***** approved. USA toll-free reservations: 1-800-462-3273 (Go Adare)

Teeing off at Dooks in County Kerry.

Darby O'Gill's

COUNTRY HOUSE HOTEL KILLARNEY

Situated just outside beautiful Killarney in the heart of the Kingdom of Kerry - it is an ideal spot for individuals or large groups to stop and enjoy the atmosphere of an Irish country house hotel. Ideal golf hotel newly refurbished and extended. New extension - 12 bedrooms. (25 bedrooms in total).

Lissivigeen, Mallow Road, Killarney.

Tel: 064 - 34168. **Fax:** 064 - 36794. **email:** darbyogill@eircom.net
Web: www.darbyogillskillarney.com

Glendalough House
County Kerry

Glendalough is an excellent base from which to tour the Ring of Kerry and Dingle Peninsula with their numerous golf courses. Killarney Dooks, Waterville, Ballybunion, Tralee, Gap of Dunloe etc. Tee times arranged. After a days golf enjoy delicious Irish cuisine in a victorian country house atmosphere.

Season: March 01 to November 30

B&B € 69 pps • Single Supplement € 20 • Dinner € 35

Caragh Lake, Co Kerry
Tel/Fax: (+353) 66 9769156
E-mail: jrb@glendaloughhouse.com
Further information look up www.glendaloughhouse.com

abbey lodge

• ★★★★ GUESTHOUSE •

Muckross Road, Killarney, Co. Kerry.
Tel: 00353 64 34193. Fax: 00353 64 35877
email: abbeylodgekly@eircom.net
Web: www.abbey-lodge.com

...anywhere else is a compromise

ROBEEN HOUSE

Robeen House is a purpose built Guesthouse where traditional hospitality and courteous personal attention awaits you.

Situated on the Muckross Road, 5 minutes from Killarney Town Centre.

✦ All rooms en suite with power shower, direct dial telephones, tea/coffee facilities, hairdryer & TV.
✦ TV lounge ✦ Private car park
✦ Wheel chair facilities
✦ Close to Killarney National Park, Ross Castle Muckross House, Golfing, Walking.

Muckross Road, Killarney, Co. Kerry.
Tel: 064 32326. Fax: 064 32334.
Email: robeenhouse@eircom.net
www.robeenhouse.com

WOODLAWN HOUSE

(off Muckross Road)

Woodlawn Road Killarney Co. Kerry

Tel: 064 37844. Fax: 064 36116
Email: awrenn@eircom.net
Web: www.kerry-insight.com/woodlawn-house/

The Killarney Oaks Inn

Enter a warm, welcoming world of true Irish hospitality, high standard of service and a delightful informal atmosphere.

A well appointed restaurant with views of the internal gardens. The restaurant is home to both local and international cuisine.

Muckross Road, Killarney, Co. Kerry.
Tel: 064 37600. Fax: 064 37619.
e-mail: info@killarneyoaks.com Web: www.killarneyoaks.co

well, and you'll be rewarded.

Nobody talks of Waterville without mentioning John Mulcahy, the Irish American visionary who gave the course, and resort, a new dimension 30 years ago.

There are so many good holes at Waterville that it's impossible to think of a weak hole. Liam Higgins, the professional there and another prodigious hitter of the ball, once holed out at the 350-yard 16th on his way to a round of 65, but Liam, now 50-plus and playing the Seniors' Tour, almost stands alone among those who can boast of breaking 70. Raymond Floyd still thinks Waterville deserves a top-ten world rating, so who are we to disagree. The eleventh there might be the best par-5 hole in Ireland!

Adare, too, is special, not only for its length (7000 yards plus) but superb hotel.

The Killarney Club enjoys two excellent courses sharing the majestic mountains of Macgillycuddy's Reeks and the atmospheric Lough Leane.

Midleton Park Hotel

Situated on the N25 East Cork road, just 16 km from Cork city, Midleton Park Hotel specialises in golf packages tailored to suit your every requirement. Just minutes away from championship golf courses Cork Golf Club, Fota Island Golf Club and other gems such as Harbour Point, East Cork and Water Rock Golf Club. Midleton Park hotel is the ideal hotel for your Golfer's paradise getaway. (Tee-off times and coach transfers can be arranged) To round off the perfect day,

Midleton, Co. Cork
Tel: 021-4631767
Fax: 021-4631605
E-mail: sales@midletonparkhotel.com

Midleton Park Hotel offers you the ideal place to relax with its luxurious recently refurbished guest rooms and award winning restaurant where you can sample local cuisine and fresh catches from scenic Ballycotton. For an informal atmosphere our "Cafe Bar" offers an extensive casual dining menu and allows you to indulge in the 'Spirit of Ireland' by sampling the famous Jameson Whiskey and Midleton Rare which is distilled here in Midleton.

Come join us
and discover a welcome as warm as the memories you will take back.

The Kingsley Hotel
Concorde Hotels Worldwide

Victoria Cross, Cork
Tel: + 353 21 4800 555
Fax: + 353 21 4800526
E-mail: resv@kingsleyhotel.com
Web: www.kingsleyhotel.com

Corks Premier Hotel, situated at Victoria Cross Cork, on the N. 22 to Killarney.

Standard, Deluxe and Suites.

A Golfers paradise within easy access to Fota, Old head, Harbour Point, Cork Golf Club, Lee Valley 1 hour from Killarney and Ring of Kerry Golf courses.

Tee times, Cadding, Transportation by road or Air arranged by The Hotels Concierge Desk.

On site Helipad
GNS: N5153.62
W00830.42

There's water and wood everywhere on this Robert Trent Jones' creation, which has already been ranked among Britain's top 10 new courses, a timely bonus.

American styled Shannon is so close to the aiport that you can almost count the rivets on a 'jumbo' coming in to land, but the trees here also grow tall and are magnificent, as indeed they are at Fota Island, and Kinsale's wonderful new gem.

Harbour Point, Muskerry, Douglas and Fota Island – how lucky Cork golfers are to have four courses of such quality right on their doorstep!

Golf is a passion, somebody said, that doesn't make a lot of sense, and in Ireland it's completely mad. Was he thinking of Lahinch, I wonder, and the goats there?. For Lahinch is where the barometer on the wall has no hands; just a note saying 'See Goats'. If they are grazing close to the clubhouse, that's a weather warning — wind and rain is on the horizon. Away from the clubhouse, and it'll be a bright and clear day, no rain gear needed.

Don't bank on it. Once a visiting golfer, happy that the goats were nicely placed, set off in short sleeves and summer slacks for a round that was soon washed out by a thunder shower.

"What happened?", he frowned. "How could the goats have got it so badly wrong?"

"Sorry," said the barman "We've just had a delivery of new goats!" Which sums up the laid-back charm of Irish golf very nicely.

The **Meadowlands** HOTEL

OAKPARK – TRALEE

Incorporating

An Pota Stoir *Restaurant*
Specialising in the Freshest of Locally Caught Seafood and Shellfish

Johnny Franks *Bar*
Bar Food Served Daily
Entertainment Wednesday & Saturday Night, Sunday Evening

Air conditioned rooms – de-luxe suites available. Easy parking facilities – wheelchair friendly hotel. Small conferences and meetings catered for.

Leisure Centre Open September 2002

EXPERIENCE AN EXPERIENCE

For Further Details Telephone (066) 7180444
Fax: (066) 7180964 • E-mail: medlands@iol.ie

GOLF DAYS
TWELFTH EDITION
GOLF COURSES OF IRELAND
FULL DETAILS OF 361 COURSES
order one for a friend!
www.golf-days.com

Get all the visitor information you need before you leave home.

www.visitor**days**.com

Dublin & The East • South West Ireland • South East Ireland • West Coast of Ireland • Northern Ireland • London • Yorkshire • Edinburgh • Glasgow • Central Scotland & Highlands

INFORMATION AT YOUR FINGERTIPS

www.visitor**days**.com

DROMOLAND CASTLE

Newmarket-on-Fergus, Co. Clare.
Tel: Hotel (061) 368144 or Golf Club (061) 368444.

LOCATION: Six miles North of Shannon Airport. Eight miles South of Ennis.
SECRETARY: John O'Halloran. Tel: (061) 368444.
ARCHITECT: Brook L. Wiggington.

This course became affiliated to the Golfing Union of Ireland although it has been in use for some considerable time. It is a course of character with natural lakes and streams, which come into play on a number of holes. Set in the grounds of Dromoland Castle Hotel the course is particularly wooded and very attractive.

COURSE INFORMATION

Par 71; SSS 71; Length 5719 metres.
Visitors: Welcome at all times.
Opening Hours: Daylight hours.
Ladies: Welcome.
Green Fees: €50 Mon – Fri; Sat, Sun & Bank Hols €60. For societies €40 Monday – Friday, €45 Saturday & Sunday. €75 for golf and meal. Caddy service, club hire and buggies available.
Juveniles: Welcome. Lessons available; Club Hire available: Caddy Service available.
Clubhouse Hours: 9.00am – 10.00pm.
Clubhouse Dress: Smart / casual.
Clubhouse Facilities: Full catering and bar, plus gym and leisure facilities. Health & Beauty salon.
Open Competitions: Ladies Open Day, Sunday 18th August.

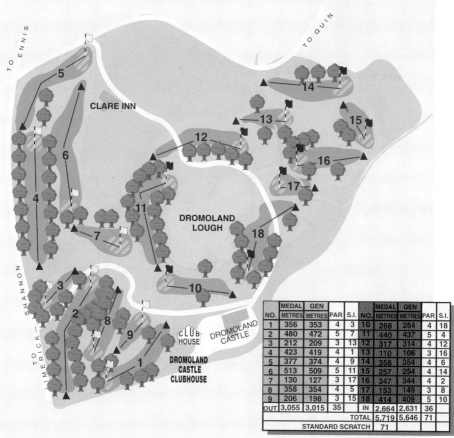

NO.	MEDAL METRES	GEN METRES	PAR	S.I.	NO.	MEDAL METRES	GEN METRES	PAR	S.I.
1	356	353	4	3	10	268	264	4	18
2	480	472	5	7	11	440	437	5	4
3	212	209	3	13	12	317	314	4	12
4	423	419	4	1	13	110	106	3	16
5	377	374	4	9	14	358	354	4	6
6	513	509	5	11	15	257	254	4	14
7	130	127	3	17	16	347	344	4	2
8	358	354	4	5	17	153	149	3	8
9	206	198	3	15	18	414	409	5	10
OUT	3,055	3,015	35		IN	2,664	2,631	36	
					TOTAL	5,719	5,646	71	
					STANDARD SCRATCH	71			

Copyright Tudor Journals Ltd.

**East Clare Golf Club,
Coolreagh, Bodyke.
Co. Clare.
Tel: (061) 921322.
Fax: (061) 921388.**

LOCATION: One and a half
miles from Bodyke Village,
situated among the rolling
hills and lakes of East Clare.
SEC MANAGER: MLO·HANLON.
Tel: (061) 921322.
ARHITECT: Arthur Spring.

All weather challenging parkland 18-
hole course with special water
features, designed with the players
satisfaction, comfort and safety in
mind.

COURSE INFORMATION

**Par 71; SSS 71; Length
5,922 metres.**
Visitors: Pay as you play.
Opening Hours: As
clubhouse.

Ladies: Welcome.
Juveniles: Permitted.
Green Fees: Weekdays €25;
weekends €30.
Clubhouse Hours:
Winter 9am – 4.30pm;
Summer 7.30am – 10pm.
Clubhouse Dress: Informal.
Clubhouse Facilities: Light
snacks always available, full
catering by arrangement.
Open Competitions: Every
Thurs from April 4th to mid Sept.

NO.	YARDS	PAR	S.I.	NO.	YARDS	PAR	S.I.
1	396	4		10	365	4	
2	204	3		11	398	4	
3	398	4		12	515	5	
4	189	3		13	197	3	
5	525	5		14	358	4	
6	510	5		15	432	4	
7	415	4		16	521	5	
8	175	3		17	191	3	
9	440	4		18	435	4	
OUT	3,252	35		IN	3,412	36	
				TOTAL	6,664	71	
		STANDARD SCRATCH			71		

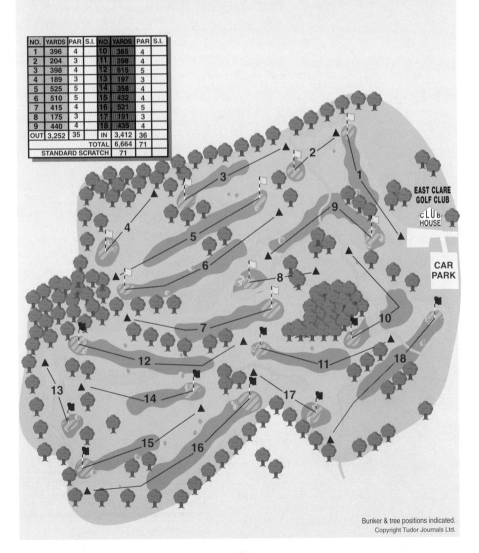

Bunker & tree positions indicated.
Copyright Tudor Journals Ltd.

**Drumbiggle, Ennis,
Co. Clare.
Tel: (065) 6824074.
Fax: (065) 6841848.
Email: egc@tinet.ie**

LOCATION: One mile west of
town.
HON SECRETARY: Ray O' Sullivan.
PROFESSIONAL: Martin Ward.
Tel: (065) 6865415.
MANAGER: Niall O'Donnell

Rolling parkland course with tree-lined
narrow fairways. The course overlooks
the town of Ennis to the east and the
green cliffs of Clare to the west.

COURSE INFORMATION

**Par 71; SSS 69; Length
5,592 metres.
Visitors:** Welcome Mon – Fri.
Opening Hours:
9.00am – sunset.
Avoid: Tuesday after 3.00pm.
Green Fees: €30.
Juveniles: Welcome (half
green fee is playing with an
adult). Lessons available;
Club Hire available; Caddy
service available by prior
arrangements. Telephone
appointment required.

Clubhouse Hours:
9.00am – 11.00pm.
Clubhouse Dress: Casual.
Clubhouse Facilities:
Snacks and á la carte.
Open Competitions:
Open Week August.
Handicap Certificate required
for Open Competitions.

NO.	METRES	PAR	S.I.	NO.	METRES	PAR	S.I.
1	312	4	5	10	351	4	12
2	114	3	18	11	310	4	11
3	305	4	13	12	420	5	2
4	250	4	15	13	158	3	16
5	333	4	7	14	383	4	3
6	419	4	1	15	299	4	6
7	140	3	17	16	176	3	14
8	360	4	4	17	304	4	8
9	492	5	9	18	466	5	10
OUT	2,725	35		IN	2,867	36	
				TOTAL	5,592	71	
	STANDARD SCRATCH				69		

Copyright Tudor Journals Ltd.

Kilkee Golf Club,
East End,
Kilkee, Co. Clare.
Tel: (065) 9056048.
Fax: (065) 9056977.
Email: kilkeegolfclub@eircom.net
www.kilkeegolfclub.ie

LOCATION: Kilkee.
SECRETARY: Patrick McInerney
Tel: (065) 9056048
ARCHITECT: Eddie Hackett.

Kilkee Golf Club is proud of its 18 hole Links. Situated on the edge of the Atlantic Ocean in a most spectacular setting overlooking Moore Bay and its famous horse-shoe beach.

COURSE INFORMATION

Par 69; SSS 68; Length 5,862 yards.
Visitors: Welcome.
Opening Hours: Sunrise – sunset.
Ladies: Welcome.
Green Fees: From €25; Half price with member.

Juveniles: Welcome. Lessons available by prior arrangement; Clubs andtrolleys for hire; Caddy service available.
Clubhouse Hours: 9.00am – closing.
Clubhouse Dress: Casual.
Clubhouse Facilities: Comfortable bar / snack bar, Restaurant with view over Kilkee Bay and Golf shop.
Open Competitions: During June, July and August. Handicap Certificate required for Open Competitions.

NO.	CHAMP METRES	PAR	S.I.	NO.	CHAMP METRES	PAR	S.I.
1	325	4	9	10	264	4	18
2	431	5	5	11	152	3	14
3	134	3	17	12	465	5	10
4	284	4	13	13	355	4	8
5	154	3	7	14	410	4	4
6	387	4	1	15	372	4	2
7	356	4	3	16	122	3	16
8	135	3	11	17	351	4	6
9	305	4	15	18	329	4	12
OUT	2,511	34		IN	2,820	35	
				TOTAL	5,331	69	
				STANDARD SCRATCH	68		

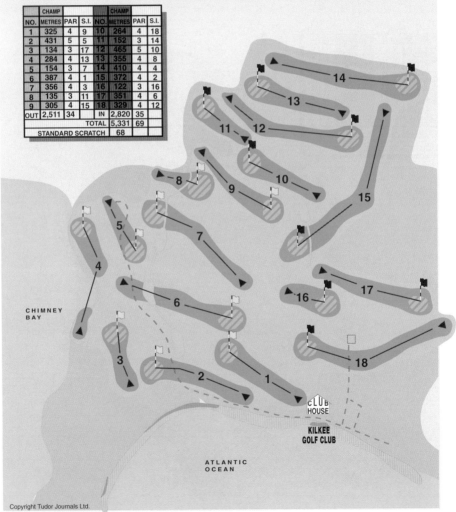

CHIMNEY BAY

CLUB HOUSE

KILKEE GOLF CLUB

ATLANTIC OCEAN

Copyright Tudor Journals Ltd.

Parknamoney, Ennis
Road, Kilrush,
Co. Clare.
Tel: (065) 9051138.
Fax: (065) 9052633
Email: info@kilrushgolfclub.com
www:kilrshgolfclub.com

LOCATION: One mile on
Kilrush – Ennis Road.
SECRETARY/MANAGER: Denis
Nagle. Tel: (087) 6237557.

Course with scenic view overlooking
Shannon Estuary. Particularly
challenging Par 3 especially the 9th
hole. The Par 5's will prove very demanding to any golfer. Further
developments to both clubhouse ancourse
recently completed.Also, an 18 hole
course was opened in July 1994.

COURSE INFORMATION

**Par 68; SSS 70; Length 4,850
metres.**
Visitors: Welcome.
Ladies: Welcome Thursdays.
Green Fees: €25 Mon – Fri;
€30 Sat/Sun & Bank Holidays;
€45 Husband & Wife.
Juveniles: Welcome if accompanied by an adult.
Club Hire available. Buggy
available for hire.
Clubhouse Hours: Daylight
hours.
Clubhouse Dress: Casual.
Clubhouse Facilities:
Spacious new clubhouse
open 2001. Lunches &
evening meals available
everyday May – September.
Open Competitions: Various
throughout the year, contact

NO.	CHAMP YARDS	MEDAL YARDS	PAR	S.I.	NO.	CHAMP YARDS	MEDAL YARDS	PAR	S.I.
1	324	313	4	5	10	285	263	4	15
2	348	324	4	9	11	421	416	4	1
3	442	438	4	2	12	338	327	4	13
4	136	127	3	18	13	504	450	5	17
5	402	391	4	4	14	176	161	3	8
6	349	338	4	11	15	505	490	5	6
7	490	483	5	14	16	398	388	4	3
8	166	158	3	16	17	196	184	3	10
9	168	159	3	7	18	338	326	4	12
OUT	2,825	2,731	34		IN	3,161	3,005	36	
					TOTAL	5,986	5,736	70	
					STANDARD SCRATCH	70	68		

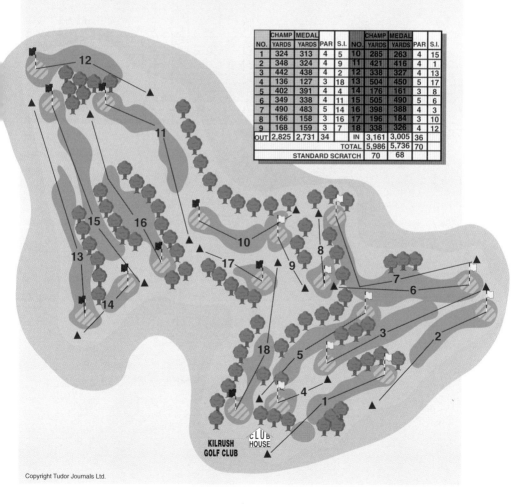

KILRUSH
GOLF CLUB

CLUB
HOUSE

Copyright Tudor Journals Ltd.

Lahinch, Co Clare.
Tel: (065) 7081003.
Fax: (065) 7081592.

LOCATION: 32 Miles North West of Shannon Airport.
SECRETARY: Alan Reardon.
Email: info@lahinchgolf.com
Website: www.lahinchgolf.com
PROFESSIONAL: Robert McCavery.
Tel: (065) 7081408.
ARCHITECT: Dr Alastair MacKenzie.

Lahinch is steeped in history and has such famous holes as 'Dell' and 'Klondyke'. The features of this famous course are carved out of natural terrain. The Old Course is the permanent home of the South of Ireland Open Amateur Championship, first played in 1895 and which annually attracts the cream of Ireland's amateur golfers to play for this most coveted title and the magnificent trophy which goes with it.

COURSE INFORMATION

Par 73; SSS 73; Length 6,687 yards (Old Course).
Visitors: Welcome most days – booking is necessary.
Opening Hours: Sunrise – sunset.

Ladies: Welcome.
Green Fees: €110 per round, €125 per day.
Juveniles: Welcome.
Clubhouse Hours: 8am – 11pm approx. summertime.
Clubhouse Dress: Casual, but smart.
Clubhouse Facilities: Full clubhouse facilities; lessons available by prior arrangements; club hire and caddy service available, but cannot be guaranteed.
Open Competitions: South of Ireland Amateur Open Championship – July.

NO.	BLUE YARDS	WHITE YARDS	GREEN YARDS	PAR	S.I.	NO	BLUE YARDS	WHITE YARDS	GREEN YARDS	PAR	S.I.
1	385	375	359	4	4	10	445	428	406	4	1
2	512	498	479	5	14	11	138	133	127	3	17
3	151	148	140	3	16	12	475	457	437	4	7
4	428	416	407	4	2	13	273	267	256	4	11
5	482	476	470	5	12	14	452	447	431	4	13
6	155	150	139	3	18	15	468	440	429	4	3
7	399	383	374	4	6	16	198	195	178	3	15
8	350	348	338	4	10	17	440	412	403	4	5
9	403	395	358	4	8	18	535	500	492	5	9
OUT	3,265	3,189	3,061	36		IN	3,422	3,279	3,159	35	
						TOTAL	6,687	6,468	6,220		
						STANDARD SCRATCH	73	71	70		

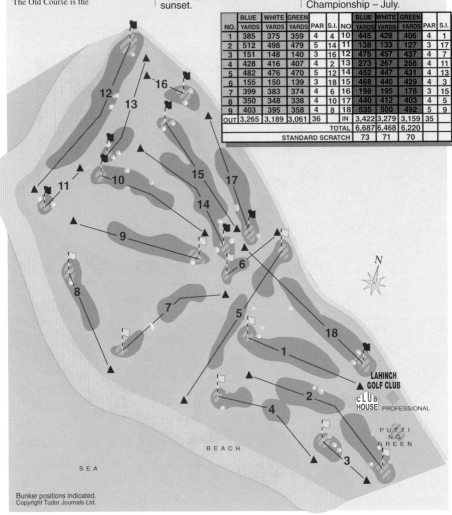

N

LAHINCH GOLF CLUB

CLUB HOUSE   PROFESSIONAL

PUTTING GREEN

BEACH

SEA

Bunker positions indicated.
Copyright Tudor Journals Ltd.

Lahinch, Co Clare.
Tel: (065) 7081003.
Fax: (065) 7081592.

Location: 300yds from Lahinch village.
Secretary: Alan Reardon.
Email: info@lahinchgolf.com
www.lahinchgolf.com
Professional: Robert McCavery. Tel: (065) 81408.

The Castle course at the famous Lahinch club has been upgraded dramatically and has hosted several championships. It is a links course and, although less daunting than the Old Course, still provides an excellent challenge to your game.

COURSE INFORMATION

Par 70; SSS 69/70; Length 5,594 yards.
Visitors: Welcome.
Opening Hours: Dawn – Dusk.
Ladies: Welcome.

Green Fees: €50 per round, €65 per day.
Juveniles: Welcome. Lessons available; Club Hire available; Caddy service available.
Clubhouse Hours: 8.00am – 11.00pm summertime.
Clubhouse Facilities: Lunches, dinners and snacks. Full clubhouse facilities.
Open Competitions: Intermediate Scratch Trophy – May.

NO.	YARDS	PAR	S.I.	NO.	YARDS	PAR	S.I.
1	345	4	6	10	149	3	15
2	182	3	8	11	344	4	1
3	303	4	14	12	439	5	7
4	347	4	2	13	138	3	11
5	227	4	12	14	277	4	13
6	125	3	16	15	348	4	3
7	115	3	18	16	282	4	5
8	203	4	10	17	381	5	17
9	323	4	4	18	291	4	9
OUT	2,170	33		IN	2,649	36	
				TOTAL	4,819	69	
STANDARD SCRATCH			68				

NO.	YARDS	PAR	S.I.	NO.	YARDS	PAR	S.I.
1	360	4	2	10	164	3	15
2	195	3	8	11	364	4	5
3	264	4	14	12	440	4	1
4	448	5	10	13	149	3	17
5	249	4	18	14	277	4	13
6	215	3	4	15	513	5	11
7	115	3	16	16	336	4	7
8	268	4	12	17	390	4	3
9	495	5	6	18	352	4	9
OUT	2,609	35		IN	2,985	35	
				TOTAL	5,594	70	
STANDARD SCRATCH			70				

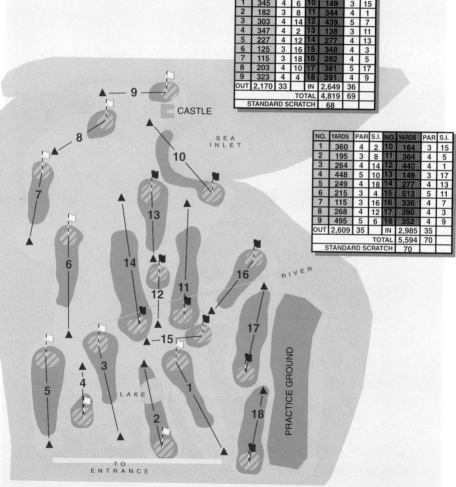

CASTLE
SEA INLET
RIVER
PRACTICE GROUND
LAKE
TO ENTRANCE

Copyright Tudor Journals Ltd.

SHANNON

MUNSTER **CLARE**

Shannon Airport, Shannon, Co. Clare.
Tel: (061) 471849
Fax: (061) 471507.
Email:
shannongolfclub@eircom.net
www.shannongolf.com

LOCATION: 200 yds beyond Airport terminal building.
SEC/MANAGER: Michael Corry.
PROFESSIONAL: Artie Pyke
Tel: (061) 471551
ARCHITECT: John D. Harris

American styled golf course with plenty of water hazards and bunkers. Tree lined fairways demand accurate tee shots. The greens are largely by protected by mounds and bunkers. Course is flat and presents a superb challenge for every category of golfer. The par 3, 17th hole is the signature hole with a carry of 185 yds over the Shannon estuary.

COURSE INFORMATION

Par 72; SSS 72: Length 6,874 yards.
Visitors: Welcome at all times, subject to availability.
Opening Hours: Dawn to dusk.
Avoid: Sunday.
Ladies: Welcome Tuesdays.
Green Fees: €35 Weekday; €45 Weekends, Bank Holidays.
Juveniles: Must be accompanied by an adult. Lessons by prior arrangement. Club Hire available. Caddy service available by prior arrangement; telephone appointment required.

Clubhouse Hours: Summer; 11.00am – 10.00pm. Winter; 11.00am – 6.00pm.
Clubhouse Dress: Casual. No shorts.
Clubhouse Facilities: Full bar and catering facilities available throughout the year. Advisable to book for 4 or more people.
Open Competitions: Open Singles each Wednesday.

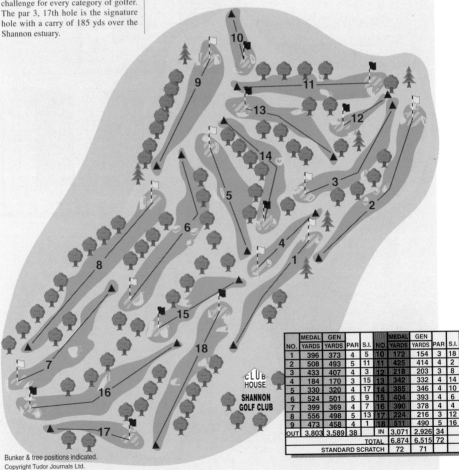

SHANNON GOLF CLUB

NO.	MEDAL YARDS	GEN YARDS	PAR	S.I.	NO.	MEDAL YARDS	GEN YARDS	PAR	S.I.
1	396	373	4	5	10	172	154	3	18
2	508	493	5	11	11	425	414	4	2
3	433	407	4	3	12	218	203	3	8
4	184	170	3	15	13	342	332	4	14
5	330	320	4	17	14	385	346	4	10
6	524	501	5	9	15	404	393	4	6
7	399	369	4	7	16	390	378	4	4
8	556	498	5	13	17	224	216	3	12
9	473	458	4	1	18	511	490	5	16
OUT	3,803	3,589	38		IN	3,071	2,926	34	
					TOTAL	6,874	6,515	72	
					STANDARD SCRATCH	72	71		

Bunker & tree positions indicated.
Copyright Tudor Journals Ltd.

298

Spanish Point, Miltown Malbay, Co. Clare.
Tel: (065) 7084198.

LOCATION: Two miles from Miltown Malbay.
SECRETARY: Dave Fitzgerald.
Tel: (065) 708 4219.

This links course overlooks the picturesque golden beach at Spanish Point. Playable all year it is renowned for its unique six Par 3's and three Par 4's. The strong Atlantic winds can make life difficult, but it is both fun to play and a challenge for any golf enthusiast.

COURSE INFORMATION

Par 64; SSS 63; Length 4624 metres.
Visitors: Welcome (restrictions on Sundays).
Opening Hours: Sunrise – Sunset.
Green Fees: Weekdays €20, Weekends €20. €15 with member.
Juveniles: Welcome if accompanied by adult. Juveniles under 14 are not allowed after 5pm or on Sat / Sun.
Clubhouse Hours: 10.00am – 11.00pm (summer); full clubhouse facilities.
Clubhouse Dress: Casual.
Clubhouse Facilities: Sandwiches and light snacks available in bar everyday during the summer.
Open Competitions: Open Week in June; Open Weekend – May. Intermediate Scratch Cup in September. Handicap certificate required for Open Competitions.

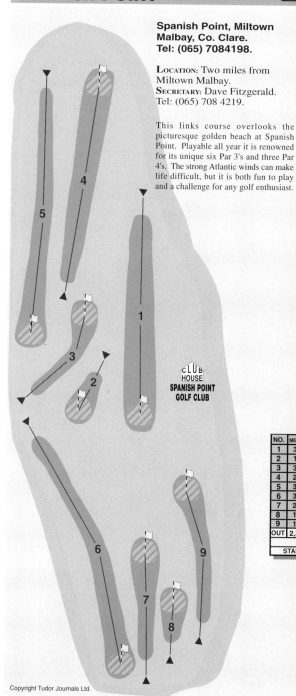

CLUB HOUSE
SPANISH POINT GOLF CLUB

NO.	METRES	PAR	S.I.	NO.	METRES	PAR	S.I.
1	307	4	13	10	307	4	8
2	180	3	9	11	180	3	12
3	371	4	7	12	371	4	6
4	205	3	5	13	205	3	4
5	387	4	1	14	387	4	18
6	339	4	3	15	339	4	10
7	287	4	11	16	287	4	16
8	100	3	15	17	100	3	14
9	136	3	17	18	136	3	2
OUT	2,312	32		IN	2,312	32	
				TOTAL	4,624	64	
	STANDARD SCRATCH				63		

Copyright Tudor Journals Ltd.

Woodstock Golf & Country Club, Shanaway Road. Ennis, Co. Clare.
Tel: (065) 6829463.
Fax: (065) 6820304.

LOCATION: Approx 2 miles from the centre of Ennis off the Lahinch Road (N85).
SECRETARY: Seamus Kolly.
ARCHITECT: Dr. Arthur Spring.

The course is championship standard with green built to the highest standard. It is built on 155 acres of free draining soil and is playable all year round. The course is challenging, yet is built so that it may be enjoyed by all categories of golfers. All who visit Woodstock will be sure of a warm welcome.

COURSE INFORMATION

Par 71; SSS 71; Length 6429 yards, 5879 metres.
Visitors: Visitors are welcome all days including weekends, but are advised to avoid members time at weekend (check with secretary).
Opening Hours: 8.00am until dusk.
Ladies: No restrictions. Have priority on Tuesdays.
Green Fees:
€35 Mon – Fri; €40 Sat / Sun / Bank Holidays
Groups of 12 or more €30

early bird specials: play before 10:30am for €18 (mon-fri)
Juveniles: Must be accompanied by an adult.
Clubhouse Hours: 9.00am until closing time.
Clubhouse Dress: Informal but neat.
Clubhouse Facilities: Club shop. Caddy cars and caddies on request. Full bar and bar menu all day everyday. Restaurant and Sunday lunch and weekend nights. Tel: (065) 6844430.
Open Competitions: Every Wednesday (Apr-Oct) & Bank Holiday Weekends

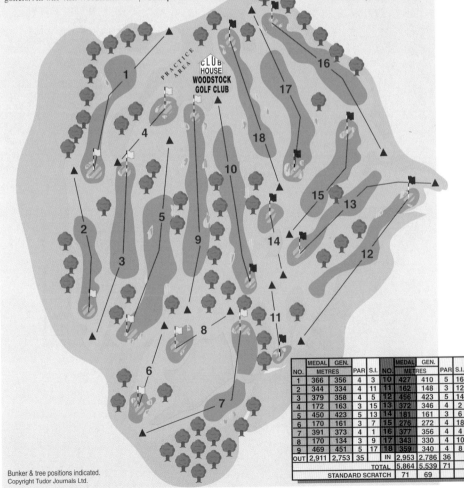

Bunker & tree positions indicated.
Copyright Tudor Journals Ltd.

NO.	MEDAL METRES	GEN. METRES	PAR	S.I.	NO.	MEDAL METRES	GEN. METRES	PAR	S.I.
1	366	356	4	3	10	427	410	5	16
2	344	334	4	11	11	162	148	3	12
3	379	358	4	5	12	456	423	5	14
4	172	163	3	15	13	372	346	4	2
5	450	423	5	13	14	181	161	3	6
6	170	161	3	7	15	276	272	4	18
7	391	373	4	1	16	377	356	4	4
8	170	134	3	9	17	343	330	4	10
9	469	451	5	17	18	359	340	4	8
OUT	2,911	2,753	35		IN	2,953	2,786	36	
					TOTAL	5,864	5,539	71	
					STANDARD SCRATCH	71	69		

**Castlebernard, Bandon,
Co. Cork.
Tel: (023) 41111 / 42224.
Fax: (023) 44690.**

LOCATION: Two miles west of Bandon Town.
SECRETARY: Noel O'Sullivan.
Tel: (023) 41111.
PROFESSIONAL: Paddy O'Boyle.
Tel: (023) 42224.

Beautiful parkland course which some consider difficult due to the sloping fairways. It is one of a few eighteen hole course in West Cork.

COURSE INFORMATION

Par 70; SSS 69; Length 6,193 yards, 5,663 metres.
Visitors: Welcome Mon – Fri excluding Wednesday.
Opening Hours: Sunrise – sunset.
Ladies: Welcome.
Ladies Day: Wednesday.
Green Fees: Mon – Fri €30; Sat €35 (€13 with member).
Juveniles: Welcome.
Competition every Monday, otherwise must be accompanied by an adult. Lessons and Caddy service available by prior arrangements; Club Hire available.
Clubhouse Hours: 10.30am; Full clubhouse facilities; Full catering facilities everyday.
Clubhouse Dress: Casual.
Open Competitions: Open Singles S/F each Thurs from May 5th - Aug 29th plus various other competitions; telephone for details. Handicap certificate required for Open Competitions.

	MEDAL METRES	GEN. METRES	PAR	S.I.	NO.	MEDAL METRES	GEN. METRES	PAR	S.I.
	271	260	4	16	10	320	320	4	11
	337	319	4	8	11	380	372	4	1
	457	447	5	14	12	179	169	3	7
	326	316	4	6	13	454	444	5	13
	155	155	3	12	14	402	392	4	3
	105	105	3	18	15	348	338	4	5
	405	395	4	2	16	315	305	4	15
	363	353	4	4	17	302	292	4	17
	348	348	4	10	18	176	166	3	9
	2,767	2,698	35		IN	2,896	2,798	35	
					TOTAL	5,663	5,496	70	
					STANDARD SCRATCH	69	68		

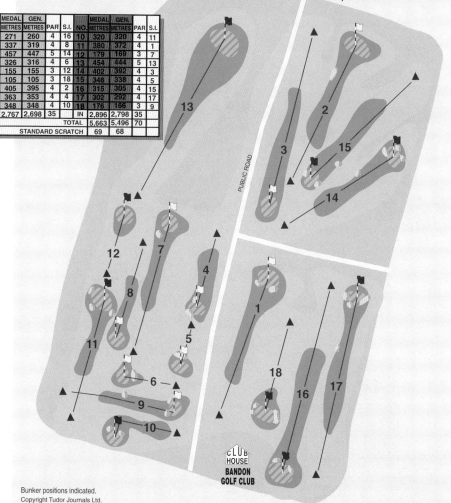

PUBLIC ROAD

CLUB HOUSE

BANDON GOLF CLUB

Bunker positions indicated.
Copyright Tudor Journals Ltd.

Bantry, West Cork
Tel: (027) 50579.

LOCATION: One mile from Bantry on Glengarriff Road.
SECRETARY/MANAGER: Liz Campbell.
Email: info@bantrygolf.com
Website: www.bantrygolf.com

Bantry Park is considered an interesting and difficult course. Several plantations are steadily coming into play, and are making the recently built 18 hole course more intriguing.

COURSE INFORMATION

Par 71; SSS 70; Length 5,910 metres.
Visitors: Contact: (027) 50579 for times of play.
Opening Hours: 8.00am – sunset.
Avoid: Days of major competitions. Prior arrangement for societies.
Green Fees: €35(L) €40(H). Group of 12+: €25(L) €30(H).
Juveniles: Welcome.

Club Hire available; caddy cars & buggy's available; telephone appointment required.
Clubhouse Hours: 9.00am – sunset during summer months.
Clubhouse Dress: Casual.
Clubhouse Facilities: Bar & catering available.

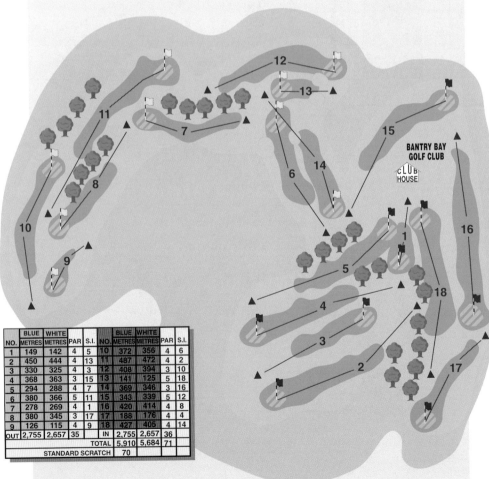

NO.	BLUE METRES	WHITE METRES	PAR	S.I.	NO.	BLUE METRES	WHITE METRES	PAR	S.I.
1	149	142	4	5	10	372	356	4	6
2	450	444	4	13	11	487	472	4	2
3	330	325	4	3	12	408	394	3	10
4	368	363	3	15	13	141	125	5	18
5	294	288	4	7	14	369	346	3	16
6	380	366	5	11	15	343	339	5	12
7	278	269	4	1	16	420	414	4	8
8	380	345	3	17	17	188	176	4	4
9	126	115	4	9	18	427	405	4	14
OUT	2,755	2,657	35		IN	2,755	2,657	36	
					TOTAL	5,910	5,684	71	
					STANDARD SCRATCH	70			

Copyright Tudor Journals Ltd.

Filane, Castletownbere, Co. Cork.
Tel: (027) 70700.

LOCATION: 3 miles from Castletownbere on the Glengarriff road.
HON. SECRETARY: Bernie Twarney.

A scenic sea-side links set on the edge of West Cork in a beautiful and quiet location. Water is a feature of the course both visually and in play. The latter features three holes where water comes into play, particularly on the Par 3 9th which requires a tee shot over the water. A new clubhouse was completed in 1994 which has

other tourist facilities such as a caravan park, picnic area tennis courts and shingle beach. 4 new greens built & open shortly.

COURSE INFORMATION

Par 68; SSS 65; Length 4,759 metres.
Visitors: Welcome at anytime.
Opening Hours: 8am – Dark.
Ladies: Welcome (no restrictions).
Green Fees: €20 per day.
Juveniles: Welcome; €10; If busy must be accompanied by

adult. Club Hire available.
Clubhouse Hours: 11.00 – 11.30pm in season, otherwise at weekends 12.00 noon – 11.00pm.
Clubhouse Dress: Casual.
Clubhouse Facilities: Full facilities from June including showers and saunas.
Open Competitions: Paddy Crowley Memorial – July; Open Week – July / August.

NO.	METRES	PAR	S.I.	NO.	METRES	PAR	S.I.
1	288	4	11	10	291	4	14
2	428	5	7	11	391	4	1
3	240	4	17	12	241	4	18
4	366	4	2	13	408	5	8
5	310	4	15	14	300	4	16
6	156	3	4	15	156	3	6
7	255	4	13	16	260	4	12
8	166	3	9	17	166	3	10
9	160	3	5	18	177	3	3
OUT	2369	34		IN	2390	34	
				TOTAL	4759	68	
			STANDARD SCRATCH		64		

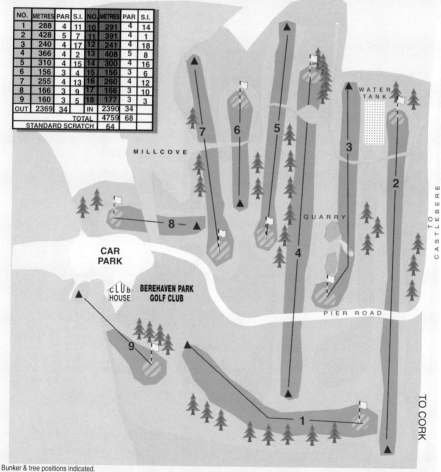

MILLCOVE

WATER TANK

QUARRY

CAR PARK

CLUB HOUSE   BEREHAVEN PARK GOLF CLUB

PIER ROAD

TO CASTLEBERE

TO CORK

Bunker & tree positions indicated.
Copyright Tudor Journals Ltd.

**Charleville Golf Club,
Charleville, Co. Cork.
Tel: (063) 81257.
Fax: (063) 81274.
Email: charlevillegolf@eircom.ie
www.charlevillegolf.com**

LOCATION: On main road from
Cork to Limerick.
SECRETARY: Pat Nagle.
HON. SECRETARY: Tony Murphy.

Both of Charleville's attractive and well
maintained parkland courses are located
in the foothills of the scenic Ballyhoura
Mountains, in the heart of Ireland's
Golden Vale. This 18 hole championship
course, renowned for its lush fairways
and excellent greens, offers relaxed
anduncrowded golf in, peaceful
surroundings.

COURSE INFORMATION

**West Course: Par 71; SSS 69;
Length 6,244 yards.
East Course: Par 72; SSS 72;
Length 6,902 yards.
Visitors:** Welcome.
Opening Hours: 9am – sunset.
Weekends telephone in advance.
Avoid major competitions.
Ladies: Welcome.
Green Fees: €25 Mon – Fri;
€32 weekends.

Juveniles: Welcome.
Clubhouse Hours:
9.00am – 12.00 midnight.
Clubhouse Dress: Casual/neat.
Clubhouse Facilities:
Full bar and catering available.
Open Competitions: Tuesdays
April - Nov. Scratch Cups -
24th, 25th or 26th May. All ROI
Bank Holidays. Ladies Open
one day each month from April
to Sept. Please telephone for
details. (entry fee for open
competitions; €15 incl green
fees.)

NO.	YARDS	PAR	S.I.	NO.	YARDS	PAR	S.I.
1	335	4	13	10	370	4	8
2	155	3	18	11	362	4	4
3	369	4	1	12	303	4	15
4	379	4	9	13	533	5	10
5	344	4	5	14	350	4	14
6	373	4	11	15	376	4	6
7	374	4	3	16	158	3	17
8	383	4	7	17	481	5	12
9	162	3	16	18	437	4	2
OUT	2,874	34		IN	3,370	37	
				TOTAL	6,244	71	
				STANDARD SCRATCH		69	

EAST COURSE

NO.	YARDS	PAR	S.I.	NO.	YARDS	PAR	S.I.
1	404	4	9	10	404	4	10
2	537	5	7	11	537	5	8
3	178	3	17	12	178	3	18
4	421	4	11	13	421	4	2
5	324	4	5	14	324	4	16
6	407	4	11	15	407	4	12
7	358	4	13	16	358	4	14
8	429	4	15	17	429	4	6
9	393	4	3	18	393	4	4
OUT	3,451	36		IN	3,451	36	
				TOTAL	6,902	72	
				STANDARD SCRATCH		72	

Bunker and tree positions indicated.

WEST COURSE

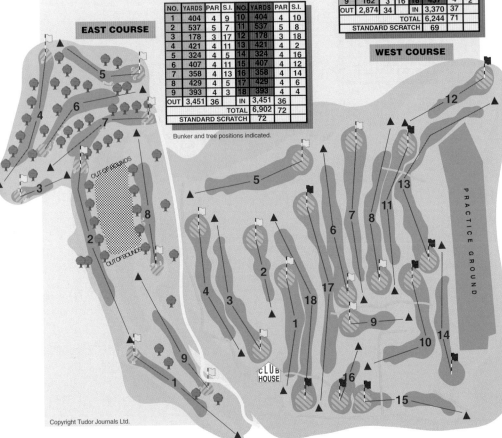

Cobh, Co. Cork.
Tel: (021) 4812399.

LOCATION:
One mile from Cobh Town.
SECRETARY: Barry Lynch.
Tel: (021) 4812399.
MANAGER: Henry Cunningham.
ARCHITECT: E. Hackett.

A pleasant course on the outskirts of Cobh, noted for the short 2nd hole which is a real card wrecker, with the out-of-bounds only feet away from the back of the green and all down along the right-hand side.

COURSE INFORMATION

Par 67; SSS 64; Length 4386 metres.
Visitors: Welcome. Telephone appointment required for weekend play.
Opening Hours: 9.00am – sunset.
Avoid: Tuesday.
Ladies: Welcome Tuesdays.
Green Fees:
€16 all week, €8 with member,
Juveniles: Welcome.

Clubhouse Hours: 12.00 noon – 11.30pm.
Clubhouse Dress: Casual but smart.
Clubhouse Facilites: Full catering and bar facilities.
Open Competitions: Open Week – August: Junior and Intermediate Scratch Cups - September.

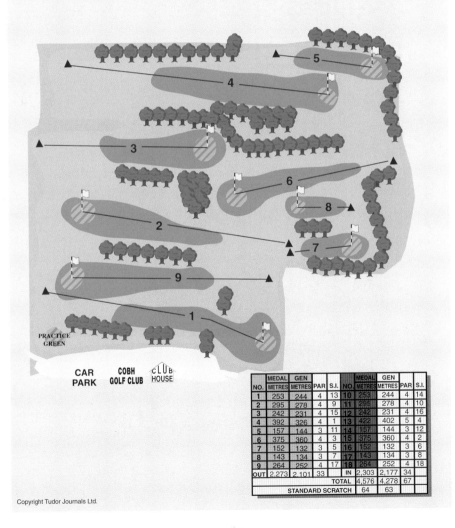

NO.	MEDAL METRES	GEN METRES	PAR	S.I.	NO.	MEDAL METRES	GEN METRES	PAR	S.I.
1	253	244	4	13	10	253	244	4	14
2	295	278	4	9	11	295	278	4	10
3	242	231	4	15	12	242	231	4	16
4	392	326	4	1	13	422	402	5	4
5	157	144	3	11	14	157	144	3	12
6	375	360	4	3	15	375	360	4	2
7	152	132	3	5	16	152	132	3	6
8	143	134	3	7	17	143	134	3	8
9	264	252	4	17	18	264	252	4	18
OUT	2,273	2,101	33		IN	2,303	2,177	34	
					TOTAL	4,576	4,278	67	
					STANDARD SCRATCH	64	63		

Copyright Tudor Journals Ltd.

**Coosheen, Schull,
Co. Cork.
Tel: (028) 28182.**

LOCATION: One and a half miles
East of Schull.
SECRETARY: Linda Morgan.
Tel: (028) 28182.
OWNER: Daniel Morgan.
ARHITECT: Daniel Morgan.

A nine hole course overlooking beautiful Schull Harbour. The faiways are tight and testing in windy conditions, especially the Par 3's, 8th and 9th holes over water. Renowned for its Par 3's.

COURSE INFORMATION

Par 60; SSS 58; Length 4,018 yards.

Visitors: (Restrictions on Sun).
Opening Hours: 8am – sunset.
Ladies: Restrictions on Sundays.
Juveniles: Restricted at weekends.
Green Fees: €16.
Clubhouse Hours: 9am – 10pm.
Clubhouse Dress: Casual.
Clubhouse Facilities: Bar/
Sandwiches. Bar open to the public.
Open Competitions: July.
Handicap Certificates required for
Open Competitions.

NO.	YARDS	PAR	S.I.	NO.	YARDS	PAR	S.I.
1	120	3	13	10	120	3	14
2	240	3	3	11	240	3	4
3	100	3	17	12	100	3	18
4	417	4	1	13	417	4	2
5	320	4	11	14	320	4	12
6	130	3	9	15	130	3	10
7	217	3	5	16	217	3	6
8	200	3	15	17	200	3	16
9	265	4	7	18	265	4	8
OUT	2,009	30		IN	2,009	30	
				TOTAL	4,018	60	
			STANDARD SCRATCH		58		

SCHULL
HARBOUR

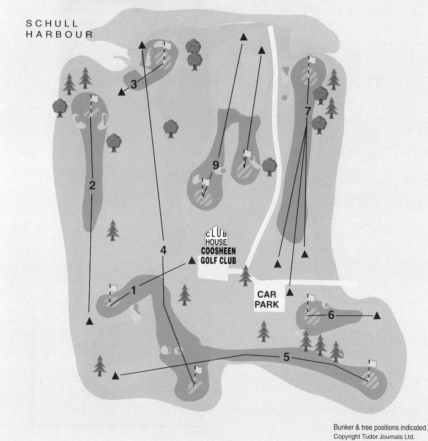

Bunker & tree positions indicated.
Copyright Tudor Journals Ltd.

Little Island, Co. Cork.
Tel: (021) 4353451.
Fax: (021) 4353410.

LOCATION: Five miles East of Cork City on N25 Rosslare Road.
GENERAL MANAGER: Matt Sands.
Tel: (021) 353451
Fax: (021) 353410.
ARCHITECT: Alister MacKenzie.

Not many clubs have such an attractive setting for a golf course with parkland running down to a rocky outcrop of land reaching out into Lough Mahon. An excellent championship test and one of the most attractive courses in Ireland.

NO.	MEDAL METRES	GEN METRES	PAR	S.I.	NO.	MEDAL METRES	GEN METRES	PAR	S.I.
1	340	335	4	8	10	374	358	4	2
2	460	442	5	16	11	454	450	5	15
3	244	244	4	18	12	289	286	4	11
4	411	402	4	1	13	157	149	3	13
5	510	504	5	6	14	397	380	4	4
6	300	272	4	14	15	383	366	4	7
7	169	158	3	10	16	323	315	4	17
8	379	374	4	3	17	360	335	4	9
9	178	170	3	12	18	387	370	4	5
OUT	2,991	2,901	36		IN	3,124	3,009	36	
					TOTAL	6,115	5,910	72	
					STANDARD SCRATCH			72	

COURSE INFORMATION

Par 72; SSS 72; Length 6632 yards; 6,115 metres.
Visitors: Welcome Mon / Tues / Wed / Fri except from 12.30pm – 2.00pm or after 4pm. Sat-Sun from 2pm.
Opening Hours: Sunrise – sunset.
Avoid: Thursday Ladies Day.
Green Fees: €70 Mon – Fri; €80 Sat / Sun.
Juveniles: Welcome. Lessons available by prior arrangement; Club Hire available, Caddy service available.
Clubhouse Hours: Sunrise – sunset.
Clubhouse Dress: Smart / casual except after 6.00pm when jacket and tie must be worn.
Clubhouse Facilities: Full bar and catering.

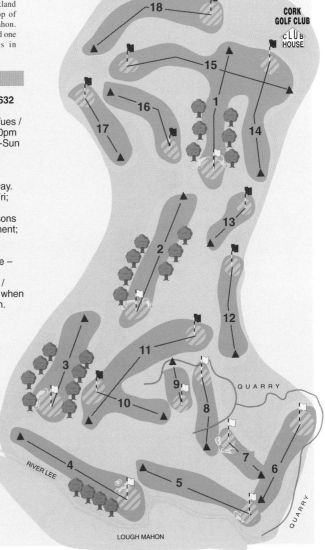

CORK GOLF CLUB

CLUB HOUSE

RIVER LEE

QUARRY

QUARRY

LOUGH MAHON

Copyright Tudor Journals Ltd.

**Doneraile Golf Club,
Co. Cork.
Tel: (022) 24137.**

LOCATION: Adjacent to Doneraile town.
SECRETARY: Jimmy 'O Leary.
Tel: (022) 24379/21522.

Attractive parkland course with many old oak, lime and beech trees. Deep and wide river valley which must be crossed twice in each nine holes. The Par 3 8th hole is a real gem. It is one of the nicest nine hole courses in the country.

COURSE INFORMATION

Par 68; SSS 66; Length 5,768 yards, 5,274 metres.
Visitors: Welcome Mon – Fri.
Opening Hours: 9.00am – Sunset.
Avoid: Saturday mornings and Sunday afternoons.
Ladies: Welcome.
Green Fees: €20.

Juveniles: Welcome.
Clubhouse Hours: Evenings only.
Clubhouse Dress: Smart casual.
Clubhouse Facilities: By prior arrangement only.

NO.	METRES	PAR	S.I.	NO.	METRES	PAR	S.I.
1	405	4	3	10	405	4	4
2	313	4	17	11	313	4	18
3	370	4	7	12	370	4	8
4	185	3	5	13	185	3	6
5	343	4	9	14	343	4	10
6	364	4	13	15	364	4	14
7	311	4	15	16	311	4	16
8	164	3	11	17	164	3	12
9	429	4	1	18	429	4	2
OUT	2,884	34		IN	2,884	34	
				TOTAL	5,768	68	
				STANDARD SCRATCH		66	

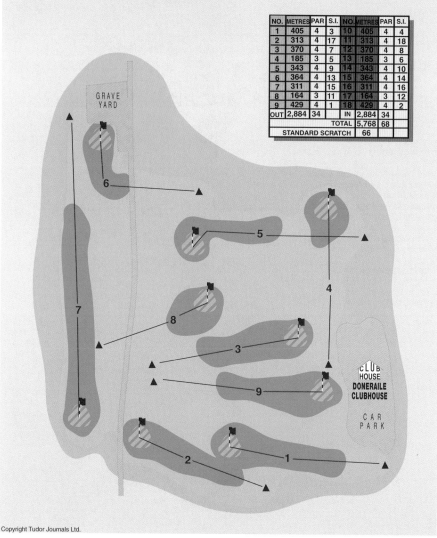

Copyright Tudor Journals Ltd.

**Douglas Golf Club,
Co. Cork.
Tel: (021) 4895297.**

LOCATION: 3 miles from
CHIEF EXECUTIVE: Brian Barrett.
PROFESSIONAL: Gary Nicholson.

We hope to provide you with a look at our newly reconstructed golf course and would welcome you to play our course on your next visit to Cork. Please contact our Chief Executive at the number below to arrange a Tee Time.

COURSE INFORMATION

Par 71; SSS 71; Length; 6,609 metres.
Visitors: Welcome,
Opening Hours:
7.00am – dusk.
Ladies: Welcome.
Green Fees: Mon - Fri €30;
Weekends €40.
Juveniles: Must be accompanied by an adult.
Clubhouse Hours: 9.00am – 11.30pm.

Clubhouse Dress: Casual.
Open Competitions:
Captain's Prize10th/11th May; President's Prize 30th/31st August; Lady Captain's Prize18th June; Captain's Prize to Ladies 28th May; President's Prize to Ladies 8th September; Lady Captain's Prize to Gents 4th May; Ladies' Christmas Hamper 22nd September; Fourball Hampers 12th/13th October; Singles Hamper (13 & Under)19th October; Singles Hamper (14 & Over) 20th Octobery.

NO.	BLUE METERS	WHITE METERS	PAR	S.I.	NO.	BLUE METERS	WHITE METERS	PAR	S.I.
1	352	324	4	2	10	311	293	4	15
2	344	281	4	8	11	346	346	4	9
3	456	445	5	18	12	358	352	4	5
4	152	138	3	14	13	352	318	4	13
5	337	308	4	4	14	374	345	4	1
6	352	342	4	6	15	134	117	3	17
7	167	148	3	12	16	381	348	4	3
8	450	434	5	16	17	363	350	4	7
9	290	290	4	10	18	453	428	5	11
OUT	2,900	2,710	36		IN	3,072	2,897	36	
					TOTAL	5,972	5,607	72	
	STANDARD SCRATCH						71	69	

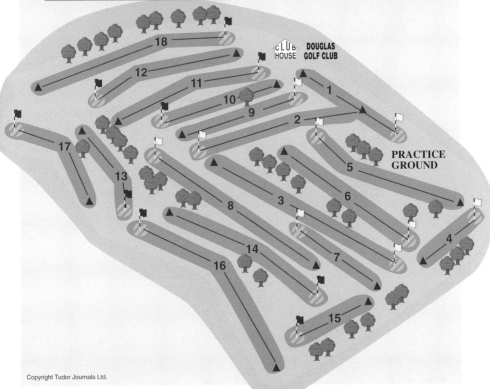

Copyright Tudor Journals Ltd.

**Dunmore, Clonakilty,
West Cork.
Tel: (023) 34644.**

LOCATION: Three miles
south of Clonakilty.
SECRETARY: L O' Donovan.
Tel: (023) 34644.

A short, tight course. Accurate
driving is called for as out-of-
bounds prevails in six of the nine
holes.

COURSE INFORMATION

**9 HOLE
Par 64; SSS 61; Length
4,464 yards, 4,080 metres.**
Visitors: Welcome avoid
Saturday & Sunday mornings.
Opening Hours:
Sunrise – sunset.
Ladies: Welcome.
Green Fees: €20
Juveniles: Welcome every day
– must be accompanied by an
adult after 6.00pm in summer.

Handicap Certificate required in
competitions.
Clubhouse Hours:
9.00am – 11.00pm.
Clubhouse Dress: Casual.
Clubhouse Facilities: In Hotel
attached to course – usual
trading hours.
Open Competitions: First
week of August.

NO.	YARDS	PAR	S.I.	NO.	YARDS	PAR	S.I.
1	270	4	9	10	270	4	10
2	346	4	3	11	346	4	4
3	159	3	13	12	159	3	14
4	440	4	1	13	440	4	2
5	109	3	17	14	109	3	18
6	303	4	11	15	303	4	12
7	275	4	15	16	275	4	16
8	160	3	7	17	160	3	8
9	170	3	5	18	170	3	6
OUT	2,241	32		IN	2,241	32	
				TOTAL	4,482	64	
			STANDARD SCRATCH	61			

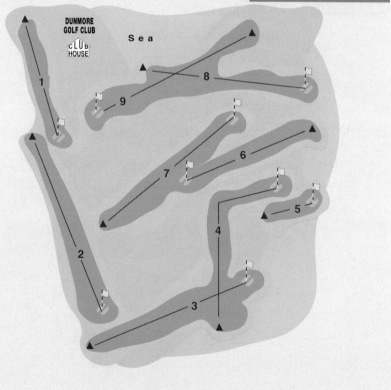

DUNMORE
GOLF CLUB
CLUB HOUSE
Sea

Copyright Tudor Journals Ltd.

**Gortacrue, Midleton,
Co. Cork.
Tel: (021) 4631687.
Fax: (021) 4613695**
LOCATION: Two miles outside town
of Midleton.
SECRETARY: Mr Maurice Moloney.
Tel: (021) 631687.
ARCHITECT: E. Hackett.

A fine eighteen hole course, very tight as
many trees planted in past years, are now
coming into play. A new clubhouse opened
in May 1992.

COURSE INFORMATION

**Par 69; SSS 67; Length 5,774
metres.
Visitors:** Welcome.
Opening Hours: 6.00am – 9.00pm.
Avoid: Saturday morning and
afternoon; Sunday morning.
Ladies: Welcome.
Green Fees: €25 daily.
Juveniles: Welcome.
Clubhouse Hours: 9am – 11pm.
Clubhouse Dress: Casual.
Clubhouse Facilities: Bar snacks, tea
and coffee.
Additional Facilities: Pro Shop.
Driving Range
Open Competitions: Contact club for
details.

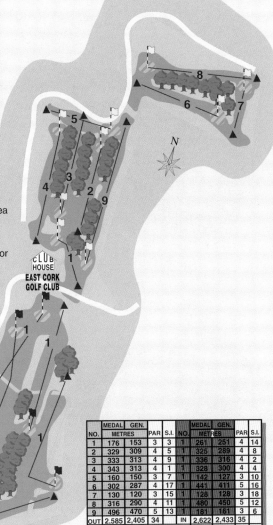

NO.	MEDAL METRES	GEN. METRES	PAR	S.I.	NO.	MEDAL METRES	GEN. METRES	PAR	S.I.
1	176	153	3	3	1	261	251	4	14
2	329	309	4	5	1	325	289	4	8
3	333	313	4	9	1	336	316	4	2
4	343	313	4	1	1	328	300	4	4
5	160	150	3	7	1	142	127	3	10
6	302	287	4	17	1	441	411	5	16
7	130	120	3	15	1	128	128	3	18
8	316	290	4	11	1	480	450	5	12
9	496	470	5	13	1	181	161	3	6
OUT	2,585	2,405	34		IN	2,622	2,433	35	
					TOTAL	5,774	4,838	69	
					STANDARD SCRATCH	67	65		

Copyright Tudor Journals Ltd.

**Corrin, Fermoy,
Co. Cork.
Tel: (025) 31472.**

LOCATION: Two miles south west
of Fermoy.
SECRETARY: Kathleen Murphy.
ARCHITECT: Commander Harris.

Heathland course with undulating terrain
approximately 700ft above sea level.
Plenty of scope with wide fairways.
There are two distinct nine holes bisected
by a road and the average width of
fairways is 25 yards.

COURSE INFORMATION

**Par 70; SSS 70; Length 5825
metres.
Visitors:** Welcome.
Opening Hours: 8.30am –
sunset.
Green Fees: Mon – Fri; €25 Sat
/ Sun & holidays; €35
Juveniles: Welcome before
5.00pm. Must be accompanied
by an adult.
Clubhouse Hours: 10.00am –
11.30pm.
Clubhouse Dress: Casual.
Clubhouse Facilities: 11.00am
– 9.00pm.
Open Competitions: Various
throughout the year telephone
for details.

FERMOY
GOLF CLUB

CLUB
HOUSE

NO.	MEDAL METRES	GEN METRES	PAR	S.I.	NO.	MEDAL METRES	GEN METRES	PAR	S.I.
1	183	161	3	18	10	458	439	5	15
2	479	479	5	16	11	159	159	3	17
3	305	305	4	8	12	380	380	4	5
4	181	152	3	9	13	339	339	4	3
5	388	348	4	2	14	366	328	4	10
6	320	320	4	14	15	328	310	4	11
7	161	156	3	12	16	158	158	3	13
8	349	308	4	6	17	349	349	4	4
9	395	395	4	1	18	527	464	5	7
OUT	2,761	2,624	34		IN	3,064	2,92	36	
					TOTAL	5,825	6	70	
					STANDARD SCRATCH		70	69	

Copyright Tudor Journals Ltd.

Fernhill Golf & Country Club, Carrigaline, Co. Cork.
Tel: (021) 4372226
E-mail: fernhill@iol.ie
Website:
www.fernhillgolfhotel.com

LOCATION: 7 miles south of Cork City on N28.
MANAGER: Mr N. Cummins
PROFESSIONAL: Wayne O'Callaghan
ARCHITECT: Mr. Bowes

18 hole tree lined course with a great variety of holes. The par 3's in particular, are very demanding, requiring accurate tee-shots if the greens are to be reached. The undulating greens require a sure putting touch.

COURSE INFORMATION

Par 69; SSS 67; Length 6,053 yards.
Ladies Day: Thursday.

Green Fees: Weekdays €20, Weekends €26.
Clubhouse Hours: 8am - 12am
Clubhouse Dress: Neat, informal.
Clubhouse Facilities: Bar (full licence), Restaurant, 20 en-suite rooms, swimming pool, sauna, 10 holiday chalets, golf-shop.
Open Competitions: Held during period May-Sept.

NO.	YARDS	PAR	S.I.	NO.	YARDS	PAR	S.I.
1	336	4	11	10	144	3	9
2	168	3	8	11	324	4	13
3	414	4	2	12	371	4	5
4	394	4	4	13	480	5	15
5	385	4	7	14	400	4	3
6	315	4	12	15	250	3	14
7	180	3	6	16	158	3	10
8	318	4	16	17	492	5	17
9	277	4	18	18	360	4	1
OUT	2,787	34		IN	2,979	35	
				TOTAL	5,766	69	
				STANDARD SCRATCH	67		

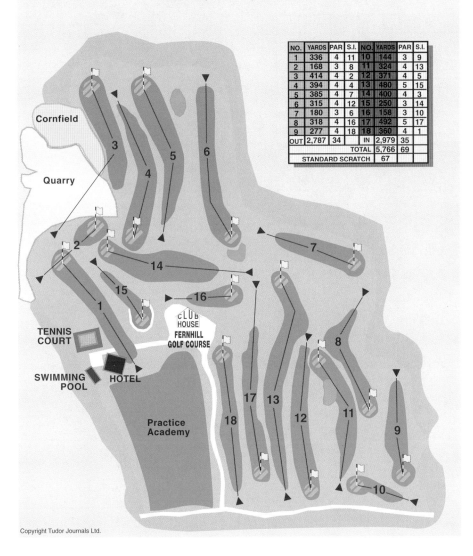

Fota Island, Carrigtwohill, Co. Cork.
Tel: 353 21 4883700.
Email: reservations@fotaisland.ie
www.fotaisland.com

LOCATION: 9 miles from Cork.
MANAGER: Kevin Mulcahy.
Tel: (021) 4883700.
PROFESSIONAL: Kevin Morris.
Tel: (021) 4532032.

Fota Island is the venue for the 2001 and 2002 Murphy's Irish Open. Fota has also hosted no fewer than three Irish Amateur Open Championships, plus the 1997 PGA Championships have been held at Fota Island. "Purists will delight at the old fashioned features......you'll stand in wide-eyed admiration." *(Golf Monthly)*.

COURSE INFORMATION

Par 71; SSS 73; Length 6,927 yards.
Visitors: Welcome.
Opening Hours: 8.30am-5pm.

Ladies: Welcome everyday.
Green Fees: €77 Tues – Thurs. €90 Fri – Sun.
Juveniles: Welcome - student rate Mon – Fri.
Clubhouse Hours: 8.30am – 7.30pm.
Clubhouse Dress: Smart / Casual.
Clubhouse Facilities: Full restaurant and bar.

NO.	BACK YARDS	MEDAL YARDS	PAR	S.I.	NO.	BACK YARDS	MEDAL YARDS	PAR	S.I.
1	409	360	4	3	10	500	487	5	10
2	461	430	4	5	11	168	156	3	18
3	165	153	3	13	12	428	394	4	4
4	548	529	5	11	13	208	194	3	16
5	544	509	5	15	14	417	397	4	2
6	376	357	4	9	15	476	428	4	8
7	179	168	3	17	16	417	400	4	6
8	478	450	4	1	17	222	203	3	12
9	424	394	4	7	18	507	479	5	14
OUT	3,584	3,350	36		IN	3,309	3,138	35	
					TOTAL	6,927	6,488	71	
		STANDARD SCRATCH	73	71					

FOTA ISLAND CLUBHOUSE

Copyright Tudor Journals Ltd.

Frankfield, Cork
Tel: (021) 4361199.

LOCATION: Two miles from Cork Airport; Three miles from Cork City.
SECRETARY: Eddie Walsh.
Tel: (021) 4361199.
PROFESSIONALS: Michael Ryan and David Whyte.
OWNER: Michael Ryan.
Tel: (021) 4363124.
ARCHITECT: M. Ryan.

Short, pleasant nine hole course on a hillside overlooking Cork City. Has a 50 bay driving range, one of the best in Muster and is a training centre used by the Irish Naitonal Coach in the Muster area.

COURSE INFORMATION

Par 68; SSS 65; Length 5137 yards; 4697 metres.
Visitors: Welcome.
Opening Hours: 9.00am – Dusk.
Avoid: Sat / Sun morning, after 2.00pm Thursdays & major competitions.
Ladies: Welcome.
Green Fees: €10
Juveniles: Welcome. Under 16's must be accompanied by an adult.

Clubhouse Hours: 10.30am – 11.00pm.
Clubhouse Dress: Casual.
Clubhouse Facilities: Lunches and snacks available at all times. Lunches Mon – Fri.
Open Competitions:
4-6 May: MS open
17-19 May: Captions Prize.
1-3 Jun: Cogans Garage Singles Competition.
30-31 Aug: Presidentz Prize.
7 Sep: Seniors (over 50's) Scratch Cup.
14 Sep: Intermediate Scratch Cup
5-6 Oct: Dennis Crawley Cup.
12-13 Oct: Club Hamper.

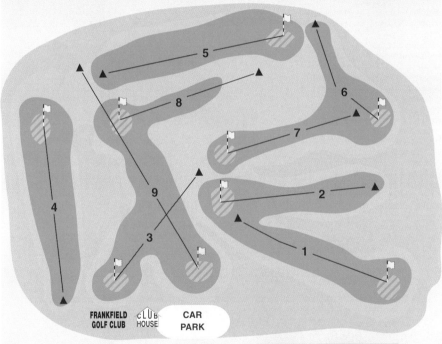

NO.	YARDS	PAR	S.I.	NO.	YARDS	PAR	S.I.
1	336	4	6	10	341	4	5
2	302	4	14	11	302	4	15
3	135	3	17	12	135	3	18
4	179	3	12	13	179	3	13
5	344	4	3	14	344	4	4
6	325	4	10	15	325	4	9
7	355	4	1	16	355	4	2
8	315	4	7	17	315	4	8
9	260	4	16	18	290	4	11
OUT	2,551	34		IN	2,586	34	
				TOTAL	5,137	68	
				STANDARD SCRATCH		65	

Copyright Tudor Journals Ltd.

**Drumgarriff,
Glengarriff, Co. Cork.
Tel: (027) 63150.
Fax: (027) 63575**

LOCATION: One mile from
Glengarriff Village.
SECRETARY: Noreen Deasy.
Tel: (027) 63150.

This is a course in a particularly
beautiful part of Ireland. There are
many breath-taking views of
mountains, forestry and sea as most of
the holes overlook Glengarriff Harbour
and Bantry Bay.

NO.	METRES	PAR	S.I.	NO.	METRES	PAR	S.I.
1	270	4	9	10	270	4	10
2	270	4	5	11	270	4	6
3	149	3	13	12	149	3	14
4	245	4	11	13	245	4	12
5	122	3	17	14	122	3	18
6	259	4	7	15	259	4	8
7	257	4	3	16	257	4	4
8	144	3	15	17	144	3	16
9	331	4	1	18	331	4	2
OUT	2,047	33		IN	2,047	33	
				TOTAL	4,094	66	
STANDARD SCRATCH				62			

COURSE INFORMATION

**Par 66; SSS 62; Length 4477
yards; 4094 metres.**
Visitors: Welcome at all times.
Opening Hours: 9.00am –
sunset.
Ladies: Welcome.
Green Fees: Jan–May €15
weekdays & €20 weekends.
Jun–Sep €20 weekdays & €25
weekends.
Juveniles: Welcome
accompanied by adult. Club Hire
available; Caddy service and
cars available by prior
arrangement.
Clubhouse Hours: 10.30am –
11.30pm.
Clubhouse Dress: Casual.
Clubhouse Facilities: Bar
snacks available all week. Full
catering available by prior
arrangement.
Open Competitions:
Quills Open May. Maple Leaf
Fourball June. Maureen O'Hara
Blair Classic June.
Open Scrambles every
Wednesday & Friday evening:
Mixed Foursomes.

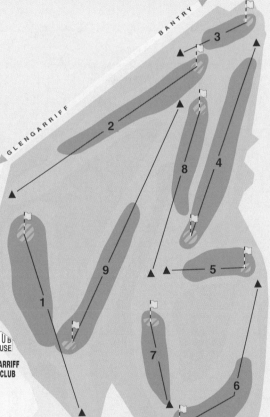

CAR
PARK   GLENGARRIFF
GOLF CLUB

Copyright Tudor Journals Ltd.

**Clash, Little Island,
Co. Cork.
Tel: (021) 353094.
Fax: (021) 354408.**

LOCATION: Seven km from
City Centre.
SECRETARY: Niamh Dwyer
PROPRIETOR: Sean O'Connell.

Little Island on the banks of the
River Lee has a particular rustic
charm. Little Island by it topography
and setting has all the natural gifts
required for a great golf course. In
fact it is more than a championship
golf course with each fairway tree
lined and each green intricately

contoured. It is a complex with an in-
built 21 bay, all weather and flood-lit
driving range positioned in acres of
ground between the 5th and 9th holes.

COURSE INFORMATION

**Par 72; SSS 72; Length
6,163 metres.
Visitors:** Always welcome.
Telephone appointment
required.
Opening Hours: 8am – 5pm.
Avoid: Sunday before 11am.
Green Fees: €33 Mon – Thurs;
€38 Fri/Sat/Sun. 'Early bird'
green fee also available before

11am Mon, Wed, Thurs & Fri.
For group rates please
telephone for information.
Juveniles: Welcome.
Clubhouse Hours: 8am –
12 midnight.
Clubhouse Dress: Neat.
Clubhouse Facilities: Full
Restaurant and Bar.
Catering hours: 10.30am –
6.00pm (winter). 10.30am –
9.00pm (summer).
Open Competitions: Open
weekend, July.

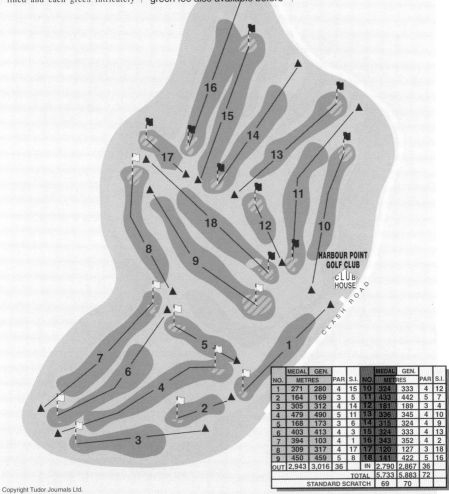

NO.	MEDAL METRES	GEN. METRES	PAR	S.I.	NO.	MEDAL METRES	GEN. METRES	PAR	S.I.
1	271	280	4	15	10	324	333	4	12
2	164	169	3	5	11	433	442	5	7
3	305	312	4	14	12	181	189	3	4
4	479	490	5	11	13	336	345	4	10
5	168	173	3	6	14	315	324	4	9
6	403	413	4	3	15	324	333	4	13
7	394	103	4	1	16	343	352	4	2
8	309	317	4	17	17	120	127	3	18
9	450	459	5	8	18	141	422	5	16
OUT	2,943	3,016	36		IN	2,790	2,867	36	
					TOTAL	5,733	5,883	72	
					STANDARD SCRATCH	69	70		

Copyright Tudor Journals Ltd.

**Fairy Hill Golf Club,
Kanturk, Boyle, Co. Cork.
Tel: (029) 50534.**

LOCATION: Location Fairyhill,
Kanturk.
SECRETARY: Tony McAuliffe.
Tel: (087) 2217510.

Lots of plantations and out-of-bounds
on several parts of the course. A
friendly atmosphere prevails at this
club whose course overlooks the
Bogeresh Mountains. 18th hole
opening soon.

COURSE INFORMATION

**Par 71; SSS 69; Length 5,527
metres.**
Visitors: Welcome.
Opening Hours:
Sunrise – sunset.
Ladies: Welcome. Ladies day
Wednesday.
Green Fees: €15 Monday –
Friday, €20 weekends.
Juveniles: Welcome.
Clubhouse Hours:
After Club Competitions.

Clubhouse Dress: Casual.
Clubhouse Facilities: By prior
arrangement. (Carmel
O'Sullivan).
Open Competitions: As
notified.

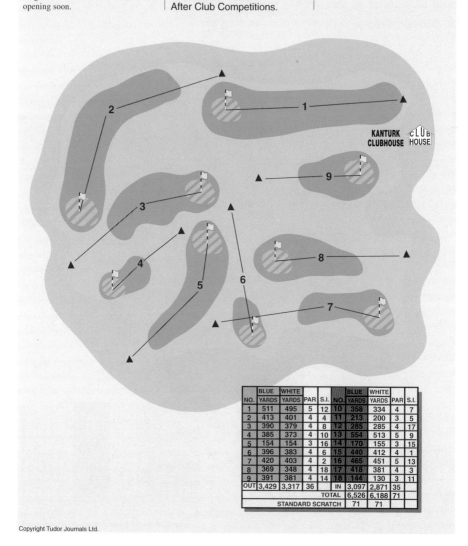

NO.	BLUE YARDS	WHITE YARDS	PAR	S.I.	NO.	BLUE YARDS	WHITE YARDS	PAR	S.I.
1	511	495	5	12	10	358	334	4	7
2	413	401	4	4	11	213	200	3	5
3	390	379	4	8	12	285	285	4	17
4	385	373	4	10	13	554	513	5	9
5	154	154	3	16	14	170	155	3	15
6	396	383	4	6	15	440	412	4	1
7	420	403	4	2	16	465	451	5	13
8	369	348	4	18	17	418	381	4	3
9	391	381	4	14	18	144	130	3	11
OUT	3,429	3,317	36		IN	3,097	2,871	35	
					TOTAL	6,526	6,188	71	
	STANDARD SCRATCH					71	71		

Copyright Tudor Journals Ltd.

Kinsale Golf Club,
**Farrangalway, Kinsale,
Co. Cork.
Tel: (021) 4774722.**

LOCATION: 3 miles from
Kinsale, turn right at Blue
Haven Hotel.
MANAGER: Pat Murray.
Tel: (021) 4774722.

An 18 hole parkland course, the first
holes maximise the roll of the land. The
back nine incorporate natural
waterways which makes for a pleasant
and testing round.

COURSE INFORMATION

**Par 71; SSS 71; Length;
6,609 metres.**
Visitors: Welcome, book at
weekends.
Opening Hours:
7.00am – dusk.
Ladies: Welcome.
Green Fees: Mon - Thurs €30;
Fri €40. Early bird 7-10am €20.
Juveniles: Must be accompained
by an adult.

Clubhouse Hours: 9.00am
– 11.30pm.
Clubhouse facilities: Bar
and restaurant.
Clubhouse Dress: Casual
but smart, no denim or
trainers.
Clubhouse Facilities:
Catering facilities all day.

NO.	MEDAL YARDS	GEN. YARDS	PAR	S.I.	NO.	MEDAL YARDS	GEN. YARDS	PAR	S.I.
1	372	365	4	13	10	405	398	4	8
2	123	118	3	17	11	216	206	3	7
3	415	407	4	2	12	438	431	4	5
4	280	274	4	16	13	395	387	4	4
5	368	358	4	11	14	421	401	4	14
6	175	163	3	18	15	183	168	3	9
7	431	419	4	3	16	368	361	4	10
8	556	548	5	12	17	411	404	4	1
9	560	550	5	6	18	492	482	5	15
OUT	3,280	3,202	36		IN	3,329	3,238	35	
					TOTAL	6,609	6,440	71	
					STANDARD SCRATCH		71		

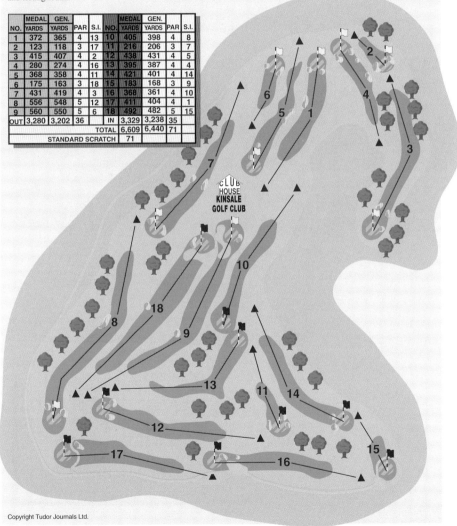

Copyright Tudor Journals Ltd.

Clashanure, Ovens, Co. Cork.
Tel: (021) 7331721.
Email: leevalleygolfclub@eircom.net
Website: www.leevalleygcc.ie

LOCATION: 10 miles from Cork City on the N22.
SECRETARY: John Savage.
PROFESSIONAL: John Savage.
ARCHITECT: Christy O'Connor

Parkland course with water featuring at several holes. One feature of note is the dry terrain whatever the weather.

COURSE INFORMATION

Par 72; SSS 72; Length 6,725 yards.
Avoid: Saturday & Sunday to 11.15am.
Opening Hours: 7am - 6pm (depending on daylight).
Green Fees: April – October: Weekday €44, Weekend €54. November – March Weekday promotions €20, Weekend €38. Juveniles €19. Early bird (before 10am) weekdays (excluding Wednesdays) €25
Clubhouse Dress: Neat informal.
Clubhouse Facilities: Bar and full restaurant.
Open Competitions: Regular throughout the year.

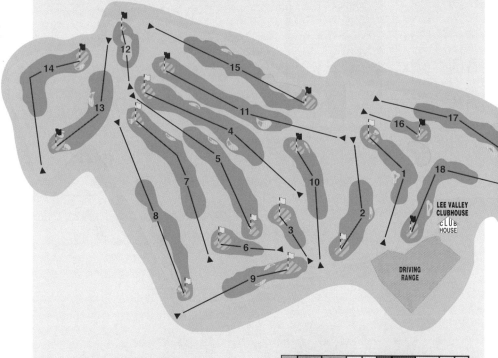

NO.	MEDAL YARDS	GEN YARDS	PAR	S.I.	NO.	MEDAL YARDS	GEN YARDS	PAR	S.I.
1	363	345	4	11	10	347	324	4	18
2	344	331	4	7	11	549	522	5	6
3	179	165	3	13	12	178	166	3	16
4	528	504	5	15	13	379	358	4	10
5	475	457	4	1	14	407	389	4	12
6	169	153	3	17	15	536	525	5	4
7	451	436	4	3	16	171	160	3	14
8	528	511	5	9	17	407	394	4	2
9	315	303	4	5	18	399	381	4	8
OUT	3,352	3,205	36		IN	3,373	3,219	36	
					TOTAL	6,725	6,424	72	
					STANDARD SCRATCH	72	70		

Bunker positions indicated.
Copyright Tudor Journals Ltd.

NO.	MTRS.	PAR	S.I.	NO.	MTRS.	PAR	S.I.
1	429	5	13	10	437	5	14
2	114	3	10	11	130	3	12
3	344	4	1	12	292	4	9
4	290	4	18	13	159	3	6
5	298	4	7	14	300	4	5
6	162	3	3	15	239	4	17
7	437	5	16	16	277	4	15
8	329	4	11	17	450	5	8
9	360	4	4	18	343	4	2
OUT	2,763	36		IN	2,627	36	
				TOTAL	5,390	72	
				STANDARD SCRATCH	70		

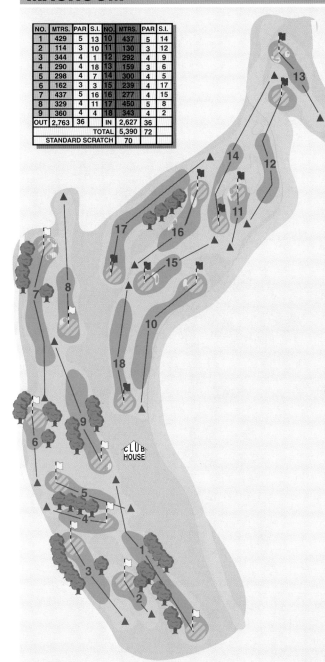

**Lackaduve, Macroom,
Co. Cork.
Tel: (026) 41072.
Fax: (026) 41391.**

LOCATION: On grounds of
Castle Demesne in centre
of town.
HON SECRETARY: Val Tupper
MANAGER: Cathal O' Sullivan

An undulating scenic 18 hole
parkland course, within the town
and constructed around the River
Sullane, natural water hazards being
a major feature of the course on the
back nine. Situated on the main
Cork / Killarney Road with entrance
through castle gates.

COURSE INFORMATION

**Par 72; SSS 70; Length
5574 metres.**
Visitors: Welcome but
advisable to phone in advance.
Opening Hours:
Sunrise – sunset.
Avoid: Days of major
competitions.
Ladies: Ladies day Wed.
Ladies full membership.
Green Fees: €25 Mon – Fri;
€30 at weekends. Early Bird
up to 11am Mon-Thur €15.
€12 juveniles/student.
Juveniles: Cannot play after
6.00pm or at weekends. Caddy
service and buggies available
by prior arrangement;
telephone appointment
required.
Clubhouse Hours: 9am –
11.30pm.
Clubhouse Dress: Casual.
Open Competitions: Open
Week: 27th July thru Aug 4th

Bunker & tree positions indicated.
Copyright Tudor Journals Ltd.

Skehard Road, Cork.
Tel: (021) 4294280.

LOCATION: Skehard Road
(Three miles from city).
HONORARY SECRETARY: Tim &
Jo O'Connor
Tel: (021) 362727.
MANAGER: Tim O'Connor.

Mahon is a municipal course and is administered by Cork Corporation. It is built on the very edge of the River Douglas Estuary and because of this has many interesting holes, the 9th especially is not a place for the faint-hearted, with a tee shot over water.

COURSE INFORMATION

Par 70; SSS 66; Length 5,192 metres.
Visitors: Welcome. Should ring in advance.
Opening Hours: Sunrise - Sunset.
Avoid: Fri/Sat & Sun mornings.
Ladies: Welcome.
Green Fees: €18 Mon - Fri; €19 Sat & Sun; Pensioners, Students and Juveniles €8 Mon - Fri; €19 Sat & Sun.
Juveniles: Welcome. Club hire available.
Clubhouse Dress: Casual.
Clubhouse Facilities: Bar and catering facilities available at the Balckrock Inn.
Tel: (021) 4291006

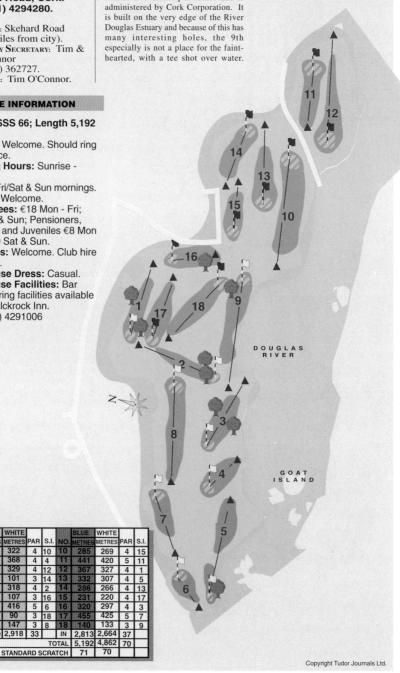

DOUGLAS RIVER

GOAT ISLAND

NO.	BLUE METRES	WHITE METRES	PAR	S.I.	NO.	BLUE METRES	WHITE METRES	PAR	S.I.
1	339	322	4	10	10	285	269	4	15
2	381	368	4	4	11	441	420	5	11
3	334	329	4	12	12	367	327	4	1
4	125	101	3	14	13	332	307	4	5
5	333	318	4	2	14	286	266	4	13
6	123	107	3	16	15	231	220	4	17
7	435	416	5	6	16	320	297	4	3
8	102	90	3	18	17	455	425	5	7
9	157	147	3	8	18	140	133	3	9
OUT	2,329	2,918	33		IN	2,813	2,664	37	
					TOTAL	5,192	4,862	70	
	STANDARD SCRATCH					71	70		

Copyright Tudor Journals Ltd.

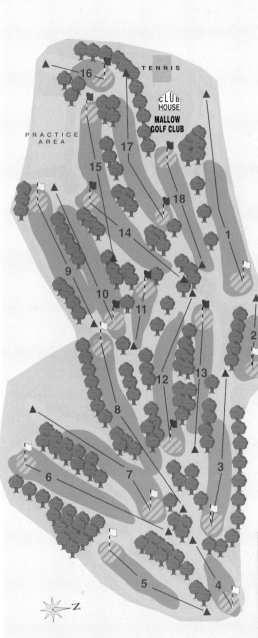

**Ballyellis, Mallow,
Co Cork.
Tel: (022) 21145.
Fax: (022) 42501.**
Email: golfmall@gofree.indigo.ie

LOCATION: One mile from centre of Mallow town on the Kilavullen Road.
SECRETARY / MANAGER: David Cortin. Tel: (022) 21145 .
PROFESSIONAL: Sean Conway. Tel: (022) 43424.
ARCHITECT: Commander John D. Harris.

This majestic parkland course, with exceptional views of both the Mushera and the distant Galtee mountains, boasts an idyllic rural setting. Set in the heart of the Blackwater Valley, Mallow's undulating treelined fairways transport the golfer from tee to green, and provide an enjoyable testing round of golf.

COURSE INFORMATION

Par 72; SSS 72; Length 5,960 metres.
Visitors: Welcome to play on weekdays but pre-booking is essential.
Opening Hours: 8am to late evening.
Avoid: Saturday and Sunday. Prior arrangement is essential.
Green Fees: €32 per day; €38 weekends & Public holidays. Caddy car hire available by prior arrangment.
Clubhouse Hours: 9.00am – 11.00pm.
Clubhouse Dress: Casual, no denim jeans.
Clubhouse Facilities: 3 tennis courts, 2 squash courts, snooker room, television lounge and sauna. Snacks at all times. Full bar and catering facilities.
Open Competitions: Open week, 3rd -7th June.

NO.	MEDAL METRES	GEN. METRES	PAR	S.I.	NO.	MEDAL METRES	GEN. METRES	PAR	S.I.
1	367	359	4	7	10	393	381	4	6
2	174	166	3	9	11	155	145	3	12
3	448	439	5	11	12	496	490	5	8
4	172	167	3	15	13	379	356	4	2
5	347	339	4	3	14	287	273	4	16
6	462	440	5	13	15	351	345	4	4
7	413	388	4	1	16	116	107	3	18
8	435	428	5	17	17	446	435	5	14
9	339	333	4	5	18	180	173	3	10
OUT	3,157	3,059	37		IN	2,803	2,710	35	
					TOTAL	5,960	5,769	72	
					STANDARD SCRATCH	72	71		

Copyright Tudor Journals Ltd.

Gurrane, Mitchelstown, Co. Cork.
Tel: (025) 24072.

LOCATION: One mile on Limerick road from Mitchelstown.
SECRETARY: Dick Stapleton. Tel: (025) 24072.

A level course which appears easy, but should not be under estimated. The main attraction to visitors are the nearby Galtee Mountains. Additional holes opening soon.

COURSE INFORMATION

Par 67; SSS 66; Length 5,148 metres.
Visitors: Welcome.
Opening Hours: Sunrise – sunset.
Avoid: Sunday.
Green Fees: €20 Mon - Fri, €25 Sat - Sun.

Juveniles: Welcome. Must be accompanied by an adult after 6.00pm.
Clubhouse Hours: 9.00am – 11.30pm.
Clubhouse Dress: Casual.
Clubhouse Facilities: Bar only in evenings. Snacks available in evenings. No lessons currently available.
Open Competitions: Contact secretary for details.

NO.	MEDAL METRES	GEN. METRES	PAR	S.I.	NO.	MEDAL METRES	GEN. METRES	PAR	S.I.
1	384	375	4	3	10	164	145	3	10
2	192	182	3	9	11	359	349	4	2
3	348	348	4	11	12	353	333	4	4
4	325	314	4	13	13	143	128	3	12
5	175	175	3	7	14	272	258	4	6
6	328	328	4	15	15	322	308	4	8
7	137	126	3	17	16	451	434	5	16
8	357	340	4	1	17	109	107	3	18
9	376	258	4	5	18	353	353	4	14
OUT	2,622	2,546	33		IN	2,526	2,415	34	
					TOTAL	5,148	4,961	67	
					STANDARD SCRATCH	67	66		

MITCHELSTOWN GOLF CLUB

CLUB HOUSE

Copyright Tudor Journals Ltd.

Parkgariffe, Monkstown,
Co. Cork.
Tel: (021) 4841376
Fax: (021) 4841722
Emai:
office@monkstowngolfclub.com.

LOCATION: Seven miles from City.
GENERALMANAGER SECRETARY:
Hilary Madden.
PROFESSIONAL: Mr B. Murphy.
Tel: (021) 4841686.
ARCHITECTS: Peter O'Hare and
Tom Carey.

A testing parkland course where, because of many trees and bunkers, accuracy is at a premium. All greens are well protected. From the first nine there are many scenic views of Cork Harbour, and on the back nine, water features on four holes. 85 bunkers were constructed and remodelled offering a great golfing challenge.

COURSE INFORMATION

Par 70; SSS 69; Length 6,199 yards; 5,669 metres.
Visitors: Welcome. Telephone bookings in advance advisable.
Opening Hours: 8.00am – sunset.
Avoid: Tues (Ladies Day); Wed afternoon; Sat / Sun mornings.
Green Fees: €37 Mon – Thurs; €44 Fri / Sun. Reductions for societies, €14 with member.
Juveniles: Must be accompanied by an adult. Lessons available by prior arrangements; Club Hire and Caddy cars available; telephone appointment advisable.
Clubhouse Hours: 8.00am – 11.30pm.
Clubhouse Dress: Casual. No denims or sneakers.
Clubhouse Facilities: Breakfast, Lunch, Dinner, a la carte. Last orders 9.00pm; tel: 4859876. Bar open 12.00 noon – 11.30pm.
Open Competitions: Intermediate, Junior and Senior Scratch Cups.

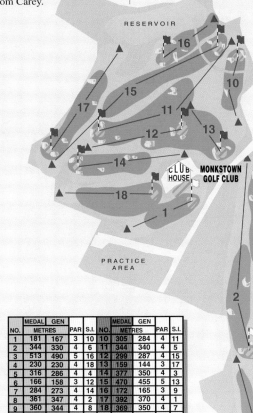

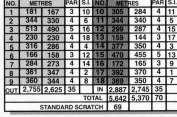

NO.	MEDAL METRES	GEN	PAR	S.I.	NO.	MEDAL METRES	GEN	PAR	S.I.
1	181	167	3	10	10	305	284	4	11
2	344	330	4	6	11	344	340	4	5
3	513	490	5	16	12	299	287	4	15
4	230	230	4	18	13	159	144	3	17
5	316	286	4	4	14	377	350	4	3
6	166	158	3	12	15	470	455	5	13
7	284	273	4	14	16	172	165	3	9
8	361	347	4	2	17	392	370	4	1
9	360	344	4	8	18	369	350	4	7
OUT	2,755	2,625	35		IN	2,887	2,745	35	
					TOTAL	5,642	5,370	70	
					STANDARD SCRATCH		69		

Bunker positions indicated.
Copyright Tudor Journals Ltd.

Carrigrohane, Co. Cork.
Tel: (021) 4385297.
Fax: (021) 4516860.

LOCATION: Eight miles north west of Cork City; Two miles west of Blarney.
MANAGER: Hugo Gallagher.
PROFESSIONAL: M. Lehane.
Tel: (021) 4381445.

Undulating on three levels. The 6th hole could be described as good a Par 3 as will be found anywhere. Last four holes provide a most challenging finish, the last two crossing a river. Precise clubbing and accuracy are demanded on this course.

COURSE INFORMATION

Par 71; SSS 70; Length 6,327 yards; 5,786 metres.
Visitors: Welcome: Mon & Tue all day; Wed up to 10.30am; Thurs from 1.30pm; Fri up to 4.00pm; Sat / Sun enquire. Telephone in advance each day.
Avoid: Members hours 12.30 – 1.30pm daily.

Opening Hours:
9.00am – sunset.
Green Fees: €35 midweek. €40 Sat / Sun (if available). Early Bird: Mon, Tue, Fri upto 10am €20.
Juveniles: Welcome. Lessons available by prior arrangement; Club Hire available; telephone in advance at all times.
Clubhouse Hours:
9.00am - 11.30pm.
Clubhouse Dress:
Neat / casual.
Clubhouse Facilities:
Full catering and bar.
Open Competitions:
Senior, Junior and Intermediate Scratch Cups.

NO.	MEDAL METRES	GEN. METRES	PAR	S.I.	NO.	MEDAL METRES	GEN. METRES	PAR	S.I.
1	385	372	4	2	10	322	292	4	15
2	243	241	4	18	11	361	344	4	11
3	356	348	4	8	12	156	144	3	13
4	444	435	5	10	13	373	351	4	5
5	339	329	4	6	14	446	433	5	17
6	182	172	3	4	15	152	132	3	9
7	425	415	5	16	16	391	346	4	3
8	165	152	3	12	17	405	377	4	1
9	309	285	4	14	18	354	352	4	7
OUT	2,848	2,749	36		IN	2,960	2,771	35	
					TOTAL	5,808	5,520	71	
					STANDARD SCRATCH	71	70		

Copyright Tudor Journals Ltd.

**Old Head Golf Links,
Kinsale, Co. Cork.
Tel: (021) 4778444.**

LOCATION: 7 miles south of Kinsale town.
DIRECTOR OF GOLF: David Murray. Tel: (021) 4778444.
GENERAL MANAGER: Jim 'O Brien

The links is situated on an Atlantic promontory rising hundreds of feet high above dramatic cliffs, surrounded by the ocean on all sides and commanding the most spectacular views. Every hole has a minimum of six tees – providing a test for all category of players.

COURSE INFORMATION

Par 72; SSS 74; Length 7,215 yards.
Visitors: Welcome at all times.
Opening Hours: 8am – 10pm.
Green Fees: €250 all week.
Juveniles: Welcome - over 12 yrs with handicap.
Clubhouse Hours: 8am – 10pm.
Clubhouse Dress: Smart/casual, denim jeans and sneakers prohibited.
Clubhouse Facilities: Bar/Restaurant and Golf Shop.

NO.	MEDAL YARDS	GEN. YARDS	PAR	S.I.	NO.	MEDAL YARDS	GEN. YARDS	PAR	S.I.
1	446	418	4	2	10	518	494	5	15
2	406	388	4	10	11	198	178	3	13
3	180	176	3	18	12	564	554	5	9
4	427	423	4	12	13	258	227	3	5
5	430	409	4	6	14	452	428	4	1
6	495	485	5	14	15	342	330	4	17
7	188	179	3	8	16	195	183	3	11
8	549	520	5	16	17	632	606	5	7
9	475	451	4	4	18	460	419	4	3
OUT	3,596	3,449	36		IN	3,619	3,419	36	
					TOTAL	7,215	6,868	72	
					STANDARD SCRATCH	74	70		

Bunker/hedge and tree positions indicated.
Copyright Tudor Journals Ltd.

Ringaskiddy, Co. Cork.
Tel: (021) 4378430.

LOCATION: Ten miles from Cork.
MANAGER: John O'Sullivan.
TREASURER: Derry Murphy.
ARCHITECT: E. Hackett.

A scenic course whose special features are tough over-water shots. Straight, accurate play will get best results. The 8th and 9th are twofearsome holes with the Lake coming into play.

COURSE INFORMATION

Par 70; SSS 68; Length 5,575 yards, 5,098 metres.
Visitors: Welcome.
Opening Hours: Sunrise – sunset.
Avoid: Competition times; Sat / Sun mornings.
Ladies: Welcome Mon – Fri.
Green Fees: €20 Mon – Fri; €25 Sat / Sun; €15 early morning Mon – Friday, €10 with member.
Juveniles: Welcome Tues-Fri up to 6.00pm, €10. Telephone appointment required.
Clubhouse Hours: 10.00am – 11.30pm.
Clubhouse Dress: Casual.
Clubhouse Facilities: Snacks available. Food served daily 12am-2.30pm.

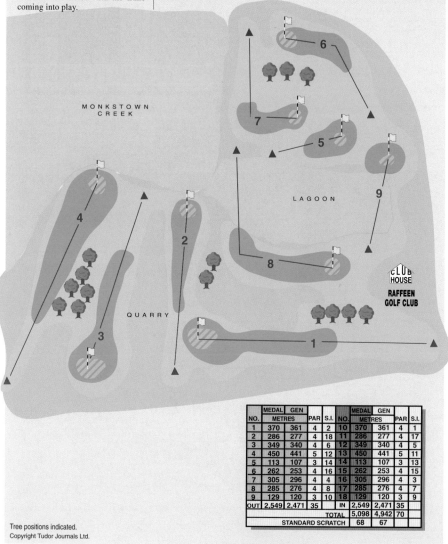

NO.	MEDAL METRES	GEN METRES	PAR	S.I.	NO.	MEDAL METRES	GEN METRES	PAR	S.I.
1	370	361	4	2	10	370	361	4	1
2	286	277	4	18	11	286	277	4	17
3	349	340	4	6	12	349	340	4	5
4	450	441	5	12	13	450	441	5	11
5	113	107	3	14	14	113	107	3	13
6	262	253	4	16	15	262	253	4	15
7	305	296	4	4	16	305	296	4	3
8	285	276	4	8	17	285	276	4	7
9	129	120	3	10	18	129	120	3	9
OUT	2,549	2,471	35		IN	2,549	2,471	35	
					TOTAL	5,098	4,942	70	
					STANDARD SCRATCH	68	67		

Tree positions indicated.
Copyright Tudor Journals Ltd.

Licknavar, Skibbereen.
Co. Cork.
Tel: (028) 28334.
Fax: (028) 22994.
Email: info@skibbgolf.com
Web: www.skibbgolf.com

LOCATION: Approx. two miles
Skibbereen.
SECRETARY/MANAGER: Séamus
Brett. Tel: (028) 21227.
PROFESSIONAL:
Christy O'Donavan.

A course with very few hazards and
wide open fairways, excellent for the
high handicapper. Extra nine holes
opened in late 1993.

COURSE INFORMATION

**Par 71; SSS 68; Length
5,967 yards; 5,279 metres.**
Visitors: Welcome.
Opening Hours: Sunrise –
sunset.
Avoid: Thursday afternoons
(Men's Competition); Friday
(Ladies Day).
Ladies: Welcome Fridays.
Green Fees: May – Sep
€30, Winter €27. Club Hire
and Caddy trolleys available.

Clubhouse Hours: 8.00am –
10.00pm (summer); irregular
hours in winter.**Clubhouse
Dress:** Casual.
Clubhouse Facilities: All day,
drinks, soups, sandwiches
(summer). Full restaurant &
bar food everyday.
Open Competitions: At fixed
dates during summer and at
Bank Holiday weekends.

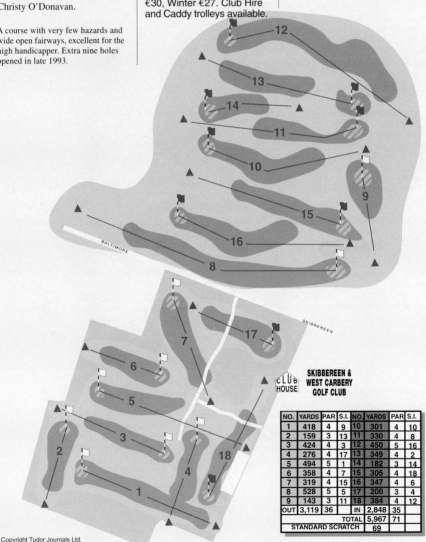

SKIBBEREEN & WEST CARBERY GOLF CLUB

NO.	YARDS	PAR	S.I.	NO.	YARDS	PAR	S.I.
1	418	4	9	10	301	4	10
2	159	3	13	11	330	4	8
3	424	4	3	12	450	5	16
4	276	4	17	13	349	4	2
5	494	5	1	14	182	3	14
6	358	4	7	15	305	4	18
7	319	4	15	16	347	4	6
8	528	5	5	17	200	3	4
9	143	3	11	18	384	4	12
OUT	3,119	36		IN	2,848	35	
				TOTAL	5,967	71	
				STANDARD SCRATCH	69		

Copyright Tudor Journals Ltd.

**Knockaveryy, Youghal,
Co. Cork.
Tel: (024) 92787.
Fax: (024) 92641.**

LOCATION: Knockaverry, Youghal.
SECRETARY: Margaret O'Sullivan.
Tel: (024) 92787.
PROFESSIONAL: Liam Burns.
ARCHITECT: Commander Harris.

Meadowland course offering
panoramic views of Youghal Bay and
Blackwater estuary. It is enjoyable for
high handicap golfers while still
offering a good test for the low
handicap golfer.

COURSE INFORMATION

**Par 70; SSS 69; Length
5,646 metres.**
Visitors: Welcome every day
except Wednesday; telephone
appointment required for
weekends.
Opening Hours:
9.00am – sunset.
Green Fees: €25 Mon – Fri;
€32 Sat / Sun.
Clubhouse Hours: 9.30am –
11.30pm. Variable in winter
months; full clubhouse facilities.
Clubhouse Dress: Casual.
Clubhouse Facilities: Snacks
available at all times; full meals
served from 10.30am – 9.00pm.
Open Competitions: One week
in July and first two weeks in
August and weekends during
summer.

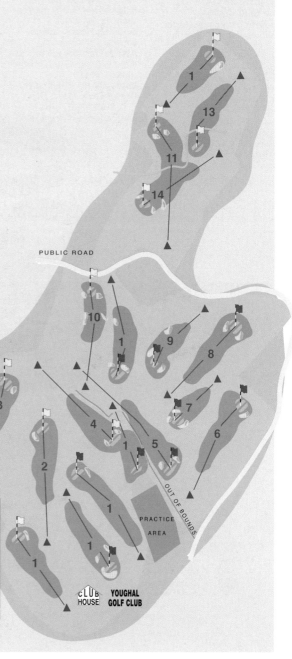

NO.	CHAMP METRES	MED. METRES	PAR	S.I.	NO.	CHAMP METRES	MED. METRES	PAR	S.I.
1	275	252	4	16	10	401	390	4	3
2	451	438	5	14	11	320	309	4	9
3	142	142	3	18	12	281	273	4	15
4	371	358	4	4	13	381	371	4	1
5	329	320	4	12	14	243	240	4	17
6	302	289	4	8	15	370	359	4	5
7	151	140	3	10	16	183	174	3	13
8	381	369	4	2	17	349	340	4	11
9	335	222	4	6	18	381	373	4	7
OUT	2737	2630	35		IN	2909	2829	35	
					TOTAL	5646	5459	70	
					STANDARD SCRATCH	69	68		

Bunker positions indicated.
Copyright Tudor Journals Ltd.

**Ardfert Golf Club,
Sackville, Ardfert, Tralee,
Co. Kerry.
Tel: (066) 34744.
Fax: (066) 34744.**

LOCATION: 6 miles from Tralee.
SECRETARY: Kathleen
O'Loughlin/ Tess Meehan.
Tel: (066) 34744.
PROFESSIONAL: Noel Cassidy
and Brian Higgins.

A nine hole parkland course greatly
compliments the scenic countryside
with a river and lake featured in its
design. It has 12 all weather driving
range bays lessons available by
appointment. Club hire is also
available.

COURSE INFORMATION

**Par 70; SSS 67;
Length 5,118 Yards.
Visitors:** Welcome.
Opening Hours: 9am –
sunset.
Ladies: Welcome.

Juveniles: Welcome, lessons
available.
Green Fees: €15 for 9 holes.
€23 for 18 holes.
Clubhouse Hours: 9.00am –
9.30pm.
Clubhouse Dress: Casual.
Clubhouse Facilities: Tea,
coffee & light snacks available
everyday.

NO.	YARDS	PAR	S.I.	NO.	YARDS	PAR	S.I.
1	180	3	10	10	188	3	9
2	338	4	14	11	362	4	13
3	511	5	2	12	542	5	1
4	352	4	6	13	360	4	5
5	306	4	16	14	320	4	15
6	328	4	4	15	340	4	3
7	452	5	18	16	465	5	17
8	163	3	12	17	180	3	11
9	130	3	8	18	155	3	7
OUT	2,760	35		IN	2,912	35	
				TOTAL	5,672	70	
	STANDARD SCRATCH				67		

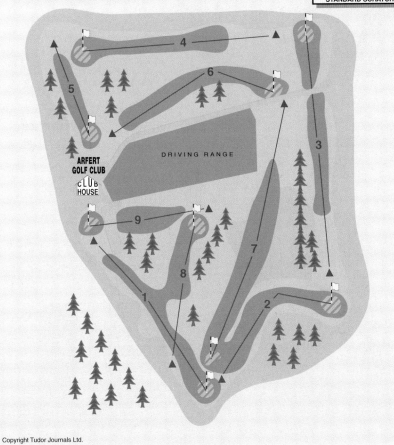

ARFERT
GOLF CLUB
CLUB
HOUSE

DRIVING RANGE

Copyright Tudor Journals Ltd.

Ballybunion Co Kerry.
Tel: (068) 27146.

Location: Ballybunion.
Secretary: Jim McKenna.
Tel: (068) 27146.
Professional: Brian O'Callaghan.
Tel: (068) 27146.

The 'Old Course' at Ballybunion is world famous and is consistently rated amonst the top ten courses in the world. A magnificent course with several holes right on the shore and towering sandhills coming into play on all. One of Ireland's greatest golfing challenges it regularly receives golfing accolades from all over the world. (The Cashen Course was designed by Robert Treant Jones and is every bit as demanding (if not more) as the Old Course).

COURSE INFORMATION

Par 71; SSS 72; Length 6,542 yards.
Visitors: Welcome.
Opening Hours: 7.00am – 4.30pm.
Avoid: Weekends.
Ladies: Welcome
Green Fees: €110 (Old Course); €135 (Both Courses).
Juveniles: Welcome. Lessons available by prior arrangement; Club Hire available by prior arrangement; Caddy service available; Handicap Certificate required; telephone appointment required for green fees times.
Clubhouse Hours: 7.00am – 11.00pm;
Clubhouse Dress: Neat.
Clubhouse facilities: Professional Shop Open; full clubhouse facilities; full catering facilities 9.00am – 9.00pm.

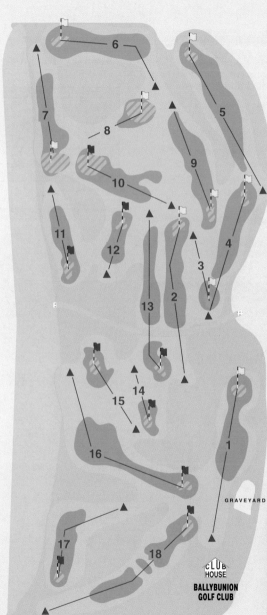

CLUB HOUSE

BALLYBUNION GOLF CLUB

GRAVEYARD

NO.	MEDAL YARDS	GEN YARDS	PAR	S.I.	NO.	MEDAL YARDS	GEN YARDS	PAR	S.I.
1	392	366	4	9	10	359	336	4	10
2	445	394	4	1	11	449	400	4	2
3	220	211	3	11	12	192	179	3	16
4	498	490	5	15	13	484	480	5	8
5	508	489	5	13	14	131	125	3	18
6	364	344	4	7	15	216	207	3	4
7	423	400	4	5	16	490	482	5	14
8	153	134	3	17	17	385	368	4	12
9	454	430	4	3	18	379	366	4	6
OUT	3,457	3,258	36		IN	3,085	2,943	35	
					TOTAL	6,542	6,201	71	
					STANDARD SCRATCH	72	70		

Copyright Tudor Journals Ltd.

Ballybunion, Co Kerry.
Tel: (068) 27146.

LOCATION: Ballybunion.
SECRETARY: Jim McKenna.
Tel: (068) 27146.
PROFESSIONAL: Brian
O'Callaghan.
Tel: (068) 27146.

The 'Cashen Course' at Ballybunion
was designed by Robert Trent Jones
and is every bit as demanding - if
not more - than the 'Old Course'.
Both courses enjoy the benefit of
the Atlantic coastline. The remote
location of the course is
instrumental in reducing the number
of casual players leaving those on
'pilgrimage' with more solitude.

COURSE INFORMATION

**Par 72; SSS 73; Length
6,278 yards.**
Visitors: Welcome.
Opening Hours: 7.00am –
5.30pm.
Avoid: Weekends.
Ladies: Welcome.
Green Fees: €75 (Cashen
Course); €135 (Both Courses).
Juveniles: Welcome. Lessons
available by prior arrangement;
Club Hire available by prior
arrangement; Caddy service
available; Handicap Certificate
required; telephone
appointment required for green
fee times.
Clubhouse Hours: 7.00am –
11.00pm.
Clubhouse Dress: Neat.
Clubhouse Facilities:
Professional Shop open; full
clubhouse facilities; full catering
facilities 9.00am - 9.00pm.

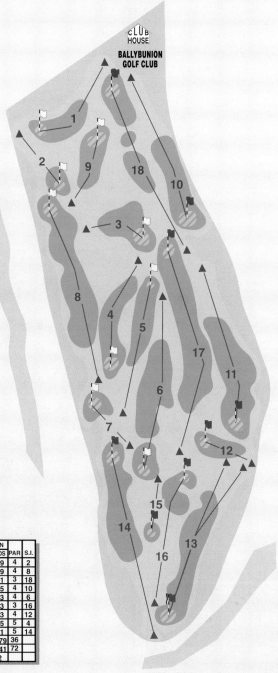

NO.	MEDAL YARDS	GEN YARDS	PAR	S.I.	NO.	MEDAL YARDS	GEN YARDS	PAR	S.I.
1	324	312	4	11	10	432	399	4	2
2	146	140	3	17	11	377	359	4	8
3	237	223	4	13	12	154	141	3	18
4	395	374	4	1	13	350	325	4	10
5	400	355	4	7	14	378	373	4	6
6	487	476	5	3	15	155	143	3	16
7	199	145	3	15	16	314	303	4	12
8	479	476	5	9	17	605	585	5	4
9	368	361	4	5	18	478	451	5	14
OUT	3,035	2,826	36		IN	3,243	3,079	36	
					TOTAL	6,278	5,941	72	
	STANDARD SCRATCH					73	72		

Copyright Tudor Journals Ltd.

**Beaufort Golf Course,
Churchtown, Beaufort,
Killarney. Co. Kerry.
Tel: (064) 44440.
Fax: (064) 44752.**
LOCATION: Seven miles west
of Killarney, just off
the N72W.
SECRETARY: Colm Kelly.
ARHITECT: Arthur Spring.
PROFESSIONAL: Hugh Duggan

Parkland, 6,587 Yds. Par 71. Situated in
the centre of South West Ireland's golfing
mecca. Just five miles from the world
famous Killarney Golf Club. Course is
surrounded by Kerry mountains and the
back nine is dominated by the ruins of
Castle Core.

COURSE INFORMATION

**Par 71; SSS 72; Length 6,587
yards.**

Visitors: At Weekends avoid
1pm – 2pm (members only).
Opening Hours: 7.30am
until darkness.
Juveniles: Permitted.
Green Fees: €45 weekdays,
€55 weekends. Society Rates
available on request.
Clubhouse Hours: 7.30am-11pm.
Clubhouse Dress:
Informal but neat.
Clubhouse Facilities: Bar food.

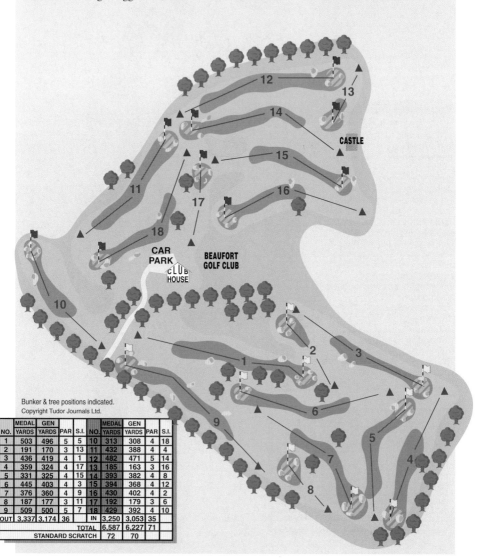

Bunker & tree positions indicated.
Copyright Tudor Journals Ltd.

NO.	MEDAL YARDS	GEN YARDS	PAR	S.I.	NO.	MEDAL YARDS	GEN YARDS	PAR	S.I.
1	503	496	5	5	10	313	308	4	18
2	191	170	3	13	11	432	388	4	4
3	436	419	4	1	12	482	471	5	14
4	359	324	4	17	13	185	163	3	16
5	331	325	4	15	14	393	382	4	8
6	445	403	4	3	15	394	368	4	12
7	376	360	4	9	16	430	402	4	2
8	187	177	3	11	17	192	179	3	6
9	509	500	5	7	18	429	392	4	10
OUT	3,337	3,174	36		IN	3,250	3,053	35	
					TOTAL	6,587	6,227	71	
					STANDARD SCRATCH	72	70		

Castlegregory Golf & Fishing Club, Stradbally, Castlegregory, Co. Kerry.
Tel: (066) 39444.

LOCATION: 2 miles west of Castlegregory.
SECRETARY: Gorretti O' Connor.
Tel: (066) 39444.
ARCHITECT: Arthur Spring.

9 hole links course, 1 par 5 and 3 par 3's. Scenically situated between a fresh water lake and the sea.

COURSE INFORMATION

Par 68; SSS 68; Length 5,880 yards.
Visitors: Welcome.
Opening Hours: Early mornings – late evenings.
Avoid: Club competitions.
Ladies: Welcome.
Green Fees: €25.
Juveniles: Welcome.
Clubhouse Hours: 9.00am – 9.00pm.
Clubhouse Dress: Casual.

Clubhouse Facilities: Catering facilities available.
Open Competitions: All summer, Mens' and Ladies' clubs.

NO.	METRES	PAR	S.I.	NO.	METRES	PAR	S.I.
1	497	5	11	10	497	5	12
2	186	3	7	11	186	3	8
3	242	4	17	12	242	4	18
4	374	4	3	13	374	4	4
5	183	3	9	14	183	3	10
6	286	4	15	15	286	4	16
7	397	4	1	16	397	4	2
8	365	4	5	17	365	4	6
9	145	3	13	18	145	3	14
OUT	2,675	34		IN	2,675	34	
				TOTAL	5,350	68	
			STANDARD SCRATCH		68		

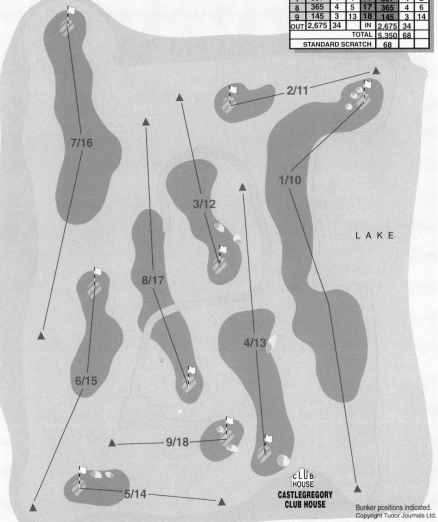

LAKE

SEA

2/11
7/16
1/10
3/12
8/17
4/13
6/15
9/18
5/14

CLUB HOUSE
CASTLEGREGORY CLUB HOUSE

Bunker positions indicated.
Copyright Tudor Journals Ltd.

Ballyoughterach,
Ballyferriter, Co. Kerry.
Tel: (066) 9156
255/408.
Fax: (066) 9156409.

LOCATION: Dingle Peninsula.
HON. SECRETARY: Padraig Foley.
MANAGER: Steve Fahy.
Tel: (066) 9156 255/408.
ARCHITECT: E. Hackett / Christy
O'Connor Jnr.

A links course with wind proving a big factor as it sweeps in from the Atlantic Ocean. The design of the course uses the natural terrain and has the advantage of the area's marvellous turf. A setting for traditional golf with panoramic surroundings.

COURSE INFORMATION

Par 72; SSS 71; Length 6,690 yards; 6,074 metres.
Visitors: Welcome at all times.
Opening Hours: Sunrise – sunset.
Avoid: Sunday afternoons.
Ladies: Welcome.
Green Fees: 18 hole: €25-€50 weekdays, €25-€57 weekends. 36 hole €45-€76 weekdays, €55-€76 weekends (prices vary with season).

Lessons available by prior arrangements; Club Hire and Caddy service available by prior arrangements.
Juveniles: Welcome (accompanied by adult June – August).
Clubhouse Hours: 8.00am – 9.00pm; Professional Shop open.
Clubhouse Dress: Casual.
Clubhouse Facilities: Full clubhouse facilities everyday. Trolly & Cart hire available.
Open Competitions: Easter Sunday; Toyota Open 1st – 3rd September.

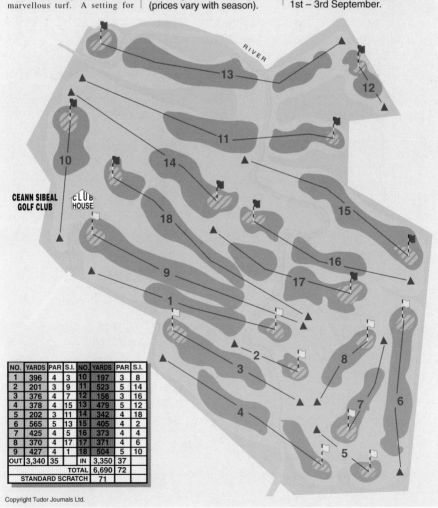

NO.	YARDS	PAR	S.I.	NO.	YARDS	PAR	S.I.
1	396	4	3	10	197	3	8
2	201	3	9	11	523	5	14
3	376	4	7	12	156	3	16
4	378	4	15	13	479	5	12
5	202	3	11	14	342	4	18
6	565	5	13	15	405	4	2
7	425	4	5	16	373	4	4
8	370	4	17	17	371	4	6
9	427	4	1	18	504	5	10
OUT	3,340	35		IN	3,350	37	
				TOTAL	6,690	72	
				STANDARD SCRATCH		71	

Copyright Tudor Journals Ltd.

**Dooks, Glenbeigh,
Co. Kerry.
Tel: (066) 9768205/9768200.
Fax: (066) 9768476.
Email: office@dooks.com**

Location: Four miles from
Killorglin.
Secretary: D. Mangan
Tel: (066) 9768205.

Dooks-a word derived from Gaelic
'drumhac' meaning sand-bank - is a

testing 18 hole links situated in one
of the most picturesque corners of the
Ring of Kerry. The golf course is laid
out on one of three stretches of sand-
dunes at the head of picturesque
Dingle Bay.

COURSE INFORMATION

**Par 70; SSS 68; Length
6,071 yards; 6,010
metres.**
Visitors: Welcome.
Opening Hours: Sunrise -

Avoid: Sundays.
Ladies: Welcome. Caddy
service available; Handicap
Certificate required.
Green Fees: €40 per round
€55 day ticket.
Clubhouse Hours: 9.00am –
11.00pm.
Clubhouse Dress: Casual.
Clubhouse Facilities:
11.00am – 7.00pm.
Open Competitions:
By invitation.

NO.	MEDAL METRES	GEN METRES	PAR	S.I.	NO.	MEDAL METRES	GEN METRES	PAR	S.I.
1	419	380	4	2	10	406	360	4	1
2	131	118	3	18	11	531	523	5	7
3	300	300	4	16	12	370	348	4	3
4	344	317	4	6	13	150	141	3	15
5	194	184	3	10	14	375	365	4	11
6	394	380	4	4	15	213	197	3	5
7	477	454	5	14	16	328	338	4	13
8	368	348	4	8	17	313	308	4	17
9	183	165	3	12	18	494	476	5	9
OUT	2,810	2,646	34		IN	3,200	3,056	36	
					TOTAL	6,010	5,702	70	
					STANDARD SCRATCH		68		

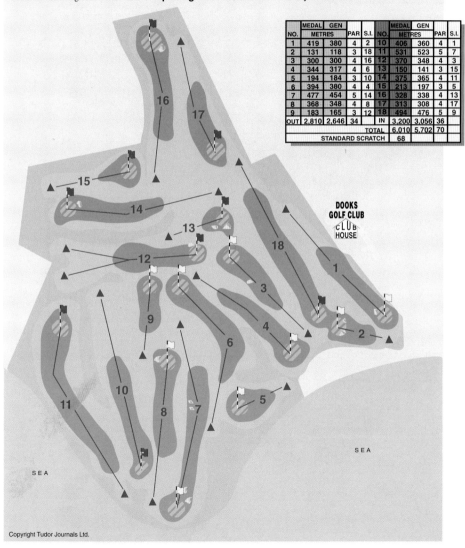

DOOKS
GOLF CLUB
CLUB
HOUSE

Copyright Tudor Journals Ltd.

Kenmare, Co. Kerry.
Tel: (064) 41291.
Fax: (064) 42061.
Email:
kenmaregolfclub@eircom.net
www.kenmaregolfclub.com

LOCATION: Turn left at top of town.
SECRETARY / MANAGER: Simon Duffield.
Tel: (064) 41291.
SECRETARY (for bookings): Siobhan O'Callaghan.

The course was increased recently from nine to eighteen holes. It is picturesque and mainly very sheltered which leaves it playable in all kinds of weather. It also has the advantage of being sited in one of Ireland's areas of outstanding scenery.

COURSE INFORMATION

Par 71/70; SSS 69/68;
Length 6,053 yards.
Visitors: Welcome any time. Booking in advance is advisable (especially weekends).
Opening Hours: Everyday, peak time May – Sept 6am – 7pm. Off peak time 9am-6pm.

Juveniles: Welcome, to be accompanied by adult.
Green Fees: €30 Mon-Sat, €35 Sun. Juveniles/with member - 1/2 price. Club hire €10; Caddy trolley €1,50.
Clubhouse Hours: 7.30am (peak time).
Clubhouse Dress: Casual but neat.
Clubhouse Facilities: Tea, coffee & snacks.
Open Competitions: Many throughout the year, contact: (064) 41291 for details.

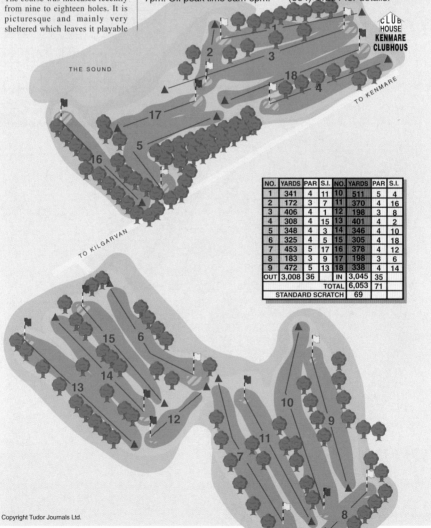

NO.	YARDS	PAR	S.I.	NO.	YARDS	PAR	S.I.
1	341	4	11	10	511	5	4
2	172	3	7	11	370	4	16
3	406	4	1	12	198	3	8
4	308	4	15	13	401	4	2
5	348	4	3	14	346	4	10
6	325	4	5	15	305	4	18
7	453	5	17	16	378	4	12
8	183	3	9	17	198	3	6
9	472	5	13	18	338	4	14
OUT	3,008	36		IN	3,045	35	
				TOTAL	6,053	71	
				STANDARD SCRATCH		69	

Copyright Tudor Journals Ltd.

The Kerries,
Tralee, Co.Kerry.
Tel: (066) 7122112.

LOCATION: 1 mile west of Tralee Town.
SECRETARY: Helen Barrett.
ARCHITECT: Dr. Arthur Spring.

9 hole Parklands course in an attractive setting overlooking Tralee Bay and the Dingle Peninsula.

COURSE INFORMATION

Par 70; SSS 68; Length 5,720 yards. Competition yds; 5,944.
Visitors: Welcome.
Opening Hours: Daylight hours.
Avoid: Sunday (8am –2pm).
Ladies: Welcome.
Green Fees: 18 holes €25; 9 holes €15. Group reductions.
Juveniles: Welcome.

Clubhouse Hours:
9am – 8pm (summer);
Clubhouse Dress: Casual.
Clubhouse Facilities: Full clubhouse facilities and winebar.

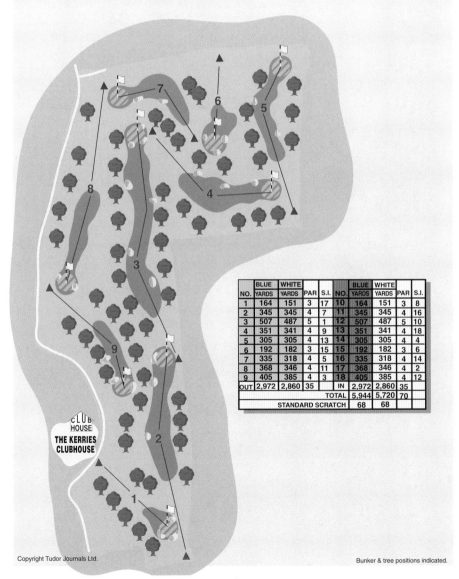

NO.	BLUE YARDS	WHITE YARDS	PAR	S.I.	NO.	BLUE YARDS	WHITE YARDS	PAR	S.I.
1	164	151	3	17	10	164	151	3	8
2	345	345	4	7	11	345	345	4	16
3	507	487	5	1	12	507	487	5	10
4	351	341	4	9	13	351	341	4	18
5	305	305	4	13	14	305	305	4	4
6	192	182	3	15	15	192	182	3	6
7	335	318	4	5	16	335	318	4	14
8	368	346	4	11	17	368	346	4	2
9	405	385	4	3	18	405	385	4	12
OUT	2,972	2,860	35		IN	2,972	2,860	35	
					TOTAL	5,944	5,720	70	
					STANDARD SCRATCH	68	68		

Copyright Tudor Journals Ltd.

Bunker & tree positions indicated.

Mahony's Point, Killarney, Co. Kerry.
Tel: (064) 31034 / 31242 / 33899.

LOCATION: Two miles west of Killarney.
SECRETARY: Tom Prendergast. Tel: (064) 31034
Fax: (064) 33065.
PROFESSIONAL: Tony Coveney. Tel: (064) 31615.
ARCHITECT: Sir Guy Campbell. (Mahony's Point).

Three excellent parkland courses occupying a site of great natural beauty. The courses are adjacent to Lough Leane, with the mountains of Kerry rising on the other side of the lake. An additional eighteen holes were completed in 1971 and the new holes were mixed with the old to form the 'Killeen' and Mahony's Point' courses.

COURSE INFORMATION

Par 72; SSS 72; Length 6,164 metres (Mahony's Point).
Visitors: Welcome..
Opening Hours: 7.30am – 6.00pm.
Avoid: Sunday.
Ladies: Welcome every day.
Green Fees: Available on request from the secretary. Certificate of Handicap required.
Juveniles: Welcome to play every day.
Clubhouse Hours: 7.30am – 11.30pm.
Clubhouse Dress: Casual.
Clubhouse Facilities: Professional shop. Lunches and dinners all day.

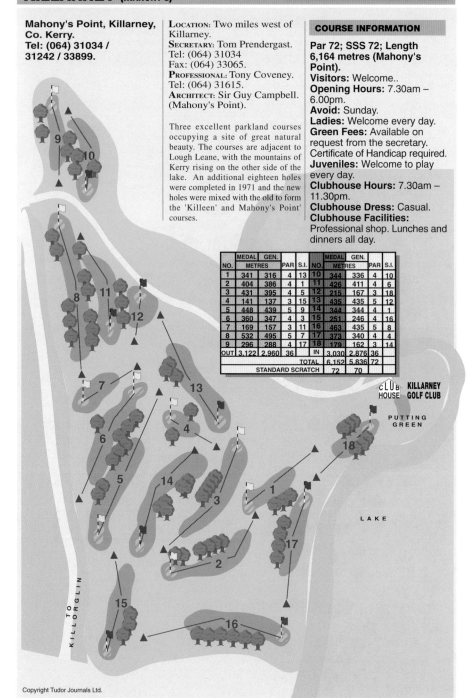

NO.	MEDAL METRES	GEN. METRES	PAR	S.I.	NO.	MEDAL METRES	GEN. METRES	PAR	S.I.
1	341	316	4	13	10	344	336	4	10
2	404	386	4	1	11	426	411	4	6
3	431	395	4	5	12	215	167	3	18
4	141	137	3	15	13	435	435	5	12
5	448	439	5	9	14	344	344	4	1
6	360	347	4	3	15	251	246	4	16
7	169	157	3	11	16	463	435	5	8
8	532	495	5	7	17	373	340	4	4
9	296	288	4	17	18	179	162	3	14
OUT	3,122	2,960	36		IN	3,030	2,876	36	
					TOTAL	6,152	5,836	72	
					STANDARD SCRATCH	72	70		

CLUB HOUSE   **KILLARNEY GOLF CLUB**

PUTTING GREEN

LAKE

TO KILLORGLIN

Copyright Tudor Journals Ltd.

Killarney, Co Kerry.
Tel: (064) 31034 /
31242 / 33899.

LOCATION: Two miles west of Killarney.
SECRETARY: Tom Prendergast. Tel: (064) 31034.
PROFESSIONAL: Tony Coveney. Tel: (064) 31615.
ARCHITECT: E. Hackett & Dr. O'Sullivan.

The second of three courses at Killarney Golf & Fishing Club the 'Killeen' is parkland, the same as its' sister courses. The main characteristics are narrow, tree-lined fairways and of course some of the holes are adjacent to the beautiful Lough Leane.

COURSE INFORMATION

Par 72; SSS 73; Length 6,474 metres. (Killeen course).
Visitors: Welcome.
Opening Hours: 7.30am – 6.00pm.
Avoid: Sat & Sun.
Ladies: Welcome.
Green Fees: Available on request from the secretary. Certificate of Handicap required.
Juveniles: Welcome. Lessons available; Club Hire available; Caddy service available.
Clubhouse Hours: 7.30am – 11.30pm.
Clubhouse Dress: Casual.
Clubhouse Facilities: Lunches and full dinners all day.

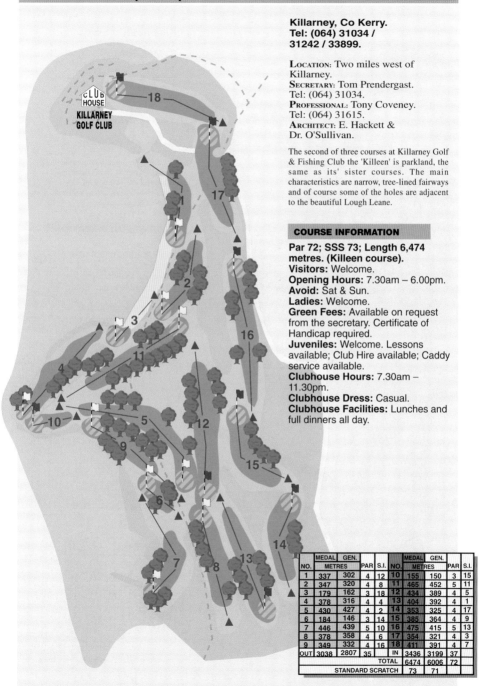

NO.	MEDAL METRES	GEN.	PAR	S.I.	NO.	MEDAL METRES	GEN.	PAR	S.I.
1	337	302	4	12	10	155	150	3	15
2	347	320	4	8	11	465	452	5	11
3	179	162	3	18	12	434	389	4	5
4	378	316	4	4	13	404	392	4	1
5	430	427	4	2	14	353	325	4	17
6	184	146	3	14	15	385	364	4	9
7	446	439	5	10	16	475	415	5	13
8	378	358	4	6	17	354	321	4	3
9	349	332	4	16	18	411	391	4	7
OUT	3038	2807	35		IN	3436	3199	37	
					TOTAL	6474	6006	72	
					STANDARD SCRATCH	73	71		

Copyright Tudor Journals Ltd.

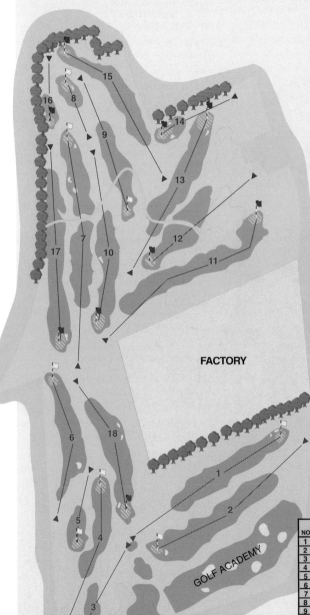

Killarney, Co Kerry.
Tel: (064) 31034/
32142/33899.

SECRETARY: Tom Prendergast.
Tel: (064) 31034.
PROFESSIONAL: Tony Coveney
Tel: (064) 31615
ARCHITECT: Donald Steel.

The third course at Killarney Golf &
Fishing Club - Lackabane - is parkland.
The main characteristics are undulating
fairways with the lake adjacent to the
3rd green and to the 11th & 12th holes.
Views of the mountains and surrounding
wood are breathtaking.

COURSE INFORMATION

**Par 72; Length 6,410
metres.**
Visitors: Welcome.
Opening Hours: 7.30am –
6.00pm.
Green Fees: Available on
request from the secretary,
certificate of Handicap required.
Juveniles: Welcome.
Ladies: Welcome
Clubhouse Dress: Casual.

FACTORY

GOLF ACADEMY

NO.	MEDAL YARDS	GEN. YARDS	PAR	S.I.	NO.	MEDAL YARDS	GEN. YARDS	PAR	S.I.
1	413	391	4	4	10	395	355	4	7
2	477	446	5	16	11	502	497	5	9
3	248	222	4	18	12	324	308	4	13
4	382	359	4	12	13	384	360	4	5
5	204	184	3	6	14	161	146	3	15
6	433	416	4	2	15	389	356	4	3
7	543	507	5	8	16	160	150	3	17
8	164	152	3	14	17	484	464	5	11
9	336	307	4	10	18	411	391	4	1
OUT	3,200	2,984	36		IN	3,210	3,027	36	
					TOTAL	6,410	6,011	72	
					STANDARD SCRATCH	72	72		

Bunker & tree positions indicated.
Copyright Tudor Journals Ltd.

**Killorglin Golf Club,
Stealroe, Killorglin.
Co. Kerry.
Tel: (066) 9761979.
Fax. (066) 9761437.
Email: kilgolf@iol.ie**

LOCATION: Two miles from
Killorglin, on Tralee Road,
14 miles from Kilarney.
SECRETARY: Billy Dodd.
RESERVATIONS: Billy/Emma
ARCHITECT: Eddie Hackett.

Eddie Hackett has made marvellous
use of the dramatic physical features
of the lands in providing golf shots
that are delightful & challenging
territory in Ireland. It offers a new &
exciting challenge to visiting golfers.

COURSE INFORMATION

**Par 72; SSS 71; Length
6,467 yards.**
Visitors: Welcome at all
times.
Opening Hours: Sunrise -
sunset.
Ladies: Welcome all times.
Green Fees: Mon - Fri €23;
Sat, Sun & Bank Hols €26.

Juveniles: Welcome if
accompanied by an adult.
Lessons by prior arrangement.
Clubhouse Hours: 8.30am –
11.30pm.
Clubhouse Dress:
Neat / casual.
Clubhouse Facilites:
Pro-shop, Bar and full
restaurant facilities, societies
welcome - special rate on
request. Caddies available by
prior arrangement. For
reservations tel: Billy.

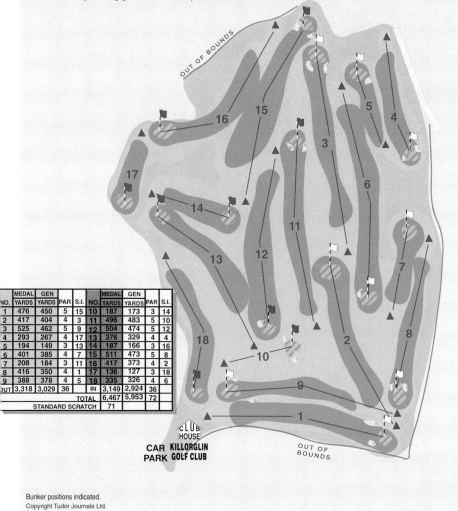

NO.	MEDAL YARDS	GEN YARDS	PAR	S.I.	NO.	MEDAL YARDS	GEN YARDS	PAR	S.I.
1	476	450	5	15	10	187	173	3	14
2	417	404	4	3	11	496	483	5	10
3	525	462	5	9	12	504	474	5	12
4	293	267	4	17	13	376	329	4	4
5	194	149	3	13	14	187	166	3	16
6	401	385	4	7	15	511	473	5	8
7	208	184	3	11	16	417	373	4	2
8	416	350	4	1	17	136	127	3	18
9	388	378	4	5	18	335	326	4	6
OUT	3,318	3,029	36		IN	3,149	2,924	36	
					TOTAL	6,467	5,953	72	
					STANDARD SCRATCH	71			

CLUB HOUSE

CAR **KILLORGLIN**
PARK **GOLF CLUB**

OUT OF BOUNDS

Bunker positions indicated.
Copyright Tudor Journals Ltd.

**Parknasilla Great
Southern Hotel, Sneem,
Co. Kerry.
Tel: (064) 45122.**

LOCATION: Parknasilla.
SECRETARY: Mr. M. Walsh.
Tel: (064) 45233.

Well laid out course in beautiful
scenery overlooking Kenmare Bay.
The course is part of the Parknasilla
Great Southern Hotel and golfers have

the added advantage of having these
facilities available to them.

COURSE INFORMATION

**Par 69; SSS 68; Length
5,284 metres.
Visitors:** Welcome.
Opening Hours: 8.00am –
7.00pm.
Ladies: Welcome.
Green Fees: €15 – 9 holes;
€25 – 18 holes.

Juveniles: Welcome. Lessons
available by prior arrangement;
Club Hire available; Caddy
service available by prior
arrangment; telephone
appointment required.
Clubhouse Dress: Casual.
Clubhouse Facilities: Full
catering facilities at hotel, a
half mile away.
Open Competitions: Small
competitions throughout
the year.

NO.	MEDAL METRES	GEN	PAR	S.I.	NO.	MEDAL METRES	GEN	PAR	S.I.
1	303	295	4	12	10	346	342	4	5
2	120	112	3	17	11	386	373	4	1
3	444	437	5	4	12	324	313	4	7
4	155	147	3	9	13	303	295	4	13
5	286	278	4	16	14	120	112	3	18
6	150	145	3	11	15	444	437	5	15
7	334	327	4	4	16	346	342	4	6
8	346	338	4	3	17	386	373	4	2
9	168	163	3	10	18	324	313	4	8
OUT	2,305	2,242	33		IN	2,979	2,900	36	
					TOTAL	5,284	5,142	69	
					STANDARD SCRATCH				

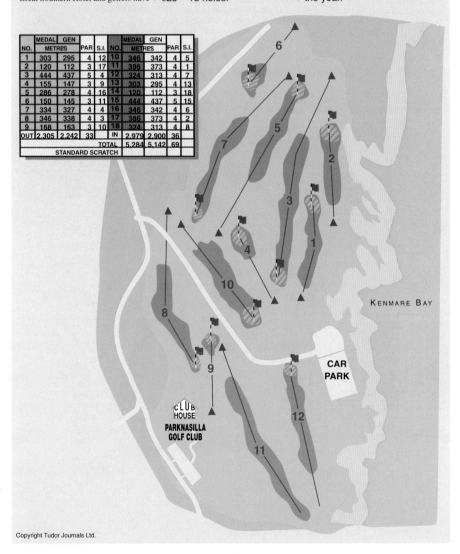

KENMARE BAY

CAR
PARK

CLUB
HOUSE

**PARKNASILLA
GOLF CLUB**

Copyright Tudor Journals Ltd.

Ring of Kerry Golf & Country Club, Templenoe, Kenmare, Co. Kerry.
Tel: (064) 42000.

LOCATION: 4 miles from Kenmare, Co. Kerry.
ORIGINAL GOLF COURSE DESIGNER: Eddie Hacket.
GENERAL MANAGER: Ed Edwards.

One of the newest additions to the Co. Kerry circuit, with panoramic views of Kenmare Bay from every hole. Described as 'world class' in Ireland

its extensive drainage and irrigation systems will ensure a year round facility. Situated just 25 miles from Killarney and 4 miles from Kenmare, this will be a popular course in the Kingdom of Kerry. Designed to test serious golfers from the back tees and provide equal enjoyment for all from the more forward ones.

COURSE INFORMATION

Par 72; SSS 73; Length 6,869 yards.
Visitors: All day every day.

Opening Hours: Sunrise to sunset.
Ladies: No restrictions.
Green Fees: €70 daily.
Juveniles: Welcome. Must be accompanied by an adult.
Clubhouse Hours:
8am – 11.30pm.
Clubhouse Dress:
Smart/Casual (no denim).
Clubhouse Facilities:
Club, trolley, cart and caddie hire available. Full dining and bar facilities.

NO.	MEDAL YARDS	GEN. YARDS	PAR	S.I.	NO.	MEDAL YARDS	GEN. YARDS	PAR	S.I.
1	386	351	4	8	10	441	419	4	3
2	374	350	4	6	11	522	492	5	5
3	179	165	5	10	12	386	366	4	9
4	581	541	5	10	13	233	208	3	15
5	469	434	5	16	14	433	404	4	1
6	383	383	4	4	15	425	385	4	7
7	186	175	3	18	16	452	430	5	13
8	469	440	4	2	17	435	397	4	11
9	307	288	4	14	1	205	185	3	17
OUT	3,294	3,115	36		IN	3,510	3,262	35	
					TOTAL	6,804	6,377	71	
					STANDARD SCRATCH	73	71		

Bunker and tree positions indicated.

Copyright Tudor Journals Ltd.

ROSS

MUNSTER **KERRY**

Ross Golf Club, Ross Road, Killarney, Co. Kerry.
Tel: (064) 31125.
Fax: (064) 31860.

LOCATION: Less than half a mile from Killarney town, Co. Kerry.
SECRETARY: Alan O'Meara.
PROFFESIONAL: Alan O'Meara.
ARCHITECT: Roger Jones.
Tel: (064) 31125.

Attractive setting in mountains, lakes and woodlands with Ross Castle and the Flesk river adjacent. Situated less than half a mile from Killarney town.

COURSE INFORMATION

Par 72; SSS 73;
Length 6450 yards.
Visitors: Welcome.
Opening Hours:
8.00am to sunset.
Avoid: Sunday mornings.
Green Fees: €15 for 9 holes & €23 per person for 18 holes. Students: €10 for 9 holes and €15 per person for 18 holes. Juveniles: €7 for 9 holes & €13 for 18 holes. Earlybird & Twilight:– €13 for 9 holes and €19 for 18 holes before 9am.
Clubhouse Hours:
8.00am – sunset.
Clubhouse Dress:
Clean attire.
Clubhouse Facilities:
Pro shop and snack bar, licensed bar.

NO.	MEDAL YARDS	GEN. YARDS	PAR	S.I.	NO.	MEDAL YARDS	GEN. YARDS	PAR	S.I.
1	340	317	4	6	10	340	317	4	5
2	537	495	5	12	11	537	495	5	11
3	410	396	4	8	12	410	396	4	7
4	401	377	4	4	13	401	377	4	3
5	395	377	4	2	14	395	377	4	1
6	116	96	3	18	15	116	96	3	17
7	271	264	4	16	16	271	264	4	15
8	154	133	3	14	17	154	133	3	13
9	600	531	5	10	18	600	531	5	9
OUT	3,225	2,988	36		IN	3,225	2,988	36	
					TOTAL	6,450	5,976	72	
					STANDARD SCRATCH	73	71		

Bunker & tree positions indicated.
Copyright Tudor Journals Ltd.

West Barrow, Ardfert, Co.
Kerry.
Tel: (066) 7136379.
Fax: (066) 7136008.
Email: traleegolf@eircom
www.tralee-golf.com

LOCATION: Barrow.
GENERAL MANAGER: Anthony Byrne.
CAPTAIN: Denis Lyons.
PROFESSIONAL: David Power.

Challenging course with the first nine
relatively flat holes, set on cliff top; the second
nine by contrast are built on dunes. The course
is set amidst the beautiful scenery associated
with the Kerry region. Tralee is the first
Arnold Palmer designed course in Europe.

COURSE INFORMATION

**Par 71; SSS 73; Length
6,252 metres.**
Visitors: Welcome up to 4.30pm,
May – October. Limited green fees
Weds / Weekends.
Avoid: Weekdays 1.30 – 2.30pm &
4.30pm onwards. Saturdays 11.00am
– 1.24pm.
Opening Hours: 7.30am – 4.30pm
(summer); 9am – sunset (winter).
Members: Wednesdays (June, July
& August) and all Sundays.
Green Fees: €110 Mon – Sat;
Sun – members & guests only.
Juveniles: Welcome. Must be
accompanied by an adult after 6pm.
Caddy service available by prior
arrangment; Handicap Certificate
required. Telephone
appointment required.

Clubhouse Hours:
7.30am – 10pm (summer);
9am – 5.30pm (winter).
Golf Shop open.
Clubhouse Dress:
Smart/Casual – no beach
wear or jeans.
Clubhouse Facilities:
Lunch, dinner, snacks
available all day everyday.

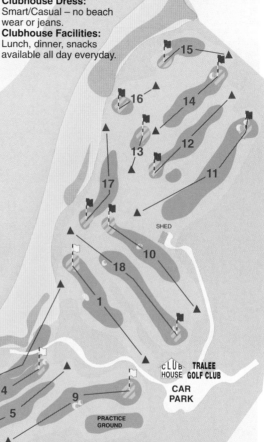

NO.	MEDAL METRES	GEN.	PAR	S.I.	NO.	MEDAL METRES	GEN.	PAR	S.I.
1	368	355	4	12	10	385	370	4	9
2	542	516	5	2	11	530	514	5	13
3	183	140	3	14	12	417	400	4	1
4	388	366	4	8	13	145	139	3	15
5	391	374	4	4	14	367	361	4	5
6	389	383	4	10	15	273	267	4	17
7	143	135	3	18	16	181	152	3	11
8	354	339	4	6	17	323	304	4	7
9	451	443	5	16	18	422	403	4	3
OUT	3,209	3,051	36		IN	3,043	2,910	35	
					TOTAL	6,252	5,961	71	
					STANDARD SCRATCH	73	71		

Bunker & tree positions indicated.
Copyright Tudor Journals Ltd.

**Ring of Kerry, Waterville,
Co. Kerry.
Tel: (066) 9474102
Fax: (066) 9474482.**

LOCATION: One mile outside
village.
SECRETARY: Noel J. Cronin.
Tel: (066) 9474102.
PROFESSIONAL: Liam Higgins.
Tel: (066) 9474237.
ARCHITECT: J. A. Mulcahy /
E. Hackett.

Waterville features finely manicured
fairways and greens with limited water
on the course. Panoramic views from
the back nine of the Atlantic Ocean and
Kerry Mountains. Spectacular Par 3's.
Driving Range on course. The course
is long, however not hilly, so a pleasant
18 hole walk is enjoyed. Each hole has
individual characteristics and every
club in the bag will be needed.

COURSE INFORMATION

**Par 72; SSS 74;
Length 7225 yards.**
Visitors: Welcome any day.
Telephone appointment
advised.
Opening Hours: 7am – 8pm.
Green Fees: €125.
Before 8am and after 4pm
Monday to Thursday €63.
Juveniles: Welcome. Lessons
available by prior arrangements;
Club Hire and Caddy service
available (May – Sept).
Clubhouse Hours: 7am-11pm.
Clubhouse Facilities:
Breakfast on request; Dining
room facilities available from
11.30am – 7pm. Bar snacks
served everyday.
Open Competitions: Open
Week June / July by invitation.
Handicap Certificate required
for open competitions.

NO.	MEDAL YARDS	GEN. YARDS	PAR	S.I.	NO.	MEDAL YARDS	GEN. YARDS	PAR	S.I.
1	430	395	4	11	10	475	450	4	2
2	469	425	4	1	11	506	477	5	10
3	417	400	4	3	12	200	154	3	18
4	179	169	3	15	13	518	480	5	14
5	595	551	5	9	14	456	410	4	4
6	387	355	4	13	15	407	365	4	6
7	178	148	3	17	16	350	330	4	12
8	435	410	4	5	17	196	153	3	16
9	445	405	4	7	18	582	555	5	8
OUT	3,535	3,258	35		IN	3,690	3,374	37	
					TOTAL	7,225	6,632	72	
					STANDARD SCRATCH	74	72		

Copyright Tudor Journals Ltd.

Abbeyfeale Golf Club
Abbeyfeale Co. Limerick.
Tel: (068) 32033.
Email: abbeyfealegolf@hotmail.com

LOCATION: The Gateway to Kerry, 40 miles west of Limerick City.
SECRETARY: Maurice O'Ríordan.
Tel: (068) 32033.
PROFESSIONAL: Ian Mowbray.
ARCHITECT: Arthur Spring.

Recognised as having some tough Par-3's. All holes are well protected by water hazards, bunkers and trees. This 9 hole course will provide a challange to golfers of all catorgories.

COURSE INFORMATION

Par 62; SSS 60; Length 4,164 yards.
Visitors: Welcome all days, Sunday by arrangement.

Opening Hours: 8am – 10pm.
Green Fees: €10. Juveniles €6.
Clubhouse Hours:
10am – 10pm.
Clubhouse Dress: Casual.
Clubhouse Facilities: Meals by pre-arrangement.
Open Competitions:
Every month from March to September. Every Thursday from mid-september.

NO.	METRES	PAR	S.I.	NO.	METRES	PAR	S.I.
1	178	3	6	10	178	3	5
2	281	4	8	11	281	4	7
3	286	4	16	12	286	4	15
4	197	3	14	13	179	3	13
5	183	3	12	14	183	3	11
6	340	4	2	15	340	4	1
7	142	3	10	16	142	3	9
8	246	4	18	17	246	4	17
9	183	3	4	18	183	3	3
OUT	2,036	31		IN	2,036	31	
				TOTAL	4,072	62	
		STANDARD SCRATCH			60		

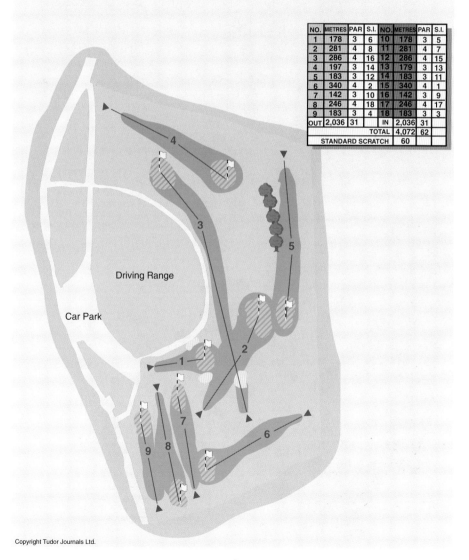

Driving Range

Car Park

Copyright Tudor Journals Ltd.

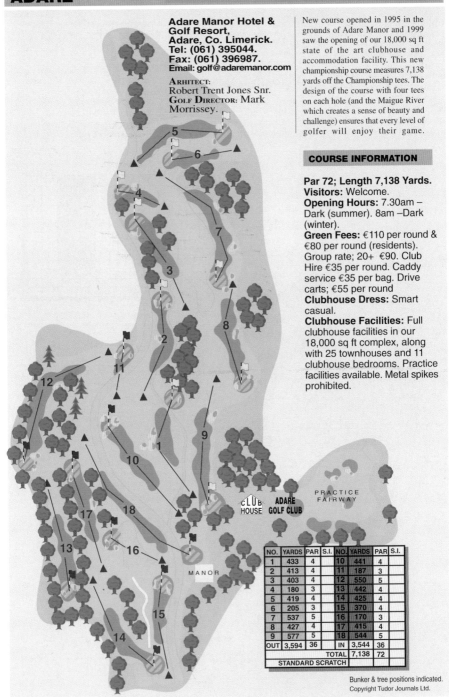

**Adare Manor Hotel &
Golf Resort,
Adare, Co. Limerick.
Tel: (061) 395044.
Fax: (061) 396987.
Email: golf@adaremanor.com**

ARHITECT:
Robert Trent Jones Snr.
GOLF DIRECTOR: Mark
Morrissey.

New course opened in 1995 in the grounds of Adare Manor and 1999 saw the opening of our 18,000 sq ft state of the art clubhouse and accommodation facility. This new championship course measures 7,138 yards off the Championship tees. The design of the course with four tees on each hole (and the Maigue River which creates a sense of beauty and challenge) ensures that every level of golfer will enjoy their game.

COURSE INFORMATION

**Par 72; Length 7,138 Yards.
Visitors:** Welcome.
Opening Hours: 7.30am –
Dark (summer). 8am –Dark
(winter).
Green Fees: €110 per round &
€80 per round (residents).
Group rate; 20+ €90. Club
Hire €35 per round. Caddy
service €35 per bag. Drive
carts; €55 per round
Clubhouse Dress: Smart
casual.
Clubhouse Facilities: Full
clubhouse facilities in our
18,000 sq ft complex, along
with 25 townhouses and 11
clubhouse bedrooms. Practice
facilities available. Metal spikes
prohibited.

NO.	YARDS	PAR	S.I.	NO.	YARDS	PAR	S.I.
1	433	4		10	441	4	
2	413	4		11	187	3	
3	403	4		12	550	5	
4	180	3		13	442	4	
5	419	4		14	425	4	
6	205	3		15	370	4	
7	537	5		16	170	3	
8	427	4		17	415	4	
9	577	5		18	544	5	
OUT	3,594	36		IN	3,544	36	
				TOTAL	7,138	72	
STANDARD SCRATCH							

Bunker & tree positions indicated.
Copyright Tudor Journals Ltd.

Adare, Co. Limerick.
Tel: (061) 396204.

LOCATION: Ten miles from Limerick City.
SECRETARY: Michael O'Donnell.
Tel: (061) 396204.

The original and more traditional course in Adare, founded in 1900, is called Adare Manor but is not the new championship course in the grounds of Adare Manor Hotel. Adare is a parkland course, which is particularly scenic. The Abbey and Desmond Castle are unique features to the course. There are three Par 5's and six Par 3's over the eighteen holes. The fairways are narrow and well maintained.

COURSE INFORMATION

Par 70; SSS 69; Length 5,743 yards.
Visitors: Welcome. Booking required for weekends.
Opening Hours: 9am-sunset.
Green Fees: €20 Mon – Fri. & €25.50 Weekends.

Juveniles: Welcome, but accompanied by an adult. Club Hire available; Caddy service available by prior arrangements (summer months).
Clubhouse Hours: 10.00am closing time.
Clubhouse Dress: Casual – no shorts or sports wear.
Clubhouse Facilities: Full catering.
Open Competitions: June & August.

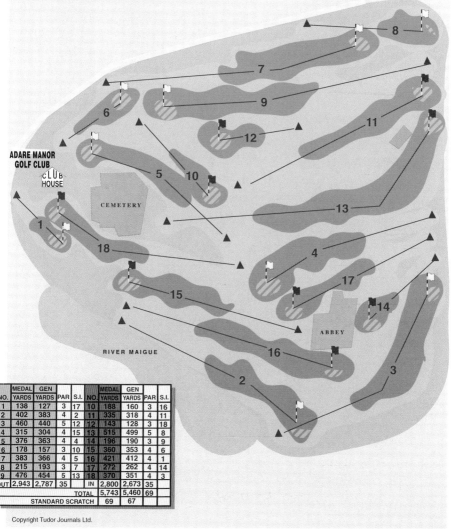

NO.	MEDAL YARDS	GEN YARDS	PAR	S.I.	NO.	MEDAL YARDS	GEN YARDS	PAR	S.I.
1	138	127	3	17	10	188	160	3	16
2	402	383	4	2	11	335	318	4	11
3	460	440	5	12	12	143	128	3	18
4	315	304	4	15	13	515	499	5	8
5	376	363	4	4	14	196	190	3	9
6	178	157	3	10	15	360	353	4	6
7	383	366	4	5	16	421	412	4	1
8	215	193	3	7	17	272	262	4	14
9	476	454	5	13	18	370	351	4	3
OUT	2,943	2,787	35		IN	2,800	2,673	35	
					TOTAL	5,743	5,460	69	
					STANDARD SCRATCH	69	67		

Copyright Tudor Journals Ltd.

Castletroy, Co. Limerick.
Tel: (061) 335261.

LOCATION: Less than three miles from Limerick City on N7 to Dublin.
SECRETARY: Laurence Hayes.
Tel: (061) 335753.
Fax: (061) 335373

Parkland course with out of bounds on the left for the first two holes. Well maintained fairways are tree lined demanding accuracy off the tee. The long Par 5 10th features a narrow entrance to the green with a stream to catch the more adventurous. The par 3 13th features a panoramic view from the tee while the picturesque 18th is a stern test to finish with the green guarded by bunkers on both sides.

COURSE INFORMATION

Par 71; SSS 71; Length 6,335 yards, 5,802 metres.
Visitors: Welcome most weekday mornings. Some afternoons may be booked by societies (check in advance).
Avoid: Thursday afternoon; Weekends; Tuesday is Ladies Day (some restriction).
Green Fees: €32 (€17 with a member). Group rate of 12+ €23.
Juveniles: Must be accompanied by an adult. Club Hire available; Caddy service available by prior arrangement.

Clubhouse Hours:
8.00am – 11.30pm.
Clubhouse Dress:
Casual but neat.
Clubhouse Facilities: Bar snacks available all day everyday; last orders for full meals 9.30pm. Bar service as per licencing hours.

NO.	METRES	PAR	S.I.	NO.	METRES	PAR	S.I.
1	339	4	4	10	458	5	11
2	323	4	10	11	326	4	9
3	337	4	8	12	306	4	5
4	335	4	12	13	159	3	15
5	396	4	2	14	312	4	13
6	420	5	18	15	407	4	1
7	134	3	16	16	116	3	17
8	339	4	6	17	367	4	7
9	329	4	14	18	399	4	3
OUT	2,952	36		IN	2,850	35	
				TOTAL	5,802	71	
			STANDARD SCRATCH		71		

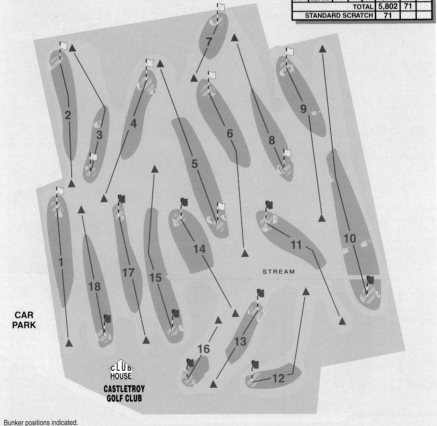

CAR PARK

STREAM

CLUB HOUSE

CASTLETROY GOLF CLUB

Bunker positions indicated.
Copyright Tudor Journals Ltd.

**Killeline Golf Club, Cork
Road, Newcastle West,
Co. Limerick.
Tel: (069) 61600.**

LOCATION: 25 miles from Limerick
City, off Killarney Road.
Tel: (069) 61600.
Fax: (069) 77792

Killeline is an 18 hole parkland course.
Wooded with over 3000 decidious trees giving
all fairways a clear definition, two good par
'5's and four challenging par '3's.

COURSE INFORMATION

**Par 72; SSS 68; Length
6,600 yards.
Visitors:** Welcome everday.
Opening Hours:
9.00am – sunset.
Ladies: Welcome.
Green Fees: €20 daily.
Juveniles: Welcome but
accompanied by adult.
Clubhouse Hours:
8am – closing time.
Clubhouse Dress:
Casual, no shorts.
Clubhouse Facilities: Hotel
on site; Restaurant and bar;
Pro Shop.
Open Competitions:
June, July & August.

NO.	MEDAL YARDS	GEN. YARDS	PAR	S.I.	NO.	MEDAL YARDS	GEN. YARDS	PAR	S.I.
1	512	458	5	18	1	315	304	4	15
2	416	411	4	3	1	300	300	4	16
3	464	423	4	1	1	500	500	5	4
4	181	165	3	13	1	332	332	4	12
5	391	335	4	8	1	175	175	3	11
6	615	545	5	5	1	424	420	4	2
7	182	182	3	14	1	346	341	4	9
8	402	400	4	7	1	486	479	5	17
9	220	176	3	6	1	194	150	3	10
OUT	3,383	3,095	35		IN	3,072	3,001	36	
				TOTAL		6,455	6,096	71	
		STANDARD SCRATCH				69	67		

TO DROMCOLLOGHER

CAR PARK CLUB HOUSE KILLELINE CLUBHOUSE

NEWCASTLE WEST 1/2 KM

Bunker and tree positions indicated.

353

Ballyclough, Limerick.
Tel: (061)
414083/415146.

Location: Three miles South of Limerick City.
Secretary: Stephen Keogh.
Tel: (061) 415146.
Professional: Lee Harington.
Tel: (061) 412492.

A parkland course with tree lined fairways. Pleasant surroundings, situated on a hill overlooking the city of Limerick.

COURSE INFORMATION

Par 72; SSS 71; Length 6,525 yards; 5,932 metres.
Visitors: Welcome up to 4.00pm Mon, Wed, Fri; Thurs am only.
Opening Hours: 8.30am – sunset.
Avoid: Tuesday and weekends.
Ladies Day: Tuesdays. Lessons available by prior arrangements; Club Hire and Caddy service available by prior arrangements; telephone appointment advisable.
Green Fees: €50 (with member €20).
Clubhouse Hours: 9.30am – 11.00pm; full clubhouse facilities.
Clubhouse Dress: Casual.
Clubhouse Facilities: Full service from 12.00 noon.
Open Competitions: Mainly holiday weekends.

NO.	MEDAL METRES	GEN. METRES	PAR	S.I.	NO.	MEDAL METRES	GEN. METRES	PAR	S.I.
1	303	297	4	9	10	397	379	4	2
2	439	426	5	15	11	341	331	4	11
3	427	419	4	1	12	372	370	4	6
4	349	337	4	5	13	281	270	4	17
5	158	149	3	16	14	140	132	3	14
6	466	456	5	7	15	344	297	4	4
7	378	362	4	3	16	305	287	4	10
8	120	107	3	18	17	344	318	4	8
9	450	438	5	13	18	318	312	4	12
OUT	3,090	2,991	37		IN	2,842	2,696	35	
					TOTAL	5,932	5,687	72	
					STANDARD SCRATCH	71	70		

Bunker positions indicated.
Copyright Tudor Journals Ltd.

354

Limerick County Golf & Country Club, Ballyneety. Co. Limerick.
Tel: (061) 351881.
Fax: (061) 351384.
E-Mail: lcgolf@iol.ie
Web: www.limerickcounty.com

LOCATION: 5 miles south of Limerick City on the R512, direction Kilmallock.
MANAGER: Gerry McKeon.
Tel: (061) 351881.
PROFESSIONAL: Donal Mc Sweeney.
Tel: (061) 351784.
ARCHITECT: Des Smyth & Associates.

18 hole championship standard golf course, set on 230 acres of undulating sand-based terrain, ensuring that it is playable 12 months of the year. The course boasts many interesting sand and water hazards. A uniquely-shaped circular clubhouse provides panoramic views of over 50% of the course and the surrounding countryside. Other facilities include driving range, three hole short-game area, 12 4 star luxury holiday cottage accommodation on site.

COURSE INFORMATION

Par 72; SSS 74; Length 6712 yards, 6116 metres.
Visitors: Welcome at all times.
Opening Hours: 7.00am to sunset.

Green Fees: Winter; Mon – Fri €26. Sat / Sun €33. Summer; Mon – Fri €33. Sat / Sun €45.
Juveniles: Welcome.
Clubhouse Hours: 9.00am – 12.00pm.
Clubhouse Dress: Neat Dress.
Clubhouse Facilities: Full bar & restaurant services. Clubhouse tuition available. Clubs, Caddy cars and caddies on request.

NO.	MEDAL METRES	GEN.	PAR	S.I.	NO.	MEDAL METRES	GEN.	PAR	S.I.
1	373	352	4	7	10	330	307	4	6
2	158	131	3	15	11	444	438	5	16
3	367	354	4	3	12	304	285	4	12
4	489	452	5	5	13	448	420	5	18
5	408	384	4	1	14	350	326	4	14
6	169	145	3	13	15	178	164	3	4
7	283	261	4	17	16	370	349	4	8
8	386	364	4	9	17	346	330	4	10
9	379	353	4	11	18	409	381	4	2
OUT	3,012	2,796	35		IN	3,179	3,000	37	
					TOTAL	6,191	5,796	72	
	STANDARD SCRATCH					74	72		

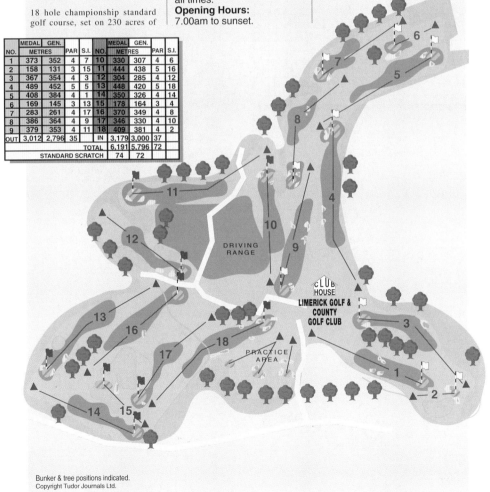

Bunker & tree positions indicated.
Copyright Tudor Journals Ltd.

Newcastle West Golf Club, Ardagh, Co. Limerick.
Tel: (069) 76500.
Fax: (069) 76511.

LOCATION: Six miles from Newcastlewest.
SECRETARY: Eamonn Cregan.
ARCHITECT: A. Spring.

Set in 150 acres of unspoilt rolling West Limerick countryside.

Newcastle West comprises an 18 hole championship course built to the highest standards on sandy soil which is playable all the year round. A practice ground and floodlit driving range are included.

COURSE INFORMATION

Par 71; SSS 73; Length 5,905 metres.
Visitors: Welcome.
Opening Hours: 9.00am – sunset.

Avoid: Saturday and Sunday mornings.
Ladies Day: Play any day.
Green Fees: €26 Mon–Fri, €32 Sat/Sun.
Clubhouse Hours: 10.00am – 11.00pm.
Clubhouse Dress: Casual.
Clubhouse Facilities: Full meals, snacks & Golf Shop.
Open Competitions: Open Week, June & Bank Holiday weekends. Wednesday open Singles.

NO.	BLUE YARDS	WHITE YARDS	GREEN YARDS	PAR	S.I.	NO	BLUE YARDS	WHITE YARDS	GREEN YARDS	PAR	S.I.
1	465	456	446	5	16	10	184	170	165	3	15
2	356	345	335	4	12	11	399	387	352	4	3
3	191	166	156	3	10	12	358	348	298	4	7
4	338	310	300	4	14	13	344	330	315	4	17
5	414	387	377	4	2	14	514	504	495	5	13
6	187	163	153	3	4	15	414	407	335	4	9
7	378	368	339	4	8	16	407	377	370	4	1
8	506	495	485	5	18	17	183	167	151	3	11
9	370	350	340	4	6	18	435	411	401	4	5
OUT	3,205	3,040	2,931	36		IN	3,239	3,101	2,682	35	
						TOTAL	6,444	6,141	5,813	71	
		STANDARD SCRATCH					72	70	70		

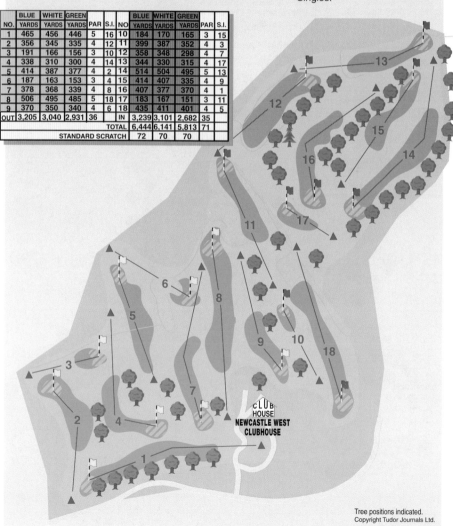

NEWCASTLE WEST CLUBHOUSE

Tree positions indicated.
Copyright Tudor Journals Ltd.

**Rathbane Golf Course
Rathbane, Limerick.
Tel: (061) 313655/313656.**

LOCATION: Limerick City.
SECRETARY: Jackie Cassidy.
Tel: (061) 313655.
PROFESSIONAL: Noel Cassidy.
ARCHITECT: James Healy.

This course was opend in April 1998. Parkland course with trees, bunkers and sand based greens. Golf lessons and clinics available. Course is situated in Limerick City and proves very popular with all types of golfers. Club hire available.

COURSE INFORMATION

**Par 70; SSS 69; Length 5,631 meters.
Visitors:** Welcome.
Opening Hours: 8am – 10pm.
Green Fees: €17 Mon – Fri; €20 Sat/Sun.

Special Concessions available to QAP's and Juniors.
Juveniles: Welcome.
Clubhouse Hours:
8am – 10pm.
Clubhouse Dress: Casual/neat.
Clubhouse Facilities: Pro-shop full catering facilities.
Open Competitions:
All competitions open and otherwise. Thursday open day.

NO.	BLUE METRES	WHITE METRES	PAR	S.I.	NO.	BLUE METRES	WHITE METRES	PAR	S.I.
1	348	343	4	7	10	330	320	4	12
2	340	335	4	5	11	147	142	3	18
3	158	153	3	13	12	348	338	4	4
4	452	446	5	11	13	179	174	3	14
5	338	333	4	9	14	360	355	4	8
6	297	287	4	15	15	146	139	3	16
7	470	459	5	3	16	490	484	5	10
8	355	349	4	1	17	344	339	4	6
9	151	147	3	17	18	378	373	4	2
OUT	2,909	2,852	36		IN	2,722	2,664	34	
					TOTAL	5,631	5,516	70	
					STANDARD SCRATCH	69	68		

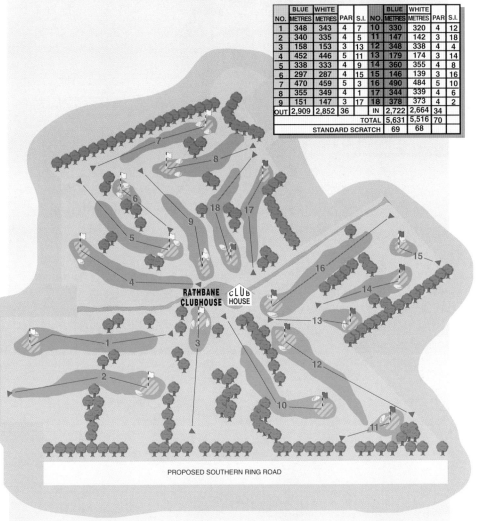

RATHBANE CLUBHOUSE CLUB HOUSE

PROPOSED SOUTHERN RING ROAD

Copyright Tudor Journals Ltd.

Ballykisteen Golf Club, Monard, Co. Tipperary.
Tel: (062) 33333.
Fax: (062) 33668.

LOCATION: Centrally located on the M24 – two miles from Tipperary Town and within a twenty minute drive of Limerick City.
SECRETARY: Josephine Ryan.
PROFESSIONAL: James Mc Bride.
ARCHITECT: Ryder Cup star Des Symth.

A parkland course, nestled in emerald green countryside in the heart of the Golden Vale. A very interesting and clever design has made this a course suitable to the high and low handicap golfer.

COURSE INFORMATION
Par 72; SSS 74; Length 6,765 yards.
Green Fees: €28 Mon - Fri €30 at weekend.

Juveniles: Club Hire available, Caddy service available by prior arrangement. Fully equipped Professional Shop, group and individual tuition and a floodlit Driving Range.

Clubhouse Facilities:
Elegant restaurant and bar – open to the general public all day everyday.

NO.	CHAMP YARDS	MEDAL YARDS	PAR	S.I.	NO.	CHAMP YARDS	MEDAL YARDS	PAR	S.I.
1	371	353	4	6	10	415	392	4	1
2	446	409	4	2	11	417	393	4	3
3	171	171	3	18	12	509	493	5	15
4	534	510	5	8	13	169	155	3	13
5	395	345	4	10	14	394	354	4	11
6	513	490	5	12	15	226	168	3	7
7	394	357	4	14	16	389	346	4	17
8	335	314	4	4	17	371	362	4	5
9	170	156	3	16	18	546	516	5	9
OUT	3,329	3,105	36		IN	3,436	3,179	36	
					TOTAL	6,765	6,284	72	
					STANDARD SCRATCH		74	72	

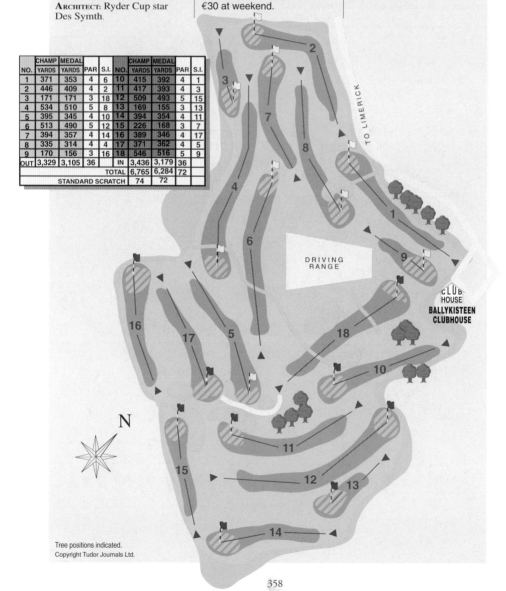

N

Tree positions indicated.
Copyright Tudor Journals Ltd.

**Kilcommon, Cahir,
Co. Tipperary.
Tel: (052) 41474.**

LOCATION: One mile from town centre.
SECRETARY: Micheal Costello Tel: (052) 41474.
PROFESSIONAL: Mark Joseph. Tel: (052) 41474.
ARCHITECT: E. Hackett.

Prime parkland, part of old Cahir Park Estate. Sloping down to River Suir which runs along the right hand side of the 7th hole, this hole is rated as one of the most difficult on the course. Holes 8 and 16 involve playing across River Suir.

COURSE INFORMATION

Par 71; SSS 71; Length 5,805 metres.
Visitors: Welcome.
Opening Hours: Sunrise – sunset.
Avoid: Major club competition days. Sat / Sun in June / Aug.

Green Fees: €20 midweek, €25 Sat/Sun.
Juveniles: Welcome at times when course is available.
Clubhouse Hours: 10.30am – 11.00pm.
Clubhouse Dress: Casual.
Clubhouse Facilities: Full clubhouse facilites, tea coffee , snacks & lunches daily.
Open Competitions: Open week July; Bank holiday weekends.

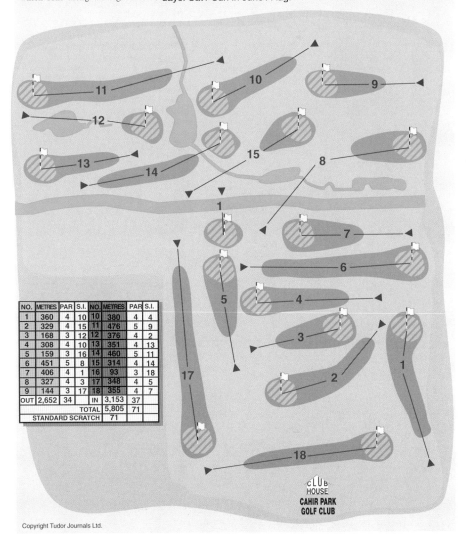

NO.	METRES	PAR	S.I.	NO.	METRES	PAR	S.I.
1	360	4	10	10	380	4	4
2	329	4	15	11	476	5	9
3	168	3	12	12	376	4	2
4	308	4	10	13	351	4	13
5	159	3	16	14	460	5	11
6	451	5	8	15	314	4	14
7	406	4	1	16	93	3	18
8	327	4	3	17	348	4	5
9	144	3	17	18	355	4	7
OUT	2,652	34		IN	3,153	37	
				TOTAL	5,805	71	
	STANDARD SCRATCH				71		

CLUB HOUSE
**CAHIR PARK
GOLF CLUB**

Copyright Tudor Journals Ltd.

Garravoone, Carrick-On-Suir, Co. Tipperary.
Tel: (051) 640047.

LOCATION: 1 mile from Carrick-On-Suir on Dargarvan Road.
MANAGER: Aidan Murphy.
ARCHITECT: E.Hackett.

Carrick on Suir is a scenic 18 hole course on elevated ground close to the town. The Comeragh Mountains are on one side as a backdrop to the first five holes and the River Suir in the valley winds its way to the sea at Waterford. The scenery will keep the golfer occupied if the game is not going to plan.

COURSE INFORMATION

Par 72; SSS 70; Length 6,061 metres.
Visitors: Welcome Mon – Sat.
Opening Hours: Sunrise – sunset.
Avoid: Mon – Wed in summer after 5pm.
Ladies Day: Wednesday.
Green Fees: €25 Mon – Fri; (€20 with member) €30 weekends (€25 with member) Group discounts. Caddy service available.
Juveniles: Welcome, telephone appointment required.
Clubhouse Hours:
10am –11pm Mon – Fri;
9am – 11pm Sat / Sun (summer);
Sat / Sun 9am – 9pm (winter).
Clubhouse Dress: Casual but neat.
Catering Facilities: Full catering available.
Open Competitions:
Open Week, July

NO.	YARDS	PAR	S.I.	NO.	YARDS	PAR	S.I.
1	367	4	8	10	351	4	3
2	166	3	16	11	447	5	15
3	297	4	2	12	379	4	1
4	154	3	18	13	328	4	7
5	497	5	6	14	439	5	17
6	180	3	4	15	321	4	13
7	332	4	12	16	167	3	9
8	335	4	14	17	418	4	5
9	495	5	10	18	338	4	11
OUT	2,823	35		IN	3,188	37	
				TOTAL	6,011	72	
				STANDARD SCRATCH	70		

Copyright Tudor Journals Ltd.

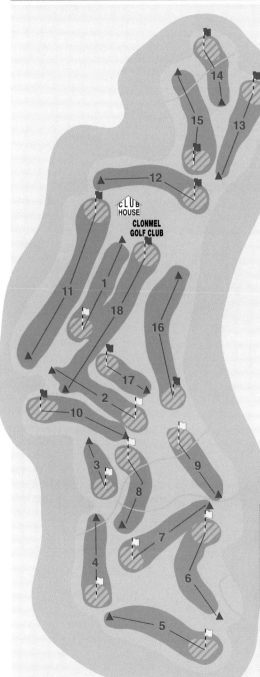

Lyneanearla, Mountain Road, Clonmel, Co. Tipperary.
Tel: (052) 21138/ 24050.

LOCATION: 3 miles from Clonmel.
SECRETARY/MANAGER: Aine Myles-Keating. Tel: (052) 24050
(052) 24050.
Email: cgc@indigo.ie
PROFESSIONAL: Robert Hayes.
ARCHITECT: Eddie Hackett.

Clonmel is a very pleasant inland course with lots of open space and plenty of variety. There is a stream that crosses three fairways and has the advantage of a picturesque setting on the scenic slopes of the pine and fir covered Comeragh Mountains overlooking the plains of Tipperary.

COURSE INFORMATION

Par 72; SSS 71; Length 5,845 metres.
Opening Hours: 8am – 10pm.
Visitors: Welcome.
Green Fees: €30 Mon – Thurs; €35 Fri Sat,Sun & Bank Hols (with member €25 anytime).
Ladies: Welcome.
Juveniles: Welcome. Lessons by prior arrangement. Club Hire available. Telephone appointment required for societies. Motorised buggy available.
Clubhouse Hours: 8.30am – 11pm.
Clubhouse Dress: Casual.
Clubhouse Facilities: Bar open everyday; Catering – Light lunch and sandwiches. Lunch and dinner by prior arrangements.

NO.	WHITE YARDS	GREEN YARDS	PAR	S.I.	NO.	WHITE YARDS	GREEN YARDS	PAR	S.I.
1	374	363	4	12	10	383	371	4	11
2	395	384	4	4	11	490	465	5	13
3	140	131	3	18	12	299	287	4	17
4	493	460	5	14	13	421	405	4	1
5	370	352	4	10	14	185	178	3	3
6	365	353	4	6	15	377	347	4	7
7	335	323	4	16	16	418	406	4	5
8	452	439	5	2	17	184	174	3	9
9	177	162	3	8	18	489	468	5	15
	3,101	2,967	36		IN	3,246	3,101	36	
					TOTAL	6,347	6,068	72	
	STANDARD SCRATCH					70			

Copyright Tudor Journals Ltd.

**Beechwood, Nenagh,
Co. Tipperary.
Tel: (067) 34808.**

LOCATION: 4 miles from town, on Old Birr Road.
HON SECRETARY: Tony Murphy.
Tel: (087) 2721852.
ARCHITECT: Patrick Merrigan.
PROFESSIONAL: Robert Kelly

Re-development completed in 2001. New design is a very fair test for every golfer irrespective of ability or experience. New sand-based greens, guarded by intimidating bunkers, are a challenge for even the most fastidious of putters. Ecellent drainage and firm surfaces allows play all year round

COURSE INFORMATION

**Par 72; SSS 72; Length
6,009 metres.
Visitors:** Welcome Mon – Fri

Avoid: Weekends.
Opening Hours:
Sunrise – sunse.t
Green Fees: €30 per 18 holes.
Juveniles: Welcome.
Clubhouse Hours: 10am-11pm.
Clubhouse Dress: Casual.
Clubhouse Facilities: Full catering available.
Open Competitions: Open week – 1st week in June; Semi-opens – most Bank Holiday Weekends.

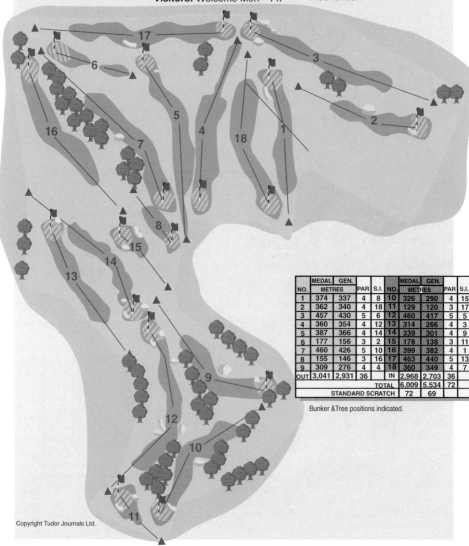

NO.	MEDAL METRES	GEN.	PAR	S.I.	NO.	MEDAL METRES	GEN.	PAR	S.I.
1	374	337	4	8	10	326	290	4	15
2	362	340	4	18	11	129	120	3	17
3	457	430	5	6	12	460	417	5	5
4	360	354	4	12	13	314	266	4	3
5	387	366	4	14	14	339	301	4	9
6	177	156	3	2	15	178	138	3	11
7	460	426	5	10	16	399	382	4	1
8	155	146	3	16	17	463	440	5	13
9	309	276	4	4	18	360	349	4	7
OUT	3,041	2,931	36		IN	2,968	2,703	36	
					TOTAL	6,009	5,534	72	
					STANDARD SCRATCH	72	69		

Bunker &Tree positions indicated.

Copyright Tudor Journals Ltd.

NO.	METRES	PAR	S.I.	NO.	METRES	PAR	S.I.
1	266	4	16	10	448	5	9
2	436	5	14	11	160	3	17
3	362	4	6	12	447	5	11
4	313	4	12	13	410	4	1
5	365	4	4	14	159	3	15
6	151	3	10	15	381	4	3
7	473	5	8	16	335	4	5
8	109	3	18	17	190	3	7
9	371	4	2	18	332	4	13
OUT	2,846	36		IN	2,862	35	
				TOTAL	5,708	71	
		STANDARD SCRATCH				70	

Derryvale, Roscrea.
Co. Tipperary.
Tel: (0505) 21130.

LOCATION: 2 miles east of Roscrea on the N7.
SECRETARY: G.P. Maher.
Tel: (0505) 21130.

A fine 18 hole course with some excellent Par 3's. The last six holes are particularly challenging.

COURSE INFORMATION

Par 71; SSS 70; Length 5,708 metres.
Visitors: Welcome Sundays by arrangement.
Opening Hours: 8am to dusk.
Ladies Day: Tuesdays.
Green Fees: €20 Mon – Fri. €25 Sat / Sun.
Juveniles: Welcome although must be accompanied by an adult. Club Hire and Caddy trolleys available.
Clubhouse Hours: 10.30am – 11.30pm.
Clubhouse Dress: Casual but neat.
Clubhouse Facilities: Full bar and catering.
Open Competitions: Open week, June. Bank Holiday weekends. Open every Wednesday (Men) April to October.

CLUB HOUSE

ROSCREA GOLF CLUB

Copyright Tudor Journals Ltd.

Clonacody, Lisronagh, Clonmel, Co. Tipperary.
Tel: (052) 32213
Fax: (052) 32040
Email:
info@slievenamongolfclub.com
www.slievenamongolfclub.com

LOCATION: 6km outside Clonmel.
PRESIDENT: Kevin Lalor.
SECRETARY: Brendan Kenny.

A Splendid 18 hole golf course overlooked by the beautiful Slievenamon.

COURSE INFORMATION

Par 66; SSS 64; Length 4,846 Yards.
Visitors: Welcome.
Opening Hours: Dawn – Dusk.

Green Fees: €10 weekdays; €15 weekends, Bank Holidays. €5 Clubhire.
Clubhouse Facilities: Full catering, á la carte, Bar. Catering & Bar Tel: (052) 30876.
Open Competitions: Regular open competitions throughout the season.

NO.	YARDS	PAR	S.I.	NO.	YARDS	PAR	S.I.
1	155	3	6	10	380	4	1
2	191	3	8	11	320	4	13
3	287	4	14	12	281	4	5
4	144	3	4	13	164	3	17
5	282	4	12	14	323	4	9
6	330	4	16	15	286	4	3
7	261	4	10	16	480	5	15
8	228	3	18	17	202	3	7
9	354	4	2	18	178	3	11
OUT	2,232	32		IN	2,614	34	
				TOTAL	4,846	66	
	STANDARD SCRATCH					64	

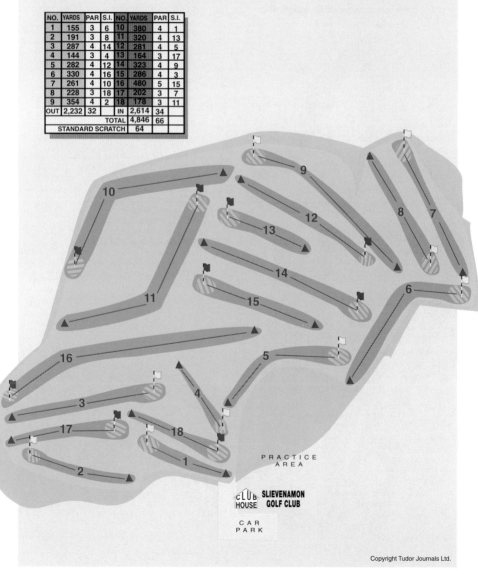

Copyright Tudor Journals Ltd.

**Manna South,
Templemore.
Co Tipperary.
Tel: (0504) 31400.**

LOCATION: 1/2 mile from town centre beside N62S.
SECRETARY: John Hackett.
Tel: (0504) 31502/32923 or (086) 8338896

This course provides a pleasant test of golf, starting with a 442 metre

Par 5. The course has five Par 3's, finishing with a very good Par 5 at the 9th and 18th. It has a very compact layout requiring only short walks from green to tees.

COURSE INFORMATION

Par 70; SSS 69 (White), 68 (Green) ; Length 5,443 metres.
Visitors: Welcome Mon – Sun.
Opening Hours: 8.00am –

Ladies: Welcome
Green Fees: €15 per day Mon – Fri. €20 per day Sat, Sun & Bank Holidays. €10 if playing with a member. Special Society Rates apply, contact secretary.
Juveniles: Welcome, new members welcome – apply Honorary Secretary.
Clubhouse Hours: 8.00am – sunset.
Clubhouse Dress: Casual.
Clubhouse Facilities: By prior arrangement.
Open Competitions: Open week July.

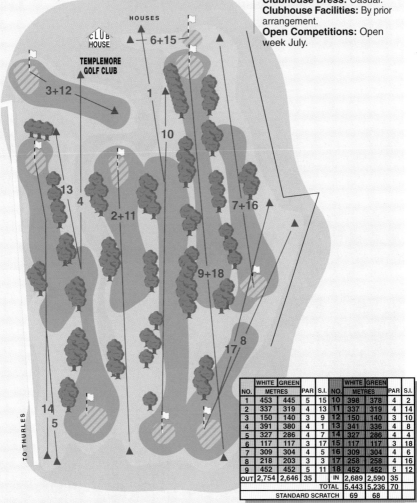

NO.	WHITE METRES	GREEN METRES	PAR	S.I.	NO.	WHITE METRES	GREEN METRES	PAR	S.I.
1	453	445	5	15	10	398	378	4	2
2	337	319	4	13	11	337	319	4	14
3	150	140	3	9	12	150	140	3	10
4	391	380	4	1	13	341	336	4	8
5	327	286	4	7	14	327	286	4	4
6	117	117	3	17	15	117	117	3	18
7	309	304	4	5	16	309	304	4	6
8	218	203	3	3	17	258	258	4	16
9	452	452	5	11	18	452	452	5	12
OUT	2,754	2,646	35		IN	2,689	2,590	35	
					TOTAL	5,443	5,236	70	
					STANDARD SCRATCH	69	68		

Copyright Tudor Journals Ltd.

**Turtulla, Thurles.
Co. Tipperary.
Tel: (0504) 21983.**

LOCATION: One mile from Thurles town.
HON. SECRETARY: Tomas Ryan.
PROFESSIONAL: Sean Hunt.
Tel: (0504) 21983.
ARCHITECT: Lionel Hewson.

Fine parkland course, with the main features being the four excellent Par 3 holes and the fearsome 18th with the out-of-bounds all the way down the left. Unusual beginning to your round with two Par 5's in a row.

COURSE INFORMATION

Par 72; SSS 71; Length 6,456 yards, 5,904 metres.
Visitors: Welcome.
Opening Hours: 9.00am – 11.30pm.
Ladies: Welcome.
Avoid: Limited availablity at weekends.
Green Fees: €25 (€12.50 with member).
Juveniles: Welcome, Club Hire available; caddy service and lessons available by prior arrangement, telephone

Clubhouse Hours: 10.00am – 11.00pm. Full clubhouse facilities which include two championship squash courts.
Clubhouse Dress: Casual.
Clubhouse Facilities: Snacks at all times; full meals as ordered.
Open Competitions: Open Week, July / Aug; Junior Scratch Cup, May; Inter. Scratch Cup, Sept.

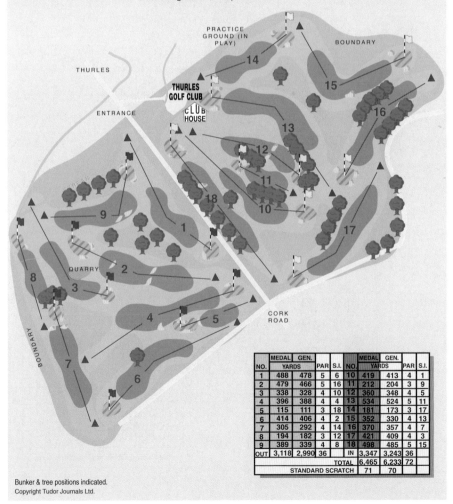

NO.	MEDAL YARDS	GEN. YARDS	PAR	S.I.	NO.	MEDAL YARDS	GEN. YARDS	PAR	S.I.
1	488	478	5	6	10	419	413	4	1
2	479	466	5	16	11	212	204	3	9
3	338	328	4	10	12	360	348	4	5
4	396	388	4	4	13	534	524	5	11
5	115	111	3	18	14	181	173	3	17
6	414	406	4	2	15	352	330	4	13
7	305	292	4	14	16	370	357	4	7
8	194	182	3	12	17	421	409	4	3
9	389	339	4	8	18	498	485	5	15
OUT	3,118	2,990	36		IN	3,347	3,243	36	
					TOTAL	6,465	6,233	72	
					STANDARD SCRATCH	71	70		

Bunker & tree positions indicated.
Copyright Tudor Journals Ltd.

**County Tipperary Golf &
Country Club,
Dundrum, Co. Tipperary.
Tel: (062) 71717.
Fax: (062) 71718.**

DIRECTOR OF GOLF: William
Crowe.
Tel: (062) 71717.
SECRETARY: Marie Lacey.
PROFESSIONAL: Available on
request.

An attractive parkland course
playable all year round that has some
interesting holes, with mature
woodland rivers and streams.

COURSE INFORMATION

**Par 72; SSS 72; Length
6,955 yards, 6,300 metres.
Visitors:** Welcome anytime
(societies included).
Opening Hours: 8am – sunset.
Ladies: Welcome.
Weekends: Advisable to book
in advance.
Green Fees: €38 midweek,
€45 weekends.
Juveniles: Welcome. Club and
Buggy Hire available.
Clubhouse Hours:
11.00am – 11.00pm.
Clubhouse Dress: Informal but
neat.
Clubhouse Facilities:
Restaurant and bar everyday.
90 bedroom hotel.
Open Competitions: Open
Week, 2nd - 12th Aug.

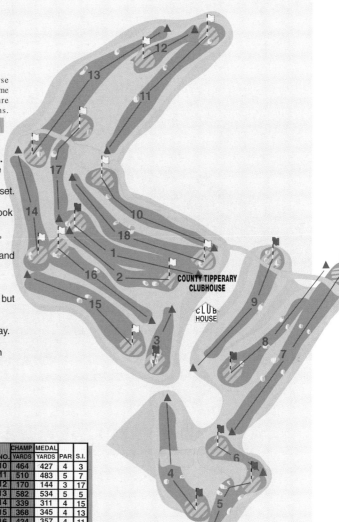

NO.	CHAMP YARDS	MEDAL YARDS	PAR	S.I.	NO.	CHAMP YARDS	MEDAL YARDS	PAR	S.I.
1	388	350	4	10	10	464	427	4	3
2	367	349	4	12	11	510	483	5	7
3	198	186	3	6	12	170	144	3	17
4	358	336	4	18	13	582	534	5	5
5	316	304	4	14	14	339	311	4	15
6	178	160	3	16	15	368	345	4	13
7	561	539	5	4	16	424	357	4	11
8	419	326	4	8	17	387	367	4	9
9	462	427	4	2	18	464	450	4	1
OUT	3,247	2,977	35		IN	3,708	3,418	37	
					TOTAL	6,955	6,395	72	
					STANDARD SCRATCH	72	72		

Bunker and tree positions indicated.
Copyright Tudor Journals Ltd.

**Knocknagranagh,
Co. Waterford.
Tel: (058) 41605/43310.
Fax: (058) 44113.
Email: dungarvangc@eircom.net**

LOCATION: Dungarvan 2 miles.
On N25 route.
SECRETARY/MANAGER: Irene Howell.
ARCHITECT: Maurice Fives.

Dungarvan Golf Club is set against the backdrop of the Comeragh Mountains and runs adjacent to

Dungavan Bay. This 6,785 yd Par 72 championship course has been architecturally designed with nine lakes and man-made hazards strategically placed to test all levels of golfer.

COURSE INFORMATION

**Par 72; SSS 73; Length
6,785 yards; 6,204
metres.
Visitors:** Welcome.
Opening Hours: 7.00am – sunset.

Green Fees: Mon – Fri €28,
Weekends €35.
Juveniles: Welcome.
Clubhouse Hours:
9am – 12pm.
Clubhouse Dress: Neat at all times.
Clubhouse Facilities: Include light meals & full dining room service. Resident PGA Professional. Snooker room.
Open Competitions: Open weeks, July and September.

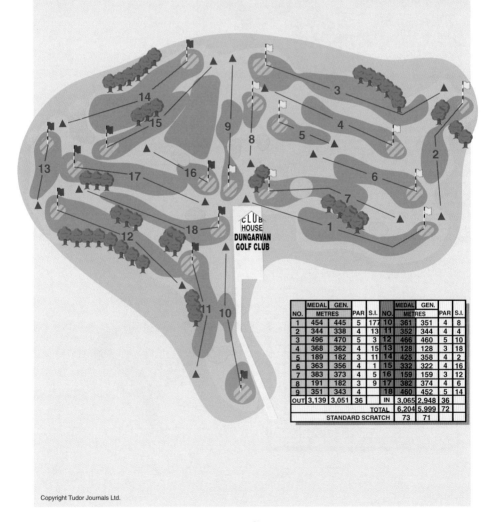

NO.	MEDAL METRES	GEN. METRES	PAR	S.I.	NO.	MEDAL METRES	GEN. METRES	PAR	S.I.
1	454	445	5	17	10	361	351	4	8
2	344	338	4	13	11	352	344	4	4
3	496	470	5	3	12	466	460	5	10
4	368	362	4	15	13	128	128	3	18
5	189	182	3	11	14	425	358	4	2
6	363	356	4	1	15	332	322	4	16
7	383	373	4	5	16	159	159	3	12
8	191	182	3	9	17	382	374	4	6
9	351	343	4		18	460	452	5	14
OUT	3,139	3,051	36		IN	3,065	2,948	36	
					TOTAL	6,204	5,999	72	
					STANDARD SCRATCH	73	71		

Copyright Tudor Journals Ltd.

**Dunmore East Golf &
Country Club,
Dunmore East,
Co. Waterford.
Tel: (051) 383151.**

LOCATION: Ten miles from
Waterford City in Dunmore
East village.
SECRETARY: Mary Skehan.
Tel: (051) 383151.
ARHITECT: William Henry Jones.

This 18 hole course overlooks the
village of Dunmore East with
panoramic views of the bay and harbour.

The course offers challenging golf, in
idyllic surroundings, with five holes on
the waters edge, and shots 15 & 16 are
played over inlets into the cliffs.

COURSE INFORMATION

**Par 72; Length 6,655
yards.
Visitors:** No restrictions.
Opening Hours: Dawn –
Dusk.
Ladies: Welcome no
restrictions.
Juveniles: Welcome.

Green Fees: €21 Weekdays;
€26 Weekends & Bank
Holidays.
Clubhouse Hours:
9am – 12pm.
Clubhouse Dress:
Neat / casual.
Clubhouse Facilities:
Full bar, light snacks and full
meals available all day. Club
Hire, caddy trolleys and golf
cart available for hire.
Open Competitions: Fourball
every Tuesday. Open Week
25th June to 1st July.

NO.	YARDS	PAR	S.I.	NO.	YARDS	PAR	S.I.
1	293	4	15	10	441	5	10
2	398	4	17	11	360	4	4
3	480	5	13	12	462	5	16
4	390	4	1	13	530	5	6
5	342	4	5	14	180	3	8
6	430	4	7	15	396	4	2
7	160	3	11	16	91	3	18
8	384	4	3	17	292	4	14
9	390	4	9	18	130	3	12
OUT	3,167	36		IN	3,167	36	
				TOTAL	6,059	72	
STANDARD SCRATCH			70				

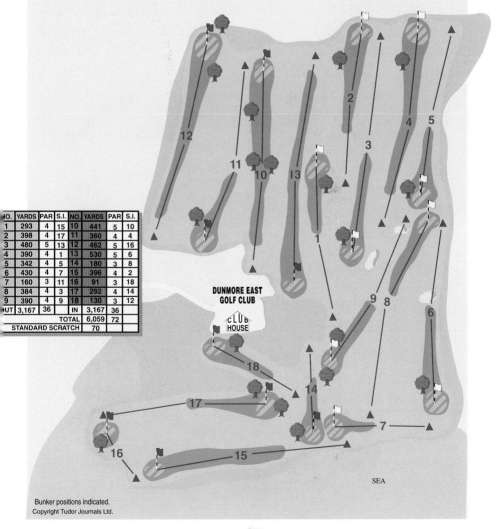

DUNMORE EAST
GOLF CLUB

CLUB
HOUSE

SEA

Bunker positions indicated.
Copyright Tudor Journals Ltd.

**Faithlegg Golf Club,
Faithlegg House.
Co. Waterford.
Tel: (051) 382241.
Fax: (051) 382664.
Email: golf@faithlegg.com
www.faithlegg.com**

LOCATION: Six miles from Waterford City, from Waterford take Dunmore East road for Cheekpoint village
SECRETARY: Mr Dick Brennan.
Tel: (051) 382241.
PROFESSIONAL: On Site.
Tel: (051) 382241

ARCHITECT: Patrick Merrigan.

Some wicked slopes and borrows on the greens and a dog-legged approach to the two tier 18th green are just some of the novel features incorporated into the course. The architect sensitively integrated the course into a landscape textured with mature trees, flowing parkland and no less than five lakes. This is a golfing tour-de-force.

COURSE INFORMATION

**Par 72; SSS 72; Length
6,690 yards; 6,285 metres.**

Visitors: Welcome. Societies always welcome.
Opening Hours:
8am – sunset.
Ladies: Welcome.
Green Fees: Mon – Thurs €35, Fri – Sun & Bank Holidays €50.
Juveniles: Permitted.
Clubhouse Hours:
8.00am – Sunset.
Clubhouse Dress: Casual but neat (no jeans).
Clubhouse Facilities: Full bar and catering facilities available, mens & ladies locker rooms, Pro-Shop. Club, Caddy cars and trolleys available for hire.
Open Competitions: Contact clubhouse for details.

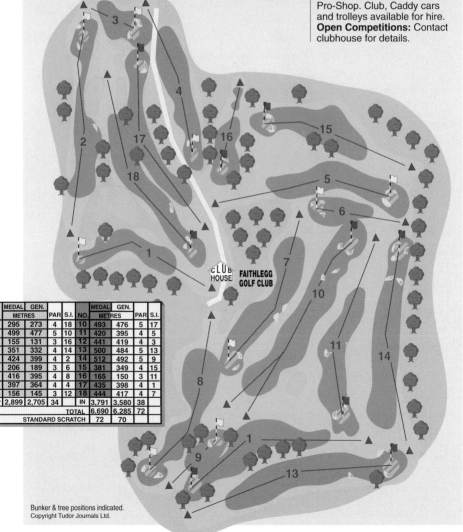

	MEDAL	GEN.				MEDAL	GEN.		
	METRES		PAR	S.I.	NO.	METRES		PAR	S.I.
	295	273	4	18	10	493	476	5	17
	499	477	5	10	11	420	395	4	5
	155	131	3	16	12	441	419	4	3
	351	332	4	14	13	500	484	5	13
	424	399	4	2	14	512	492	5	9
	206	189	3	6	15	381	349	4	15
	416	395	4	8	16	165	150	3	11
	397	364	4	4	17	435	398	4	1
	156	145	3	12	18	444	417	4	7
r	2,899	2,705	34		IN	3,791	3,580	38	
				TOTAL		6,690	6,285	72	
		STANDARD SCRATCH	72				70		

Bunker & tree positions indicated.
Copyright Tudor Journals Ltd.

**Gold Coast Golf Club,
Ballinacourty,
Dungarvan.
Co. Waterford.
Tel: (058)
42249/44055.
Fax: (058) 43378.**

Location: Three miles East of
Dungarvan.
President: Dave Clarke.
Secretary: Eugene Collins.
Captain: Billy Power.

A parkland course bordered by
Atlantic Ocean with a scenic
background of Dungarvan Bay and
Comeragh Mountains.

COURSE INFORMATION

**Par 72; SSS 72; Length
6,171 metres.**
Visitors: Welcome.
Opening Hours: Sunrise –
sunset.
Avoid: Advisable to book in
advance for weekends.

Ladies: Welcome.
Green Fees: Mon–Fri €30;
Sat/Sun €40.
Juveniles: Welcome. Club
and trolley hire available.
Clubhouse Hours:
8.00am – 12.00pm.
Clubhouse Dress:
Casual, neat.
Clubhouse Facilities: Hotel &
catering services, including
leisure centre & swimming
pool on site.

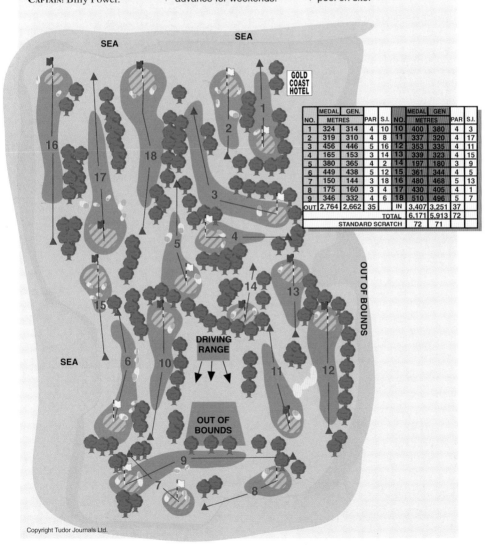

NO.	MEDAL METRES	GEN. METRES	PAR	S.I.	NO.	MEDAL METRES	GEN. METRES	PAR	S.I.
1	324	314	4	10	10	400	380	4	3
2	319	310	4	8	11	337	320	4	17
3	456	446	5	16	12	353	335	4	11
4	165	153	3	14	13	339	323	4	15
5	380	365	4	2	14	197	180	3	9
6	449	438	5	12	15	361	344	4	5
7	150	144	3	18	16	480	468	5	13
8	175	160	3	4	17	430	405	4	1
9	346	332	4	6	18	510	496	5	7
OUT	2,764	2,662	35		IN	3,407	3,251	37	
					TOTAL	6,171	5,913	72	
					STANDARD SCRATCH	72	71		

Copyright Tudor Journals Ltd.

Lismore Golf Club,
Ballyin, Lismore,
Co. Waterford.
Tel: (058) 54026.

LOCATION: 1Km north of town,
off R.666.
SECRETARY: Stephen Hales.
Tel: (058) 54026.

Undulating parkland course with
mature hardwood trees, on the estate of
Lismore Castle, in the Blackwater
Valley.

COURSE INFORMATION

Par 69; SSS 67; Length
5,790 yards.
Visitors: More than welcome.
Opening Hours: Dawn – dusk.
Avoid: Saturdays and Sundays.
Ladies Day: Wednesday.
Green Fees: €16 weekdays,
€20 Saturday, Sunday Bank
Holiday Monday.
Juveniles: Accompanied by
an adult.
Clubhouse Hours:
9.00am – close.
Clubhouse Dress:
Neat / Casual.
Clubhouse Facilities: Bar,
snacks, changing rooms.
Open Competitions: Open day
every Thurs. Open Week
May/July. Bank Holiday weekend
– August.

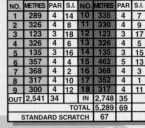

NO.	METRES	PAR	S.I.	NO.	METRES	PAR	S.I.
1	289	4	14	10	335	4	7
2	326	4	8	11	330	4	9
3	123	3	18	12	123	3	17
4	326	4	6	13	326	4	5
5	135	3	16	14	135	3	15
6	357	4	4	15	462	5	13
7	368	4	2	16	368	4	3
8	317	4	10	17	352	4	1
9	300	4	12	18	317	4	11
OUT	2,541	34		IN	2,748	35	
				TOTAL	5,289	69	
			STANDARD SCRATCH		67		

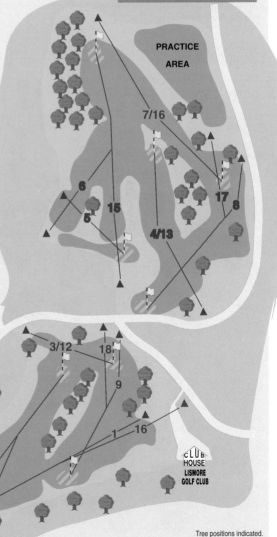

Copyright Tudor Journals Ltd.

Tree positions indicated.

**Newtown Hill,
Tramore.
Co Waterford.**

LOCATION: On the Dungarvan coast road.
SECRETARY: James Cox.
Tel: (051) 386170.
PROFESSIONAL: Derry Kiely.

18 hole championship course with generous fairways. In a recent survey, by Sports Columnist John Cowyn, two holes — the 4th and the 6th were rated in the top eighteen in Ireland.

COURSE INFORMATION

Par 72; SSS 73; Length 6,055 metres.
Green Fees: €40 Mon – Thurs. €45 Weekends.

Visitors: Welcome, lessons available by prior arrangements; Club Hire and Caddy service available; telephone appointments required.
Clubhouse Hours: 11.00am – 11.30pm;
Clubhouse Dress: Casual but neat.
Open Competitions: Open Weeks 24th Aug – 8th Sept (1st week gents; 2nd week ladies).

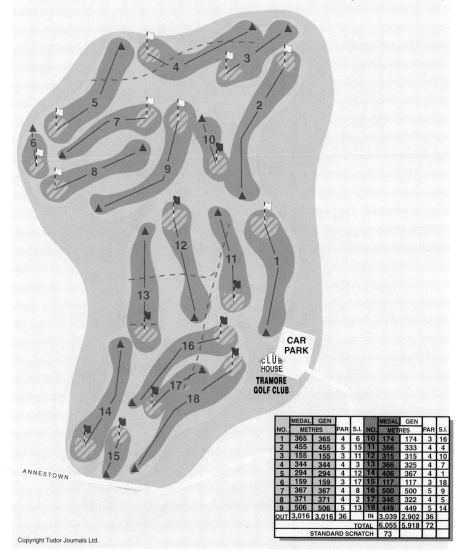

NO.	MEDAL METRES	GEN METRES	PAR	S.I.	NO.	MEDAL METRES	GEN METRES	PAR	S.I.
1	365	365	4	6	10	174	174	3	16
2	455	455	5	15	11	366	333	4	4
3	155	155	3	11	12	315	315	4	10
4	344	344	4	3	13	366	325	4	7
5	294	294	4	12	14	406	367	4	1
6	159	159	3	17	15	117	117	3	18
7	367	367	4	8	16	500	500	5	9
8	371	371	4	2	17	346	322	4	5
9	506	506	5	13	18	449	449	5	14
OUT	3,016	3,016	36		IN	3,039	2,902	36	
					TOTAL	6,055	5,918	72	
					STANDARD SCRATCH		73		

ANNESTOWN

CAR PARK
CLUB HOUSE
TRAMORE GOLF CLUB

Copyright Tudor Journals Ltd.

Waterford Castle Golf Club, The Island, Ballinakill, Waterford.
Tel: (051) 871633.
Fax: (051) 871634.
Email:golf@waterford castle.com
LOCATION: Waterford City.
DIRECTOR OF GOLF: Micheal Garland.
ARHITECT: Des Smyth & Associates.

Ireland's only true island golf course. A unique 310-acre island golf course surrounded by the river Suir and accessed by private ferry. A mature parkland course and a commendable test of golf.

COURSE INFORMATION

Par 72; SSS 73; Length 6,231 Metres.
Visitors: Welcome.
Opening Hours: 8am – dusk.
Avoid: 8.30am – 10.30am (Sat & Sun).

Ladies: Welcome.
Juveniles: Permitted with adult.
Green Fees: €38-€41midweek. €45-€49 weekends.
Clubhouse Hours: 8am-dusk.
Clubhouse Dress: Casual, no jeans etc.
Clubhouse Facilities: Bar snacks available. Full meals with pre-booking.
Open Competitions: Open week: July.

NO.	MEDAL MTRS	GEN. MTRS	PAR	S.I.	NO.	MEDAL MTRS	GEN. MTRS	PAR	S.I.
1	385	361	4	7	10	160	152	3	18
2	176	154	3	17	11	346	318	4	6
3	372	346	4	3	12	415	397	4	2
4	356	338	4	5	13	463	427	5	12
5	476	432	5	15	14	343	306	4	10
6	337	320	4	11	15	468	454	5	14
7	193	176	3	9	16	187	173	3	8
8	452	443	5	13	17	368	344	4	4
9	381	360	4	1	18	353	326	4	16
OUT	3,128	2,930	36		IN	3,103	2,897	36	
					TOTAL	6,231	5,827	72	
					STANDARD SCRATCH	73	71		

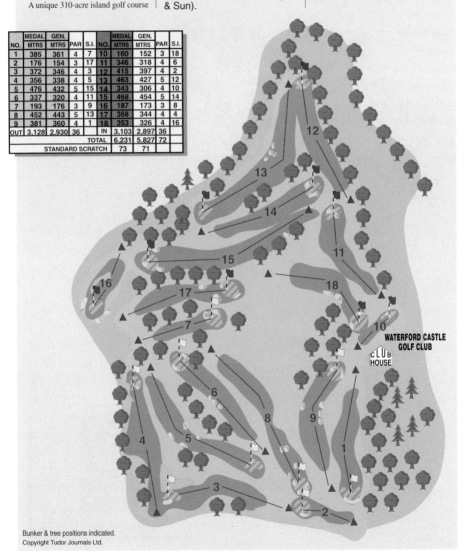

WATERFORD CASTLE GOLF CLUB

CLUB HOUSE

Bunker & tree positions indicated.
Copyright Tudor Journals Ltd.

Dungarvan.
Co. Waterford.
Tel: (058) 43216.
Fax: (058) 44343.
Email: info@westwaterfordgolf.com
www.westwaterfordgolf.com

LOCATION: 3 miles from Dungarvan, 30 miles from Waterford city.
SECRETARY: Tom Whelan.
ARCHITECT: Eddie Hackett.

The course extends over 150 acres of magnificent rolling topography taking in the beautiful panoramic views of Co. Waterford. An interesting feature of the course is that the first nine holes are laid out on a large plateau featuring a lovely stream which comes into play at the 3rd and 4th holes. The course extends to 6802 yds, but it was built to suit a wide range of players with a minimum interference to the natural characteristics and vegetation. Playable all year round.

COURSE INFORMATION

Par 72; SSS 72:
Length 6,732 yards.
Visitors: Welcome.

Opening Hours:
Sunrise – sunset.
Green Fees: €26 Mon – Fri. €32 Sat – Sun. Discount for societies.
Juveniles: Welcome. Clubs and caddy cars available for hire.
Clubhouse Hours:
8.00am – sunset.
Clubhouse Dress: Casual / neat.
Clubhouse Facilities: Full bar & catering facilities all day, every day.

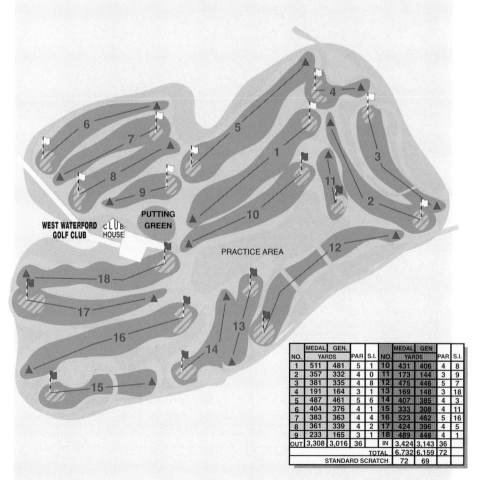

NO.	MEDAL YARDS	GEN. YARDS	PAR	S.I.	NO.	MEDAL YARDS	GEN YARDS	PAR	S.I.
1	511	481	5	1	10	431	406	4	8
2	357	332	4	0	11	173	144	3	9
3	381	335	4	8	12	475	446	5	7
4	191	164	3	1	13	169	148	3	18
5	487	461	5	6	14	407	385	4	3
6	404	376	4	1	15	333	308	4	11
7	383	363	4	4	16	523	462	5	16
8	361	339	4	2	17	424	396	4	5
9	233	165	3	1	18	489	448	4	1
OUT	3,308	3,016	36		IN	3,424	3,143	36	
					TOTAL	6,732	6,159	72	
					STANDARD SCRATCH	72	69		

Copyright Tudor Journals Ltd.

CONNACHT

BY JACK MAGOWAN

Cecil Ewing was a big man – feisty, humorous, opinionated and hopelessly in love with golf. He wore an 'extra large' label in personality, and was the kind you thought would live for ever. When he died at 63, it was as though the game had lost a grand uncle.

Cecil had not only played in six Walker Cup teams and for Ireland over 90 times, he won the West of Ireland championship ten times and was beaten finalist on another eight occasions, a record almost without parallel in the days when the BBC of amateur golf, Burke, Bruen and Carr, were in their prime.

Ewing could play left-handed as well as right, and often did, usually for a happy wager.

Nobody loved an audience as much as he did, and his favourite party piece would be to challenge somebody to a match over the last three holes of his beloved Rosses Point links.

If the reply was "no thanks, you're too good", Cecil would propose a compromise "OK. I'll play left-handed and you right-handed," he would tease. And nine times out of ten the result would be the same — he won!

Like O'Connor Senior, he revelled, too, in wind and rough weather. "I learned the game in a good school," he used to say. "When it blows at Rosses Point, the only hiding place is in the clubhouse!"

Cecil had a gift for making the game look easy, and was 45, and over 17 stone, when he played against the United States for the last time in the Walker Cup at St. Andrews. Three years later he was Irish Close champion again, a surprise winner over one of the toughest courses in the game, Ballybunion.

Ewing was also a Cup selector and captained Ireland to two European championship victories, one of them in Italy. The ball he used for an exciting win against Ray Billows in Britain's historic Cup victory of 1938 is on display in Sligo's splendid clubhouse and still sparks many potent memories, especially of some of the great names who've played under the shadow of Ben Bulben.

Like Walter Hagen, who took two days to get there from London. And

Westport course has an attractive mixture of
tree-lined fairways and superb views.

GARVEY'S HOTEL

With Garvey's impressive stand overlooking Galway's focal point - Eyre Square, this hotel and bar has become a landmark in Galway City. Due to its location in the heart of Galway City, Garvey's is in close proximity to all amenities and local attractions.

The family-run hotel opened its doors in February 2000, following a huge redevelopment of the whole building. All the rooms have been furnished to the highest standards and include the following facilities: All en-suite with Multi-channel television, Tea/Coffee making facilities, Direct-dial telephone, Iron and Ironing board, Trouser-press and fabulous views of Galway City.

Eyre Square, Galway.
Tel: (091) 562 224 Fax: (091) 562 526
Email: info@garveyshotel.com
www.garveyshotel.com

Meadow Court Hotel

Welcome to one of Ireland's finest hotels. Done to 5 star standard. Winner of 16 awards. Tucked into the scenic country side. Two restaurants and two bars, old world style. Fine dining and casual. Ideal hotel to relax during a golfing trip. 5 minutes from golf club, many golf greens to choose from. Lakes, fishing, horse riding, boating all close by.
Dublin 2 hrs, Shannon 45 mins, Galway 20mins.

Clostoken, Loughrea, Co. Galway.
Tel: 091 841051. Fax: 091 842406.
E-mail: meadowcourthotel@eircom.net
Web: www.meadowcourthotel.com

Salthill HOTEL

Tel: (091) 522 711

Salthill Hotel, is situated on Ireland's Premier Seaside resort and Promenade overlooking Galway Bay. Galway City Centre is just five minute drive and within thirty minutes you can be in the heart of Connemara or fly/sail to the Aran Islands. There are four golf clubs with easy reach of the hotel. Salthill has a number of lively pubs, restaurant and cafes all located within walking distance of the hotel. Salthill Hotel has 75 en-suite bedrooms.

BAR
The Bar overlooks Galway Bay with a lively night trade and bar food available throughout the day.

RESTAURANT
Our restaurant offers an extensive a la carte menu and is popular with local trade.

BEDROOMS
Each of our 75 en-suite rooms are equipped with the following: • Direct Dial Telephone • Multichannel TV • Tea & Coffee Facilities • Hair Dryer • Parking for up to 150 cars

e-mail: salthillhotel@eircom.net

Visitor information at your fingertips

www.visitordays.com

NEXT TIME GET ALL THE INFORMATION BEFORE YOU LEAVE HOME

With views over Galway Bay and beyond, Galway Golf Club compliments a
good challenge with superb scenery.

Bobby Locke and Henry Cotton, and
more recently Bernhard Langer. "I went
there to play one round and stayed two
weeks," says Langer of the 100 per cent
links course that would almost surely
covet a world rating were it not so isolated.

If it wasn't the sea air and scenery
that captivated Langer, then it must
have been the loudest silence in golf.
Along the corridors of these exposed
and barren fairways, all you hear is the
grass growing!

Sligo can boast several star-studded
holes, but the pick of them by far is the
17th. Tucked among high dunes, this
classic hole spans 450 yards off the

tiger tees, and in O'Connor Senior's
book is one of the finest two-shot holes
in the country. "It carries a knock-out
punch like the Tyson of old," smiles
fight-fan O'Connor.

Ireland now has over 350 golf courses,
and if there's a bad one anywhere, somebody once said, they're keeping it a
secret. Inexpensive, underplayed and
welcoming – that's how they beat the
drums for Connacht courses, the cream
of which are always special.

Nothing beats the birth of a new
course, and if two here could be awarded
a rosette for quality they are Carn, in Co.
Mayo, and O'Connor Junior's wonder-

ASHFORD CASTLE

EXCELLENCE SINCE 1828

Set on the shores of Lough Corrib, this magnificent undulating parkland course with mature trees, hundreds of years old and generous greens, is a challenging par 70 which is very user friendly.

This nine hole course measuring 3,000 yards is exclusive and complimentary to the guests of the hotel and designed in a way that everyone – beginning and advanced golfers, female or male are all very welcome.

There is club hire and tuition facilities for ladies and gents in this tranquil location which is perfect for learning the wonderful game of golf at your leisure.

Ashford Castle has established itself as a premiere venue for golf and corporate entertainment.

If you would like some information on our new *"VIP Golf Programme"* please contact golf Pro Tom Devereux.

Cong, Co. Mayo, Ireland.
Tel: 353 92 46003
Fax: 353 92 46260
e-mail: ashford@ashford.ie
Website: www.ashford.ie
Booking in the
U.S.A.: 1 800 346 7007

fully ambitious layout at Galway Bay.

Have you ever been to Belmullet? That's where Carn is – in the back of beyond. Or as *Golf World* so aptly put it in their choice of Britain's Top 10 new courses a couple of years ago, "It's not the sort of place you can pop in to on the way to somewhere else!"

Some holes there are truly majestic, and there's the odd one or two that push the realms of respectability a bit too far. But it's a challenge and fun to play.

German and French golfers are drawn to Ireland's west coast like fruit flies to a ripening. The piano in the lounge at Connemara is a gift from a German diplomat who came for a fishing holiday some years ago, but never even got rod and line out of his car. Instead, he hired a set of clubs and had a ball in the company of some of the most remote, yet hospitable, people on earth.

Connemara, like Waterville, is an Eddie Hackett creation, and like Waterville, the second nine there are better than the first. In fact, the last six holes at Clifden is as tough a finishing stretch as there is anywhere, a veritable no-man's land of sand and wilderness. In May and June, the links are a tapestry of yellows, blues and purples.

It doesn't surprise me that Enniscrone is now in Ireland's top-30 rankings, for here, too, is a links course that can both exhilarate and terrify. It's about ten miles from Ballina on the shore of Killala Bay, and looks like a lunar landscape among dunes that dip and roll and disappear out of sight.

Eddie Power won the Irish title there in '93, beating Liam Higgins' son, David in a thrilling final, and calls

Enniscore "a sleeping giant". It's the real thing, that's what he means!.

Westport has also hosted the Close championship and makes a fuss of visitors in a town where hotel beds are not expensive and there are plenty of them.

After a benign start, Westport picks up momentum, with the long 15th the pinnacle hole. The tee-shot here is not for the faint-hearted, not with a carry over an inlet of Clew Bay that must be all of 170 yards. And just for added mischief, there's an out of bounds fence along the port side.

Again, the welcome at Westport has been known to trip up the unsuspecting, so go prepared.

No two golf courses play the same, and in the west of Ireland they are all different. From Achill to Athlone to the sylvan setting of Athenry — they're all nature's own design, a playground for those who like to compliment their golf with scenery and atmosphere. As Henry Longhurst once wrote, Irish golf has that indefinable something which makes you relive again and again the days you played there!

Don't take my word for it. Go and see for yourself!

The nine hole course at Ashford Castle on the shores of Lough Corrib and beside the village of Cong.

ATHENRY

**Athenry Golf Club,
Palmerstown, Oranmore,
Co. Galway.
Tel: (091) 794466.**

LOCATION: 5 miles from
Athenry town. 8 miles from
Galway.
SECRETARY/MANAGER:
Padraig Flattery.
ARCHITECT: Eddie Hackett.

This eighteen hole parkland course
sports two ruined forts amidst dense
wooded backdrop. It was extended

from a nine hole to an eighteen hole
course in 1991 taking on a completely
different layout, but not detracting
from its sylvan setting.

COURSE INFORMATION

**Par 70; SSS 70; Length
6,200 yards.
Visitors:** Welcome.
Opening Hours:
Sunrise – sunset.
Avoid: Sundays.
Green Fees: €15 Mon – Fri;
€32 Sat/Sun.

Ladies: No restrictions.
Juveniles: Permitted, must be
accompanied by an adult after
5.00pm.
Clubhouse Hours: Flexible.
Clubhouse Dress: Casual.
Clubhouse Facilities: Full meals
at all times.
Open Competitions:
All Bank Holidays;
Open Week, 22nd–30th July.
Contact club for more details.

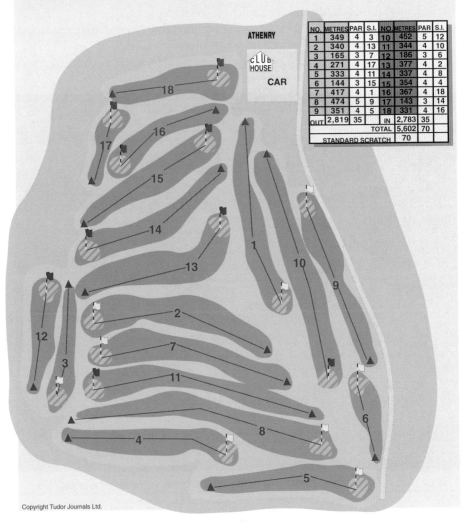

NO.	METRES	PAR	S.I.	NO.	METRES	PAR	S.I.
1	349	4	3	10	452	5	12
2	340	4	13	11	344	4	10
3	165	3	7	12	186	3	6
4	271	4	17	13	377	4	2
5	333	4	11	14	337	4	8
6	144	3	15	15	354	4	4
7	417	4	1	16	367	4	18
8	474	5	9	17	143	3	14
9	351	4	5	18	331	4	16
OUT	2,819	35		IN	2,783	35	
				TOTAL	5,602	70	
	STANDARD SCRATCH				70		

Copyright Tudor Journals Ltd.

Rossgloss, Ballinasloe, Co. Galway.
Tel: (0905) 42126,
Fax: (0905) 42538.

LOCATION: Off the Ballinasloe Portumna Road. Two miles from the town centre.
SECRETARY: Conor Carr. Tel: (0905) 42126.
ARCHITECT: Eddie Connaughton.

Ballinasloe Golf Club was established on the Cloncarty Estate, now Garbally College, in 1894. Originally a nine hole parkland course, major redevelopment of the club was undertaken in 1970 and the course was extended to eighteen holes in 1984. The course is invariably playable all year round.

COURSE INFORMATION

Par 72; SSS 70; Length 5,865 Metres.
Visitors: Welcome.
Opening Hours: 8am – Dusk.
Avoid: Major Sunday competitions.
Ladies: Welcome Tuesdays.
Green Fees: €20 Mon–Fri. €25 Sat&Sun. Societies €20
Clubhouse Dress: Neat and tidy.
Clubhouse Facilities: Full catering facilities Monday to Sunday.
Open Competitions: Open day every Thursday. Open week 6th – 14th July; Open Weekends 4th - 5th May; 3rd - 4th Aug; 29th - 31st March; 18th March. Keller Mix Am; 31st - 1st Sep; Special Olympics fundraiser; 15th - 16th June. All Ireland Inter Pubs 31st May - 1st June

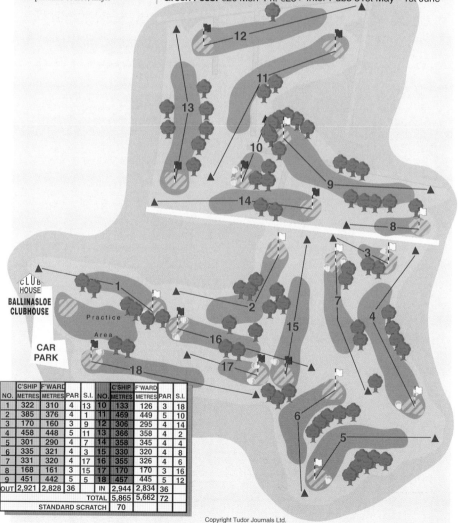

NO.	C'SHIP METRES	F'WARD METRES	PAR	S.I.	NO.	C'SHIP METRES	F'WARD METRES	PAR	S.I.
1	322	310	4	13	10	133	126	3	18
2	385	376	4	1	11	469	449	5	10
3	170	160	3	9	12	306	295	4	14
4	458	448	5	11	13	366	358	4	2
5	301	290	4	7	14	358	345	4	4
6	335	321	4	3	15	330	320	4	8
7	331	320	4	17	16	355	326	4	6
8	168	161	3	15	17	170	170	3	16
9	451	442	5	5	18	457	445	5	12
OUT	2,921	2,828	36		IN	2,944	2,834	36	
					TOTAL	5,865	5,662	72	
	STANDARD SCRATCH					70			

Copyright Tudor Journals Ltd.

Ballyconneely, Co. Galway.
Tel: (095) 23502,
Fax: (095) 23662.

LOCATION: 27 hole championship links, nine miles from Clifden.
SECRETARY/MANAGER: Richard Flaherty.
Tel: (095) 23502.
PROFESSIONAL: Hugh O'Neil.

Situated on the edge of the Atlantic Ocean in a spectacular setting with the Twelve Bens Mountains in the background, this championship course is a challenge as good as any golfer would wish for. Established in 1973 the course has a popular reputation with big hitters, who relish the long meandering fairways.

COURSE INFORMATION

Par 72; SSS 73; Length 6,173 metres.
Visitors: Welcome.
Opening Hours: Dawn – Dusk.
Avoid: Sunday mornings.
Green Fees:

	Weekday	Weekend
Jan - Apr	€30	€32
Oct - Dec	€30	€32
May - Sept	€45	€50

Lessons available by prior arrangement. Club hire and caddy car available. Golf carts available.
Juveniles: Welcome but may not play weekends, Bank Holidays or Open Weeks. Handicap Certificate required.
Clubhouse Hours: 8am – 11pm.
Clubhouse Dress: Casual (no spikes).
Clubhouse Facilities: Bar Snacks and a la carte restaurant.
Open Competitions: Open Weeks, June and September. Handicap required for open competitions.

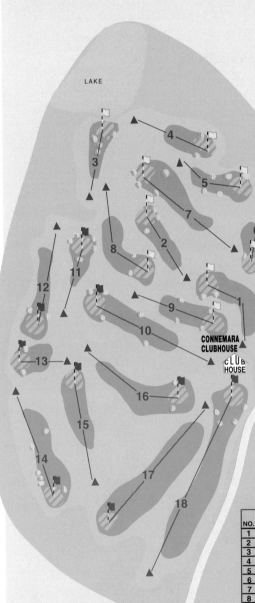

LAKE

CONNEMARA CLUBHOUSE

CLUB HOUSE

NO.	CHAMP METRES	MEDAL METRES	PAR	S.I.	NO.	CHAMP METRES	MEDAL METRES	PAR	S.I.
1	349	331	4	6	10	398	383	4	7
2	385	366	4	8	11	171	151	3	17
3	154	145	3	18	12	416	399	4	1
4	358	335	4	14	13	196	180	3	5
5	360	342	4	12	14	483	460	5	15
6	193	175	3	10	15	367	349	4	9
7	531	482	5	16	16	417	370	4	3
8	438	418	4	2	17	491	468	5	11
9	408	344	4	4	18	496	475	5	13
OUT	3,176	2,938	35		IN	3,435	3,235	37	
					TOTAL	6,611	6,173	72	
					STANDARD SCRATCH	75	73		

Copyright Tudor Journals Ltd.

Bunker positions indicated.

Connemara Isles Golf Club, Eanach Mheain, Leitir Moir, Connemara.
Tel: (091) 572498

LOCATION: Annaghvaan Island, Leitir Moir via Causeway from Beal A'Daingin.
SECRETARY/MANAGER: Tony Lynch.
Tel: (091) 572 498.
ARCHITECT: Craddock & Ruddy.

Unique Island course located in the heart of the Connemara Gaeltacht. The course is distractingly beautiful – where ocean inlets and rocky outcrops provide natural hazards, demanding steady nerves. After the game relax in the friendly atmosphere of Ireland's only thatched clubhouse, which is warmed by an open fire.

COURSE INFORMATION

Par 70; SSS 67; Length 4770 metres.
Visitors: Welcome (appreciated if able to contact office).
Opening Hours:
9.30am – 11.30pm.

Avoid: Sunday afternoon.
Ladies: Welcome any day.
Green Fees: €15 or €10 with member.
Clubhouse Hours:
9.30am – 11.30pm.
Clubhouse Dress:
Informal / casual.
Clubhouse Facilities:
Full bar, catering available by arrangement.

NO.	YARDS	PAR	S.I.	NO.	YARDS	PAR	S.I.
1	314	4	12	10	314	4	11
2	340	4	5	11	340	4	7
3	170	3	9	12	170	3	10
4	280	4	18	13	280	4	8
5	380	5	6	14	380	5	2
6	165	3	16	15	165	3	17
7	282	4	14	16	282	4	15
8	425	5	13	17	425	5	4
9	165	3	3	18	165	3	1
OUT	2,521	35		IN	2,521	35	
				TOTAL	5,042	70	
	STANDARD SCRATCH				67		

Bunker positions indicated.

Copyright Tudor Journals Ltd.

Dunmore Demesne Golf Club, Dunmore, Co.Galway. Tel: (093) 38709.

LOCATION: 9 miles from Tuam, 30 miles from Galway.
SECRETARY: Carmel Hawley. Tel: (093) 38159.
COMPETITION SECRETARY: Padraig Donlon. Tel: (093) 38692.
COURSE DESIGNER: Eddie Hackett.
COURSE BUILDER: Peter Casbalt.

A short but difficult course located in mature parkland. Rewards accuracy and skill around the greens. 5th tee features a spectacular view of the entire course. Unique in that the 1st tee is loocated within 200 metres of the town centre.

COURSE INFORMATION

Par 70; SSS 68; Length 5,278 metres.
Visitors: Welcome.

Opening Hours: 8.30am – darkness.
Green Fees: €13.
Juveniles: Monday evenings in Summer (with adult).
Clubhouse Hours: 8.30am onward.
Clubhouse Dress: Informal.
Clubhouse Facilities: Dressing room & showers only.
Open Competitions: First week in August. First week in June.

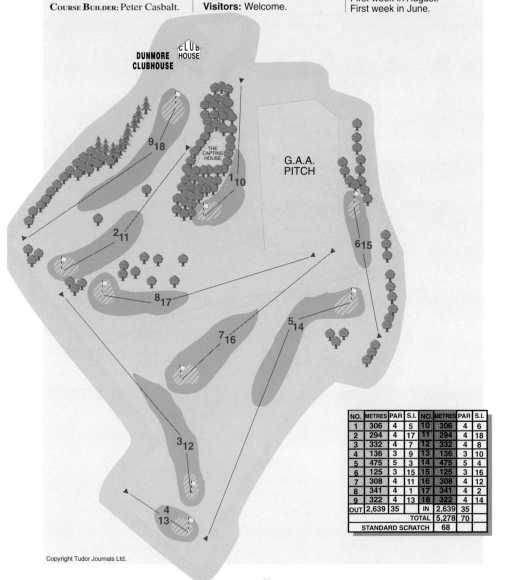

NO.	METRES	PAR	S.I.	NO.	METRES	PAR	S.I.
1	306	4	5	10	306	4	6
2	294	4	17	11	294	4	18
3	332	4	7	12	332	4	8
4	136	3	9	13	136	3	10
5	475	5	3	14	475	5	4
6	125	3	15	15	125	3	16
7	308	4	11	16	308	4	12
8	341	4	1	17	341	4	2
9	322	4	13	18	322	4	14
OUT	2,639	35		IN	2,639	35	
					TOTAL	5,278	70	
				STANDARD SCRATCH		68	

Copyright Tudor Journals Ltd.

Galway Golf Club, Blackrock, Galway. Tel: (091) 522033.

LOCATION: 3 miles west of Galway city.
SECRETARY: Padraic Fahy.
Tel: (091) 522033 (office).
PROFESSIONAL: Don Wallace.
Tel: (091) 523038.

A tight tree lined course. Some tiered greens make it very important to accurately place your drives and a good short game is necessary to score well. The course has excellent views of Galway Bay, the Burren and the Arran Islands.

COURSE INFORMATION

Par 70; SSS 71; Length 5,912 Metres.
Visitors: Welcome.
Opening Hours: 8am – Dusk.
Avoid: Tuesday, Saturday and Sunday.
Ladies: Welcome.

Green Fees: €35 weekdays, €45 weekends; Group rate (minimum 25) €25.
Clubhouse Hours: 11am – 11pm.
Clubhouse Dress: Informal.
Clubhouse Facilities: At all times.

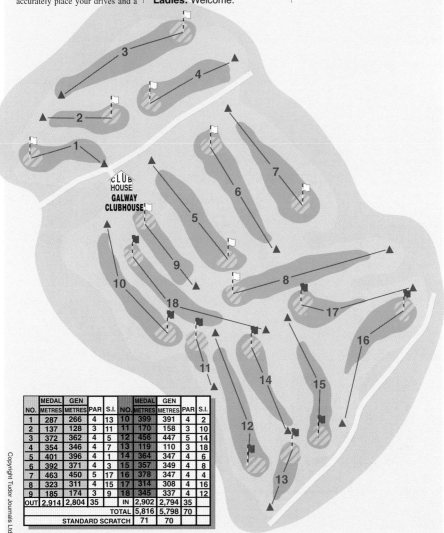

NO.	MEDAL METRES	GEN METRES	PAR	S.I.	NO.	MEDAL METRES	GEN METRES	PAR	S.I.
1	287	266	4	13	10	399	391	4	2
2	137	128	3	11	11	170	158	3	10
3	372	362	4	5	12	456	447	5	14
4	354	346	4	7	13	119	110	3	18
5	401	396	4	1	14	364	347	4	6
6	392	371	4	3	15	357	349	4	8
7	463	450	5	17	16	378	347	4	4
8	323	311	4	15	17	314	308	4	16
9	185	174	3	9	18	345	337	4	12
OUT	2,914	2,804	35		IN	2,902	2,794	35	
					TOTAL	5,816	5,798	70	
		STANDARD SCRATCH				71	70		

Copyright Tudor Journals Ltd.

**Galway Bay Golf & Country Club,
Renville, Oranmore, Co. Galway.
Tel: (091) 790503.
Fax: (091) 792510
Web: www.gbaygolf.com**

LOCATION: Six miles south of Galway City.
PROFESSIONAL: Eugene O'Connor.
Tel: (091) 790503.
ARCHITECT: Christy O'Connor Jnr.

Christy O'Connor Jnr, Ryder & world cup player, designed this 18 hole course to highlight and preserve the ancient historic features of the Renville Peninsula. The spectacular setting on Galway Bay is distractingly beautiful and the cleverly designed mix of holes presents a real golfing challenge which demands total concentration.

COURSE INFORMATION

Par 72; Length 6,537 metres.
Visitors: Welcome.
Opening Hours: 8am – 7pm.
Ladies: Welcome.
Green Fees: Apr–Oct: €55 weekdays, €60 weekends & bank hols; Nov–Mar: €25 weekdays, €32 weekends & bank hols. Group discounts available, tel for details.
Clubhouse Hours: 8am – 11pm.
Clubhouse Dress: Informal.
Clubhouse Facilities: Restaurant, Spike Bar & Cocktail Bar – all day.
Open Competitions: Yes.

NO.	MEDAL METRES	GEN METRES	PAR	S.I.	NO.	MEDAL METRES	GEN METRES	PAR	S.I.
1	506	486	5	14	10	411	367	4	5
2	409	362	4	2	11	377	356	4	7
3	387	370	4	10	12	400	372	4	1
4	155	136	3	16	13	162	148	3	15
5	336	323	4	8	14	501	464	5	13
6	481	434	5	12	15	172	160	3	17
7	138	126	3	18	16	496	481	5	11
8	418	386	4	6	17	349	323	4	9
9	400	374	4	4	18	439	423	4	3
OUT	3,230	2,997	36		IN	3,307	3,094	36	
					TOTAL	6,537	6,091	72	
					STANDARD SCRATCH	73	71		

GALWAY BAY CLUB
CLUBHOUSE HOUSE

Copyright Tudor Journals Ltd.

Bunker positions indicated.

**Glenlo Abbey Golf Course,
Bushypark, Galway.
Tel: (091) 519698
Email: glenlo@iol.ie
Web: www.glenlo.com**

LOCATION: 2.5 miles from Galway city.
DIRECTOR OF GOLF/SECRETARY: Mr. Bill Daley.
PROFESSIONAL: Philip Murphy.

Lakeside - 9 hole - double green layout. Very picturesque and a good challenge, in a particularly attractive part of the country.

COURSE INFORMATION

**Par 71; SSS 70; Length 6,174 yards.
Green Fees:** €15.50 Midweek, €20 Weekend.
Juveniles: Welcome.

Clubhouse Hours: Dawn to Dusk. (Timesheet daily).
Clubhouse Dress: Neat dress essential.
Clubhouse Facilities:
5 star Hotel facilities on site. Murphy Sweeney Golf School on site, floodlit Driving Range.
Open Competitions:
Every Thursday/ Sunday.
Open Week - Jul 31st - Aug 7th.

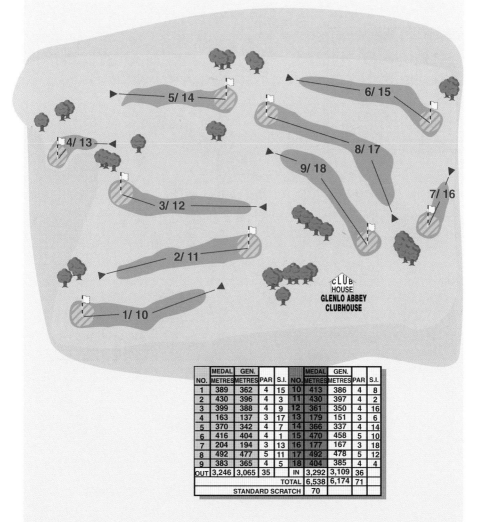

NO.	MEDAL METRES	GEN. METRES	PAR	S.I.	NO.	MEDAL METRES	GEN. METRES	PAR	S.I.
1	389	362	4	15	10	413	386	4	8
2	430	396	4	3	11	430	397	4	2
3	399	388	4	9	12	361	350	4	16
4	163	137	3	17	13	179	151	3	6
5	370	342	4	7	14	366	337	4	14
6	416	404	4	1	15	470	458	5	10
7	204	194	3	13	16	177	167	3	18
8	492	477	5	11	17	492	478	5	12
9	383	365	4	5	18	404	385	4	4
OUT	3,246	3,065	35		IN	3,292	3,109	36	
					TOTAL	6,538	6,174	71	
					STANDARD SCRATCH		70		

Copyright Tudor Journals Ltd.

**Gort Golf Club,
Castlequarter,
Gort, Co. Galway.
Tel: (091) 632244.
Fax: (091) 632244.**

LOCATION: Kilmacduagh
road, Gort.
HON. SECRETARY: James B.
Hannigan. Tel: (091) 632244.
ARCHITECT: Christy O'Connor Jnr.

A parkland course opened in 1996.
Set in an area of rare beauty,
surrounded by world famous Burren,
Coole Woods & Aughty mountains. A course
for every club in your bag.

COURSE INFORMATION

**Par 71; SSS 69; Length
5,705 metres.
Visitors:** Welcome to play
everyday.
Opening Hours: Dawn to dusk.
Avoid: Sunday mornings
to 11.00am.
Ladies: Tuesdays is Ladies Day.

Juveniles: Welcome before
3.00pm.
Green Fees: €23 Weekdays,
€26 Weekends
Clubhouse Hours:
10.00am – 11.30pm.
Clubhouse Dress: Casual.
Clubhouse Facilities:
Light meals.
Open Competitions:
Open Week: 16th – 23th June,
11th – 18th August.

NO.	METRES	PAR	S.I.	NO.	METRES	PAR	S.I.
1	339	4	9	10	298	4	6
2	397	4	5	11	360	4	2
3	373	4	3	12	295	4	8
4	325	4	7	13	160	3	14
5	126	3	15	14	482	5	16
6	271	4	17	15	303	4	10
7	407	4	1	16	156	3	18
8	151	3	13	17	440	5	12
9	478	5	11	18	344	4	4
OUT	2,867	35		IN	2,838	36	
				TOTAL	5,705	71	
				STANDARD SCRATCH	69		

Copyright Tudor Journals Ltd.

NO.	MEDAL METRES	GEN METRES	PAR	S.I.	NO.	MEDAL METRES	GEN METRES	PAR	S.I.
1	336	330	4	11	10	368	351	4	2
2	375	347	4	8	11	146	124	3	12
3	392	381	4	3	12	445	427	5	7
4	187	178	3	9	13	307	291	4	6
5	388	383	4	1	14	134	121	3	18
6	354	340	4	5	15	267	242	4	4
7	260	243	4	14	16	421	415	5	13
8	120	105	3	15	17	160	135	3	16
9	259	242	4	17	18	342	332	4	10
OUT	2,671	2,549	34		IN	2,590	2,438	35	
					TOTAL	5,261	4,987	69	
			STANDARD SCRATCH			69	69		

Loughrea Golf Club, Craigu, Loughrea, Co. Galway.
Tel: (091) 841049.

LOCATION: One mile south east on the Loughrea to Bullaun road.
SECRETARY: Danny Hyne.
Tel: (091) 841049.
ARCHITECT: Eddie Hackett.

The course has wide grassy fairways with smooth greens and has a generally quiet atmosphere. The main course difficulties are the lush rough and the fact that second shots need great accuracy.

COURSE INFORMATION

Par 69; SSS 67; Length 5,261 metres.
Visitors: Welcome.
Opening Hours: 9am – Dusk.
Avoid: Sundays & major competition days.
Green Fees: €20 daily.
Juveniles: Welcome (before 6pm). Lessons available by arrangement.
Clubhouse Hours: Open all day.
Clubhouse Dress: Casual.
Clubhouse Facilities: New clubhouse, full catering facilities all day.
Open Competitions: Most Bank Holiday Weekends and Open Weeks in June and August. Open day every Wendsday.

New Clubhouse opening in 1999.

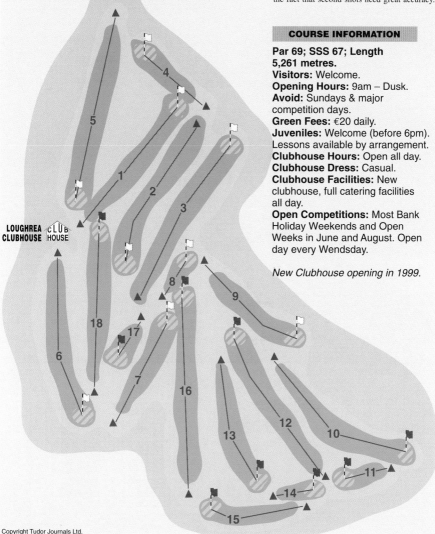

LOUGHREA CLUBHOUSE

Copyright Tudor Journals Ltd.

**Mountbellew Golf Club,
Mountbellew, Ballinasloe,
Co. Galway.
Tel: (0905) 79259/79274.
Fax: (0905) 79274.**

LOCATION: Ballinasloe 17 miles,
Galway 30 miles and Roscommon
20 miles.
HON. SECRETARY: Michael Dollan
Tel: (0905) 79274.

Parkland course in sylvan setting. Ideal
for a casual, leisurely round or a day of
golf. Generous fairways on all holes
with the greens always in good
condition.

COURSE INFORMATION

**Par 69; SSS 66; Length
5,143 metres.
Visitors:** Wecome to play, no
special arrangements required.
Opening Hours:
Daylight hours.
Avoid: Saturday afternoons
(Ladies competitions).

Green Fees: €15 every day;
€60 per weekly ticket.
Clubhouse Hours:
3.00pm – 9.00pm.
Clubhouse Dress: Informal.
Clubhouse Facilities: Light
snacks in bar. Outings catered
for by arrangement.
Open Competitions:
Open Week – June.

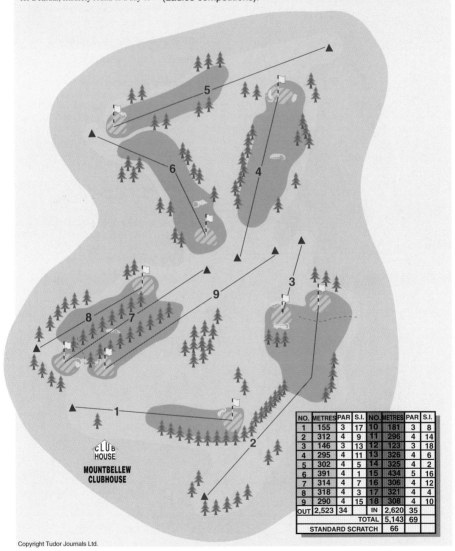

NO.	METRES	PAR	S.I.	NO.	METRES	PAR	S.I.
1	155	3	17	10	181	3	8
2	312	4	9	11	296	4	14
3	146	3	13	12	123	3	18
4	295	4	11	13	326	4	6
5	302	4	5	14	325	4	2
6	391	4	1	15	434	5	16
7	314	4	7	16	306	4	12
8	318	4	3	17	321	4	4
9	290	4	15	18	308	4	10
OUT	2,523	34		IN	2,620	35	
				TOTAL	5,143	69	
				STANDARD SCRATCH	66		

**MOUNTBELLEW
CLUBHOUSE**

Copyright Tudor Journals Ltd.

Gortreevagh, Oughterard, Co. Galway
Tel: (091) 552131.
Fax: (091) 552733.
Email: oughterardgc@eircom.net

LOCATION: Fifteen miles west of Galway City en route to Connemara.
SECRETARY: John Waters. Tel: (091) 552131,
PROFESSIONAL: Michael Ryan. Tel: (091) 552626.
ARCHITECT: Patrick Merrigan.

A beautiful and mature parkland course on the shores of Lough Corrib, Oughterard is renowned for its friendly and welcoming atmosphere. Always in pristine condition with a variety of trees and shrubs to punish wayward shots to otherwise generous and lush fairways.

COURSE INFORMATION

Par 71; SSS 69; Length 6,005 metres.
Visitors: Welcome. Restricted at weekends, due to competitions.
Opening Hours: Sunrise – sunset.
Avoid: Telephone in advance.
Ladies: Wednesday.
Green Fees: €30 standard, €40 husband & wife, €15 student.
Clubhouse Hours: 8.00am –12.00pm (except Winter). Full clubhouse facilities.
Clubhouse Dress: Casual.
Clubhouse Facilities: Breakfast from 8.00am – 10.30am; full dinner menu everyday all day until 10.00pm.
Open Competitions: Open Week 29th July - 2nd Aug. Many Open Weekends throughout the year. Handicap Certificate required for Open Competitions.

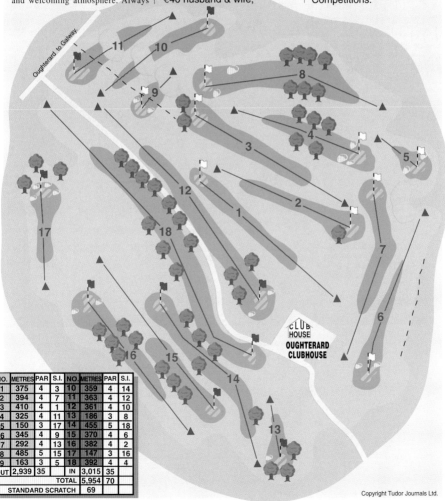

NO.	METRES	PAR	S.I.	NO.	METRES	PAR	S.I.
1	375	4	3	10	359	4	14
2	394	4	7	11	363	4	12
3	410	4	1	12	361	4	10
4	325	4	11	13	186	3	8
5	150	3	17	14	455	5	18
6	345	4	9	15	370	4	6
7	292	4	13	16	382	4	2
8	485	5	15	17	147	3	16
9	163	3	5	18	392	4	4
OUT	2,939	35		IN	3,015	35	
				TOTAL	5,954	70	
	STANDARD SCRATCH				69		

Copyright Tudor Journals Ltd.

PORTUMNA

Portumna, Co. Galway.
Tel: (0509) 41059.

LOCATION: Less than two miles west of Portumna on the Woodford Road

HON. SECRETARY/PROFESSIONAL: Richard Clarke. Tel: (0509) 41214.
CAPTAIN: Eamonn Nihill.
Tel: (0509) 47033.

Located in Portumna Forest Park, this is a very attractive woodland course with plenty of mature trees. Deer can sometimes be found on the course. The finishing Par 3 hole is the most difficult of the round, playing to an elevated green.

COURSE INFORMATION

Par 72; SSS 71; Length 6,225 metres.
Visitors: Welcome to play every day.
Opening Hours: 9am – Dusk.
Avoid: Sunday.
Ladies: Welcome.
Green Fees: €25.
Juveniles: Welcome.

Clubhouse Hours: 9.00am – 10.00pm. (Summer).
Clubhouse Dress: Casual.
Clubhouse Facilities:
Catering facilities available.
Open Competitions:
Handicap Certificate required for Open Competitions. Open week – July.

NO.	METRES	PAR	S.I.	NO.	METRES	PAR	S.I.
1	406	4	3	10	241	4	2
2	166	3	13	11	350	4	10
3	405	4	1	12	332	4	4
4	300	4	15	13	149	3	14
5	140	3	17	14	368	4	6
6	327	4	11	15	453	5	16
7	374	4	5	16	161	3	18
8	235	4	9	17	362	4	7
9	345	4	12	18	160	3	8
OUT	2,798	34		IN	2,676	34	
				TOTAL	5,474	68	
	STANDARD SCRATCH				67		

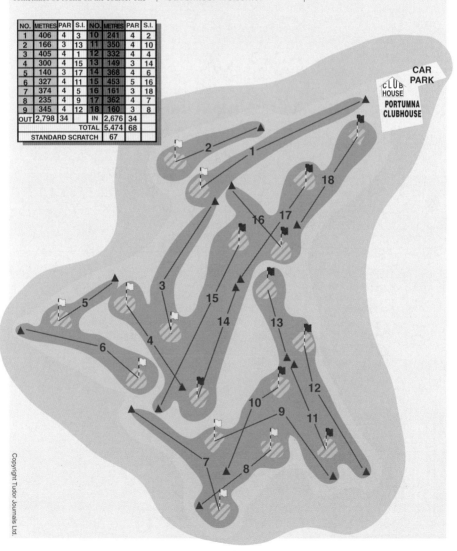

CAR PARK

CLUB HOUSE

PORTUMNA CLUBHOUSE

Copyright Tudor Journals Ltd.

	CHAMP METRES	MEDAL METRES	PAR	S.I.	NO.	CHAMP METRES	MEDAL METRES	PAR	S.I.
1	368	361	4	5	10	331	311	4	18
2	469	464	5	15	11	340	335	4	16
3	384	374	4	3	12	183	172	3	6
4	312	307	4	9	13	478	468	5	12
5	484	454	5	13	14	309	303	4	8
6	172	166	3	11	15	346	326	4	4
7	381	358	4	1	16	152	142	3	14
8	133	131	3	17	17	486	456	5	10
9	349	339	4	7	18	368	358	4	2
OUT	3,052	2,954	36		IN	2,993	2,871	36	
					TOTAL	6,045	5,825	72	
					STANDARD SCRATCH	71	70		

Tuam Golf Club, Barnacurragh, Tuam, Co. Galway.
Tel: (093) 28993.
Fax: (093) 26003.

LOCATION: Twenty miles north of Galway.
SECRETARY/MANAGER: Vincent Gaffney. Tel: (093) 28993.
PROFESSIONAL: Larry Smyth. Tel: (093) 24091.

Fine parkland course. The fairways are guarded by plantations and trees, with greens well bunkered. Tuam recently completed their new clubhouse development.

COURSE INFORMATION

Par 72; SSS 71; Length 6,045 Metres.
Visitors: Welcome any weekday.
Opening Hours: 8.00am – Sunset.
Avoid: Saturday mornings and Sundays.
Ladies: Welcome.
Green Fees: €25 daily.
Lessons available, groups on request Club Hire, Caddy service, buggies.
Clubhouse Hours:
9am – 12 midnight (except winter).
Clubhouse Dress: Casual / neat
Clubhouse Facilities: Bar and Catering facilities everyday (full restaurant).
Open Competitions:
Open Weekends: March, July, October. Open week: June.
  Open Wed Apr - Oct.

Bunker positions indicated.

Copyright Tudor Journals Ltd.

**Ballinamore Golf Club,
Ballinamore, Co. Leitrim
Tel: (078) 44346.**

LOCATION: Two miles north
west of Ballinamore.
SECRETARY: Martin McCartin.
Tel: (078) 44346/7673471.

Redesigned by Arthur Spring with new
sand based greens well bunkered with
water coming into play on 1st and 2nd
fairways. The Canal comes into play
on the 1st, 2nd, 6th and 7th holes. A
warm and friendly atmosphere awaits
you at Ballinamore.

COURSE INFORMATION

**Par 70; SSS 68; Length
5,514 metres.
Visitors:** Welcome except on
Captain's or President's Day.

Opening Hours: 8am-sunset.
Ladies: Welcome.
Green Fees: €15.
Clubhouse Hours:
9.00am – 11.00pm.
Clubhouse Dress: Casual.
Clubhouse Facilities:
Catering facilities – soup and
sandwiches.
Open Competitions: Open
Week and certain weekends.

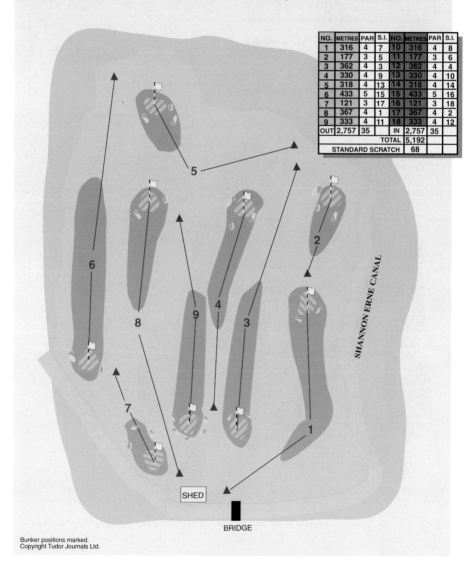

NO.	METRES	PAR	S.I.	NO.	METRES	PAR	S.I.
1	316	4	7	10	316	4	8
2	177	3	5	11	177	3	6
3	362	4	3	12	362	4	4
4	330	4	9	13	330	4	10
5	318	4	13	14	318	4	14
6	433	5	15	15	433	5	16
7	121	3	17	16	121	3	18
8	367	4	1	17	367	4	2
9	333	4	11	18	333	4	12
OUT	2,757	35		IN	2,757	35	
				TOTAL	5,192		
				STANDARD SCRATCH	68		

SHANNON ERNE CANAL

SHED

BRIDGE

Bunker positions marked.
Copyright Tudor Journals Ltd.

Achill Golf Club, Keel, Co. Mayo.
Tel: (098) 43456.
Fax: (098) 43265.

LOCATION: Keel, Achill.
MANAGER: Dominic Vesey.
SECRETARY: Sean Connolly.

A scenic links course situated beside a large beach. Achill course is of a level and open nature – continuously grazed by sheep. Fairways marked by white stones.

COURSE INFORMATION

Par 70; SSS 67; Length 5,416 metres.
Visitors: Welcome.
Opening Hours: Dawn – Dusk.
Ladies: Welcome.
Green Fees: € 15.
Juveniles: Must be accompanied by an adult (under 14's).

Clubhouse Hours: Same as course.
Clubhouse Dress: Casual.
Open Competitions: Handicap Certificate required for open competitions.

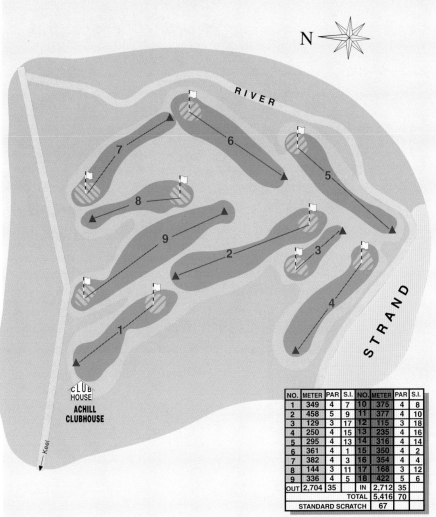

NO.	METER	PAR	S.I.	NO.	METER	PAR	S.I.
1	349	4	7	10	375	4	8
2	458	5	9	11	377	4	10
3	129	3	17	12	115	3	18
4	250	4	15	13	235	4	16
5	295	4	13	14	316	4	14
6	361	4	1	15	350	4	2
7	382	4	3	16	354	4	4
8	144	3	11	17	168	3	12
9	336	4	5	18	422	5	6
OUT	2,704	35		IN	2,712	35	
				TOTAL	5,416	70	
				STANDARD SCRATCH		67	

Copyright Tudor Journals Ltd.

Cong, Co. Mayo.
Tel: 353 92 46003
Fax: 353 92 46260
E-mail: ashford@ashford.ie
Website: www.ashford.ie

SECRETARY: Tel: 092-46003
PROFESSIONAL: Tom Devereux
ARCHITECT: Eddie Hackett.

Beautiful matured 9 hole golf course set on the shores of Lough Corrib, with panoramic views of Ashford Castle, where some of the world's top professionals have stayed and played.

COURSE INFORMATION

Par 70; SSS 68; Length 3,000 yards.
Opening Hours: 9am to 6pm.
Green Fees: €57 per person.

Juveniles: By prior arrangement.
Clubhouse Hours: 9am to 6pm.
Clubhouse Dress: No jeans.
Clubhouse Facilities: Coffee shop.

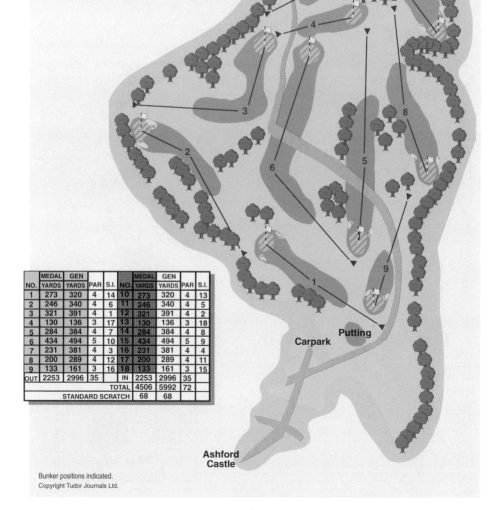

NO.	MEDAL YARDS	GEN YARDS	PAR	S.I.	NO.	MEDAL YARDS	GEN YARDS	PAR	S.I.
1	273	320	4	14	10	273	320	4	13
2	246	340	4	6	11	246	340	4	5
3	321	391	4	1	12	321	391	4	2
4	130	136	3	17	13	130	136	3	18
5	284	384	4	7	14	284	384	4	8
6	434	494	5	10	15	434	494	5	9
7	231	381	4	3	16	231	381	4	4
8	200	289	4	12	17	200	289	4	11
9	133	161	3	16	18	133	161	3	15
OUT	2253	2996	35		IN	2253	2996	35	
					TOTAL	4506	5992	72	
	STANDARD SCRATCH					68	68		

Carpark

Putting

Ashford Castle

Bunker positions indicated.
Copyright Tudor Journals Ltd.

Ballina Golf Club,
Mossgrove, Shanaghy,
Ballina, Co. Mayo.
Tel: (096) 21050.
Fax: (096) 21718.

LOCATION: Bonniconlon Rd, Ballina. 1.5 KM from town centre
SECRETARY: V. Frawley.
Tel: (096) 21050.

A flat inland course, with fairways guarded by plantations.

COURSE INFORMATION

Par 71; SSS 69; Length 6,103 yards.
Visitors: Welcome.
Opening Hours: 8am –10pm (summer); 9am – 6pm (winter).
Avoid: Sunday mornings.
Green Fees: Oct to Mar– Mon/Fri €16, Sat/Sun/Bank Hols €20; Apr to Sept – Mon/Fri €25. Sat/Sun/Bank Hols €32. H/Wife (Oct to Mar) daily €25. H/Wife (Apr to Sept) daily €50.

Societies rates available.
Juveniles: Welcome.
Clubhouse Hours:
9am –11pm.
Clubhouse Dress:
Neat / Casual.
Clubhouse Facilities:
Catering and bar facilities available.
Open Competitions: Whit Weekend; Open Weekend – August. Handicap Certificate required for Open Competitions.

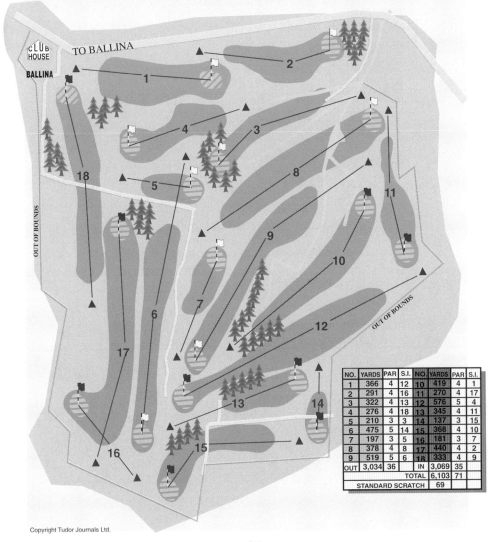

NO.	YARDS	PAR	S.I.	NO.	YARDS	PAR	S.I.
1	366	4	12	10	419	4	1
2	291	4	16	11	270	4	17
3	322	4	13	12	576	5	4
4	276	4	18	13	345	4	11
5	210	3	3	14	137	3	15
6	475	5	14	15	368	4	10
7	197	3	5	16	181	3	7
8	378	4	8	17	440	4	2
9	519	5	6	18	333	4	9
OUT	3,034	36		IN	3,069	35	
TOTAL					6,103	71	
STANDARD SCRATCH					69		

Copyright Tudor Journals Ltd.

Ballinrobe Golf Club,
Cloonacastle,
Ballinrobe, Co. Mayo.
Tel: (092) 41118.

LOCATION: 30 miles from Galway. 20 miles from Castlebar and Westport.
SECRETARY/MANAGER: Tom Moran. Tel: (092) 41118.
ARCHITECT: Mr Eddie Hackett..

This scenic parkland course will offer a challenge to any golfer with its mature trees, man-made lakes, lush fairways and traditional stone walls. The greens are notable with their sweeping contours and good drainage. "This is probably the finest course in the West of Ireland" Padraic Harrinton.

COURSE INFORMATION

Par 73; SSS 73; Length 6,234 metres.
Visitors: Welcome.
Opening Hours: 8am – Sunset
Avoid: Sunday and Tuesday evenings.
Ladies: Welcome.
Green Fees: €30 High Season, €20 Low Season.

Juveniles: Welcome.
Clubhouse Hours: 10.00am – 6.00pm (June – August).
Clubhouse Dress: Casual.
Clubhouse Facilities: The clubhouse is a fully restored 250 year old estate house. Which offers golfers a restaurant with full bar, comfortable and well appointed changing rooms.
Open Competitions: Contact club for details.

NO.	METRES	PAR	S.I.	NO.	METRES	PAR	S.I.
1	336	4	15	10	365	4	2
2	410	4	1	11	364	4	8
3	175	3	9	12	348	4	10
4	478	5	11	13	156	3	12
5	354	4	7	14	491	5	16
6	484	5	5	15	348	4	6
7	158	3	13	16	156	3	14
8	490	5	3	17	376	4	4
9	302	4	17	18	443	5	18
OUT	3,187	37		IN	3,047	36	
				TOTAL	6,234	73	
	STANDARD SCRATCH				73		

Bunker positions indicated.

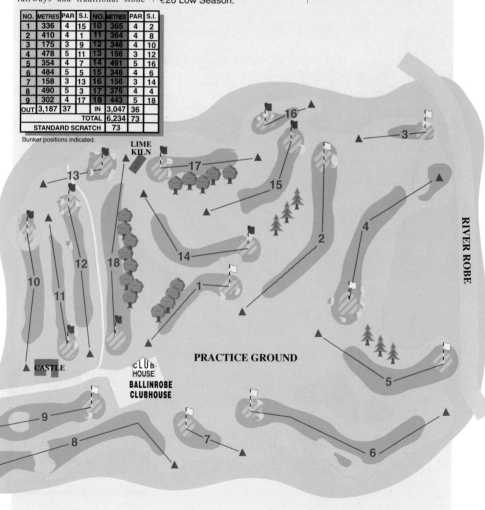

**Ballyhaunis Golf Club,
Coolnaha, Co. Mayo.
Tel: (0907) 30014.**

LOCATION: 2 miles north of Ballyhaunis
on the Charlstown Road. 7 miles from
Horan International Airport.
HON. SECRETARY: John Mooney.
Tel: (0907) 30060.
CAPTAIN:: John Collins.

An interesting parkland course situated close to
the famous Knock Shrine. The main features of
Ballyhaunis are its pleasant elevated greens
protected with well positioned bunkers.

COURSE INFORMATION

**Par 70; SSS 69; Length 5,801 yards,
5,413 metres.**
Visitors: Welcome at all times.
Opening Hours: 9.00am – sunset.
Avoid: Members competitions on
Sundays & Thursdays.
Ladies: Welcome Thursdays.
Green Fees: €15 per day.
Juveniles: Welcome (Handicap
Certificate required). Must be off the
course by 3.00pm unless accompanied
by an adult. Caddy service available by
prior arrangement summer only.
Clubhouse Hours: Licencing hours.
Clubhouse Dress: Casual. During
presentations – jacket and tie.
Clubhouse Facilities: Full catering
facilities by prior arrangement. Snacks
available normally.
Open Competitions: Open Competition
5th July. Open Week 13th - 20th July.
Handicap Certificate required.

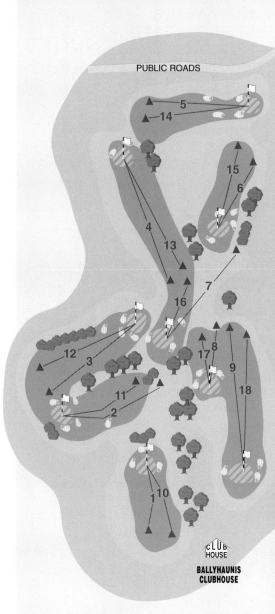

PUBLIC ROADS

BALLYHAUNIS
CLUBHOUSE

CLUB HOUSE

NO.	MEDAL METRES	GEN METRES	PAR	S.I.	NO.	MEDAL METRES	GEN METRES	PAR	S.I.
1	359	355	4	3	10	372	364	4	4
2	309	304	4	9	11	337	334	4	6
3	447	442	5	11	12	412	410	5	14
4	360	355	4	1	13	354	347	4	2
5	282	278	4	15	14	273	269	4	16
6	153	149	3	13	15	149	145	3	18
7	322	317	4	7	16	301	295	4	10
8	126	121	3	17	17	148	143	3	12
9	359	354	4	5	18	350	345	4	8
OUT	2,717	2,675	35		IN	2,696	2,652	35	
					TOTAL	5,413	5,327	70	
					STANDARD SCRATCH	69			

Bunker/hedge and tree positions indicated.
Copyright Tudor Journals Ltd.

**Carne Golf Links, Carne,
Belmullet, Co. Mayo.**
Tel: (097) 82292.
Fax: (097) 81477.
Web: carnegolflinks.com
Email: carngolf@iol.ie

LOCATION: On the Mullet
Peninsula near Belmullet,
Co. Mayo. 2.5KM from
Belmullet.
SECRETARY: Evelyn Keane.
ARCHITECT: Eddie Hackett.

This new exciting links has a
natural setting of considerable
beauty. Splendid sand dunes on
ancient commonage. Elevated tees
and plateau greens exploit the
magnificent backdrops over
Blacksod Bay. Voted No.5 in
Ireland by *Golf World* Jan 2000.

COURSE INFORMATION

**Par 72; SSS 72; Length
6,090 metres.**
Visitors: Welcome anytime.
Green Fees: €40 per day
Mon - Fri. €40 per round
Sat/Sun.
Club Facilities: Practice
range, Caddy and Car Hire.
Clubhouse Facilities: Bar
and restaurant.

NO.	MEDAL METRES	GEN METRES	PAR	S.I.	NO.	MEDAL METRES	GEN METRES	PAR	S.I.
1	366	356	4	9	10	465	432	5	16
2	183	149	3	11	11	332	302	4	6
3	376	370	4	5	12	300	280	4	14
4	473	463	5	17	13	482	446	5	8
5	378	327	4	15	14	133	129	3	12
6	363	355	4	1	15	366	356	4	2
7	162	154	3	13	16	154	142	3	18
8	365	360	4	3	17	399	392	4	4
9	327	320	4	7	18	495	486	5	10
OUT	2,993	2,854	35		IN	3,126	2,965	37	
					TOTAL	6,119	5,819	72	
					STANDARD SCRATCH	72	71		

PRACTICE AREA

CLUB HOUSE

**BELMULLET
CLUBHOUSE
& CARPARK**

ATLANTIC OCEAN

Copyright Tudor Journals Ltd.

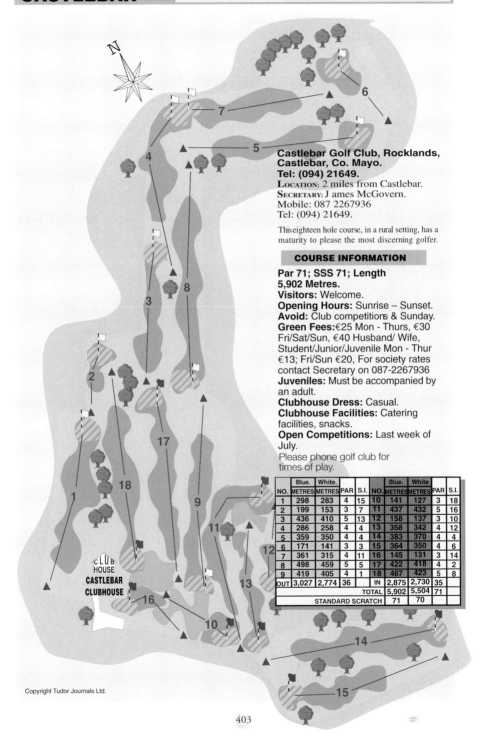

Castlebar Golf Club, Rocklands, Castlebar, Co. Mayo.
Tel: (094) 21649.
LOCATION: 2 miles from Castlebar.
SECRETARY: James McGovern.
Mobile: 087 2267936
Tel: (094) 21649.

This eighteen hole course, in a rural setting, has a maturity to please the most discerning golfer.

COURSE INFORMATION

Par 71; SSS 71; Length 5,902 Metres.
Visitors: Welcome.
Opening Hours: Sunrise – Sunset.
Avoid: Club competitions & Sunday.
Green Fees: €25 Mon - Thurs, €30 Fri/Sat/Sun, €40 Husband/ Wife, Student/Junior/Juvenile Mon - Thur €13; Fri/Sun €20, For society rates contact Secretary on 087-2267936
Juveniles: Must be accompanied by an adult.
Clubhouse Dress: Casual.
Clubhouse Facilities: Catering facilities, snacks.
Open Competitions: Last week of July.
Please phone golf club for times of play.

NO.	Blue. METRES	White. METRES	PAR	S.I.	NO.	Blue. METRES	White. METRES	PAR	S.I.
1	298	283	4	15	10	141	127	3	18
2	199	153	3	7	11	437	432	5	16
3	436	410	5	13	12	158	137	3	10
4	286	258	4	4	13	358	342	4	12
5	359	350	4	4	14	383	370	4	4
6	171	141	3	3	15	364	350	4	6
7	361	315	4	11	16	145	131	3	14
8	498	459	5	5	17	422	418	4	2
9	419	405	4	1	18	467	423	5	8
OUT	3,027	2,774	36		IN	2,875	2,730	35	
					TOTAL	5,902	5,504	71	
					STANDARD SCRATCH	71	70		

Copyright Tudor Journals Ltd.

**Claremorris Golf Club,
Castlemagarrett,
Claremorris, Co. Mayo.
Tel: (094) 71527.**

LOCATION: Galway Road, 2 miles from town.
SECRETARY / MANAGER: Chris Rush.
Tel: (094) 71527.

An 18 Hole Championship parkland Course designed to the highest standards by Tom Craddock (designer nof the Druid's Glen) Claremorris consists of many eye-catching water features, bunkers, trees and wooded backgrounds. It has been highly praised by golfers of all descriptions for its layout, the variations on each hole, the eye-catching features and above all the excellent quality of our sand based greens.

COURSE INFORMATION

Par 73; SSS 71; Length 3,136 metres.
Visitors: Welcome to play at any time.
Avoid: Competitions for members.
Ladies: Welcome.

Juveniles: Welcome
Green Fees: Weekdays – €23 Weekends and Bank Holidays – €25 ; €13 with a member.
Clubhouse Dress: Casual.
Clubhouse Facilities: Catering and bar facilities by prior arrangement.

NO.	MEDAL METRES	GEN METRES	PAR	S.I.	NO.	MEDAL METRES	GEN METRES	PAR	S.I.
1	320	320	4	7	10	140	136	4	4
2	123	130	3	17	11	346	346	4	6
3	432	405	5	9	12	344	344	5	14
4	345	315	4	5	13	360	360	4	2
5	487	452	5	13	14	320	300	4	16
6	402	370	4	1	15	330	330	3	18
7	178	158	3	11	16	470	446	4	10
8	364	336	4	3	17	380	345	3	12
9	310	310	4	15	18	485	450	4	8
OUT	2,961	2,796	36		IN	3,175	3,058	37	
					TOTAL	6,136	5,854	73	
					STANDARD SCRATCH		69		

CLUB HOUSE

CLAREMORRIS CLUBHOUSE

Copyright Tudor Journals Ltd.

**Swinford Golf Club,
Barbazon Park, Swinford,
Co. Mayo.
Tel: (094) 51378.**

LOCATION: Beside Swinford
town.
HON SECRETARY: Tom Regan.
Tel: (094) 51378.
HEAD GROUNDSMAN:
Michael Farrelly.

There are quite a number of trees on the
course which adds considerably to the
difficulty of wayward shots.

COURSE INFORMATION

**Par 70; SSS 68; Length
5,542 metres.
Visitors:** Welcome everyday.
Opening Hours: All day
everyday.

Ladies: Welcome.
Green Fees: €15 per day.
Juveniles: Permitted.
Clubhouse Hours: Open all day.
Clubhouse Dress: Casual.
Clubhouse Facilities: Bar.
Catering by request.
Open Competitions: Open
weekends: on bank holidays.
Open Week; 27th July - 4th Aug.
Handicap certificate required.

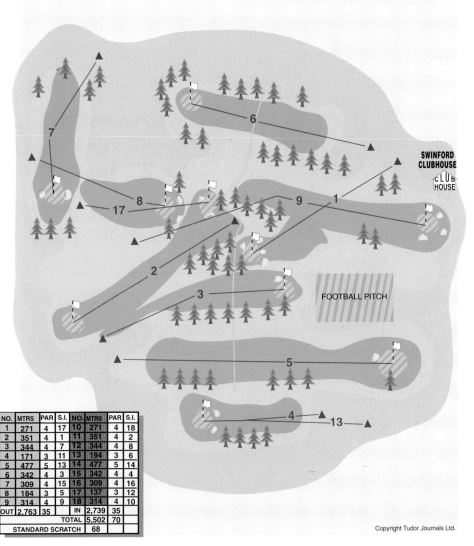

NO.	MTRS	PAR	S.I.	NO.	MTRS	PAR	S.I.
1	271	4	17	10	271	4	18
2	351	4	1	11	351	4	2
3	344	4	7	12	344	4	8
4	171	3	11	13	194	3	6
5	477	5	13	14	477	5	14
6	342	4	3	15	342	4	4
7	309	4	15	16	309	4	16
8	184	3	5	17	137	3	12
9	314	4	9	18	314	4	10
OUT	2,763	35		IN	2,739	35	
				TOTAL	5,502	70	
STANDARD SCRATCH		68					

Copyright Tudor Journals Ltd.

NO.	CHAMP YARDS	MEDAL YARDS	PAR	S.I.	NO.	CHAMP YARDS	MEDAL YARDS	PAR	S.I.
1	344	335	4	14	10	537	498	5	11
2	345	330	4	8	11	437	420	4	3
3	168	142	3	16	12	220	208	3	5
4	502	488	5	18	13	455	412	4	1
5	360	343	4	10	14	191	180	3	7
6	463	445	4	4	15	580	515	5	9
7	529	511	5	12	16	363	350	4	15
8	472	455	4	2	17	378	343	4	13
9	208	196	3	6	18	520	499	5	17
OUT	3,391	3,252	36		IN	3,695	3,401	37	
					TOTAL	7,086	6,653	73	
			STANDARD SCRATCH			72	73		

Westport Golf Club, Carrowholly, Westport, Co. Mayo.
Tel: (098) 28262/27070.
www.golfwesport.com

LOCATION: 2½ miles from Westport town.
MANAGER: Pat Smyth.
Tel: (098) 28262/27070.
PROFESSIONAL: Alex Mealia.
Tel: (098) 28262.
ARCHITECT: Fred Hawtree.

Situated on the shores of Clew Bay and set in 260 acres of parkland, Westport offers golfers a memorable challenge. The course commands a wonderful view of Clew Bay and is dominated by the Holy Mountain, Croagh Patrick. The best known hole on this course is the Par 5 fifteenth which reaches 580 yards (535 metres) and features a long carry from the tee over an inlet of Clew Bay. Designed by the noted golf architect Fred Hawtree, who also designed the new course at St Andrews.

COURSE INFORMATION

Par 73; SSS 72; Length 6,653 yards.
Visitors: Welcome (phone first).
Opening Hours: Sunrise to sunset.
Avoid: Competition days.
Ladies: Welcome.
Green Fees: Weekdays – €35/€38; weekends & Bank Holidays – €41/€47. Special rates for societies.
Juveniles: Welcome. Lessons and Caddy service available by prior arrangement. Club hire available.
Clubhouse Hours: 9.00am – 11.30pm.
Clubhouse Dress: Informal.
Clubhouse Facilities: Catering facilities – meals available 9am – 10pm.
Open Competitions: July 20th - 27th

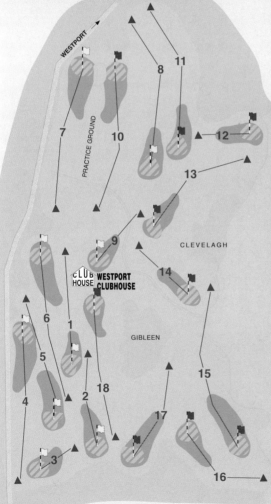

Copyright Tudor Journals Ltd.

**Athlone Golf Club,
Hodson Bay, Athlone,
Co. Roscommon.
Tel: (0902) 92073.**

LOCATION: 6 km from
Athlone.
HON. SECRETARY: Johnny
Bracken.
Tel: (0902) 92073.
PROFESSIONAL: Martin Quinn.
Tel: (0902) 92073 / 92868.
CAPTAIN: Jimmy Fox.
LADY CAPTAIN: Maura Cleary

Athlone has a commanding view of
Lough Ree from an elevated
Clubhouse. Undulating terrain and
tree-lined fairways make it a true test
of golf. Out of bounds exists on the
right of ten fairways. Course well
equipped with strategically placed
bunkers.

COURSE INFORMATION

**Par 71; SSS 72; Length
5,935 metres.**
Visitors: Welcome.
Opening Hours: 7.30am –
10.00pm.
Ladies Day: Tuesday.
Green Fees: €27 Mon – Fri;
€30 Sat / Sun / Bank Holidays.
Juveniles: Must play with an
adult before 3.30pm. Special
times on noticeboard.
Lessons available by prior
arrangements. Club Hire
available. Caddy service
available by prior
arrangements. Handicap
Certificate required.

Clubhouse Hours: 7.30am –
11.30pm.
Clubhouse Dress: Casual –
no shorts.
Clubhouse Facilities: Full
catering facilities available,
restaurant hours 9.30am –
10.00pm open all year round.
Open Competitions: Open
Week first week in June;
Lough Ree Open July and
August.

NO.	MEDAL METRES	GEN. METRES	PAR	S.I.	NO.	MEDAL METRES	GEN. METRES	PAR	S.I.
1	346	289	4	7	10	354	319	4	10
2	152	148	3	11	11	475	439	5	12
3	265	259	4	15	12	393	369	4	3
4	390	367	4	4	13	326	302	4	8
5	503	490	5	9	14	300	288	4	16
6	425	414	5	17	15	188	160	3	14
7	390	374	4	5	16	408	388	4	1
8	400	366	4	2	17	121	114	3	18
9	172	163	3	13	18	365	357	4	6
OUT	3,043	2,870	36		IN	2,930	2,736	35	
					TOTAL	5,973	5,606	71	
	STANDARD SCRATCH		71	70					

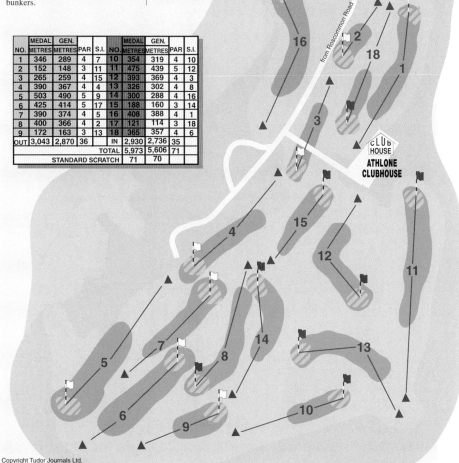

Ballaghadereen Golf Club,
Aughalustia,
Ballaghadereen,
Co. Roscommon.
Tel: (0907) 60358.

LOCATION: Three miles from Ballaghadereen town.
SECRETARY: John Corcoran.
Tel: (0907) 61092.

A relatively flat course but trees which are maturing are becoming a great asset both visually and also coming into play. A trip to the rough can quite easily cost a shot. The 5th hole in particular requires great accuracy to a very small green, well protected with bunkers.

COURSE INFORMATION

Par 70; SSS 68; Length 5,840 yards.
Visitors: Welcome at all times.
Opening Hours: 9am – Dusk.
Ladies: Welcome.
Green Fees: €15 daily. Handicap Certificate required for open competitions.

Juveniles: Welcome. Must be off course by 6pm. Caddy service available by prior arrangement.
Clubhouse Hours: Saturday & Sunday evenings
Clubhouse Dress: Casual.
Clubhouse Facilities: Bar. Catering by prior arrangement.
Open Competitions: Open week June 3rd to 10th. Seniors Open, 1st, 2nd, 3rd May.

NO.	METRES	PAR	S.I.	NO.	METRES	PAR	S.I.
1	304	4	15	10	305	4	15
2	313	4	6	11	313	4	7
3	353	4	2	12	421	5	12
4	342	4	3	13	335	4	4
5	145	3	9	14	105	3	17
6	426	5	16	15	367	4	1
7	150	3	10	16	150	3	11
8	238	4	18	17	284	4	13
9	314	4	5	18	314	4	6
OUT	2,585	35		IN	2,595	35	
				TOTAL	5,180	70	
	STANDARD SCRATCH	67					

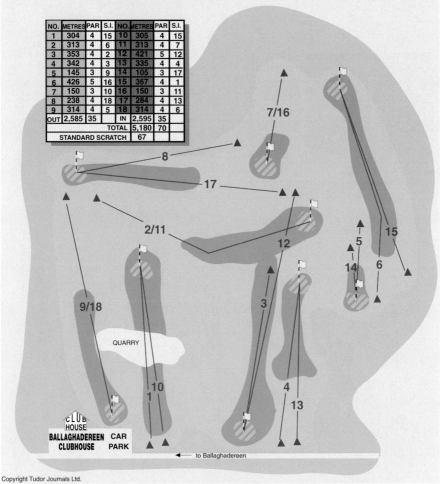

Copyright Tudor Journals Ltd.

Boyle Golf Club, Knockadoobrusna, Boyle, Co. Roscommon.
Tel: (079) 62594.

LOCATION: 1 mile from Boyle.
SECRETARY:Jim Mooney.
Tel: (079) 62594.
HANDICAP SEC: Bartly Moran.
Tel: (079) 62102/63075.

A feature of the course is the views of Lock Key, Curlew Mountains, Sligo Mountain and the Mayo Mountains from the 8th green and 2nd tee. The course is also within easy reach of Loch Key and Forest Park, Boyle.

COURSE INFORMATION

Par 67; SSS 64; Length 4,865 metres.
Visitors: Welcome at all times.
Opening Hours:
Sunrise – sunset.
Ladies Day: Tuesday.
Green Fees: €15 per round. Special rate for families €20; Gentleman & lady €15; Juvenile €5.
Juveniles: Welcome. Must be accompanied by an adult and off the course by 5pm during the summer.

Restricted at weekends, Saturday mornings 10am – 12 noon only.
Clubhouse Hours:
4.00pm – midnight.
Clubhouse Dress: Casual.
Clubhouse Facilities:
Catering facilities: bar snacks.
Open Competitions: Open Week July; 12 hole open every Thurs from May – Dec; Open Scramble every Friday from May – Sept.

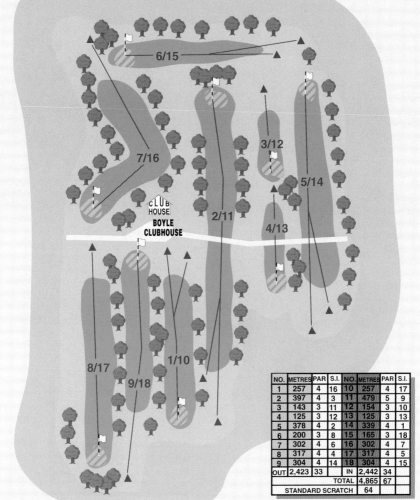

NO.	METRES	PAR	S.I.	NO.	METRES	PAR	S.I.
1	257	4	16	10	257	4	17
2	397	4	3	11	479	5	9
3	143	3	11	12	154	3	10
4	125	3	12	13	125	3	13
5	378	4	2	14	339	4	1
6	200	3	8	15	165	3	18
7	302	4	6	16	302	4	7
8	317	4	4	17	317	4	5
9	304	4	14	18	304	4	15
OUT	2,423	33		IN	2,442	34	
				TOTAL	4,865	67	
				STANDARD SCRATCH		64	

Copyright Tudor Journals Ltd.

**Carrick-on-Shannon,
Co Roscommon.
Tel: (079) 67015.**

LOCATION: Beside N4 route four miles west of Carrick-on-Shannon.
HOUSE SEC: Jim Newcombe. Tel: (078) 20525.
CLUB SEC: Tommie Kenoy. Tel: (078) 37068.

A pleasant inland course overlooking the River Shannon, that provides a good test of golf for any low or high handicappers. Course currently being extended to 18 holes.

COURSE INFORMATION

Par 70; SSS 68; Length 5,545 metres.
Visitors: Welcome to play at any time (except competitions).
Opening Hours: Daylight hours.
Green Fees: €15 husband & wife €20 (with member €12)
Juveniles: Welcome (restricted at weekends).
Clubhouse Hours: 9.30am – 11.00pm.

Clubhouse Dress: Informal.
Clubhouse Facilities:
Coffee and snacks at bar plus full meals.
Open Competitions: Open Weekends April, June, July & August. Handicap Certificate required for Open Competitions.

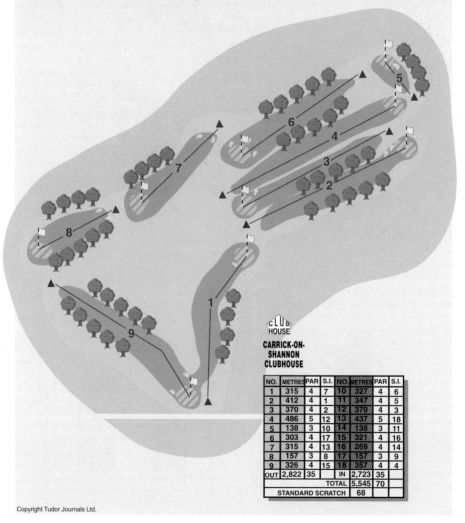

CARRICK-ON-SHANNON CLUBHOUSE

NO.	METRES	PAR	S.I.	NO.	METRES	PAR	S.I.
1	315	4	7	10	327	4	6
2	412	4	1	11	347	4	5
3	370	4	2	12	370	4	3
4	486	5	12	13	437	5	18
5	138	3	10	14	138	3	11
6	303	4	17	15	321	4	16
7	315	4	13	16	269	4	14
8	157	3	8	17	157	3	9
9	326	4	15	18	357	4	4
OUT	2,822	35		IN	2,723	35	
				TOTAL	5,545	70	
				STANDARD SCRATCH		68	

Copyright Tudor Journals Ltd.

**Castlerea Golf Club,
Clonailis, Castlerea,
Co. Roscommon.
Tel: (0907) 20068/21214.**

LOCATION: Town of Castlerea.
Between Castlebar and
Roscommon.
HON. SECRETARY: E. O'Laughlan.
Tel: (0907) 20072
CAPTAIN: Willie Gannon.

This is a short parkland course with
three Par 3 holes. River comes into
play on 4th, 5th and 8th holes. Narrow
fairways make accuracy important,
although the light rough does not cause
too much frustration for errant shots.

COURSE INFORMATION

**Par 68; SSS 66; Length
4,974 metres.
Visitors:** Welcome.
Opening Hours: Sunrise –
sunset.
Ladies: Welcome.
Green Fees: €15.
Juveniles: Welcome. Caddy
service available by prior
arrangement. Trolleys for hire.
Clubhouse Hours: 10.30am
to closing time. Bar open from
5pm weekdays and all day
weekends.

Clubhouse Dress: Casual.
Clubhouse Facilities: By
prior arrangment.
Open Competitions: Open
Week June. Handicap
Certificate required for Open
Competitions.

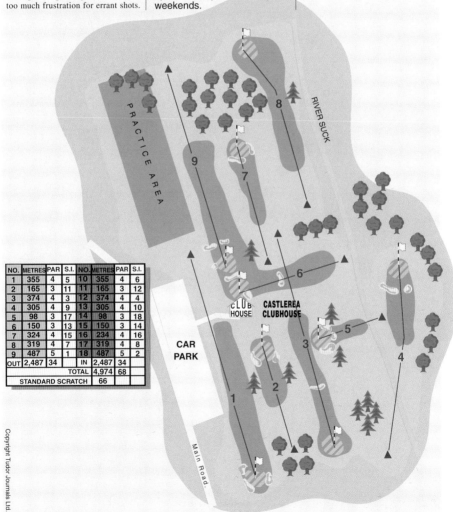

NO.	METRES	PAR	S.I.	NO.	METRES	PAR	S.I.
1	355	4	5	10	355	4	6
2	165	3	11	11	165	3	12
3	374	4	3	12	374	4	4
4	305	4	9	13	305	4	10
5	98	3	17	14	98	3	18
6	150	3	13	15	150	3	14
7	324	4	15	16	234	4	16
8	319	4	7	17	319	4	8
9	487	5	1	18	487	5	2
OUT	2,487	34		IN	2,487	34	
				TOTAL	4,974	68	
	STANDARD SCRATCH				66		

Copyright Tudor Journals Ltd.

**Roscommon Golf Club,
Mote Park, Roscommon,
Co Roscommon.
Tel: (0903) 26382.
Fax: (0903) 26043.
Email: rosgolfclub@eircom.net**

LOCATION: Roscommon Town.
SECRETARY: Cathal McConn.
Tel: (0903) 26062.
CAPTAIN: Gerry Keegan.

Roscommon is one of the more challenging golf tests in the Midlands and West. With a standard scratch score of 70, it requires long and accurate hitting on some holes, while others will test the short game skills of the golfer.

COURSE INFORMATION

Par 72; SSS 70; Length 5,901 metres.
Visitors: Welcome to play any time. Tuesdays and Sundays by arrangement.
Opening Hours: Sunrise – sunset.
Avoid: Summer evenings.
Ladies Day: Tuesday.
Green Fees: €25 per day. €20 1st Nov to 15th March. Weekly tickets on request, and society rates available.

Clubhouse Hours: 11am – midnight.
Clubhouse Dress: Informal but neat.
Clubhouse Facilities: Bar and catering available everyday.
Open Competitions: Open Weeks: June & Sept.

NO.	METRES	PAR	S.I.	NO.	METRES	PAR	S.I.
1	285	4	13	10	404	4	1
2	343	4	6	11	124	3	18
3	300	4	14	12	455	5	10
4	466	5	9	13	132	3	17
5	363	4	4	14	365	4	5
6	149	3	16	15	357	4	7
7	418	5	12	16	456	5	11
8	408	4	2	17	329	4	15
9	163	3	8	18	384	4	3
OUT	2,895	36		IN	3,006	36	
				TOTAL	5,901	72	
				STANDARD SCRATCH		70	

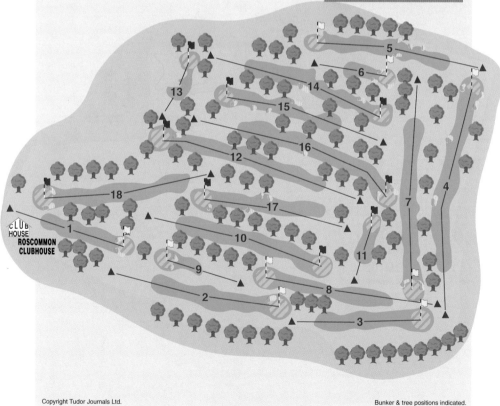

ROSCOMMON CLUBHOUSE

Copyright Tudor Journals Ltd.

Bunker & tree positions indicated.

Ballymote, Co Sligo.
Tel: (071) 83089/83504.

LOCATION: 15 miles south of Sligo town, 12 miles west of Boyle, between the N4 & N17.
CAPTAIN: Sean Henry.
PRESIDENT: Roy Hewitt.
HON SECRETARY: D. Mullaney.
SECRETARY/MANAGER: J. O'Conner.

The Club is based 1 mile outside the town on the Castlebaldwin road. The course offers a fine test of golf over undulating parkland.

COURSE INFORMATION

Par 68; SSS 67; Length 5,302 metres.
Visitors: Welcome at all times (some restrictions Jul & Aug).
Opening Hours: Dawn – Dusk.

Ladies: Welcome.
Green Fees: €10 per day or, €5 with member.
Clubhouse Dress: Casual.
Clubhouse Facilities: Practice putting green, practice range, training bunker & training net.
Open Competitions: Contact club for details.

NO.	METRES	PAR	S.I.	NO.	METRES	PAR	S.I.
1	164	3	12	10	164	3	12
2	328	4	16	11	328	4	16
3	350	4	6	12	350	4	6
4	222	3	8	13	222	3	8
5	438	5	14	14	438	5	14
6	318	4	10	15	318	4	10
7	338	4	2	16	338	4	2
8	142	3	18	17	142	3	18
9	351	4	4	18	351	4	4
OUT	2,651	34		IN	2,651	34	
				TOTAL	5,302	68	
				STANDARD SCRATCH		67	

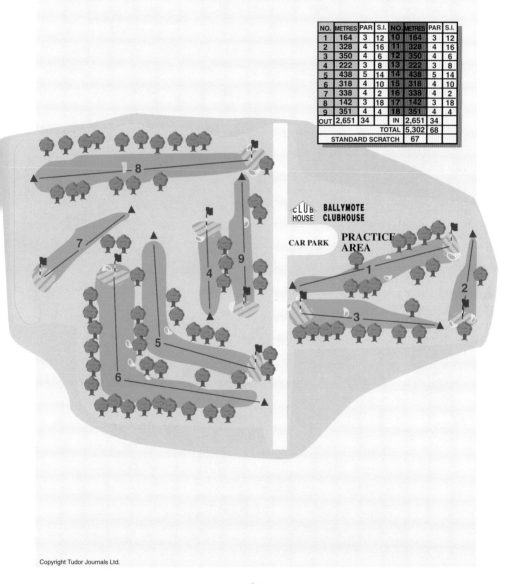

Copyright Tudor Journals Ltd.

County Sligo Golf Club, Rosses Point, Co Sligo.
Tel: (071) 77186/77134
Fax: (071) 77460.

LOCATION: Eight km. west of Sligo.
MANAGER: Jim Ironside
SECRETARY: Teresa Banks.
Tel: (071) 77134.
PROFESSIONAL: Jim Robinson.
Tel: (071) 77171.
ARCHITECT: Colt & Allison.

Situated under the shadow of famous Benbulben, the County Sligo Golf Club, or Rosses Point as it is more popularly known, is one of Ireland's great championship links. Home of the West of Ireland Championship held each year since 1923. Set among vast sand dunes on the cliffs overlooking three large beaches. Constant winds are an added factor to its many challenges, not least of which are some of its elevated tees. A burn meanders through the course and comes into play on a number of holes.

COURSE INFORMATION

Par 71; SSS 72; Length 6,043 metres.
Visitors: Welcome to play, except during major championship competitions.
Opening Hours: Daylight.
Avoid: Advisable to check tee time available before travel.
Ladies: Welcome.
Green Fees: Mon-Thur €55, Fri/Sat/Sun/Bank Holidays €70; Lessons available by prior arrangement. Club Hire available. Caddy service available by prior arrangement.
Clubhouse Hours: 8.00am - 11.30pm.
Clubhouse Dress: (Casual Neat).
Clubhouse Facilities: Full facilities. Snacks during day, a la carte after 6pm, and any other requirements by arrangement.
Open Competitions: Open week August. Handicap Certificate required. 9 holes Bowmore Course.

NO.	CHAMP METRES	MEDA METRES	PAR	S.I.	NO.	CHAMP METRES	MEDAL METRES	PAR	S.I.
1	347	339	4	8	10	351	348	4	1
2	278	273	4	11	11	368	368	4	0
3	457	448	5	15	12	486	479	5	3
4	150	150	3	12	13	162	150	3	1
5	438	424	5	17	14	394	358	4	4
6	379	365	4	6	15	367	358	4	1
7	393	385	4	1	16	196	172	3	8
8	374	373	4	5	17	414	385	4	4
9	153	140	3	13	18	336	325	4	7
OUT	2,969	2,897	36		IN	3,074	2,943	35	
					TOTAL	6,043	5,840	71	
					STANDARD SCRATCH	72			

Bomore Card

NO.	METRES	PAR	S.I.	NO.	METRES	PAR	S.I.
1	305	4	15	10	305	4	16
2	322	4	12	11	322	4	11
3	348	4	5	12	348	4	6
4	127	3	17	13	127	3	18
5	457	5	9	14	457	5	10
6	364	4	2	15	364	4	1
7	365	4	8	16	365	4	7
8	177	3	3	17	177	3	4
9	320	4	13	18	320	4	14
OUT	2,785	35		IN	2,785	35	
		TOTAL	5,570	70			
		STANDARD SCRATCH	69				

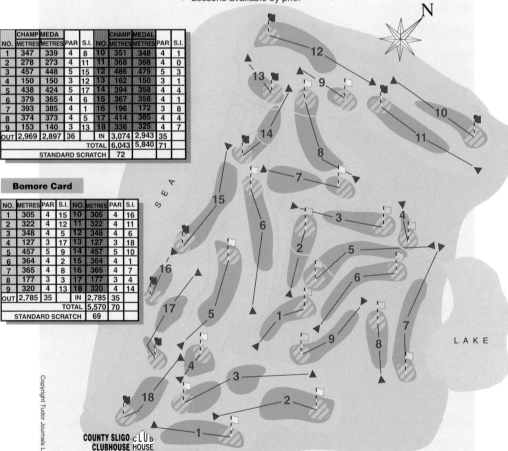

N

SEA

LAKE

COUNTY SLIGO CLUBHOUSE CLUB HOUSE

Copyright Tudor Journals Ltd.

Enniscrone Golf Club, Enniscrone, Co. Sligo. Tel: (096) 36297. Fax: (096) 36657.

LOCATION: Ballina Road, south of Enniscrone.
HON. SECRETARY: Brian Casey. Tel: (096) 36414.
PROFESSIONAL: Charles McGoldrick.
SECRETARY/MANAGER: Micheal Staunton
ARCHITECT: E. Hackett/ Donald Steel.

This links, on the shore of Killala Bay, is one of the many marvellous tests of golf which can be found in Ireland. The quality of the golf is matched by the surroundings, with the Ox Mountains close at hand. Killala Bay reaches out to the broadAtlantic within miles of sandy beaches surrounding the course. *"This is certainly a course not to be missed... the club is very keen to encourage visitors, so a warm welcome is assured"* (Golf World). Enniscrone was a venue for the Irish Close Championships and the West of Ireland Championship.Now a 27 hole championship complex.

COURSE INFORMATION

Par 73; SSS 72; Length 6,671 yds.
Visitors: Always welcome. (telephone at weekends).
Opening Hours: Sunrise – sunset.
Avoid: Bank Holidays; Sundays 8.00am – 11.00am and 1.30pm – 4.00pm.
Ladies: Welcome.
Green Fees: €45 weekdays, €60 weekends, Monday - Friday €35 for societies (12 or more people).
Juveniles: Must be accompanied by an adult. Club Hire is available. Caddy service and lessons available by prior arrangements. Telephone appointment required.
Clubhouse Hours: Open at all times.
Clubhouse Dress: Casual but neat.
Clubhouse Facilities: Catering facilities: snacks at all times. Meals by arrangement.
Open Competitions: Open Week 24th-28th June.

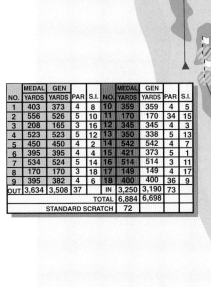

NO.	MEDAL YARDS	GEN YARDS	PAR	S.I.	NO.	MEDAL YARDS	GEN YARDS	PAR	S.I.
1	403	373	4	8	10	359	359	4	5
2	556	526	5	10	11	170	170	34	15
3	208	165	3	16	12	345	345	4	3
4	523	523	5	12	13	350	338	5	13
5	450	450	4	2	14	542	542	4	7
6	395	395	4	4	15	421	373	5	1
7	534	524	5	14	16	514	514	3	11
8	170	170	3	18	17	149	149	4	17
9	395	382	4	6	18	400	400	36	9
OUT	3,634	3,508	37		IN	3,250	3,190	73	
					TOTAL	6,884	6,698		
					STANDARD SCRATCH		72		

Copyright Tudor Journals Ltd.

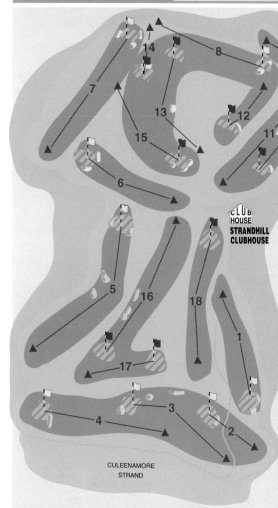

CLUB HOUSE
STRANDHILL CLUBHOUSE

CULEENAMORE STRAND

Strandhill Golf Club, Strandhill, Co. Sligo.
Tel: (071) 68188.
Fax: (071) 68811.
Email: strandhillgc@eircom.net

LOCATION: Five miles west of Sligo City.
SECRETARY: Christy Hennessey.
ARCHITECT: E. Hackett

Strandhill is a links course, playable all year round and situated in a most scenic area with views of Knocknarea and Benbulben Mountains. It has some very interesting holes, with the final three providing a sting in the tail.

COURSE INFORMATION

Par 69; SSS 68; Length 6,032 yards, 5,516 metres.
Visitors: Welcome.
Opening Hours: 8.30am – sunset.
Ladies: Welcome Thursday.
Green Fees: €35 Mon – Fri; €45 Sat / Sun & Bank Hols.
Juveniles: Welcome. Prior arrangement is required for groups.
Clubhouse Hours: 8.30am – 11.30pm.
Clubhouse Dress: Casual.
Clubhouse Facilities: Snacks at any time, lunch by prior arrangement.
Open Competitions: Most Bank Holiday Weekends.

NO.	MEDAL METRES	GEN METRES	PAR	S.I.	NO.	MEDAL METRES	GEN METRES	PAR	S.I.
1	397	380	4	2	10	304	285	4	14
2	158	155	3	8	11	300	263	4	12
3	375	330	4	17	12	304	260	4	16
4	291	270	4	10	13	338	305	4	7
5	480	460	5	18	14	132	111	4	13
6	355	336	4	11	15	306	270	4	3
7	352	335	4	5	16	386	362	4	6
8	308	275	4	15	17	178	141	3	9
9	186	140	3	4	18	384	329	4	1
OUT	2,902	2,681	35		IN	2,614	2,326	34	
					TOTAL	5,516	5,007	69	
	STANDARD SCRATCH					68			

Copyright Tudor Journals Ltd.

**Tubbercurry,
Co. Sligo.
Tel: (071) 85849.**

LOCATION: 10 minutes walk
from town centre.
SECRETARY: Tommy Clarke.
Tel: (071) 81135.
ARCHITECT: Eddie Hackett.

A challenging nine hole parkland
course with spectacular views of the
Ox Mountains and surrounding
countryside. It features a magnificent
elevated 8th tee box to the difficult
185 yard par 3, (169metres).

COURSE INFORMATION

**Par 70; SSS 69; Length
5,490 metres; 6,004 yards.
Visitors:** Welcome everyday.
Opening Hours:
Dawn – dusk.
Avoid: Sundays by
appointment.
Ladies: Welcome – active
ladies committee.
Green Fees: €15.
Juveniles: €10.
Clubhouse Hours:
12.00 noon – 11.30pm.

Clubhouse Dress: Neat dress.
Clubhouse Facilities: Newly
built clubhouse – full bar and
restaurant.
Open Competitions:
Christmas, Easter, bank holiday
weekends and Open Week in
July.

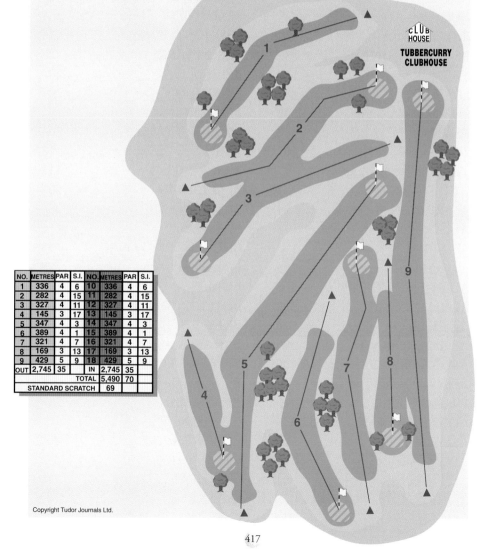

TUBBERCURRY
CLUBHOUSE

NO.	METRES	PAR	S.I.	NO.	METRES	PAR	S.I.
1	336	4	6	10	336	4	6
2	282	4	15	11	282	4	15
3	327	4	11	12	327	4	11
4	145	3	17	13	145	3	17
5	347	4	3	14	347	4	3
6	389	4	1	15	389	4	1
7	321	4	7	16	321	4	7
8	169	3	13	17	169	3	13
9	429	5	9	18	429	5	9
OUT	2,745	35		IN	2,745	35	
				TOTAL	5,490	70	
	STANDARD SCRATCH				69		

Copyright Tudor Journals Ltd.

INDEX

ADVERTISERS INDEX